A Benn Study · History

Nations of the Modern World
Iraq: International Relations
and National Development

Edith and E. F. Penrose

Iraq:
International Relations and National Development

London · Ernest Benn
Boulder · Westview Press

First published 1978 by Ernest Benn Limited
25 New Street Square, Fleet Street, London EC4A 3JA
& Sovereign Way, Tonbridge, Kent TN9 1RW
and Westview Press
5500 Central Avenue, Boulder, Colorado, 80301

Distributed in Canada by
The General Publishing Company Limited, Toronto

Printed in Great Britain by The Anchor Press Ltd
and bound by Wm Brendon & Son Ltd
both of Tiptree, Essex

A Nations of the Modern World Book

British Library Cataloguing in Publication Data

Penrose, Edith Tilton
Iraq. – (Nations of the modern world).
1. Iraq – History
I. Title II. Penrose, Ernest Francis III. Series
956.7 DS70.9

ISBN 0–510–39040–4

Library of Congress Cataloging in Publication Data

Penrose, Edith Tilton.
Iraq: international relations and national development.
(Nations of the modern world)
Bibliography: p. 592
Includes index.
1. Iraq – History – 1921– 2. Iraq – Economic conditions. I. Penrose, Ernest Francis, joint author. II. Title. III. Series.
DS79.P396 1978 956.7 77–16007

ISBN 0–89158–804–3 (Westview)

Contents

Part Two The Years of an Independent Monarchy, 1932–58

Part Three The 14th of July Revolution, 1958–63

Part Six The Summing-up

List of Illustrations

Inserted between pages 204 *and* 205

Maps and Charts

Charts

Spelling of Names

We have avoided the use of diacritical marks and have used a simplified English spelling for most proper names. We have also followed a usage common in the Arab world of frequently referring to individuals by their first names only, when the context permits it. Thus, Nuri al-Said is often referred to as 'Nuri'; Rashid Ali al-Gaylani as 'Rashid Ali'. Similarly, when we refer, as we often do, to Saddam Hussain al-Takriti (and the numerous other al-Takritis in the Baath hierarchy) by their first names only, it is in accordance with this custom and not because we observe the instructions of the Baath government disapproving the use of last names referring to places of origin or tribal affiliation.

A dispute has existed between Iran and some of the Arab states over the appropriate name to be given to the Gulf bordered by Iran, the United Arab Emirates, Saudi Arabia, Kuwait, and Iraq. Historically it has been known as the 'Persian Gulf' and when discussing historical events we have used this name. More recently there has been an insistence by some Arab governments that it be called the 'Arab Gulf'. We do not want to get involved in this dispute and hence we refer to this body of water either as 'the Gulf' or (if a distinction from other Gulfs is required) as the 'Arab/Persian' Gulf.

Acknowledgements

This study has been long in the making, and accordingly we have acquired a heavy indebtedness to many people, but it is fitting that we first acknowledge an obligation not directly connected with it. Professor Isaiah Bowman, an eminent and original geographer with a special interest in international relations, a long-time friend who was President of the Johns Hopkins University when we joined that institution in 1947, foresaw even then that the Middle East was destined to become an increasingly important focus of international affairs. He turned our attention to the area, and this prescient stimulation from him set in motion an interest on our part which has culminated in this work almost exactly 30 years later.

Next we want to thank the many Iraqis who have been helpful in our researches into the history of their country, especially since the Second World War. Some are, or have been, in prominent positions in Iraq and elsewhere; others have been students, teachers, small businessmen, or civil servants. Most have specialized personal knowledge of Iraq or have made a special study of some aspect of Iraq's modern economic or political history. None bears any responsibility for, and indeed many would probably disagree with, a number of our judgements. For research assistance we are grateful to Dr A. K. Guzine Rasheed, who helped in our historical research in uncovering needed materials, especially for the years before the 1958 Revolution. Similarly we would like to thank Dr Albertine Jwaideh for her help in collecting materials on the period after the Qassim Revolution and for her work on Iraqi land tenure.

The books and published articles, the doctoral theses and seminar papers of our many students, have been used and cited, and we want to thank them all warmly for their scholarly contributions, for their friendship, for the many hours of discussion on topics of interest to us, and for their unfailing willingness to help us find the elusive document, to interpret the deceptive statistic. To the many friends and officials in Iraq and outside it who took the trouble to answer our questions and discuss our work with us, we express our deep obligation. Some of these friends are not alive to read these words: in particular Abdul Rahman al-Bazzaz, whose death a few years ago was undoubtedly hastened by his incarceration and ill-treatment, and Nasir al-Hani, murdered in 1968.

Our debt to 'oilmen' both Iraqi and foreign is similarly very great. Officials of the Iraqi Ministry of Oil in its various manifestations through the years, officials of the Organization of Petroleum Exporting Countries and of the Organization of Arab Petroleum Exporting Countries, and officials of the oil companies who were operating in Iraq, have all been most helpful. We are particularly grateful to Ronald Ferrier, historian of British Petroleum, for reading parts of the manuscript dealing with the history of the oil industry, and to A. W. Willcocks, Head of Trade Relations of BP, as well as to many others in that company, in Shell, Exxon, and in the old IPC group, for information and criticism; and to an old friend, E. Hartshorn.

Students, colleagues, and others who have been members of the seminars on the international petroleum industry originally started by Edith Penrose (with Peter Odell) in the London School of Economics in the early 1960s and later continued under her direction in the School of Oriental and African Studies (in the last few years in association with Robert Mabro at St Antony's College, Oxford) are also among those to whom we are indebted. The papers, criticism, and discussion in seminars have over the years been of inestimable value to us. To other colleagues in the School of Oriental and African Studies, some of whom have read and criticized parts of the manuscript, while others have discussed issues with us, we offer our thanks, and in particular to Abbas Kelidar and his wife Madge Salibi (who did some research for us a few years ago), and to P. J. Vatikiotis. A. K. Selby, Keith McLachlan, and Heino Kopietz made some of their work available, which we much appreciated. We must also thank C. J. Edmonds, Elizabeth Monroe, and Elie Kedourie not only for discussions but especially for their published work. Of very great importance to all who work on Iraq is that grand old scholar of Iraqi history whose work will never be dated, Stephen H. Longrigg. To Humphrey Trevelyan and Waldemar Gallman, former ambassadors in Iraq, our thanks again for their published works as well as discussions. In North America, Ragaei El-Mallakh of the University of Colorado made some of his research available to us and enabled us to talk with some of his students, and Phebe Marr of the University of Tennessee gave us information on many of the early Iraqi leaders. Elizabeth Collard of the *Middle East Economic Digest* has been most helpful and the reader will see from the use made of their work how much we owe to Fuad Itayem, Ian Seymour, and the staff of the *Middle East Economic Survey*.

Our indebtedness extends to other parts of Europe besides Britain. A very large part of the political sections of the work was done in Paris and Vincennes. Paris is rich in materials on the Middle East, and we have been indebted for some 15 years to Marcel Colombe whom we first met in L'École Nationale des Langues Orientales Vivantes, Université de Paris, for our first personal connections with French Middle East scholars, for many long discussions on contemporary history, and for his invitation to contribute specialized articles on Iraq to *Orient*, the French quarterly which he directed and which brilliantly combined contemporary history with literature until 1969 when, apparently for financial reasons, it ceased publication, much to the regret of scholars of the Middle East in many countries. Marcel Colombe's most recent work, in two volumes covering intra-regional events during part of our period, has been indispensable to an understanding of what went on in a single country. For insight into the role of the Soviet Union in the Middle East we thank Hélène Carrère d'Encausse. Our indebtedness to her published work, the most recent addition to which came at a most opportune time for us, has been increased by the generosity with which she gave of her time in conversation. The articles of Hamid al-Shawi in *Maghreb-Machrek* have been extremely valuable and, again, have been supplemented by long discussions with him, which we much appreciated. We are also grateful to Eric Rouleau of *Le Monde*, especially for his facility in getting behind outward appearances and official versions in times of crisis. To Pierre Rondot of the Centre des Hautes Études Administratives sur l'Afrique et l'Asie Modernes we are similarly grateful. For the period before 1963 we have benefited from Bernard Vernier's published work and for several years afterwards for conversations on subsequent events.

We are particularly grateful to Jean Meyriat for access to the Services de Documentation of the Fondation Nationale des Sciences Politiques. The greater part of the political chapters was written in this institution, first in the Salle de Travail des Messieurs les Professeurs and later in the Salle de Consultation des Dossiers, making use also of the excellent library and the index covering 3,000 periodicals organized in sub-headings to cover not only countries but also numerous aspects of politics and economics in each. Jack Bizeray, Monique Michaud, Maria Th. Deretz, and Madame Le Therizien were particularly helpful in our fields. We owe much to the skill and kindness of the staff as a whole. We would add our thanks to Nadine Dada, of Science Politique, for innumerable acts of friendship in helping us in various ways.

Within the Fondation we have also been greatly aided by frequent conversations with members of the staff of the Section du Monde

Arabe of the Centre d'Étude des Relations Internationales, of which Jean Meyriat is director, on Middle Eastern countries having relations with Iraq: including Nicole Grimaud, Olivier Carré, Elisabeth Picard, and the director of the section, Louis-Jean Duclos, from whom we have profited greatly in conversations over three years.

Without the courteous assistance of the staffs of the Libraries of the School of Oriental and African Studies, the Institute of Historical Research, both of the University of London, of the Library of the Institute of International Affairs, of the London Library, and of the British Library, this book could not have been written and we accordingly acknowledge their help. We are particularly grateful to the Director of the Institute of Historical Research, Professor A. G. Dickens, who not only welcomed us to the Institute but introduced us to libraries in Paris. Our thanks are also due to the staff of the Salle de Travail in the Bibliothèque Nationale in Paris.

We have had no financial assistance in the preparation of this book except for research leave financed by the School of Oriental and African Studies, and a small grant from the Ford Foundation. We are grateful to both institutions.

Finally, everyone who has produced a book knows how much its successful completion has depended on the devoted and almost always under-rewarded assistance of those responsible for the physical preparation of the typescript. In our case we owe much to Janet Marks, the secretary of the Department of Economic and Political Studies of the School of Oriental and African Studies, to Rosemary Stride who over many years has lived with successive drafts, and a very great deal to June Foxlee who took charge of the final draft and the preparation of the bibliography, who was zealous in discovering inconsistencies and errors and stern in seeing that they were corrected. At considerable inconvenience to herself she saw us through to the end—and all we can say is 'thank you'—a hopelessly inadequate acknowledgement. It is fitting also for us to thank the publishers, and in particular John Collis for his skill in detecting defects and for his almost unbelievable patience in the face of almost intolerable delays on our part.

Neither of us can appropriately offer the usual apologies for personal inattention to the other. To be sure, each of us suffered from each other's activity: how much and why, however, is best kept in the family archives. We should like to thank our children, and especially Perran, Trevear, David, Joan, and Margaret, as well as our grandchildren, for their understanding in accepting our inability to devote as much time to them as we should have liked during their visits to us, and to Douglas and his family for our inability to visit them. To

Trevear we are indebted for drawing the map and the charts; and to Joan for help in preparing the manuscript.

We alone are responsible for the use made of the help we have received.

London
January 1978

Edith Penrose
E. Francis Penrose

Plates 5, 6, 7, 18 are by courtesy of *MEED*; 9, 10, 12, 23 by courtesy of Camera Press Limited; 11, 14, 22 by courtesy of Nik Wheeler; 26 by courtesy of Robert Harding Associates.

Abbreviations

BP	British Petroleum Company
EXXON	Formerly Standard Oil Company (New Jersey) (SONJ)
RD/S	Royal Dutch Shell Group
CFP	Compagnie Française des Pétroles
ENI	Ente Nazionale Idrocarburi
TPC	Turkish Petroleum Company
IPC	Iraq Petroleum Company
BOD	British Oil Development Company
BPC	Basra Petroleum Company
INOC	Iraq National Oil Company
ICOO	Iraq Company for Oil Operations
APOC	Anglo-Persian Oil Company
AIOC	Anglo-Iranian Oil Company
NIOC	National Iranian Oil Company
KPC	Kuwait Petroleum Company
KNPC	Kuwait National Petroleum Company
OPEC	Organization of Petroleum Exporting Countries
OAPEC	Organization of Arab Petroleum Exporting Countries
ICP	Iraq Communist Party
KDP	Kurdish Democratic Party
RIIA	Royal Institute of International Affairs
PIW	*Petroleum Intelligence Weekly*
MEED	*Middle East Economic Digest*
MEES	*Middle East Economic Survey*
b/d	barrels per day To convert b/d to t/y multiply by 50:
t/y	tons per year to convert t/y to b/d multiply by .02
Ha.	Hectare = .25 Iraqi donums
ID	Iraqi Dinar = 1,000 fils = £1 until 1971. 1972 = \$3.04; 1973 = \$3.35; 1974 = \$3.38

Preface

The present study aims at an interpretation of the political and economic development of Iraq from her foundation as a state. To borrow a phrase used by a distinguished scholar of the Middle East, 'Analysis, not comprehensive narration, is the interest of this study'.[1]

Our interpretation has given particular attention to influences, coming both from within and beyond the Middle East and affecting Iraq's intra-regional as well as her wider international relations. As a new state carved out of the territories of the former Ottoman Empire, Iraq came into being at a time when changes in the sources of energy used in modern transport and in industrial development created a growing international demand for the refined products of the most abundant of her economic natural resources. However, her economic development has shown that finance capital and foreign exchange alone are inadequate to ensure development.

Moreover, economic influences have been intermingled with political influences, some of ancient origin, some arising out of the relations of the new states created in the Middle East after two world wars, and some emerging with the changing relationships among the great powers at the end of each world war. Thus our study becomes a study of international relations as well as a study of internal developments in one country.

1. C. Ernest Dawn, *From Ottomanism to Arabism* (London, 1974).

1 Introduction

The establishment of the state of Iraq was an outcome of the fall of the Ottoman Empire. It was not, however, an inevitable outcome. The passing of the Empire was a necessary but not a sufficient condition for the establishment of Iraq as a new state. There were other conceivable ways of disposing of the territories which had lost their overlord. Their actual disposition was largely determined by the rivalries of the great European powers. From the beginning it was not to them a question of mere 'sovereignty' so much as a question of 'spheres of influence'. Already they had imposed these in varying degrees on parts of the Empire.

In the post-war period world conditions had changed. The Asian peoples were beginning to assert themselves. The Mandate System was designed to modify colonialism and prepare the way for independence, but the disposition of territories under it revealed the great power rivalries. These in turn were affected by far-reaching economic changes which had begun to penetrate the Middle East, to give a new significance to its natural resources, and to exert a far-reaching influence on its intra-regional and international relations.

The area with which we are concerned in this study had for long been contained within the Ottoman Empire. Assigned under mandate of the League of Nations to Great Britain, it displayed special physical characteristics which affected both its economic and its political development.[1]

The mountain ranges close to and almost parallel with the eastern Mediterranean coastlands to the west of Iraq intercept the westerly and south-westerly winter winds from the Mediterranean and only allow weak depressions to extend into Iraq mainly between November and April, which yield an average rainfall of 150–200 mm. in the plains. Except in close proximity to the mountains rainfall diminishes rapidly to the east, though at first more slowly in the area which extends from the latitude of Homs northward where rain-fed agriculture is possible. Deserts appear all the way to and across Iraq, covering more than half the country west and south of the Euphrates river. The traveller crossing the Great Syrian Desert from Damascus to Baghdad reaches the frontier of Iraq at Rutba—an isolated desert post at which traffic, mainly lorries and buses, coming from Syria on the west, Baghdad on the east, and Saudi Arabia on the south, meet. Following the frontier formalities he continues a long distance in equally barren territory until he reaches the vicinity of Ramadi on the Euphrates from which he goes on through populated lands to Baghdad on the Tigris.

These twin rivers and the elaborate irrigation network which over many centuries has grown up around them, allow the designation 'Fertile Crescent' to be extended from the Mediterranean coastal areas to include the Mesopotamian Plain as well, notwithstanding the great expanse of desert that lies between the eastern and the western segments of the Crescent. The human geographer, however, cannot afford to neglect either the economic or the political effects of this intervening desert on Iraq and on her relations with her neighbours, for it has formed a great land barrier to close contact—and is still important in spite of the modern forms of travel.

Just as the internal political and economic history of the Iraqi people can only be interpreted after taking equally into account the developments among its neighbours and even beyond, so the physical geography largely takes its form and finds its origin in the land and sea forms of surrounding areas. To the north lie the high lands of eastern Anatolia with the Taurus range, and the Armenian highlands in the Zagros range from which the twin rivers derive their waters, particularly from the melting of snows which reaches a maximum in the early spring. The course of the rivers is then determined by the contours and by the nature of the materials which at certain points include lava flows.

The twin rivers have been the subject of great interest and considerable investigation. They enter Iraq after crossing part of the Kurdish areas in Turkey further north, and a part of Syria. The differences in the land forms through which they move to the Arab/Persian Gulf, however, have produced marked differences in their regimes. The Zagros mountain range which roughly parallels the Tigris on its left bank gives rise to substantial tributaries which augment the rate of flow of the river. The Euphrates, on the other hand, has no tributaries in Iraq. The gradients of both rivers are steep and the currents fast-moving during much of the year, while the loss by evaporation is great during the hot months, temperatures reaching 45°C in July and August, and the levels fall rapidly. The Tigris is faster and fluctuates more frequently and widely than the Euphrates, causing extensive flooding in some areas. The flooding of the Baghdad area in 1954, for example, aggravated the political disturbances of the times, and, with substantial oil revenues by then available, large capital works were undertaken to prevent repetition.

Between Baghdad on the Tigris and Ramadi on the Euphrates near Lake Habbaniya, the two rivers come closer together before opening up again towards the south-east until they reach the delta. In the southern section the character of the flow changes and drainage takes place into extensive marshlands and lakes where highly specialized forms of habitation have developed. Here the problem of dealing with an excess of water has required as much ingenuity as the problem of dealing with deficiency has done in the central and northern areas, with the reservation that the water characterized as excessive is too saline for use and may be described as a negative resource. Marshland prevails over a far greater length in the lower courses of the Tigris and Euphrates than on the Nile. The rate of fall in the level of the river beds is very low, especially for the Euphrates. Iraq has a poor south associated with special and peculiar natural resources.

The limitation on agricultural development relates more to the availability of fresh water than to the supply of land. In the irrigated areas the existing supply must be rationed among alternative crop uses. But these limitations are not wholly fixed by nature. The use made of natural resources to meet human demands depends on human knowledge and human skill, and these, though they advance in the long run, may at times retrogress in certain areas during certain periods. The larger populations maintained in the Abbasid period between the area of Takrit and Baghdad-Ramadi appear to have been supplied largely through the extension of irrigation works based on the difference between the levels of the Tigris and the Euphrates, which, as long as the channels were kept clear, could be exploited both for watering and for draining lands, thus stimulating cultivation and repressing salinity. The subsequent decline has been sometimes attributed to the savage attacks of Hulagu Khan in 1258, but while these were important, the failure to maintain adequate drainage and prevent the salinization of the soil seems to have played a leading part up to the present day in Iraqi agricultural history.

Thus the natural resources in the eastern part of the Fertile Crescent could only be transformed into and maintained as *economic* natural resources by human skills and sustained human management and supervision designed to meet the special conditions of a unique area. A high degree of skill is required to apply modern technology effectively in the economic exploitation of Iraq's limited range of natural resources. Although political disasters like the Mongul invasions are no longer to be feared, political misjudgements on economic policies concerning land use and management have been a constant danger in recent years. The part of the Fertile Crescent represented by Iraq's irrigated areas may easily pass from fertility to infertility in a short time, both in the narrower area of the Jezirah and in the central and southern plains. Then, beyond the irrigated areas to the north lies an area of sufficient rainfall for cultivation merging into the foothills of the Kurdish mountains. These lands also require careful management in view of the fluctuations in rainfall and the possibilities of pump irrigation from wells, taking advantage of different levels of contour lines.

The political boundaries of Iraq remained indefinite during the Ottoman period and, as we shall see, their determination later led to international difficulties which, in respect to Turkey, Syria, and Saudi Arabia, were not settled until the inter-war period; in the case of Iran and Kuwait, boundaries continued to raise controversy after the Second World War.

Turkish influence, however, was less marked in Iraq than in the regions of the Empire lying to the west and north. The number of Turkish people in Iraq was small and the officials and men of affairs who were stationed there looked forward to their eventual return to Turkey much as, a hundred years later, the Iraqi officials sent from Baghdad to the marshlands of southern Iraq looked forward to an eventual return to Baghdad. Thus the Turkish influence which played an important role in the thinking of some of the prominent Iraqi politicians during the Mandate and the earlier period of independence, came from temporary outward migration to Turkey rather than from permanent inward migration from Turkey. It was brought back by Iraqis from Constantinople rather than implanted in Iraq by residents of Turkish origin.

Nonetheless, the eastern segment of the Fertile Crescent was important to Constantinople. It stood as a buffer between the western segment and Persia and the areas to the north-east and beyond, through which the old inpourings from the steppes had come and where Russia subsequently held sway, arousing fears in the west. Here, then, was an interest shared from different viewpoints by Great Britain and the British-dominated government of India, an interest which was later supplemented by the economic and 'strategic' importance of oil supplies, both giving special significance to the security of communications between Britain and India. On the eve of the First World War the role of the Middle East as a source of fuel for the outside world had begun and Iraq was soon to be among the foremost of its oil-producers.

The population of the *vilayets* of Baghdad and Basra in the Ottoman period remained Arab. Iraq did not acquire her present bi-national, Arab/Kurdish, character until 1926, when the League of Nations confirmed, over the opposition of the new Turkey, the addition of the *vilayet* of Mosul to those of Baghdad and Basra, thus bringing a large slice of Kurdistan into Iraq. Looking at the composition of the Arab population and of the smaller sects and minorities within it, however, we find traces of the successions of invasions and migrations which passed over its territory in historic times. We also find divisions within Islam as well as, on a far smaller scale, within Christendom, which arose out of the heresies which broke with the orthodoxies of their time of birth. In Islam the chief heresy originated in disputes over the legitimate religious line of succession to the Prophet, although there were others associated with elements of mysticism applied to the central interpretations of the Koranic message. In a quantitative sense the great schism was between Sunni and Shia.

In Iraq, the Arab population is divided: the Shia are in a majority of between 50 and 60 per cent, but the Sunni have traditionally held most of the leading economic, social, and political positions in the country. As we shall see, however, the Shia are growing in influence and status as a result of educational advance, migration from the rural areas in the south to Baghdad, and increasing income.

This religious split within Islam has intra-regional as well as domestic consequences. On the north of Iraq, Turkey is predominantly Sunni. On the east, Iran is almost completely Shia and the sacred Shia centres in Kerbela and Najf draw large numbers of pilgrims and considerable trade as well as, in the past, a large quantity of metals for the mosques. Sunni-dominated governments in Baghdad have frequently been on bad terms with the Shia centres at Kerbela and Najf (as they were at the time of writing). To the west, Syria has until recently been largely dominated by the Sunni, centred in Damascus, but more recently they have been displaced in government by a group dominated by the Alawi, a sect that might be described roughly as a Shia deviation. This difference may be given a place, though not an exclusive place, among the causes of the difficult relations between Iraq and Syria in the 1960s and early 1970s.[2] Another geographical source of disharmony lies in the problem of equitable distribution of the waters of the Euphrates between the agricultural areas of the two countries.

The schisms within Islam were matched by schisms within Christianity, and here a major part was played by different conceptions of the Godhead—the subject also of theological conflict between Islam and Christianity. At the Councils of Ephesus in 431 and 449 the influence of the Alexandrian theologians, who gave predominance to the divine nature of Jesus, prevailed over the Nestorian point of view, which was formulated in terms that left a much larger place for the human Jesus. But at the second of these gatherings the Patriarch of

Alexandria pressed his advantage too far and aroused fears in Rome and Constantinople of heretical leanings. This led to the famous Council of Chalcedon in 451, which, without lifting the ban on Nestorius, excluded equally the opposite doctrine, which came to be known as Monophysite and established itself in the Eastern Coptic Church. Thus the Middle East harboured a variety of heresies, Christian as well as Muslim.

Some among the deviationist sects were impelled for political reasons to re-establish relations with Rome by slightly modifying their formulations of doctrine and by recognizing the Papacy as head of Christendom. Two widely separated events, the Mongol invasions of the thirteenth century and the First World War in the twentieth, contributed indirectly to these reconciliations. In Iraq practically all these groups are represented, though in small numbers. They include the Armenian Catholics, the Syrian Catholics, and the Nestorians, who became Chaldean Catholics. The Assyrians in Iraq have been mainly, though not exclusively, refugees from war and boundary changes. The minorities are represented in the large cities and in some of the country districts in the north of the country. In the northern areas there are also non-religious differences arising out of the displacements of the past, as in the case of the Assyrians, and the establishment of a disputed northern frontier, as in the case of the Kurds who, though Sunni Muslim, like the dominant class in Iraq, are not Arab but cherish a separate national sentiment whose adherents also overlap into Turkey and Iran.

Iraq is not only a crossroads lying between Europe and the Mediterranean to the west and Inner Asia to the east, but is also a connecting route to the Indian Ocean and its bordering countries to the south-east. It was this geographical position which drew the area into the military operations of both world wars in the twentieth century, and brought it subsequently into the scope of rivalry between the Soviet Union and the United States.

Beyond the influence of mere location, special geographical characteristics, belonging partly to those of arid lands in general, have circumscribed Iraq's social and economic development, calling for special skills to exploit the natural resources and overcome or circumvent the natural obstacles of the country. Archaeological remains testify to the early appearance of some of these skills, and in the Abbasid period in the eighth and ninth centuries both the skills and, for a time, the ability to organize their application were highly developed in the control of water and its uses to extend the area of cultivation and to increase food production to meet the needs of a growing population.

In the Ottoman period Baghdad appeared as a distant part of an

Empire preoccupied with difficult issues in its European and Mediterranean areas. Consequently, at a time when European advances in technology were spreading to a number of other parts of the world, assisted by European capital, Iraq lagged behind, apart from limited advances in the period of Midhat Pasha.[3] Most educated Iraqis, if asked when modern economic and social influences first began to appear in Iraq, would probably name this period when he was Governor of Baghdad in 1869–72 and serious attempts were made to reform the administrative system, to create a system of land registration, and to enforce enlightened policies regarding land settlement and reclamation, tribal pacification, and river transport. During Midhat Pasha's regime a hospital, a number of new primary schools, and a woollen-textile factory were built and a newspaper was established. Although much that he attempted was short-lived or abortive, many of his policies took root and had a significant impact on future developments. This was possible only because the ground had already been prepared in preceding decades.

Throughout the whole of the final century of the Ottoman period Iraq had increasingly been opened to the wider world. A slow process of change, which began with the destruction of the Stambul Janissaries by Sultan Mahmud II in 1826, had clearly set in as Iraq was pulled along behind the changes in Turkey itself. The creation of the 'New Army' in Iraq under Europeanized officers was accompanied by the introduction of European-trained doctors and engineers and even of modern clothing factories. From then on European ideas, manners, clothing, and customs increasingly influenced the urban classes. In government, there were a number of attempts, even before Midhat Pasha came to Baghdad, to introduce reforms, to reduce corruption, and to improve the countryside. A class of officials with some degree of education and 'civil service' outlook grew up, to be known as 'Effendis', and these brought some order and administrative competence into government. Because of British interests in trade, transport, and the 'route to India', British officials of various kinds began to exert considerable influence in the nineteenth century, as we shall see in the next chapter.

In Iraq, as elsewhere in those countries in Asia, Africa, and Latin America which were soon to attempt a rapid development of their people and resources with a view to achieving economic progress along the lines of the rapidly industrializing world, it was necessary to absorb much of the scientific and technological knowledge associated with the application of modern methods in agriculture and industry. This in turn called for the use of foreign technical assistance, the establishment of new educational institutions, advances in organizing and managerial capacities, and, perhaps the most difficult, for changes in the attitudes and attributes of the local working population. Economic change both required and induced political change. In the following pages we shall trace both types of change with special reference to the way in which the economic and political development of Iraq has been influenced and shaped by both the international and intra-regional relationships of the country.

Notes

1 For an excellent discussion of the physical and human geography of Iraq see W. B. Fisher, *The Middle East* (London, 6th ed., 1971). Also Peter Beaumont, Gerald Blake, and J. M. Wagstaff, *The Middle East: A Geographical Study* (London and New York, 1976), especially, Ch. 12.

2 For the history, geography, and doctrines of the Alawi see particularly J. Weulersse, *Le Pays des Alaouites* (Tours, 1940).

3 See S. H. Longrigg, *Four Centuries of Modern Iraq* (Oxford, 1925), pp. 276–320; and Bernard Lewis, *The Emergence of Modern Turkey*, 2nd edn. (Oxford, 1968), pp. 160–9, 390f.

Part One

The New State is Formed

Eve of First World War to 1932

2 The Origins of the State of Iraq

On the eve of the First World War Iraq was no longer the isolated backwater of a hundred years previously. Although the way of life of most of her people had scarcely changed, the country was supporting an increasing population and improvements in living standards, especially in the cities, were discernible.

Neither education nor medical science had touched the majority of people, and village and tribal activities continued in their age-old patterns. Apart from the appearance of a few oil-driven pumps, agricultural techniques and the management of the land had advanced little from biblical times. Tribes were still asserting their independence, defiant of government; the government writ ran fitfully in the Kurdish highlands, and the tax-collector everywhere was still avaricious and often brutal.

To this society modern warfare came suddenly. The Christian Europeans drove out the Ottoman Turks who, though disliked, had nevertheless been Muslim and less alien, and their activities had begun to lay the foundation for the formation of a modern state in Mesopotamia. The formal establishment of the state was associated with the collapse of the Ottoman Empire following its entry into the First World War on the side of the Central Powers, and with the rivalries and bargaining among the great powers which preceded, accompanied, and followed the war and which resulted in the division of the dismembered territories into spheres of influence and of territorial administration according to the new formulas of Mandates under the League of Nations. The net outcome was not all that the victors had designed or desired, and the imperialist powers sustained a decisive check from a resurgent Turkish nationalism which, like a later Arab resurgence in the 1970s, demonstrated the limits to the ability of the Great Powers to dictate the terms of political settlements in international relations. But a number of new states were formed; some of them, like Saudi Arabia, were independent, others, like the mandated territories, were placed under tutelage but set on the road to independence.

Great Britain had long shown an interest in Mesopotamia.[1] In the early nineteenth century the area was looked on from time to time as a possible route to India via the Arabian Gulf and an alternative to the isthmus of Suez. This presupposed navigation along the Euphrates, which at first was believed to be practicable. A series of brilliant pioneering surveys of the route was carried out for the Admiralty between 1830 and 1837 which ultimately showed that the Euphrates was not navigable along its whole length and could not therefore be used as a route for commerce with India. But it was subsequently found that considerable stretches of the Tigris could be used for river transport and a British company had a long and successful career in river commerce and transport, with the approval of the British and Indian governments and the tacit unwritten approval of the Ottoman authorities in Constantinople, who had scant knowledge of the area concerned.

Britain's Early Imperial Interests

One of the foremost strategic aims of imperial Britain had long been, and at the end of the First World War continued to be, that of safeguarding the route to India. Before the Suez Canal was built, the isthmus of Suez, and after it the Canal itself, were the leading routes apart from the long journey around the Cape of Good Hope. But whatever the difficulties of navigation on the Euphrates, the importance of Mesopotamia from the point of view of India continued to be rated high in both London and Delhi. Commerce was not the only consideration: the danger that the route might be dominated by rival powers, particularly from Baghdad to Basra and the Red Sea, was always in the minds of officials in the two capitals.

The concern over the route to India began to find expression well over a century before the First World War. The imperialist rival or rivals which, it was feared, might seek to use or dominate this route changed from time to time, but the possibility was by no means fanciful. During the Napoleonic Wars four different projects were prepared for an invasion of India overland through the Near or Middle East. Three of them would have passed through some part of Mesopotamia. That of Bonaparte would have followed the Euphrates to near Basra, then crossed the river and entered Persia, thereafter following a line near the coast to the border of India. Two other projects envisaged collaboration between France and Russia against British India, though they would only have been practicable in certain short periods during the shifting systems of alliances and counter-alliances between 1793 and 1815 which are loosely described as the Napoleonic Wars. The more important of these was the project designed to be shared by France, Russia, and Persia following the Treaty of Tilsit between Napoleon and the Tsar Alexander in 1807, which was concluded after French military successes at Jena over the Prussians and over the Russians at Friedlund. With Russia transformed from an enemy to an ally of Napoleon, the prospect of a Franco–Russian attack on India suddenly appeared as a serious contingency and an early threat. This time, however, the assent and co-operation of the Shah of Persia was sought and the plan envisaged a two-prong attack, one part of which would sweep through Baghdad and northern Iraq, *en route* to India via Persia. The Shah's fears of British and British–Indian imperialism were exploited.

But British diplomacy played on Persian fears of Napoleon's strength and his expansionist aims, and by skilful representations both in Persia and in Turkey as well as in a European context, Britain was able to block Napoleon's aims. It should be added, however, that plans drawn up under Napoleon's supervision were detailed and covered much of the 'logistics' of the military operation envisaged. It is not surprising that, following these experiences, British and British–Indian circles continued to take a serious view of the problem of 'safeguarding' the route to India.[2]

After the Napoleonic Wars, the fears of Russian pressure on Turkey and Persia recurred, particularly from the later 1820s. The rise of Mohammed Ali in Egypt and his efforts to become more and more independent of the Sultan Mahmud II, and to extend his rule into Palestine, Syria, and part of Arabia, reawakened the rivalries among the European powers and Russia. British governments tended to take a hostile attitude towards Mohammed Ali, particularly after his success in 1807 in preventing the attempt to land British forces in Alexandria. Metternich, in accord with his policy of opposing change, also attempted to arouse the great powers to support Constantinople against Mohammed Ali. France, however, from an early stage after the war, diverged sharply on this issue. Mohammed Ali was above all a modernizer and innovator and became known as the 'father of modern Egypt'. He sought and obtained French experts to effect a reorganization both of the army and of civilian activities and institutions, and accorded monopolies to a number of French enterprises.

Thus France remained outside, while Palmerston and Metternich failed to agree on the form of intervention which both of them desired. Meanwhile Mohammed Ali advanced towards his goal of dominating much of the Fertile Crescent, and, incidentally, the 'route to India':

> Il avait conquis une parti du Soudan et le pays noir lui donnait une pépinière de soldats. Des reconnaissances avait été poussées jusqu'au Golfe Persique. Une flotilla pénétrait dans les bouches du Chatt-el-Arabe. La voie à Bagdad était ouverte et les principales routes de l'Inde allaient être commandées par ce nouvel empire.[3]

Failing to obtain help from London or Vienna the Sultan turned to Russia. A Russian fleet was sent to Constantinople and troops were landed. Hostilities ceased and terms were accepted by the Sultan and Mohammed Ali which left the latter in Syria, Adana, and Tarsus. The Treaty of Unkiar Skelessi was then drawn up, in 1833, in one of the clauses of which Turkey agreed to exclude armed vessels from the Dardanelles in the event of war. In the same year, the Tsar and the Austrian Emperor, under Metternich's influence, agreed on measures of mutual aid to suppress any liberal uprisings. Britain and France opposed these moves, but owing to clashes of interest arising out of commercial competition they could not agree on common action. Thus when Mohammed Ali declared his independence of the Sultan in 1838 and the latter retaliated by sending an army against him, the powers were disunited. When the Sultan's army was decisively defeated and his navy deserted him, Mohammed Ali became the dominant force in the Ottoman Empire.

In 1839, however, the European powers, in face of this emergency, agreed, on Metternich's initiative, on the need for intervention. Russia, however, refused to accept Vienna as the centre of negotiation and approached Palmerston, who then took a new initiative which led to a quadruple agreement with the Eastern powers. Mohammed Ali was forced to abandon his hold on the Fertile Crescent. But French opinion continued to support him, and the government refused to join in this coercive action.

The chief motive of Britain was again the safeguarding of the route to India via Mesopotamia and the Persian Gulf. But the wisdom of Palmerston's action was not self-evident. It was later questioned by Sir Valentine Chirol, the outstanding director of *The Times* Foreign Department, and others, on the ground that Britain would have found a more reliable ally in Mohammed Ali than in the Sultan and his successor, and would have established harmony with France at the same time.

In the early 1850s the British and French governments allowed themselves to be drawn into one of the recurring conflicts between the Russians and the Ottoman Empire. The issues were complicated and some of them had little to do with the route to India. The Turks refused to accept a series of Russian demands and for the first time Britain and France were ready to give them more than diplomatic support. The question of the continuance of a buffer state between Russia and Central and Western Europe was raised. For a number of reasons public opinion was more than usually aggressive in Great Britain. Lord Palmerston's diplomatic judgement was unsteady. The terms imposed on Russia after the Crimean War were subsequently repudiated unilaterally at the time of the Franco–Prussian War in 1870–71. But the continuance of the Ottoman Empire was ensured up to the First World War.

As we have seen, British interest in Mesopotamia was maintained, through the development of her commercial interests and through the continued activities of the Lynch Company up to the First World War. A large part of the trade of the area was in British products and through British commercial channels. France concerned herself little with the area, and her chief difficulties in relation to Britain arose out of the relations of the two countries with Egypt, particularly the unilateral British occupation of Egypt and control over the Egyptian external indebtedness.

Eve of the First World War: European Rivalries

On the eve of the First World War, the source of British fears over the route to India was above all to be found in Germany. The misplaced and indeed absurd suspicions of France had at last given way to growing fears of the immensely powerful military machine which the German General Staff had created, and the vigorous naval competition that had sprung up in the decade before the war. The English Channel had finally given way to the North Sea as the most dangerous area of potential conflict. Although the newer and growing rivalries of great powers within Europe were centred more and more on European questions, and Germany was comparatively indifferent to overseas empire, fears concerning the route to India, south-east Asia, and the Far East had by no means diminished, and Mesopotamia came most prominently into the overseas picture through German economic and commercial enterprise directed towards Anatolia and beyond it into Mesopotamia towards Basra and the Persian Gulf. The British attempt to develop a through water route using the Euphrates had failed. The obvious alternative was to construct a railway route. Here, however, British initiative and British enterprise were lacking and late in the century German financial and business interests took the lead.

Britain, Germany, and the Baghdad Railway

In 1899 German railway and financial interests obtained a concession to construct an extension of the railway in Anatolia to

Baghdad and Basra; in 1903 a concession for 99 years was given to a new company whose shares were mostly owned by the railway company in Anatolia. The construction of a port at Basra was included in the scheme.

The discussions and controversy on the Baghdad railway remain of great interest to the historian of Mesopotamia. They reveal clearly the intense rivalry among the great powers of the day over the Near East. The weakness of the Ottoman government encouraged competitive demands for economic concessions in Anatolia and beyond. A close examination shows that Britain, notwithstanding her unique record as a country practising free trade unilaterally, did not follow her own principles when it came to economic penetration of other countries. Her record of long opposition to the Baghdad railway reflects, among a mixture of strategic and other economic motives, the desire to protect monopolistic British interests already established in the area. These interests were usually able to find spokesmen in the House of Commons, sometimes in both parties, as well as in the press. The government of the day did not generally initiate defensive action on their behalf, but it was subject to pressure from vested interests, which were frequently brought to bear on it through members of Parliament who had been influenced by businessmen and by shareholders in foreign enterprises. Other members of Parliament, unconcerned over vested interests, enlarged on the strategic considerations to which, in their view, priority should be given over purely economic factors.

For some years the phrase 'Berlin to Baghdad' became almost a slogan. It coincided with a period of Anglo–German naval rivalry and aroused strong feelings in some circles in London. Germany was also regarded as a rival in international trade, at a time when Britain was losing some of her initially long lead in the Industrial Revolution in face of the rise of Germany and, behind her, the United States, as industrial powers. In contemporary circles the competitive aspects of Germany's rise were overemphasized to the exclusion of the parallel effects of the expansion of her domestic market. The crude oversimplifications of the popular press aggravated these misconceptions in both Britain and Germany.

The British government, however, contained wiser heads than those responsible for aggravating Anglo–German rivalry. They correctly saw in the Baghdad railway plan an opportunity for profitable economic co-operation between Britain and Germany. At the same time, some financial circles in Germany favoured British participation in the scheme, for German capital was hardly equal to financing such a large scheme. The saying 'Berlin veut et Londres peut' was a terse way of summarizing economic realities. Balfour and a number of members of his Cabinet, in contrast to the crude outlook of the popular press, took an intelligent view of the matter and, if they had been free to move, would have agreed to participation on the latest terms proposed. Unfortunately, the public attitude, the opposition of a few members of the Cabinet and of more in his party, blocked their efforts, some on strategic grounds, others from a desire to protect a few British-built local railway-lines from competition. Balfour was unable to carry all his Cabinet with him. On this issue as well as the later free trade and protection controversy, the unstable Joseph Chamberlain worked strongly against him and the prospect of British participation was destroyed.

As with the Suez Canal earlier so with the Baghdad railway, Britain opposed initiatives and projects, accomplished later by others, to which she had been invited to contribute and which offered greatly improved communication with India and with the British colonies in Southern and South-east Asia and with the Far East. The motive behind this shortsighted policy was a desire to obtain or retain as high a degree of monopoly as possible, in both a political and an economic sense. There were not wanting highly intelligent statesmen, and outstanding public men who were opposed to such exclusive attitudes, but their influence was smothered by narrow imperialists who desired British domination of all routes to India and the suppression if possible of any initiatives Britain could not dominate,[4] even when they would have shortened the time and reduced the expenditures required to convey goods and passengers between Britain and India. The development of the areas along these new routes, one of which was to pass through Iraq, while the other greatly shortened the journey from Basra to Europe and beyond it, was hindered by the delays created through Britain's failure to co-operate.

Other Economic Rivalries

After the Young Turks had seized power in 1908, the new Ottoman government played a more active part in the control of concessions, recognizing that the great powers were concerned only with their own competitive interests, not with Turkey's domestic needs. The new leaders understood better than their predecessors the advantages of distributing concessions in a more balanced manner among the competing applicants and thus checking the attempts of any single country to establish a commanding position, and Turkey's own interests were asserted more actively than they had been under the old regime. The competitors were numerous enough—Great Britain, France, Germany, and Italy—to offer, if not safety in numbers, at least pressure coming from within their own ranks, against any one of their number who might appear to be accumulating a disproportionate share.

The scramble for concessions, in which the territories of the future state of Iraq were among the leading objects, was not an edifying spectacle. The European democracies were as ready as the European autocracies to engage in it. There were 'Liberal imperialists' as well as 'Conservative imperialists'[5] and the criteria by which the public judged the actions of their government in Asian and African territories were radically different from those by which they judged them in domestic affairs. It was in this spirit that the first approaches to the disposition of Ottoman territories after the war were made. But, as we shall see, after the shock of war had been widely felt, newer currents of thought and sentiment developed which modified the approach towards the future of Mesopotamia and Syria.

Historians in the later twentieth century have often been preoccupied with the idea of 'East–West' rivalry and conflict of interests. The counterpart of these, in the opening years of the century, might be better described as a triple rivalry of East–Central–West. The expansion of German economic interests into Anatolia and Mesopotamia had aroused Russian fears that the establishment of German control over communications might be prejudicial to the Russian need of outlets to the Mediterranean. In August 1911, an agreement was reached by which the Baghdad line would be linked to the future plan for a network of new Russian and Persian lines which would be joined to a German–Persian network, the whole providing an outlet for goods to the Mediterranean and the Gulf. In return for this concession, Germany recognized that the north of Persia was a Russian sphere of influence in which Russia would have priority in the construction of new lines.

In dealing with the foreign scramble for concessions, the Ottoman governments after 1909 were faced with difficult choices. Their leaders recognized the necessity of modernization. The age of the internal combustion engine and of petroleum was in its early dawn and there were as yet no huge revenues to be derived from exports of oil. The concession-hunters were always a political danger. But they brought with them capital and skills which were essential to modernization. This applied particularly to rail transport in areas where the main centres of population were separated by large stretches of desert. In these circumstances, it is difficult, and often impossible, to make a railway enterprise profitable in the short run, and private capital can be attracted only when large public subsidies are granted in the form either of funds or of land or of financial inducements such as tax exemption or remission. Some of these inducements were given to the Deutsche Bank in the Baghdad railway enterprise. The scarcity of domestic capital and skills would have long retarded even the beginnings of modernization in such an area as Mesopotamia, as well as in other extensive areas of a loose empire, much of which had not yet emerged from medieval economic conditions.[6]

In making terms with modern European imperialism the Ottoman government was therefore opening the way to earlier modernization than could be achieved in any other way at the time, and this advantage had to be weighed against the serious political dangers in granting foreign concessions, some of the conditions of which impinged on the independence of the country. Customs duties had been regulated by a concert of European powers, which, however, had allowed the imposition of a surtax in 1907 in connection with reforms in Macedonia. As compensation, Turkey had agreed to the German construction of the Baghdad line, to the Austrian annexation of Bosnia and Herzegovina, and to the Italian acquisition of Tripolitania. Turkey, France, and Britain were suspicious of the contents of the German–Russian agreement: in 1913 they eventually obtained from Germany a renunciation of the exclusive rights which she had been given for the construction of the line between Baghdad and the Gulf. France received concessions from Turkey for the construction of lines leading to the Black Sea. Turkey gave a new concession to Germany for the construction of the line joining Nisibin to Baghdad across Kurdistan, passing Zakho, Arbil, and Kirkuk. She obtained also the authorization to construct a branch from Samara to Khanaqin and to the Persian frontier. In the future, this would join the Russian–Persian network, thus opening Kurdistan and the eastern part of Mesopotamia.

Finally, Anglo–Turkish agreement was reached in the spring of 1914. Britain had been particularly concerned over the section of the Baghdad railway which was to be constructed between Baghdad and Basra at the head of the Gulf, and which was of especial interest to the government of India. Britain recognized Turkish suzerainty over Kuwait, but Turkey agreed to respect the independence of the Shaikh—to whom a British 'adviser' was attached.

Entente between France and Britain from 1904 had still left a difference between them regarding railway developments in Syria. The early British ambition to construct a line from the Mediterranean, which would have traversed a part of Syria to join the projected British-controlled route to India, was now out of the question. This obstacle being removed, the Foreign Office recognized the special interests of France in Syria, and in 1913 Turkey agreed to the extension to Ramleh of the French Aleppo–Rayet line, as well as concessions in the ports of Tripoli, Haifa, and Jaffa. These concessions disposed of earlier rumours that Britain aspired to annex

Syria and join her to Egypt. Britain, having failed earlier in the century to carry out proposals for an all-rail, all-British route from the Mediterranean to the Gulf, was now left with the route Port Said–Basra or Kuwait as the only remaining possibility. Moreover, it had long been clear that British interests in Mesopotamia could only be achieved by recognition of French interests in Syria. As we shall see later, the relationships of Britain and France with reference to Syria played a leading role in the establishment of Iraq within boundaries, and under a head of state, on which agreement was obtained only with difficulty.

The Struggle for an Oil Concession

Although the maintenance of a paramount position in Mesopotamia was for Britain central to the strategic needs of empire, and commercial interests, including oil, were of secondary moment, nevertheless as time went on the two imperial motives—strategy and commerce—increasingly reinforced each other, particularly as far as oil was concerned. As the first decade of the century drew to a close, the future importance of oil, especially as fuel for the navy, was increasingly appreciated and fears were rising that a great imperial power would be extremely vulnerable if it did not control its own supplies of oil. To be sure, British interests had discovered and controlled Persian oil, but Britain still depended for over four-fifths of her oil on the United States. What if at some time that country became unfriendly? Of the British government departments, the Admiralty took the closest interest in such questions. For the Foreign Office, oil was not the central issue affecting British Mesopotamian strategy, but nevertheless its policy was to support British groups in the search for concessions.

The Turkish Sultan, Abdul Hamid, had in 1888 taken all revenues from mineral and oil concessions in the *vilayets* of Mosul and Baghdad under the 'civil list', thus, in effect, making them his private property. In the same year the first foreign concession relating to oil in Mesopotamia was obtained from him by the Anatolian Railway Company (owned and organized by the Deutsche Bank) in connection with its railway concession in Turkey. Later, when the company received permission to extend its railway to the Persian Gulf, it obtained a promise of special treatment for mining rights. The Baghdad Railway Convention of 1903 gave the German company preferential rights to oil on each side of this proposed railway, and in 1904 the company, on behalf of the Deutsche Bank, obtained a one-year option to explore the area and report. The German company did not meet the conditions imposed for the extension of the option which, after some inconclusive correspondence, was deemed in 1907 to have lapsed.[7] At that time, the Germans let things drift, but later, when others, and particularly the British, represented by the William Knox D'Arcy group,[8] came on the scene, they insisted that their claim under the 1904 contract was still valid. Between 1904 and 1912, amidst considerable confusion and Turkish procrastination, German, British, and American groups jockeyed for position in the negotiations with the Turkish government for oil rights. The D'Arcy group believed that it had established a 'moral' claim, while the German group, knowing its case was very weak, nevertheless maintained that it still had rights under the 1904 contract.

In 1912 it became known that still another group, consisting of the National Bank of Turkey (and an 'English group' associated with it), the Asiatic Petroleum Company (a subsidiary of the Royal Dutch Shell group), and the Deutsche Bank, had joined to form the Turkish Petroleum Company and was seeking a concession in the Mosul area, the National Bank of Turkey having a 50 per cent share and the others 25 per cent each. This group constituted a powerful new rival, including as it did the strong influence of the Deutsche Bank and the Turkish connections of the National Bank which, however, had a British president and several British directors, and in its origins had been strongly supported by the Foreign Office. For the Foreign Office the most worrying aspect of the new group was the presence of the Royal Dutch Shell subsidiary.

The Foreign Office had become convinced, as had other government departments (notably the Admiralty), not only that Britain should control the areas from which she expected to obtain the bulk of her future oil supplies, but that the companies supplying the oil should also be British-controlled. The Royal Dutch Shell group (hereafter simply called 'Shell' according to custom) was composed 60 per cent of the Royal Dutch Petroleum Company and 40 per cent of the Shell Transport and Trading Company (a British company). The group was therefore non-British in the eyes of the Foreign Office and, worse, it was Dutch, for the Dutch were believed to be under strong German influence. Shell and Anglo–Persian were commercial rivals and the former had made several attempts to effect a merger of the two groups. These had been refused by Anglo–Persian, which was much the weaker company financially; there were always fears that Shell, through severe price competition, might some day force the merger it desired.[9]

The prospect that Shell might obtain a strong position in Mesopotamia alarmed the Anglo–Persian company, and its managing director convinced the Foreign Office that access to cheap oil in that area could give Shell an irresistible advantage over Anglo–Persian which eventually could threaten British control not only of Mesopotamian oil, but of Persian oil as well. Anglo–Persian persuaded the Foreign Office to oppose the efforts of the new group to obtain an oil concession. In the event, neither the D'Arcy group nor the TPC was able to obtain the desired concession from the Turkish government, and it eventually became necessary to consider an amalgamation of all the interests to present an agreed offer to the Turks. The Foreign Office finally, and very reluctantly, accepted this necessity. The negotiations were long and convoluted, with the Turkish government, within the British government, and between the TPC and the D'Arcy group, each wanting a controlling position within the company.[10] The outcome was an agreement entitled 'Arrangements for Fusion of the Interests in Turkish Petroleum Concessions of the D'Arcy Group and of the Turkish Petroleum Company' (known briefly as 'The Foreign Office Agreement'), which was signed on 19 March 1914 by representatives of the German government, the British government, the National Bank of Turkey, the Anglo-Saxon Petroleum Company (a Shell subsidiary), the Deutsche Bank, and the D'Arcy group.

Under the Agreement, the 50 per cent interest of the National Bank of Turkey was divided equally between the Deutsche Bank and Anglo-Saxon; new shares equal in number to the existing shares were created and allocated to the D'Arcy group, thus giving the group 50 per cent of the new company. C. S. Gulbenkian obtained a 5 per cent non-voting beneficiary interest, contributed equally by Anglo-Saxon and the D'Arcy group. (Gulbenkian had had a 15 per cent interest in the National Bank of Turkey's share of the original company and had played a considerable role in the negotiations. He had no intention of being manoeuvred aside.) The so-called 'self-denying clause' (later to become the 'Red Line Agreement'), which had been in the original Deutsche Bank–TPC agreement, was maintained. In this clause each of the participating groups undertook not to be interested directly or indirectly in the production or manufacture of crude oil in the Ottoman Empire otherwise than through the Turkish Petroleum Company.

The problem for the reconstituted TPC was now to decide the area over which it should apply for a concession and how far it should attempt to obtain monopoly rights. Old rivalries reappeared and both the Turkish and British governments were preoccupied with the monopoly problem. To grant a monopoly concession was against the Turkish mining law, but the TPC wanted to prevent the emergence of future rivals. The dispute over the validity of the old German concession rights and of the status of the D'Arcy negotiations was revived, for the grounds on which a concession could be demanded needed to be resolved. The story is complicated, but finally on 18 June 1914 the Grand Vizier gave a formal promise of the concession and confirmed it in writing to the British and German ambassadors on 28 June.[11] Negotiations over its form continued, the most difficult point being the desire of the Turkish government to participate in the exploitation of the concession. The issue was not settled before the outbreak of the war, which disrupted the negotiations and changed the positions of all parties involved.

The Ottoman Empire and the Powers at the Outbreak of War

The competing European imperialist powers had obtained, or, it could be said, exacted, a variety of economic concessions from a weak and loosely organized empire. During much of its history it had also been a corrupt empire in which corruption often came near to being a way of life for high administrators and for *fonctionnaires*. A combination of despotism and maladministration had left a weak government to face and bargain with the most advanced countries of the world. These had allowed the Empire to survive in its existing form only because its existence helped to keep the peace among themselves by serving as a buffer state separating rival groups from contact which would increase the risks of conflict.

The seemingly paradoxical situation, in which disputes and friction between the rival holders of and claimants for concessions in the Ottoman Empire were on the point of being resolved when war broke out in 1914, has received less attention than might have been expected. It may be asked what light, if any, this situation throws on disputes over the role of economic factors in imperialism and war. Professor E. M. Earle, an able American historian, in one of the most penetrating histories of the international ramifications of the Baghdad railway, expressed the view that:

> Had the agreement been reached 10 years earlier it might have avoided estrangement between the two nations. Had it come at almost any other time than on the eve of the Great War, it would have been a powerful stimulus to an Anglo–German *rapprochement*.[12]

This statement appeared in 1923, when the materials on the First World War and the events leading to it were inadequate, and the one-sided selection of German documents in *Die Grosse Politik*[13] was being published. In 1926 Luigi Albertini's great work appeared,[14] but was ignored in Germany.

After the Second World War the new documents which came to light, the fresh examination of neglected German critical works written during the First World War, and the evidence of the way in which the documents in *Die Grosse Politik* had been deliberately selected with a view to representing Germany in a favourable light, have shown clearly that Imperial Germany and not Austria–Hungary nor Russia, was chiefly responsible for the outbreak of the First World War. Germany's readiness to join other powers in compromises, and division of interests in areas of economic penetration of the Ottoman Empire between 1910 and the outbreak of war in 1914, does not change this conclusion.

The German government had no desire to provoke closer relations between Russia, France, and Britain by disregarding their several economic interests in the territories of the Ottoman Empire. Far more important to its strategic aims was the further expansion of the German navy and the improvement of its comparative position in relation to the British and French navies. Under existing conditions, German interests would not have been served by alarming other powers and driving them into closer alliance. If, however, Germany had obtained a superior naval position, the arrangement into which she entered in 1913–14 with regard to the Baghdad–Basra section of the railway would not have been allowed to block whatever means German expansionists might have wished to use in the pursuit of their aims.

Thus, it cannot be said that the disputes over rights in the territory of Iraq played a leading role in the genesis of the First World War. Earle's thesis demonstrates the dangers of attempting to estimate the wider significance of a regional event without reference to and examination of the whole ensemble of which it forms a part, and not necessarily the leading part.

These qualifications may be made without minimizing unduly the role of great power rivalries in the Near and Middle East, and in territories in Asia beyond them. The position in Iraq as part of a route between Europe and Asia certainly drew her into what may, in a somewhat different sense from that held by neo-Marxist historians, be described as a clash of imperialisms. Within a wider framework of the Fertile Crescent than Iraq alone, this viewpoint was well developed by Jean Pichon in two studies published in 1937 and 1938.[15] Pichon's viewpoint on the war is closer than Earle's to that which is sustained by recent research. In different ways, however, they both find it necessary to analyse the rival imperialisms of European great powers as the chief influences determining the external relations of the western Orient, and particularly of Syria and Egypt.

Signs of these rivalries had already appeared at the opening of the nineteenth century, but were affecting the coastal and riverain areas of the eastern Mediterranean rather than the greater part of Mesopotamia. The revolution in transport, on land and on sea, in the second half of the nineteenth century, and the second Industrial Revolution, which had opened the way not only to the methods of mass production which raised living standards, but also to those which provided more and more deadly methods of destruction, were drawing more distant inland areas into the scope of these rivalries in the early twentieth century. In any case the future territory of Iraq, whether independent or part of a wider unity, would have been drawn into the conflict among the great powers: its one very short coastline stood at the head of the Gulf and was of commercial and strategic importance to the Indian peninsula and to Britain's maritime interests in Southern and Eastern Asia. India, even if it had been independent, would have been actively interested in questions relating to control of the area: as it was, the historical circumstances which had placed Britain in a dominating role in the Indian peninsula had given a special importance to the geographical position and resources of Mesopotamia.

The questions remain, how far did Germany herself view the Baghdad railway as a political instrument aiming at the expansion of German power over land and sea, and how far as a commercial instrument facilitating the expansion of German trade and international economic influence?

The answer, it would seem, varied with the groups within, and to a lesser extent outside, the German government, which shaped German policy and actions. Certainly von Moltke and his staff looked on the railway as a useful means of moving troops rapidly in a future Middle Eastern campaign. For its own purposes, so also did the Ottoman government. But the German civilian groups and a number of civilian statesmen were concerned primarily with civilian economic aims, and we are inclined to accept Pinon's conclusion as representing the majority viewpoint: 'La ligne de Baghdad n'est pas, pour elle, un outil de conquête, c'est une soupape de dureté par où elle éspère écouler le trop-plein de sa production industrielle'.[16]

European imperialism had already affected many parts of Western Asia and North Africa when the First World War began. Even in areas where formal independence remained, its economic penetration had in some cases limited the autonomy and sovereignty of the state. An important difference between the Middle East and Latin America illustrates well the two different situations in which the peoples of territories subject to imperialist encroachments at this time found themselves. The Latin American countries had to contend with one great power alone in a political sense. Although European countries were economic competitors with the United States, they had long abandoned any attempt at political intervention in the affairs of that continent. In the Near and Middle East (including North Africa), however, a number of European powers were arrayed against each other, not only in economic but also in political competition. This gave the Ottoman Empire and Persia an advantage over the Latin American countries in so far as they could offset one imperialist country against another and derive gains from each in its attempt to outbid the other. But with the advantage inevitably came the risk that the rivalries among the great powers might explode into wars that would draw in the weaker powers of the region and bring contending foreign armies on their soil.

If the Ottoman governments of the period had maintained a more even balance in their policies towards the rival imperialisms, they might have preserved their empire beyond the First World War, and there might never have been a state of Iraq. But, although there were differences within the Ottoman government, those who leaned towards Germany for reasons that went beyond economic considerations prevailed in the end and sealed the fate of the Empire. The decision of Enver Pasha and his associates to plunge their country into the war at Germany's side was destined to snap the slender links that had so long held together an extensive, diverse, and imperfectly co-ordinated imperial structure. On the one side, it was the culmination of a series of official visits during half a century by German and Turkish political leaders and by German technical and military missions to Turkey. On the other, it was the product of far-reaching political changes in the Empire after 1909.

The early promise of the revolution of the Young Turks in 1908 had not been fulfilled. The attempt to transform a corrupt, antiquated, and weak autocracy into a modern representative regime had largely miscarried. The parliament was manipulated by one party. The Council of Ministers merely reflected the Committee of Union and Progress, the three most active members of which were Mehmed Talaat Bey, the President of the Committee and the Minister of the Interior; Enver Pasha, the Minister of War and Chief of the General Staff; and Djemal Pasha, Minister of the Navy and Governor of Constantinople. In later years Iraq was to become familiar with political conditions in which young officers (Enver was only 32 years old at the outbreak of war) who had proved themselves to be adept at conspiracy and the seizure of power, could raise themselves in a single move to posts that enabled them to decide between peace and conflict in the relations of their country with the outside world. The very existence of Iraq as a political state today was made possible by just such an action.

The decision to form an alliance with Germany by the treaty of

2 August 1914, committed the Ottoman Empire to enter the war on the side of the Central Powers.[17] The Grand Vizier had come under the influence of Enver and the German ambassador, who had worked untiringly to commit Turkey to German aims in the Near and Middle East. Enver was the leading spirit in the final act. His complete faith in the ultimate victory of Germany can be better understood in the context of the times than it can be in a more objective view gained in retrospect. The rise and rapid development of Germany after her union in the 1870s and German efficiency in military and economic spheres had greatly impressed the peoples of the less-advanced regions of the world. Talaat and Djemal—himself an opportunist—accepted Enver's designs and the decision was made; only after it had become a *fait accompli* was it communicated to the rest of the Committee of Union and Progress and to other political circles.

The First World War

The sudden onset of the war, and the critical position of the French army and the small British force that joined it, forced attention to questions of short-run interest. But the great French victory on the Marne, which in retrospect appears as the decisive battle of the war, practically stabilized the western front for a long period. And the agreement of the three great powers arrayed against Germany not to make peace separately with the Central Powers inevitably turned attention to some extent towards the political lines of the post-war world. Then Turkey's alliance with Germany, and later her formal entry into the war, raised questions that went beyond the Near East into the Middle East. Pan German plans had laid down ambitious goals for Turkey to pursue: among them was the task of instigating revolts in Persia and Transcaucasia, creating independent states in the latter, and organizing an attack on India through Afghanistan. As General Liman von Sanders pointed out in his memoirs,[18] the expectations which the German Staff had formed of the role of Turkey in the war far exceeded the means at the disposal of Constantinople, both economic and military. Nevertheless, though these aims were not attained, the progress made towards the achievement of some of them, and the knowledge of the direction which the others would have taken if sufficient means had been available to carry them out, reinforced the British government's earlier intentions to obtain control over Mesopotamia, particularly in the south.

Rivalries among the Allies

Pressed by the government of India, even before Turkey had declared war, the British government took the precaution of sending a strong force of Indian troops to Bahrain. The German–Turkish plans, formed by the German General Staff, were designed to seize the oil of lower Mesopotamia, block the Suez Canal and the Straits of Bab-el-Mandeb, and prevent the dispatch of Indian forces to Europe. The government of India pressed early for the occupation of Basra and the head of the Gulf. This operation was approved by London when it became clear that Turkey was entering the war: it was accomplished by a mixed naval and military force. Thus the territory of the future state of Iraq began early to be drawn into the war, confirming what appeared to be its future strategic importance to Britain and the British Empire, from the point of view both of the British navy's fuel supplies and the Empire's network of communications.

From this point onwards, however, serious doubts and differences of opinion arose in Whitehall, and between Whitehall and outlying centres concerned with the direction of the war, on the question how far the Allied campaign in the Near and Middle East should be carried. First, the division of opinion was centred on the general question whether practically all resources should be concentrated on the western front in Europe, where the main enemy attack had come, or whether a considerable force should be directed against a weaker spot on the enemy flank or rear. The expedition to the Dardanelles was then, and has been since, widely regarded in this sense. The same general issue arose in the Second World War and was the subject of sharp controversy between the British and the United States military authorities. In both cases the Middle East, including Iraq, was affected, and, as we shall see, it would hardly be too much to say that, but for the British decision to place large forces in the Middle East and in campaigns in the Fertile Crescent, Iraq in her present boundaries would not have come into existence.

There were two preliminary questions to be considered. First, was the Ottoman Empire to be dismembered? Enver's uncompromising total commitment to Germany and his force of character largely determined the outcome. But in 1915 voices were still heard in Whitehall, in both military and civilian circles, which favoured the retention of a reformed and decentralized Empire as a buffer state. Although Russia as well as France were in the war as allies, British political and military circles had not advanced beyond late nineteenth-century ideas of imperialism. They wished to avoid any common frontier between Russian and British spheres of influence and the early planning in 1915 took account of this aim, scheming to use France as a buffer.

The divergencies of view were not divergencies between those who wished to dismember the Ottoman Empire and those who wished to preserve it as a sovereign state. The opponents of dismemberment envisaged a post-war Ottoman Empire in the different regions of which spheres of influence would be divided or shared among the European great powers—Germany excluded. It would be a satellite, not of a single but of a collective imperialism. These spheres of influence would ensure that each country holding one of them would be protected from economic competition from outside, while at the same time the Ottoman government would undertake to exclude or limit domestic competition. Thus the Mesopotamian scene would not have been changed in principle from that which existed in the first decade of the twentieth century, except that Germany would have been eliminated.

If Turkey had remained strictly neutral, there seems to be little doubt that the Empire would have survived in some such form. But when she entered the war, the Russian government made it clear that after the defeat of Germany it would demand a post-war disposition of the Straits and of Constantinople in accordance with Russian interests. These demands started a competition among the Allies for shares in a dismantled empire. France, which desired the neutralization of the Straits, was inclined to resist Russian demands at the outset, but Britain accepted them in principle with surprising readiness in return for Russian consent to the British annexation of Egypt, which was then under consideration in London, though it was later rejected. This reversal of an historic British policy which had influenced British governments in the direction of war in the past, was a result of growing fear and anxiety over the position of the Russian armies, especially on the Polish front. The Tsar stressed the need to hold out to the Russian people the prospect of returns for the sacrifices they were making. France weighed the consequences more carefully before accepting the Russian demands with qualifications. Her economic, and especially her financial, interests in the Ottoman Empire were greater than Britain's, and her historic role as protector of religious minorities was also greater.[19]

This accord lapsed when Russia abandoned the war. Its repudiation by the Russian government under Lenin was superfluous. But it had played an important part in setting the two leading Western *Entente* Powers on the way to dismemberment of the Ottoman Empire.

Tensions within the Area

Internal and external developments exercised complementary roles in shaping the post-war world. Here again, however, the future of Mesopotamia was bound up with a wider area which was largely peopled by Islamic groups but within which considerable divergencies existed to hinder unity of outlook and solidarity of political aims.

In the early stages of the war the Allies were apprehensive of the proclamation of a *Jihad* (or Holy War) by the Caliph if Turkey came into the war on the side of Germany. German leaders cherished hopes corresponding to the fears of the British and Indian governments. The precise significance of such a measure was not well understood, and the fears on the one side, the hopes on the other, that such a proclamation, when it came, would lead to uprisings among Islamic populations elsewhere were ill-founded. The Allies had issued counter-proclamations emphasizing that they were in no sense acting against Islam, but only against German aims of domination and the Panturanian aims of the Sultan and the Young Turks.

Internal developments of much greater importance in the Ottoman Empire had arisen through the restiveness of the non-Turkish populations in face of Constantinople's centralized autocracy. The conquering Turks had originally subjugated groups that did not share their traditions, their ethnic composition, and many of their modes of life. In Mesopotamia we are concerned mainly with the Arab peoples and with certain minority groups which entered it, mainly from the north and east. But, as we shall see, the extension of the area, later to be included in Iraq, to the north of what was generally considered to be Mesopotamia, gave, and at the time of writing still gives, added importance to non-Arab minorities. But at the outbreak of the war the most important of the non-Turkish peoples desirous either of greater or of complete independence of Turkish rule were the Arabs, particularly in Mesopotamia and Arabia. An Arab nationalist movement had come into existence before the First World War.

Islam claimed to be a universal religion. But its founder and the early disciples who had spread it widely were Arabs, and its sacred scriptures, its laws and precepts, and the documents in its great seats of learning had been written in Arabic. Under the Ottoman Empire the Caliph had ceased to be recognized as the spiritual leader chosen by the *umma* in the line of direct succession to the Prophet and inheriting part of his functions and legitimate powers. Rather he had come to be considered as the political head of Islam whose position had been acquired by the power of his temporal office.

The proclamation of a *Jihad* in November 1914 failed to unite followers of Islam throughout Asia and Africa against Britain and France and behind the Turks and Germans. Within the Ottoman Empire, the disparate elements in different regions were not led into greater unity by the war. On the contrary, the non-Turkish peoples who had sought to maintain and to increase whatever *de facto* local autonomy they already enjoyed, and, in some cases to transform it into *de jure* autonomy as well, suffered instead a setback. The organization of an empire for war, particularly when it had to undertake military operations on its own soil against invasion in some areas and the threat of invasion in others, rendered imperative a greater centralization of control and direction. This was a move in the opposite sense to that of granting greater autonomy to regions inhabited by non-Turkish peoples with a view to reconciling them to acceptance of a place within the Empire.

In fact, however, the movement away from the early ideas of some of the Young Turks towards the grant of more regional autonomy had begun before the war to be displaced by the aim of creating a unified state with equal rights for all and a common patriotism. This in turn encountered the growth of a stronger Turkish nationalism on the one hand, and the intensification of regional sentiments among a large part of the non-Turkish population on the other. From the point of view of the Empire both these tendencies acted in a centrifugal direction, and even without war they would have weakened and possibly dissolved it. The Young Turks who seized power in 1919 were junior military officers bent on the elimination of the corrupt rulers of the day and all their practices. It does not appear that they were moved by any strongly held political doctrines.[20] It would have required abler thinkers and much more experienced politicians to have dealt successfully with the grave questions of integration and disintegration with which they were faced in both the European and the Asian territories of the Empire.

As it was, they assumed power at the least favourable time for the realization of their original aims. The peoples of the European territories of the Empire were in a state of nearly chronic unrest. The Balkan peoples were on the verge of combining to attack Turkey, and two successive wars followed which went badly for the Turks, the second seriously weakening their position on the European side. The European powers viewed the conflict largely from the point of view of the effects produced on their own rivalries. As these wars were fought on European and not on Asian territory, they did not increase the pressure from Constantinople on the people to the same extent as the later wars, fought partly in Anatolia, Mesopotamia, and areas further east, could not fail to do. But the effects of Turkish reverses and losses of territory in Europe were unfavourable to earlier aims of liberalization of the Empire and they strengthened the position of those Young Turks who leaned towards Germany against those who favoured France and to a lesser extent Britain.

Imperial Interests and Local Attitudes

Still, in the earlier planning in Whitehall it was felt that proposals affecting the post-war position of the Middle East which were based on the assumption that the Ottoman Empire would be eliminated might create dissension among the Western Allies. When a committee was formed in April 1915 under Sir Maurice de Bunsen, its proceedings were kept secret and its report was not made available to the public or to research workers until half a century later.[21] As Russia was still in the war in 1915, much of it became obsolete from the point of view of post-war policy. Mesopotamia played a large role in it, again from the point of view of the route to India and to some extent of petroleum. The scheme for an all-British railway from a Mediterranean port to join the Baghdad railway was again raised but not strongly pressed.

The two outstanding features of British and French planning for the post-war period were, first, a readiness to dispose of the territories of the Ottoman Empire without adequate—in some cases without any—consideration of the wishes of the indigenous inhabitants, and, second, an unwillingness of the two countries—particularly marked on the British side—to end their own pre-war rivalries even though they were engaged as allies in a life-and-death struggle with the Central Powers.

At some points British policy was influenced by the regional centres for the direction of war operations in Delhi and Cairo. Moreover, throughout the war the ideas and preconceptions of a number of individuals played a considerable role in, and exerted much influence on, the policies that were followed and the measures that were adopted by the government. Thus, when General Townsend and his mainly Indian forces were sent early in the war to protect the sources of oil and to safeguard Basra, lower Mesopotamia, the Shatt-al-Arab, and Kuwait against Turkish advances southward, he interpreted his own mission more loosely and widely when he found little resistance before him as his advance guards probed the country further north than he had been directed to go. In the past Russia had been feared as the greatest danger to the security of this route to India. Since Russia had now become an ally, the diversion of large military forces to Mesopotamia seemed to the military and to the majority of political leaders in London and Paris to be a diversion to post-war objectives of resources needed to ensure survival against Germany. General Robertson, when he became Chief of the General Staff, saw matters in that light.

When, however, Britain and France (the latter reluctantly) believed that it was necessary to accept Russian demands on Constantinople, competition was intensified among the Allies for annexations and for the creation of 'spheres of influence' over the greater part of the Asian territories of the Ottoman Empire, including all the territory of what now constitutes Iraq. To each of the Allies some areas within the Empire appeared to be of special importance to its interests, economic or strategic. At some points their several priorities overlapped. The ultimate boundaries of each of the successor states to the Empire were determined by compromises which offset some claims against others by mutual concessions based on the different scales of priority of each claimant in accordance with its different geographical and historical relationships.

In the Anglo–French–Russian secret negotiations and agreements in 1915–16, first exposed to the world by the Russian revolutionary government, certain territories ultimately included in Iraq were originally an objective of all three competitive imperialisms.[22] In the early stages, Russia aspired to annex Kurdistan and extend its frontiers beyond Mosul. On no account would Britain have accepted this.

But the Anglo–French secret agreements reached in the negotiations between Mark Sykes and François-Georges Picot between December 1915 and May 1916, which later gave rise to so much controversy among historians as well as politicians, were based on different conceptions of British 'strategy' from those adopted later. However, for the first time they included, in however rudimentary a form, some recognition of the sentiments of the peoples whose territories, according to their plans, were to be so summarily disposed of after the war.

Although British imperialism had a wider geographical range than any other imperialism of its day, it sometimes showed more perception than French imperialism did of the political and not merely the cultural characteristics and aspirations of the colonial peoples.[23] While the French cultural contribution to the Middle East has been far greater than the British, the recognition in a practical sense of a dawning Arab nationalism came more readily from British than from French political circles. This recognition, however, was not in itself a sure guide to the selection of spokesmen and future leaders in the emerging national communities concerned. In the most important case affecting the future state of Iraq, the wisdom of the actual choice has never ceased to be a subject of dispute among historians.

In the early moves leading to the Sykes–Picot agreement, the guiding motive was to encourage an Arab nationalist rising against the Ottoman Empire which would weaken the Turkish leaders and help to eliminate Turkey from the war. But along with this aim went another which was primarily defensive. Constantinople was the seat of the Caliph. The leading personalities in the government of India, as well as many British statesmen, feared the effects on the Islamic world generally of the entry of Turkey into the war. To them it appeared necessary to establish a new centre of the Islamic faith under independent Arab control, and Mecca, the centre from which the Founder of the religion established it firmly, and which was the objective of pilgrims from all Islamic areas of the world, seemed to be the most appropriate choice. But this required the agreement and co-operation of the Sharif of Mecca.

In the negotiations of 1915–17 the British undertaking to the Sharif of Mecca to support the creation of an independent Arab kingdom in and around Arabia created new difficulties. Britain, partly under the influence of Delhi and Cairo, was resolved to establish and maintain a special and exclusive relationship with Mesopotamia. At the same time she had promised to support the establishment of an independent state in the Arab world, and Arab leaders were unlikely to content themselves with one whose writ did not run beyond Arabia proper.

But from the beginning Britain had also resolved to extend her influence, and even her administration, farther than Mesopotamia. While Asquith and Grey had wisely given priority to the Anglo–French *Entente,* the aggressive imperialist ministers and Lord Kitchener envisaged Egypt as a permanent British protectorate in the future and set themselves against any disposition of Palestine that would place it under French influence which would thus reach the borders of Egypt. As long as Russia remained in the war her insistence on an international status for a Palestine area around Jerusalem curbed British ambitions.

The earlier plans for partitioning the Middle East in accordance with the respective interests of Britain and France as they conceived them at the time provided for a line extending from a point on the eastern boundary of a sector to be created around Jerusalem to near Lake Urmia to the north-east on the Persian frontier. This line was to divide two spheres of influence in Mesopotamia, of which the northern part, including Aleppo, Homs, and Damascus on its western side and Mosul and Ruwanduz on its eastern, was to be French; while the southern part, bounded by a line which appeared convex when looked at from the north, and which divided it from an independent Arabia, was to be British. North and west of the French sphere and east of the British were areas marked for direct administration by the two countries respectively. The north-east part of the French border was to face an area of eastern Turkey to be annexed by Imperial Russia.

This scheme of partition, which was the subject of secret agreements in 1915 and 1916, reflected dominant historic and strategic conceptions of the time. The British aim to control lower Mesopotamia directly came from the desire to safeguard a possible route to

India which, it was hoped, would become more important in the future, and, to a lesser extent, from a concern for the safety of the sources of oil for the British navy.

The French preoccupation with Syria and Lebanon was a compound of historic links: first, of those arising out of the role of France as protector of Christian groups, acknowledged from time to time since the days of Charlemagne and Haroun al-Rashid and, on a larger scale, in the convention of 1536 between the Sultan and Francis I; and second, of contemporary links between the silk merchants of Lyons and the sources of supply of raw silk.[24] In Lebanon, the French government had led an Allied intervention in 1860 after the massacre of Christians by the Druze in the Lebanon and fanatical Muslim sects in Damascus, and had landed forces in Beirut to ensure the safety of surviving Christians.

Russian claims were of wide scope, embracing not only Constantinople and the new zones around it but also territories in the east and north-east of Turkey. Russian suspicions were aroused by the extension of the area of the French zone, which included part of the future Iraq, to the Persian frontier. But in compensation the assigned Russian zone, which extended south from the Black Sea to near Diarbekir, was enlarged.[25] If Imperial Russia had survived the war, she would have been a much closer neighbour to Iraq than revolutionary Russia became.

The Sykes–Picot agreement, and the later changes reached with difficulty, which largely displaced it, envisaged two areas in one of which British, and in the other French, influence would be predominant, and in each of which a part would be reserved for direct British or French administration while the other would be left free for direct Arab administration. But in the original agreement, Mosul, where the prospects for oil were held to be great, was included in the French sphere of interest. This aspect of the agreement very much disturbed the Admiralty and others, including, of course, the Anglo–Persian Oil Company, but the insistence of the War Office on the importance of inserting a wedge between the British zone and Russia was the decisive consideration.[26]

The turning-point came with the collapse of the Imperial Russian armies and the withdrawal of Russia from the war in 1917. That event, which created great military difficulties for the Western members of the alliance against Germany, gradually led to the disintegration of the earlier plans for the partition of Asia Minor and the Fertile Crescent. The replacement of three competitive imperialisms by two gave opportunities for Britain to seek radical changes in the form of partition. Britain and France were relieved at the nullification of the Russian demand for Constantinople. But a fundamental rift between the Allies came when British advisers in London, Cairo, Delhi, and Mesopotamia disagreed among themselves and tended to undermine Anglo–French agreements without adequate consultation with France. Many of them unilaterally assumed that the former agreements were rendered obsolete as a whole when Russia left the scene.

The initiative towards the change in the British position came partly from personalities in the governments in Cairo and Delhi. In Whitehall the Foreign Office was more concerned to maintain Anglo–French solidarity in a war on which the survival of the British Empire depended and in which France had withstood the greater part of the German offensive, but the pressure grew from those wanting to ensure that Mosul with its oil should be secured under British influence. Not only did the Admiralty and the Anglo–Persian oil company now press more strongly than ever in this direction, but Sir Maurice Hankey, Secretary to the Imperial War Cabinet, the Chief of Air Staff, and others added their voices. Although Balfour, the Foreign Secretary, felt that to insist on obtaining the oil lands as a 'War Aim' was too imperialistic, he nevertheless accepted that the Sykes–Picot agreement was out of date. Moreover, he held that there was a 'vital necessity . . . to secure a settlement which would not endanger our facilities for obtaining oil from this region'.[27]

The Anglo–French declaration, issued four days before the Armistice, could reasonably be interpreted as committing the two countries to support the real independence of an Arab state or Arab states after the war. It explicitly stated the Anglo–French aim to be ' . . . the complete and final liberation of the peoples who have so long been oppressed by the Turks, and the setting up of National Governments and administrations that shall derive their authority from the free exercise of the initiative and choice of the indigenous populations'.[28] It was indeed difficult later to maintain that the subsequent actions of either country were consistent with this. But an advance was certainly made at the Peace Conference.

Imperialism and colonialism did not die during the First World War. But a step was taken on the road towards decolonization. The elaboration and adoption of the Mandates system under the League of Nations represented progress. Even if some of the principles behind it would not command assent today, they were certainly a retreat from annexation, at least in respect of Class A and B Mandates. A leading military officer of liberal outlook expressed the changed mood of the times when he said:

> There are indications that the attractions which are keeping us in the Mosul *vilayet* are the possibilities of developing oil fields and

> of opening up railway communications with Persia, but we no longer live in times when the occupation of territory for the sake of painting the map red, or for the possible benefit of oil and railway concessionaires is held to be desirable, while even the most ardent imperialist does not suggest that we should absorb Caucasia.[29]

Both Britain and France, however, adhered after the war to their conceptions of national and imperial interests, even when these were clearly not in line with the expressed wishes of the inhabitants of the areas affected. The elimination of Germany from the competitive imperialisms in the Middle East was to reduce but not to eliminate the great power rivalries and their impact on the indigenous people of the area.

Sir Edward Grey, British Foreign Secretary from 1905 to 1916, had shown a scrupulous regard for understanding with France and for her position on Syria, but among many officials in other centres, including Sir Mark Sykes and Colonel T. E. Lawrence, there was much dislike of France and many pressures in favour of ignoring earlier engagements Britain had entered into with France. Sykes had also become an enthusiast for the Zionist cause, and when Britain espoused this cause in the Balfour Declaration in 1917, she violated the earlier Allied agreement on the internationalization of Jerusalem. In a number of British circles it was assumed that Russian defection had relieved her of any obligation towards France. For the rest of the century Britain has had reason to regret her action and France to be thankful for having escaped direct embroilment in the Palestine controversy which brought such disaster to the Middle East: but this could not have been foreseen at the time, and the survival of ancient suspicions of her neighbour, even after she had become an indisputable ally, still left Britain anxious to exclude France from influence in territories adjoining Egypt.

French historic links with Syria had given French statesmen and some French interests the feeling that a special relationship should take a practical form after the fall of the Ottoman Empire. In Syria, both Syrian and Arab nationalist movements had looked on France before the war as the supreme example of a country upholding freedom and the rights of peoples everywhere. At a conference in Paris in 1913 a warm reception had been given to Syrian aspirations for independence. In some French circles it was not appreciated at the end of the war that Syrian attachment to French culture and French democracy did not carry with it a willingness to come under French rule, even with the safeguards of a Mandate. Moreover, the population of Syria, a Mediterranean country with coastal peoples, contained more influential Christian minorities and larger non-Arab groups than that of Iraq.[30] French opinion may have given more weight to these minorities than to the large Muslim majority.

This situation may be compared with that of the future Iraq, in which Britain had no comparable cultural links but only riverain trading interests. However, the addition of a substantial area of Kurdistan, hardly a part of Mesopotamia, and the implantation of a displaced group of Assyrians, created minorities which, like the Christian minorities in Syria and Lebanon, were more favourably disposed to a mandatory power because of its possible protective role, than were the Arab majorities.

It seems clear, however, that objections to French rule, mandatory or otherwise, were only one manifestation of a general objection to the substitution of any European or outside rule for that of the Ottoman Empire, from which they were glad to escape. Many British writers have tended to attempt to justify, either directly or by implication, British, while condemning French, intervention. The contrast between the future Iraq and the future Syria and Lebanon, from the point of view of their assignment to the influence and, for a time, to the rule, of great powers after the war, lies chiefly in the occupation of a large part of Iraq during the war itself by a British and British–Indian army and the establishment of a framework of administration in some areas. Some British politicians and writers have maintained that the British military campaigns, with their losses in lives and materials in Mesopotamia and the Fertile Crescent, entitled Britain to have the final word. The French, they argued, have no such claim. This viewpoint overlooks the reason for the discrepancy: France placed far greater forces on the western front against Germany—the decisive area of the war. The campaign in Mesopotamia was not part of the planning of the Supreme Military Command and General Robertson, the Chief of Staff, had not favoured it. To France, therefore, the British attitude seemed indefensible.

Such were the conflicts which, in large part, determined the nature of the regime which was to govern Iraq until 1958.

Notes

1 See Zaki Salah, *Mesopotamia (Iraq) 1600–1914: a Study in British Foreign Affairs* (Baghdad, 1957), for a valuable introduction to the English reader. Space does not permit listing of the large amount of material that is available on this subject, but further references can be found in the Bibliography.

2 The best general view of the projects for the invasion of India is contained in Jean Pichon, *Les origines orientales de la guerre mondiale* (Paris, 1937) which contains an excellent chart of the projected routes, and a concise historical and geographical analysis.

3 Roger Lambelin, *L'Egypte et l'Angleterre vers l'indépendance de Mohamed Ali au roi Fouad* (Paris, 1922). This is a particularly valuable work with useful sidelights on the Fertile Crescent.

4 Tigris navigation was long dominated, but not monopolized, by the Euphrates and Tigris Steam Navigation Company, a British company which had been founded by H. B. Lynch in 1859. Partly because of Lynch's willingness to co-operate with German interests in the Baghdad Railway Company before the First World War and thus threaten a British monopoly, the company lost favour with the British government, which subsequently arranged with Inchcape to extend its interest in river shipping. See S. A. Cohen, *British Policy in Mesopotamia, 1903–1914* (Oxford, 1976), pp. 256–61. See also Helmut Mejcher, 'Oil and British Policy towards Mesopotamia, 1914–18', *Middle Eastern Studies,* Vol. 8, No. 3 (October 1972) for a discussion of Inchcape's private interest in shipping and his public position in oil matters, which raised problems for the British government after the war.

5 'Liberal' and 'Conservative' in the British political party sense.

6 For a discussion of the contribution of foreign capital and enterprise in this context see Orhan Kurmus, *The Role of British Capital in the Economic Development of Western Anatolia, 1815–1913* (unpublished Ph.D thesis in the University of London, 1974).

7 Much of this discussion of the scramble for oil concessions and confusions of oil policy in Turkey and Mesopotamia is based on Marian Kent's detailed, scholarly, but very readable book, *Oil and Empire: British Foreign Policy and Mesopotamian Oil, 1900–1920* (London, 1976). The reader is referred to that book for references to official documents and other material supporting the interpretation accepted here. See pp. 20–1 for discussion of the point in text. See also Helmut Mejcher, *Imperial Quest for Oil* (Oxford, 1976). This book covers much the same material as Kent, but was published after this chapter was completed.

8 D'Arcy had obtained the Persian concession in 1901 and established the Anglo–Persian Oil Company in 1909. The Burmah Oil Company subsequently had taken shares in Anglo–Persian when D'Arcy ran into financial difficulties. If D'Arcy had obtained the Mesopotamian concession, therefore, Britain would have secured control of the oil in both Iraq and Persia.

9 The British government took a controlling interest in the Anglo–Persian Oil Company in 1914 and the Admiralty made a long-term supply contract with it, partly to ensure the company's financial viability, and partly to remove any risk that it might be absorbed into some other company (and Shell was the only likely candidate at the time). See Kent, op. cit., p. 48.

10 It is important to note that it was the D'Arcy group and not the Anglo–Persian Oil Company (which was to come under British government control in 1914) that obtained shares in the TPC. The British government was not itself involved in the TPC and took pains to make clear that APOC funds would not be used to finance oil developments. Had the British government taken a direct financial interest in the TPC, the political objections would have been serious: ibid., p. 100.

11 Throughout all the negotiations the British were in a strong position because the Turkish government urgently needed finance and to this end wanted to increase their customs duties, for which British permission was required. The Foreign Office refused to conclude the financial agreements much wanted

by the Turks until the concession issue was settled. This was the chief reason why the British interests obtained the favourable treatment they did.

12 E. M. Earle, *Turkey, The Great Powers, and The Baghdad Railway: a Study in Imperialism* (New York, 1924), p. 264. For more detail on the question of the Baghdad railway based on more recent papers, see Cohen, op. cit.

13 *Die grosse Politik der europäischen Kabinette, 1871–1914,* ed. J. Lepsius, *et al.* (Berlin, 1922–27).

14 Luigi Albertini, *Le origine della guerra del 1914* (Milan, 1926).

15 Jean Pichon. op. cit.; and *Le Partage du Proche-Orient* (Paris, 1938). Like most historians of the present time Pichon recognized fully the dominating role of Germany in precipitating the First World War, and he devoted a chapter to 'Le plan pan-germaniste' which, like Fritz Fischer, Immanuel Geiss, and others, he regards as the key to an understanding of the genesis of the war.

16 René Pinon, *L'Europe et L'Empire Ottoman* (Paris, 1913), p. 335.

17 In the event of Russian intervention, 'le causus foederis vis-à-vis l'Autriche-Hongrie . . . entrer également en vigeur pour la Turquie'. The German military mission was to be left at the disposition of Turkey on the understanding that it would be assured an effective influence on the conduct of the war. For a well-organized account of events see M. Larcher, *La guerre turc dans la guerre mondiale* (Paris, 1926), pp. 37–8.

18 L. von Sanders, *Five Years in Turkey* (London, 1927; trans.).

19 The French and British positions are well summarized in A. Pingaud, *Histoire diplomatique de la France pendant la grande guerre* (Paris, 1938).

20 See especially the excellent work of Bernard Lewis, *The Emergence of Modern Turkey,* 2nd edn. (Oxford, 1968).

21 Report of the Committee on Asiatic Turkey, which was set up by Asquith, the Prime Minister, under the chairmanship of Sir Maurice de Bunsen. It reported at the end of June 1915. This report was strongly influenced by a memorandum of Sir Arthur Hirtzel, Secretary of the Political and Secret Department, India Office. Hirtzel suggested a boundary for Mesopotamia which would include Mosul. See Kent, op. cit., pp. 120–1; and J. Nevakivi, *Britain, France and the Arab Middle East, 1914–1920* (London, 1969).

22 There is an extensive literature on this subject, some of which is cited in the Bibliography. See especially, *Les Documents diplomatiques sécrets russes* and the works of M. Paléologue, Jean Pichon, Viscount Grey, Elie Kedourie, Jukka Nevakivi, and for implications for oil, M. Kent.

23 Possibly this characteristic contributed to the comparatively peaceful course of decolonization in British dependencies in the second half of the twentieth century.

24 See particularly Dominique Chevalier, 'Lyon et la Syrie en 1919; les bases d'une intervention', *Revue historique,* Oct.–Dec. 1960.

25 See Pingaud, op. cit., Vol. 3, pp. 230–1.

26 See Kent, op. cit., pp. 120f.

27 Quoted Kent, op. cit., p. 124.

28 Quoted J. C. Hurewitz, *Diplomacy in the Near and Middle East: a Documentary Record* (Toronto and New York, 1958), Vol. II, p. 30.

29 Maj.-Gen. Sir Frederick Maurice, 'Our Commitments in Mesopotamia', *The New Europe* (18 March 1920), p. 227.

30 On these questions see the viewpoints in Abdulla Sfer Pacha, *Le mandat français et les traditions français en Syrie et au Liban* (Paris, 1922); Nadra Moutran, *La Syrie de demain* (Paris, 1916); Berthe-Georges Gaulis, *La question arabe* (Paris, 1930).

3 The Formation of the State: Mandate and Independence 1918–32

The Ottoman Empire had irretrievably collapsed. The Anglo–French Declaration had unambiguously pledged support for the independence of the Arab peoples. The British were in effective occupation of much of Mesopotamia as well as of Mosul further to the north into which, in order to strengthen their bargaining position,[1] they had moved after the armistice of 30 October 1918 signed at Mudros with the Turks. At the same time, Britain had a number of international commitments and imperial interests for which acceptable arrangements would have to be made. Consistent solutions had to be sought within a short time for an intricate set of problems within four interrelated areas. First, the establishment and operation of an internal administrative and political structure in the area for which Britain was now responsible; second, the determination of the international political status of the new state; third, the determination and international acceptance of the boundaries of the new state; and fourth, the protection of British economic interests in the area, especially oil.

Decisions taken in any one of these areas affected the others and the interests of many groups were involved, including British, French, American, the League of Nations as an institution, the Iraqi government, and the very divergent interests of the different peoples in Iraq (especially Shia, Sunni, Kurds, and Assyrians) as well as private Iraqi economic interests. Not surprisingly, many of the difficulties in formulating and executing British policy arose out of conflicts of interests within Britain itself: among government departments, among governments of other areas in the Empire, among private economic interests, and between the latter and the government. Running through all of these for all countries, of course, were the ambitions and idiosyncrasies of politicians! It is impossible to find a solution for an over-determined set of simultaneous equations.

British Administration

The first priority of any occupying civilian authority following the termination of conflict is to ensure the maintenance of law and order while dispensing as quickly as possible with military measures of enforcement. Although military responsibility for the area was not formally ended until October 1920, in practice the British Civil Commissioner administered the country. The problems were enormous and British administrators and their families flowed into the country to remould the bureaucracy along more efficient lines, to establish a tax and revenue system, to set up fair and accessible courts of justice and ensure an appropriate police organization, to organize the necessary public services and the thousand and one aspects of civil life essential in a reasonably modern state.

But Iraq was not yet 'reasonably modern' and the British attempts at efficiency, the efforts of administrators to change the established and ancient ways of doing things, to reduce the customary as well as unacceptable corruption, and in general to modernize the processes of government were not particularly well received by the local peoples, and especially by the local notables whose authority, customs, and 'perks' were thus undermined. No matter how self-sacrificing and devoted the administrators were, they were alien, infidel, non-Arabs.[2] Much of their work was, of course, appreciated and many a close friendship was made. But clearly Iraq would not long accept administration by foreigners. Nor did the British particularly want to administer her with British personnel—and funds. The process of turning as much as possible over to Iraqis with British 'advisers' went very fast indeed, as did the effort to raise local revenue to finance the government. On the other hand, some of the minority groups in the country, particularly the Kurds and Assyrians, feared an Arab administration and preferred the British—with good cause, as we shall see.

The task of establishing a reasonable administration went remarkably well under the circumstances,[3] but it would have been much easier and more acceptable had so many Iraqis not feared that the British were in the process of consolidating their own position as rulers of the country instead of arranging the promised independence. Rumours that a 'mandate system' was being worked out in Paris which would effectively leave the country under foreign tutelage for an indefinite period were spreading and creating unrest. The well-meaning paternalism of Sir A. T. Wilson, who was in charge until the return of Sir Percy Cox as High Commissioner in October 1921, combined with his insensitive attitudes towards Iraqi politicians and Iraqi aspirations, intensified a popular dissatisfaction which would have grown in any case as the impossibility of satisfying the post-war economic, and the difficulties in the way of meeting post-war political, expectations became increasingly evident.

The economic problems of Britain after the end of the war reinforced the general British policy that her overseas territories should pay their own way. The administration in Iraq, running the country from Baghdad, was short of funds and it made every effort to increase the efficiency of tax collection. Although taxation was undoubtedly fairer and less arbitrary than that of previous regimes, its very efficiency intensified all the other new pressures on the people to change familiar ways, and the subsequent resentment could only be ameliorated if the people clearly saw that large and immediate benefits were forthcoming. This was not possible in the nature of things. The British administrators became a visible and popular scapegoat for all grievances. Arrests and deportation of political 'troublemakers' relieved immediate problems but were no solution.

On the political side, the paternalistic Wilson wanted to demonstrate that the Iraqis preferred British tutelage to immediate independence. He thought that the Anglo–French Declaration of November 1918 which held out the promise of independent freely chosen governments was a disaster. He organized a confused and not entirely fair plebiscite to test local opinion; from the results it was concluded that the people wanted a united Iraq (i.e., including Mosul, over which there was still diplomatic dispute), with an Arab ruler, but under British control.

On 28 April 1920 Britain was awarded a Mandate over Iraq under the San Remo Agreement. This immediately provoked widespread protest in the country and a serious insurrection broke out in July, which was not completely suppressed until early 1921.[4] Nevertheless, the British High Commissioner moved formally to terminate the military government and rapidly to set up an Iraqi government and civil service. The search for a suitable Arab ruler to install in Iraq finally settled on the Amir Faisal, son of Sharif Hussain of Hijaz.

Faisal had taken part in the Arab Revolt and had represented his father at the Peace Conference in Paris to plead unavailingly for Syrian independence. He had resisted the French in Damascus in Syria and lost. The British persuaded him to make himself available for the Iraqi throne and promised, in response to his refusal to accept it under a Mandate, that the relationship between the two countries would take the form of a treaty of alliance. The British then persuaded the Iraqi Council of Ministers to nominate him and the choice was confirmed by a popular referendum. Although the hand of Britain was very evident in the arrangements, and there was therefore much suspicion and criticism in Iraq, the evident capability and personal qualities of Faisal soon made him acceptable to the Iraqis. In August 1921 he was officially installed as King Faisal I.

The constitutional position of the territory, in Longrigg's words, was as yet

> . . . singularly unclear. Its elements were a Turkish sovereignty still existing, though dormant: an unratified Mandate, accepted by Great Britain but unwelcome to Iraq itself: a constitutional monarchy, with no Constitution; and an intended treaty relationship with Great Britain, but as yet no treaty.[5]

The Mandate posed the most serious political problem.

The Mandate in Principle and Practice

None of the post-war plans for the dissolution of the Ottoman Empire and the disposition of its territories took adequate account of the movements of opinion and the changes in sentiment among the peoples of the area. The early years of the twentieth century had marked the peak of European imperialism and colonization. Almost all the southern hemisphere as well as North and Central America had already fallen under the domination of European peoples and their descendants. But the establishment of Iraq came at a time when the tide was on the turn.

The First World War had demonstrated the necessity of far-reaching changes in the international order and gave an impetus to the change that was to reach a decisive stage from the middle of the century onwards. President Wilson, with his emphasis on the necessity of permitting the self-determination of peoples, had made a deep impression, which had spread at least to the educated minorities in dependent as well as independent countries. This impression was strengthened by the work of outstanding British and French liberal thinkers, some of them with wide experience of less-developed lands. Resistance to imperialism had been strengthened. Hence, the residual imperialist ambitions among the European powers at the end of the First World War had to contend with an outflowing tide which represented a reversal of the historical trend of the preceding half-century in the relations of Europe with Asia and Africa.

In this changed political atmosphere the Mandate System was devised. The system was based on the view that the peoples in a large proportion of Africa and a smaller proportion of Asia who had been in a dependent or colonial status were entitled to self-determination, but as yet were insufficiently developed in a material and educational sense to stand wholly by themselves in the modern world. A great power would therefore be given a Mandate by the League of Nations over each of the territories brought within the system.

In principle, the system should have been applied to all existing colonies and dependencies, but for the most part the colonial powers were not prepared to accept such a far-reaching change. Two leading questions with which the Allies were faced at the end of the war, however, opened the way for an application of the system in framing the structure of the new world after the war. The first of these was the disposition of the German colonies in Africa and the second the establishment of new states in the Fertile Crescent after the disintegration of the Ottoman Empire.

In both cases the rivalries of the great powers played a leading part. But the changed temper of the post-war world precluded the Allies from dividing the German colonies among themselves and then annexing them outright. As Professor F. H. Hinsley has pointed out,[6] and as General Sir Frederick Maurice emphasized in relation to colonization at the time, public opinion was playing a larger part in international relations around the turn of the century. The changed sentiment was tempered by a form of paternalism which, though it became less acceptable later, was sincerely held at the time; it was one which placed mandated territories under the tutelage of great powers or their offshoots while they were being prepared for independence.

The African mandated territories merely underwent a change of supervisory power, though, except perhaps in practice for the Class C Mandates, they now came under new rules. Thus the change represented a rise in their status, a liberalization of 'colonialism', without changes in boundaries. But in the Fertile Crescent the adoption of the Mandate System represented a more radical change. For the peoples concerned it was a passage from loosely integrated territorial areas of administration, corrupt and inefficient by modern standards, leaving opportunities for evasion by many of its regulations and impositions, to separate political states with defined boundaries and more modern types of administration largely following European lines, bringing greater efficiency and touching the life of the individual at more points. The area of administration was also widely extended into fields hitherto only scantily developed in the Ottoman Empire.

The movements loosely described as 'nationalist' were unevenly spread among the Arab peoples. Nationalism in the full sense probably animated only a comparatively small number of people, mainly among the more educated classes which had some acquaintance with European conditions. But it did not follow that the rest of the population was willing to accept a colonial status. On the contrary, the absence of a sentiment corresponding to nationalism as it was conceived in European circles was consistent with a strong desire for independence, or perhaps more precisely, an opposition to foreign interference, especially when this came from distant peoples of different religions and cultures. These sentiments harmonized, up to a point, with those felt by the educated classes: both were directed towards independence from the great European powers, and this was the dominant aim after the First World War.

But all these points of view left ambiguities in respect to their practical application. The sentiment of Arab nationalism cut across divisions of culture and of interests within the Arab world, which was spread over a wide geographical area. Communications between and even within many parts of the area were slow and difficult. Transport of goods was costly, and the routes restricted. It was inevitable that, in spite of the desire in all the areas to be free of foreign domination, there should be divergencies of interest and differences of outlook which would render impossible the creation of a single Arab state after the end of the Ottoman Empire.

But the philosophy behind the Mandate System was unfamiliar and extremely distasteful to the Arabs. It might be true that large sections of the Arab peoples appeared to be little more developed than some of the groups in tropical Africa. But the Arab leaders, and the political class generally, felt themselves part of a great Islamic heritage with an ancient history associated with the very birth of human civilization. They resented domination from European powers and were fully prepared to take charge of their own destinies.

It cannot, however, be said that any agreement could have been found among the leaders of the various parts of this vast area on the nature and the nomination of a single government for all the Arab peoples in the Ottoman Empire that had collapsed. In Arabia a civil war was raging at the time when the Iraq Mandate was under discussion; one regime was displaced by another, representing a different form of Islam. As it was after the Second World War, so it was after the First: independence frequently coincided with internal conflicts associated with the passage from older to more modern economic and political structures. These conflicts made it all the more difficult to obtain agreement on the appropriate government to establish at the time of independence.

Nor, as subsequent history has shown, could the differences among the different groups of Arab peoples in the Fertile Crescent alone be overlooked. That they are by no means a matter of past history we have had ample opportunity to note over the decades since the end of the Second World War. To them must be added the problems of minorities, both non-Arab minorities and minorities resulting from past theological controversies in Islam and, to a lesser extent for present purposes, in Christianity.

When all these aspects of the post-war problem are taken into account, it would be difficult to suppose that the aftermath to independence would have followed a smooth course even if the Allies had kept to the assurances in the Anglo–French Declaration. Moreover, the Mandate System, however little it may have been liked by Arabs, did put limits on the periods and the types of tutelage by the mandatory powers and made them responsible to the international community. It subjected the political leaders to cross-examination and supplied information on internal affairs.

There is, however, no doubt that neither the idea of British rule, even for a limited period, nor the idea of a League of Nations Mandate, appealed to the Iraqi political leaders or to the Iraqi public. The peoples of Syria, Lebanon, and even Turkey had long been familiar with international intervention and regulation of special aspects of their political life. But the mountains of the north and the Great Syrian Desert on the east stood between these areas and Iraq. The opposition to the application of the Mandate System to Iraq was therefore in no way surprising, even when it could be argued that an earlier start and more rapid progress in modernization could be achieved by accepting it for a limited period.

Iraqi opposition, together with the restraints placed on 'imperialism' as a result of changes in the international political atmosphere, which were powerfully reflected in official attitudes within Britain, effectively destroyed the possibility of an acceptable application of the principle of the Mandate in Iraq. As we have seen, King Faisal refused the throne unless assurances were given that he would not remain ruler of a country under a mandate. One of the first moves of Britain, therefore, was to fulfil her promise and establish treaty relationships with Iraq.

This 'fulfilment' took the form of a twenty-year treaty which effectively incorporated in a different form the terms of the Mandate, but with no mention in it of the Mandate. Faisal complained 'This is not the kind of treaty which Mr. Churchill promised me in London',[7] but, with pragmatic calculation, he accepted it in October 1922 and weathered the subsequent political outcry, fully intending to continue to press for the independence the country demanded. The following year the treaty was revised, its term being reduced from twenty to four years, for by this time the British were also beginning to want to reduce their responsibilities in Iraq (as well as the cost of their involvement). The treaty was formally accepted by an elected Constituent Assembly, which opened in March 1924, but with much stormy opposition and in a somewhat irregular manner. Further unsatisfactory attempts at compromise over treaties were to be made during the remainder of the decade. But before discussing these and the progress of Iraq to independence, we must turn to the question of the boundaries of Iraq, which raised thorny issues but clearly had to be definitely settled before the geographical area over which the new government's writ was to run could become clear.

The Geographical Extent of the State

The original aim of giving preponderant influence and perhaps administrative supervision over Mesopotamia to Great Britain had to be given content in precise geographical terms when it became a practical possibility in the post-war world. In the north the state of Iraq, when it was eventually delimited, included more than was included in the term Mesopotamia. As we saw earlier, Mosul and an appreciable part of the northern territory ultimately included in Iraq, were earmarked for French administration or influence in the days when it was expected that Russia, with westward claims of her own, would be a powerful force in determining the shape of the Near and Middle East after the war. It was largely on British initiative that this undertaking was adopted, not indeed out of consideration for the leading ally in the operations which broke the mighty German offensives on the Marne and at Verdun, but rather as a British device to avoid what was expected to be direct boundary contact with post-war Russia by having French-controlled territory as a buffer between Britain and Russia.

When it became clear that the new Russia would recede to the east, Britain's imperial ambitions in the area were reawakened and under the dubious claim that her engagements made in 1916 with France were rendered inoperative by the collapse of Imperial Russia, she determined to evade them. The Quai d'Orsay resisted, but when the question became the subject of direct discussions between Lloyd George and Georges Clemenceau, the latter gave it a priority lower than the vital issue of providing for France's future protection along the Rhine. There can be no doubt that Clemenceau was correct in his scale of priorities, but the support which he believed that he had gained on European security was not forthcoming, either in the 1920s or in the critical 1930s when British governments refused to co-operate in any French measures to check Hitler's advances. Such are the 'ironies of history' that led to the transfer of a considerable section of territory from Turkish to British instead of French influence and determined the northern boundaries of Iraq.

But if France and the new Russia had given up their claims to the

Mosul area, the new Turkey which had emerged from the dissolution of the Ottoman Empire had not, and the determination of the boundaries of Iraq was a long and arduous task.

The decision by the Council of the League of Nations to award a mandate, and its formal acceptance, did not in all cases imply that a definitive settlement had been made of all its frontiers. In some cases, difficult problems arose over the precise boundary lines to be drawn in deserts. In other areas disputes remained over the lines to be drawn between the older states and the new states being created on their frontiers.

In the case of Iraq both types of difficulty and dispute arose in acute forms. The deserts were the habitations and the transit routes of nomadic tribes. Both their seasonal movements and their trading routes often crossed the lines where boundaries would be drawn. Treaty arrangements were concluded with the new Wahabi regime in Saudi Arabia to enable the Muntafiq, Dhafir, and Amarat tribes to enter the new state of Iraq. The Iraq–Syria frontier was the subject of negotiations between the British and French High Commissioners in 1922–23, dealing especially with conflicts between the tribes and with questions of the waters of the Euphrates and Tigris, but final agreement was not reached until 1932.

The Turks presented a far more serious problem. British views of the northern frontiers of Iraq had been radically changed by the discussion between Lloyd George and Clemenceau. The French agreed to give up their claims to the *vilayet* of Mosul in exchange for British concessions in Syria and a share in any Mosul oil concession. As we have seen, the British had proceeded to occupy Mosul after the armistice at Mudros in order to strengthen their post-war bargaining position. But the inclusion of the former *vilayet* of Mosul within Iraq was resisted by the new Turkey, which had triumphantly emerged from the conflict over the Treaty of Sèvres and the war with Greece. The question, well defined by Arnold Toynbee, was

> . . . whether the new frontier should be drawn at the southern extremity of the former Mosul vilayet, along the Diyalah and the Jabal Hamrin, or at its northern extremity, either along the actual line of its former administrative boundary or along one of the parallel ranges to the north or the south of it, or should cut across the vilayet along some intermediate line.[8]

The unsettled conditions in the area, the movements of Kurdish and, to a smaller extent, Assyrian groups, and their disputes, both with the Turkish authorities on one side of the *de facto* line of separation and with the occupying British forces on the other, created a great variety of what may be termed sub-conflicts, on which adjudication was sometimes extremely difficult. The number of Europeans with knowledge of the peoples of the area was extremely small. A small group of British officers, with a representative of the Foreign Office, established excellent relations with the Kurds among whom they lived for a time.[9] They developed a genuine interest in the Kurds and their wellbeing. In turn, many Kurds in the area came to trust Britain and to look to her for protection against Arabs as well as Turks.

From a more general point of view, however, the opposing forces among the powers were concerned with what they conceived to be their own national interests in the disputed areas. Both Turkey on the one side, and the new Iraqi leaders as well as the British on the other, believed that possession of the area was essential to their security. Certainly a Turkey whose southern borders extended to the borders of the *liwa* of Mosul would have had easy direct access to the Mesopotamian plain.

To the mandatory power and to the emerging indigenous government it seemed of the greatest importance to establish the boundary on a line less vulnerable from the point of view of the new Iraqi state. But the new Turkey, having successfully challenged and subsequently nullified the Treaty of Sèvres, was not disposed to yield lightly, and the negotiations were difficult,[10] for the British position had aroused the fury of Kemal Pasha (later Atatürk) whose first impulse was to resist it by force.

Attempts at direct agreement between Britain and Turkey failed and the issue came before the League of Nations, which in the 1920s was a more effective instrument than the United Nations became after the Second World War since it did not suffer from domination by two rival and disproportionately large powers. Both Britain and, after some hesitation, Turkey agreed to accept its verdict.

The League dispatched a Commission of Inquiry to Mosul to examine the territories in dispute. Taking a broad view of their task, they endeavoured to balance a number of different considerations, which included both the economic effects of hypothetical alternative boundary lines, and also their effects on minority groups in the areas concerned. The different criteria in the two cases sometimes pointed in opposite directions: for example, the city of Mosul was predominantly Arab, but in the surrounding country Kurds outnumbered Arabs. A line drawn on an ethnic criterion would therefore have separated Mosul from its hinterland.

To appreciate the strenuous resistance of the Turkish leaders to the separation of the Mosul *liwa* from Turkey, account must be taken of the National Pact which had been adopted by the Turkish parliament at the end of 1919 and which had specified the area to be retained as part of Turkey, thus overturning the Treaty of Sèvres.[11] To give way on the Mosul *liwa* would represent an encroachment on this area. The Turkish delegates fought long and hard at every stage of the negotiations.

The League Commission, however, reporting in December 1925, came out in favour of not partitioning the *liwa,* citing particularly the interests of the peoples of the area. They considered that the sentiments of the majority supported union with Iraq. The award of the Commission, accepted by the Council, therefore went in favour of the British case, with, however, two important qualifications.

The first specified the continuation for a further 25 years of the League Mandate. This they regarded as necessary to safeguard the rights of minorities in the area. The second specified the appointment of Kurds in administration, in the judicial system, and in teaching.

The first of these intrinsically sound qualifications clashed directly with the aspirations both of the Iraqis and of the British. Though subsequent history has proved that the apprehensions of the Commissioners were well founded, the safeguards proposed resembled, metaphorically, an attempt to propel the ship of state upstream against a torrential outflowing tide. Attempts were quickly made to find a way around it. The Council of the League, in confirming the allocation to Iraq of all the territory south of the so-called 'Brussels Line',[12] laid down, as a condition, that Britain should present a new treaty with Iraq guaranteeing the continuance of the Mandate for 25 years unless Iraq was admitted as a member of the League at an earlier date.

The opening which this qualification left for early independence was a blow to Kurdish hopes. No effective means had been devised by which the League of Nations could ensure the fair treatment of minorities by its members. There was no convincing evidence that the Iraqi governments of the future would be more tolerant of and more willing to recognize other nationalisms than their own within the borders of the new state. Where old countries had shown intolerance which had led to conflict, was it likely that Iraq would show greater enlightenment? The League had been faced with the same problems in Europe and it attempted to provide safeguards, but without conspicuous success. The misgivings of some members of the Mandate Commission and some of the League delegates were well founded.

The Treaty of 1930 and the Progress to Independence

With the arrival of King Faisal and the establishment of the new structure of government under the Mandate and the 1922 treaty, the grouping of departments and their functions assumed new forms which displaced those of the regime of Sir A. T. Wilson, which had been influenced by Indian precedents and which were a closer approximation to those of colonialist regimes. However, British advisers, who included some able civil servants, continued to exercise much power and an unacknowledged period of tutelage followed. In view of the comparatively backward state of material development in the country this had its uses, although they could not be acknowledged publicly in face of nationalist sentiment which had never accepted the British role. Necessarily the role and importance of the British advisers diminished as time passed.

The ministers in the early governments inherited some of the Turkish or Ottoman traditions and types of administration. It appears that legal forms and administrative organization were much less corrupt than they had been in the Ottoman Empire and that British models had improved the structure and functioning of the courts. Under the ministries during the period of the Mandate the British advisers performed functions that in practice went beyond mere advice. However repugnant this may have been to nationalist sentiment, it had its uses for the future Iraq in supplying European models of administration that corrected or supplemented Turkish precedents. The system of British advisers, who were for the most part experienced political officers, was extended to the *liwas,* with varying degrees of acceptability and of success. Such an arrangement could not last long; dual responsibility, differential salaries, and administrative costs, most of which had to be borne locally, rendered it unpopular, both in Iraq and with the British public, which was more concerned with economic conditions at home than in Iraq.

Nevertheless, much useful work was accomplished and a considerable number of able Iraqis were brought into administrative posts. The Iraqi Ministry of Foreign Affairs was founded in 1925. Consuls to Iraq were appointed by a number of countries, and Iraq was recognized as a state by leading European powers. The Organic Law was established in the spring of 1925, and in 1926 a period began of parliamentary governments which were now based on elections. By this time, too, a great deal of the administration was under Iraqi control.

Even apart from certain practical advantages of the Mandate to the development of Iraq as a state, there was a distinct political gain for Iraq from an international point of view. The accord reached between Britain and France on the inclusion of the Mosul *liwa* in Iraq was not extended to Turkey and it is difficult to see how, without British influence, the new Arab leaders of Iraq could have gained control over the area. However little this was recognized in public, it was well understood by the King and his responsible advisers.

But by the end of the 1920s Britain was ready to agree to Iraqi independence and to support her admission to the League of Nations. Facing strong pressures at home and abroad, the British government expedited the treaty of 1930 with Iraq, which gave Iraq most of what she wanted and paved the way for Iraq's entry as an independent state into the League of Nations. It was a twenty-five-year Treaty of Alliance between independent states and was aimed to satisfy Iraqi aspirations, but the British retained a number of privileges and especially military concessions: in case of the involvement of either in war with a third party it bound each to come to the aid of the other, subject to obligations under the League Covenant. Iraq would grant the use of railways, rivers, ports, aerodromes, and means of communication. Sites would be given to Britain for an air base near Basra and another west of the Euphrates. Britain would maintain forces in those areas for five years.

As for naval and military forces, Iraqi officers would be trained in Britain, arms would be provided by Britain, and military instructors from outside would be British, while training of Iraqi personnel sent abroad was to be in Britain. British military equipment was to be used.

In the spirit of the times it did not appear strange to Britain or open to adverse criticism that an independent Iraq should be limited in these ways in her freedom of choice with respect to allies and to technical assistance. Nor was it unacceptable to the Mandates Commission.

In most European and North American circles the subsequent vehement protests of certain political groups in Iraq and the Middle East seem to have been regarded as the work of 'extremists'. Contemporary opinion seriously underestimated the long-run effects of treaties of this character. When living in Iraq about a quarter of a century later we found that widespread resentment of the treaty still survived. It was not confined to 'extremists' or to the 'left wing'. King Faisal and his advisers were themselves genuine Arab nationalists, but they considered that acceptance of these questionable clauses was a price worth paying for the great extension of independence in the treaty as a whole. In this their judgement was correct, but it reduced their popularity among younger political elements and may have contributed to the ultimate downfall of some of the advisers, in particular Nuri al-Said, the Prime Minister from March 1930 to October 1932, who had signed the treaty.[13]

In a characteristically brilliant discussion of Iraq's admission to membership of the League of Nations published two years later, Arnold Toynbee noted

> . . . this political emancipation of an Oriental country from the control of a Western Power signified the reversal of a previous process of Western imperial expansion which had been at work for the best of two centuries beginning with the *de facto* establishment of the British East India Company in A.D. 1764.[14]

It was not always realized in Britain, however, that many, if not most, Iraqis, taking into account the continued economic and political links through the treaty which were a condition of the settlement, did not share the view that the end of the Mandate signified 'emancipation' from the control of Britain, on either the political or economic side. The members of the Mandates Commission, on the other hand, having started from the assumption of a need for an initial tutelage to establish successful independence, were less perturbed by certain remnants of it in the terms of settlement.

The two great issues on which doubts remained among a number of observers, in the League of Nations and the Mandates Commission, were concerned first with the willingness of Iraqis to accept, and their ability to operate, the institutions of representative government, and second with the position of minorities in an independent Iraq. On both issues the doubts were, unfortunately, well founded. But strong forces impelled the British government to aim at a date for independence which, though later than that sought by the Iraqi government, was much earlier than the Mandates Commission had envisaged at the outset. At the same time the British government was well aware of the serious danger that the League might refuse Iraq; for if so, Britain alone would be blamed by the Iraqis, with disastrous consequences.

The first of these difficulties was common to many other cases of accession to independence. A strong current of public opinion and sentiment had developed around the demands for independence; it was difficult to resist it for long without provoking serious conflict. In the case of Iraq, public opinion in Britain reinforced this difficulty. The drive for independence and the questions surrounding the revision of the treaty tended to overshadow other proceedings and other issues in the period of the Mandate.

Plainly, however, the political development of the Iraqi politicians generally failed to match the very substantial progress made in the construction of the political institutions that they were expected to operate. One of the factors behind the political instability of the government, however, was a tendency for the resentment over the Mandate and the treaty to overshadow other issues and cause politicians to quarrel with each other over the best means of attacking what they saw as an external humiliation and dependence, instead of devoting their minds and energies to ways of making the new institutions work. The largely Western-devised political 'forms'[15] were imported into a tribal society ethnically and theologically fragmented, with an urban crust of sophisticated, largely Turkish-educated leaders.[16] It took all of Faisal's diplomatic and political skill and judgement to guide politicians and governments along anything like a smooth passage. He, along with some others, well understood the complexity of Iraq's international position, and also understood that the way was indeed open to independence, which could be progressively enlarged. He could wait while keeping up a steady pressure. But others were impatient and either struggled intemperately for power or uncompromisingly for their own versions of appropriate policy. Between 1921 and 1932 Iraq had 14 Cabinets (including the 1920 Provisional Government).[17]

At the time of independence, when the expectations of many were high, the fears of those who knew Iraq well were also great. But to focus on the internal political weakness of the Iraqi ruling class, on their deficiencies as politicians genuinely caring about the development of their country, and on the too-often self-seeking nature of their patriotism and the ambiguity of their nationalism, would be to concentrate on only one blade of a pair of scissors, which would not help much in explaining the method of operation. The underlying pressures on the men at the top of the social and political structure were intensified by the frustrations created by resentment and bitterness over the foreign tutelage. The big powers had been, and still were, using the countries of the Fertile Crescent as instruments in their own larger rivalries and as means of advancing their own economic interests. To be sure, the great age of imperialism may have been on its way into history, but one could hardly expect this to be perceived by the Iraqis, and even if perceived, to be contemplated with patient resignation as they picked in the debris left in its wake. The goodwill and, indeed, the solid contribution to the country's welfare of the British was considerably greater than most nationalist Iraqis were (or are now) willing to acknowledge, but equally great, and equally unrecognized by the British, was the Iraqi need to be free of even a well-meaning paternalistic interference. Unfortunately the shadow of nationalist resentment was to hang over the land and the fires of resentment were to burn for a period much longer than might normally have been expected, largely because Iraq was to be one of the major oil-exporting countries of the world and host to the great international oil companies.

The second issue on which serious doubts about Iraq remained related to the adequacy of measures to protect minorities. Judging from the extremely imperfect census statistics of 1920 it would appear that not less than one-quarter of the population of the new state consisted in non-Arab minorities, of which the Kurds were the most important. Britain had been responsible for the inclusion of Iraqi Kurdistan into the new state. The resulting difficulties and conflicts are discussed in later chapters. At the outset an optimistic note was sounded by the final British report on the administration of Iraq.

The optimism was ill-founded.

Finally, the question arises whether the end of the Mandate brought genuine political independence to Iraq. Many Iraqis deny that it did on the ground that certain clauses of the treaty of 1930 narrowed the choices open to her in planning future developments. These we have discussed critically, but they are not an answer to the broader question. We prefer to accept the verdict of an outside observer who did not hesitate to criticize the treaty.

> Quant au calcul de la politique britannique il est aisé à comprendre. En effet, lier la mise en vigueur du traité à la seule cessation du régime mandataire exposerait le gouvernement britannique aux remonstrances des autres Puissances qui pourraient lui reprocher d'avoir voulu profiter du mandat pour sauveguarder ses propres intérêts, et soulèverait peut-être même la question de la non-validité d'un tel acte par suite de l'incapacité du pays sous mandat. Par contre, dans le cas où cette mise en vigueur découlerait automatiquement de l'admission de l'Irak à la Société des Nations personne n'aurait le droit de parler pour l'Irak, puisqu'il y serait lui-même.[18]

Such was the situation resulting from the admission of Iraq to membership of the League of Nations by a unanimous vote, 3 October 1932.

The Oil Concession

During most of the period we have been discussing, the question of the terms on which the oil resources of the new state were to be exploited occupied much of the time of the Iraqi ministers and of the King, and was a major preoccupation of the British government as well as of the oil companies of at least four foreign powers. The disintegration of the Ottoman political framework and the defeat of Germany created not only the opportunity for the victorious powers to displace German and Turkish interests in the (presumed) oil resources of the area but also the necessity of reconciling their own divergent interests. International rivalry was thus intensified as the governments of the Allied powers each struggled with undisguised ambition and some bitterness to gain as much control as possible over any Mesopotamian oil that might be discovered. In Britain, control of oil supplies by national companies was treated as a strategic necessity after the conversion of the British navy from coal to oil just before the war. During the war also, France had been almost totally dependent on the United States for her supplies and the United States government had imposed stringent regulations as a condition of supply.

The First World War had dramatically demonstrated the military importance of oil and of owned supplies to all participants; even the American authorities became concerned about the country's domestic reserves, fearing that they were becoming dangerously low. They expressed considerable alarm over the prospect that oil resources elsewhere in the world were coming increasingly under British or British/Dutch control. Before the war a few American concession-hunters had been active in the Turkish Sultan's ante-rooms, notably Rear-Admiral Chester, who had had some illusory success, but the large companies showed little interest. After the war, however, the situation changed and Mesopotamia was seen not only as a potential source of oil of great importance and an area in which a British/French monopoly might well be established, but also as an area in which the United States could present a legitimate claim for consideration since she had been an ally in the defeat of Germany. The terms of the oil concession obtained in Iraq and the structure of the company set up to exploit it, reflecting as they did the rivalry and suspicion of the allied partners, were the result of compromises which, as time went on, proved to be increasingly unsatisfactory from the point of view both of the Iraqi government and of the participants themselves.

Conflicts of National Interests

As we have seen, there were pre-war claims and acquired rights relating to Mesopotamian oil concessions that had to be reconciled with the new interest of France and the United States as well as with those of the emerging Iraqi state. The first step involved agreement between Britain and France on the delineation of their respective spheres of influence in the area and specifically in its oil resources. Neither the APOC nor the Royal Dutch Shell, let alone C. S. Gulbenkian, were at all eager to admit French participation, but this was clearly a political necessity determined by governments as part of the wider arrangements for the area. Since, however, no agreement governing the relations between the parties could be worked out entirely independently of the demands of the American government and the American companies, complicated and interrelated sets of negotiations continued side by side for a decade after the end of the war.[19]

France claimed the pre-war German share in the Turkish Petroleum Company, which had been taken over by the British Custodian of Enemy Property in 1915, and early in 1919 an agreement was made between Walter Long, First Lord of the Admiralty, and Senator Bérenger, French Commissioner-General of Petroleum Products. This provided for a French interest of 20 per cent in the TPC, with 70 per cent for British interests and 10 per cent for a native government. Moreover, if a subsidiary company were to be formed to work the oilfields, 10 per cent would be made available for other native interests by the other shareholders. In return, the French government was to facilitate the construction of pipelines for the transport of Mesopotamian and Persian oil across Syria to the Mediterranean.

Although the Long–Bérenger agreement was ratified by the Foreign Office, it was not accepted by Lloyd George. The main principles were nevertheless embodied in the San Remo oil agreements of 24 April 1920 which provided for permanent British control of any company set up to exploit Mesopotamian oil, the French to have 25 per cent and, if wanted, native interests 20 per cent if the company were private. The French were to contribute one-half of the first 10 per cent of the native interest and the balance was to come from each participant in proportion to its holding. In effect, the San Remo agreement maintained the TPC arrangement of 1914, substituting French for German, and adding native, interests.

Both the Italian and the American governments quickly sent protests to the Foreign Office complaining that this agreement established an Anglo–French monopoly in the areas to be mandated. The American diplomatic drive to obtain access to Mesopotamian oil, which had begun even before the San Remo agreement, now took the form of an insistence on what was called an 'open door' policy—equal opportunity for nationals of all countries in the mandated territories with no concession to be granted so large as to be exclusive. In her attack on the San Remo oil agreement, the United States challenged the validity of the promise given by the Turkish Sultan in 1914 (which was the basis of the TPC claim to the right to the oil concession) on the ground that the right to grant any such concession could not be derived from a Turkish grant but rested with the people of the new country. This same issue was also raised in the British Parliament, where questions were asked as to how the San Remo agreement and French participation could be reconciled with the promise to the new Arab state to be created that it should own its own oil.

In the, at times caustic, diplomatic exchanges with the State Department the British government defended its position with vigour, not only pointing out that the United States had long adopted oil policies that were not devoid of exclusiveness but also insisting that the United States had such a dominant position in world oil markets that she could afford to permit British companies to benefit from the arrangements they had been able to make in 1914. Moreover, the British government did not deny the right of the new Arab state to the ownership of its resources and to determine how they should be developed. The United States government at one time proposed that the validity of the TPC claim to concession rights should go to arbitration, but the American oil companies themselves began to negotiate directly with the British and French companies and this proposal was not pursued.

The San Remo agreement had left open the question whether Mesopotamian oil should be developed by private companies or by a state company. The British government officials strongly argued that it was not appropriate for a government short of funds and with many urgent needs to engage in an enterprise as risky as oil production when it could obtain royalties without any risk by permitting foreign companies to invest their own money. At the same time the government could prevent such companies from making excessive profits if it wished. They noted also that even if the Iraqi government did undertake the task of oil exploration and development, it would have to rely on the expertise and co-operation of the private foreign companies in any case.

Although consideration was given to these and many other issues, the course of events was consistent: the TPC participants—APOC, Shell, and the Compagnie Française des Pétroles (CFP; the company formed by the French at that time to hold the French shares in the TPC)—proceeded to draw up a draft agreement in consultation with the American group with which they were negotiating on the side. This agreement was to be presented to the Iraqi government as the basis for a separate negotiation for the grant of a concession. The insistence of the State Department on some kind of 'open door' policy had to be respected, and negotiations between the TPC group and the American companies dealt with the practical aspects of the form its implementation should take.

Seven American companies were interested in a share in the TPC in the beginning and the Standard Oil Company of New Jersey (SONJ) acted as negotiator for the group. Negotiations on a proposal drawn up by SONJ began in the middle of 1922. Using as a precedent for the implementation of the principle of the 'open door' the way in which the United States government had dealt with the sale of the lands of the Osage Indians, the SONJ scheme proposed that the TPC would select within two years not more than 12 blocks of 16 square miles each (192 square miles) for its own exploitation out of the entire concession area and make the rest of the area of 159,000 square miles available for leasing to any other companies, *including* the partners in the TPC.

As might be expected, Gulbenkian reacted sharply to such a proposal, since clearly it would enable the partners of the TPC to ensure that his 5 per cent interest in that company would relate only to oil won in the original 12 blocks, whereas he believed that he had rights to the exploitation of all the oil of the *vilayets* of Mosul and Baghdad. Even worse, it would also permit the partners, who in his view would be the only serious contenders for the plots put up for sub-leasing, to agree to sell to each other the leases at nominal prices, thus even depriving him of revenues from the sales. Gulbenkian had been instrumental in putting the original TPC together and he had every intention of maintaining his position intact. In this he often had the support of the French, who were also determined that any arrangements between the British and Americans should not reduce the French share in all Iraqi oil.

Negotiations for a Concession

But before any of the ambitions of the companies or of the foreign governments could be realized, the Iraqi government had to grant an oil concession, for it was recognized that the ownership of the oil resources and the right to determine the terms of their exploitation lay with the Iraqi government. With the establishment of the Iraqi state and the installation of Faisal on the throne in 1921 negotiations could begin, even though the Iraqi parliament was not yet in being. Negotiations among the companies, and especially between the TPC group and the American companies, over a 'working agreement' which would govern the relations among the shareholders as well as the internal operations of the TPC were also soon to begin.

The negotiations with the government for a concession were protracted, largely because of bitter disagreement over the question of the 20 per cent share in the company that had been promised to the Iraqis at San Remo in 1920. The companies were completely unwilling to accept Iraqi ownership in the TPC and the Iraqis were equally unwilling to relinquish their right to ownership. The TPC, as planned by the parent companies, was to be a company with the sole purpose of holding a concession and producing oil for its parents. The companies had no intention of putting oil into the hands of the Iraqi government nor of permitting the government to interfere in the management of what was to be a wholly-owned subsidiary (apart from the Gulbenkian interest, for which special arrangements would be made).

The working agreement being negotiated between the European and the American companies provided that oil should be available to the parents in proportion to their shares in the Iraqi company. Moreover, in order to avoid the double taxation of the American companies which would occur if the profits of the TPC, a British registered company, were taxed by the British government while the American companies would at the same time also have to pay taxes to the American government on their share of the profits, the agreement provided that no profits should accrue to the TPC. Oil was to be taken by the parents at cost plus a nominal fee. Clearly if the Iraqi government were admitted as a shareholder on a par with the others, this carefully negotiated arrangement among the partners would have to be recast, for the Iraqis would be entitled to a share of the oil, or at the least, to dividends from their share of profits. The Iraqis were not told of these arrangements.

Jealous and very conscious of its newly attained political status, the Iraqi government was determined to assert its sovereignty in oil matters. Not only did it feel that the international prestige of the country was involved, but it knew that its own domestic prestige was at stake, for the first elections were pending. The political consciousness of the Iraqi population, and the nationalist protests which were rising in stridency over the British hegemony implied by the Mandate, considerably weakened the bargaining position of the companies *vis-à-vis* the Iraqi negotiators since, if the desired concession was to be obtained, it would be necessary to arrive at an agreement quickly, otherwise to the approval of the Cabinet would have to be added that of a newly elected parliamentary assembly. Britain was the mandatory power and the northern boundaries of the country had not as yet been settled. Hence Britain had (in principle) a strong bargaining position. The position was not so strong that terms could be dictated to the Iraqis since the British company badly wanted a concession but could hardly force a parliament to grant it, and the British government was not willing to attempt coercion on the company's behalf.

Apart from the question of whether or not Mosul would be included in the territory of the new state—and there were attempts to create uncertainty over this issue to soften the Iraqi insistence on some of their demands—perhaps the primary counter in the hands of the TPC lay in the Iraqi need for government revenues and for the expertise of the companies in winning the oil. Iraq needed to give a concession even more than the oil companies needed to have one; the only alternative to the TPC lay in the possibility that other foreign oil groups might be interested. There were proposals from other concession-hunters who offered rather better terms than the TPC was offering, but their ability to do the job was by no means proved; both the British High Commissioner and the TPC group took the opportunity to make this clear.

The British government urged the Iraqis not to insist on an ownership share, arguing that the country would do better to accept royalties which would provide revenues with no risk and with no commitment of its own resources. Every effort was made by the High Commissioner to persuade the Iraqis to accept the company proposals; he even allowed them to believe that the political future of the Mosul *vilayet* and Britain's willingness to support the new state might depend on the signature of the concession agreement.

Nevertheless, both the companies and the British government consistently recognized that the Iraqi demand for an ownership share was legitimate. As negotiations dragged on and most other issues became resolved, the High Commissioner strongly urged his government to put severe pressure on the Iraqis to accept the company position. The British government refused and instead decided to put pressure on the TPC. Press attacks and popular demonstrations during the course of the negotiations underlined the political risk that the whole concession could be endangered if negotiations were much longer protracted. At the same time the Iraqi Cabinet, which also wanted an agreement, was divided. Early in March 1925 the British government advised the TPC to agree to a compromise under which Iraq would receive free of charge special non-voting shares equal to 20 per cent of the total shares. These shares would be entitled to dividends, but would confer no right to interfere in the commercial policy or general management of the company, and royalties would be reduced by the amount of dividends paid. The company had already told the Iraqis that if they insisted on participation, their royalties would be reduced, and that the 'high rate' already offered was on the assumption that ownership rights would be relinquished.

The company negotiators delayed presenting this proposed compromise to the Iraqis; before learning of it, the King and his Cabinet authorized the Minister of Works to sign the new Convention as already negotiated, but subject to agreement on some minor points and including the company's proposed clause with respect to Iraq's participation. This clause read: 'whenever an issue of shares is offered by the Company to the general public, subscription lists shall be opened in Iraq simultaneously with lists opened elsewhere, and Iraqis in Iraq shall be given preference to the extent of at least twenty per cent of such issue' (Art. 34). The companies must have known that the clause had no practical significance except as a political gesture to Iraqi sensitivity. Nor were all the Iraqi negotiators deceived, and two cabinet ministers resigned rather than accept it.

It is by no means certain, however, that the Iraqis would have gained financially had they obtained an ownership share in the TPC at that time under the compromise terms proposed by the British government. The profits to be attributed to the TPC would still have depended on the policy of its international parents with respect to the price at which they decided to buy the TPC oil, for there was no appropriate open market price for crude oil and the international industry was almost entirely dominated by the vertically integrated large companies. It seems likely that the companies would have so arranged matters that they would not have become liable to payments greater than the royalty proposed and that the Iraqi government would have been in no position to do much about it.[20] In view of the great depression that was to hit the industry in the 1930s and of the Second World War which quickly followed, the Iraqis might have found, as the Persians did, that they would have been worse off had they depended on dividends rather than on a fixed royalty.

On the other hand, the political advantages of obtaining the promised equity participation would have been great, and such an arrangement in Iraq would undoubtedly have been copied elsewhere in the Middle East. Moreover, a 20 per cent ownership in the company might have made it possible for the government to bring effective pressures for substantial increases in oil revenues much earlier than in fact occurred. Almost all Iraqis, knowledgeable or otherwise, are even now firmly convinced that Iraq suffered greatly in being denied participation in the exploitation of her oil in 1925. They look at the 20 per cent equity they might have had as a lost opportunity to learn the oil business, to gain enough knowledge at least to enable the government effectively to control the foreign companies, and in general to develop the necessary expertise to permit them to manage their own resources.

Although defeated on this central issue of participation, the Iraqi negotiators gained points on other matters on which the company was forced to compromise. They defended Iraq's interests intelligently and with a persistence which more than once provoked expressions of great irritation and annoyance from the High Commissioner as well as from the company negotiators. The Iraqi team, led by the Minister of Finance, Sassoon Hiskail, who was a Jewish financier with experience of high position in the Ottoman government,[21] recognized the disadvantages to Iraq if an exclusive monopoly were given to the TPC for a long period. In particular, they wanted to see rapid development of Iraq's oil and it was obvious to them that more rapid progress as well as additional revenues might be gained if the government had areas at its disposal for which it might grant new concessions. They met with limited success for a time with the so-called 'plot system'.

This 'system' was proposed by the American companies as a means of meeting the State Department's insistence on an 'open door' which, for the American government of the day, was put forward as a matter of high international principle; but it also had the effect of ensuring that American companies would have access on equal terms with others to world resources. Wilsonian principles and private commercial interests coincided—but only up to a point. The oil companies had to observe the principle, but at the same time they knew that it would be much against their interests if the open competition implied in the concept of an 'open door' in fact materialized because too many people walked through the door. The American companies wanted to ensure that they were admitted into the club of Middle East oil-producers, but, as we shall see, they also soon ensured that it was very difficult indeed for anyone else to follow them in.

The final arrangements retained the principle: the TPC was to select within 32 months from the date of the agreement, 24 plots (instead of the 12 originally proposed under the American plan) of 8 (instead of 16) square miles for its own exploitation. But the government demanded, and obtained, the right to offer the 'outside areas'—areas outside the 24 plots—for leases to newcomers instead of leaving this entirely in the hands of the company as had been proposed in the company draft. Within four years the government was to select an additional 24 plots and to invite sealed bids from any responsible bidder for the leases. The TPC was not excluded from bidding and in any case would receive the proceeds from the sale of leases, although the lessees would pay the appropriate royalties to the government and assume specified obligations. The Americans were not entirely happy with this provision. It clearly put the TPC as a company in a stronger position than outsiders since the company could, if it wanted to, outbid any others at no cost to itself, receiving back any price it paid out. Moreover, the American companies did not control the TPC.

The TPC had originally asked for a concession of 99 years; the Iraqis demurred and suggested 30 years. The compromise was for 75 years, after which the government was entitled to acquire the ownership of the fixed assets. The area of the concession—called the 'defined area'—included all of Iraq except the 'transferred territories'[22] and the *vilayet* of Basra. But since the final boundaries of Iraq had not yet been settled, the agreement provided for the later execution of a convention which would expressly delimit the defined area.

The company had offered royalties at the rate of 4*s*. a ton, which was supposed to be comparable to the rate offered in the United States where royalties were a percentage of the well-head value of oil. It was argued that a fixed royalty rather than one related to the value of oil was appropriate in the Middle East because there was no established market value for crude oil in the Persian Gulf. On the other hand, the Iraqis wanted the possibility of sharing in the future profits made by the companies on Iraqi oil. They did succeed in obtaining an arrangement which would link royalties to profits, defined to include the estimated profits on refined products made from Iraqi oil, with a minimum royalty of 2*s*. and a maximum of 6*s*. (gold) per ton, but the arrangement was not to come into effect for twenty years. In the meantime a royalty of 4*s*. (gold) per ton was to prevail.

It was important for the Iraqis to link the royalty payment to gold in order to avoid a loss in its value due to a depreciation of sterling, and they proposed a precise formula which would have specified the payment with reference to the weight and fineness of a sovereign. The TPC argued that such specification was not necessary and agreed only to accept the phrase 'four shillings (gold)', which they insisted would be adequate to meet the Iraqi objective of protecting their royalties against a fall in the value of sterling. The absence of a clear specification was to cause difficulties when the company later attempted to evade the gold requirement.

The company also attempted to obtain exemption from the normal Iraqi tax system, but finally agreed to accept the right of the government to impose the same taxes on it, its property, and its employees, as were imposed on other industrial undertakings in Iraq. It agreed to build a refinery to meet Iraq's internal requirements and to build a pipeline for export shipments as soon as practicable, but in any case within four years after its plots were fully tested.

It is clear that later Iraqi attacks on the negotiators of the original oil concession for 'betraying' Iraq's interest without a struggle were unfounded. Moreover, the Iraqi insistence that because Britain was the mandatory power, the Iraqi government had no freedom of action very much overstates the weakness of the Iraqi position. Both allegations are now accepted as unchallengeable historical truth in nearly all Iraqi interpretation of their country's history, but they are both unjustified.

It is true that some of the points gained by the Iraqi negotiators turned out to be of no significance as events unfolded (the shortening of the length of the concession, the linking of royalties to profits after twenty years); some were later nullified by company action (the taxation arrangements, the right of the government to select plots for new bidding); but some were useful (provision for local refining); and at least one was of great importance (the gold clause). It is also true that they lost the main issue of participation on which even the British government in London had decided, too late, that the company should compromise.

The oil companies were in a strong negotiating position partly because the Iraqis needed money and partly because there was uncertainty in the King's mind over what would happen if the TPC did not get the concession before the parliament convened. His difficulty did not relate primarily to the settlement of Iraq's northern boundary but to the unpredictability of Iraqi politics, given the widespread resentment over the Mandate and over the dominating British presence in the country. But equally the Iraqis had considerable bargaining power because the company badly wanted the concession, and wanted it before parliament was elected. It is easy to understand the Iraqi national feelings, and had they obtained an *effective* participation in the company, the history of the oil industry in the Middle East would have been very different.

But in our judgement, even a 20 per cent equity interest would not have brought significantly greater revenues to Iraq over the subsequent twenty-five years, while the companies would have been able to contain attempts at effective Iraqi interference with the management of the company. The most that can be said is that a concession in 1925 on the ownership terms demanded by the Iraqis might have led to a more rapid disintegration of the control of the international companies than in fact took place, but not until after the end of the Second World War in any case. By then, however, the whole international petroleum industry was already on the road to very rapid change as the newly developed oil resources of Kuwait and Saudi Arabia began to enter world markets in an ever-accelerating flow. As we shall see, the Iraqi oil industry suffered from the *structure* of the Iraq Petroleum Company (as the TPC was called after 1929), but this was unrelated to the concession terms and would have been reduced only if Iraqi government participation had been accompanied by actual Iraqi involvement in the company's plans. This was not seriously contemplated by the companies.

The 'Group Agreement' among the TPC Shareholders

The TPC concession agreement was ratified by the King and Cabinet on 14 March 1925. The American companies had not yet been formally admitted into the company and negotiations over the agreement between them and the existing shareholders, Anglo-Persian,

Shell, CFP, and Gulbenkian, had yet to be completed. Since there was no provision for an Iraqi shareholding and only a fixed royalty was stipulated, the tax status of the TPC that was insisted on by the American companies in their parallel negotiations over a working agreement with the TPC shareholders was implicitly taken into account; and by accepting the 'plot system', a version of the 'open door', albeit considerably diluted in view of the privileged position of the TPC in dealing with bids, had been provided for. Thus, two main requirements of the American companies had been met by the concession agreement.

There were other important issues to be settled among the shareholders that did not involve the agreement itself. The first was the question of the so-called 'self-denying' clause that had been accepted by the TPC shareholders in the Foreign Office Agreement of 1914;[23] the second was the distribution of shareholding among the TPC participants and the position of APOC. In addition, there were a variety of legal and other matters regulating the obligations and rights of the shareholders and the internal organization of the TPC and its subsidiary bodies, which had to be settled and embodied in a group agreement.

Prolonged negotiations over these questions did not, however, force inactivity upon the TPC itself.[24] It immediately set up an exploration and drilling programme, bringing in equipment, recruiting labour, and building facilities. Most of the initial exploratory drilling was disappointing, but on 15 October 1927 the Baba No. 1 well at Baba Gurgur just north of Kirkuk came in with enormous force, flowing wild and inundating the countryside with tons of oil before it could be controlled after a week of effort. Here clearly was the area on which the TPC would concentrate for a considerable time to come.

This success, in addition to other promising reports on the prospects of Iraqi oil resources, very much increased the incentive for the American companies to come to an agreement over their entry into the TPC. They had consistently refused to accept the restrictions imposed on all shareholders of the TPC by the Foreign Office Agreement of 1914 which prevented them from having any interest in the production or manufacture of oil in the Ottoman Empire except through the TPC. Both the French and Gulbenkian insisted on the maintenance of the self-denying clause for the same reason as they had opposed the acceptance of an 'open door' policy within the area of the TPC concession. They were afraid that the other shareholders of the TPC, if permitted to obtain oil elsewhere in the area other than through the TPC, would to that extent have their incentive to develop the production of the TPC reduced. Gulbenkian was not interested in more oil, but he was interested in as much money as possible from the TPC; the French wanted oil and felt that they would be at a disadvantage in relation to other shareholders when it came to bidding for oil concessions. Their interest would be best protected by ensuring that all had to work through the TPC itself.

A compromise among the conflicting interests was eventually reached under which the Americans agreed to accept the application of the self-denying clause within the area of the old Ottoman Empire as outlined in red by the French on a map, and to work only through the TPC or on a 'share and share alike' basis. (Because of this the Group Agreement of 1928 is generally known as the 'red line agreement'.) In return, the American companies were permitted to bid independently for leases in the 'outside areas' of the TPC concession.[25]

Although the TPC shareholders, partly at the insistence of the Americans, had obtained a concession which gave the Iraqis neither an ownership interest nor a share in profits and thus made it possible for the company to be organized as a non-profit making enterprise simply producing oil for its shareholders, the 'working agreement' which would give effect to such an organization was not accepted by Gulbenkian until 1927. Only after CFP agreed to buy his share of oil (or refined products) at a price determined as 'fair' by experts selected by both sides, did Gulbenkian accept the working agreement. (A subsequent arrangement was made between the CFP and the other shareholders to share the costs and benefits attached to the purchase of Gulbenkian's share of the oil.) The American group was also unwilling to sign an agreement until Gulbenkian's position was definitely settled.[26]

Finally, the groups had to agree on the distribution of the shareholdings. This too was highly contentious. APOC controlled 47.5 per cent of the shares, Anglo-Saxon Petroleum (a Shell subsidiary) 22.5 per cent, CFP 25 per cent, and Gulbenkian 5 per cent. To let the Americans in, the largest contribution would clearly have to come from APOC, which wanted to retain the largest interest. But other groups did not want a distribution which would let any two shareholders together exercise control. Eventually, an equal distribution giving 23.75 per cent of the shares to each group, with 5 per cent for Gulbenkian, was agreed upon, APOC being compensated with an overriding royalty of 10 per cent of the oil produced from the 24 plots.

In February 1928 the American Group, now containing only five of the original seven companies, organized the Near East Development Corporation to hold their interest in the TPC.[27] The Group Agreement was signed on 31 July 1928 settling all these issues as well as a variety of lesser questions dealing with the company organization, pipeline, refining, and marketing arrangements, and regulations for the relationships among the shareholders which bound them to enforce the agreement not only among themselves but on any subsidiary companies they might set up. Refining by the TPC was to be confined to Iraq's internal needs and the TPC was not allowed to market except in Iraq. The agreement thus ensured that the TPC itself could not enter into competition with other companies in the international oil industry, and competition among its own parents throughout the 'red-line' area was also prevented.

Revision of the Concession: the 1931 Agreement

The painfully negotiated 'plot system' was not to last long. In November 1927 the 32 months within which the TPC was to have chosen its 24 plots would have passed, yet the Group Agreement would clearly not be completed and only in July 1926 had the frontier settlement, which was necessary for any exploration to take place in northern areas, been accepted. A one-year extension of the time for choosing the plots was asked of the government and was granted in August 1927. When, in the middle of the following year, the company again asked for an additional extension of five years on the ground that it had not yet been able thoroughly to evaluate the geological structures in the area it had obtained, it found itself enmeshed in political complications. Although the King and government were apparently not averse to accommodating the company, they had received a request from a newcomer, a British–Italian syndicate called the British Oil Development Company (BOD), that the government should select the plots on which it would be able to bid in accordance with the concession agreement.

The BOD offered, as part of its proposal, to build a railway to the Mediterranean at no cost to Iraq—a project desired by the Iraqis and so far refused by the TPC; the government was naturally attracted. Moreover, there was considerable suspicion in many quarters that the TPC was dragging its feet in the matter of selecting plots, not because it had insufficient information to do so, but because it in fact wanted a larger concession area for its exclusive exploitation. Whether or not this was the important reason behind the request for an extension of time, it was in fact true that the TPC shareholders felt that the area open to them was too small to permit adequate evaluation of oil resources and to ensure their economic exploitation, especially in view of the cost of building the pipeline to which they were committed, let alone a railway. This problem was raised with the government and, in addition to requesting an extension, the TPC made it clear that it would like a revision of the concession agreement. The government was not unsympathetic, but the BOD intervention made it politically difficult for the government to grant yet another extension of time to the TPC. Nevertheless it also gave the government an opportunity to bargain for the railway it wanted and for improved financial arrangements, as well as on other matters.

It is not clear how far the IPC (Iraq Petroleum Company, as the TPC was now known) considered the BOD to be a serious rival; there was considerable doubt whether its financial capacity and its technical competence could match the IPC's ability to develop the country's oil resources. Nevertheless, the IPC's desire for a revision of the concession convention and the government's desire to improve some of the terms and to obtain a commitment for the railway as well as specific arrangements for the pipeline to the Mediterranean, led to the opening of negotiations, with the BOD as an 'embarrassing third party at the door', in Longrigg's words.[28]

Clearly the IPC would, at the least, have to offer terms which would make it politically possible for the government to reject the BOD proposals. This time the government did not have as free a hand as it had had in 1925, for a revised concession agreement would have to be submitted to parliament, many of whose members were very suspicious of the IPC and opposed to any strengthening of its monopoly. Among the opponents to any revision of the concession was Muzahim al-Pachachi, the Minister of Communications and Public Works. The *Hisb al-Ikha al-Watani* (National Brotherhood party) led by Yasin al-Hashimi, a leading critic of the treaty with Britain, was strongly opposed, and Rashid Ali al-Gaylani, along with two of his colleagues, resigned their seats in the Chamber of Deputies in protest against the signing of a revised oil agreement with the IPC.[29]

In negotiating the revised convention the primary aims of the government were first to obtain clear commitments for the pipeline and railway (with the pipeline to terminate at Haifa rather than Tripoli, since for political reasons it did not want to have the terminal in Syria; another 'irony of history'); second, substantial dead rents with a guaranteed minimum revenue; third, lower product prices for internal consumption; and fourth, the maintenance of the right to tax the company as provided in Article 27 of the original 1925 concession.[30] The IPC's primary objectives were to obtain a larger area for its exclusive use, the elimination of the plot system, and the elimination of the tax provisions of Article 27.

The negotiations continued for three years. In the new concession agreement signed on 24 March 1931 to run for 70 years, the IPC had to move some way towards the government's position. The company obtained exclusive rights to an area of some 32,000 square miles in the provinces of Mosul and Baghdad east of the Tigris,[31] but gave up all territory west of the Tigris. The plot system was abandoned, and the 'open door' was thus firmly closed for the area of the IPC, but was opened even wider elsewhere for the moment.

The taxation question was a source of great controversy and even bitterness, since the Iraqis felt that a restriction on their ability to impose ordinary taxation on the company was an unacceptable interference with their national sovereignty; the company felt that the absence of restrictions on the rate at which taxes could be imposed would leave it unacceptably vulnerable to the financial demands of the government. At times it seemed as if negotiations would break down over the issue. The Prime Minister, Nuri al-Said, on a visit to London, had agreed to a revision of Article 27 of the 1925 concession, since he appreciated the company's position that it could not make large expenditures in Iraq unless it could ensure that it would not be subject to undefined tax liabilities. But the opposition in Iraq on this issue was so strong that he had to insist on adequate compensation if Iraq were to forego her sovereign rights to tax as she wished. In the end the government agreed to commute the taxes it might have imposed under Article 27 into fixed annual payments of £9,000 (gold) up to the commencement of commercial export, and thereafter £6,000 (gold) on the first 4 million tons produced and £20,000 (gold) on each additional million tons.[32]

In return, the company agreed to complete by 1935 a pipeline from Kirkuk to the Mediterranean, with two terminals[33] and a capacity of not less than 3 million tons a year. No commitment to build a railway was given. Until the commencement of exports, the company agreed to pay the government £400,000 (gold) of which half would be dead (i.e., non-recoverable) rents and half recoverable from later royalties. Royalties were to remain at 4*s*. (gold) a ton, with a minimum annual payment of £400,000 for twenty years beginning with the first exports, regardless of the level of exports. Supplies of products for internal consumption were to be secured by the company and sold at specified prices.

Such were the chief changes in the new agreement, although there were some other consequential and relatively minor alterations as well. The area west of the Tigris could now be bestowed on some other company by the Iraqi government. In April 1932 the BOD obtained a 75-year concession for the entire area west of the Tigris and north of the 33rd parallel (46,000 square miles) on terms similar to those of the IPC concession, but improving on them in one notable respect—the Iraqi government was given the right to take free of charge up to 20 per cent of the oil for local consumption or for resale to the company, in lieu of royalty.

Appraisal of the Oil Agreements

On the eve of her entrance into the League of Nations as a fully independent country, therefore, Iraq had made arrangements with the oil companies for the development of her resources which, in their general provisions, were to last until the middle of the century. It is not easy to evaluate the gain (or loss) to Iraq from the 1931 agreement in relation to that of 1925. Gains for the companies were not necessarily losses to Iraq, which far too many observers, especially Arab observers, tend to assume. The 'game' was not a 'zero-sum' game in which one side inevitably lost if the other gained, and it was played in conditions of great uncertainty. But even with the illegitimate advantages of hindsight, evaluation is not easy since we have only one actual outcome and cannot know what would have been the alternative outcomes if different terms had been agreed on.

The cold reality was that the great international companies had the finance and expertise to do the job of finding, developing, and selling the oil, and Iraq did not. These companies had to be paid what was necessary to induce them to do it, but it was to the advantage of Iraq that the job be done and done well. One cannot know whether the government could have paid less, and if so, how much less for the services desired. Even with hindsight, but in the light of the information available, the uncertainties prevailing, and the objectives sought at the time, one cannot reasonably say that the Iraqi government made a bad agreement.

The restrictions accepted on the government's right to tax were undoubtedly the most substantive concessions made by the Iraqis, but there is little question that a tax arrangement which gave *carte blanche* to the government to impose whatever taxes it chose would not have been acceptable to the companies in view of the emotional and unstable political environment and the anti-British sentiments of many of the leading politicians. The danger for the companies of giving hostages to the government in the form of large fixed investments would very likely have led them to minimize their investment in the country, and to explore more assiduously elsewhere, to the detriment of a rapid development of Iraqi oil. This the cooler heads, such as Nuri al-Said and the King, fully understood. Moreover, in view of the urgent need for money by the new state it was not foolish of its leaders to place a relatively high discount on the future and favour lump sums in the present.

The other useful gain for the companies was the elimination of the plot system, although it had already been substantially undermined in practice. Moreover, it is not clear that the country would have gained much even if there had been open competition for new areas, in view of the very few foreign companies that at the time had the resources and willingness to undertake the development of Iraqi oil.[34] There were, of course, some American companies, such as Standard Oil of California and Gulf Oil, which were looking for concessions in the Middle East and willing to explore, but whether these would have been prepared in the 1930s and 1940s to compete effectively with the established American companies in Iraq is more than doubtful. Thus, while it is possible that the retention of the plot system in a more effective form might have produced some improvement in the financial provisions of concession terms, it might equally have created even greater problems for the Iraqi government than those that it had with the IPC. To be sure, the removal of the plot system and the assurance of a larger area for exploration was a great advantage to the companies, enabling them to plan their work over a longer period and wider horizon. And it eliminated unwanted competition on their doorstep.

In our judgement, the disadvantages suffered by Iraq rose more from the terms of the group agreement among the companies, which governed the production and offtake of oil, than from the terms of the concession agreement itself.[35] Iraq might have been better off if the concession had been given to a single international company, large, oil-hungry, and financially well-provided—or perhaps two. But this would surely have given rise to even greater criticism of monopoly and imperialistic exploitation than was provoked by the IPC—and in any case where was there such a company that could be attracted?

Unfortunately, the IPC quickly acquired a reputation for dragging its feet in the development of its oil concession, and there is evidence that the charge was justified. A portion of the original cartel report of the Federal Trade Commission had been classified and withheld from publication when the rest of the report was published in 1952, on the ground that it was prejudicial to the national security of the United States. The classified material was finally declassified and published in the United States Senate hearings of the Church Committee in 1974.[36] It contained excerpts from reports and letters of J. Skliros (General Manager of the IPC during 1934–49) taken from SONJ files by the Commission, which makes it clear that in Syria the IPC used a variety of devices to delay the laying of the pipelines, had held its exploratory activities 'in abeyance' after the discoveries in Kirkuk, and had deliberately 'sat on' the Qatar concession for a period, because there was already too much oil in the Gulf area.

We do know, and we shall see further examples later, that oil discoveries in the Middle East proved to be so prolific that the companies found it desirable to hold back their development in order to prevent a very great fall in prices. Some companies, in particular Anglo–Persian (later Anglo–Iranian and still later British Petroleum), Standard of California, Gulf, and for a while SONJ, had very much more owned oil available than they could use in their own operations; others, notably Mobil Oil and the French CFP, wanted a great deal more than they had. The last two companies would have had incentives to develop their oil much more rapidly than the oil-surplus companies. When the two groups were combined in the same consortium, as they were in the IPC, it is not surprising that the oil-surplus companies would attempt to slow down the rate of development.

It must be remembered, however, that if the kind of competitive expansion of output envisaged by the Federal Trade Commission as desirable had prevailed throughout the region, prices would have been much lower and overall output only slightly, if at all, higher, since demand, which was already rising very rapidly, would not have tended to expand very much faster in response to even lower prices. Consumers would have benefited, but producers as a whole probably would not, although some of the lower-cost producers might have gained at the expense of the higher-cost producers. The Federal Trade Commission Report and other evidence of the monopolistic activities of the oil companies has been, and still is, used by the oil-exporting countries to charge the oil companies (and their governments) with 'imperialist exploitation', but it seems likely that had the free competition desired by the FTC prevailed instead of 'oligopolistic restraint', the consumers (in whose interest the FTC purports to operate) would have been the gainers, not the producers—and the consumers reside largely in the industrialized countries. It is probably true that competition for oil concessions would for a while have made it possible for the host governments to obtain better concession terms, but if competition in oil markets had forced down prices and thus profitability, the demand for concessions would have soon been damped and any boom short-lived. That this would have led to an early 'OPEC' is very doubtful in view of the political conditions of the countries at the time.

Notes

1 The British advanced into Mosul after the armistice. This was, strictly speaking, within the terms of the armistice. But, as Marian Kent reports, '. . . the minutes of the War Cabinet meetings . . . show clearly that it was undertaken also to put Britain in as strong a bargaining position as possible

for negotiating peace with Turkey and a reorganization of the Sykes–Picot Agreement with France. Oil was not specifically mentioned at these meetings, but the discussions that took place beforehand, and the succeeding negotiations with France, make it plain that it was an important factor in Britain's wish to regain influence over Mosul'; op. cit., pp. 126–7. Longrigg notes that without this British action Mosul would probably today form part of Turkey instead of Iraq. S. H. Longrigg, *Iraq, 1900 to 1950* (London, 1953), p. 92.

2 Because of the difficulty in finding qualified Iraqis and because there was an easy supply of experienced junior Indian civil servants, Britain tended to use large numbers of Indians in the clerical and lower administrative grades in her Iraqi administration. This was widely resented by the Iraqis.

3 Longrigg, op. cit., Ch. IV presents a lively and knowledgeable discussion of the trials and tribulations of British administrators in Iraq in this period, largely from their point of view. Ghassan Atiyyah, *Iraq, 1908–1921: A Political Study* (Beirut, 1973), discusses the British administration more from the point of view of the local population. Atiyyah's analysis of the fragmentation and heterogeneity of the Iraqi population is of particular interest; esp. pp. 213ff.

4 See ibid., pp. 307ff. for a discussion of the rising and its suppression from an Iraqi point of view.

5 Longrigg, op. cit., p. 134.

6 F. H. Hinsley, *Nationalism and the International Order* (London, 1973), Ch. 8.

7 Quoted M. Khadduri, *Independent Iraq, 1932–1958*, 2nd edn. (London, 1960).

8 A. Toynbee, *Survey of International Affairs* (London, 1925), Vol. I. *Islamic Affairs,* p. 473. Footnotes have been eliminated from this quotation.

9 See C. J. Edmonds, *Kurds, Turks and Arabs* (London, 1957).

10 For an excellent account of the negotiations see Arnold Toynbee, *Survey of International Affairs, 1925. The Islamic World Since the Peace Settlement* (London, 1927), pp. 471–531. In addition, the relevant documents of the League of Nations are available.

11 Bernard Lewis, *The Emergence of Modern Turkey,* 2nd edn. (Oxford, 1968), pp. 248, 250–1, 255.

12 This line was so called because it had been accepted as a provisional line at a League Council meeting in Brussels on 25 July 1924, separating the areas occupied by the Turkish and Anglo-Iraqi forces respectively at the time when the Commission of Inquiry began its work.

13 Major General Nuri al-Said dominated the Iraqi political scene from the Arab Revolt until 1958. He was born in 1888 and educated at the Military and Staff College in Istanbul. During 1912–13 he fought in the Balkan War; espousing the Arab cause, he escaped from Istanbul and went first to Egypt and then to Basra, where he resumed his work for Arab independence. He joined the Arab Revolt and was appointed Chief of Staff to Hejaz and the Syrian front. He fought the desert campaign with Lawrence of Arabia 1916–18. Accompanied Faisal to Europe in 1921 after the Armistice. In 1921 was appointed Chief of the General Staff and later acting Commander-in-Chief of the Iraqi army. Between 1930 and 1958 he was Prime Minister 14 times, six times Minister of Defence and six times of Foreign Affairs. Went into exile twice, first when the army killed his brother-in-law and political colleague, Jaafar al-Askari, after the Bakr Sidqi *coup,* and secondly after the Rashid Ali *coup.* He was assassinated on 15 July 1958 after the Qassim *coup.*

14 A. Toynbee, *Survey of International Affairs* (London, 1934), pp. 109–216.

15 An admirably concise summary of the machinery of government in Iraq can be found in Chapter II of Majid Khadduri, op. cit. The central institutions were similar to those of Britain; a constitutional monarchy with, unlike

Britain, a written Organic Law, and a Cabinet and parliament. Local government was organized in three tiers: 14 governorates (*liwas*), then subdivided into *qadas* and further subdivided into *nahiyas*. An independent judiciary was provided, in which some British judges were to be employed under a supplementary agreement to the 1930 treaty. (This permitted enough confidence in the justice of the courts for Britain to accept the abolition of the extra-territorial privileges of the capitulations of Ottoman times.) But religious courts were also provided for.

16 Many of the leading Iraqi political figures in this period had had their education in Turkey. They included Nuri al-Said, Yasin al-Hashimi, Rashid Ali al-Gaylani, Hikmat Sulayman, Jamil al-Midfai, Muzahim al-Pachachi, Ali Jawdat al-Ayubi, and Sassoon Hiskail, all of whose names will figure in these pages. Nuri, Yasin, and Ali Jawdat were educated at the Military College in Istanbul; Hiskail, Rashid Ali, and al-Pachachi were educated at the Turkish Law College, while Hikmat was at Istanbul University and Midfai at the Royal Engineering School in Istanbul.

17 Khadduri, op. cit., p. 27.

18 Hassan Aaref, *La Grande Bretagne en Egypte et en Irak* (Paris, 1939), p. 234.

19 The history of these negotiations has been summarized by numerous authors whose books appear in our Bibliography, including Longrigg, Schwadran, Stocking, and, notably, the Federal Trade Commission Report, in English, and by Faure and Murat in French. Many of the relevant documents are published in the various volumes of the *Foreign Relations of the United States,* and in *Documents on British Foreign Policy, 1919–1939,* E. L. Woodward and Rohan Butler (eds.), as well as in J. C. Hurewitz, *Diplomacy in the Near and Middle East: a Documentary Record: 1914–1956* (Toronto and New York, 1958). Documents in the British Public Records Office have been used in the preparation of a number of unpublished theses, especially C. Davies, *British Oil Policy in the Middle East, 1919–1932* (University of Edinburgh, 1973), and B. R. N. al-Haidari, *The Development of the Iraq Oil Industry and the role of Iraq National Oil Company, 1925–1974* (Unpublished Ph.D thesis prepared in the Polytechnic of Central London, 1976). See also H. Mejcher, *Imperial Quest for Oil. Iraq 1900–1928*; and M. Kent, *Oil and Empire.*

20 The parent companies arranged to buy Gulbenkian's share of TPC oil and provided for an outside expert to help determine a fair price for it. In 1950, when profit-sharing arrangements were being made with the Middle Eastern governments, crude oil was valued for tax purposes at a price which had no necessary relation to 'market' prices. This was the result of the vertical integration of the companies. For an analysis of this situation see E. T. Penrose, *The Large International Firm in Developing Countries: the International Petroleum Industry* (London, 1968).

21 Sassoon Hiskail was one of the most astute of the early Iraqi political leaders and diplomats. He was born in 1860 of a distinguished Jewish family, was educated in Europe and Istanbul and spoke six languages. He held high office in the Ottoman government. In 1908 he was elected a member of the Ottoman parliament for Baghdad and held the seat until the end of the First World War. In 1921 he attended the Cairo Conference to establish the Iraqi Kingdom under Amir Faisal and was one of the three members of the Iraqi Committee formed to examine the draft of the country's Organic Law in 1922. From 1925 until his death in Europe in 1932, he was a member of the Iraqi parliament, and many times Minister of Finance.

22 The 'transferred territories' referred to the areas on the Persian–Turkish frontier which were the subject of the 'Transferred Territories' protocol of

December 1913 signed by representatives of Britain, Russia, Persia, and Turkey. The area around Khanaqin in eastern Iraq, where APOC had oil interests, was awarded to Turkey which subsequently recognized the APOC concession. Subject to negotiation of the terms, the Iraqi government also agreed to recognize the APOC concession after oil was discovered in commercial quantities at Naftkhana in 1923. This territory was excluded from the TPC concession area.

23 See above, Chapter 2.

24 Although in December 1925 the Council of the League of Nations had endorsed the recommendation of its investigative commission that the Mosul *vilayet* should be awarded to Iraq, the Frontier Treaty between the United Kingdom, Iraq, and Turkey which settled the frontiers, was not ratified until July 1926. This treaty provided, as compensation to Turkey, that the Iraqi government would pay to the Turkish government 10 per cent of the royalties it received under the oil concession for 25 years.

25 This privilege, given with one hand, was effectively taken away with the other since the American companies were required to notify the TPC of their intention to bid, thus giving the other TPC shareholders plenty of time individually or collectively to outbid them. For a discussion of CFP interest in these questions see R. F. Kuisel, *Ernest Mercier, French Technocrat* (Berkeley, Calif,. 1967), Ch. 3.

26 The evolution of this agreement has been fully discussed in the Federal Trade Commission Report, *The International Petroleum Cartel* (Washington, D.C., 1952). See also the account of the history of negotiations leading to participation of American companies in the Iraq Petroleum Company in *Multinational Corporations and United States Foreign Policy,* Hearings before the Subcommittee on Multinational Corporations of the Committee on Foreign Relations, United States Senate (93rd Congress, 2nd Sess., Part 7, pp. 508–16). (Church Committee Hearings.)

27 Later three other American companies withdrew, leaving only Mobil Oil and Standard Oil Company (New Jersey) as shareholders in the Near East Development Corporation, the subsidiary organized to hold the shares of the American participants in the IPC.

28 S. H. Longrigg, *Oil in the Middle East,* 2nd edn. (London, 1961), p. 74.

29 Yasin al-Hashimi played a leading role in Iraqi politics up to 1935 when he was overthrown in the first military *coup d'état* and exiled to Syria, where he died. Born in 1884, he was educated at the Military College of Istanbul and held various appointments in the Ottoman army. After the occupation of Damascus in the First World War he joined the Arab army and was later Chief of Staff to the military governor of Syria. Banished by the British to Palestine in 1919, he returned after popular demonstrations in protest. He returned to Baghdad in 1922 and subsequently held several cabinet posts; he was five times Minister of Finance and twice Prime Minister.

Muzahim al-Pachachi, who had taken part in the oil negotiations, was a member of the original Constituent Assembly in 1924; also several times a minister from 1924 on and one of Iraq's leading diplomats. Rashid Ali al-Gaylani was to prove a stormy petrel in Iraqi politics and we shall hear much more of him. Born in 1892, he was a Turkish-educated lawyer, and became first a judge, and then Minister of Justice, followed by the Ministry of the Interior, and President of the Chamber of Deputies in 1925–26. He first became Prime Minister in 1933.

30 This permitted the government to impose such taxes on the company as were ordinarily imposed on other industrial enterprises in Iraq.

31 Because a larger area was now reserved to the IPC, the APOC in 1934 accepted

a reduction in its overriding royalty from 10 per cent to 7.5 per cent of the oil produced.

32 Just how 'gold' was to be interpreted was for a long time to be a source of controversy between the company and the Iraqi government. The first disagreement occurred in 1932 after the devaluation of sterling when the IPC refused to pay the royalties due at the beginning of January at the previous gold rate. On taking legal advice, however, the British government advised the company to pay the sterling equivalent of gold at the old rate. (See below, Ch. 6.)

33 Haifa was not specified, but, in the event, the pipeline went both to Tripoli in (then) Syria and Haifa. The Iraqi political objection to Tripoli in Syria proved unjustified (until 1976) and Haifa turned out to be the politically more risky, that arm of the pipeline having to be closed after 1947.

34 See, for example, the Iraqi experience with the BOD discussed below in Ch. 6.

35 See below, Ch. 6.

36 *Multinational Corporations and United States Foreign Policy,* Part 7, pp. 529–32.

Part Two

The Years of an Independent Monarchy 1932–58

4 Independence and a Faltering Democracy: 1932–45

Iraq entered on her newly attained independence as a full member of the League of Nations in 1932 with the machinery of representative government under a constitutional monarchy. The King came from a ruling house which had been ejected from Saudi Arabia by a rival and from Syria by the French forces. His views had been profoundly modified by his experiences in Damascus, which had predisposed him for the future to reject the advice of 'all or nothing' schools of thought and to accept piecemeal advances towards desired goals rather than run head-on into 'confrontations' in which the chances seemed to favour his opponents.

But it takes more than a wise monarch to make a success of a democratic system under a constitutional monarchy. A well-qualified contemporary observer, Arnold Toynbee, correctly pointed out in 1934 that

> The differentiation in the Mandatory Powers' treatment of Iraq on the one hand, and the Syrian territories on the other, was a political paradox . . . there could be no doubt that the Syrian Arabs were more ripe than the Iraqi Arabs for managing their own affairs.
>
> . . . On the other hand . . . neither the British nor yet the French Government had yet shown any intention, in regard to Palestine Proper and the Lebanon, of even going so far as to translate the tutelage of the mandatory regime into treaty form, though Palestine and the Lebanon were undoubtedly the least immature of all the Arab-speaking countries under mandate. . . .[1]

This does not necessarily support the view that immature countries should be held under tutelage for a time by foreign powers, but it does suggest by implication that the political authorities of the great powers were giving precedence to what they conceived to be their own interests over what, on their own criteria, they conceived to be the interests of the smaller powers concerned.

King Faisal proved to be a fortunate choice for Iraq; his wise and moderating influence was essential to mediate among the contending politicians and contending political attitudes. The politicians and the politically conscious Iraqi public early became torn between two points of view. One was a moderate Iraqi nationalism stressing the importance of the economic and political development of the Iraqi state, affirming Arab brotherhood and solidarity but not accepting that Iraq should engage in militant international action in support of 'unity and independence' of all Arab states, and supporting friendly links with Britain. The other espoused a militant and, in practice, extremely intolerant Arab nationalism, was resentfully anti-British, strongly attacking the Mandate as a remnant of British imperialism (which, as we have seen, it was in part), and was, even in principle, impatient of democracy. This second group was represented by the Ikha al-Watani (National Brotherhood) party which was fiercely hostile to any concessions to, or even recognition of, any other sentiment than that of Arab nationalism. Their intransigence was even wider in scope: they had opposed King Faisal for his readiness to mediate between the British government and other outside influences and they had declared that they would never recognize as binding the 1930 treaty with Britain.

Upon independence the King attempted to find a coalition Cabinet, but the Ikha declined, since they refused to accept the treaty with Britain. A transition government was then formed headed by Naji Shawkat, a neutral politician. It was attacked by the Ikha so strongly that the King then turned to Rashid Ali al-Gaylani, one of their leaders, to head a government and appealed to him to consider the unfortunate international consequence for the new state if a treaty just recently negotiated were abrogated so quickly. Because he accepted the King's argument, however, Rashid Ali came under furious attack from the militant nationalists. The consequent weakening of the government encouraged a reopening of the agitation of the Shia against Sunni domination, for the Ikha party consisted primarily of Sunni, who, though in a substantial minority in the country, were politically dominant and discriminated against the Shia.

In the meantime, there had broken out a conflict in the north of the country where a group of Assyrians had demanded that the state should provide them with territory large enough for them to settle in. Nationalist passions were running high and the Ikha party seized on this affair, allegedly to divert public attention from the country's political divisions.[2] The 'Assyrian Affair' was the first of the several serious conflicts between the Iraqi government and Iraqi minority groups, and showed how fiercely intolerant the dominant group could be.

The Assyrian Atrocity

Since Iraq was a new state, created by outside forces within boundaries that were a compromise among these forces, it was not surprising that one of its first critical issues, though domestic in principle, originated on other sides of the new frontiers and was a legacy of war.

The settlement of the dispute over the frontier between the new Turkey and the new state of Iraq had left in Iraq about three-quarters of the Assyrians who had aided Britain during the war. They were refused re-entry into their mountain homes in Turkey, and nothing remained open to them but resettlement in Iraq. Since they lived in regions largely inhabited by Kurds, it had been disastrous for their post-war relations in Iraq that the British army during the war had on certain occasions used them in retaliatory operations against Kurdish opponents of the wartime or early post-war British regime in the north. Other unfavourable influences on the prospects of resettlement in independent Iraq came from the Arab side and from disappointed expectations among the Assyrians themselves. In addition the Assyrian Patriarch, the Mar Shamun, was inexperienced and used poor judgement throughout of political possibilities. The Assyrians demanded a region in which they could resettle as a homogeneous group and they maintained this demand even after the Iraqi government had declared, and Great Britain and the League Council had subsequently agreed, that no unoccupied area large enough could be found. On the other hand, the British and Iraqi governments showed poor diplomacy in flatly and formally rejecting the right of the Patriarch to exercise any form of temporal authority, since the former had used that authority as one of the means of maintaining the loyalty of the Assyrian troops in the service of the British army. The transition from conditions normal under the Ottoman Empire to those appropriate to a state establishing itself on modern European lines was too abrupt.[3]

The independent Iraqi government, in retaliation for the opposition coming from the Patriarch, held him, in effect, as a prisoner in Baghdad in mid-1933, in spite of efforts by the British High Commissioner and urgent messages from King Faisal, then in London on a State visit. The condition of his release was to be the signature of a document renouncing all temporal power. This clumsy and incompetent approach inevitably led to a crisis in Mosul and the north. The British Administrative Inspector in Mosul, Colonel Stafford, and Major Thompson, the British expert on resettlement, made every effort to avert disaster. There were in principle two possible courses before the Assyrians. The first was to co-operate in the realization of a scheme for land settlement that Major Thompson proposed; the second was to leave the country. Iraqi ministers in Baghdad declared their readiness to facilitate the second course, but this had no meaning unless other countries could be persuaded to accept the Assyrians.

The responsibility for the final disaster must, we believe, be placed on the Iraqi government: its imprisonment of the Patriarch and its demand for a formal written statement repudiating all authority over his followers showed a lack of political sense. It led to the migration across the Tigris of a number of Assyrians and later to the return of some of them after the French authorities had shown themselves unwilling to accept them permanently. By this time the Iraqi government, in the absence of King Faisal and largely under the influence of the Interior Minister, Hikmat Sulayman, who was perhaps as much Turkish as Arab in outlook,[4] had reversed its former position and adopted a policy aimed at the elimination of the Assyrians. This was facilitated by the presence of a Kurdish officer, General Bakr Sidqi, who was noted for his hatred of the Assyrians and was in command of the Iraqi troops in the area. In August 1933 when the Assyrians recrossed the frontier, clashes occurred and on the order of Bakr Sidqi the Iraqi army deliberately carried out in cold blood a systematic massacre of the Assyrians at the village of Simmel, in which women and children as well as men were among the victims.[5] All this was a severe blow to King Faisal himself, and a foretaste of the attitudes of later independent Iraqi governments towards minorities.

Because of the Assyrian tragedy, King Faisal had returned from his State visit to London on 2 August 1933, but he was a very sick man and finding that he was helpless in the face of the fanaticism whipped up by the Ikha among the Iraqi people, and his counsel virtually ignored, he returned on 2 September to Berne for medical treatment. A few days later, on 8 September, he died. In death he received the homage denied him by his people in the last weeks of his life.

The Failure of a Political Legacy[6]

Britain, and the League of Nations, had attempted to endow Iraq with a constitution and the rudiments of a parliamentary system on lines that had originated and evolved through centuries in Britain. The transplant was rejected by the body politic of Iraq. Embedded in the system itself was an alien body around which festered inflamed and bitter agitation—the unequal treaty relation with Britain, the foreign power which had, in the view of very many Iraqis, denied the Arabs their birthright.

Between independence and the Second World War there were 12 Cabinets. To a considerable extent the instability of Cabinets reflected instability in the country: to some extent it was a consequence of the rivalries of individual politicians and of political groups, the lines between which were not always clearly drawn. The fanatical nature of extreme Pan Arab nationalism, the inability to treat minorities humanely or sectarian groups other than the ruling Sunni wisely, the dominance of warring personalities willing to use the army to advance their political cause—all became clearly evident. Turkish authoritarianism clashed with anarchical tribalism and both with moderate nationalism and democratic government eventually to produce government by military oligarchy.

Faisal was succeeded by Ghazi, his 21-year-old only son, who asked Rashid Ali to form a new government. Faced with the necessity of establishing confidence abroad in the new regime, Rashid Ali expressed his government's intention to follow in the path of King Faisal and to maintain the friendship and alliance with Britain. He realized that it would be damaging for Iraq and for the new King, after having acquired independence on terms acceptable to the League of Nations as well as to Britain, to initiate a new diplomatic move that would reopen all the old differences. This provoked a clash with some of the other Ikha politicians, and the Prime Minister met this new internal opposition by a request for the dissolution of parliament; the electoral process in Iraq had already become grossly distorted by the ability of those in power so to manipulate it as to ensure the return of a majority of their supporters to the subsequent parliament. The new King refused this request, and the Ikha ministers in the Cabinet, including Rashid Ali, resigned on 28 October 1933.

Non-party political leaders provided the alternative to an Ikha Prime Minister. The King appointed Jamil al-Midfai, an independent politician who had served under Faisal and had taken part in the 1916 Army Revolt. Four Cabinets followed in quick succession. His first Cabinet broke down as a result of factional infighting among its members and Sunni–Shia divergencies; his second was weak and administrative affairs deteriorated, for which he was blamed by the Ikha. The third Cabinet went to Ali Jawdat, Chief of the Royal Diwan, whose request that parliament be dissolved was granted by the King. The subsequent elections were not only 'managed', but badly managed in that too many powerful men were excluded from parliament, and the government had too many enemies in too many quarters.

The resentment of the Ikha at being excluded from power led them to abandon peaceful means of fighting the government and they plotted to arouse the tribes of the middle Euphrates against it (an idea apparently suggested by Hikmat Sulayman). Aided by the anger of certain of the shaikhs who had also been excluded from parliament, by tribal land disputes, and by Shia grievances, the revolt of the tribes spread rapidly throughout the whole area south of Hilla. Ali Jawdat resigned, and al-Midfai succeeded, to last only 12 days.

The failure of the four Cabinets headed by independent Prime Ministers finally opened the way for a government based on the Ikha al-Watani party with its forcible demands for treaty revision and for the removal of British influence. Headed by Yasin al-Hashimi, it included Rashid Ali as Minister of the Interior, which gave him control of the police, but omitted Hikmat Sulayman. Two independent ministers, Nuri al-Said and Jaafar al-Askari, were included as Foreign Minister and Minister of Defence. (Thus did al-Hashimi secure his rear.)

The Ikha ministry was stronger and lasted longer than the ministries of independent politicians which it succeeded, and it was able to introduce a number of economic and social measures, as we shall see later. But the tribes of the middle Euphrates were stirred against it by disappointed politicians in Baghdad; the same weapons that the Ikha had used against the governments of their predecessors were now to be turned against them. Incitements from Baghdad politicians and occasionally from *ulema* in Najf, land disputes, and attempts to enforce the conscription law which had been passed in 1934, all contributed to the unrest and occasional outbreaks in the middle Euphrates. Both diplomacy and, later, bombing and military repression were employed without any serious attempt at reform or serious efforts to deal with genuine grievances. Bakr Sidqi, profiting by an ordinance of 1935 legalizing resort to martial law, disposed of a number of those arrested in his customary manner.

In October 1935 another discreditable episode occurred against a minority group again in the north. The conscription law encroached on the central tenets of a sect of Kurdish origin, the Yazidis, who followed an heretical deviation from Islam which probably embodied elements derived from pagan cults and, more doubtfully, from Zoroastrianism. By the orthodox they have sometimes been assailed as 'devil-worshippers', but this seems an absurd travesty of their view that Allah in his infinite mercy will pardon even the angel who was cast out, and will let him return. Unlike the Kurdish people generally, they inclined to the Shia rather than to the Sunni. Their doctrines precluded them from participating in military service. The Ottoman regime had exempted them. Not so the government of Iraq. When the Yazidis resisted recruitment, mainly by passive means, a brigade of troops was used to meet an unresisting population; martial law was declared; hundreds of men were seized; nine of them were hanged and the rest imprisoned.

The First Military Usurpation of Power

Prime Minister Yasin al-Hashimi soon revealed a tendency, widely followed by his successors, to concentrate power in his own hands, dispensing with party support. As he became increasingly autocratic, the Ikha party increasingly lost cohesion and al-Hashimi finally announced its dissolution, claiming that he himself represented all groups. There were serious clashes with Hikmat Sulayman, who maintained his unrelenting opposition to the government which had excluded him from its ministerial ranks. Disorder in the country grew and Hikmat carried on secret discussions with General Bakr Sidqi and other army officers with a view to overthrowing the government. The army had a high prestige in Iraq, but the failure of the civilian governments to establish effective parliamentary institutions, and the suppression of civilian expressions of opinion, finally left the governments of Iraq heavily dependent on the army for support.

The army was extremely nationalist and contained officers who believed that a strong military regime in Iraq was necessary to eliminate foreign control, to establish Pan Arab solidarity, to help sister Arab countries against imperialist domination (notably Syria), and to bring about the reforms necessary to ensure law and order in the country. The political leaders of independent Iraq had already called on the army several times to suppress resistance or opposition by minority groups, and the savage methods of Bakr Sidqi against minorities had been widely popular in Arab circles. Moreover, one of Hikmat's brothers had been prominent in the rising of the Young Turks before the First World War: thus military conspiracies by young officers were not unfamiliar to him. But wider support, including civilian support, would be needed to form an alternative government. This Hikmat sought among leaders in the *Ahali* (or 'Reformist') group and he carried on secret discussions with them as well as with Bakr Sidqi and other army officers.

The *Ahali* group, not yet formed into a party, represented a different viewpoint from that of the Ikha. Its organ *Ahali* had in spite of censorship become by far the most influential newspaper in Baghdad, serving as the mouthpiece of the most constructive, the most modernized, and the most progressive minds in Iraq. It rejected both political conservatism and authoritarian communism or socialism based on class war. It concentrated on social reforms, including land reform, and improvements in the conditions of the workers in both rural and urban areas. Some of its members were liberal and re-formers, some socialists in the social democratic sense; one was a Marxist socialist, but there were also 'opportunists'.[7] To the *Ahali* leaders Hikmat could point to the failure of Yasin to carry out social reforms. These men had suffered in the past from the severe censorship exercised by Yasin over the Baghdad press, which had suppressed their first paper, *Al-Bayan,* after two issues and which now fell heavily on *Ahali.* Like the civilian Baathists in Syria in the 1950s, they had yet to learn the pitfalls of alliances with army officers.

Hikmat Sulayman was an intermediary between Bakr and the army group on the one hand and the *Ahali* group on the other. But the plot formed by Bakr and the rebel officers for the revolt of the army was not disclosed to the *Ahali* group until the last minute; they only reluctantly accepted, fearing that the result would be a government run by officers. Hikmat assured them that the army would withdraw after the overthrow of the government and he informed them that Bakr had asked that they should draw up the proclamation and the letter to the King. Convinced that the repressive measures of the Yasin government, particularly the suppression of dissenting opinion, the arrests on political grounds, and the dismissal of civil servants on mere suspicion, left no alternative to force, the *Ahali* group consented. On 29 October 1936 the army entered Baghdad and Iraq suffered her first military *coup d'état.*

The Minister of Defence, Jaafar al-Askari (brother-in-law of Nuri al-Said), had at the last moment appealed to the King to arrest the march on Baghdad, which had by then become unnecessary since Yasin had agreed to resign on hearing of the *coup.* But Bakr, determined to profit by a big military demonstration in the capital, instigated the murder of Jaafar.

Because of the co-operation of the *Ahali* group and the nature of the Yasin government, the *coup* was not a clear case of the overthrow of a genuine parliamentary regime by the army. Nor did it represent the overthrow of an autocratic regime with a view to the establishment of a true parliamentary democracy. Undoubtedly the *Ahali* group wished it to take that form. But an examination of the ideas of the military officers and the civilian leaders other than the *Ahali* shows that none of them desired a free press or open, unmanaged elections, or freedom of opposition parties.

The elements which supported this first military *coup d'état* were thus hopelessly at variance among themselves and inevitably fell apart during the formation of a new regime. The immediate open clashes were between the Arab nationalists and the *Ahali* group.

When the former observed the prompt call by the latter in the press and at the Speaker's table in parliament for land reform, for changes in social conditions, and for trade unions, and saw the precedence given to these reforms over Arab nationalism, they at once launched forcible attacks on what they described as 'socialism' and 'communism'. The reformers, particularly Kamil Chadirchi and Muhammed Hadid, were the only unmistakable believers in parliamentary democracy.[8] The groups more loosely described as Arab nationalists, which included the Istiqlal, tended towards conservatism in internal economic matters and in many cases towards authoritarian rather than parliamentary government. Some of them were sympathetic towards the army officers around Bakr Sidqi, who was increasingly to create fears that he aspired to establish a military government in Iraq.

Many features of the first *coup d'état* foreshadowed the pattern of what was to follow in independent Iraq. No real unity existed in the army as a whole. Even less unity existed in the mixed army-civilian ranks of those who overthrew the previous regime, except on the desire to end it. The ambitious individual leaders of the *coup* pledged themselves to satisfy incompatible aims of the groups whose support they had sought.

The regime of Hikmat Sulayman soon became as autocratic as that of Yasin had been, and the progressive forces were left as far away as ever from the realization of their aims. Almost immediately a vendetta against members of the previous government was instituted, the leading members of which were deported or persecuted. Widespread charges of communism were laid against reforming groups. The shaikhs of the middle Euphrates particularly feared that the government's land policies would damage their interests. Disputes over land boundaries, combined with the government moves to enforce conscription and taxation on the tribes, enabled the shaikhs to bring their tribesmen to revolt against the government.

The tribal problems in the Diwaniya area brought to a head the growing tensions between the reformist group in the Cabinet and the Prime Minister, who, by now completely dependent on the army and Bakr, separated himself from his reformist colleagues. The army had emerged as the only strong political vested interest in the country and in June 1937 the Prime Minister had no choice but to agree to a military attack on the tribes without reference to the Cabinet. The four reformist ministers, a majority in the Cabinet of seven, then resigned. Hikmat reconstituted his Cabinet, bringing in nationalist and Istiqlal leaders. Some of the opposition leaders were deported (including Yasin al-Hashimi who died later in Damascus of a heart attack), others were banished, persecuted, or disgraced, the Reformist

Society was abolished, and parliament was dissolved in order to purge them from that body.

Continued *Coups d'État*

The Government had now lost all support from the progressive and even from the moderately conservative forces in the country. The Prime Minister was obviously dominated by Bakr and his army associates who could veto any measure of which they disapproved. Change came, however, from within the army which, though it was the strongest group in the country, overshadowing civil power, could never escape the weakness of divisions within its own ranks. The anti-Bakr faction of the army plotted his assassination and on 11 August 1937 he was murdered by a soldier while resting at the Mosul airport. Hikmat's government could not survive the defeat of Bakr's party in the army and he resigned on 16 August. In effect, Hikmat Sulayman was overthrown by a second *coup d'état*.

Then, as later, what there was of public opinion was strongly opposed to army rule and army interference in civil government, and concessions were made to this by the recall on 17 August of Jamil al-Midfai as Prime Minister of a new government, with assurances from army leaders that they would not again interfere in government. The new premier declared that his policy was to 'forget the past' and to avoid reprisals. But the animosities which had been aroused since the army had forsaken its proper role in the state in order to dominate and exercise veto powers over governments could not be allayed by declarations and appeals. The divisions—some would have called them feuds—among the officers continued and were intensified in the next few years by external events.

The army ostensibly withdrew from politics, but with the disappearance of the reformist civilian leaders and of the relatively moderate group around Yasin al-Hashimi, the army continued to exercise power behind the scenes, different factions supporting different groups in government. Majid Khadduri summarizes this aspect of the situation as follows:

> The army became virtually the sole deciding factor in the rise and fall of almost all Cabinets from 1937 to 1941. This naturally created instability in administration and led to the recurrence of military coups d'état. The first coup, while it was welcomed as a means of getting rid of an undesirable Cabinet, set a bad precedent for the intervention of the army in politics; the move indeed became impossible to stop and led to six more military coups up to 1941. The seventh, culminating in a conflict in the application

of the Anglo–Iraqi Treaty of 1930, met utter failure in a war with a foreign Power.[9]

Memories of the past did not die. Personal animosities and feuds were still openly pursued in public life. Though the chief instigator of the murder of Jaafar was dead, the desire to bring to justice others concerned in the Bakr group was still expressed in the parliament. Army interests were still active and the pledge against army intervention in politics was not effective in practice. Generals Nuri al-Said, who had been appointed as minister to Egypt, and Taha al-Hashimi were opposed to the government and secretly plotted against it. At the same time four colonels, who came to be designated as the 'Golden Square', formed a mutual pact to stand together, of which much was to be heard in the future. For a long time behind the scenes and later openly in association with other military and political leaders these four men exercised a dominant influence on Iraqi politics. They were Salah al-Din al-Sabbagh, Commander of the Third Division of the Iraqi Army, Kamil Shabib, Commander of the First Division, Mahmud Salman, Commander of the Air Force, and Fahmi Said, in charge of mechanized forces.

The Approach of World War

The shadows of the coming World War were already beginning to fall over the Middle East. The state of Iraq owed its origins to the First World War, in which the enthusiasm of the Young Turk officer Enver Pasha for the German military class had drawn the Ottoman Empire into the war on what was destined, in spite of its early victories, to be the losing side. In the latter 1930s there appeared in Iraq elements among the 'young officer' class who, possessing only the sketchiest knowledge of the First World War, were nourishing a similar enthusiasm, not solely for the German army, but beyond it for the authoritarian regime which had seized power in 1933. Like the Young Turks, they had at first subscribed to democratic and liberal principles as a useful ideology in combating European imperialism. They had also tolerated the continuation of limited and indirect British control after independence had been declared formally. But outside this sphere their ideas were authoritarian, having no place for the restraints of a legislature on the executive. The aim of the majority of their leaders was to gain power and to keep it indefinitely, preferably without the need to submit themselves to a free voting electorate. If that were impracticable, then the alternative for them was to manage the elections to the extent necessary to keep in power. This had been standard practice up to a point since 1932, but it had not been enough to prevent the rise and fall of ministries according to which was the dominant faction in the army.

Such was the position as the Second World War approached. It was complicated and aggravated by the increasing difficulties in Palestine. The Mandate, which Britain had originally sought largely as a means of keeping the influence of French liberal thought at a distance from Egypt, had brought nothing but trouble. The Hitler regime had adopted in a much-aggravated form the discrimination against Jewish people which Imperial Russia had practised from 1884 to the First World War. That problem was concerned primarily with Eastern European Jews: under Hitler it was extended to German Jews.

Sharp divisions were opened among officers and political leaders by the critical events in Europe in 1938, especially by the Munich agreement between Neville Chamberlain and Adolf Hitler. Those in Iraq who sympathized with Germany and Italy took little account of the probable designs of those powers on North Africa and Western Asia after the war.[10] But even among the more sophisticated military leaders and politicians resentment over conditions in Palestine was an almost unsurmountable obstacle to a balanced view of future international prospects.

Jamil al-Midfai, the new premier, was soon frustrated in his attempts to persuade political circles to turn their backs on the past and he was not able to control the feuding and factional infighting of the army. He was a civilian politician who believed in a sort of parliamentary government without political parties, and he attempted to control the army officers by a variety of checks and balances. The pretext for deposing him was his appointment of a Defence Minister who did not belong to the group formed by the colonels and their associates. Generals Nuri and al-Hashimi, who were the colonels' candidates for Prime Minister, secretly approved their enterprise, disregarding its effects in reinforcing dangerous precedents already set.

Preparations were made for a military *coup d'état* and the officers informed the King that they had lost confidence in the premier, and demanded a new government headed by Nuri al Said or Taha al-Hashimi. On 25 December 1938 al-Midfai resigned and the King called on Nuri to form a new government with al-Hashimi as Minister of Defence; Rustum Haydar, a strong Minister of Finance; and Rashid Ali al-Gaylani as Chief of the Royal Diwan. Nuri called for support of the democratic rather than the Nazi or Fascist powers and for a constitutional order of government at home with political parties and a free press, but he also showed considerable vindictiveness in the pursuit of personal animosities, particularly towards Hikmat Sulayman, whom he had accused of plotting against the state. Hikmat was tried and condemned to death under dubious procedures and with dubious evidence.[11]

Feuds of long standing continued to occupy army and political circles more than constructive efforts at reform. Meanwhile international conditions, both in Europe and in the Middle East, deteriorated rapidly, and Nuri, who had a clearer understanding than most of his colleagues and most of his opponents of international affairs, became increasingly preoccupied with them.

At a time when the Nazi and Fascist powers were gaining ground, the former in Central and Eastern Europe and the latter in North Africa, there appeared to many Iraqis to be a shift in the balance of power, unfavourable to the British and the French who had imposed their control on much of North Africa and the Fertile Crescent. The prospects opened by this change were pleasing to some Iraqi politicians and to more Iraqi officers. On the one hand, neither the case for parliamentary democracy nor the indispensable conditions of its attainment were yet accepted or even understood in Iraq. On the other hand, some civilians and many military officers failed surprisingly to realize the imperialist and colonialist aims of Mussolini and the Italian Fascists. Most of those who were aware of these aims looked to Germany to control the Italians. They failed to realize that Hitler's aspirations were directed towards expansion in Central and Eastern Europe and that he could be expected to support Mussolini's aims so long as they did not conflict with his own.

Here, however, differences arose among the Iraqi leaders. Nuri al-Said had spent more time outside Iraq and knew more of Britain than other leaders. Although he was himself an Arab nationalist, he believed that Iraq had more to gain and less to fear from Britain than from any other great power. In this he shared broadly the attitude towards the two great European democracies, Britain and France, of the more liberal section of the Turkish leaders of the revolution of 1909. Although he himself shared in and was partly responsible for the shortcomings of the Iraqi parliamentary system, he saw the dangers from Hitler and Mussolini.

A further grave issue complicated relations with Great Britain. The Palestine question had arisen much earlier, but the Nazi regime had greatly magnified it. The flow of Jewish refugees in the 1930s had intensified the conflict over the demand for unlimited immigration into Palestine. A strong reaction from the Arab population led to an early and serious conflict with the mandatory administration. In the face of her inconsistent commitments to Arabs and Zionists, Britain attempted to find a way out by limiting immigration while maintaining a single state to which independence could be granted, or alternatively by partition into two states, one Arab, the other Zionist. Neither solution satisfied either party concerned.

Nuri al-Said recognized the dangers of the Palestine impasse to the whole Middle East and, unlike most of his colleagues, was ready to take an initiative and seek a practical solution. He had clearly perceived that it was in the Arab interest to support the democratic rather than the totalitarian powers on the one hand, and to seek Palestinian independence while the Arabs constituted a substantial majority of the population on the other. Being of a more constructive mind than his colleagues, he sought to integrate these two desirable aims by holding out the prospect that Arab co-operation with the democratic powers would be facilitated by a favourable British response on Palestine.

In April 1939, King Ghazi was killed in a driving accident. The Amir Abdul Ilah was appointed as Regent during the minority of his nephew, Ghazi's son, King Faisal II. Ghazi had succeeded to the throne at too early an age to influence events as his father had done. He had occasionally intervened in favour of compromises falling short of some of the aims of the more aggressive officers. Although in principle the constitutional monarchy might have served as a check on military usurpation of power, just as kings in earlier days had sometimes controlled the barons, the hazards of personal character opened the way for periods of weakness that might occur in critical times. So it was in Iraq in the troubled times preceding and during the Second World War.

Nuri held elections on the eve of the new World War in the usual corrupt way, producing an obedient parliament. His policy was to maintain the alliance with Britain in the coming war, giving Britain facilities in accordance with the treaty in respect of transport and communications inside Iraq, but accepting a belligerent role only if Iraq were attacked. Within the army this position was acceptable to some officers but opposed uncompromisingly by the four colonels who had now separated themselves from the three officers with whom they had been joined in the actions that had brought Nuri to power. Their faith in the ultimate triumph of Germany and in the efficacy of government under army direction in Iraq remained undiminished. Their actions continued to reveal their intellectual limitations and the shortness of their vision. But they excelled in the art of intrigue and no ministry which incurred their hostility could endure. Although they had been instrumental in bringing Nuri to power, their co-operation had rested on a negative basis rather than on a political accord, a common dislike of the preceding regime rather than the pursuit of a common constructive purpose. When, three months after the election, war became a reality instead of a threat, it was inevitable that co-operation would turn to enmity, for the parties held opposite views both on its outcome and on Iraq's interests in it.

Attention was diverted from international to domestic affairs by the murder in January 1940 of Nuri's Finance Minister, Rustum Haydar, who had been one of his best and strongest ministers, and a powerful influence making for harmony in the Cabinet. The war aggravated domestic differences and divisions and Nuri, with a seriously weakened and divided Cabinet, decided to resign in favour of a Cabinet headed by Rashid Ali as Prime Minister and himself and Taha al-Hashimi as Ministers of Foreign Affairs and Defence respectively. Nuri hoped thus to bring Rashid in support of his position on international affairs. But this proposal created a severe division of opinion within the army and a threat of civil war between army factions. The Regent therefore asked Nuri to form a new government which, however, he could only do with the support of the four colonels and the removal of the officers, including the Chief of the General Staff, who had opposed their views in the army. Nuri returned, but only because of the insistence of the stronger group in the army—in effect another army *coup*.

Nuri's reconstituted government proposed a series of reforms dealing with the electoral laws and with reform and settlement of land disputes in the Diwaniya area, but dissension within the government, fanned by the intrigues of the colonels, frustrated him at every turn. His concessions brought no returns from the colonels; they perceived that he still gave precedence to relations with Britain—which to them appeared as Iraq's greatest enemy. The position of Rashid Ali was more qualified, and the colonels believed that they could influence him in the direction which they wished Iraq to take. Nuri was subject both to pressure from this direction and also to criticism from others who distrusted his attacks in general terms on his personal enemies and his failure to deal directly with the central problem of military domination of government. Faced with opposition from all sides, Nuri resigned in March 1940, but it was agreed between the Regent, Nuri, and Rashid Ali that Rashid Ali should succeed him, for Nuri still hoped to bring Rashid's support to his foreign policy. As Rashid's Foreign Minister Nuri continued to try to influence policy from within, but with little effect.

Rashid Ali and Conflict with Britain

Rashid Ali, who had succeeded Nuri somewhat reluctantly in view of the clear dependence of the government on the four colonels, may be described as an impulsive, ambitious, and opportunist, rather than doctrinaire, Arab nationalist. Like Nuri he allowed his opportunism to lead him at times into ambiguous positions in which he appeared to be attempting to reconcile contradictory viewpoints. He had been known as a sharp opponent of the Anglo–Iraqi treaty, but he now called for stronger friendly relations and alliance with Britain, conforming to the mutual interests of both countries. If the last phrase was meant to imply changes in the treaty, the hint was too subtle to placate his followers who, having no responsibilities themselves, maintained unchanged their opposition to the treaty as it stood—some of them, like the colonels, to any treaty with Britain. He was not alone among Iraqi politicians and military officers in desiring a double insurance for Iraq aimed at protecting her interests whichever side came out of the war in a dominating position. He was much less naive than the officers, but, like all the actors on the war stage, he was faced with uncertainties on every side. If his aim was to maintain himself in power, he knew that this was possible only with the consent of the dominant army officers, which would never be given in support of the British cause. Nuri had already discovered this, but, correctly estimating the outcome of the war, he could afford to wait.

Caught between the opposite but confidently held views of Nuri and the colonels, Rashid Ali sought arms and, if it should be required, air support from Germany. Iraq was a small power whose interests were unlikely to receive high priority in the plans of the belligerents. Her geographical position hindered the delivery of supplies, and Rashid Ali was insufficiently informed on the factors influencing Hitler's ability and willingness to deliver the goods. In the earlier stages, the German agreement with the Soviet Union and Hitler's agreement with Mussolini precluded German interference in the Middle East: later, the secret plans to attack Russia and the Mediterranean war left no appreciable surplus arms for new adventures.

Since the fall of the French army came in the early stage of Rashid Ali's first ministry, the uncertainties as to which side would prevail in the war reached their height; critical issues between Britain and Iraq began to move towards the climax which was to come in the spring of 1941. The interpretation of these developments must begin with a short analysis of the underlying factors influencing the attitudes of both sides.

British diplomacy, as it seems to us, lacked subtlety in its appraisal of conditions in Iraq, partly because it came under the purview of the armed services, but still more because it drew the attention of the 'top level' politicians with little background in the Middle East. Only a few perceptive British observers, including former administrators in Iraq, realized the depth of the feeling among Iraqi and other Arabs that Britain had not fulfilled her promises, but, in company with France, had sought to divide the Arab peoples for her own purposes. Most of all, the Palestine conflict alienated the Arabs, particularly at this time when Nazi persecution had intensified the demands of Zionist organizations for unlimited immigration of German Jews and Eastern Europeans into Palestine. Not surprisingly, this appeared to the Arabs as a renewal of European imperialism in the Middle East, coming now from Eastern instead of Western Europeans, but using the British Mandate in Palestine as an instrument.

On the eve, and during the early stages, of the war, the Foreign Office and the able High Commissioner for Palestine, Malcolm MacDonald, showed a clear appreciation of the difficulties and dangers of the Palestine question. In May 1939 a White Paper was issued on policy, containing three main points: first, independence for Palestine in ten years; second, annual Jewish immigration of 75,000 in the following five years, to be continued subsequently only with Arab consent; third, powers to be given to the British High Commissioner to regulate the sale of land to non-Arabs to the extent necessary to preserve the rights and the position of the Arabs.

Nuri al-Said had grasped the possibilities of this paper as a basis for negotiation. He had tried to follow it up and to draw in other Arab leaders with him with a view to linking Arab co-operation in the war with the fulfilment of an agreed policy on Palestine.

This statesmanlike view was frustrated from the British side. The Foreign Office and Malcolm MacDonald continued to hold the same views on Palestine as they had held under the Chamberlain ministry. For the change on Palestine that was to bring such disastrous consequences later, the primary responsibility must go to the new Prime Minister, Winston Churchill, whose foresight on the dangers of Hitlerism had not been matched by a modernization in his outlook on Asia and Africa, or in his understanding of the psychology of their peoples. Moreover, he retained certain sympathies with Zionist sentiments which he and a few other British ministers had formed during the First World War, arising partly out of the overlapping of some of the elements in Jewish thought and Protestant Christianity, in contrast to the rather hazy, but unfavourable, impression of Islam so long retained in Europe in the popular mind.

Whatever the underlying springs of action may have been, Churchill overruled the well-thought-out policies adopted under his predecessors, largely on the plea that support from Zionist groups would make a more important contribution to the war effort. If this was so, it was chiefly because the great majority of Zionists were Eastern Europeans and therefore more modernized than the Arabs. But this fact, as the Foreign Office quickly perceived, carried with it risks for operations in the Middle East: the reactions of the indigenous peoples could not be ignored.

The replacement of the Chamberlain by the Churchill attitude towards Zionism and the collapse of Nuri's efforts on Palestine, weakened his attempts to offset the colonels in their anti-British aims and aggravated British political difficulties in Iraq. The first fruits of it were to be revealed during the war, the second very quickly in the early post-war period.

Thus developments in the critical period on which Iraq was about to enter in the spring of 1940 had been deeply affected in advance by changes in British policy which had been unfavourable to Arab interests in Palestine. As Iraq enjoyed more independence than Egypt and the other countries in the Fertile Crescent had then acquired, the repercussions would show themselves most clearly there. Other events in the early months of the Rashid Ali administration further weakened the supporters of the British alliance, notably events in Norway and France and the entry of Italy into the war. It is hardly surprising that Iraqi doubts over Britain's chances were intensified, or that hesitation was shown over Britain's demands to break with Italy, beyond stopping the flow of oil to Tripoli into the, by then, Vichy French territory.

That ministers were widely divided on important questions was neither new nor surprising; that Naji Shawkat, the new Minister of Justice, was convinced of a German victory and Nuri, the Foreign Minister, of a British victory, with Rashid Ali temporizing in between, was known at the time, within Iraq and in Italy, Germany, and Britain. British experts had broken the Italian code. But with a longer view of history it cannot be said that the breaking of the Italian code, any more than the breaking of the Japanese code by American experts in 1941, was beneficial to British wartime policy. It incited the British government to demands and interventions that ultimately alienated sections of Iraqi opinion that would otherwise have taken a more qualified attitude. The failure of the Italian attack in North Africa in September 1940 and that on Greece in October, followed by the decisive defeat inflicted by General Wavell's forces in December, strengthened General Nuri's belief in an ultimate British victory. But the opposing group, including the colonels and the Mufti of Jerusalem, had put their faith in Germany rather than in Italy.

At this critical period in late 1940 and early 1941 clumsy British diplomacy aggravated the crisis. The British ambassador, Sir Basil Newton, stated that the British government had no confidence in the Iraqi Prime Minister and demanded his resignation. This public interference in Iraq's internal politics turned a precarious state of affairs into a crisis. Nuri, in a well-directed memorandum to his Prime

Minister, showed the strength of the British position with its firm United States support, and, with excellent foresight, exposed the unnatural and temporary character of the Russo–German Pact. Turkey and the United States also put pressure on the Prime Minister. The British Foreign Office finally removed the ill-adapted British ambassador from Baghdad—only to leave the post vacant for nearly two months!

Secret information on discussions between the Germans, Naji Shawkat, and the Mufti of Jerusalem, together with the activities of the Italian embassy in Baghdad, seem to have been misinterpreted in Britain through inadequate insight into the divisions and reservations among the opposing Axis powers. The Italian Fascists were colonialists and imperialists and would not collaborate with Germans desiring to pose as anti-colonialists to gain Arab support.[12] Moreover, the difficulties of transport of German weapons to Iraq, even if they could have been spared from the coming attack on Russia, could not be surmounted. The Soviet Union would not have been prepared to allow the movement through its territories. Reliance on air routes sharply limited the quantity.

Naji Shawkat and the young colonels held political views of a fascist totalitarian type, but in general the Iraqis were inclined towards a sort of double insurance aimed at avoiding confrontation with whoever came out uppermost. If Britain had been in a losing position, Nuri would also have joined those seeking accommodation with Germany. The psychological approach of so many British writers towards the so-called 'Rashid Ali uprising' or 'revolt', conceived in terms of 'loyalty to the Treaty', overlooked the methods by which, with British support, the treaty had been pushed through the Iraqi parliament in the face of strong opposition.

In the first half of 1941 the Near and Middle East comprised an area of particular concern to both sides in the war. General Wavell's brilliant offensive against the Italian forces at the turn of the year had been followed by that of the German *Afrika Korps* under Rommel, which retook much of the lost ground and was investing Tobruk in April. Rommel was aiming at the Suez Canal. In Europe the German armies swept through Yugoslavia and Greece and in May they took Crete in an airborne invasion.

In these months of anxiety, when Britain stood alone, with some help from the Dominions, in armed resistance to the Nazi–Fascist powers, the British political and military authorities turned their attention to Iraq as an area of strategic importance. With the Suez Canal threatened and Egypt, the base of the British army, resisting German–Italian attacks, the possibilities of the route Basra–Baghdad–Palestine took on special importance, and the question of

British rights under the treaty arose in an increasingly acute form. In Britain there were differences of opinion on the best method of presenting demands, and in Iraq, as we have seen, there were fundamental differences over the national interests in the matter. That the danger from a strategic point of view was real seems to be borne out by a directive from Hitler on 22 May 1941, in which he concluded:

> I have therefore decided to advance developments in the Middle East by giving assistance to Iraq. Whether and how the English position between the Mediterranean or Persian Gulf—in connection with an offensive against the Suez Canal—shall later be definitely defeated is to be decided only after Barbarossa.[13]

In practice, however, the problem of transporting military supplies to Iraq was never satisfactorily solved, for Turkey refused to permit them to pass through her territory. Even the Iraqis who favoured the German cause were disillusioned over the failure.

It was not until war with Britain was already in progress that arrangements were made by Admiral Darlan, in response to German pressure, to release some supplies in Syria for dispatch to Baghdad by rail. General Dentz, the French High Commissioner, however, limited these supplies further.

The crisis which led to the Anglo–Iraqi War of 1941 arose over disputes in the interpretation of the treaty with respect to landing rights for British troops and their disposition in Iraq. Both sides shifted their interpretations as the dispute continued. Both were influenced also by the external developments in the Great War which have been outlined above, and which raised difficulties over the interpretation of the Anglo–Iraqi treaty in relation to military operations.

The treaty in Article 4 committed Iraq to furnish in wartime 'all facilities and assistance, including the use of railways, rivers, ports, aerodromes and means of communication'. The British government, in making representations under this clause of the treaty, held that Rashid Ali was not acting in conformity with it and demanded his displacement as Prime Minister. This appeared, as it was, a direct interference at the most sensitive point of domestic policy. Then and later the demand strengthened the position of the colonels and of the reactionary elements within Iraq. It came at a time when the differences of view between Nuri and Naji Shawkat were the centre of growing dissension within the government.

This dissension ended the Rashid Ali government at the close of January 1941, and a new government was formed by General Taha al-Hashimi with Tawfiq al-Suwaydi as Foreign Minister. The choice of premier seems to have been dictated by the colonels. They were not satisfied with Rashid, who preferred to maintain relations with both sides in the war until the outcome was discernible. The judgement of most Iraqi and of some British contemporary observers seems to have been that he did not wish to provoke a crisis with Britain.

Nor, apparently, did his successor, who aimed on the one hand to maintain relations with Britain, but at the same time to conciliate the colonels by explaining the practical necessities in the existing international situation.

While these internal discussions were proceeding, Anthony Eden visited Cairo and engaged in discussions with Tawfiq al-Suwaydi early in March. The Foreign Minister, like Nuri before him, held a realistic view of the war and recognized that Iraqi interests, while not completely in harmony with the interests of either side in the war, had much less to fear and more to gain from Britain than from Germany and Italy. Eden pressed him to break diplomatic relations with Italy, and, according to some reports, demanded the resignation of Rashid Ali and the removal of certain army commanders. Suwaydi again requested the adoption of some additional provisions of the White Paper on Palestine. All through the Anglo–Iraqi controversy, the Palestine question was a dominant influence in shaping the attitudes of Arab circles. The interview with Eden seems from several accounts to have been one of the most important factors among those leading to the war which soon followed. The dominant military officers, believing that the Foreign Minister had come to an agreement with Eden, decided on another military *coup d'état*. Taha al-Hashimi was forced to resign after the colonels had moved forces to strategic points in Baghdad.[14] The Regent escaped in disguise from his palace, which had been surrounded by the army, and with the assistance of the American legation and of the British, he left Baghdad for Habbaniya and then Basra and thence to Transjordan, where he was later joined by General Nuri, Jamil al-Midfai, and Ali Jawdat. Rashid Ali, supported by the army, assumed power, arranged for the recall of parliament, which appointed a relative of King Faisal II to act as Regent and endorsed the necessary changes in government to give effect to the military *coup*. Rashid Ali was anxious to acquire legitimacy, but the colonels left him limited room for manoeuvre.

These events, coinciding with the German attack on Greece and the offensive in Cyrenaica by Rommel, were met by a British request to land British forces in Basra. Rashid Ali wanted to accept on condition that he obtained British recognition. His first response was therefore favourable. He would permit the landing of 3,000 troops on condition that they were directly moved through the country towards their destinations in Egypt or Palestine. But the colonels intervened, disapproving any concessions to Britain. On the British side also the nature of the demands changed. Rashid Ali had publicly declared his intention to fulfil Iraq's international obligations. In response to the British ambassador he appears to have agreed to an open route for British forces through Iraq, provided the forces in Iraq at any one time were kept within specified limits and kept on the move. It would seem that Britain accepted these conditions at first.[15]

The initial exchanges between Sir Kinahan Cornwallis (who had succeeded Sir Basil Newton as ambassador but had not presented his credentials) and Baghdad led, then, to a tentative understanding that did not last. On the British side, later instructions sent from London raised British demands above the original position. As Sir Llewellyn Woodward, in his *British Foreign Policy in the Second World War,* based on the Foreign Office documents, says:

> Mr. Churchill pointed out that our chief interest in sending troops to Iraq was to establish and cover a great assembly base at Basra. We had invoked our treaty rights to ensure a peaceful landing, but, if necessary, we should have used force. Our position at Basra did not rest solely on the treaty with Iraq, but also on a new event arising out of the war. We could not undertake to send the troops northwards or to move them through to Palestine, and we could not recognise a right to require such undertakings 'in respect of a Government which has itself usurped power by a *coup d'état* or in a country where our treaty rights have so long been frustrated in the spirit'.[16]

The British ambassador was 'not to entangle himself in explanations'. The note of urgency in this utterance reflects Britain's critical situation at the time. But it reflects also a profound misreading of Iraqi internal conditions. The era of decolonization had not dawned for Winston Churchill, who had always opposed independence for India. British governments had already turned a blind eye on frequent military *coups* in Iraq. Only seventeen years later, after the 1958 Revolution, did Britain at last treat Iraq as an independent state, *de facto* as well as *de jure*.

London's attitude naturally convinced the Iraqi leaders that they faced a British occupation of Iraq. It was not merely the colonels and Naji Shawkat who feared a loss of independence. The far-reaching extension of the original British demands appeared to many Iraqis to be the preliminary step to British military occupation, and this aroused among Arab nationalists a renewed feeling of resentment over the role of Britain in the Middle East during and after the First World War. German and Italian radio propaganda was intensified. The decision was taken to resist Britain by force in what was believed to be the impending reoccupation of the country.

Rashid Ali's political judgement was often erratic and impulsive, as events during the Qassim period were later to show, but suspicion of and opposition to Britain were widespread in the country among Arab nationalists, although some of them would have preferred British to German and Italian success in the war. But even when the dangers of the British position are fully appreciated, the fact remains that in manner and timing British diplomacy was hardly of a high order at this stage. Except perhaps to some extent for Cornwallis, there was a failure of those who made the decisions on the British side to place themselves imaginatively in the position of Iraqi ministers.

The Anglo–Iraqi War

Neither in a military nor in a psychological sense was Iraq prepared for war. Her armaments were inferior, her troops inadequately trained in recent methods of warfare. Rashid Ali had few of the qualities needed to lead the country in military operations. The colonels, who in the background had been largely dictating the course of external policy, were mediocre and ineffective. As always the army itself was divided in its allegiances, and, partly in consequence, its morale was low.

After all the stiff demands requiring military landings in the Basra area, the forces that were landed there on 29 April 1941 played only a small role when the crisis came. For the flooding of the area was an effective check on any rapid movement to the theatres of war. When Rashid Ali gave the signal for armed action, Iraqi troops moved on Habbaniya, where small British forces with Assyrian detachments guarded the air base. Reinforcements were essential and a small force came in by air, but the main force had to come from Palestine. The internal Iraqi weaknesses were not all evident on the outside, and the British position appeared precarious. The Italian diplomats in Baghdad as well as German representatives in Turkey exaggerated Iraq's strength and prospects.

At Habbaniya these illusions were quickly dispelled. The British commander took the offensive, first in the air, throwing the Iraqi forces into panic, and later by a sortie, following which they retreated to Falluja. The main reinforcements came in two columns from Palestine along the Amman–Mafraq–Baghdad route. Rutba was taken early, Habbaniya was reached, and the way opened to Baghdad when behind air bombing Falluja was taken. In a bold advance with slender forces the British commander pushed on to Baghdad, seizing a radio transmitter to broadcast defeatist propaganda and exaggerated reports on the size and strength of the British columns moving on the capital. Here again larger forces gave way to smaller and by the end of May Baghdad had fallen and the Rashid Ali regime was at an end. The premier, several leading ministers and army officers left for Tehran or Turkey and a new chapter had opened.

The forceful action of Churchill and the Chiefs of Staff has drawn favourable comment from British writers. When on 5 May General Wavell still urged that a negotiated settlement should be sought, the Chiefs replied abruptly:

> Settlement by negotiation cannot be entertained except on the basis of a climb down by Iraqis, with safeguards against future Axis designs on Iraq. Realities of the situation are that Rashid Ali has all along been hand-in-glove with Axis powers, and was merely waiting until they could support him before exposing his hand. Our arrival at Basra forced him to go off at half-cock before the Axis was ready.[17]

This is an oversimplification leading to serious inaccuracy in the interpretation of events. It misreads the character of Rashid Ali by confusing his aims and policies with those of Colonel Salah al-Din al-Sabbagh. Like al-Midfai and Nuri before him, Rashid Ali was dependent in the last resort on the colonels for continued retention of office. It by no means followed that he and al-Sabbagh were in agreement at every point. The shifts in British policies regarding the introduction of troops into Iraq explains how he came to be 'convinced without doubt, that Britain aimed to occupy the country'.[18]

A Turkish offer of mediation after war had started, which was rejected out of hand by Churchill and the Chiefs of Staff, against Wavell's advice, brought out a fundamental difference between Rashid Ali and the colonels. On 8 May, four days after the Turkish offer, Rashid Ali and Naji Shawkat—who, as we have seen, leaned further towards Germany than Rashid Ali did—held discussions with the Turkish government in Ankara. According to information given to Khadduri by Naji Shawkat himself and supported by his memoirs of the time as well as those of the Mufti's secretary, both Rashid Ali and Shawkat were willing to accept an agreement providing facilities for British forces and fulfilling treaty obligations generally, in return for recognition of the existing government and an undertaking not to violate the independence of Iraq. It was most significant that

Shawkat recommended acceptance of these conditions and Rashid Ali agreed.[19] Only the colonels, still believing in the certainty of German victory, as Enver had done in Turkey during the First World War, threatened the life of Rashid Ali if he accepted.

This put an end to hopes for a political settlement. But in itself it does not justify laudatory references to the actions of Churchill and the Chiefs of Staff at the expense of General Wavell. For the consequences of high-handed actions taken in wartime may endure long after the war has ended, becoming a source of embarrassment to a succeeding generation in both combatant countries. If we assume that, owing to the veto of the colonels on all compromise, the war, once it had started, would in any case have taken the course it did, it does not follow that a continued search for diplomatic solutions would have been superfluous. Wavell was obviously more conscious of and sensitive to the sentiments of the Arab peoples than the political and military leaders in London were. If his advice had been followed, and Britain had been willing to discuss a settlement in Ankara without necessarily suspending her military activities in the meantime, she would have placed herself in a more favourable position in the eyes of succeeding generations of Iraqis. If, at the same time, she had confined her demands within the level of a reasonable interpretation of the treaty and if, later, she had taken particular care to avoid giving ground for the charge that the Iraqi Royal House and some of the chief ministers were instruments of Britain, the post-war history of Iraq would have started with happier prospects.

Security in the war did not require high-handed expressions such as those referring to a public 'climb-down', nor did it require the abandonment of diplomacy for tactlessly phrased ultimata. The complicated interplay of conflicting motives, sentiments, and beliefs, arising out of past history and contradictory anticipations of future events, is hardly reflected in Churchill's slapdash appraisal: 'Rashid Ali, who was working with the Germans, and began a conspiracy with three prominent army officers . . .'[20]

Aftermath of War

At the cessation of hostilities the leaders of the regime fled from the country. Rashid Ali eventually reached Germany where he stayed for a time; later he was received by King Ibn Saud. Three of the colonels were given up to the new Iraqi government, and in 1942 were hanged under the directions of the Regent and Nuri. The fourth, Colonel al-Sabbagh, escaped but was eventually caught, and in 1945 he was handed over and also hanged. This did not end the feuds and reprisals among Iraqi political and military leaders.

The Iraqi leaders who had engaged in the Anglo–Iraqi War had been moved by an Arab nationalism the aims of which they believed had been frustrated by Britain after the First World War. In this cause they had been willing to ally themselves under certain contingencies with Nazi Germany and Fascist Italy in the hope that by doing so their own cause could be more easily advanced. The relations between the Nazis and the Iraqi leaders who had now fled from the country had been loose and fragmented. Each side had desired to use the other for its own purposes. This had rendered impossible the synchronization of movements which alone could establish genuine co-ordination.[21]

Any successor regime during the war had to make difficult external as well as internal decisions. Extensive riots in Baghdad were hardly a sign of popular rejoicing at the outcome of the war. The heavy loss of life under intense British bombing had brought the war home to many Iraqi families. Troops had to be used to restore order. In June 1941 Jamil al-Midfai was again nominated to step in as Prime Minister after the crisis, and he attempted to repeat his formula based on 'forgetting the past'. This policy had many advantages. If followed, it would at least have broken the cycle of feuds and personal antagonisms. As before, al-Midfai made no attempt to prosecute the defeated leaders. At the same time he reversed their policies and permitted a defined role for British ground and air forces during the war and British control over a base area at Basra. He also severed relations with Italy. The actions of the preceding government were declared illegal on the ground that the parliament which had ratified them had been summoned in an unconstitutional manner. He agreed to establish censorship of the means of communication.

Thus, whatever forms of independence were preserved, Iraq was in an important sense an occupied country during the war; she paid the penalty of her geographical position in relation to great powers in conflict. Her history in this period was shaped in the main by forces operating far away from her territory and over which she could exert no control. The Prime Minister was uneasily aware of the psychological resentments arising in some quarters and began to resist any further British demands. After four months, he made way for the return of Nuri al-Said, who was ready to collaborate more closely with Britain, with less regard for popular reactions.

With the disclosure of documents long held secret in archives, including German documents of which copies were taken over by the Allies, it is now possible to envisage more accurately than before the role which Iraq and the Middle East played in the calculations of both sides in the war. The role of the Middle East in Hitler's eyes was particularly affected by his motives in attacking the Soviet Union.

Speculations on these has ranged from ideological fanaticism to anticipatory strategy concerned with safeguarding his gains from flank attack in the future, and to continuation of an historic German 'drive to the East' perhaps accompanied by colonization. It now appears, however, that Hitler's motive was much simpler. Enraged by unexpectedly strong British resistance, which he believed to be based on the hope that Russia would yet enter the war, he decided that Russia must be 'shattered to its roots with one blow'. Then, 'With Russia smashed Britain's last hope will be shattered. Germany will then be master of Europe and the Balkans'.[22]

As Britain had chosen to take risks on home defence in order to conserve a strong position in the Middle East which would protect the routes to Asia, Africa, and Australasia, Germany was forced to take account of the area if she were to overcome Britain. When the campaign against the Soviet Union was designed as a step in the conquest of Britain, it followed that if it had gone according to plan, the next step would have made the Middle East an even more vital centre, with Iraq in a leading place in a German attack from the north through Bulgaria and Turkey and from the east through Iran, opening further routes for an invasion of India and other grandiose schemes comparable to the dreams of Napoleon. Though not all these schemes of Hitler were known to the British authorities, there were grounds for anxiety concerning Iraq and Egypt at stages where the Russian military position seemed precarious.

During the ministries of Nuri al-Said from October 1941 to June 1944, Iraq was in a sense under British control, particularly in her international relations. Her position resembled that of Egypt at certain points and would have resembled it more closely if the paths of the campaigns had come nearer. The reactions of the populations in both countries were, broadly speaking, similar, ranging among politicians from those of Nahas Pasha in Egypt and Nuri al-Said in Iraq to those of opposition groups whose activities under the war-time restrictions were severely limited; that is, from those who feared German and Italian more than British imperialism to those who, indifferent to the radical contrast between the Nazi and Fascist regimes and the British and French democracies, were more concerned to shake off a domination which they had known, than to guard in advance against a possible but speculative domination from a source hitherto unknown to them.

These elements, as well as more liberal opposition elements which rejected Nazi and fascist philosophies and practices, were silenced during the war. As George Kirk remarks of the Nuri ministries during the war: 'political effervescence in the towns had been kept within prudent bounds by the collaboration of the Iraqi and British security authorities, a vigilant press censorship, and the presence of British ground forces since May, 1941'.[23]

If to the British authorities in Iraq during the war the bounds set to political activities seemed 'prudent', they appeared less so in the longer run. Even those who had not opposed the treaty regarded the British 'occupation' as going far beyond its stipulations. Those who observed Iraq from within during the next two decades were in a position to appreciate the longer-run effects of this reoccupation of 'independent' Iraq.

The question remained, how to treat those associated with the preceding regime. Here, al-Midfai's policy of forgetting the past was set aside by Nuri who, not for the first or the last time, pursued his opponents relentlessly, arresting several hundred of them to be confined in remote areas to the south.

The limitations on domestic turbulence in this period enabled some progress to be made with much-needed reconsideration of the constitution which had been based on a number of instruments, national and international, which were no longer active operating forces in the world. A new government committee had been appointed at the end of 1941: its proposals were discussed in both houses of parliament and a Draft Amendment Law was passed in the middle of 1943. This work is only at present of interest because of some of the issues raised in the debate. Some of the leading participants were concerned chiefly to curb the *coup* as a method of changing governments, and the question arose whether the King should be clearly authorized to dismiss a Prime Minister and Cabinet. Associated with this issue was the question how far Cabinets should be in a position to maintain themselves in power when they had lost the confidence of parliament. It was widely felt that parliament had not been able to fulfil the role that it had been intended to fill. But as Khadduri aptly remarked, 'Parliament could never be strengthened simply by weakening the Cabinet'.[24] What was needed was an amendment of the electoral system to introduce direct individual voting.[25]

All these labours were nullified when, later, the entire structure was abolished and parliament disappeared.

With the checking of the Nazi offensive and the entry of the United States into the war, it became clearer which side would emerge victorious, and the Nuri ministries faced fewer obstacles than their predecessors had done to measures supporting Britain. Not all the right-wing nationalist groups, however, shared this change of attitude. But the focus of controversy changed. Left-wing and even some of the centre groups began to reflect widespread currents of thought and sentiment in the late war and early post-war periods which demanded reforms leading to an amelioration of the conditions of life of the masses. In Iraq these demands were accompanied by agitation coming from the *Ahali* group for a genuinely democratic parliamentary system based on direct individual voting.

On domestic affairs the lines of cleavage now changed sharply. A number of the 'moderates' who had opposed the colonels and Rashid Ali on international affairs were also opposed to progressive democratic groups in domestic affairs. Personal differences also arose from time to time between Nuri and the Regent. Nuri's resignation in the middle of 1944 came at a time when the prospect of a German–Italian victory had faded and Nuri's confidence in the ultimate victory of the Western Allies, joined by the Soviet Union, was seen to be justified.

But the danger of civil war at home had grown and here also, Nuri, in one of his last acts before resigning, had shown prevision. A few weeks earlier he had visited Kurdistan and attempted to reach a durable political settlement by carving out a new Kurdish governorate to which a representative Kurdish minister in the Cabinet would appoint the civil servants. Realizing the error of attempting to enforce Arabic as the sole recognized language in the area, he proposed the appointment of a Kurdish Deputy Director of Education in the Ministry of Education. This was a timely attempt to meet the strong Kurdish desire to maintain a proper place for the Kurdish language and literature in the educational system, including institutions of higher learning.

It was an ominous foretaste of later developments that this statesmanlike effort to remove a constant danger to the unity of Iraq was quickly frustrated by the intense opposition of the Regent and of a number of cabinet ministers to any such concessions to Kurdish nationalism. This stubborn refusal to recognize that Iraq could only achieve harmonious unity as a bi-national state has been responsible for much loss of human life together with a weakening of Iraq in international affairs. We ourselves had noted a little over a decade later how the attempts to achieve this aim were still deliberately frustrated by Arab administrators.

The Regent remained critical of Nuri and attempted to set up a government independent of him. In June 1944 he requested Hamdi al-Pachachi to form one whose composition he influenced. Al-Pachachi remained at the head of two succeeding ministries which lasted about eighteen months, during the second of which the war ended. Attempts were made to improve administration, but the growing demands for social reforms brought little or no response from the government.

On the international scene another crisis, also largely the result of events in Europe, was rapidly coming to a head with consequences which would prove disastrous for the Middle East—the immigration of European Jews into Palestine and the Jewish demand to take over Palestine.

Notes

1 Arnold Toynbee, *Survey of International Affairs* (London, 1934), pp. 286–7.
2 Khadduri, op. cit., p. 39.
3 Toynbee did well to raise some aspects of this question (op. cit., pp. 152–4), though his consistently strong personal dislike of nationalism in itself often coloured his treatment of the subject.
4 Hikmat Sulayman was the brother of Mahmud Shavkat Pasha, the Prime Minister who ousted the Sultan in Turkey in 1909. During the 1920s he held several ministerial posts in Iraq. He was reputed to have admired Atatürk as a 'progressive' and considered himself in the same category.
5 See especially R. S. Stafford, *The Tragedy of the Assyrians* (London, 1935) for an authoritative account of the affair; also a good treatment by Toynbee, op. cit., pp. 135–74. Majid Khadduri reports that Hikmat Sulayman, in an interview with him, said that he approved the general line of policy which General Bakr adopted: op. cit., p. 42.
6 For the discussion in this and the following section we have relied heavily on the works of P. W. Ireland, *Iraq* (London, 1937); Majid Khadduri, *Independent Iraq* and S. H. Longrigg, *Iraq, 1900–1950,* already cited. We have little to add to their discussion of the various *coups* and the political manoeuvring, the army intrigues and clashes of personalities and doctrines that characterized Iraqi politics between independence and the outbreak of war. For a detailed and informed discussion of this aspect of Iraq's political history the reader is referred to these works. That of Longrigg is in some ways more comprehensive, but Khadduri adds much as a result of his extensive personal interviews with the officers and politicians concerned.
7 The chief founding members in 1931 of the *Ahali* group were Abdul Fattah Ibrahim and Muhammed Hadid. Kamil Chadirchi joined in 1933 and brought in Abu al-Timman, who became the group's leader. As a result of his quarrel with the Yasin–Rashid Ali group, Hikmat Sulayman joined in 1935. One member, Abdul Qadir Ismail, was a Marxist. See Khadduri, op. cit., pp. 69–74.
8 Kamil Chadirchi and Muhammed Hadid were the two leading social democrats throughout Iraq's modern history. Chadirchi was the elder, born in 1897, and was a lawyer educated at the Baghdad Law College. He was Minister of Economic Affairs in the Hikmat Sulayman Cabinet of 1936, but was primarily a newspaper editor and independent politician, and was president of the National Democratic party. He was a strong opponent of Nuri al-Said and one of the chief intellectuals working for the 1958 Revolution. Muhammed Hadid, born in 1906, came from a wealthy Mosul family. He was educated at the American University of Beirut and the London School of Economics, where he took a BSc(Econ). He held numerous economic and financial posts in the Iraq Civil Service between 1931 and 1939 and was elected deputy to the Assembly from Mosul in 1937, 1948, and 1954. He was vice-president of the National Democratic party, 1946–54. Abdul Fattah Ibrahim (born in 1907) was also educated at the American University of Beirut, and later went to Columbia University in the United States. He advocated a kind of popular democratic socialism.

9 Khadduri, op. cit., p. 124.
10 For a discussion of Hitler's aims in Africa see Alexandre Kum'a N'Dumbe III, 'Les buts de guerre de l'Allemagne hitlérienne en Afrique', *Revue d'histoire de la deuxième guerre mondiale,* avril 1977, pp. 37–60.
11 His sentence was, however, commuted to life imprisonment by King Ghazi, but he was soon set free because of his illness. See the account in Khadduri, op. cit., pp. 137–40.
12 As Hirszowicz perceptively remarks, this resembled the government of India's opposition to the use of Arab liberation as a weapon against the Ottoman Empire. Lukas Z. Hirszowicz, *The Third Reich and the Arab East* (London and Toronto, 1966), p. 117.
13 Quoted Hirszowicz, ibid., p. 166.
14 See especially ibid., pp. 136–7.
15 ibid., pp. 143, 343. Also Khadduri, op. cit., 217ff.
16 Llewellyn Woodward, *British Foreign Policy in the Second World War,* Vol. I (London, 1970), p. 577.
17 Winston Churchill, *The Second World War,* Vol. III (London, 1950), p. 229. See also G. E. Kirk, *The Middle East in the War* (Oxford, 1953), pp. 71–3.
18 Hirszowicz, op. cit., p. 153.
19 Khadduri, op. cit., p. 228.
20 Churchill, op. cit., p. 225.
21 British sources, with some support from Hirszowicz (op. cit., pp. 166–72), claim that the prompt British intervention forced the issue before the Germans had time to intervene adequately. This, however, raises the question whether more German war material could have been spared from the offensive against Russia which was to commence about three weeks later and which failed to achieve its objective.
22 See G. L. Weinberg, *Germany and the Soviet Union, 1939–41* (Leiden, 1954), pp. 115–16, where the notes of a German officer are reproduced.
23 Kirk, op. cit., p. 147.
24 Khadduri, op. cit., p. 297.
25 ibid., pp. 302–5, for a discussion of the electoral laws.

5 Adjustment to the Post-war World: Internal Tensions and External Pressures

The end of the war left Iraq in a confused and unsettled state. The economic hardships which shortages of goods and inflation of prices had imposed on the people, together with the dislocation resulting from wartime activities and the immediate effects of troop withdrawals, had created much popular unrest. Politically, however, the liberal and modernizing groups had been strengthened by the defeat of the Axis powers and, in particular, by international developments such as the declaration of the Atlantic Charter, the creation of the United Nations, and the general international atmosphere giving promise of progressive, democratic development. Not surprisingly, such an atmosphere encouraged demands in Iraq for greater freedom and for more effective and representative parliamentary institutions, including free political parties. But what Khadduri calls the 'elder politicians' resumed their old game of combating reforms which undermined their interests, of manipulating parliamentary elections, and of attempting to suppress dissent, sometimes by force.

The first two ministries that followed Nuri al-Said's resignation in 1944 and those headed by Hamdi al-Pachachi (June 1944 to January 1946) were marked by conservative policies unfavourable to the admission of political parties to a place in parliamentary life. They were followed by the short-lived but liberal and progressive ministry of Tawfiq al-Suwaydi (23 February to end May 1946) which was brought down by manoeuvres of the oligarchic grouping of the older politicians who were 'moderate' in external policy but highly conservative in domestic affairs, being opposed to any development of parliamentary life on party lines which could open the way for far-reaching social and economic changes. However, there was freedom from censorship and al-Suwaydi succeeded in obtaining the legalization of political parties, the passage of a new electoral law, and a reform of the law on the administrative powers of provincial governorates. These were notable achievements even though some of the reforms were undone after the fall of his ministry as a result of intrigues in the Senate and the influence of the Regent, whose undoubted flashes of liberalism were apt to be short-lived. The Regent then called on one of the most authoritarian politicians of the oligarchy, Arshad al-Umari, who quickly suppressed newspapers, restricted parties, forcibly repressed demonstrations even when they were peacefully conducted, and arrested party leaders whose unions had engaged in strikes. These policies failed to gain support and Arshad was obliged to resign after less than seven months in office. Nuri returned temporarily (21 November 1946 to 11 March 1947) to organize a general election which he was able to manage under the corrupt electoral system in such a way as to eliminate representation of most of the parties, including all the Istiqlal.

Thus, the older politicians (including Nuri al-Said who, although Prime Minister in only six of the 22 Cabinets between May 1946 and July 1958, was the guiding eminence behind the scenes for most of the period) continued their traditional roles much as before, with Nuri in the forefront of those who pressed for the maintenance of Iraq's special relationship with Britain and of those who distrusted the intentions of both the Soviet Union and Egypt.[1] After the election, Nuri resigned and Salih Jabr, a moderate politician and a supporter of Anglo–Iraqi co-operation, became Prime Minister. Jabr had the task of presiding over the negotiations to revise the treaty with Britain which opened in early 1947.

Unfortunately for Britain's friends in Iraq, the negotiations over the treaty took place at the same time as the Zionist drive to establish a Jewish state in Palestine was achieving success. These two issues—Palestine and the revision of the treaty—dominated the immediate post-war years, the former strongly influencing attitudes towards the latter.

It was a strange, and to the Arab peoples of the Middle East a grim, paradox that just at the time when they were celebrating the end of the Western European occupation of their countries, they were faced with a determined drive from Eastern Europe, not only to force an entry into, but also to colonize rapidly, a Middle Eastern country which for many generations had been settled by an overwhelming majority of Arab peoples. The hopes of improved relations between Europe and the Middle East after the passing of Anglo–French imperialist rivalries, and the collapse of Italian imperialism in the Maghreb, were shattered by the new danger of unlimited influx from Eastern Europe backed first by American money and political support, later by Russian aid through Czechoslovakia, and made possible by ambiguous and vacillating British policy.

Attacked on every side, Britain announced her intention of abandoning the Mandate she had originally sought with such determination. The measures she had taken against Zionist agitation in Palestine and her efforts to protect the Arab peoples there by limiting both Jewish immigration and the right of Jews to purchase land from the Arabs, now gained her little credit in the Arab world in view of this failure to stand firm against Zionist pressure, amounting to terrorism. She refrained from voting on the November 1947 partition scheme of the United Nations, insisting she would accept no solution that had to be imposed by force, but she held to her decision to abandon the Mandate in May 1948. Conditions in Palestine deteriorated quickly, with guerilla warfare and terrorist activities mounting amid rising fear, resentment, and bitterness in the Arab world. Since Britain was the country responsible for the Palestine Mandate and as she was abdicating her responsibilities to the newly created and as yet untried machinery of the United Nations, it was inevitable that forcible opposition would arise to any renewal of the treaty. But the strength of the opposition was gravely underestimated by Salih Jabr and by Nuri as negotiations proceeded in both Baghdad and London in the spring of 1947.

The Iraqi government rejected the first set of British proposals, largely because they included unacceptable military provisions and did not provide for Iraqi control over the military bases, but after some six months of talks, agreement was reached and a draft treaty was finally initialled in January 1948 at Portsmouth, where Ernest Bevin, the British Foreign Secretary, was on holiday. The offending military proposals had been dropped and a Joint Defence Board was provided for on which consultations would take place on defence and strategic matters, and on the training and equipment of Iraq's army. The Iraqi delegation and the government declared themselves satisfied that the new treaty was a genuine agreement between equals and in the interest of Iraq.[2]

But the politically conscious classes in Iraq, with wide support among the whole public, thought otherwise. All the stored grievances against Britain—the Balfour Declaration of 1917, the selection of the Hashemites as monarchs of Iraq, the Mandate, the terms of the original 1930 treaty, the Anglo–Iraqi War only six years previously—found forcible public expression. Demonstrations, street riots, and violent combats with the police in Baghdad were accompanied by widespread, though less intense, disturbances elsewhere. The later practice of parading army tanks through the streets had not yet started and civilian ministers correctly suspected that if the army were drawn in to exercise police functions, they might be tempted to take the reins of government into their own hands. Retreating all the way, the Jabr government declared that the treaty was unacceptable and, when the disorders continued, it made way at the end of January

1948 for another ministry led by an Arab nationalist, like Jabr of Shia origin, Muhammed al-Sadr, which confirmed the rejection of the treaty but held out the possibility of another. Preparations were then made for another election, during which demonstrations and disorders recurred, aggravated by economic difficulties.

The new government remained uneasily in power up to the middle of the year. The conflict in Palestine grew more menacing than ever. Money from Zionist sources in the United States facilitated the flow of arms from Czechoslovakia to the militant Zionist forces under Ben Gurion. Resentment in the Arab world grew, and external issues took precedence over internal affairs in public controversies.

Arab Defeat in Palestine

The failure of Britain in the face of Zionist terrorism to discharge her obligations in terminating her Mandate opened the way for the war between Israel and the Arabs in May 1948. The Iraqi army, which had suffered heavy losses in the Anglo–Iraqi War of 1941, and which was still poorly equipped, was handicapped by long lines of communication. Nevertheless it made better progress for a time than any other Arab army except the Jordanian Arab Legion. Martial law was imposed in Iraq, but the widespread unrest which accompanied the defeat of the Arab forces and expressed itself in violent opposition to unpopular governments pushed them into positions where none could maintain itself except by censorship and suppression. Domestic issues were as always a source of fierce controversy, but all political life was embittered by the consequences of the Eastern European invasion of the Middle East. As usual, retaliation, when it could not reach its real object, was exercised on third parties which bore no responsibility for the wrongs in question. The drive against Iraqi Jews was indefensible in itself. Jews had early begun to emigrate to Israel illegally and in 1950 a law was passed permitting them to leave Iraq legally but depriving them of their Iraqi nationality if they did so permanently. Thus, they were permitted freely to emigrate or to remain Iraqi subjects, as they chose. There was a mass exodus as many thousands chose to leave for Israel. Many had to dispose of their property at depressed prices in order to do so. Too often discrimination against them amounted to persecution.

The results of this war continued adversely to affect every aspect of Middle East political life. If Iraq was not affected in a territorial sense, she nonetheless became inextricably entangled in the intra-regional controversies which followed the failure of the Arab armies. The decisive factor in the outcome had been the continued flow of arms and supplies to the forces of Ben Gurion through Russian and

American efforts. The diplomatic initiatives of both the largest powers were directed to obtaining recognition of Israel and condonation of her actions. British efforts to restrain Israel were nullified by President Truman and Stalin. This, however, did not restrain Iraqi Arab nationalist circles from continuing to represent Britain as the leading culprit.

The two international organizations which had played parts in the affair were both caught in their formative stages; as yet they were inexperienced and inadequately organized. The United Nations was the most important, but it was only what its members allowed it to be, particularly the small proportion of them that possessed the power of veto. The barbarous massacres of Jews in Nazi Germany had predisposed the representatives of many of the countries in the United Nations to accept in 1947 the Zionist demands for a state of Israel, and the sub-committee appointed to examine these claims reported in favour of partition of Palestine.

With both the United States and the Soviet Union throwing their weight on the side of Israel, the one for internal political reasons and the other out of a desire to reduce British political influence in the Middle East, the outcome was not long in doubt. But the United Nations went beyond its legitimate powers in recommending partition, as the great international lawyer Professor Hans Kelsen, who, because he was a Jew, had been obliged to flee from his own country, pointed out.[3] In addition, it weakly permitted the lines of partition to be determined by force in place of those laid down in its own resolutions. In accepting partition the peoples of many other powers were moved by compassion for the Jewish victims of a European massacre; they overlooked the inequity of penalizing the Palestinian Arabs to compensate for European misdeeds.

The other international organization, the Arab League, which had been created only in 1946, was in no position to arouse, let alone organize, unified Arab action. It too suffered from the same disunity among the Arab peoples that had been exposed in the war with the Zionist forces and contributed to their defeat. Its very origins illustrated the rivalry that made for internal disunity.

Disunity Among the Arabs

Egypt, which had long hesitated between Egyptian nationalism and Arab nationalism, had by the mid-1940s become ardently Arab nationalist—at least among her governing classes and 'intellectuals'—and already, under Nahas Pasha, displayed aspirations towards leadership of an Arab nationalist movement with its headquarters in Cairo, where Egypt could influence its secretariat.

The original impulse towards Arab nationalism seems to have come largely from Syria while she was still in the Ottoman Empire.[4] The fragmentation of Greater Syria by imperialist rivalries intensified Arab nationalism among Syrians, but for a time its full expression was limited by the French Mandate. With the end of the British Mandate over Iraq, Baghdad became the more important centre of discussion in the early post-war years. Iraq was in a more prominent position among Arab countries than she occupied later. Syria and Lebanon were only just disentangling themselves from French control and Egypt was engaged in disputes with Britain over her treaty, the Sudan, and particularly military bases. Leaders in the Arab nationalist movement had been freer to meet and discuss their views in Baghdad than in some of the other Arab capitals. At the end of the Anglo–Iraqi conflict of 1941 Anthony Eden openly gave British encouragement and support to the idea of Arab unity.[5]

During the war exchanges of views within parts of the Arab world had taken place on how to give effect to plans for unity formed in Baghdad, Damascus, and Cairo; in its fullest sense Arab nationalism logically implied for many the eventual emergence of a single unified Arab state. Between this and the conception of a league of independent states, a number of schemes for union in limited parts of the region were proposed.

All the movements towards unity were affected by the continuous and rapid changes taking place in the Middle East bringing it, unevenly but unmistakably, from a medieval to a modern order. Some of the changes, particularly those following each of the World Wars, gave rise to difficulties for the leadership of any unified state to be established, as well as for the form and the composition of its government. Largely through British initiative the more traditional form of dynastic rule had been chosen for Iraq and Transjordan, to be combined with the machinery of representative government as a 'limited monarchy'. The coincidence of these steps with the displacement of the Hashemites by the Wahabis in Arabia created an internal dynastic conflict which inhibited movements towards Arab unity on traditional lines, at least up to the time of the Iraqi Revolution of 1958.

After the Second World War attention was directed towards schemes for a Greater Syria and for the Fertile Crescent as a whole.[6] Iraqi politics up to, and including, the 1958 Revolution were influenced by these schemes and their repercussions. The Regent seems to have been the moving spirit in them rather than Nuri, for both King Abdullah of Jordan and the Regent of Iraq aimed at unification on the dynastic lines planned earlier when the former had been marked by his father, the Sharif of Mecca in the First World War, as the future King of Iraq, while Faisal I was to be King of Syria. Since French intervention had thwarted the second of these plans and Faisal I had taken the Iraqi throne on British initiative, Abdullah saw a Greater Syria as a compensation for himself.

Nuri al-Said's plan for an Arab union, which had been formed in 1942 and published in 1943, was very different from the original dynastic views of the Hashemites. His proposal contained provisions more in line with modern ideas. In a union of Syria, Transjordan, Lebanon, and Palestine the form of government would be chosen by the peoples and might be republican; special protection was to be provided for Christians in Lebanon and Jews in Palestine.

In the Arab discussions on the forms of unity, however, it was an Egyptian proposal that prevailed. The Egyptian parliamentarian Nahas Pasha presided over a meeting in Cairo in 1944 which accepted a protocol embodying a concrete plan which, with modifications, was adopted in March 1946 and created the League of Arab States. The League took the form of an association of states, each of which maintained its own character as an independent entity. The Iraqi delegates would have favoured stronger provisions for future steps towards closer union. Egyptian diplomacy succeeded in gaining the headquarters for Cairo, with an Egyptian Secretary General.

The dislike of the Iraqi monarchy by the Arab nationalists was deep-seated and could not be remedied. Opposition in Iraq to the British treaty was, as we have seen, long-standing; for many, and especially for the young, its denunciation had become an emotional symbol of Iraq's assertion of independence. The Anglo–Iraqi War had concluded with the restoration of the Hashemites by the British army and this removed any hope there might have been of reconciling any Arab nationalist movement with the Hashemite dynasty, even though, led by the Sharif Hussain, it had been at the centre of Arab nationalism in the First World War. The hanging of Colonel al-Sabbagh in front of the Ministry of Defence in 1945, following the earlier hanging of the three colonels, put the final touches on the hatred which had been aroused.

Nuri himself had also lost all credit with the nationalists by his role in the war of 1941. To the new generation, particularly to the politically active sections of the student class, both left-wing radical and nationalist, he appeared as a reactionary consorting with imperialists. His great services, and those of some of the Hashemites, to the earlier development of Arab nationalism were forgotten: many in the newer generation had never heard of them. His repeated efforts to arouse political circles at home and abroad to the need of a solution to the Palestine question were ignored. Even after the failure of the Arab forces in the 1948 war, Nuri wished to hold out against acceptance of any form of partition in Palestine that went beyond the United Nations plan, and in addition, to insist on retaining Jerusalem, on making Haifa an international port, and on the repatriation of the Palestinians who had been driven out. It was only when other Arab countries, except Jordan, refused to join in a collective Arab demand on these lines that the Iraqi troops were withdrawn in the middle of 1949.[7] But all this meant little in the face of the attempts to renew the treaty with Britain, the unwillingness or inability of successive governments to introduce adequate political and economic reforms, the implacable drive against communists, and other measures of repression. In consequence, Iraq's position was seriously weakened as Egypt asserted her claim to the leadership of Arab nationalist sentiment, which had been raised to new heights and imbued with new bitterness after the humiliations suffered at the hands of the Zionists and their foreign allies and the consequent loss of Arab rights in Palestine.

The decade of the 1950s was a momentous one in the modern history of the Arab world. Economically, very large oil revenues began to become available at an ever increasing rate and economic and social development became a central object of policy. Politically, however, dissension and conflict, both internally and internationally, increased.

Within Iraq domestic unrest erupted in widespread public disturbances. In November 1952 as violence increased the police were unable to maintain order and the Regent turned to the army. General Nur al-Din Mahmud, Chief of the General Staff, was invited to form a government and martial law was declared. The army had to use considerable force to restore order, but at the same time General Mahmud attempted to initiate some of the reforms demanded by the opposition and, in particular, to provide for freer and more direct elections. In January 1953, after civil peace had been achieved and the elections held, he was content to resign and to make way for civilian government.[8]

Although order was restored, political stability was not; from 1953 to the Iraqi Revolution there were 11 Cabinets and 9 different persons held the office of Prime Minister. Only the two successive ministries of Nuri al-Said (August 1954 to June 1957) lasted even one year. Reforming and modernizing influences in internal political life were continually frustrated by the oligarchic tendencies of the older politicians, by the tactical incompetence of some of the reformers, and by the political immaturity of Iraqi society in a modern age. The genuine believers in representative government continued to come from the *Ahali* group of the National Democratic party, particularly Kamil Chadirchi and Muhammed Hadid (neither of whom headed a ministry), and the battle for free elections and individual voting continued. Nevertheless, it should be recognized that the course of politics in some of the years in this period compared favourably with much of what went before and with what followed, and military officers in the main pursued their vocation instead of aspiring to usurp the functions of government. It was Nuri's foreign policy rather than domestic policy that was most bitterly criticized both at home and abroad, although Nuri's anti-communism led him to take excessively repressive measures against communists, or reputed communists, within Iraq.

Nuri al-Said and Communism

The strong support of Great Britain and the virtual boycott of Russia and the communist countries generally which characterized Nuri's foreign policy were not based on mere prejudice and a spirit of reaction, as the opponents of the regime implied. As to Britain, Waldemar Gallman, United States ambassador in Baghdad during 1954–58, has well expressed the position:

> Nuri . . . never lost sight of the role the British played in the struggle to break the Turkish hold on the Arabs and to make Iraq independent. . . . He saw clearly the advantages of having Iraq allied with a big power like Britain. It had both protective and material advantages. There was no other big power prepared to do for Iraq what the United Kingdom was willing and anxious to do.[9]

To Nuri, Britain was much closer to being a model than the United States. At first sight, then, it may seem paradoxical that he should have taken such an intransigent view towards Russia and other communist countries. For Britain was herself conspicuously free from fanatical anti-communism and maintained diplomatic relations with China as well as Russia and other communist countries. Since in general Nuri was not a doctrinaire and had shown much flexibility in advancing the cause of Arab nationalism throughout his career, we must look beyond doctrinal influences to account for his uncompromising attitude towards Russia and Eastern European countries.

A predisposing influence may be found in Nuri's early associations as an officer in the Ottoman army. The Turkish regions of the Ottoman Empire were always conscious of the dangers of Russian expansion to secure unilateral command over the Straits. With such a background it was not surprising that Nuri should be profoundly impressed by Stalin's demands on Iran and by the prolongation of the wartime Russian occupation of her zone after British troops had withdrawn promptly in accordance with the wartime agreement. Equally, he grasped the implications of Stalin's demands on Turkey for a revision of the Montreux Convention in some ways favourable to the Soviet Union. Fundamentally these were questions, not of communism as opposed to capitalism, but of the imperialistic tendencies of a great power, which, even though the Russian actions may be regarded as a form of defensive imperialism aimed at safeguarding the frontiers of Russia and at extending southwards the policy of controlling the Eastern European countries, were nonetheless disturbing to Iraq. She had long boundaries with the two countries thus subjected to Russian pressure.

Within Iraq the Communist party was a small minority among the opposition groups arrayed against the regime, but it was better organized than most of them. The Arab nationalist groups and the Social Democratic party were also opposed to the regime and desired its removal, as did the extreme right-wing Muslim Brotherhood. In Iraq, as in the majority of Asian countries in this period where the party was illegal, the communists engaged in underground activities and evidence of revolutionary plotting on their part was from time to time brought to light. But they were not strong enough to be a serious danger. In 1948 the clandestine Communist party had been active along with the other parties and groups which had organized large-scale political demonstrations against the Portsmouth Treaty. Further demonstrations and outbreaks alleged to be communist-led in this period occurred and Nuri reacted strongly. In 1949 four Iraqi communist leaders were hanged. The effect was to confer martyrdom on them in the eyes not only of communists but also of a number of other sections of opinion in the country. Year after year their deaths were commemorated and their fearlessness in the face of execution was held up as a noble example in revolutionary circles. Again in 1952 the communists were active in the renewed political demonstrations demanding direct elections and the recognition of political parties. But it would be incorrect to say that any of these were 'communist plots'.

To summarize, in our view the explanation of Nuri's attitude lies mainly in historical events dating from much earlier. The first of these was Stalin's demands on Teheran after the war, which had support from the Tudeh party inside Iran, and which, if accepted, would have made Iran a satellite of the Soviet Union. The second was Stalin's demands on Ankara for a revision of the Montreux Convention on the Straits. The third was the end of the policy adopted by communist parties in non-communist countries of furthering the military cause of the Allies, and the substitution for a few years beginning in 1948 of a policy of revolutionary actions, sabotage, and guerilla activities in a number of Asian countries. A supplementary historical factor consisted in memories of the long-continued Russian quest in Tsarist times for control of the Straits to safeguard full access between the Black Sea and the Mediterranean.

The first two of these events impressed Nuri al-Said: he believed that Iraq, being in close proximity to Iran and Turkey, had a deep interest in their security, and should clearly side with those great powers which had supported them against Stalin's demands.

At this time, however, the wartime alliance between the United States and the Soviet Union had given way to a rivalry so intense that it became known as the 'Cold War', in which the underlying conflicts of interest of these great imperialist world powers were magnified and distorted by the fanatical anti-communism of John Foster Dulles, Secretary of State under Dwight Eisenhower who became President of the United States in 1952, and by the obsessive fear of Soviet communism in the United States. Nuri's policies inevitably entangled Iraq in this Cold War against the preponderant sentiment in the country.

Also at this same time, changes were taking place in Egypt which were to have the effect of ensuring that Nuri's involvement in the struggle between the United States and the Soviet Union would further weaken his position in Iraq as well as Iraq's position in the Arab world.

Iraq, Egypt, and the Cold War

In 1952 the Egyptian monarchy was overthrown by a group of young officers and for a while it looked as if a return to representative government might be effected. But in 1954 the emergence of Gamal Abdul Nasser as the unchallenged leader in Egypt presaged the introduction of a new type of doctrinal controversy into Middle East politics which was admirably adapted to serve Nasser's ambition to establish Egypt (and also himself) as the leader of the 'progressive' Arab world.

In countries under traditional authoritarian rule in the nineteenth and early twentieth centuries the modern revolutionary ideal had been representative government. From the First World War this gave way in many parts of the world to newer forms of autocracy, some of them thinly disguised with a populist exterior but managed from the top largely by army officers. The Young Turks began to move in this direction a few years after they had seized power, and some Iraqi governments in the 1930s and 1940s moved in the same direction. But from 1954, under the influence of Nasser, a new and stronger current began to appear which mingled the claim to a 'socialist' political ideology with an administration dominated by military officers and directed in the last resort by a single figure among them.

Within Egypt, political competition at the top was excluded by a number of devices. Abroad, President Nasser's ambition to create a parallel position as 'Leader of the Arab World' led to direct conflict with Iraq when Nuri al-Said was a leading influence in her government and, as we shall see, with those who succeeded Nuri. The rivalry between Egyptian and Iraqi leaders was not new: but 'Nasserism' heightened and gave a new edge to old rivalries. It appealed widely to those in Iraq who had become disappointed with parliamentary government after seeing it manipulated by an oligarchy of politicians and army officers who in their view were determined to stay in power, serving the interests of feudal landlords, rich merchants, and also of 'imperialists' who still deprived Iraq of genuine independence, and who were also responsible for the loss of Arab rights in Palestine.

An immediate aim of the 'young officer' group under Nasser was to remove foreign military bases from Egyptian soil. This was soon accomplished. The prestige of Nasser rose in Arab nationalist circles in Iraq. Nuri and his associates came under increasing attack, which reached a crescendo when in February 1955 Iraq signed a defence agreement with Turkey (known as the Baghdad Pact). The pact was designed as part of a 'Northern Tier' defence line against Russia; and Britain, Pakistan, and Iran joined later. Turkey and Iran feared their mighty neighbour; Britain joined because she saw the pact as a convenient substitute for the unpopular 1930 treaty (which was then replaced by a 'Special Agreement'), and because Nuri was anxious to include great powers in it, of which Britain would be the first and, as he hoped, the United States the second. But the United States played an equivocal role: she did not join the pact although she encouraged it and participated in some of the activities associated with it.

Nuri al-Said's political judgement in bringing Iraq into the Baghdad Pact was defective in two respects: he misjudged first the appropriate relation between Iraq and the Soviet Union and second the effect on Iraq's position in the Arab world.

The premise that Russia constituted a continual threat to the independence and territorial integrity of Iraq was a doubtful one then: in retrospect it appears still more doubtful. But regardless of the weight that might be given to it, the best riposte to the potential danger was not a close alliance with the leading great powers that were at odds with Russia. Such an alliance aggravated the danger without significantly adding to the security of Iraq. If Russia had invaded or threatened to invade Iran or Iraq, it is hardly conceivable that the other great powers would have remained idle in face of a move that would have appeared to them as a first step towards the control of the Mediterranean and the Persian Gulf. Whether Iraq was aligned with them or maintained a neutral policy, it can safely be presumed that their response would have been the same.

By forging intimate links with Britain and the United States and by severing all relations with Russia, China, and the Eastern European countries, even denying them diplomatic representation, Nuri intensified Russian suspicions; from the time of the Suez affair he also outraged the feelings of many of the Arab peoples in Iraq and abroad by failing to react strongly enough against European and North American encroachments on the sovereignty of Egypt. He did not learn from India or Yugoslavia the advantages of non-alignment for a country in the position of Iraq, nor did he recognize the disadvantages of allowing a great power to maintain an armed base on Iraqi soil. He overlooked the effects on the Russians of military and political links between the United States and smaller countries close to the borders of Russia, particularly during the early American monopoly of atomic weapons. He exaggerated the aggressive, and underestimated the defensive, elements in Russian policy after Stalin's death.

Nor did Nuri grasp fully the relation between Russia's international strategy and the policies and actions of the Iraqi Communist party. When Said Qazzaz, his Minister of the Interior, informed him of the nature of communist underground activities, he seems to have assumed that the attitudes of local communists were linked to an unchanging doctrinaire revolutionary policy and tactic in Moscow as well as among local communists. In fact, however, the primary interest of the Russians would have been served by a government in Baghdad that remained neutral and unaligned.

Nuri remained inflexible in his attitude to the communist countries even after the death of Stalin, when important changes had begun.[10] He persisted in his view that a neutral policy would have exposed Iraq either to direct aggression or to pressures that would have undermined her independence. He seemed not to understand those policies and forms of diplomacy by which small states situated between larger rivals may yet survive and at the same time avoid exposing themselves to those intense propaganda blasts which an alliance with one of the rivals inevitably draws from the other. Disdaining to reply to such attacks coming from abroad as well as at home, and underestimating their effects on the politically conscious classes, he, who had been a foremost Arab nationalist before most of his critics had been born, left the way open to charges of treason to the cause of Arab nationalism and in this lay his second misjudgement.

From the start the Baghdad Pact was violently attacked by Egypt as inconsistent with the Arab League Security Pact and as an attempt to isolate Egypt in the Arab world.[11] It was strongly opposed by most Arab nationalist circles in Iraq, by right-wing Islamic groups, and in left-wing liberal and socialist circles alike. Nuri and his associates underestimated the intensity of the opposition. The British political leaders on their side had failed to grasp the radical changes which the Second World War had brought in the world. The Bandoeng Conference in April 1955, which Nasser attended, with its resolutions condemning imperialism and opposing military alliances, was a foretaste of the impending acceleration of the drive for decolonization and independence of action by the countries of Africa and Asia. But the worst blunders of the Western powers in the Middle East were yet to come.

In July 1956 Egypt nationalized the Suez Canal and seized the assets of the Canal Company when the United States, followed by Britain and the World Bank, refused to go ahead with a promised loan to enable Egypt to finance the construction of the High Dam on the Nile. Britain, together with Israel and France, thereupon decided to attack the Canal, apparently in the belief that they could in this way bring about Nasser's downfall. The attack took place in October without the approval, or even the foreknowledge, of the United States. Anthony Eden, British Prime Minister, seemed to hold the outmoded view that the Canal was an 'economic lifeline' for Britain; the French under Guy Mollet were reacting against the Arab countries' support for Algeria in the bitter struggle between France and her former North African possession. President Eisenhower was furious at the tripartite action and the United States insisted that it be called off, joining with the Soviet Union in supporting a United Nations resolution calling for prompt evacuation of the territories overrun. The aggressors were forced to retreat.

For Iraq, and for Nuri al-Said in particular, the repercussions of these events were far-reaching. Nothing could have been more discreditable to Britain in the eyes of Arabs than joint military action with Israel, and it came just after Nuri and his associates had drawn Iraq into the Baghdad Pact to which Britain was a party. No matter that Nuri had been an active and consistent opponent of Zionism who had tried unsuccessfully to arouse Arab circles to the need of united action in resistance to it; no matter that he had publicly supported Egypt in the controversy over the nationalization of the Suez Canal, and later broke off diplomatic relations with France—these actions could not influence Arab opinion in face of his continued adherence to the Baghdad Pact.

The favourable effects of President Eisenhower's firm action over the Israeli–Anglo–French attack on Egypt were soon overshadowed by an intensified anti-Soviet attitude in Washington. In January 1957 the 'Eisenhower Doctrine' was proclaimed, publicly denouncing the Soviet Union as seeking to 'communize the world', and declaring that Russian interest in the Middle East was for that purpose. The United States was obsessed with this view of Soviet intentions in the Middle East, for which there was little evidence and which at best was a gross oversimplification.[12] The implicit assumption behind Dulles's international policies as a whole seemed to be that the countries of the Third World were more or less helpless before the great powers and would inevitably fall victim to a Russia aspiring to world domination unless the United States stepped in and 'guaranteed their independence'. The Congressional resolution which gave legal form to the 'Eisenhower Doctrine' authorized the President, when requested by any nation (or group of nations) in the Middle East, to commit the armed forces of the United States to its defence against aggression from any country under the 'control of international communism' and to extend aid to, and generally co-operate with, countries endeavouring to maintain their independence from 'international communism'.

This American initiative further aggravated the divisions in the Arab world and the tension between Iraq and Egypt. It also, as we shall see, exacerbated the political controversies in Syria and complicated her relations with Iraq and Egypt. It was naturally looked on by many as an attempt by the United States directly to interfere in Arab affairs (as it was) and, through the offers of aid, to 'bribe' Arab countries not only to join with the United States in the Cold War against the Soviet Union but also to encourage the suppression of what the United States might look on as 'subversion' at home, in which 'Nasserism' might well be (and in many quarters was) included. The offers of aid attracted the so-called Northern Tier of states bordering on the Soviet Union which, without taking seriously the 'doctrine' as a whole, felt genuinely apprehensive of border infringements and pressures. To these Nuri and some of the senior Iraqi politicians with earlier Ottoman associations could be added, and after a United States mission came to the country in April 1957 headed by James Richards, Iraq received direct grants for the equipment of the army and police, while over $12 million was to be made available to support projects under the Baghdad Pact. The Richards mission was greeted by hostile demonstrations in Iraq. The then American ambassador later commented:

> Press coverage of this largess was limited and coldly factual. Three newspapers used the occasion to address an 'open letter' to Richards, warning that the way to secure better U.S.–Arab relations was to withdraw United States 'support' for Israel.[13]

The Eisenhower Doctrine, stated as it was in provocative language, was forcefully challenged by Egypt. Nasser was able to reach the masses by his oratorical appeal. He called, and untiringly continued to call, for Arab unity in resistance to encroachments from outside. He proclaimed, and continued to proclaim, non-commitment to any of the contending international blocs. He denounced, and continued to denounce as unfaithful to the Arab cause, the leaders in those countries which had aligned themselves with any of the great power blocs. In Iraq Nuri was censured and Nasser praised with equal vehemence. The government, it was said, had made Iraq a satellite of Britain and the United States. Nominally independent, she was in fact still under colonialist domination. These criticisms, which could daily be heard in the colleges, in the schools, in the coffee-shops, and even in the houses of the middle-class opponents of the regime, were reinforced by incessant attacks from Cairo and Damascus radio and from communist 'voices' beamed on Iraq from outside.

There were those among the middle and upper classes who generally supported, or at least accepted, the regime, who were uneasily conscious of its vulnerability in these matters. But Nuri was the dominating influence. While the Foreign Office in London and the State Department in Washington counted on Iraq as a counterweight to Egypt in the Middle East, the support which they gave to Nuri contributed only to his downfall, and the system which they aimed to establish in the Middle East in support of their interests in wider world rivalries among the great powers aggravated, instead of relieved, the instability in the region and sharpened the internal quarrels which hindered its development.

Thus the two militant forces in the international affairs of the Middle East at this time were represented by Nasser on the one hand and by John Foster Dulles, working through Eisenhower, on the other. Nasser held the advantage: he could appeal to deep-running currents of national and cultural pride, to long-felt resentments over historical grievances, to a people's inchoate longing for greater respect, greater freedom, greater independence—and in a language which lends itself to powerful oratory with great emotional appeal. By contrast the United States could only rely on fears of the Soviet Union and of 'communism', and on promises of economic and military aid.

Struggle over Syria

In the midst of these international and intra-regional rivalries of the 1950s, Syria had become the centre of intense political conflict. It was inevitable that attention not only on the international level, but on the intra-regional, inter-Arab level as well, should become focussed on Syria: Patrick Seale has remarked, not without reason, that 'whoever would lead the Middle East must control her'.[14] Notwithstanding the contemporary ideological veneer which covered them, traditional rivalries in a world still lacking in a rule of law survived below the surface. On the one side the Iraqi Hashemites persisted in their designs, which they had shared with King Abdullah of Jordan, for Greater Syria to be ultimately absorbed in their kingdom. On the other, Egyptian defensive–offensive imperialist instincts with respect to Syria persisted, and hastened Egypt's adoption of Arab nationalism, overshadowing though hardly extinguishing an Egyptian nationalism based on an ancient civilization and remaining strong among the masses who were much less affected than the political classes by the newer ideologies. Thus, the struggle for influence in the Arab world between Iraq and Egypt became focussed on Syria.

Syrian Arabs were among the most politically conscious of all Arab nationalists. Damascus was the centre of the Baath movement which had been established after the departure of the French in 1946 by two French-educated teachers, Michel Aflaq, a Christian, and Salah al-Din al-Bitar, a Muslim. Aflaq, the philosopher of the movement, preached a doctrine of 'Arab unity, freedom, and socialism'. Arab unity was conceived of as the moral and spiritual foundation of the Arab peoples liberated from communal conflict, a kind of regenerative nationalism (hence the name 'Baath' meaning 'resurrection'). Freedom encompassed both individual freedom and national independence (hence the Baath dislike of communism, which they saw as endangering Arab national independence in a subservience either to a foreign power or to a foreign philosophy). Socialism was an ideal form of social organization existing in some sort of mystic unity with nationalism, giving a progressive character to it. The teaching and philosophy of the Baath supplied most of what there was of systematic thought and doctrine among Arab nationalists. As expounded by Aflaq it rested on great idealism and an almost religious reverence for the greatness of the Arab peoples once they had experienced the regeneration of a genuine unity, a true freedom, and a just socialism. But power and influence could only be gained through the negotiation of successful alliances, and ends had to be subordinated to means. Because the Baath were a small minority passionately eager to gain influence and power, they became involved in military as well as civilian intrigue, for the quickest short cut to power was through the dangerous expedient of enlisting support in the army.

In Syria, the Baath party, the Communist party under Khalid Bagdash, a politician of outstanding ability, and a number of inde-dependent progressive politicians were strongly opposed to the Hashemites and to Nuri. (The Baath had supported the Rashid Ali revolution in 1941.) The right-wing groups in the National party and the People's party, as well as the independent conservative members of the parliament, were favourably disposed to the Iraqi regime. One of the central issues between the rival groups became whether or not Syria should allow herself to be drawn into the Baghdad Pact. Pressures were brought to bear on Syria from both the United States and the Soviet Union, the former desiring to block the development of Syrian political, military, and trading relations with the Soviet Union, and the latter anxious to restrain Syria from joining anti-Russian alliances. The Regent and Nuri and his associates became entangled in the plots and counter-plots formed around these issues,[15] and some of the army leaders were charged with missions to bribe Syrian politicians to overturn governments unfavourable to Syrian alignment in the Cold War.

As the records later showed, private meetings were held between agents of Syrian right-wing groups and Iraqi agents of the Regent and Nuri, at which agents of the United States Central Intelligence Agency and, in a less active capacity, British intelligence agents were present. The aim of the leading participants, or at least of the principals for whom they acted, was to use bribe money with a view to securing the return of a Syrian government that would co-operate with the Iraqi regime in rejecting neutralism and in joining the Baghdad Pact or, as the Americans preferred, a 'Northern Tier' alliance.[16] All this time Nasser was becoming increasingly alarmed at these events.

From 1955 to 1958 Syria was the centre of unceasing intrigue at home and of pressures coming from near and far from abroad. Some circles, particularly among a section of the National party, still leaned towards Iraq and the Hashemites. Against these forces were arrayed the Egyptian regime under Nasser and its growing number of followers in Jordan, in Iraq, and in Syria itself, all of them impressed by Nasser's successes in achieving independence of the great powers. The United States had been ready to sell arms to the Middle Eastern countries and to supply economic aid only under limited and discriminatory conditions based on political criteria related to the rivalries between the two largest world powers. In practice access to arms sometimes depended on willingness to join pacts directed against the Soviet Union, although at one point Jordan succeeded in avoiding this condition. Egypt's success in obtaining arms from Czechoslovakia was widely looked on as a great step towards the achievement of independence by removing the unbalanced dependence on the Western powers. On the north Turkey and on the east Saudi Arabia added their pressures, exercised through diplomatic, through other official, and through private channels. The Saudi monarchy, although intensely conservative and traditional in politics, had a long history of rivalries with and hostility towards the Hashemites. All these forces were directed against Iraqi aims in Syria.

As the political conflicts between the Baath and the communists, between the conservatives and the radicals, intensified in Syria, the United States became increasingly alarmed at what she saw as an accelerating drift towards communism and growing Soviet influence. Also in Jordan domestic conflicts, exacerbated by the pressures from outside the region, were acute. A nationalist government came to power in October 1956 in the aftermath of the attack on Suez and of the dismissal of the British General Glubb from the Arab Legion by King Hussain. This government brought an end to the Anglo–Jordanian treaty, denounced the Eisenhower Doctrine, and moved to establish relations with the Soviet Union.[17] King Hussain reacted strongly: he dismissed the government, dissolved the parliament, purged the army, imposed martial law with the aid of his bedouin regiments, and accepted the financial and political support of the United States. This strengthened relations with Iraq, but Jordanian relations with Syria further deteriorated.

The pressure from the United States mounted (at one time she even considered military intervention). Russia took a different line, insisting that her economic relations were on a business basis and not aid, and that her political support was to help ensure the independence of the Arab countries from imperialism; she warned the United States not to interfere.

Harassed by external pressures, the Syrian government turned towards President Nasser, who had successfully resisted Britain's desire to retain a military footing on the Canal and that of the United States to control Egypt's trade in arms and supplies. But even this aroused controversy within Syria and Iraq alike, for while Egypt's independent stand against the great powers won approval in both countries, the deeply rooted historic fears of domination from the Nile had not been extinguished. Nevertheless, the Syrian President, Shukri al-Quwatly, pressed by army officers, urged union on Nasser. Al-Quwatly was an independent politician who feared that Syria would fall under the sway of one or the other of the rivals in the Cold War; he was supported in this by the Baath, who feared any increase in communist influence. Within the Baath the role of the Syrian military, however, was even more pronounced than that of the Baath civilian leaders in the government, and this led to uneasy internal relations between leading civilian and military leaders.

Such was the situation at the formation of the United Arab Republic announced on 1 February 1958, an event of major importance for Iraq. President Nasser was thought to have been reluctant to embark on the union with Syria, and only agreed to it under considerable pressure and on conditions that would in practice leave him in a dominant position. He did not command the political *souplesse* that would have been necessary to work out a constitutional relationship likely to reconcile Syrians to the union which had been sought only by a minority. The Baathist leaders expected that, as they had taken a strong initiative in the union, they would be in a position to take part in the formation of policies and to exercise some measure of administrative power in Syria. They were to be disappointed. President Nasser was never willing to share power.

The union was a serious blow to the ruling regime in Iraq and it was not long before a riposte came. The dream of a 'Greater Syria' under the Hashemite dynasty had ended. But it remained to determine the role of Jordan, and the Hashemite counterblast took the form of an announcement on 12 February of union between Iraq and Jordan. At the time of the Iraqi Revolution the members of the Iraqi and Jordanian Cabinets were engaged in giving effect to the outlines of such a union.

Looked at superficially, the proposal to unite Iraq and Jordan might appear to be only a simple riposte to the creation of the United Arab Republic. Although the latter had abruptly ended the hopes of joining Syria with Iraq, the Iraqi rulers had to consider the possibility that in Jordan an internal 'Nasserite' rising might conceivably carry that country into the United Arab Republic with Syria and Egypt. Nevertheless, the initiative for an Iraq–Jordan union seems to have come more strongly from Jordan, and from King Hussain personally, than from Iraq. Nuri al-Said had set his hopes above all on the economic development of Iraq. In a union, Jordan would be a very weak partner from an economic point of view, and Nuri and his ministers hesitated before they agreed to assume the burden for political reasons. King Hussain and his advisers were uncertain of the allegiance of certain army officers, who might, as once before, attempt a *coup d'état,* perhaps on Nasserite lines.

But this was not the only consideration. The idea of Arab unity on more traditional lines, resembling in some respects that which prevailed in the later stages of the First World War, had considerable appeal to them. A Hashemite unity embracing Jordan and Iraq and perhaps extending to the Gulf States might be united in some fashion with Saudi Arabia and her adjoining shaikhdoms. Such ideas were ambitious but vague. But since unity was in the air and the two countries that had taken practical steps towards it were doing so on revolutionary, *progressiste* lines, it was natural that others, in which there had been no 'young officer' *coups d'état,* should try to compete on the lines, and in the spirit, of an earlier Arab nationalism.

Thus the move to create a union of Iraq and Jordan was an expression in part of ideas that had long antedated the establishment of the United Arab Republic and it would be an oversimplification to characterize it as a simple riposte to the latter. Nevertheless, its timing was undoubtedly influenced by what was considered in some Iraqi and Jordanian circles to be a danger arising out of the establishment of the United Arab Republic and out of the Lebanese civil war.

Crisis in Lebanon

In the 'Greater Syria' area a sharp division emerged. In Syria proper the forces of Arab nationalism were predominant, but in Lebanon they were tempered by the presence of Christian and of Druze minorities, and by the prudence of responsible heads of Islam in the country who desired to avoid religious conflicts. However, while Syria was more actively seeking wider Arab nationalism, the election in 1952 of Camille Chamoun to the presidency of Lebanon brought in a semi-autonomous landed feudal magnate associated with an intolerant Christian sect. Chamoun was opposed to Arab nationalism and to Nasser. He aimed to turn Lebanese policy from one of neutralism and balance, both internationally and within the Middle East, to one openly aligned with the West. This contributed to the civil conflict which broke out later and which indirectly influenced the instigators of the Iraqi Revolution.[18] Thus here, as at other leading centres in the Middle East, the impact of pressures from outside played a leading part in the internal conflicts.

Among the gravest of all President Chamoun's many misjudgements was his agreement in 1957 to co-operate with the United States in the application of the Eisenhower Doctrine.[19] Apparently his Foreign Minister, Charles Malik, persuaded him that by doing so Lebanon would gain large amounts of economic aid. Chamoun also departed from the accepted distribution of offices which had been designed to preserve a balance among the sects and groupings in Lebanon and he allowed the suspicion to grow that he desired a second consecutive term of office, which was prohibited by the Lebanese constitution. There developed a political atmosphere in which it took only the murder of a political journalist to start a civil war.

On 8 May 1958 the assassination of a Christian newspaper editor opposed to Chamoun ignited an armed insurrection of both Muslims and Christians in Tripoli and in other areas of the country dominated by Muslims and Druze. The army refused Chamoun's demand that it suppress the rebellion, but it did maintain reasonable order and prevented the outbreak of large-scale civil war.

In accepting the Eisenhower Doctrine the Lebanese government not only overturned the delicate internal balance of power, but also undermined the position of the country in the Middle East by aligning it on one side in an internal schism in the area over the foreign policies to be adopted towards the outside world. Egypt could hardly remain aloof in face of Lebanon's adherence to an arrangement by which her government could, if it thought fit, call in United States armed forces to deal with internal conflicts alleged to be the outcome of interference by outside agents, including Egyptians. Middle East tension rose steadily.

But the first external appeal of President Chamoun was to the United Nations, not to the United States. It led to the dispatch of United Nations observers to establish a watch on the frontiers of Lebanon. The Lebanese Foreign Minister charged Egypt and Syria (then the United Arab Republic) with promoting the disorder, and supporting the rebellion with arms. The charges were denied by Egypt and controversy continued until the observers were able to take up positions in the areas held by the insurgents as well as in government areas. The report of the observers did not substantiate the charges made by the government.[20] If agents and materials had crossed the frontier earlier, their numbers and quantity appear to have been grossly exaggerated. In some cases local smuggling activities of long standing were mistaken for or misinterpreted as underground political activities. No *prima facie* case was made out for UN police intervention.

Nuri al-Said became entangled in the controversy and looked with increasing disquiet on the weakening position of President Chamoun; he misjudged the preponderant political sentiment in Lebanon as he had misjudged it in his own country, where the chronic underlying dissatisfaction with the ruling group was heightened by events in Lebanon and the Iraqi government's attitude towards them. The students and professional classes in particular, as well as a number of other elements among the politically conscious groups in Iraq, were overwhelmingly on the side of the Lebanese opposition. Yet

Nuri gave no more attention to the Iraqi opposition than President Chamoun did to the Lebanese opposition. Even when Chamoun belatedly declared that he would not seek re-election, Nuri's position remained unchanged. The American ambassador, recording his last conversation with Nuri on 12 July 1958, noted that

> He was unhappy about our [the United States] failure to adopt a more positive line of action on the Lebanon. Even at this late date he felt that if Chamoun were 'actively' supported by friendly governments, he would change his mind and stand for re-election. Any action that Iraq might take would be for the sole purpose of maintaining the independence of Lebanon. Iraqi military action on behalf of Lebanon would, he was convinced, have strong popular support. 'But Iraq cannot act alone because of the lack of adequate air coverage'. If only he knew what the United States contemplated doing, he could make his own plans. Would there be intervention? he asked. I had to tell him that I did not know. He looked very dejected and pre-occupied as I left him.[21]

This revealing passage strikingly illustrates both the magnitude of the gulf between rulers and ruled in Iraq on the eve of the Revolution, and the limitations of Nuri's understanding of the political temper in other Arab countries.

The conflict was kept at a simmer in Lebanon with the army preventing it rising to a boil, and keeping Beirut under dawn to dusk curfew. When, however, in July 1958 the Iraqi Revolution swept away the monarchy and the Iraqi government, Chamoun, fearing that the Lebanese rebellion would be intensified, called on the United States for help and 10,000 American marines were flown in and landed immediately.

The Americans took the occasion to mediate between the contending parties and as a result General Chehab, the Lebanese army commander, was decided upon as Chamoun's successor, although he was strongly opposed by many Christians and the right wing. The United States occupation of Lebanon was soon ended, but the effects of the landings at Beirut were much more serious and far-reaching than had been anticipated at the outset. The American military authorities had used the opportunity to land troops and materials on a much larger scale than was necessary to deal with conditions in Lebanon alone. The effects on the Soviet Union were serious: the Middle East, from a strategic point of view, was comparable in Russian eyes to the Caribbean in American eyes. The narrow technical point of view from which the American military looked on the exercise took insufficient account of the concern with which the Soviet military and civilian authorities watched events so close to their boundaries. It is difficult to escape the probable conclusion that the expansion of Russian naval and aircraft construction in the next decade, which has been the subject of widespread concern and frequent complaints, was greatly hastened by the technical success of the Beirut landing.

Notes

1 In addition to the works from which we have quoted, Lord Birdwood's *Nuri al-Said* (London, 1959) is a useful personal account relating to Nuri al-Said.

2 See Khadduri, op. cit., pp. 262–7.

3 'To decide that the United Nations shall administer a territory for the purpose to establish on it two new states is hardly within the competence of the General Assembly or other organ of the United Nations': Hans Kelsen, *The Law of the United Nations* (London, 1950), p. 197.

4 A useful brief discussion of this can be found in C. Ernest Dawn, *From Ottomanism to Arabism: Essays on the Origins of Arab Nationalism* (Chicago, 1973), Ch. 6. See also George Antonius, *The Arab Awakening* (London, 1938).

5 The British government had striven to minimize the hardships that wartime shortages imposed on the Middle East by establishing the Middle East Supply Centre as a means of achieving an equitable and efficient distribution of the diminished supplies available. At the outset the secretariat of the Centre found that economic information about the area was seriously deficient. They set out to improve this and it seemed clear to them that the continuance of the Centre in some form after the war would serve the interests of the people of the region. Unfortunately the resentments, especially in Iraq, over the British–Iraqi War of 1941 were unfavourable to the realization of this idea. The establishment of the Arab League offered an alternative.

6 For a brilliant treatment of the issues arising from the schemes to unify the Fertile Crescent viewed from the Syrian angle, see Patrick Seale, *The Struggle for Syria* (London, 1965). There is of course a considerable literature on this subject. See also M. Khadduri, 'The Scheme of Fertile Crescent Unity: a Study in inter-Arab Relations', in R. N. Frye, ed., *The Near East and the Great Powers* (Cambridge, Mass., 1951), p. 137.

7 On this question see especially Longrigg, *Iraq, 1900 to 1950*, p. 357. In some other accounts it is passed over.

8 The Regent and the succeeding government were shortsighted in failing to return General Mahmud to his position as Chief of Staff after he resigned. He deserves a distinguished place in Iraqi history as a competent soldier who in an emergency accepted a political position but refused to use it to usurp the role properly assigned to civil power. Some of his successors were less patriotic. See M. Khadduri, *Independent Iraq*, pp. 302ff. for an account of the elections and of Mahmud's role.

9 Waldemar J. Gallman, *Iraq Under General Nuri, My Recollection of Nuri al-Said, 1954–58* (Baltimore, 1964), p. 223.

10 See, for example, J. H. Brimmell, *Communism in South East Asia* (Oxford, 1959).

11 See P. J. Vatikiotis, *The Modern History of Egypt* (London, 1969), pp. 390-1.

12 The disagreement arose from a fundamental divergence of outlook which existed not only among the countries of the Middle East but also within a number of the countries vaguely classified as 'Western'. The issue was clearly stated by G. Barraclough and R. Wall in the RIIA *Survey of International Affairs 1955–1956* (Oxford, 1960), pp. 23, 24: '. . . apprehension of Soviet intentions was the dominant note in Anglo–American policy. In fact events in 1954 provided little evidence of direct Soviet interest in the Middle East; but, in western eyes its military weakness constituted a standing invitation to Russian intervention, and western effort was largely concentrated on combating this potential but at this juncture still largely hypothetical "danger" . . .

'. . . Whether western policy was wise in viewing the Middle East primarily in military terms as an anti-Russian base and an area to be closed to communist influence, is another question . . .'

13 Gallman, op. cit., p. 81.

14 Seale, op. cit., p. 1. See also Malcolm H. Kerr, *The Arab Cold War: Gamal 'Abd al-Nasir and his Rivals, 1958–1970*, 3rd edn. (New York, 1971).

15 There is a considerable scattered literature on this. An excellent treatment is in Seale, op. cit., Chs. 19 and 20. See also Marcel Colombe, *Orient Arabe et le non-engagement* (Paris, 1973), II, 9–13, 60–3, 81-90; and H. Carrère d'Encausse, *La politique soviétique au Moyen Orient 1955–1975* (Paris, 1975), pp. 89–100; and R. El-Sayed, *The Baghdad Pact in World Politics* (Geneva, 1971), pp. 104–8.

16 On this see particularly El-Sayed, op. cit., Ch. IV, pp. 33–42; and Russell Brines, *The Indo-Pakistani Conflict* (London, 1968).

17 In Jordan, with her Hashemite links with Iraq but with fewer surviving earlier links with Ottoman influences, the renewed drive of Arab nationalism in the 1950s had been strongly reflected in the ministries of premiers sympathetic to it and hostile to the intensified American penetration into the Middle East. See especially *Orient* (juillet 1957), pp. 211–32 for a detailed account of events in Jordan at this period.

18 For a convenient summary of contemporary views on these political controversies in Lebanon see *Orient* (juillet 1957), pp. 234–45.

19 For his own defence see Camille Chamoun, *Crise au Moyen-Orient* (Paris, 1963), pp. 219–313. This lucidly written apologia unfortunately becomes thinner and increasingly one-sided as it approaches the events of 1958.

20 See especially Security Council: *Official Records. Supplement,* July, August, September 1958, p. 80; and for the type of charges see United National Front's statement of 14 May 1958 reproduced in M. G. Agwani, *The Lebanese Crisis of 1958* (London, 1965), pp. 62–3. This is an extremely useful collection of records bearing on the crisis and illustrating it from many angles.

21 Gallman, op. cit., p. 165.

6 The Oil Industry Comes of Age: a Changing Economy, 1932–52

The course of political change within the framework of a constitutional parliamentary monarchy was, as we have seen, erratic and frequently retrogressive, displaying only few characteristics which could be described as 'development'. This most difficult of political forms was, of course, a foreign intrusion into the traditional social and political framework of a Middle Eastern country and would necessarily have had to be digested by the local society and adapted to its own social and political culture. This in itself would give rise to uneven and precarious political development, for which success would perhaps have been more to be wondered at than failure. But economic development, also bringing a strong infusion of foreign and non-traditional elements, proceeded more evenly. Although beset by difficulties of its own, deflected by the impact of war, and at times and in certain of its aspects distorted by political constraints and disruptions, nevertheless the course of economic change, in contrast to the course of political change, was characterized by important elements of progress appropriately called 'development'.

Those who speculated on the future of Iraq as an independent country invariably commented on her bright economic prospects: oil had been discovered and the outlook for the country as a major oil-producer was encouraging. And quite apart from oil, the land and water resources of the country once supported a prosperous agriculture and could easily do so again. Suffering neither population pressure nor extreme underpopulation, the vigorous and talented people of Iraq were widely expected to move rapidly forward to create a flourishing economy and an effectively functioning society.

At independence oil had already been discovered in the north, but there had been little exploration in other parts of the country. Oil was not yet a dominating force in the economy nor were oil royalties the chief source of government revenues. As we have seen, a new revised oil agreement had been made with the IPC in 1931 for the area east of the Tigris in the *liwas* of Mosul and Baghdad, in which the most important fields were of course near Kirkuk. The British

Oil Development Company (BOD) obtained a concession for the area west of the Tigris. But this arrangement was not to last long and the IPC was soon to obtain a monopoly over the country.

The IPC Obtains a Monopoly

The BOD was originally a British syndicate which became associated with Italian interests and then with German and French interests. In 1931 the company had needed additional capital which the British were unable or unwilling to contribute. Italian and German capital was increased and the British share was reduced to 40 per cent. To organize the interests of existing shareholders and to accommodate the new capital, the BOD group set up Mosul Oilfields Ltd (MOF), a holding company with British, Italian, German, Dutch, French–Swiss, and Iraqi shareholders. A number of wells were drilled with sufficient success to encourage the company, although the oil was heavy and of relatively low quality.

In spite of the new capital, the company's financial resources proved inadequate to the task. Over a quarter of a million sterling was due as dead rent to the government at the end of March 1936 and the company had difficulty finding the money. By then the Italian group had a majority shareholding. Italy had much welcomed the access to Iraqi oil that her holding in the BOD had provided, for the Italians saw in this venture some compensation for their exclusion in 1920 when the powers had staked out their interests in Mesopotamia. A suggestion from the Italians that if the company did not pay, the concession might be taken over by the Italian State Company (AGIP) was rejected by the Iraqi government. An Egyptian group at this time was also given an option to purchase shares, but nothing came of it. To save the BOD concession the Italian group paid the rent due. But affairs were cloudy below the surface: American interests were alleged to be behind the Italian payment, while at the same time discussions were also being held between the Italians and the managing director of the IPC. It later appeared that the IPC itself had put up the money through the Italians, and that negotiations were in progress to enable the IPC to take over Mosul Oilfields and thus acquire the BOD concession.

The board of Mosul Oilfields was reorganized and among the new directors was the managing director of the IPC. By the beginning of 1937 the IPC had obtained effective control. The MOF shares were acquired from the other interests, the Italians thus giving up their position in the company, which they had hopefully seen as their gateway to Middle East oil. The IPC then organized the Mosul Petroleum Company as a wholly-owned subsidiary, and liquidated

Mosul Oilfields. By 1941 it had formally taken over the BOD concession. This move eliminated an unwelcome competitive group and gave the IPC a monopoly over the exploitation of all Iraqi oil in the Baghdad and Mosul provinces. In taking over the BOD concession, the IPC also accepted terms more stringent than those in the 1931 IPC agreement. The latter had not imposed drilling obligations on the company, while the BOD concession required the company to maintain a minimum number of drilling rigs in operation and gave it 7½ years to begin exports, which then had to be maintained at at least one million tons a year, with the government entitled to 20 per cent of the oil produced as part of its royalty.

Although within Iraq the many political opponents of the IPC were critical of the newly extended monopoly, the government itself accepted the argument, not without controversy, that its oil resources could be more effectively developed in the hands of the technically experienced and financially strong group of oil companies which the IPC represented. Although oil had not been spared the effects of the great depression (the international groups elsewhere were attempting to negotiate a cartel agreement to contain competition and to maintain prices[1]), the IPC pushed ahead with its expansion programme. Some 150,000 feet were drilled in the old BOD concession west of the Tigris by the middle of 1938, but results were meagre. East of the Tigris, however, attention was concentrated on delimiting and developing the Kirkuk field, which was clearly one of the most important in the world.

While the Kirkuk field was being prepared for large-scale production, the IPC group began to consider the problem of the pipeline, and after the 1931 agreement began to move rapidly to construct it. In addition to the physical and technical problems of acquiring land, transporting materials, organizing labour supplies and accommodation, water, food, power, communications, and other supporting facilities in the great barren desert which had to be crossed, were the political considerations posed by differing views as to the appropriate choice of route and port. The French preferred a northern route to Tripoli in Syria (now Lebanon) while the Iraqis and British wanted a southern route to Haifa in Palestine. To satisfy both, the pipeline branched at Haditha, one part going to Tripoli and the other to Haifa. A 12-inch line was completed in 1934 with a capacity of 4 million tons a year. Iraqi exports, which had risen little since 1930, suddenly jumped from less than a quarter of a million to over a million metric tons between 1933 and 1934 and then nearly quadrupled again by 1935. Payments to the government doubled between 1933 and 1934, reaching nearly £1.5 million.

The discovery of oil in Bahrain by Standard Oil of California

(Socal) in 1932, and later in the al-Hasa region of Arabia, rekindled the IPC's long-standing interest in the southern region of Iraq.[2] There was some competition for a concession in the Basra area, but none of it was sufficient to present a serious threat to the IPC's position since once again the government, although aware of the criticism,[3] and indeed of the possible disadvantages, of granting one group a monopoly of the country's oil, nevertheless preferred the devil it knew to be financially and technically capable of developing and marketing its oil. Its experience with the BOD had not encouraged it to risk another unknown. A concession was granted in 1938 to the Basra Petroleum Company,[4] a sister company of the IPC group, on terms very similar to those of the BOD concession, including drilling obligations, minimum royalty payments, dead rents until the export of oil, and a government entitlement to 20 per cent of the oil produced. If oil resources comparable to those of Kirkuk were discovered, both payments and export obligations were to be increased.

The prospects of high-quality commercial oil discoveries in Basra were very promising, especially after the discovery in April 1938 of the great Burgan field in Kuwait not very far away. The concession terms, which were more favourable to the government than those in the north, seemed reasonable also to the company in view of the excellent outlook. But the area covered by the BOD concession, on which the Basra terms were modelled, was in a different category. In that concession the oil finds were very disappointing and the oil of low quality. The company did not want to give the priority to the development of this area which would be necessary to fulfil the obligations laid on it by the concession terms, in particular the drilling obligations and the requirement to produce commercial oil within 7½ years from the beginning of the concession (i.e., by 1938). The IPC sought and obtained a modification of these terms in return for a substantial interest-free loan to the government recoverable in part out of future royalties. The IPC group would have liked to consolidate the obligations of all three affiliates and to concentrate on the development of the more attractive oil reserves, but this was not at that time acceptable to the government, which wanted as rapid an increase as possible from all sources.

Knowing that the shareholders in the IPC, with the exception of CFP and Gulbenkian, had extensive interests in oil elsewhere, the Iraqis were always fearful that the development of their own oil would be prejudiced. The government had always to balance conflicting considerations in deciding its concession policy. There was a danger in granting a monopoly to one group, yet the alternative contenders had neither the financial strength nor the proved capacity of the big established companies. On the other hand, the potential ability of these companies to bring rapid development and large revenues to the country might not be fully realized if they gave a higher priority to their interests in other countries while their monopoly in Iraq was protected from competition. Hence, the government did the best it could to impose obligations which would encourage rapid exploitation of its concessions and was always loath to modify them.

Oil Company Policies and Iraqi Fears

The Iraqi fears were soundly based. The French and Gulbenkian saw the dangers even more clearly; their reason for insisting on the red-line agreement was to ensure that the expansion of IPC oil production was not retarded by the acquisition of interests in Arabia by their partners or, if it was to be so retarded, that they would share fully in these other interests.[5] The 'big three' in the IPC—Anglo–Iranian, Shell, and Jersey Standard—were the largest oil companies in the world and were very much concerned that world oil production should expand as demand expanded, but not faster, for faster expansion would only bring competition and falling prices. The emerging productive potential of the Middle East was clearly a potential threat to the hoped-for stability of markets if the oil fell into many and 'weak' hands. Hence it was not only to expand their 'empires' that the big companies attempted to gain control over potentially rich resources everywhere in the world, but also to protect the profitability of their existing interests. At the same time, the profitability of taking oil from any one source depended on the cost of doing so and new fields might be more profitable than existing ones. Once they became established in a country, however, the companies had to consider the political sensitivities of the host governments. Thus they too had to balance a large number of political and economic considerations while attempting to maintain overall control of the international development of the industry. In such circumstances Iraq, like every host government, was correct in her own interest in attempting to tilt the balance in her own favour by restricting the freedom of action of the IPC. CFP and Gulbenkian were correct, in their own interests, in doing the same by insisting on the red-line agreement.

Nevertheless, the red-line agreement did leave the vast potential of the circumscribed area open to others, and when in the 1930s Socal moved to obtain concessions therein and Gulf defected from the IPC, the 'big three', and especially the American group, saw their position threatened. The divergence between their interests and those of CFP and Gulbenkian widened. Not surprisingly, therefore, extensive and involved overt negotiations and covert intrigues characterized the relations among the shareholders and between some of the shareholders and other companies and governments as all strove to maintain or improve their existing positions. Because the individual interests of the IPC shareholders were so divergent, the IPC as a group was not effective in the cut and thrust of the concession-hunting in Arabia, and the French and Gulbenkian succeeded in preventing the American shareholders from obtaining Arabian interests until the latter forced the elimination of the red-line restrictions after the Second World War.

In spite of these differences among the partners, however, the IPC could not neglect Iraq, and the company laid plans for a large expansion in the 1930s. The size of the pipelines was the factor limiting production and export, for the capacity of the Kirkuk field, the development of which proceeded steadily, greatly exceeded existing pipeline capacity. Accordingly, in 1938–39 plans were made to double the pipeline to the Mediterranean, but the outbreak of war not only forced the temporary abandonment of that project but also forced the company to subordinate its activities in Iraq to the military and political requirements of war and the exigencies of British policy.

It is often argued, especially by Iraqis and those who are particularly outraged at the restrictive conditions and monopolistic arrangements imposed by the oil companies in the Middle East, that the interests of the host countries were seriously damaged by the activities of the companies. Appraisal is of course difficult because it can only be done by comparing what actually happened with what might have happened had circumstances been different; the tendency of the critics is to compare the imperfections of reality with some idealized situation, often clearly impossible of realization in the conditions of the time. So far as Iraq is concerned, there are four aspects of the position which are worth examining.

First, there is the simple question of monopoly by one company as contrasted to a situation in which there are several competing companies. As we have already noted, there were very few companies in the world capable of developing oil in the Middle East at that time and the assumption that if a number of them entered the country, they would in fact have competed and would not have acted in collusion is probably unrealistic. But if we do make it, the issue is still by no means clear, for if a number of companies entered and attempted to produce Middle East oil as rapidly as possible, prices would have been lower, the industry would probably not have been as profitable as it was, and the oil-producing countries would probably not have been able to obtain the amount of income from it that they did, since the amount of oil demanded would probably not have been very much greater at lower prices. It is possible that larger total revenues might have been obtained from a somewhat larger output even if revenues per ton had been less, but this would have meant a more rapid depletion of oil resources. In any case, given the extremely low levels of educational attainment, industrial skills, and administrative expertise, and the still rudimentary political administration in the early period, it is not obvious that rapid increase in oil revenues would have led to a more rapid rate of economic development. In these circumstances, one can plausibly argue that the monopolistic control by the companies, with all its disadvantages, even including the occasions when the host governments were imposed upon, not to say cheated, was nevertheless in the long-run economic interest of the countries when compared with alternatives reasonably likely to have emerged at the time. In Iraq the threat of competition from potential newcomers was sufficient to give considerable bargaining power to the Iraqis in the 1930s, which they used skilfully, while the internal political opposition to the government and to the Anglo–American companies, made not only the companies but also the British mandatory power fully aware of the desirability of arriving at agreements satisfactory to the government.

Secondly, the structure of the IPC with its mixture of companies of four different nationalities each with strongly divergent interests and led by men with different national outlooks did create special problems for the development of Iraqi oil and put Iraq at a disadvantage compared with Iran and the more homogeneous consortia elsewhere. The American companies were very suspicious of the French. CFP was not a large international company with extensive marketing outlets and the Americans feared that if it had abundant and cheap Middle East oil, it might indulge in price competition in Europe. The American partners in the IPC had their eyes on Arabia and from 1933 to the outbreak of war they tried hard to secure a relaxation of the restrictions of the red-line agreement in order to obtain access to Bahraini and Saudi Arabian oil through Standard of California. They never succeeded in overcoming the opposition of the French and of Gulbenkian, both of whom wanted a rapid expansion of Iraqi oil.[6]

Moreover, Shell and SONJ had had their properties in Mexico nationalized in 1938 and they had to consider the political implications for their other Latin American concessions, especially Venezuela, should expansion there be reduced in favour of the Middle East. Anglo–Iranian, with its large and exclusive concession in Iran, had also to balance diverse interests. The Iraqis frequently expressed their dissatisfaction with the slow rate at which their production increased compared to that of Iran following the completion of the pipeline to the Mediterranean. Iranian output increased by 36 per cent between 1935 and 1938 while that of the IPC rose by only 16 per cent.

Thirdly, the fact that one single company had a dominant economic position in the country and that this company was British, the nationality of the mandatory power and of the power held responsible for Palestinian affairs, focussed the burning rays of nationalist feeling on the oil industry in a more intense way than might otherwise have occurred. Many Iraqis firmly believe that had there been more oil companies of different nationalities operating in the country, the effect on Iraqi political life of foreign operations would have been less resented and the end results in the 1960s and early 1970s less disruptive. It is difficult to form a judgement on this in view of the uninhibited contentiousness and the violence of Iraqi politics in which the oil company was not for the most part a really major issue—at least until the 1960s.

Finally, as we shall see in the next section, the IPC group, being British, had necessarily to conduct its affairs during the war in a manner consistent with British policies, which many Iraqis did not consider in Iraq's interest. Again, however, it is probable that in one way or another the Allies would have been able to prevent the use of Iraqi oil to benefit the Axis powers regardless of the ownership of the company—at least in the later years of the war when such matters were crucial.

It is easy to understand, and to sympathize, however, with much of the Iraqi bitterness towards the oil companies, whether or not it was all well-founded. There is no question but that the Iraqis felt dominated by the foreign companies and especially by the British government; they felt that their government was not only too much under the influence of the British but that Britain had in some way too much power over the country to enable them to consider their independence a reality. As we have seen, the exercise of British power was clear during the war; but, as we have also seen, it does seem likely that the direct influence of Britain in Iraqi politics has been much exaggerated, especially by the nationalists, in comparison with the divisions within the country itself and with the activities of self-seeking politicians and army officers, as an explanation of the unsatisfactory political development of the period. The charge of imperialism was used without scruple by ambitious politicians to attack their enemies and mislead the public. Imperialism there clearly was; the difficulty is to judge its significance correctly.

War and Post-war Oil Policies

The outbreak of war did not result in any immediate fall in the demand for Iraqi oil. Although the British government prohibited shipment of oil to other than British and French sources, these could take all that could be delivered. But when Italy entered the war in the middle of 1940, the Mediterranean was closed to Allied shipping, confining Iraq's Mediterranean exports to those products that could be refined by the AIOC–Shell refinery at Haifa and the small refinery at Tripoli. Iraq's oil production then fell from 3.9 million metric tons in 1939 to 1.4 million in 1941. Revenues did not fall so heavily (from £2.2 to £1.4 million), being kept up by dead rents, minimum royalties, and tax commutation payments. After the German occupation of France and the establishment of the Vichy puppet government, the CFP shares in the IPC were sequestrated by the British Custodian of Enemy Property[7] and the group was not allowed to take IPC oil, which was sold f.o.b. Haifa to other groups at a price equal to that of Texas oil at the Gulf of Mexico less a quality differential.

For a short period during the regime of Rashid Ali al-Gaylani in May 1941, oil production was stopped completely. The company's property and equipment suffered some damage and looting. The virtual occupation of Iraq by British troops in the summer of 1941 made heavy calls on the company to maintain supplies of oil products for the British army, but from 1942 on exports continued to rise in spite of the destruction in that year of all but six of Kirkuk's producing wells to ensure their denial to the enemy in the event of a German attack. By the end of the war in 1945 exports were already greater than in any year before the war.

The war interfered with the planned development of the IPC's oil resource and, by the same token, created problems for the company in fulfilling the obligations to explore, produce, and export, which it had assumed under the concession for both Mosul and Basra. In 1943 it asked for a moratorium on the fulfilment of these obligations. The Iraqis were loath to consent in spite of the company's plea of *force majeure,* especially in the south, but after much negotiation and some recrimination, agreement was reached in 1943 permitting a suspension of the company's drilling, production, and export obligations until two years after the armistice. As recompense to the Iraqi government the company made an interest-free loan of £500,000 immediately and promised an additional £1 million when an armistice was reached, the whole to be repayable out of royalties on terms similar to those of the 1939 loan.

The fact that Britain was directly involved in the war, and that the IPC was a British company, did have some adverse consequences for Iraq during the war in that exports were affected by British government policy and by the position of the Allied powers in the Mediterranean. It is probable that at least early in the war Iraqi exports might have been greater had the IPC been able to sell to the Axis powers. Nevertheless, the British military activity in Iraq was not related to the nationality of the IPC, and Britain would undoubtedly have taken the same political and military action in the country in any case. Iraq, no more than other countries, could expect to escape the repercussions of conflicts among the powerful.

As soon as the war was over, the IPC promptly moved not only to restore war damage and bring its operations back to full normal operations, but also to fulfil the concession obligations for the Mosul oilfields and for Basra in the south. It also had to reconsider the problem of supplying refined products for Iraqi internal consumption, since the Iraqi government, even before the war, had stated its dissatisfaction with the existing refining and distribution arrangements. At the same time, the partners in the IPC were quarrelling bitterly over the insistence of the American companies that they be permitted to pursue their own interests in the rest of Arabia freed from the restrictions of the 1928 group agreement. In addition, the IPC had to settle the claims of CFP and Gulbenkian arising out of their inability to lift their share of oil during the war.

The problem that caused the greatest difficulty among the partners and eventually forced a new group agreement arose from the unilateral denunciation of the red-line agreement by the American group in 1946. The Americans, having successfully demanded before the war, with the backing of the State Department, that the door be opened to them in Iraq, had no intention after the war of opening the door to Arabia for either the French or the British. Both the French and Gulbenkian reacted strongly against the American withdrawal from the red-line agreement and legal action was initiated. Negotiations involving all the companies, the State Department, and the British government continued during 1946 to 1948.

Nobody wanted the affairs and arrangements relating to the IPC to be paraded in public. The State Department was worried about the deteriorating diplomatic relations with the French; the British did not want to rock the boat. British resistance to the American demands may have been weakened by American offers to British Petroleum of a long-term contract for its Kuwaiti (or Iranian) oil; the French (and Gulbenkian) were mollified by an agreement to make new arrangements for the expansion of IPC output which would also give them the opportunity to take more oil than their proportionate shareholding would have permitted under the old group arrangement.

In November 1948, a general accommodation was finally reached among the partners which removed the restrictions preventing the operation of individual companies outside the red-line area, thus meeting the chief demands of the American companies. SONJ and Mobil could now enter Aramco and undiluted American control of Aramco was assured. The new group agreement affirmed Anglo–Iranian's right to its 7 per cent overriding royalty, thus satisfying this company (which had also by separate agreement obtained market outlets for its Kuwaiti oil). Gulbenkian was assured profitable outlets for his oil; arbitration was arranged for CFP's war claims; and procedures were agreed for the expansion of IPC output. The last was of primary concern to Iraq. The entry of both American companies into Aramco, which the lifting of the red-line restrictions made possible, meant that the only companies in the IPC with a strong incentive to expand Iraqi output rapidly were first CFP, since it was the only one with no oil elsewhere, and to a lesser extent Shell.

The new arrangements were an attempt to reconcile the desire of CFP for rapid expansion and that of Anglo–Iranian and the American companies for a slow one. The procedures were clumsy; there was an unduly long planning period between the request of a partner for oil and the actual production of it; total output was governed by a complicated formula the effect of which was to restrict total planned investment and production as well as the amount of oil any partner could take.[8] Although the new programme envisaged a large expansion of Iraqi oil production, and did permit partners short of crude to buy additional amounts at reduced costs, it was nevertheless to prove inadequate to overcome Iraq's resentment at the failure of the IPC to expand output as rapidly as that of other major producing countries. There is little doubt that the composition of the IPC group, together with the absence of competition, did result in relatively unfavourable treatment of Iraq in this respect.

An expansion was, however, already under way when the new agreement was made. Freed from wartime restrictions and subject only to the post-war difficulties of acquiring materials and finance, the IPC went ahead with the work of repairing and restoring facilities, further developing and delimiting the Kirkuk field, and exploring in both the Mosul and Basra concessions. As indicated earlier, the major restraint on Kirkuk production was the capacity of the pipeline. By 1946 work had begun on a 16-inch line, the northern branch of which would terminate at Tripoli and the southern at Haifa along almost the same route as the old 12-inch line. A line larger than 16 inches was ruled out because neither Britain nor France could produce larger pipe and the IPC was not permitted to acquire dollars (another disadvantage of the company's British nationality). On completion, total pipeline capacity from Kirkuk would be more than tripled to nearly 13 million tons a year.

Unfortunately the southern branch of the line had to be abandoned when it was nearly finished in 1948 as a result of the Arab–Israeli conflict, and has never been used. Even before the completion of the northern branch in 1951, work had begun on the even greater project of a 30- to 32-inch line from Kirkuk to Banias, a terminal in Syria north of Tripoli. The pipe for this was imported from the United States (Longrigg tells us that even 24-inch pipe was not produced in 'sterling mills' until 1954) and the line, with a capacity of 14 million tons a year, was completed by 1952. The whole system could then deliver nearly 16 million tons a year. Total IPC output jumped to 18 million tons in that year, including around 2.5 million tons from Basra and Mosul, for by this time exploration and development in those areas was well advanced.

Of the two, the old BOD concession at Mosul was still the least attractive. The pre-war extension of time for the fulfilment of the concession terms plus the wartime moratorium would run out by early 1953 when the company would be required to begin exports. When the war ended, oil had not yet been discovered in commercial quantities and it was necessary to accelerate the rate of exploration.[9] In spite of early discouraging results, for the oil discovered was heavy and viscous and in relatively small deposits, the company pressed ahead. By 1952 it had found enough to permit export. The fields, though not by any means great by Middle East standards, were worth having.

Basra was a different story and expectations were high for the south of the country. Oil of good quality was soon discovered and commercial exports began in December 1951 after completion of a pipeline to Fao at the mouth of the Shatt al-Arab in the Gulf. The BPC was clearly to be an important producer in the IPC group, and it expected to approach some 8 million tons a year by 1955.

The impressive results of exploration and development, and the rapid expansion of pipeline capacity, resulted in a more than four-fold increase in output between the end of the war and 1952. During the same period there were even more far-reaching changes in the financial arrangements. As a result, government oil revenues, instead of merely quadrupling as output increased, rose more than fifteen times in the period.

Economic and Social Change After Independence: 1932–52

The dramatic jump in financial resources consequent on the new arrangements for oil revenues at the beginning of the 1950s tends to dominate discussions of Iraq's economic history up to the 1970s. But economic and social development in the preceding two decades since independence, though slow and hesitant, was by no means negligible. It was not to be expected that the termination of the Mandate and the entry of Iraq into the League of Nations as an independent state late in 1932 would bring about any marked change in economic policy, let alone economic activity. Iraqis had for most practical purposes been taking increasing charge of their own internal affairs ever since 1925, when the constitution was adopted and a parliamentary regime established. British advisers were much in evidence and British influence was great, but Iraqi politics and policies came increasingly to dominate the decisions of government on domestic matters. To be sure, the government did not want any serious clashes with the mandatory power, but King Faisal was a man of considerable stature, with a mind of his own, and he had some able and formidable advisers. In any case, the British for their part wanted to influence, but not to run, Iraq's internal affairs.

In both oil and foreign affairs, however, British views were of particular importance, although, as we have seen, in oil negotiations the company did not always get its own way—indeed it did not always get British government support. Independence was not to change the position in this respect very much for a considerable time to come. British influence on the economic life of the country continued, although on a different basis and perhaps in diminished strength. Special treaty arrangements remained and the links between the two countries in trade, financial, oil, and economic matters generally continued to develop. The oil company remained British, and in both import and export trade Britain remained Iraq's most important supplier and customer. During the Mandate Iraq was part of the Indian monetary system and early in 1932 the dinar replaced the rupee as the country's currency, but was at parity with and linked to sterling and managed by a currency board in London, which invested its assets in sterling securities. Monetary independence was not part of political independence, although at least until the war Iraq undoubtedly benefited, considering the conditions of the times, from the confidence that the link with sterling engendered. British advisers were widely used in government, and the courts continued to rely on British judges.

The death of King Faisal in 1933 was probably more important for the country's immediate future than was the acquisition of formal independence. Iraq lost a leader who might have been able to contain in some sort of balance her turbulent political forces and undisciplined politicians. As we have seen, cabinet changes were frequent, and 1936 saw the first military *coup d'état*. The jockeying for position among the politicians, and the general political instability, could not fail to have consequences for economic affairs, for government programmes changed frequently and government energies were diverted from constructive tasks. With the changes in government often came changes in the more senior civil servants which clearly interfered with the continuity necessary for successful administration. Between 1927 and 1945, for example, there were fourteen different Directors-General of Education, a politically sensitive civil service post, for students were a significant political force. But in most economic matters, government was not yet the dominating influence that it was increasingly to become from the 1950s. Oil revenues paid directly to the government were only around £3 million as late as 1949 (or 11.8 per cent of total government receipts), having risen from less than £1 million in 1933 and £2 million a decade later.[10] Customs duties were nearly four times oil revenues. Direct attempts by the government to control economic life were still of minor importance.

Total government revenue rose moderately from an average of slightly over 4 million dinars a year in the period 1931–35 to nearly 28 million dinars a year in the period 1946–50, around 12 per cent coming from oil, another 25 to 26 per cent from import duties, and the rest from indirect taxes of various kinds, including agricultural taxes. The *istihlak* tax alone, which replaced an ineffective and unjust land tax in 1931, and was a tax on the sale of agricultural products, brought 19 per cent of total government revenues in 1946–47. This was the main agricultural tax, but it fell largely on urban consumers who paid it through increased prices of agricultural products.[11] Between 1935 and 1940 around 29 per cent of total government expenditure was devoted to capital works and the still meagre revenues from oil went largely for such investment. The railways and the port of Basra had independent budgets. The army, as might be expected, absorbed a large share of budgetary expenditure. During the war the government budget maintained surpluses, but deficits reappeared in 1945–46 to 1949–50, almost two-thirds of which were incurred in 1948–49 because of harvest failures and the Arab–Israeli war.[12] In real terms both receipts and expenditures were lower until 1952–53 than before the war because of the large rise in prices.[13]

Exports of cereals, dates, cotton, and other agricultural products, added to the growing oil exports, permitted rising imports; except for the immediate post-war years 1946–49, Iraq's trade accounts were in surplus. During the war years Iraq suffered an inflationary boom under the impact of wartime expenditures, especially spending by British troops stationed in the country, which was estimated to have reached £64 million in the period 1941–44. Prices rose rapidly, the consumer price index reaching 636 (1938–39 = 100) in 1943. Since imports were severely curtailed by war conditions, most of this money (some £58 million in both public and private accounts) accumulated as sterling balances in London. Altogether, on public and private account Iraq accumulated in London an estimated £70 million. Although the British authorities released the balances only gradually after the war, it was possible by drawing on reserves to finance a post-war upsurge in the value of total imports, which more than doubled between 1945 and 1948, but the shortages of goods and other economic hardships imposed on the country during the war intensified many Iraqi grievances against Britain.

In 1947 provision was made for the establishment of a Central Bank, which was finally set up in 1949, to take over the management of the currency from the Currency Board. In principle the rigid links with sterling were modified and the Iraqi authorities obtained the power to influence the domestic money supply. Iraq remained in the sterling area, however, and in practice the dinar remained at par with sterling and was devalued with it in 1949.[14]

Land and Agriculture

In agriculture, the most important, and at the same time the most difficult, sector to develop, slow progress was made. Until the 1950s government revenues were not sufficient to finance the large engineering works required to control the rivers, to prevent flooding, and to bring the water into use, although the Kut barrage on the Tigris, the first to be completed since the Hindiyah barrage on the Euphrates of 1914, was opened in the late 1930s. This, together with the building of feeder canals and other small systems, and the continuation of private investment in pumps, made possible a substantial increase in land under irrigation in the south of the country. The wartime boom, during which prices rose rapidly to reach in 1945 a level six times that of 1936, stimulated agriculture. Between 1934–38 and 1950 the area under wheat and barley expanded by nearly 40 per cent and that under rice somewhat more, largely in the south. By 1944 the total cultivated area in the irrigated zone had risen some four times over that in 1918, but even then only amounted to slightly over 17,000 square kilometres. Inadequate drainage, the curse of the countryside, remained the outstanding and largely neglected problem. The World Bank mission found that 'The drainage of existing irrigated land would make the most important single contribution to increasing the productivity of agriculture'. It reported that 20 to 30 per cent of the cultivated land of the country had been abandoned 'over the last few decades' because of salt, while in a large part of the rest, yields had declined by 20–30 per cent.[15]

Investment in agricultural machinery continued to grow, especially in pumps. During the war tractors and combines were increasingly seen in the north. An Agricultural Machinery Administration was set up in the Ministry of Economics to control and make machinery available to farmers, but the total number of private and government combines and tractors was well short of a thousand in 1950 and their life was short. Modern grain silos also began to appear.

Apart from locust control, however, where some progress could be clearly seen in the considerable reduction of damage to crops from this pest, the measures to assist agricultural productivity were slight. Advances were made, however, in date-packing, wool-dipping, grain-cleaning and storage, and in handling and distribution, but yields remained very low and techniques of cultivation remained unchanged in most areas. Little was done to remedy the human and social problems of Iraqi agriculture arising from the ignorance, ill-health, and poverty of the peasants and the conditions of land tenure. The Agricultural Department had in 1950 only 108 officers with a base pay of over 15 dinars a month, and the Veterinary Department only 40. A Ministry of Agriculture was established only in 1952. The expansion of the cultivated area and the investment that did take place were largely due to the activities of private landlords and urban financial interests who saw opportunities in agriculture.

Land registration, the drawing of boundaries, and land settlement continued slowly. By the early 1950s it was reported that title had been settled to over two-thirds of the land area of the country excluding desert, although southern Iraq was still largely neglected. At least one important settlement scheme for small farmers was started in 1945 on the Dujaila Canal below Kut in which over a thousand families were given plots of land by 1950 and for which model educational, health, and cultural amenities were planned. But the settlement was not solely designed to give land to existing landless farmers, for retired army and police officers, civil servants with at least eight years' service, and unemployed graduates of religious institutions were, among others, entitled to land. Inevitably a certain amount of absentee ownership and even sharecropping resulted. The project was not nearly so successful as had been hoped, partly through bad planning and largely through neglect of drainage. Salt, accumulating in the soil, quickly caused yields to fall and in some areas forced land out of cultivation.

Over the country generally, however, continued official registration of land titles permitted greater and greater areas of land to become the property of tribal shaikhs who had acted as agents of the government in the tribal areas before independence. As we have seen, after independence disputes over land titles continued to be a potent source of conflict in the countryside, which urban politicians used or attempted to use to their own advantage in their struggles for power in Baghdad. The powerful influence of shaikhs on weak and vacillating governments resulted in tribal lands becoming in effect the private property of the shaikhs, who thus became the largest landowners in the country. The categories of Iraqi land tenure have frequently been described elsewhere[16] and it is not necessary here to outline them once again. The old system was completely swept away by the 1958 Revolution. Had the British administrators understood the local situation more clearly while they still retained effective control over the country after the First World War, they might have been able to introduce a system for settling land titles which gave the great tribal shaikhs, who now often lived in the cities, smaller opportunities to acquire tribal lands for themselves and form a large class of absentee landlords.[17] But one must also recognize the strong likelihood that the politicians of an independent Iraq would nevertheless have been unable or unwilling to adopt policies with respect to land tenure that went against the interests of the more powerful tribal shaikhs.

In any event, the policies adopted destroyed prospects for the development of a class of small or medium-sized independent farmers and laid the foundations for extensive absentee landownership throughout the country and severe exploitation of tenant farmers in many areas, especially in the south. The position of the actual cultivator, usually a small sharecropper, probably deteriorated in most places in the inter-war period. The landlords virtually escaped taxation; attempts to charge them for drainage improvements and impose taxes on income, inheritance, and land were continually defeated in the parliament they dominated. Migration of the impoverished farmers to the cities continued, again primarily from the south. As the cultivation of cash crops spread, the dependence of the farmer on the landlord for both the marketing of his crop and for his agricultural needs further increased. In spite of a law passed in 1933, which was designed to prevent peasants indebted to their landlords from obtaining employment elsewhere until the debt was paid off, many continued to leave illegally. According to one estimate, about a quarter of the population of Amara *liwa* in the south moved to other *liwas,* primarily Baghdad and Basra, in the middle 1940s. The problems of land tenure were well known and there had been groups advocating reform (notably the *Ahali* group) from the early 1930s, but the landed interests blocked reform until the violent overthrow of the parliamentary monarchy in 1958.

An Agricultural and Industrial Bank was established in 1936 to provide credit for agriculture (the two sides were divided into two separate banks in 1946), but it was of little help to the small farmer.

In the summary of 25 years of operation issued in its Annual Report of 1959–61, the Agricultural Bank pointed to the problem of land titles as the chief difficulty:

> The Land Settlement Departments were new to the task entrusted to them, and the problems besetting arable land in the various areas caused the settlement of rights in it to be delayed and consequently made it impossible for the actual usufructuaries to benefit from the services of the Agricultural Bank. There is no doubt that influential persons were given preference in the settlement of their right in the land, so that it was quite easy for them to secure the documents and deeds which enabled them to obtain loans from any quarter, including the Agricultural Bank, while small cultivators remained in the grip of problems arising from disputes over the establishment of their right in the land under their usufruct, so that they remained incapable of making use of the services of the Bank. Anyhow, the Agricultural Bank itself, in giving advances to cultivators, accepted only certain securities, such as real estate, movable properties represented by pumps and other agricultural machines and implements, and collateral securities. No other securities were ever accepted.[18]

Industrial and Other Public Expenditures

As part of government policy to encourage industry, the industrial side of the bank, and after 1946 the separate Industrial Bank, was empowered to invest directly in industry, but it was never given enough money to make much of an impact. Government agencies continued their attempts to improve the quality of agricultural products for processing as well as the quality of processing itself, but progress was slow except in the date industry. Industrial investment was very small, hardly exceeding half a million dinars in the period 1946 to 1950. Out of some 60,000 people employed in industrial enterprises in 1950, only 2,000 were in modern industrial plants. The oil industry employed around 12,000 and had advanced rapidly in spite of the delays caused by the war.

Most public investment went into irrigation, flood control, transport and communications, and construction projects. Road-building was pushed forward, but by 1950, out of the 8,000 km. of roads only 500 km. were metalled and much of the rest of the system was impassable for much of the year. The number of registered passenger cars rose from over 4,500 to nearly 11,500 between 1942 and 1950, trucks from nearly 2,000 to over 6,000, and motor-cycles from under 100 to over 1,500. There was considerable expenditure on urban amenities and the face of the larger towns changed rapidly, but by 1950 only 40 towns had piped water (as contrasted, however, to only one in 1920). No town had a municipal sewage system, and although electricity was more widely available, its costs were among the highest in the world. Outside of Baghdad and Basra the management of electricity enterprises was extremely inefficient. In Baghdad the Light and Power Company was British-owned and was efficient, but profits were very high as a proportion of gross receipts and taxes were paid to the British government as well as to Iraq.

Budgetary allocations for education rose from less than one million to over 2 million dinars between 1938–39 and 1949–50, but even then less than a quarter of the country's school-age children were in school and illiteracy was estimated at nearly 90 per cent of the population, with very few women able to read and write. In 1950 there were only about 3,000 pupils in colleges. During the thirty years before 1950 the number of doctors had risen from 25 to nearly 800, but some three-fifths were to be found in Baghdad alone.

Thus, at mid-century a visitor from Europe, if he left the better-off sections of Baghdad, would have been appalled at the poverty of the people, the primitive state of agriculture, and the condition of the towns. Only if he had visited the country thirty years earlier would he have been able to appreciate the advances made, and even then most of these would probably have had to be pointed out to him. Nevertheless, some progress had been made in nearly every sector of the economy and especially in the cities. There had probably been a distinct improvement in living standards generally, and the necessary administrative foundations for further development had been laid. Agriculture was the country's greatest industry and its greatest weakness; but by 1950 oil was clearly beginning to take the lead and was expected to remove the financial restraints under which Iraq had suffered for so long.

But social and political unrest was growing. It had been aroused, or at least intensified, by two broad influences. The first was the triumph of the Western democratic countries and the downfall of Germany and Italy. In its wake came demands for a more equitable social and economic order. Second, the more left-wing circles, recognizing the leading role of Russia in the war and in the post-war period, demanded freedom to take part in the political life of Iraq.

Underlying these discontents, and extending far beyond the politically conscious classes, which constituted only a small proportion of the total population, lay the discontents of the masses of people, both in the urban slums of the small as well as the large cities and in extensive rural areas to the south, whose chronic conditions of poverty had been aggravated by the shortages created by the war.

Their commerce had been disrupted and their needs had been subordinated to those of the great powers in the most destructive war in all history, a war which they had done nothing to provoke and over which they had no control. It was hardly surprising that the peoples of the Middle Eastern countries should give priority in the post-war world to the aims of political independence from the great powers and to their own economic development. In Iraq new arrangements with the oil companies were to bring the promise of rapid development nearer to realization. A new era was soon to be proclaimed on all sides, but within the decade its promise was to wither.

The Oil Industry Comes of Age

A system for paying royalties satisfactory to both company and government had not been achieved before the war and remained a continual source of argument and friction. Although the government had acquiesced in a fixed tonnage royalty unrelated to the profits of the company, a compromise had been included in the 1931 concession agreement under which at a future date arrangements would come into effect relating royalties to profits. The formula accepted was unwieldy and completely unworkable: twenty years after the beginning of exports the rate of royalty was to be increased or decreased in proportion to the extent to which the profit or loss of the company was greater or less during the immediately preceding 5 years than it had been during the first 15 years of the 20-year period. Profit and loss were defined to include the cost of refining and distributing the products made from Iraqi crude oil. A minimum of 2*s*. and a maximum of 6*s*. a ton was stipulated.

Commercial exports began in 1934; hence by 1954 the change in royalty payments would be due for consideration under the above provision. The 15-year period which would set the base for the new calculations would begin in 1939. The Iraqi government was not to be caught napping, and it early queried any decisions of the IPC which might affect the calculations, including the price to be charged to the IPC parents for oil. For example, when in 1935 the IPC imposed the price of 18*s*. a ton before putting a 'cost-price' formula into effect, the Iraqi government asked for an explanation, only to be told that this was an arbitrary price. Dissatisfied with such replies, the government persisted over the years in attempting to get information out of the IPC relevant to the calculations that would be required. It had no success at all; the IPC insisted that the information simply could not be provided since Iraqi crude was blended with other crudes in the process of manufacture and there was no way of determining the profits which could be attributed to a particular crude. Moreover, there was no unambiguous market price for crude oil because very little was sold in the open market. Almost all the oil entering into international trade was transferred by the international companies from their own producing subsidiaries to their own refining affiliates. Hence it made little sense to talk of 'free market' prices. The IPC suggested that the problem be resolved either by accepting some agreed price at the Mediterranean terminals or by using an expert adjudication, as was done, for example, for the pricing of Gulbenkian's crude. The issue was still unsettled at the outbreak of war. Immediately after the war the Iraqi government raised it again, since by then the matter was becoming urgent.

Along with this longer-term problem of calculating royalties was the more immediate 'gold question': just exactly how should a '4*s*. (gold)' royalty be calculated? The question first arose after the devaluation of the pound in 1931 when the IPC attempted to refuse to pay the sterling equivalent of the new price of gold in spite of the fact that the concession agreement had explicitly stipulated '4*s*. (gold)'. The world 'gold' had been inserted expressly to deal with the contingency that the gold value of sterling might change. The company was not supported by either the British or French governments in their shabby effort to avoid the payment clearly due, and subsequently it had to agree that royalties would be calculated in sterling at the 'current price of gold'. This apparently straightforward solution was, however, adequate only when there existed an unambiguous price for gold. During the war the price of gold in the bazaars of the Middle East far exceeded the Bank of England price in London and the Iraqis insisted on the use of the free market price to calculate royalties due. The sterling debt of the IPC to the government, which was further increased by another devaluation of the pound in 1949, would on this basis be very large indeed. The Iraqis prepared to take the company to court, refusing arbitration.[19]

The acrimonious controversy over these genuinely difficult issues was soon overshadowed and swept aside by the impact of a new approach to the determination of oil revenues for the host government—that of an equal sharing of profits. Such a method of payment had long been in use in Venezuela, and in 1950 Aramco and the Saudi government negotiated an agreement which provided for profit-sharing in the form of a 50 per cent tax. The principle quickly spread in some form to all the major oil concessions in the Middle East. In Saudi Arabia such an arrangement was advantageous to the oil company, for Aramco was itself a corporation chartered in the United States and its shareholders were all American companies. Aramco was thus subject to the United States income-tax laws. The United States Treasury agreed to permit the company to deduct from its United States income-tax liability all income taxes paid to the Saudi government. Consequently the company, in effect, simply transferred the tax that it had previously paid to the United States government to the Saudi government at no cost to itself. As we have seen, the IPC and its shareholders were in a very different fiscal position. Extensive negotiations were required among the shareholders and with their own governments before acceptable arrangements could be arrived at, and the British government had to be persuaded to grant British oil companies similar deductions on their British tax liabilities. But Iraq could not be given less favourable terms than Saudi Arabia, and a new agreement was signed in February 1952 effective from 1 January 1951.[20]

The agreement dealt with a number of matters on which the Iraqi government had been pressing the company, but its most dramatic result was the increase of oil revenues from around 18*s*. to 40*s*. a ton. Since the IPC itself made no profits, it was necessary to create a system by which profits could be attributed to the production of crude oil; the device of the 'posted price' was taken over from the procedure established in Saudi Arabia. The companies posted (or published) the prices at which they would offer specified crudes for sale from specified export terminals. In the 1952 agreement posted prices were prices f.o.b. seaboard terminals to be determined with reference to free market prices for individual commercial sales of full cargoes according to a procedure agreed between company and government, or by the use of 'fair prices' fixed by agreement in the absence of such free market prices; alternatively arbitration could be resorted to. The first of these was generally accepted. The *procedure* was thus agreed, but in practice the parent companies of the IPC, which actually posted the prices, arrogated to themselves the freedom to set the actual prices they posted. This soon brought them into conflict with the government.

The price of Kirkuk oil for the purpose of calculating profits to be shared with the government was determined by its 'border value'—the value of the oil at the point of export from Iraq, which would take into account transport costs to seaboard terminals and the posted price of oil at those terminals. A discount of 17*s*. 6*d*. a ton at the Iraqi–Syrian border and of 13*s*. a ton at the port of Fao in the south was given to 'facilitate' exports.

Profits were calculated as the difference between the border value and the actual or 'fixed' (=agreed) costs of production. Costs could be agreed (or 'fixed') in advance for administrative convenience with the proviso that in any year actual costs would apply if they differed from fixed costs by more than 10 per cent. The state was entitled to a royalty of 12½ per cent, which it could take in kind or sell back to the company at posted prices, but the value of the royalty would be included in the government's 50 per cent share of profits calculated before the deduction of royalty. Thus, the strictly income-tax element in the government's revenue was less by the amount of the royalty than 50 per cent of the calculated profits. The government was guaranteed minimum payments of not less than 25 per cent of the seaboard value of IPC and MPC exports and 35 per cent of the value of BPC exports.[21] A minimum output was guaranteed subject to *force majeure*.

Attempts were made to deal with some of the other persistent complaints of the government regarding the advancement and training of Iraqis within the company. More extensive training and education abroad of Iraqi employees and the appointment of more Iraqis to higher positions in the company were agreed, and a second Iraqi director was also to be appointed.

The Iraqi government had long wanted a state-owned refinery to provide oil products for local consumption. It was not happy with the existing arrangement under which the Anglo–Iranian Oil Company supplied the products for northern and central Iraq from its refinery on the Alwand river (which was owned by its subsidiary, the Khanaqin Oil Company) and marketed them through another subsidiary, the Rafidain Oil Company.[22] Anglo–Iranian thus fulfilled the IPC obligation to secure Iran's internal requirements. It was not surprising, however, that this arrangement was unacceptable to Iraq. The case at that time for permitting foreigners to develop the country's crude-oil resources for export to world markets, though not convincing to all Iraqis, was nevertheless strong, and was accepted by the government. A similar case could not be made for giving foreigners the task of supplying Iraq's internal demand for oil products.

In 1935 the Iraqi government had asked the British government to provide an expert to advise and make recommendations on the construction of a refinery in Iraq and on the sale and distribution of products by the government. The expert reported unfavourably, and it seems highly probable that he was right from an economic point of view. The Iraqi market was not large, the north and central parts of the country could easily be supplied from Alwand, while the large Abadan refinery just south of Basra in Iran was the most efficient source of supply for the south. But in such circumstances economic factors are not, nor should they necessarily be, the ruling considerations, and the Iraqis wanted a locally-owned refinery.

The issue, like so many others, was shelved during the war, but revived just after it, the revival being much hastened by the improved financial resources of the government consequent upon the new agreement about revenues. The government decided to go ahead with plans to take unto itself all refining for the local market and a good deal of distribution as well. In 1951 it engaged an American contractor to build a small refinery at Dora, a southern suburb of Baghdad, which would draw its supplies from the IPC pumping-station on the Tigris nearly 150 miles to the north. This refinery would be entirely capable of supplying all of Iraq's needs for some time to come.

In addition, the government decided to take over (with compensation) the refinery at Alwand and the assets of the Rafidain Oil Company, leaving the Khanaqin Oil Company's producing operations alone for the time being. The KOC organization was retained for a time to operate the facilities as agent for the government. In 1951, when Iranian oil exports disappeared from the world market consequent on the nationalization of the Anglo–Iranian operations in Iran, urgent measures had to be taken to expand Iraqi refining capacity to serve the south.

Between 1952 and 1958 Iraqi oil output nearly doubled and revenues slightly more than doubled, the biggest increase in output occurring between 1951 and 1953 when the completion of the pipelines coincided with the steep decline in Iranian output. The government quickly made arrangements to channel oil revenues into the economic and social development of the country.

Notes

1 In 1928 Standard Oil of New Jersey, Royal Dutch Shell, and Anglo–Persian drew up plans to stabilize the world market shares of the major oil companies and eliminate price competition. The agreement is known as the 'as is' or Achnacarry agreement, for it was drawn up at Achnacarry Castle where Sir Henri Deterding, Chairman of Royal Dutch Shell, Walter Teagle, President of Standard Oil of New Jersey, and Sir John Cadman, Chairman of Anglo–Persian, had gathered 'for the grouse' in 1928.

2 In 1927 the Gulf Oil Corporation, while still a member of the American group negotiating for entry into the TPC, acquired rights to the Bahrain concession. In accordance with the red-line agreement the company proposed that either the TPC take over these rights or permit Gulf to continue alone. Both proposals were refused and Gulf withdrew from the American group, but subsequently sold the Bahrain rights to Socal. In Arabia, also, Socal obtained the now famous Saudi concession, assisted by the limitations imposed on the other companies by the red-line agreement. The IPC made a somewhat half-hearted effort to bid for the concession, apparently more to keep it out of the hands of others than because it wanted to extend its own activities. See Longrigg, *Oil in The Middle East*, p. 107.

3 Not surprisingly the government's attitude towards the IPC has always been a central issue of political conflict in Iraq. In 1938, it will be recalled, Jamil al-Midfai was Prime Minister, but was forced out by pressure from the army

and other political groups. Taha al-Hashimi and Rustum Haydar, who became Ministers of Defence and of Finance respectively in the succeeding government headed by Nuri al-Said, were strong critics of the hegemony established by the IPC.

4 The IPC group now consisted of the Iraq Petroleum Company proper with the Kirkuk concession east of the Tigris, the Mosul Petroleum Company west of the Tigris, and the Basra Petroleum Company in the south. Until 1960 the three companies operated essentially as one group with the same ownership, and will here be referred to collectively as the IPC (or IPC group) unless there is reason to distinguish them.

5 See Ch. 3 above for discussion of the red-line agreement.

6 CFP also wanted a low price of IPC oil, but this was resisted by the American companies for the above reasons. As we have seen, the IPC was set up as a non-profit-making company, the parents to acquire oil in proportion to their shareholding at cost, plus a nominal fee per ton. This arrangement was not immediately put into effect and when exports began in 1935 an arbitrary price of 18*s*. a ton was charged. This price was queried by both the Iraqi government and CFP. But even the 'cost price' formula was a source of disagreement, for 'cost' is an elastic concept that includes depreciation, amortization, and other items which can be spread over a longer or shorter period, thus reducing or raising current costs. The more rapid the rate at which write-offs are made and the greater the items charged to current expenses, the greater are current costs. The French wanted slower write-offs and lower current costs and therefore a lower current price for oil. In their attempts to obtain French agreement to modifications of the red-line agreement, the IPC partners agreed to the French request for lower prices, but failed to get the modifications desired. The formula agreed in 1936 was a price equivalent to the cost accepted by the United Kingdom for income-tax purposes plus one shilling a ton. This did not affect Iraqi revenues, which were received as rents and royalties.

7 C. S. Gulbenkian was also classed as an enemy alien for a short period since he lived in Paris, and his shares also were sequestrated. He moved to Lisbon in 1942, and in 1943 his previous status was restored.

8 The outlines of this agreement have been presented and its importance discussed in a number of works cited in the Bibliography, notably the *Report* of the Federal Trade Commission and in E. T. Penrose, *The Large International Firm,* pp. 157–9.

9 The IPC had repeatedly pressed the government to permit a pooling of the obligations of all three concessions, but this would have allowed the IPC to concentrate on Kirkuk. In the Mosul and Basra concessions, but not in Kirkuk, the government was entitled to 20 per cent of the oil produced. It naturally refused to give this up by accepting pooling.

10 See Zuhayr Mikdashi, *A Financial Analysis of Middle Eastern Oil Concessions: 1901–65* (New York, 1966) for data on oil revenues up to 1965.

11 Guzine A. K. Rasheed, 'Development of Agricultural Land Taxation in Modern Iraq', *Bulletin of the School of Oriental and African Studies* (Vol. XXV, Part 2, 1962), pp. 262–74.

12 The modern theories of economic development, in which budget and trade deficits are considered desirable ways (within limits) of accelerating development, had not yet become widespread in this period. Hence surpluses, or at least balanced accounts, were treated as a mark of sound economic management.

13 We have drawn on the work of Kathleen Langley, *The Industrialization of Iraq* (Cambridge, Mass., 1961) for data on this period. See also Longrigg,

Iraq, 1900 to 1950, where an account marked by acute personal observation and a deep knowledge of the country in the period may be found.

14 See discussion in F. Shehab, 'Iraq', *Bulletin of the Oxford Institute of Statistics* (Vol. 21, No. 4, 1959), pp. 292–307.

15 International Bank for Reconstruction and Development, *The Economic Development of Iraq* (Baltimore, Md., 1952), p. 17.

16 See especially the discussion of Doreen Warriner, *Land Reform and Development in the Middle East,* 2nd edn. (London, 1962), pp. 142ff. Longrigg, *Iraq, 1900 to 1950*, pp. 260–2 briefly and less critically describes early policy.

17 An extremely valuable discussion of the development of the land system of lower Iraq under the Ottomans in the nineteenth century can be found in Albertine Jwaideh, 'Midhat Pasha and the Land System of Lower Iraq', *St. Antony's Papers,* No. 16 (1963), edited by Albert Hourani.

18 Agricultural Bank, *Annual Report,* 1959–61, p. 9.

19 A compromise was reached in February 1932 under which the Iraqi government agreed to accept payment at the current price of gold in London. This increased the current January payment due (of £409,000 at the old rate) to £578,000. Some Iraqis have been critical of the government for accepting this compromise, believing that the 'bazaar price' would have been accepted as the appropriate price in the courts.

20 In spite of the large increase in revenues, a number of Iraqi politicians were dissatisfied with the agreement. The Istiqlal leaders demanded nationalization, having been encouraged by the example of Mossadeq (who had not yet been shown to have failed) and five members resigned in February 1952 when the agreement was introduced into parliament.

21 It was also separately agreed between the government and the IPC that should any of her neighbours receive higher revenues per ton of oil produced than Iraq received, the company would consider and discuss a revision of financial terms. The Iraqis considered that this 'most favoured company' agreement entitled her to receive treatment at least as favourable as that received by any neighbour.

22 Anglo–Iranian had been granted a concession in 1925 to exploit oil at Naftkhana in the Transferred Territories where it had made a discovery in 1923. (The agreement under which the rights to this area were acquired by Anglo–Iranian was unrelated to TPC affairs.) The concession required it to build a refinery near Khanaqin. The Khanaqin Oil Company was organized to operate the concession and in 1927 the Alwand refinery, a simple topping plant with a capacity of some 150,000 tons a year, was completed on the Alwand river. In March 1932 Anglo–Iranian organized the Rafidain Oil Company to undertake the marketing of KOC's products. Southern Iraq was supplied by Anglo–Iranian from the Abadan refinery in Iran.

7 Development with 'Unlimited Finance', 1950–58

> Specify the type of residence . . . which you occupy, whether it is a remshackle, or a house (bricks) or a house (sun-backed-bricks) or a sarifa, or a hair tent, or a hut, or an apartment (flat), or a rest-house, or a palace, or a building, or a boat, or a bridge-stop, or a garage, or a restaurant, or a shop, etc. [*sic*]

Here, in a single sentence copied literally from the official English version of the instructions for the 1957 census schedules, are neatly illustrated the great disparities in the conditions of living of the people of Iraq. 'Do you live in a "remshackle" [i.e., a ruin] or a palace, a "bridge-stop" or a flat?' The contrast between the standards represented by the mud and reed dwellings of the poor and the mansions and palaces of the rich has always been and still is a recurring theme in most discussions of the social and economic position of the Iraqi people.

Yet a similar disparity between the poorest and the richest will be found in even the most affluent of the industrialized countries (including the advanced communist countries) and *mutatis mutandis,* similar questions could be asked. It is not the contrast as such that is the chief target of most development programmes but rather the large numbers of people living in conditions of great poverty. For nearly 30 years Iraq has had a large flow of oil revenues and, in consequence, there have been very great advances in the standard of living of the people, in industrial development, and in the provision of economic and social 'infrastructure'. Although we have little knowledge about the distribution of income in the country until very recently and only fragmentary estimates of consumption expenditure, all evidence we do have indicates that not more than 20 per cent of the population had by the early 1950s attained a standard of living that could by any stretch of the imagination be described as either healthy or comfortable, while a very few had access to all of the luxuries that cheap human services, ancient skills, and modern technology could provide.

There were of course great regional variations in the economic conditions of the people. The populations in the rain-fed agricultural regions or in the high mountains of the north, in the irrigated regions of the central and southern alluvial lands or in the vast reed marshes of the south-east, and the nomadic peoples in the great arid deserts of the west and south, all lived under very different conditions. Housing and clothing are dictated in part by climatic conditions, and food by its local availability; medical services, education, roads, other transport facilities, and other aspects of public expenditure are determined in part by the degree of local prosperity and in part by the extent to which the central government can be persuaded to assist; both conditions varied widely over the country. Dwarfing the regional differences are the differences between the rural and urban populations, for by and large the urban dwellers of all classes are, and always have been, better off than those in the countryside. Even the reasonably well-off people in the villages and smaller towns have had few of the amenities of even the lower-middle class living in the cities and this, among other things, has made it difficult for the authorities to persuade doctors to settle in the smaller towns and has caused school-teachers to look eagerly for transfers.

In only four cities was there any appreciable industrialization at the beginning of the decade: Greater Baghdad, Greater Basra, Mosul City, and Kirkuk City. Kerbela and Najf were pilgrimage centres. All other towns were market towns looking to agriculture. The agricultural population congregated in villages, and whole villages would sometimes move when the soil became too salty or the watercourses changed their direction, especially in the south. Although there had always been considerable movement in Iraq by nomadic tribes and pastoralists who returned at fixed times to their home villages, Fenelon, the chief government statistician, noted in 1957 that

> There is now, however, a new form of restlessness influencing the rural communities, and that is a movement from the countryside to the towns. In almost every Liwa, there is a tendency for the capital town to grow at the expense of the villages.[1]

Extensive migration continued. Between 1947 and 1957 it has been estimated that nearly half a million people left the *liwa* in which they were born for another *liwa*. And the movement to the big cities continued, Baghdad alone receiving a net increase of nearly 200,000 immigrants in the period and Basra absorbing another 28,000, primarily from Amara.[2] In 1952 and 1953 there had been serious trouble with the cultivators in the south because of a new law which on the one hand gave the cultivators a right to 15 donums (3.75 ha.), but, on the other, contained provisions which could be manipulated by the shaikhs to enable them to acquire all the land for themselves.[3] Not unnaturally there were riots as the peasants saw their legal right denied, and the police had to be called in. As a result there was almost an exodus of cultivators from the area: nearly 96,000 people left Amara in the period 1947–57, of which over 18,000 went to Basra and 68,000 to Baghdad. Altogether the six southern *liwas* (Kut, Hilla, Kerbela, Diwaniya, Amara, and Nasiriya) lost a total of nearly 169,000 people, and this in spite of laws imposing severe penalties on peasants who tried to leave the estates to which they were attached: they might be returned home by force, or members of their families might be expelled from their homes and their livestock and property confiscated by the landlord. In a 1957 survey in Baghdad migrants were asked why they had left their place of birth and their answers clearly showed that the conditions in the rural areas were more important than the attraction of the city. Common reasons given for emigrating were 'we did not have enough to eat', 'hunger', 'oppression by the landlord', 'dispute with the landlord over the size of our share', 'we could not get enough water for our crops', 'our land was flooded and the crop died', etc. In spite of low incomes (40 per cent of those interviewed received less than ID 90 per year) most of the migrants believed themselves to be much better off, with better housing and better diet than they had had before.[4]

According to the 1956 housing census, four-fifths of the houses in the country as a whole were made of mud or of reed matting or a combination of the two, or consisted of tents, and were without electricity or piped water; toilets were available to less than one-third. On the other hand, in half of the fifteen largest cities electricity was laid on in more than 50 per cent of the houses and piped water was widely available. The typical house of the great majority of the people was a windowless one- or two-room hut of mud or reeds and surrounded by a high mud or reed wall perhaps pierced by a reasonably stout door. It contained little furniture other than the blankets and quilts which could cover all the family in winter as they huddled together on the floor at night, some sort of receptacle for the babies to sleep in, a chest for miscellaneous belongings, an earthen water jug, and a cooking pot or two. The family generally lived in a courtyard behind a wall and in this area most household chores would be done and the chickens, or perhaps a goat, if the family were fortunate enough to have one, also sheltered. Unleavened bread baked in mud ovens fired with sun-dried cakes of dung or brushwood, collected by the women, was the chief food, supplemented by sweet tea and occasionally by meat, vegetables, or dates and rice, the combinations differing according to locality. Meat and vegetables were more widely consumed in the cities than in the rural areas, although there were some rural areas where meat was an important supplement to the staple diet of unleavened bread for the peasants. On the average the smaller houses contained between 4 and 5 people per room, but the national average density was 2.75 people per room. The ease with which the mud and reed houses can be constructed and moved meant that there was a relatively high percentage of owner-occupied houses and that the density per room even in the cities was lower than in the slums of many of the large cities in much wealthier countries.

Few of the peasants wore shoes and their outer clothing consisted of a simple gown-like garment of cotton, a black cloak for the women, and perhaps a jacket for the men. The Kurds and some of the Christian communities adopted much more colourful dress, especially for the women, than the Muslim Arabs.

It is important not to exaggerate the degree of Iraqi poverty in the period before development began to accelerate. Clothing, food, and shelter were all primitive, and the crowded hovels jumbled tightly together like a ragged crazy quilt, their inhabitants plastered with mud in wet weather and with flies in dry, exuded the aroma of extreme poverty. Yet it should be noticed that even twenty-five years ago one rarely saw starvation and not even very much gross deficiency disease. Shelter was generally physiologically adequate—the walls of mud or mud and reed huts are very thick and keep out heat, cold, and sand, and in summer these huts were often more comfortable than the brick or cement houses of the better-off workers. In other words, except for a small minority, consumption of food, shelter, and clothing were above, and probably considerably above, subsistence levels. It is perhaps significant that 'peasant riots' —rural disturbance and revolts arising from intolerable poverty—have been rare in Iraqi history and this in spite of the high proportion of the crops taken as rent and of oppression in other ways by the landlord in many areas, especially in the south.

On the other hand, if we look at the consumption of public health, medical, and educational services we find the greatest source of the discomfort, misery, illness, and premature death associated with poverty. It is here that the condition of living of perhaps the majority of people was truly abysmal and where the vicious circle of poverty–illness–ignorance–poverty begins without end. Yet from the point of view of the peasants, and perhaps of most of the lower-income groups in the cities, these services, when new and unfamiliar, are often difficult to introduce quickly; as many a social worker or health official will testify, it is often difficult to persuade people to consume them even when they are available and free. But insofar as the 'physical' condition of the Iraqi worker was responsible for his low productivity, diseases due fundamentally to filth, flies, poor sanitation, and polluted water were probably the greatest source of his physical debility. Mortality, especially infant mortality, was extremely high. Although malaria had been substantially reduced and even wiped out in some areas, water-borne diseases such as amoebic and bacillary dysentery, diarrhoea, bilharzia, and hookworm were very common, together with trachoma, tuberculosis, and venereal diseases. Progress in reducing the incidence of such diseases can be made partly though the provision of social facilities and services and partly through reduction of ignorance, both of which may, however, require considerable government investment and expenditure. At the beginning of the 1950s the way was suddenly opened to the government to initiate an extensive and sustained programme of expenditure on industrial and agricultural investment, on housing, and on the provision of education, health, and other social services. For in 1951 the severe financial restraints on Iraq's economic development were lifted.

In 1950, with the increase in the rate of oil royalty from 4*s*. to 6*s*. per ton, oil revenues a little more than doubled to reach £6.8 million; when royalties were superseded in 1951 by profit-sharing, revenues again more than doubled to £15.1 million. The progression continued: £40.8 million in 1952, £84.6 million in 1958. Oil exports and revenues had magnificent prospects, and Iraq was not expected to have any balance of payments difficulties in her attempts to develop the economy: it was widely assumed that she only needed to spend her revenues wisely and her people would be rapidly lifted out of poverty and ignorance as the conditions of economic life changed in response to productive investment.

But in Iraq, as everywhere else in the 1950s, there was a very great underestimation of the difficulties of development and a consequent serious overestimation of the speed with which change could be effected. Moreover, since export receipts from oil took the form of tax revenues to the government and not income payments to individual producers and exporters, as in the usual case of ordinary exports, their productive use depended almost entirely on government action, and there were no precedents to guide a government seeking wisely to use such very large inflows of foreign exchange to develop a country where environmental conditions were often difficult, disease widespread, the majority of the population illiterate, local skills of all kinds in very short supply, and social, economic, and political institutions ill-adapted to the task.

The knowledge that large revenues were being received raised the expectations of the people, but the form in which they were received did not directly give individuals (apart, perhaps, from certain officials) any means of immediately improving their economic conditions. And since Iraq was an underdeveloped country, in a political and administrative as well as an economic sense, an unreasonably heavy responsibility was bound to be placed on an inadequate government administration. Moreover, government from now on was destined to dominate economic activity.

The Development Board

Aware that the task was difficult, and of the fact that careful organization of expenditure was required, the government established in 1950 an independent Development Board. The Board was designed to be insulated from political pressures and be independent of changing Cabinets. The Prime Minister and the Minister of Finance were *ex-officio* members and maintained liaison with the government. The other six members, three of whom were to be 'experts', were to be appointed for five years. One of the experts chosen was British and one American. The Board was charged with preparing and executing a 'general economic and financial plan for the development of the resources of Iraq and the raising of the standard of living of her people' and was given its own budget to which all oil revenues were at first allocated. In 1952 total oil revenues had risen so fast that the Board's share was reduced to 70 per cent, where it remained until 1959. To reinforce its independent and expert character, the Board had its own secretariat, who were not civil servants, but it was required to submit reports and budgets to the Cabinet and these, together with the general programme, were subject to parliamentary approval.

The establishment and organization of the Development Board were widely approved, especially by foreigners who saw in it the continuity, the efficiency, and the freedom from politics that would ensure the optimum spending of Iraq's revenues. Although the political dangers of appointing foreigners as executive, voting members of the Board were appreciated, their impartial contributions to efficient and wise planning were expected to more than compensate. It was assumed that at least this aspect of government administration and policy would be free from the widespread corruption and nepotism which so often reduced the effectiveness of Iraqi policies, and that a superior secretariat, whose remuneration exceeded that of the civil service, could be relied on to be more hardworking and efficient than was usual.

The attempt to give an independent executive body so much power and so much control over so much money proved to be impracticable. The Board's budget soon exceeded that of the government, expectations were great, and immediate achievement was necessarily limited. Politically motivated newspapers and resentful politicians made telling attacks, and ministers, without control and sometimes even with little information, found themselves in an anomalous position in meeting parliamentary criticism. In 1953, therefore, a Ministry of Development was set up, and the Minister of Development was made a member of the Board and responsible to parliament for its decisions. The secretariat of the Board was absorbed into the civil service and transferred to the Ministry, which was given the task of executing the Board's decisions. The position of the Development Board was thus fundamentally altered: it was still primarily 'non-political', that is, it made its decisions with reference to 'expert' rather than to political considerations, but it became dependent on the co-operation of a government department and its freedom of action was curtailed in a number of ways. The Iraqi civil service was poorly paid and the assimilation of the Board's secretariat into the civil service involved both resignations and a lowering of morale, as well as the loss by the Board of its control over the execution of its decisions.

On the other hand, from the point of view of development in the broadest sense, there were serious disadvantages in insulating the plans for the spending of oil revenues from the rest of the government administration, and even from those 'political' considerations which alone could reflect the extent to which the Board's operations were acceptable to the Iraqi people. There are clear limits to which either the planning or the administration of economic development can be successfully imposed from the top. Development is a seamless web, inevitably involving the entire society. The insulation of the administrative machinery of the development programme, although modified by the establishment of a Ministry of Development, still influenced significantly the policies adopted for the expenditure of the oil revenues. The clear separation of 'development' from other government expenditures, a separation of the kind implied by the existing 'capital works' budgets, tended to cause the Board to confine its expenditure to fields which were qualitatively different from those which were the subject of 'normal' government expenditure, and which were often very short of funds. In other words, the use of revenues under the control of the Board for expenditures on continuing activities such as education and health tended to be frowned on, both because the funds would have had to be administered by an existing government department and not by the Board and because the activities were qualitatively similar to familiar 'non-development' expenditures.

The Board preferred to keep its programmes in its own hands. Its insulation from the politics reflecting popular opinion encouraged the Board to resist 'easy popularity' and to develop programmes concentrating on projects with a long gestation period, bringing little immediate or widespread direct benefit to the ordinary people. That part of the Board's terms of reference charging it with 'the development of the resources of Iraq' was given much more emphasis than the 'raising of the standard of living of her people'. To be sure, it was presumed that the latter would naturally follow from the former, but in economic matters at least, it is not good policy to ignore time lags. As we shall see, however, the more serious deficiencies in the Board's programme had their roots deep in the political and social conflicts within the country and in its failure to press for action with respect to many things that money could not buy.

It could hardly be expected that the Board would be able to spend productively at short notice such large sums of money as clearly would be available, but it did not start from zero. It could take over the programme of capital expenditure already in operation under the previous capital works budgets; it had available extensive reports on irrigation, notably the Report of the Haigh Commission,[5] which had been presented in 1949, as well as a variety of expert reports on lesser projects; and it soon had the Report of the Mission of the International Bank for Reconstruction and Development which had visited the country for nearly four months in 1951.[6]

The early reports inevitably stressed irrigation and flood control: over half the proposed expenditures on capital works for the period 1949–53 had been allocated to these purposes, while the Haigh Commission had recommended the building of the great storage reservoir in the Wadi Tharthar Depression to drain off the flood water of the Tigris and ensure the protection of Baghdad—an enormous project which was not to be completed before the next two decades.

The IBRD Mission had recognized the necessity of flood control, irrigation, and drainage and had allocated about one-third of its proposed development programme to these items, but it had also stressed the importance of such slow-yielding activities as agricultural extension, teacher training, and community development. The IBRD programme suggested considerably larger allocations for housing and community facilities than those actually adopted in the period by the Development Board.

Total annual expenditure for the five years 1951–56 envisaged under the programme of the Board averaged around ID 25.7 million, or more than twice that planned for the 1949–53 capital budget, and made provision for investment in industry and transport as well as in irrigation and flood control. As we have noted, plans exceeded achievement, especially in the earlier years. For example, only about one-third of the expenditures planned for 1951 were actually spent in that year, but the proportion rose in the later years of the period to a peak of over two-thirds in 1955, the highest percentage achieved in the decade.[7] The Board was most successful in spending money on the construction of buildings, on irrigation and flood control projects, and on communications; it was least successful in industry. This was partly because the former types of investment had been given greater study earlier, and partly because straightforward construction which could be done almost entirely by contractors was easier than more complicated projects. The Board was very cautious in adopting large programmes, such as a chemical project based on natural gas which had been suggested by the IBRD. Nevertheless, within the first five years the construction of a bitumen refinery, a cotton-spinning and weaving mill, and two cement plants was begun, and final specifications for a large power plant in the north of the country were being prepared. A small oil refinery at Dora near Baghdad was completed.

Criticism and Response

Apart from the flood-control projects—the importance of which must not be underrated—there was not much to show from the spending on development before 1956, although many projects and surveys were in preparation, including a survey of the country's mineral resources and possible power projects and a general survey of industrial potentialities. As awareness spread among the population of the very large and growing income which the country was obtaining from oil, the slowness with which it was being reflected in the standard of living gave rise to increasing criticism. The need for pure-water supplies, better housing, health services, and educational facilities was great; and while the Board could not even spend the money allocated to it on long-run projects, it seemed indefensible to many that more attention was not given to the immediate needs of the present. It should be noted, however, that 30 per cent of the oil revenues were available for current expenditure under the ordinary budgets of the ministries, including education and health.

As a result of mounting criticism, the Board invited Lord Salter, a noted British economist and former international civil servant, to examine its activities and to advise. His appraisal found grave fault with the Board's implicit preference for 'bricks and mortar development' and its tendency to get bogged down in the details of engineering at the expense of a clear delineation of its broader priorities; and he flatly attacked the irrigation policy of the government which laid stress on the opening-up of new lands instead of on improving the productivity of the old, although he realized the political reasons for it. He saw, and did not hesitate to state forcefully, the real political danger of a development programme that did not take sufficient account of the aspirations of the people:

> . . . policy must be such as to assure sufficient popular support to enable it to be carried out without interruption either through parliamentary or extra-parliamentary methods of protest and resistance. There is a strong and widespread resentment against the Development Board among many sections of the population. . . . It is complained that the large oil revenues are bringing no benefit to the country as a whole; and it is no effective answer to say that after many years the water-schemes and other long-term projects will enrich the country.
>
> There is therefore the strongest reason for substantial expenditure of a kind which will bring quick and clearly visible benefits. Among these housing, pure-water systems, and detailed and immediate help to farming and husbandry are among the most obvious. All these can give quick results. The benefits can be dispersed throughout the country; and their effect can then be greatly increased by suitable publicity.[8]

Lord Salter also recommended, as had the IBRD Mission before him, that the Development Board should recognize the importance of recurrent expenditures as well as capital expenditures in many fields, especially health, education, agricultural extension, etc., and that it should work through the appropriate government departments. Perhaps one of the most serious defects of the Board's procedures, as mentioned above, and one that inevitably brought about a substantial curbing of its independence, was its failure to follow the advice of the Bank Mission and

> . . . enlist the aid and cooperation of other government ministries and agencies and of the provincial and municipal administrations in the task of planning and carrying out a development program. It should actively encourage them to submit suggestions and plans for development, integrate these plans with each other and the Board's own, and, to the maximum extent feasible, allocate money and responsibility for the execution of these plans and projects to other agencies. The establishment of a Community Planning

Office and a Housing Authority . . . would be in line with this suggestion.[9]

Lord Salter escaped the fate of most authors of reports and recommendations on economic development. His report was not 'pigeon-holed' and forgotten. It was taken seriously by all the ministries between the time when it was delivered and the Revolution in mid-1958. Well-organized and written with distinction, it clearly analysed the leading issues in a wide range of topics and did not shrink from criticisms of existing policies and concrete proposals for future action. Partly as a result of this report and partly because of the ever greater revenues, the second development programme put forward by the Board in 1955 was superseded by a new and much-enlarged programme in 1956 which was intended to run until 1960. The allocation for housing was quadrupled and its share of the total nearly tripled, reflecting the priorities suggested by Salter. Allocations for health and welfare were greatly increased as well as the absolute sums to be spent on industrialization. Expenditures again fell far short of allocations and, although total investment expenditures rose, the rate of increase fell.

In the period 1951 to 1958, however, about 229 million dinars had actually been spent on capital investment, excluding administrative expenses, and the annual rate of current expenditure in the government budget had more than doubled, reaching nearly 74 million dinars a year by 1957. About a third of the Development Board's expenditure had gone into 'agriculture'—primarily dams, barrages, and other large flood control/irrigation projects—over half into building and communications, and nearly ID 30 million, or 12.5 per cent, into industry. The Development Board and the government together thus put large new sums of money into the Iraqi economy, most of which were derived from oil revenues. Oil revenues are foreign exchange and confer the power to import; accordingly total imports (excluding imports by the oil companies) rose from ID 29 million in 1950 to over ID 100 million in 1957, with imports of capital goods rising faster than those of consumer goods. The demand for domestic goods and services also rose and domestic production increased, although at a disappointing rate.

Calculations of the national income of the country (in 1950 prices), which are very rough, especially for the earlier years, showed a compound annual increase of some 11 per cent in the period 1950 to 1956. This is very high, but may not be far off in view of the tremendous surge in oil revenues and of government expenditures in the early years, for government expenditures alone ranged between a quarter and a third of the national income. Later estimates put the rate of increase of national income between 1953 and 1958 at around 7 per cent per year.[10] In the middle 1950s crude-oil extraction and agriculture each contributed around a quarter of the national income, with the result that the impact of the strongly upward thrust of the former was continually reduced by the stagnation and uncertainty of the latter, for the large expenditures on water control and irrigation did not have any noticeable impact on agricultural production.

Agriculture and Land

Surveys and discussions of Iraqi agriculture have always emphasized the great productive potential of the Tigris–Euphrates river valley on the one hand, and on the other, the appallingly low productivity of the farmer, the abuse of the land, the primitive nature of the techniques used, and the extremely uneven distribution of landownership. As we have seen, in the transition from largely tribal to private tenure during the first few decades of the country's existence, a very large proportion of the privately owned cultivated area came into the hands of the wealthy tribal shaikhs and town merchants. In general, land was cultivated by sharecropping tenants from whom the landlords took a large proportion of the crop in rent. Many of the landlords lived in the cities and took little interest in the improvement of the land, the sharecroppers lacked security of tenure, were very poor, and in any case had little incentive themselves to invest in the land or to improve the techniques of cultivation.

Over most of the country, the earth was ploughed superficially with an iron-tipped wooden plough drawn by animals. The seeds were broadcast by hand. Crops were largely harvested as in biblical times, but a few combines and tractors had appeared, especially in the rain-fed areas of the north, but also in irrigated zones. In most areas half of the land was left fallow every year to maintain fertility, and summer cropping was not the rule.

The division of the crop between landlord and tenant varied widely depending on the type of crop, the method of irrigation, and the nature of the land title, the contribution to production made by each party, and also on custom, for tribal custom was still important in many areas. In the flow-irrigated areas in the centre and south of the country the tenant (if he supplied the seed) commonly obtained between one-third and one-half of the crop, the smaller landlords not infrequently taking a greater proportion than the larger ones. When irrigation was by pump, the pump-owners commonly took 20 per cent, the landlord 40 per cent, and the tenant 40 per cent, but in the four northern *liwas*, Mosul, Arbil, Sulaimaniya, and Kirkuk, the tenants' share was much higher, usually two-thirds on irrigated land

and 60 per cent, 80 per cent, and even as high as 90 per cent, on the rain-fed land, the higher share occurring on the land farthest from the cities. Part of the northern rain-fed zone was farmed in large mechanized units using hired labour.

Sometimes land was owned jointly by a number of farmers who divided the crop according to the number of shares held by each, and in many of the irrigated areas of south and central Iraq there were large holdings jointly farmed by several farmers under the active management of the landlord. In the villages farmers were often organized in groups linked by family ties, each group sharing the work of maintaining the canals under the leadership of the *sirkal* (or manager) who himself was often related to the farmers. In the appointment of a *sirkal* the shaikh frequently had to respect the old tribal custom which required that he be acceptable to the farmers. Thus, the role of the landlord varied widely among the different regions, according to the size of the landholdings, the tribal relationships between him and the cultivators, the nature of the crop, and the competence and interest of the landlord and his local *sirkal*.[11]

General agricultural improvements—extension work, model farms, improved seeds for plants, and breeding stock for animals—received very small allocations under the development programmes, although, after drainage, these were the greatest needs of Iraqi agriculture. The government concentrated on water control and storage projects, but often appropriate arrangements were lacking which would ensure the use of the stored water, and especially the provision of adequate drainage, for Iraq had little effective natural drainage in the river valleys. The Food and Agriculture Organization pointed out that the water stored by the great dams for summer flow

> . . . did not so much offer a new promise of prosperity in agriculture as represent an immediate menace to the future well-being of Iraq. An unsound system of irrigation, especially of intensive summer irrigation, represents a deadly threat to the productivity of the soil . . . irrigation may ruin the land by salination, if systematic drainage is not carried out.[12]

Some experts held that 70 per cent of the remaining irrigated areas were acutely threatened by such ruin.

Direct attempts to use development funds to improve and extend drainage and irrigation and to raise productivity on lands already in cultivation were resisted, except where they directly benefited, by the large landowning shaikhs whose political power and influence were not only dominant in their own localities but were also important in shaping, or rather limiting, the scope of central government policies.

They blocked attempts to frame measures of land reform and effective land taxation. They even prevented the government from imposing charges for drainage and irrigation services, from which they were the leading beneficiaries. The Crown Prince, Abdul Ilah, is reported to have replied to a request that he should support a land reform bill in parliament with: 'The town is already against me. Do you want to turn the countryside against me too?' Neither he nor Nuri al-Said felt strong enough to risk antagonizing the landlords, even when they recognized the desirability of reform.

Under existing economic and political structures, expenditures to raise agricultural productivity appreciably would have benefited landlords above any other groups. Not only would landlords have obtained the resulting services free, but most of the gains in productivity would probably have also been retained by them. The fear that sharecroppers would not benefit may indeed have been exaggerated. But the government attempted to bypass the whole issue by moving in a different direction. First it put its main effort into opening up new lands for cultivation where the farmers would be owners and not sharecroppers or tenants. In this way it was hoped that the landlords would be forced to improve the position of their own tenants in order to retain them on their estates. Given time, such a policy might have had some effect, but results were slow—too slow to be acceptable. Nevertheless, in some areas there was evidence that urban migration had forced some landowners to improve the terms offered tenants in order to keep them on the land.[13]

A similar measure to improve the lot of the agricultural worker without direct confrontation with the shaikhs was that of spending development funds on projects situated in or close to some of the agricultural areas, particularly in the south where the conditions of the farmers were most unfavourable. Such projects would create a demand for local labour and it was assumed that landlords in order to retain their tenants and farm workers would have to improve conditions. Both this policy and that of opening up new lands worked too slowly, the benefits were spread too unevenly, and their total volume was too small, to obviate the necessity of land reform.

Thus, although most of the reports of foreign experts, including those of Lord Salter and the Food and Agriculture Organization of the United Nations, urged a high priority for agriculture, and the Development Board consistently allocated more of its funds to agriculture than to any other sector [42.5 per cent in the First Plan (1951–54) and 37.6 per cent in the Second (1955–59)] and was able actually to spend about half the amount allocated, little progress was visible beyond the great water projects. And no practical steps were taken to deal with the organization of agriculture or the problem of land tenure. The FAO in an interim report in 1957 insisted that the great disparity between urban and rural incomes could only be removed if the pace of industrial development were quickened, and it attacked the argument that high-cost industrialization in the short run was necessarily uneconomic when account was taken of improved efficiency in the longer run.[14] The report noted that tax and land reform, together with a system of charges that made landlords pay proper prices for the water and drainage services they received, might be more efficient methods of improving income distribution, but added that

> . . . such reforms are highly unlikely in the short run, because they would depend on very drastic, perhaps undesirably drastic, prior political changes. The policy of creating new land settlements, the alternative favoured at the moment, cannot, as we have already argued, solve the problem. Thus counsels of economic perfection seem futile and calculated to permit the present dangerous trend towards an increasingly under-employed and unemployed urban population to continue.[15]

The general emphasis on the necessity of developing agriculture and particularly of raising productivity, was unexceptionable. Agriculture, although contributing 30 per cent of the national income, accounted for 70 per cent of employment. But the warnings against attempts to force the pace of industrialization seem to us to have been carried too far. The extremely optimistic outlook on the scope for increasing the area of cultivable land and for absorbing more labour was not, apparently, based on a detailed examination of the conditions of land use, especially the problems of water supplies and of salination, and the probable extent of population growth. Nor was sufficient account taken of the restraints on agricultural expansion imposed by the system of landownership. In the event, however, industry fared better than agriculture.

Industry and Construction

While the value of agricultural output, if any credit can be given to the estimates, fluctuated widely and showed no distinct trend,[16] the value of manufacturing output rose steadily and in 1958 showed an estimated increase of some 85 per cent over that of 1953, but still accounted for less than 10 per cent of the national income, as contrasted to between a fifth and a third for agriculture.[17] By far the greater part of Iraqi manufacturing activity was, as might be expected, devoted to the processing of local agricultural materials for consumption in local markets. But factories were rapidly established to provide materials for the booming construction industry. Brick factories expanded and many new ones were established. In 1949 no cement was produced in Iraq, but by 1957 private cement companies had a capacity of around 800,000 tons a year and the Development Board was constructing two additional plants with an annual capacity of 200,000 tons.[18] Oil refining also increased with the establishment of a government refinery near Baghdad and the expansion of existing plants. Among consumer goods, foods and beverages, furniture, metal products, and shoes increased significantly.

Thus Iraqi entrepreneurs responded in a modest way to the increased spending of the Development Board (which itself was modest, amounting only to some ID 30 million in 1951–58), but rather slowly. In some cases, for example, in cement and textiles, private entrepreneurs feared that the entry of the government into production would prejudice their own position, whereas the government, noting hesitancy on the part of private business, took this as an indication of the necessity for government action. It is probably true, as one student of Iraqi industry has pointed out, that the response of businessmen, especially in the production of building materials, showed that 'Iraqis possessed a latent desire to enter business', but that much of this response 'was evoked by the possibility of a quick profit, rather than by the prospect of long-term success'.[19]

The establishment of an industrial middle class prepared to invest capital for long periods in countries where rents from land and profits from trading have been the chief ways of making money takes a long time. The desire for quicker results leads the government to enter industry and this in itself inhibits the emergence of private entrepreneurs. But in Iraq, the development programmes were centred primarily around construction and infrastructure and the expenditures created conditions usually favourable for private entrepreneurship. Laws had been passed for the 'encouragement of industry', providing various types of exemption from taxation. An Industrial Bank had been created very early to make loans to industry, but its finance was grossly inadequate and its policies were extremely conservative. It was of little help in promoting general credit facilities, and capital markets and other means of financing industrial development were inadequate or non-existent. In spite of the high level of liquidity in the banking system, neither the Central Bank, nor the government-owned Rafidain Bank, nor the commercial banks offered sufficient facilities to the smaller industrial firms. In addition, of course, industry was handicapped by the scarcity of skilled labour, and even of literate workmen, foremen, accountants, and all of the middle management skills necessary for modern industrial activity.

It was in the field of construction that the Development Board's activities made their greatest impact, with the exception of low-cost housing for the people. 'Construction' includes not only buildings but all construction activity in agriculture, industry, transportation, communications, public utilities, dams and flood control, etc. 'Projects' of this kind absorbed nearly all of the Development Board's effort and funds. The theory was, of course, that this type of infrastructure would lay the foundations for future development and it was also hoped that expenditures would stimulate the economy. Almost inevitably, the Board became dominated by an engineering 'bricks and mortar' approach to development, with a heavy bias towards the large projects. It lost sight of the fact that factories and projects were merely inanimate 'tools for the people to work with'—to use Ionides's phrase[20]—and it failed to provide the administration and managerial expertise required to enable the people to work them. The task of the Board was to construct projects, which were then handed over to the appropriate government agencies in completed form, but these agencies were more often than not ill-equipped to deal with them. Iraqi civil servants were notoriously underpaid in comparison with the professions outside the civil service, and it was often difficult to keep those of high quality. Ionides, a leading British engineer and a member of the Development Board for several years, noted that

> The overloading of the administration was shown up most clearly in the Irrigation Department. Dams, barrages, canals and drains accounted for by far the biggest slice in the programme. All these works, when completed, were being handed over to the Irrigation Department. But for several years, no new professionally qualified young Iraqis had joined the Department; they found more agreeable and better paid jobs with contractors, consultants, or in businesses working for the Development Board. What was worse, several of the senior Iraqi engineers had left the Irrigation Department for similar reasons.[21]

In other words, the problem of administration and management, in the best of circumstances likely to be the most difficult to overcome in the implementation of a large development programme, was exacerbated by the refusal of the government to pay its civil servants adequate salaries.

Administration and Management

The Development Board was unable to spend all of the money allocated to it largely because of the time taken to plan, organize, and implement construction projects. Even when these were completed, additional delays and wasted effort occurred because the government agencies whose task was to operate them had not been prepared for the job. This difficulty became more acute as the work of the Development Board accelerated and projects began to roll off the assembly line, so to speak. This process intensified around 1956, when an annual 'Development Week' was started in which the

> King, his Ministers, and dignitaries, the Development Board and a bevy of Notables, ambassadors and visitors from abroad went on a round of ceremonial tape-cutting. There were speeches and celebrations inaugurating the year's crop of completed projects—dams, roads, bridges, flood escapes, canal systems, factories, houses, buildings, power stations, and the like. The streets were lined with cheering schoolboys and girls, tribesmen, citizens; after each ceremony with its speeches and recitals of poems, there was a feast. It was encouraging and stimulating but it could not but divert attention away from aspects of development which by their very nature cannot be inaugurated with trumpets and feasts: humdrum things like administration, training, legislation. Many such problems were piling up.[22]

In a 1956 report a leading firm of economic consultants recommended that the construction and planning of industrial projects should not take place until the senior persons who would be responsible for their management had been designated. The consultants found that in the absence of a close association of future management with the building of the plant there was a tendency for management taking over a new plant to

> . . . absolve itself from the major responsibility of making a success of the operation. A claim could be made that the plant was of an inappropriate size or that the design was unsuitable for the products it had to make, and that the possibility of achieving profitable operating results had been precluded by incompetent planning for which the new management was not responsible.[23]

To make arrangements of this sort, however, required a much more complicated programme of planning than either the Development Board or the Iraqi administration contemplated.

In planning and construction great reliance was placed on foreigners and foreign technical assistance, but in a sense, as Ionides notes, the foreigners had the easier job. They were largely technical experts of one kind or another and were employed to do specific jobs, after which they left. Consultants such as A. D. Little came and advised, but to choose and train managers and other local personnel, associate them with particular projects from the beginning, and ensure continued good management, required a co-ordinated effort from many branches of the Iraqi administration and implied a type of planning that went far beyond the construction programmes on which the Development Board centred its activities. The need was not met, with the result that the effective contribution of the Board could not be measured by money spent and projects completed. A great deal more money would have had to be devoted to improving and enlarging the administrative capacity of the ministries concerned with plan implementation. Between 1951 and 1958 the sums in the government ordinary budget devoted to plan administration slightly more than tripled, but they still only amounted to around 3.6 per cent of total ordinary expenditure.[24] All evidence indicates not only that administration was inefficient, but also that very little serious effort was devoted to attempting to improve it. All expert advisers in the period emphasized this point, but without effect.

Advances in Social Welfare

The activities of the Development Board and the scope of economic planning did not, with one exception, deal with social policies and with investments in the development of health and education, which are at least as important for the development of a country as capital investment in dams and factories (if not more so). The exception, of course, related to the construction of the houses, schools, hospitals, and social welfare centres which were within the scope of the Development Board. Lord Salter's comment that 'The Development Board has so far made its contribution to the health services of the country in the form of providing hospitals, dispensaries and clinics'[25] might equally have been applied to schools for education. This is not unreasonable in that the appropriate ministries, with a broader scope than that of the Development Board, were charged with the provision of education and health services, although, as has been pointed out above, the financial dichotomy in the allocation of oil revenues was not necessarily desirable. Housing, however, was in a somewhat different category, for although deficiencies in housing are not less important in their effects on public wellbeing than are deficiencies in public health, inadequate housing, like inadequate nutrition, is largely a problem of personal income distribution and of social policies to aid the poorer sections of the community.

Laws providing for various kinds of social security (old-age benefits, marriage, death, sickness benefits, etc.) and for unemployment benefits, as well as for minimum wages, were passed, but their application was limited; less than 16,000 people were in receipt of social security benefits of all kinds by 1967.

Housing

In the development programme, housing had been given a very low priority until the appearance of the Salter Report in 1955. The political as well as the economic value of improved housing was strangely overlooked. Here was a form of development which would at once have created a favourable impression of the activities of the government on behalf of the poorer classes in the community. Poverty takes many forms, some of which are not easily seen by any but trained observers. But housing makes a direct daily visual impression.

Around the cities, particularly Baghdad, lay the *sarifa* (or 'shanty town') areas, where the migrants from the countryside congregated in mud huts, or, in the poorest sections, in shelters improvised from light branches cut from trees and bushes. These areas grew very rapidly in the post-war period. Washash Village, a suburb of Baghdad, east of the fashionable Mansour area, was one of the better-off examples of a rapidly expanding migrant suburb. In 1946, the area was still vacant land partly used for agriculture, but the availability of land began to attract people from Baghdad whose houses had been demolished as new streets were opened. During the Second World War a great wave of immigration to the area took place and again in 1954, after the high flood of the Tigris which destroyed the *sarifa* houses and mud huts behind the bunds of Baghdad. The 1947 census had reported only 2,400 people and 350 houses in the village; in 1956 the housing census showed a population of some 12,000 people in 1,555 houses. Less than one-third of the people had been in the village more than 8 years; over half had been there less than five. Nearly 90 per cent of the wage-earners had found work as soldiers, policemen, workers, porters, peddlers, servants, guards, and cleaners in Baghdad. Electricity and water were laid on, there were schools for boys and girls, and evening classes for adults, a dispensary, and both doctors and midwives. The main endemic diseases suffered by the population were bilharzia, malaria, and trachoma.[20]

The sharp contrast between the conditions in the poorest *sarifa* areas just outside the city and the conditions in the suburban areas just inside it gave political importance to the issues raised by the growing migration from poor rural areas to Baghdad. Again and again the voices of the active elements in the student and professional classes were raised against what appeared to be government inaction in face of the conditions in the *sarifa*. On one occasion, our students, when we accompanied them to a picnic near Lake Habbaniya west of Baghdad, directed the driver of the bus to make a detour first to show the excellent modern housing conditions of the British and Iraqi officers at the Air Force base there, and then, by contrast, to view the poor streets and houses in which ordinary Iraqis in Habbaniya, including the servants of the army officers, lived.

The housing question, however, was more complicated than it appeared to be on the surface. A closer look at the *sarifa* in some areas disclosed that some of the houses were comparatively large, with 2 to 5 rooms, in some places with piped water and electricity. In 1956 more than half of the *sarifa* in Basra had more than one room and some were verging on the elegant.

In Baghdad people could be seen building their own improvements and extensions. There could be little doubt that a large proportion of the *sarifa* inhabitants in and around Baghdad had raised their standard of living substantially by migration to the city. Indeed, just as one reads occasionally in the Western press of some individual in a slum area leaving on his death a fortune in hoarded notes, so after the 1958 Revolution, it was reported that when the old currency was called in to be exchanged for the new, *sarifa* dwellers were among those bringing thousands of dinar notes to the banks to be exchanged. Nevertheless, for the mass of the people the gap between them and the middle, let alone upper, classes was wide and, by juxtaposition, conspicuous.

After 1955, the Development Board began to take a serious interest in housing and produced a housing programme to be implemented in stages, the first of which included the creation of new settlements, research on building materials, and training of personnel. During the programme new houses were to be built, old ones improved, and foundations laid on which people could build for themselves. Plans for the resettlement of the *sarifa* population on plots of land on which they would be assisted in building new houses were also formulated by the Board. But around Baghdad difficulties were encountered in inducing private landowners to sell land from which they aimed at obtaining a growing unearned increment as the city expanded and land values rose steeply. No spectacular progress had been made up to the time of the Revolution. The government was not prepared to take strong measures that might alienate the landowners and the new Five-Year Plan, which was to run from 1956 to 1962, and would have met the needs of some 256,000 families had it been completed, had barely got under way when the Revolution of 1958 overtook it.

Health

In public health, impressive advances had been made, especially in the towns. The great epidemic diseases, which at the end of the First

World War took a large toll of life and working capacity, had been brought under effective control, and malaria was declining in most rural as well as in urban areas. During the First World War the word 'Mesopotamia' to British soldiers and administrators evoked a vision of dangerous epidemic diseases taking a heavier toll in deaths and sickness than in battle casualties. General Maude, in the hour of victory over the Turkish armies, died suddenly of cholera in Baghdad. Yet in 1957 one could live in Baghdad, or Mosul, or Basra without special precautions beyond attention to food hygiene and especially to the dangers of contamination from flies. However, in the poorer parts of the cities, although piped and purified water was frequently available, public sewage systems had not been installed and open drains ran through narrow streets and alleys. Refuse collection in Baghdad and some of the larger cities was fairly regular, but the inhabitants of all sections dumped their refuse in the streets where it attracted animals and flies while awaiting collection.

On the other hand, little had changed in the rural areas. Infant mortality was very high and sanitation almost non-existent. Water was drawn from the irrigation canals, stagnant pools, and the rivers, near which pits served as latrines. The irrigation ditches were used for bathing, laundering, and other purposes and were often polluted with human and animal wastes. The hot sun and dry climate of the plains reduced the dangers to health arising from rotting refuse and filth, but flies and dust were still spreading infant diarrhoea and dysentery, and trachoma was widespread. Tuberculosis was associated particularly with congested housing conditions. Typhoid occurred from time to time, particularly in rural areas. A variety of intestinal parasites impaired the working capacity of most of the peasants.

Clinics, hospitals, and dispensaries were, however, beginning to reach the rural areas and medical officers were to be found in the provinces and districts. By 1958 there were 123 hospitals in the country containing over 9,000 beds, and over 500 dispensaries and clinics, but nearly 700 of the country's 1,200 doctors were to be found in Baghdad and nearly half of the 770 nurses. Iraqi doctors and medical personnel were reluctant to work in the countryside and government expenditures on hospitals, public health, and preventive medicine were inadequate.

Unfortunately, we have little knowledge of the changes in the amounts and quality of foodstuffs consumed in the preceding decades. The statistics of agricultural production were almost worthless. Nor had any nutritional surveys nor even surveys of food consumption been carried out on a significant scale, at least outside Baghdad.

From observation on the streets of Baghdad and other cities where cooked products, both animal and vegetable, were sold for immediate consumption, and in shops, in restaurants, in canteens attached to the higher educational institutions, in houses and in mud huts of the poor, it appeared that the middle and upper classes were abundantly supplied, and that many manual workers consumed considerable amounts of animal products. It was difficult to find evidence of serious widespread deficiencies of energy intake at any income level.[27] Salad products appeared in the diets of many workers as well as of the well-to-do classes in the large towns, but less often in small towns and villages, in some of which at least there appears to have been a shortage of fresh vegetable products. Fish and dates were widely consumed in the south and in most areas the farmers kept some livestock or poultry, although milk yields were low and eggs too valuable to eat on the farm.

We were impressed by the comparative absence of the nutritional diseases which we had observed in earlier years in parts of Eastern and South-Eastern Asia. Even among the poorest classes the plain unleavened bread which provided a main source of energy was an adequate protection against beri-beri—the most important disease resulting from nutritional deficiency in parts of the Far East and South-Eastern Asia. Another common bread was made from more refined flour of about 75 per cent extraction and, consequently, lower vitamin B content, but still appreciably above that of the bleached flour. The peoples of the Middle East have been fortunate in avoiding the major deficiency in the diets of rice-eating peoples after the seventeenth century and of the peoples who are dependent on cassava for their chief source of energy. In recent years citrus fruits have been supplemented by the spread of tomatoes, and the intake of ascorbic acid appeared adequate except possibly in some of the very poor rural areas. Whether the intake of vitamin A and calcium was adequate in the latter is more doubtful. Probably the most serious shortages were those in the energy intake of the population in the overcrowded and poverty-stricken areas of the south, particularly in the vicinities of Amara and Nasiriya.

Education

Simultaneously with the urban–rural migration the number of students coming to Baghdad for free higher education, and drawn by a quota system from all over the country, increased markedly. In the provinces from which they came the proportion which the comparatively well-to-do formed of the total population was much lower than in Baghdad. The poorer sections of the *sarifa* reminded them of the rural conditions in their home areas. But in the capital the contrast was heightened by the sight of so much more wealth than many of the provincial students had ever seen before. This experience intensified their political consciousness and their resentment against the well-to-do and the political leaders drawn from their ranks. Some of the most active students on the political left wing came from the south.

The spread of education was playing an important role in the development of a social and political consciousness, particularly among the younger age-groups of the population. Education was limited at all stages, but was spreading quickly in the last years before the Revolution. The government had rapidly increased its expenditure on education. But the total amount remained low, rising from a little over 3½ million dinars in 1950–51, or 14 per cent of total government expenditures, to nearly 13 million in 1957–58, or over 18 per cent. Even then, there were only slightly over 2,000 elementary schools in the country, and somewhat less than 13,000 teachers for about 417,000 students. In the government secondary and intermediate schools in 1957–58 there were only about 2,500 teachers and 51,000 students. Altogether in the six-year period the number of schools and teachers almost doubled and the number of students slightly more than doubled. Nevertheless, illiteracy was almost universal in the countryside and high in the towns.

Higher education had for a number of years been concentrated in Baghdad, in a group of autonomous specialized colleges, under the general control of the Ministry of Education, and dealing with Law, Arts, Sciences, Teachers' Training, Engineering, Commerce, Agriculture, Medicine, Pharmacy, Dentistry, and Veterinary Medicine. By 1958 over 5,000 students were registered in these institutions.

In 1957 an act was passed to establish the University of Baghdad out of these colleges, or such of them as were considered to have reached adequate standards. The task was a difficult one: there were some who considered it to have been undertaken prematurely, before the quality of instruction in secondary schools and colleges had improved sufficiently to lay a sound foundation for university work. However, the prospects of improvement appeared to the authorities to be better in a university which would absorb and integrate the colleges than under the existing system. If political stability could have been established in the country and stricter conditions of entry into higher education imposed, these hopes might well have been realized.

Appreciable progress was made in the university year 1957–58. Professor Matti Akrawi, the first president of the University, proved to be a vigorous and able organizer of wide experience and temperate judgement. The government failed to give him all the financial support that it might have done without detriment to national economic development: apart from the construction of buildings, education was not included as part of 'development', entitled to a contribution from the oil revenues earmarked for development. The expenditures on books for a new university library were deplorably low. But in spite of many handicaps, good progress was made in the six months before the Revolution. Akrawi was assisted by a council which included a number of able scholars, among them Dr Abdul Jabar Abdullah, Dr Abdul Aziz al-Duri, Dr Salih al-Ali, and Dr Zaki Salah, all of them well known in academic circles in Europe and North America. In the spring and early summer of 1958 Akrawi appointed a small committee of the council, including one of the authors, to inspect each of the colleges and to determine whether its qualifications entitled it to be included in the new university. This work was proceeding steadily when the Revolution came.

The difficulties faced in Iraqi higher education were by no means peculiar to Iraq: they were found widely in the Middle East and in many other parts of Asia and Africa. There was above all the problem of quality. Since higher education rests on a foundation of secondary education, and secondary education rests upon a foundation of primary or elementary education, the weakness of the foundation is inevitably reflected in the weakness of the superstructure. From a long-run point of view it might appear wiser to reform and expand from the bottom upwards, beginning with the elementary school. But this was out of the question. The politically conscious section of the public would not have accepted a standstill in higher education. An increase in the supply of technicians and skilled labour was a prerequisite of economic development. An increase in the supply of doctors, pharmacists, nurses, and laboratory technicians was essential to further advances in public health. And, not least, an increase in the supply of trained teachers was a condition for an extension and improvement of elementary and secondary education.

Unfortunately, it was much easier to increase the quantity than to improve the quality of education. To extend the existing types of education it was necessary only to train more teachers and to construct more buildings. To improve the methods and raise the standards of education, far-reaching changes in the attitudes both of teachers and students were needed. The methods of teaching, which still lingered in much higher education, consisted in the dictation of lectures, passively received by students and committed to memory. Examination questions required only the return to the teacher, often in the same words, of that which he had given out. The considerable number of old-fashioned Egyptian teachers in Iraq seem to have encouraged these practices. Students performed astonishing feats of memory, repeating by heart long passages the import of which they often did not grasp. Such a travesty of true learning exercised a baneful effect on the whole educational system; it extended even into medical education, where, for example, some of the students memorized complicated descriptive passages on anatomy taken from textbooks or lecture notes, without properly understanding them.

But vested interests had been created among both teachers and students. The former were civil servants inadequately paid in relation to other professional and business occupations. They supplemented their incomes by mimeographing their lectures, sometimes consisting largely of translated foreign texts, and selling them to their students. The latter expected their teachers to set examination questions that could be answered by reproducing from memory sections of the lectures; independent reading by students was not often expected by either the students or their teachers. To a rational observer it might appear superfluous that in these conditions classes should have been held at all or lectures given. In some departments attempts to change this system were made, but these were resented by the majority of students, though some of the abler ones recognized that the change was in their interests. Reform was a slow process; the reformer was unpopular with the many and appreciated only by the few.

Even within the limits of the existing system the course of education did not run smoothly. Notwithstanding the urgent need of improvement in quality and standards, instruction in some of the colleges and secondary schools was frequently interrupted by strikes and demonstrations on the part of the students. In our experience the motives behind these interruptions were normally political, but genuine grievances relating to the quality of education also sometimes played a part. Some observers held that the leaders of strikes were drawn from the duller students who endeavoured to hide their scholastic inadequacies behind a screen of political activities. We found this charge justified only in a limited number of cases: many of the abler students held strong political convictions, and, whether mistakenly or not, believed that it was their duty to engage in political activities. One of our students asserted 'As the educated group in the country, it is our duty to lead the people'. In all cases education suffered from the intense political preoccupations of students, and teachers were often intimidated.

The Position of Women

The introduction of modern education, however imperfect may have been the forms that it took, hastened the social changes that would in any case have taken place sooner or later once Iraq had been brought into closer touch with the rest of the world. Perhaps this was nowhere more noticeable than in the relations between the sexes. The history of Islam records a number of earlier changes in the position of women, both in law and in actual practice. In Europe it is sometimes supposed—and this view appears to have been general up to near the middle of the nineteenth century—that Muhammed and his successors believed in the subordination of women and that the institution of polygamy was evidence of this belief. But this superficial and prejudiced view has long since changed among serious students of history. Muhammed appears to have held women in high respect and to have raised their position over that which they occupied in the society of pagan nomads. It would have been impracticable to have attempted to abolish polygamy, but the limiting conditions with which he tried to surround it, so far as they were accepted in practice, greatly restricted it. His own marriages, after the death of his first wife, Khadijah, appear to have been contracted partly for political motives. But his successors fluctuated in their interpretations of the Koran's pronouncements on the position of women. If, in the early history of its expansion, Islam was in advance of contemporary opinion and law, there have been periods since in which it has failed to keep pace with the evolution in more liberal directions of the attitudes of other societies, and of secular attitudes within societies predominantly Islamic.

The survival in Iraq of the veiling of women was widely regarded among the younger generation in Baghdad as a mark of female servitude. On the eve of the Revolution the full face veil was not often seen within the city, and when it appeared, it was usually among the poorer classes or among visitors from other Muslim areas, particularly Iran. It aroused anger among the students, who felt that it placed the country in an inferior light in comparison with modern societies outside the Middle East. However, since most of the institutions of higher education were in Baghdad, it was only there that the collective influence of the students could be brought to bear strongly on social practices, though in a more dispersed sense they influenced the country generally through their effect on their own families and through the influence of some of them subsequently as schoolteachers in various parts of the country. In Baghdad the more important issue was not concerned with full veiling, but with the wearing of a voluminous black cloak (*abaya*) outdoors over European clothes. Many, if not most, female students in the colleges came from homes in which it was not customary for women to go into the streets without the *abaya* over their indoor clothes and their parents often objected to their doing so. But as many of the male and some of the female students were opposed to the practice, the women students, whose families insisted on their leaving the house covered in this way, would often walk up to, or descend from a car in front of, the colleges and hastily discard their *abaya* immediately after entering the gates, carrying them to cloak-rooms where they would remain until students left for home in the evening.

The position of women had changed less in the home than in the institutions of higher learning. The 'conflict of the generations' was nothing new in itself. But in the mid-twentieth century it took on new forms and attained a scope and intensity greater than it had ever reached in the past. It was an inescapable accompaniment of wider changes in the structure of society. In some circles, and particularly among the student and professional classes, the inferior status of women had come to be regarded as a survival of what was loosely described as 'feudalism', which was as much an object of doctrinal antagonism as 'imperialism' was. This viewpoint was reinforced from two directions: on the one hand, Egypt, which aimed at the elimination of polygamy and supported the reinterpretation of Islam in more modern terms, and on the other Russia, which presented a more advanced model in some respects—for example, in occupational opportunities for women—than many other industrialized countries could show.

On the eve of the Revolution it was already clear that, particularly among the professional classes and to some extent among younger women from poorer homes, the transformation to a modern outlook on the position of women was taking place more swiftly and smoothly than would have been predicted earlier. But, as with most social changes, it was much faster and more widespread in Baghdad than elsewhere in Iraq, and more among some classes than others, and it cut across political attitudes. A left-wing or radical Arab nationalist attitude did not always carry with it a belief in sex equality in public affairs or even in the home (although it seems to have done so more among the communists where women were to be found in leading political positions). Nor was a conservative attitude necessarily accompanied by opposition to changes in the status of women. Actually the regime which fell in 1958 had taken a liberal attitude towards the education of women, and some, though not all, of the regimes which followed it were less progressive than it had been in this field.

Conclusion

The discovery and development of oil led to a rapid increase in the national income of Iraq. Revenues began on a modest scale in the early 1930s, but did not reach a million pounds until exports began in 1934–35 and only reached £3 million in 1949. But with the new agreement in 1951, Iraq began to be relieved of the shortages of capital and foreign exchange that had previously impeded the finance of development programmes. The government was able and willing to call extensively on foreign advice and direct technical assistance in the development of the country. There were frequent cabinet changes, extensive political unrest at times, unpopular governments, but political instability as such did not seriously interfere with the development programme except through the administrative confusion created by frequent changes of civil servants when ministers changed. A kind of 'spoils system' was traditional in Iraqi politics.

It is common to measure economic development by changes in *per capita* national income, and on this basis Iraq was 'developing' rapidly with increasing oil revenues. The measure is used for want of a better one, for its defects, both statistical and conceptual, are widely appreciated, especially with reference to the less-developed countries, where national income statistics can be especially misleading as indicators of changes in the standard of living of the people or in their productivity. The large oil revenues of Iraq made development possible, but they did not ensure it, and apart from the control of the great rivers, which eliminated the ravages of floods, and the creation of a variety of public utility and industrial projects, there was little spectacular change in the economic condition of the country. Economic development, defined as improvement in the skills and welfare of the people, and in the efficiency with which they used the country's resources, and as the investment of capital in productive projects to yield a stream of output for the future, undoubtedly continued, but at what rate we cannot know, for many of the crucial ingredients cannot be appraised against the measuring rod of money, which alone enables us to combine the disparate elements in homogeneous indexes.

We saw that there were many signs of economic advance in the country after its formation following the First World War, and indeed even in the preceding half-century. This advance continued, but apart from the capital investments mentioned above which added enormously to the productive physical endowment of Iraq, the expenditure of the oil revenues does not seem to have raised substantially the underlying rate of growth in productivity of the economy—but little can be expected in a period of less than a decade. The standard of living of the Iraqi people was still very low. Mortality and morbidity rates were high. Workers were unskilled, illiterate, and inefficient. Agriculture—the country's greatest industry, apart from oil—was the most backward economic sector and showed few signs of substantial progress. The distribution of income was grossly unequal; the few were very rich, the many very poor, with only a small (but growing) middle class, largely composed of government employees, the professions, and small merchants.

The picture, however, is only gloomy against the background of the unrealistic expectations that accompanied the beginning of Iraq's oil fortunes. Should it have been expected that the expenditure of large sums of money could markedly change the rate of advance in a country so recently emerged from its tribal structure, with such an ancient and yet primitive agriculture in a harsh and difficult environment? The creation of attitudes adapted to modern education, training, industrial and agricultural technology, the inculcation of habits of hygiene and child care, all take time. The expenditure of money is necessary to bring about the requisite changes, but its effects can only appear slowly. Moreover, to spend large sums of money efficiently already presupposes the existence of efficient administrators, just as rapid expansion of education presupposes the existence of qualified teachers, and the spread of medical care the availability of doctors and nurses. It is simply not possible to use foreigners for all these purposes, especially in a country with a language little known by non-Arabs. It seems likely that if the Development Board and the government had taken a different line in their development plans and had from the beginning put large sums into attempts directly to improve agriculture and the standard of living of the farmers and of the urban workers, and to develop the necessary human skills hand-in-hand with the 'projects', the country would have made somewhat greater progress. This would, however, have been an even greater task than that undertaken and, given the limited skills available, one can only assume that accomplishments would also have fallen short of expectations.

On the other hand, there is also no doubt that the political structure of the country, and particularly the agrarian structure, was an impediment to the adoption of effective policies for agriculture, on which the successful development of Iraq depended, and still depends. It was no longer possible to attribute the low rate of economic development to lack of capital, and the critics of the government eager for greater progress found the trouble in the agrarian structure (feudalism) and in the monopolistic position of the oil companies (imperialism). Those who insisted that 'imperialism' was the great influence retarding industrialization were merely demagogues; those who stressed the necessity of land reform were correct, but they greatly underestimated the magnitude of the task.

The political power and the wealth of the shaikhs were derived from their economic position as landlords and from their control over the peasants and over the agricultural income of the country. It was widely believed that, when water supplies were available and the rivers controlled, the reform of landownership alone would remove the chief obstacles facing agricultural development in Iraq. It was an article of faith that if only landlords were deprived of the greater part of their land and the peasants relieved from paying a large proportion of their produce as rent, the incomes of the latter would rise, their incentive to develop agriculture would be raised to the point where, with government help, especially in the provision of credit, the countryside would become prosperous. Land reform was seen primarily as a political need whose economic consequences could not fail to be beneficial.

The failure of successive governments to undertake adequate measures to increase productivity on the land, to improve the position of the farmer, and to reform the social and political structure under which in some areas, particularly in the south, landlords were almost a law to themselves, was undoubtedly one of the most serious political issues of the time. It coincided with the expansion of education, which brought numerous students from the countryside to Baghdad, increased political consciousness, and hastened the passing of traditional attitudes, including the attitude of resignation to conditions of deprivation and class oppression. The plight of the farmers was taken up by all political opposition groups. Political consciousness on this subject also extended to some of the officers in the armed forces who came from poor rural areas.

Neither the farmer's immediate material needs nor the means of raising his efficiency as a producer were taken adequately into account in the formulation of plans for and expenditure on development, but above all the changes taking place in his social and political attitudes were seriously neglected.

As we shall see later in more detail, however, the urban political agitators, including a considerable part of the student class, held oversimplified views of the agricultural situation, underestimating the important economic role of the landlords in a number of areas, especially in the north, and overestimating the ability of the peasant farmers and agricultural workers to take over such functions efficiently if the landlords were suddenly removed. Even an observer as experienced and knowledgeable as Doreen Warriner failed fully to understand the complexities of Iraqi agriculture when she wrote:

> . . . land reform is worth doing, even if it is not done with administrative efficiency, simply because redistribution of land can bring immediate improvements in the living standard. Reform need not wait on better farming: the agriculture of south Iraq is so primitive

> that there is no risk that a decline in production could follow a division of the big estates. There is no need to aim at perfection in equipping the farmers, or in the organization of services. If Iraq has to wait for land reform until the Government can provide schools, experts, health services, and co-operatives, it will wait too long. These good things can come, and will come, once ownership has been redistributed. What is wrong with Dujaila can be put right, but what is wrong with the big estates cannot be remedied except through a general measure of reform, including the redistribution of ownership.[28]

It does not follow that reform in the land system and new measures aiming at the improvement of productivity would have produced quick results or would necessarily have saved the country from political revolution. The most that can be said is that revolutionary agitation might have been moderated if the governments before the Revolution had been seen by the public to entertain serious intentions to effect land reform—if they had at least made a beginning on it and pledged themselves to complete it in stages. Their failure to do so heightened the feeling that only revolution could solve Iraq's problems.

Notes

1 K. G. Fenelon, in the *Iraq Times*, Annual, 1957.

2 We have drawn on the statistical and field work of Atheel al-Jomard, a research student at the School of Oriental and African Studies, University of London, and a Lecturer at the University of Mosul, who has made a special study of rural–urban migration in Iraq in the period 1947–65. We acknowledge with thanks his permission to use his as yet unpublished data.

3 For a description of the conditions in Amara and a discussion of the effects of the 'Amara Law' (No. 42 of 1952) see Doreen Warriner, *Land Reform and Development in the Middle East*, pp. 150 ff.

4 Atheel al-Jomard, paper presented at the Development Seminar of the School of Oriental and African Studies, December 1976. D. G. Phillips, in *Economic Development and Cultural Change*, Vol. 7 (1959), p. 413.

5 Iraq Government, Irrigation Development Commission [The Haigh Commission], *Report on the Control of the Rivers of Iraq and the Utilization of their Waters* (Baghdad, 1951).

6 International Bank for Reconstruction and Development (IBRD), *The Economic Development of Iraq* (Baltimore, 1952).

7 For a detailed discussion of government investment activity see F. Jalal, *The Role of Government in the Industrialisation of Iraq, 1950–1965* (London, 1971).

8 Lord Salter, *The Development of Iraq: a Plan of Action* (Iraq Development Board, 1955), p. 37. Salter's strictures on the dangers of attempting to spend

too fast could be read with profit today by the Iraqi authorities. See below, Chapter 18.

9 IBRD, op. cit., p. 80.

10 The first detailed estimates of the Iraqi national income were made by the Government Expert on Statistics, K. G. Fenelon, *Iraq: National Income and Expenditure, 1950–1956* (Baghdad, 1958). His was the pioneering work, which was followed by the much more comprehensive and detailed research of Khair al-Din Haseeb undertaken while he was preparing his doctoral dissertation in Cambridge University and published in 1964. K. Haseeb, *The National Income of Iraq, 1953–1961* (London, 1964).

11 The conditions of tenure, crop-sharing, and position of the cultivator generally, have been discussed in numerous works. Of the works cited in the Bibliography, see especially D. Warriner, S. H. Longrigg, Doris Adams, Abdul Salih H. Alwan (which gives a very good summary of variation in crop-sharing), and the FAO reports. A particularly useful study which illustrates how dangerous it is to generalize is that of A. P. G. Poyck, *Farm Studies in Iraq: an Agro-Economic Study of the Agriculture of the Hilla-Diwaniya Area in Iraq* (Wageningen, 1962). Poyck shows that in a number of areas the income of tenants on the larger estates was greater than that of independent farmers on small plots of land. The latter had to farm their land too intensively and yields suffered in consequence.

12 Food and Agriculture Organization, *Mediterranean Development Project, Country Study: Iraq* (Rome, 1959), p. 128.

13 In a study of the area along the Daghghara Canal in the Diyala region Fernea found that 'The conditions of tenancy in 1958 varied somewhat from landowner to landowner. A "good" landlord charged no more than half the tenant's crop for the use of his land, claimed no interest on the seed which he provided at the beginning of the season and placed no restriction on the use of fallow land for grazing the tenant's flocks. Some landlords tried to charge higher rents or demand a few animals from the sharecropper in exchange for grazing rights on fallow land. However, the rising tide of urban migration had created a labour shortage here during the period in question [1956–59] and even the most rapacious landowners were being forced to offer favourable tenancy terms, lest they be altogether without cultivators'. Robert A. Fernea, 'Land Reform and Ecology in Post-revolutionary Iraq', *Economic Development and Cultural Change* (Vol. 17. No. 3, April 1969), p. 363.

14 For example, the Arthur D. Little report, though proposing a comprehensive programme of industrial projects most of which were related to the processing of the natural resources or the agricultural production of Iraq, and intended for the local market, nevertheless warned that for the present at least proposed industries should be able to produce 'at a cost below the landed price of comparable imported goods or materials before import duty is levied. . . .' Arthur D. Little, Inc., *A Plan for the Industrial Development of Iraq* (Cambridge, Mass., 1956), p. 9. Later, they suggest, a less stringent test might be used.

15 In a variety of ways the interim report of the FAO echoed the criticisms of the left-wing and the nationalists. It appeared in Arabic under the authorship of Thomas Balogh, in a translation by Mohammed Salman Hassan, but only after the 1958 Revolution. The final report of the FAO published in 1959 was modified to take account of the changes brought about by the Revolution, particularly the land reform, and struck a note of considerable optimism. Although the report rejected many of the popular ideas about industrialization, it somewhat uncritically accepted the claims regarding the

beneficent effects of the land reform. FAO, op. cit. (Interim Report 1957), Chapter VII, para. 19.

16 See Charts I–IV pp. 492–5.

17 Haseeb, op. cit., p. 23, Table 6.

18 Kathleen M. Langley, *The Industrialization of Iraq* (Cambridge, Mass., 1961), p. 191.

19 ibid., p. 203.

20 M. G. Ionides, *Divide and Lose: The Arab Revolt, 1955–58* (London, 1960), p. 200. This criticism is even more valid today (1977) than it was in 1956.

21 ibid., p. 201.

22 ibid., p. 199.

23 Arthur D. Little, Inc., op. cit., p. 363.

24 Jalal, op. cit., p. 91.

25 Salter, op. cit., p. 83.

26 A sociological survey of the area was made in 1957 by Doxiadis Associates, a consulting firm particularly concerned with housing. The above information is taken from their mimeographed report.

27 In 1954 a sample survey of household budgets was carried out for the lower- and medium-income groups of workers in Baghdad which produced some information on total expenditures on food and other items of consumption. Defective as it was, it did indicate some of the differences between the expenditure of *sarifa* dwellers and others, and notably the larger proportion of income spent on food, and especially on cereals, by the former. A useful survey of the information can be found in Hashim al-Dabbagh, *Études statistiques sur le développement économique de l'Irak* (Baghdad, 1960), pp. 386 ff.

28 Doreen Warriner, *Land Reform and Development in the Middle East: A Study of Egypt, Syria and Iraq*, 2nd edn. (London, 1962), p. 169.

Part Three

The 14th of July Revolution 1958–63

8 The Seizure of Power 1958

In the year preceding the Iraqi Revolution of 14 July 1958 an outward calm and appearance of stability reigned over most of the country, broken only by occasional disturbances within and near some of the schools and colleges. People could travel without restriction in all parts of the country. Near the end of 1957 and early in 1958 we travelled in the north, even beyond Dohuk in the Kurdish lands, and over a wide area in the central and southern parts without restriction and without encountering any outward signs of unrest or revolutionary ferment.

But in turning from the outward and visible signs in daily life to the private expression of views among individuals, a striking contrast appeared in many circles. Among the politically conscious classes from the far right to the far left it was difficult to find many, except those whose personal fortunes depended on the continuation of the regime or who were associated with it, who were not in some degree in opposition to it. The Amir Abdul Ilah, the King's uncle, and Nuri al-Said, were the objects of particular animosity, the first because he was believed to be the real power behind the throne and opposed to social reform, the second because he had dissolved political parties and suppressed the main channels of political opposition, and both of them because of their role in the Anglo-Iraqi War in 1941, their determination to align Iraq with Britain and the United States and to exclude diplomatic and economic relations with the communist countries, and their opposition to the newer currents of Arab nationalism.

The feeling among the politically active students in many of the colleges and even secondary schools, and among a large part of the professional classes, including lawyers, doctors, and artists, ranged from strong disapproval of, to almost fanatical hostility towards, the existing regime. But these classes did not comprise the whole opposition. The conservative sections of the *ulema*, and the more extreme Muslim Brotherhood, looked askance on the government, and the peasants in those rural areas which were dominated by autocratic landed proprietors laboured under heavy grievances which the regime had done little to redress.

The underlying motives and aims which inspired the miscellaneous groups, open and clandestine, of which the opposition was composed, varied widely, and included incompatible elements. But as long as the groups were all in opposition, their divergencies remained in the background. Even Arab nationalists and communists were content to accept each other as tacit allies in a common cause which each group believed to be in its own interests. This disposition to maintain in practice a truce, not always formally acknowledged, was encouraged by the varied and perverse interpretations of the common terms used in political discourse throughout the world of the mid-twentieth century.

The extreme Arab nationalists who, if they obtained power, would have denied political freedom to all who did not share their central ideas, the more conservative Islamic groups which opposed modernization of law and social customs, and hankered after a theocratic state, the communists who, if they could ever have gained power, would have suppressed all but their own party and satellite parties, were ready without exception to join in denouncing the government for limiting the rights of parties, for 'managing' elections, and for failing to grant full political freedom and to put the provisions of the constitution fully into effect. The terms 'democracy' and 'freedom' were on the lips of all, but were far from the hearts of the majority of the opponents of the existing regime.

The seeds of future troubles had long been sown, and the harvest was destined eventually to bring widespread political disillusionment. But in 1957 and most of 1958 the expectation was widespread that 'revolutionary' change would bring with it greater political freedom, faster economic development, and a deeper social transformation. But the discontent over domestic policies and conditions formed only a limited part of the causes of the Revolution. It was the regime's foreign policy, both in the Middle East and beyond it, which aroused the deepest passions and alienated the widest circles of opinion. Individuals and groups, seriously divided among themselves on domestic affairs, came much nearer to unity on matters of external relations with other Arab countries and with the great powers.

Nuri very much misjudged the temper and the aspirations of his people. In conservative Islamic quarters he appeared in some respects to be too modern in his domestic aims, while his international aims appeared to be leading Iraq into alliance with, and dependence on, imperial Christian powers which had formerly dominated much of the Islamic world. He was regarded by the radical Arab nationalist section as a traitor to the Arab cause and an instrument used by the imperialists in their efforts to re-establish domination over the Middle East. The left wing, which put less emphasis on Arab nationalism, particularly resented his exclusion of the Eastern European countries from all relations—diplomatic, commercial, or cultural. In this respect he went much further than the Western great powers whose alliance he sought.

On Nuri's behalf it has been argued that he was justified in believing that links with Great Britain and, to a lesser extent, the United States were in the interests of Iraq, bringing a greater contribution to her economic development than could be obtained elsewhere, while links with Eastern countries would only encourage underground communist activity and might expose Iraq to the sort of pressures that Iran had faced at the end of the war.

Experience after the Revolution threw some light on these arguments, and we shall return to the subject in later chapters. Whatever the merits of Nuri's position, however, the Israeli–Anglo–French attack on Suez, and the failure of Nuri, in the eyes of the Arab world, to react adequately to it, may fairly be said to have settled the fate of the Iraqi regime. Its downfall was only a matter of time and opportunity; with such wide disaffection, the end could hardly have been far off.

Both Nuri and his opponents, in different ways, believed that they were following the only road that would safeguard the independence of Iraq and of the Arab world as a whole, while each was convinced that the other was prejudicing that independence by establishing, or proposing to establish, closer links with one side or other of the rival great powers. Whether there was any justification for Nuri's intense fears of communism will appear in the discussion of the post-Revolution period.

The Iraqi Revolution took place at a time when the forces making for modernization were not only impinging on traditional lines of cleavage in the Middle East but were also suffering sharper cleavages in their own ranks. Thus, to traditional lines of disunity, modern lines of disunity were added, and, since the traditional and the modern could not be separated, and the divided counsels in each case overlapped those in the other, the pattern of disunity became more and more intricate and confused and gave rise to deeper conflicts in which rival modern political doctrines were intermingled with traditional sectarian doctrines. It was on this strange, and yet familiar, world, in which a babel of voices competed to proclaim a variety of ways to salvation, that the Iraqi Revolution broke.

The *Coup d'État*

Rumours of a coming attempt to overthrow the regime had been circulating in Baghdad for some weeks before the blow came on the night of 13 and 14 July 1958. Even at a degree-giving ceremony of the University of Baghdad early in July, at which King Faisal II distributed the diplomas, the atmosphere was tense. The speech of the president of the University outlining the progress which had been made, and the plans for the first year of an integrated university programme that was to commence in the autumn, was received by students and staff in silence. At the close of the ceremonies the Iraqi teachers hastened to a staff room to listen to the latest broadcasts from Cairo Radio. One member of the staff, who was not in sympathy with the revolutionaries, remarked that the atmosphere resembled closely that on the eve of Rashid Ali's *coup d'état* in 1941, and that an attempt might be made at any time. But if this was the atmosphere in the Waziriya district of Baghdad, where most of the higher educational institutions and some of the professional institutes were situated, it found less reflection in the south of the city, where many of the foreign residents and the more well-to-do Iraqis lived.

For some time groups of 'Free Officers' had been meeting in secret to devise means of overturning the regime. A central organization had been formed with Brigadier Abdul Karim Qassim as its chairman. The subsequent accounts of these activities, given by members of the group, naturally differ widely. Each of those who later became prominent in the public eye desired to place his role in the most favourable light, while the less prominent witnesses of the activities of the leaders showed their personal preferences for one or other of the latter. It would be as unjust to dismiss the various accounts as fictitious as it would be unwise to accept any of them as conclusive.[1]

The circumstance that gave the conspirators the opportunity for which they had long waited was the outcome of the three events in the first half of 1958 that we discussed in chapter 5: the first was the formation on the initiative of some Syrian army officers of the United Arab Republic, bringing President Nasser's jurisdiction to the borders of Iraq; the second was the civil conflict in Lebanon which led to a division of opinion in Iraq among the army officers as well as among civilians; and the third was the declaration of a union between Iraq and Jordan.[2]

On the eve of the Revolution some of the ministers and officials in the Iraqi and Jordanian governments, and a number of the leading army officers, were occupied in preparing the framework of the new 'Arab Union' between them. A number of senior army officers had gone to Amman to take part in the organization of a Joint General Staff to serve a unified army. Nuri himself and some of his ministers were preoccupied with the formation of the new government of the union. Nuri seems to have been less closely in touch for a few days with details of affairs in Baghdad.

When orders came to a brigade situated north-east of Baghdad to move to Jordan on the night of 13–14 July, some of the Free Officers suspected that the government was planning to use it in President Chamoun's support against the Lebanese opposition. They were aware of the preoccupation of staff officers and ministers with the affairs of the new union. Later, in retrospect, Colonel Abdul Salam Arif, in the course of a speech in Damascus, referred to the decision that the leaders of the *coup* made:

> Compatriots, the great night of 13–14 July was a fateful night in history. Imperialism had ordered forces to implant its criminal plans. However it did not realise . . . that these forces were the forces of the people. . . . These forces advanced on Baghdad while imperialism thought that they were advancing towards the objective which it had assigned them . . .[3]

The brigade would have moved along the outskirts of Baghdad without entering the main part of the city if it had followed the normal route to Jordan which it had been directed to take. Its commander was not one of the Free Officers. Colonel Arif and some of the other younger officers persuaded him to take an advance party to Falluja, west of Baghdad on the Euphrates, where they would meet him with the main body of the brigade. By a series of manoeuvres Colonel Arif succeeded in getting control of the entire brigade.[4]

At 4.30 in the morning on 14 July, he entered Baghdad at the head of the brigade. At 5 o'clock he crossed to the east bank of the Tigris and seized the radio station, where he announced the downfall of the regime and, pouring out a violent stream of abuse on its leading members, urged the mob to come out on the streets. 'Noble people. go to Rihab Palace and other palaces of humiliation . . .' This and later incitements led to the appearance of mobs on the streets, many of whom were politically motivated and animated by hatred of the leading personages in the governing regime, but some were ready also to take advantage of any opportunities of loot.

Detachments had been sent to surround the Rihab Palace (residence of the King and Crown Prince), to seize the Department of Defence, to occupy the nearby South Gate police station, to establish communications with Free Officers in the Rashid Army Camp to the south of Baghdad, and to seize control of the west bank of the Tigris. For the most part these plans were successfully executed, and with very little resistance the whole of the city speedily came under the control of the military revolutionaries. However, Nuri al-Said was warned in time to leave his house and cross the river. Two days passed before he was betrayed and murdered and his body dragged through the streets.

The first detachment sent to dispose of the royal family was checked, but the second broke into the palace and shot dead all the members of the family except one young female relative, who was sheltered secretly. Neither sex nor age restrained the assassins. Mobs seized the body of Abdul Ilah and dragged it through the streets before hanging it in front of the Ministry of Defence.

The arrival of Brigadier Qassim in Baghdad brought a more sober note into some of the broadcasts, but the violent utterances continued for some time. Contrasting types of appeal succeeded one another rapidly. An example of the more extreme type follows:

> Noble Iraqi people, here are the happy tidings you have long been waiting for. Listen to them. My noble Iraqi brother and my brave Iraqi sister, go out into the street. . . . You will see him who wanted to fly high. . . . Look at him in the street: he has been eliminated, together with his strange master Abdul Al-Ilah, the enemy of God. They have been dragged like dogs in the street. Your noble people refuse to hand over their bodies. They will probably be purified by burning, though burning is not good enough for them. What great joy this is and what great tidings these are.[5]

In contrast, a responsible statement, beginning with an injunction to maintain order, continued as follows:

> The affairs of the country must be entrusted to a Government emanating from the people and working under its inspiration. This can only be achieved by the formation of a popular republic to uphold complete Iraqi unity, to bind itself with bonds of fraternity with Arab and Muslim countries to work in accordance with U.N. principles, to honour all pledges and treaties in accordance with the interests of the homeland, and to act in compliance with the Bandoeng Conference resolutions. This national government shall be known from now on by the name of the Iraqi Republic.[6]

There was a short period of uncontrolled ferocity after the *coup*. Colonel Arif's forces had apparently released the inmates of a prison

Faisal being welcomed to his kingdom in August 1921

King Faisal I (1885–1933)

King Faisal II (1935–58) with King Hussain of Jordan in 1953

Nuri al-Said (1888–1958) and Crown Prince Abdul Ilah in 1957

Abdul Karim Qassim (d. 1963)

Left: Colonel Fadhil Abbas al-Mahdawi presides over a session of the People's Court. On trial are pro-Nasser elements accused of trying to assassinate Qassim

Demonstration at the Ministry of Defence in Baghdad after the Mosul revolt in spring 1959

Right: Abdul Rahman al-Bazzaz, Prime Minister 1965–66

Below right: President Abdul Salam Muhammed Arif (d. 1966), Qassim's successor in February 1963

The Kurdish leader Mustafa Barzani

Left-wing Iraqi workers and students demonstrating on the Day of the Baath, 14 April 1977

Saddam Hussain al-Takriti, appointed vice chairman of the Revolutionary Command Council in November 1969

Field Marshal Ahmed Hasan al-Bakr, President since 1968

Parade of the 'Youth Vanguard' (*futuwwah*), a paramilitary organization for boys, in Baghdad

Kurds in the typical terraced town of Aqra

A local craft, the *gufa*, used for fishing on the Tigris

Preparing a *masguf*, the traditional method of grilling large fish on the banks of the Tigris near Baghdad

Members of the Yazidi sect near the Iraqi-Syrian frontier do not cut their hair, but wear it in pigtails

Above right: A crude oil seepage at Pulkhana, near Kirkuk

Right: A natural gas seepage at 'Baba Gurgur', Kirkuk, known as the 'Eternal Fires'

Above left: Dohuk in northern Iraq

Left: The mosque courtyard at Kerbela, a famous Shia shrine

Marsh Arabs of southern Iraq

Above left: A *sarifa* outside Baghdad, with mud houses

Above: The back entrance to the Suq al-Shurjah in Baghdad. The cakes in the foreground are *zlabiah*, next to them *baqsam*

Water wheel at Hit, 160 kilometres north of Baghdad, on the Euphrates

A fertilizer factory in Basra

near Baquba, north of Baghdad, and had allowed them to move into Baghdad behind the troops. His own provocative broadcasts after the seizure of the radio station brought out many inhabitants from the slums of the city. Mobs ransacked the British embassy, overturned the statue of General Maude,[7] and, invading Rashid Street and the Saadoon area, where many foreigners lived, seized a vehicle which was conveying some foreign visitors to the Ministry of Defence, presumably for their safety, dragged them from it into the street, and murdered them, in full public view. It was said that this revolting deed was committed in the belief that the victims were ministers in the Cabinet of Nuri al-Said. Three of the murdered men were Jordanians, one was a German, and another an American businessman.

These acts of savagery were long commented on and deplored in other parts of the Arab world and by Iraqis. They were short-lived. When Brigadier Qassim and his forces arrived, Brigadier Ahmed Salih al-Abdi was appointed and took up his duties as Military Governor of Iraq.[8] On the afternoon of 14 July martial law was proclaimed. Tanks were stationed at important points in the city. A series of proclamations gave stern warnings to violators of the peace, and it was not long before the police, at first demoralized by the sudden takeover, were re-established with some changes in higher personnel. After two or three days order had been completely restored.

The Role of the Mob

The horrifying murders committed in the first days of the Revolution are still shrouded in uncertainty. The discussion on the motives behind the massacre of the royal family has centred chiefly on the question whether the operation was planned in advance or whether it was the outcome of a sudden impulse on the part of a single officer, possibly even a junior officer. Contradictory assertions have also been made about the conduct of Abdul Ilah, one account alleging that he provoked the fire of the soldiers by first shooting at them with his revolver. But the opposite assertion has been made, from a very different point of view, that he ordered the guards and others not to fire. We believe that the latter suggestion carries more weight than the former, but even if it is accepted, it is not a major point.[9]

We strongly incline towards an explanation in historical terms. The Revolution was planned, not hastily improvised, even though opportunism shaped some of the details of its execution. During the planning the memory of the unsuccessful attempt of Rashid Ali in 1941 to establish himself with army support was still strong. The failure of that attempt was attributed above all to the escape of the young King and the Prince Regent and of Nuri al-Said, which gave 'the imperialists' an opening to represent their intervention as an act of restoration of a legitimate government. The same thing might happen again. The conspirators believed that Great Britain or the United States would not hesitate to intervene again in order to prevent the establishment of a government which they could not hope to control and which would end Iraq's links with them. If to British people this seems far-fetched, it should be remembered that the invasion of Egypt had taken place only two years earlier, and that the majority of Iraqis had never been ready to interpret the intervention in 1941 as a mere outcome of wartime emergencies in the British and Russian struggle for survival.

In view of this attitude there is nothing improbable in the supposition that the assassination of the royal family was planned by the conspirators as a regrettable necessity. Whether it was planned to include the female members of the family in the massacre is more doubtful. It now seems almost certain that the majority of the Free Officers did not approve of it, but the exact instructions given by Arif to the contingent which carried out the murders are not known. Our own later conversations with persons who had discussed some of the outrages of the first few days with some of those who took part in them disclosed the highly abnormal state of mind, amounting at times to frenzy, of the junior officers and rank and file who were sent to hunt down the leading persons in the regime, as well as the street mob who participated in the dragging of bodies.

The next question is concerned with mob violence, to which we have already made brief reference. The role of the mob is extremely difficult to determine in retrospect after any revolution. The Iraqi Revolution consisted above all in a *coup* by a section of the army, which accepted the leadership of a few young officers who had been influenced to some extent by the politically conscious class which formed a small proportion of the total population, and the majority of whom lived in Baghdad. This class, which included the professional groups and many of the students in higher education, had grown considerably since independence. Political unrest had been chronic among these groups from an early stage. But there was little sign of serious organized revolutionary agitation among the masses of people, apart from a few areas in the country where local grievances flared up at times. The conditions did not exist in which street orators could hold forth in public and incite mob disturbances; nor was it apparent that the poorer sections of the community were seething with discontent on a scale likely to produce a spontaneous uprising.

The mobs which had been responsible for the violence on 14 July were no doubt influenced by the deliberate incitements broadcast by Arif and others, but many seem to have been spurred on by the hope of private gain. Before the Revolution we had witnessed on several occasions the rapidity with which a crowd would gather with much less provocation when any unusual incident, unrelated to politics, occurred. The British embassy, on the west bank of the river, faced on two sides densely populated slums interlaced with numerous alleys and narrow streets. It was not surprising that mobs gathered quickly, and that they should contain many whose objectives were not political.

Order Restored

The authors of the military *coup* could not afford to permit prolonged chaos and damage to property, particularly the property of foreign missions. Having their hands full with the domestic problems of creating a new government and extending its authority over the entire country, they realized that to enter into conflicts with other countries would risk the loss of all their unexpectedly easy gains. With modern military equipment, rampaging mobs can be quickly dispersed. Order was soon re-established, and broadcasts announced from the first day that all foreign commitments would be honoured and the rights of foreign enterprises respected.

This concern to avoid offence to other countries was fully justified. For, on the day after the *coup*, American troops occupied Beirut, and British soldiers entered Jordan soon afterwards. The idea in some foreign circles, especially in the United States, that the revolutionary government might be tempted to invade its neighbours at a time when it had yet to consolidate its hold on the army as a whole and on the country outside Baghdad was far-fetched, if not ludicrous. It is true that the Jordanian government feared that some elements in its own army, influenced by President Nasser, might seek to emulate the authors of the successful Iraqi *coup*.

For a few days wild rumours circulated in Jordanian and Lebanese circles that some of the troops outside Baghdad disapproved of the *coup* and were moving on the city. Actually, there was little trouble in the provinces, and first impressions in Kurdistan seem to have been favourable to the Revolution. No organized large-scale resistance showed itself in Iraq in its immediate aftermath. Some regretted the passing of the old regime, mainly among the upper and middle classes, but not exclusively so. The animus against the regime was not shared by all the lower-income groups, many of whom had little, if any, awareness of political affairs. Only a short time earlier standing among a group of Iraqis gathered to see King Faisal's Egyptian fiancée who was to visit a hospital in Baghdad, an Iraqi who obviously belonged to a very modest income group turned with an approving smile to tell us, 'She will be our Queen'. But such people remained discreetly silent after the Revolution in face of the overwhelming chorus of approval with which it was greeted. Although carried out by a small, and young, military group, the *coup*, demonstratively approved in Baghdad, seemed to win the immediate acclaim of a large majority in the army and was apparently popular among the people of Iraq of nearly all political points of view.

The attempt to define closely the idea of revolution seems unprofitable. But in a broad sense the events of mid-July 1958 appear to have more claim to the term than any of the numerous military *coups* before or since, at least up to the time of writing. The general approval and rejoicing that followed the overthrow of the government revealed a genuine desire for new lines of development, particularly in international (including intra-regional) policy, in political development at home, and in some aspects of economic development, particularly in agriculture. Of no later *coup* could these things be said.

Following the proclamation of martial law, a series of proclamations and decrees were published and broadcast in succeeding days. It was announced that a Council of State was to be established, consisting of three members. Though not explicitly so stated, this was designed as an institutional replacement, within the republic, for the monarchy. A new Cabinet was then announced, with Brigadier Qassim as Prime Minister; Colonel Abdul Salam Arif as Deputy Prime Minister and Acting Minister of the Interior; Muhammed Hadid, a liberal merchant and prominent figure in the National Democratic party, as Minister of Finance; Abdul Jabar al-Jomard, a well-known Mosuli, as Foreign Minister; Ibrahim Kubba, a college teacher of reputedly 'Marxist' views, as Minister of Economy; Siddiq Shanshal, a prominent figure in the Istiqlal (Independence) party, who had been associated with the Rashid Ali uprising, as Minister of Guidance; Jabir Umar, who favoured strong links with Egypt, as Minister of Education; Fuad al-Rikabi, a well-known and very young Baathist, as Minister of Development; Hudayb al-Hajj Hammud, a liberal landowner who had been severely criticized by his class, as Minister of Agriculture; and other ministers drawn mostly from political groups known to have been opposed to the preceding regime.

The complete change of ministers was accompanied by extensive changes among the higher army officers. Since the revolutionary officers had broken their allegiance with the preceding regime, the precedent thus created might be used against them in the future. The primary concern of the new rulers was to select officers who could be trusted to support them in power. Personal loyalty was given priority over military efficiency. The changes included the appointment of a new Chief of Staff and of new commanders for the four army divisions, and the retirement of a long list of officers.

Changes in higher army personnel for purely political reasons were by no means new in Iraq. Militarism had been a foremost evil in political life from an early stage after independence. But Nuri al-Said had done much to curb it and in the early and mid-1950s no military *coups* had taken place. Civilian ministers had controlled the departments, and some of them had been experienced and capable men. A few officers had been lowered in rank or moved to distant positions on suspicion of political disloyalty, but there had been no extensive purges since the Second World War.

The Revolution brought a sharp change in the role of the military. The return of the army to the centre of politics quickly affected its professional efficiency. More than ever in the following period, precedence was given to political over military criteria in the selection and promotion of higher officers. From this time onwards the most efficient military officers were passed over if any doubt was felt of their allegiance to the particular officers or military group which had carried out the last *coup*. Since this was characteristic of a number of other Arab countries besides Iraq it was not surprising that later their armies were ineffective against Israel.

In the early days after the Revolution the developments in this direction were not foreseen and the army enjoyed a period of popularity during the rejoicing over the fall of the old order. For a time it was looked on as the instrument of a successful change which many had desired, but none had been able to achieve.

Notes

1 A useful discussion can be found in M. Khadduri, *Republican Iraq* (London, 1969), Ch. II.
2 ibid., pp. 56–9; Gallman, op. cit., pp. 210–11.
3 BBC, Summary of World Broadcasts, Part IV, 21P7, p. 6 (1958).
4 For accounts of the planning and execution of the *coup* see Uriel Dann, *Iraq Under Qassem* (London, 1969), chapter 2, and Khadduri, op. cit., chapter III.
5 BBC, Summary of World Broadcasts, Mediterranean and the Middle East: N.601, p. 6.
6 ibid.

7 To the historian, the wrecking of the statue of General Maude seems an irony of history. When, in his campaign against the Turks, the general liberated Baghdad, all he desired was to continue his victorious march northwards as quickly as possible. His view was that the British aim should be to liberate the Arabs from the Turks, not to take the place of the latter and rule Iraq. Sir Percy Cox found difficulty in persuading him even to take measures to establish a local administration in Baghdad pending a post-war settlement.

8 Discussing these events with the late General Ghazi al-Daghistani, who was Chief of Staff before the Revolution, we asked his opinion of Brigadier Abdi, who had been under his command at one time. 'He did not impress me as an outstanding officer', he replied, 'but he remained loyal to Qassim and took no part in political movements.' Unlike many officers in Iraq, then and since, Abdi confined himself to his military duties.

9 See the somewhat differing accounts of Dann, op. cit., p. 30, and Khadduri, op. cit., p. 44.

9 The Early Qassim Period, 1958–60: Political Upheaval

The enormous enthusiasm with which the new Iraqi regime was greeted by the people was simply the obverse of their discontent with the old, and they expected changes which would eliminate the sources of their discontent. They had been told that the obstacles blocking the emergence of a prosperous and modern Iraq, in which justice, brotherhood, and equality reigned, were the creation of 'feudalism', 'imperialism', and 'exploitation'. These were to be abolished by the 'blessed revolution' led by Abdul Karim Qassim, soon to be known as the 'sole leader', and a new start was now to be made, the past wiped out. The expectations of the people, including the students, were high; so also were the fears of those who had responsible positions in business affairs, in public administration, and education. It was not clear how far, and in what manner, the past was to be wiped out; no man could be sure exactly where he stood.

In the sphere of international politics, the new regime immediately announced the establishment of diplomatic relations with the communist countries, including China, and also with the United Arab Republic, but remained silent about the Baghdad Pact. The federal union with Jordan was abandoned. Internally the new leaders had to purge their 'enemies' from the courts, the civil service, and the military, but at the same time they had to allay the fears and reduce the uncertainty of the business community and others whose co-operation was required to maintain the level of economic activity: they had to retain the enthusiasm of the people by some immediate action in order to buy the time required to make the fundamental reforms which had been promised, but for which no serious preparation had been made.

Dissident students, teachers, and other political opponents of the old regime were released from prison and many of the older politicians who had not fled the country took their place. Numerous senior government officials, including the members of the Development Board, were dismissed; army officers joined the Cabinet and were placed in many senior posts in the civil service. Landlords, urban as well as rural, are always popular targets to attack and rent is a heavy item in the consumer budget. Almost at once, therefore, the government reduced all rents by from 7 to 20 per cent, depending on the type of house or building and the year in which it was first leased. Similarly the prices of bread and gas were reduced. For the students, Qassim decreed that there should be no failures; all students in the schools and colleges were permitted to pass their courses in 1958 and to graduate or go forward to higher classes. Presumably the students had been working hard for the Revolution, and in any case had allegedly been unfairly treated and unable to give of their best in the conditions prevailing under the former regime. Many were the jokes told about the need to choose one's surgeon according to the year of his degree!

At the same time, soothing words were addressed to the oil industry and to the business community. A 'Provisional Constitution' promulgated within two weeks of the Revolution stated that private property would be safeguarded and confiscation would only be in the public interest against fair compensation and according to law.[1] The Minister of Economy declared that industry would be supported, given greater customs protection, and supplied with necessary technical help. The oil companies were assured that the government intended to abide by its agreements and Qassim openly stated that 'mutual interest' made Iraq and the Western industrialized countries in need of each other. The government took care to protect the oilfields against sabotage by irresponsible activists. It seemed that, apart from agriculture, the new regime intended to adopt conciliatory and moderate economic policies, although the political rhetoric was intense. 'Feudalism' and 'imperialism' along with the 'feudalists' and domestic 'imperialists' were to be abolished forthwith and the people were urged to be on constant alert to root out the 'enemies of the Revolution'. Immediate steps were to be taken to raise the standard of living of the Iraqi people and to accelerate the pace of development.

Feudalism was to be dealt with through the agrarian reform. Imperialism was to be attacked through changes in trade and international financial policy as well as through control of foreign interests in Iraq, and the 'wresting of Iraq's rights' from the oil companies. Economic advance and improvement in the standard of living were to be brought about by a thoroughgoing overhaul of the development programme and of development planning, which the Minister of Development asserted had so far been conducted primarily in the interests of the ruling class and of the imperialists, and by giving special attention to housing, health, education, and social security.

The revolutionary leaders had promised and threatened much, but both the promises and the threats were vague, in accordance with the customs of Iraqi *coups*. None among the military, and few among the new civilian leaders, had any real comprehension of the task they had undertaken. Everything had to be improvised. Unfortunately, the policies had to be formulated and practical steps taken under conditions of continuous and growing disunity in the country, a disunity which, as in the past, was seriously exacerbated by external conditions.

Early Disunity

The various groups which had enthusiastically hailed the Revolution had been united only in a common desire to eliminate the old regime. The ties which held them together fell apart as soon as that aim had been accomplished. The underlying divergencies were deep-seated and based on issues of substance. They arose out of incompatible aims and reflected mutually exclusive expectations. The moderate right, the centre, and the social democratic left wing wished and expected that parliamentary life would be restored, this time without restrictions on parties and without government manipulation of elections. The communist left and the extreme right, however, desired a more and not less authoritarian regime than that which had been overthrown.

On the economic side differences were also very wide wherever economic questions involved political doctrines. They were not closely parallel to the differences over the forms of government to be established, but they were connected closely enough to entangle the economic discussions and economic plans in doctrinal political controversies at a number of points. The civil servants who strove to give new content and fresh drive to the economic policies of the country were severely handicapped by the political controversies and rivalries which led to fluctuations in the personnel of government departments and ministries. The inability of Qassim from the beginning to organize adequate machinery for reaching collective decisions, his assumption of personal power of decision over many economic and technical matters of which, as an army officer, he had little knowledge and experience, and the day-to-day improvisations that had in consequence to be made—all these things hindered efforts to pursue consistent and constructive lines of action in economic and administrative affairs.

The domestic clashes, which appeared from the early stages of the post-revolutionary period among the groups which had rejoiced in the Revolution, were closely associated with two related external influences. Ideological differences interacted with differences in the interests of the individual member countries of the Arab League both within the Middle East and in the wider international setting beyond the Middle East.

The differences were deepened by the ambiguity of the conceptions embodied in their political doctrines. Among these conceptions, that of Arab nationalism particularly lent itself to confusion in interpretation. The ambiguities were not new; they had existed from the birth of the idea in the Ottoman Empire. But the sudden transformation of the political position of Iraq and of her ideological relations with other Arab countries, and especially with Egypt, had raised new issues concerning the application of the concept of 'Arab nationalism' and 'Arab socialism' to internal and intra-regional affairs. It was speedily to become a major source of conflict within Iraq and between her and her neighbours. Within Iraq the conflict emerged in a clear-cut contest between Qassim and some of his associates on the one hand, and a group of parties and individuals on the other who, while not wholly in harmony with one another, were combined in opposing Qassim. This ideological clash was intimately associated with intra-regional conflicts and with the ramifications of the Cold War.

Iraq, Arab Nationalism, and the United Arab Republic

From an intra-regional point of view the history of Iraq in this period must be viewed in the light of the changed and changing relations between Egypt and Syria. The proclamation of the Egyptian–Syrian 'union' only five months before the Iraqi Revolution had greatly affected the expectations of what would follow the downfall of the Hashemite regime in Iraq. The most striking, and to many the most surprising, development was the extraordinary rapidity with which antagonism between Iraq and Egypt reopened after a brief lull following the fall of the royal regime. Cairo had welcomed the Revolution unreservedly, but in both Cairo and Baghdad there were, as there had been from the beginning, widely different and even conflicting interpretations of its nature circulating side by side. It was confidently assumed by many that the Revolution would open the way for the absorption of Iraq into the United Arab Republic. For others, some form of federation would serve better to reconcile the interests concerned. But for many, and especially for the communists, and, as a minority in the Arab state, the Kurds, neither alternative was acceptable. The question was one of fundamental importance, and was the most immediately urgent political issue confronting the military officers who had seized power and whose first entrance into political life was to take over the entire responsibility for the functions of government.

On this central political question—Arab nationalism with its corollary of Arab unity—the two chief rivals for power among the Free Officers, Qassim and Arif,[2] held opposite views. Both had played leading roles in the seizure of power. Each had used his influence to obstruct the formation of a Revolutionary Council, which would have led to the collective government of the Free Officers and which had been agreed to by most of them before the Revolution and was therefore expected by most of them after the fall of the old regime. Both were personally ambitious and neither thought of handing over power to a constitutional civilian government. Each felt that, having risked not only his career but also his life in clearing the way for a new government, he was entitled to play a leading role, perhaps *the* leading role, in it.

At the time of the Iraqi Revolution the prestige of Egypt under President Nasser was at its height in the Arab world. Nasser had eliminated foreign military bases and successfully resisted an armed intervention by Israel, France, and Great Britain. On the initiative of the Syrian military officers who had embraced the Baathist creed in vague, general terms, President Nasser had been drawn into the project of uniting Syria with Egypt, ostensibly as a first step towards the unification of the whole Arab world, actually as an opportunist move to save the domestic political position of the Baath party, which had failed to gain the support of the majority of the Syrian people and faced further reverses.

Qassim perceived that Nasser aimed at a 'leadership' of the Arab world which prejudiced independent action by Iraq in external affairs and, if it should lead to the absorption of Iraq into the United Arab Republic, would place Iraqis, as it had already placed Syrians, completely under the control of Egyptians. Qassim was certainly correct, as events later demonstrated, in feeling that this would be neither in the interests nor according to the wishes of a great majority of the Iraqi people. Very early Nasser perceived that Qassim was challenging his position as leader in the Arab world by clearly asserting in his speeches and by his actions an interpretation of Arab nationalism which ran sharply counter to his own, and which above all was designed to maintain Iraq's independence from Egypt. Without explicitly stating it, Qassim unmistakably implied the equality of Iraq with Egypt within the framework of Arab nationalism. In a speech to army officers at the end of February 1959 Qassim pointed out that 'Iraq is part of the Arab nation. It is part of a whole, not part of a part'.[3]

Arif, on the other hand, felt a deep emotional attachment to the idea of Arab nationalism, and this attracted the very small number of Baathists, and the larger number of Pan Arab nationalists, towards him as a better hope than Qassim as leader of an early spectacular move towards unity with Egypt. The two men could not survive in the same government. Qassim, the more mature, the more resourceful, and the more politically astute soon outmanoeuvred Arif, gradually stripped him of his positions, and then, when Arif was goaded to attack, or seem to attack, his person, had him arrested, tried, and imprisoned.[4] He remained in prison until the autumn of 1961.

It does not appear certain in retrospect that the Baathists' judgement of Arif was accurate even at the outset. In the light of later events, it seems doubtful whether, if Arif had gained the upper hand at this stage, he would have gone so far as to carry Iraq into the United Arab Republic. But he would certainly have made gestures towards Nasser and would have tried to associate Iraq more closely with Egyptian policies. At the outset he seems to have had no clear, concrete view of how the idea of Arab nationalism could be interpreted in practical, political, and economic measures which would draw the Arab countries into closer and closer relations.

From the start, the United Arab Republic, as we have seen, embodied a contradiction. The two elements of which it was composed entertained irreconcilably different conceptions of the ways in which power should be distributed and government should be conducted. President Nasser's firm conviction that an Egypt directed by him should be the 'leader of the Arab world' could never be adjusted to the conviction of the Syrian Baathists that they should supply the ideas and the philosophy of the government of the UAR. Most calamitous of all, from their point of view, was Nasser's demand that the Baath party, along with all other parties in Syria, should be disbanded and replaced by a single Arab Socialist Union on Egyptian lines, in which Egyptian direction would prevail.

But the student of the Iraqi Revolution and its *sequelae* cannot safely assume that what is known to him at a later date concerning Egypt and Syria was known widely to Iraqis in the early part of the Iraqi Revolution. It is in fact quite clear that the Iraqi Baathists were at the start, and remained, wholly untutored on these matters and innocently believed that should Iraq join with Nasser in the UAR, he would be ready to co-operate with rather than to dominate them. They threw in their lot with what they thought was the Nasser version of Arab nationalism. Nasser, they believed, was adopting what the Baath had earlier initiated. The Iraqi Baathists were for the most part very young and without practical experience of politics. At the outset their estimate of Nasser was naive, and, with characteristic impetuosity, they called for the immediate adhesion of Iraq to the United Arab Republic, apparently then and later quite unconscious of the underlying dissent among the Syrians themselves.

Their enthusiasm for Nasser was accompanied by an intense hatred of communists, which the latter reciprocated. Very early in his attempts to formulate a Baathist philosophy, Michel Aflaq, the leading Baath theoretician, had sketched in very general terms the outlines of a socialism which stood in sharp contrast to communism in so far as it was linked with a creed of Arab nationalism and was regarded as an 'Arab' socialism distinct from internationally linked socialisms and communisms which emphasized the solidarity of workers as a class against capitalist governments. Communism was regarded in Baathist ideology as an enemy of Arab nationalism, no matter whether it was defined in Marxist terms, or by the actual practice of communist parties outside Russia in accepting the Soviet Union as an object of allegiance. In the first case it was hostile to nationalism in principle; in the second it could be represented as serving a Great Russian nationalism.

Reasoning on these lines may have been influential only among the intellectuals of the party, but the whole issue had come to life in Syrian politics on the eve of the establishment of the United Arab Republic, when Khalid Bagdash, an experienced parliamentarian as well as secretary of the Syrian Communist party, had taken the lead in opposing the interpretation of Arab nationalism in terms of total union between different Arab countries. Khalid al-Azm and a number of other non-communist Syrian politicians had held the same view, though not for identical reasons, and it was to forestall this combination of forces that the Baathist leaders and the army officers, the latter carrying the former further than they ultimately wished to go, went to Cairo and persuaded Nasser to join in proclaiming the United Arab Republic.[5]

Thus had Iraq been drawn into the bitter struggle over union. The young Iraqi Baathists, poorly acquainted with the mounting disillusionment in Syria, regarded Qassim as a traitor to Arab nationalism for not joining Nasser and for giving scope to the communists. The historic rivalry between Cairo and Baghdad, which in the few years before the Revolution had reached an intense phase under Nasser and Nuri al-Said, now returned in an equally intense form. Its external aspects had changed. Nasser and Nuri had been divided with Nasser on the 'left' and Nuri on the 'right'. Nasser and Qassim were divided, with Nasser on the 'right' and Qassim on the 'left'. Before the Revolution Nuri had appeared to Nasser to be attempting to drag the Arab countries into the Cold War by aligning them as satellites of Britain and the United States through the Baghdad Pact. This viewpoint could be given powerful support on objective grounds. Soon after the Revolution Qassim seemed to Nasser to be encouraging the Arab countries by example to align themselves with the Soviet Union and the Eastern bloc and thus drawing Iraq into the Cold War from the other side. This interpretation of Qassim's attempts to redress the balance found support in the United States, though not very much in Britain nor in other parts of Europe, but it was without foundation.[6]

Forms of Internal Dissension

The disintegration of the revolutionary forces into warring factions began almost at once. Immediately after the *coup*, of which civilians seem to have had no exact foreknowledge, the different groups were in very different states of preparedness. The Communist party, small though it was, proved to be the party most ready to act. Its leaflets, often in mimeographed form, circulated widely in Baghdad. The place where they attracted most attention was along Rashid Street, traditionally the main thoroughfare of the city, colonnaded in the old Turkish style. Here the leaflets were often pasted on the pillars of the colonnades.[7] Among the first of these was what came to be described as the 'anti-God leaflets', which in rather crude, primitive terms, poured ridicule on all religious beliefs, dismissing them as childish superstitions and inventions designed to reconcile the common people to their lot under the capitalist system.

This leaflet was soon removed by the authorities, but it left its mark and contributed to the unpopularity of the Communist party in the country. It was a major blunder which showed how far out of touch with the 'masses' the communists really were: while in theory they were the spokesmen of the 'proletariat' and the peasantry, in practice they represented a small minority in the country. Indefatigable in the production of statements, in the formulation of policies on paper, in the preparation and distribution of leaflets, in the organization of meetings, demonstrations, and petitions, they gave an outward impression of larger numbers and greater strength than they were actually able to command.

In a number of areas of Baghdad where particular political groupings were dominant, troubles arose, especially at night, from the influx of members of hostile political groups from other districts. It was not safe for the partisans of the far left, for example, to enter after dark certain districts where the nationalist groups were dominant. Different parts of the city, which covers a very large area, were strongholds of different political groups and the sympathies of people in different districts were displayed through the pictures of politicians in the windows of houses and shops.

At the outset Nasser's picture was shown prominently as well as Qassim's, but by the autumn friction had already been revealed and the left wing were condemning Nasser and acclaiming Qassim as the 'Sole Leader'. In the sectors where the left predominated among active political groups Nasser's pictures disappeared: no one would venture to show them. On one occasion we found many pictures of Nasser still displayed in a district west of the Tigris at a time when not one could be found in Rashid Street and nearby areas. About ten days later a demonstration organized by left-wing groups went in procession through this district calling for the removal of the pictures. A riot began; a shot fired from a roof-top killed one of the demonstrators. The victim was given a spectacular funeral in a demonstration by a reputed 100,000 people, and ringing denunciations of imperialist plotters, with implications that Nasser was at work aiding them, were heard and repeated on the radio and in some of the newspapers.

For some time, no shop or institution could afford to abstain from showing somebody's photograph. But those—the majority—which did not approve of the left wing and its activities sometimes showed the picture of the President of the Sovereignty Council, General Najib al-Ruba'i, as well as that of Qassim. This was a decisive indication of a position which supported the Revolution to the extent that it was not taken over by the extreme left political elements and so long as it was not dominated by the cult of a 'sole leader'. We had the impression that this represented the attitude of the majority of the middle class, though they were less vocal than the minorities of the extreme left and the extreme right. The poorer classes were attracted to Qassim, believing, with reason, that he sincerely cared for them.

The various strands of public opinion were well reflected within the educational institutions in Baghdad, particularly in the colleges of higher education being selectively included with the university. The Revolution had led—for a time—to the loosening of political restraints on the student body and to the participation of students in political agitation and political activities to a greater extent than under the preceding regime. If this aided the leaders of the Revolution in some directions, it was ultimately to prove embarrassing to them in others. The college students were an important influence on social and political change. They were drawn from every section in the country on a quota system which modified in a downward direction the principle of selectivity according to attainments in secondary education. This made them all the more representative of the diverse groups in the whole country. Coming to Baghdad from the provinces, the students from poor agricultural areas, for example around Nasiriya and Amara in the south, were brought under modern influences which affected their outlook, creating a greater awareness of the deficiencies of their home areas and the need of reform. The call for far-reaching changes in agriculture was thus brought home to many urban dwellers, particularly in Baghdad. At the same time, however, the students were poorly equipped to propose remedies. They oversimplified the problem of agricultural reform, for example, and much overrated the capacity of the peasants to take over the functions of the landlords.

But greater political scope for the students was to prove more embarrassing than helpful to the new authorities when divisions appeared among the revolutionary groups. Bitter animosities arose among the different political groups: the Arab nationalists of the Nasserite type and the Baathists at one extreme; in the middle the more moderate and much less well-organized Arab nationalists who desired a resumption of parliamentary government, and the National Democrats, who aimed at socialism on British or Scandinavian lines within a party system of representative government; finally, at the other extreme, the communists, who aimed not only at removing landlords but also rich merchants and private owners of industry, replacing all of them by collective farms in agriculture, and state ownership and operation in industry and large-scale trade.

The sharpest antipathies were between the Baathist and Nasserite students on the one hand, and the supporters of Qassim and his conception of Arab nationalism, including the communists, on the other. While the communists claimed to be supporters of Qassim, many of them during the autumn and winter of 1958–59 went far beyond government policy and committed excesses that aroused wide resentment in the colleges as well as among the general population. These will be discussed later in other contexts. The group antagonisms sometimes led to affrays in the grounds of the colleges where weapons, usually knives, were drawn. The combatants were separated by members of staff and other students, for the body of students as a whole was always in the last resort against violence.

In August 1958 Qassim established a Special Supreme Military Court, generally known as the 'People's Court', presided over by his cousin, Col. Fadhil Abbas al-Mahdawi. Its purpose was to try anybody charged with acting against the interests of the Iraqi 'homeland' or of other Arab countries. It was a military tribunal with the widest possible powers, presided over by a president with no qualifications of any kind; in its proceedings little attention was paid to legalities or to 'natural justice' in any form. It was a purely political organ. The first group of people brought before the court were members of the old regime. The conduct of the court was far from judicial, but the accused were represented by counsel and were given a chance to defend themselves, which some did with spirit and courage. The proceedings were later published in several volumes and provide a valuable historical source.[8] In addition to this contribution to the historical record, however, was the more immediate function of providing a focus for the emotions and resentments of the people. The trials were televised, the 'evil' behaviour of the 'imperialists', 'feudalists', and other 'enemies of the people' infesting the old regime was paraded and roundly condemned. Undoubtedly the trials were a useful and convenient way of allowing the people to 'let off steam', much less harmful than riots and mob action. None of the death sentences then passed was carried out by Qassim.

In the later part of 1958 and in early 1959 there were serious attempts to overturn the new regime. The first of these was associated with the return to Iraq of Rashid Ali al-Gaylani, in the expectation of being received with honour as an early opponent of Britain.[9] He got no post in the new government, but his residence became a centre for meetings with a number of dissidents. He disliked the prominence of the communists in the early months and leaned further towards Egypt than was acceptable to Qassim, although he seems to have favoured Iraqi independence in economic matters, presumably not wishing to share the oil revenues of Iraq with Egypt. Adhering to older conceptions of the distribution of political influence in the country, he attempted to use the tribes of the middle Euphrates in a rising against the new regime. But the plotters failed to maintain adequate secrecy and the police arrested them in advance of the date fixed for it. In any case, the changes in the techniques of warfare during and after the Second World War had made tribal rising ineffective, and his attempt '. . . to repeat as closely as possible the coup which had brought him success and power in the entirely different circumstances of 1934–35 . . .' failed.[10]

Rashid Ali was tried in the People's Court, but in private. This was the first time the court had had to deal with an attack on Qassim's regime instead of with the alleged enemies of the old regime. Rashid was tried on two charges, armed conspiracy and inciting a foreign power to attack Iraq. On the latter count he was sentenced to death. He remained in prison until July 1962 when he was pardoned by Qassim.

Unrest in the North: the Mosul Revolt

The unrest in Baghdad in late 1958 and early 1959 had its counterparts elsewhere in Iraqi cities, including areas whose peoples showed such diverse characteristics as those of Najf and Kerbela, where the

Shia Muslims predominated, and Mosul, where the majority were Sunni. Broadly speaking, and with many individual exceptions, it may be said that the Shia tended to be more favourably disposed towards the political left, and the Sunni towards the political right and centre.

The Kurdish population in the vicinity to the north of Mosul, like the majority of the Arabs and almost all the great Arab families of the city, were Sunni Muslims. But this religious affinity coexisted with marked social divergencies and with sharply different political outlooks. It has been widely noted that the Arabs of the Mosul area have generally taken a harder attitude towards the Kurds and their aspirations than the Arabs of Baghdad have done. The great Arab families of Mosul had shown in their outlook the limitations of religious affiliation and practice as an indication of political relationships. Less sympathetic to the Sunni Kurds to the north than to Sunni Arabs to the south, they were also extremely critical of, and often opposed to, the dominant Sunni Arabs in the Baghdad establishment, believing them to have taken advantage of their central position to divert an undue proportion of national resources and especially oil resources to the capital at the expense of Mosul and the north.

The city of Mosul contained a number of leading merchants and others of old Arab families with a conservative Islamic outlook, who formed a strong upper-class social group. They were not themselves a centre of disturbance, and among them were a number of moderate leaders who had aimed at establishing harmony between Muslims and the Christian groups in and around Mosul. But their conservatism clashed with some of the new influences let loose by the Revolution. The streets of Mosul showed contrasts with those of Baghdad. The veil had not wholly disappeared there, and the *abaya* was almost universally worn by women in the streets. The women of many of the more well-to-do conservative Islamic families were rarely seen on the streets after marriage and some spent their years mainly within the precincts of the house and garden. In some families polygamy was still practised and the design of the houses provided for the harem and the separation of the sexes.

The old customs and practices were being modified slowly by the new education, which was being extended to all classes and to both sexes. The conception of women's position was changing. New occupations carried on under more modern conditions were transforming conditions of work in some sectors. New forms of amusement and recreation were spreading. The quality of education was usually poor, but such as it was, it changed the outlook of the young and introduced ideas of the modern world beyond. The average standards reached by Mosul students in examinations for the Baghdad colleges were higher than the national average. New generations were rising and the normal divergence of outlook between the new and the old was widened and deepened by the changes in the conditions of life and work. In many families where parents had received scanty education or none at all, the younger members were studying in the colleges and others had qualified a few years before and were studying abroad or had returned to work as technicians.

The people of Mosul had taken no active part in the Revolution, but the economically dominant groups had hoped and expected that it would usher in a more pronounced Arab nationalist policy and enable them to restore and strengthen their commercial ties with Syria. They had been unprepared for the apparent rise in the influence of elements of the left, including especially the communists, who seemed to exert a disproportionately large influence in a number of directions. Locally, the extreme left formed only a small proportion of the Arab population, though perhaps a larger proportion of the Kurdish and Turkoman minorities. But a left-wing minority in Mosul, encouraged by, and to some extent sheltering under, the rise of the left to greater importance in the capital, had shown increased activity, which had aroused the fears and resentment of the conservative Arab elements, for there were deep economic and social divisions within the city. The inhabitants of the densely populated and extremely poor working-class sections did not share the inordinate suspicion of the left held by the rich merchant and landowning classes, but rather shared the enthusiasm for Qassim and the Revolution which was evident among simple working people elsewhere.

Hence it was hardly surprising that, in the temper of the times, the unrest came first to a head in Mosul, where the influential leading Muslim families had been aroused partly by developments in the capital itself, partly by local developments, and partly from outside. It was here that the second and most serious attempt to organize the overthrow of the regime was made.

The Mosul outbreak cannot be discussed wholly in terms of the forces at work within Iraq. The evidence is clear that the United Arab Republic had a hand in it. The brusque rebuffs which President Nasser had sustained in the months since the Revolution had disappointed the high expectations and upset the ambitious plans which had been formed in Egypt in the immediate aftermath of the downfall of Nuri al-Said. With Rashid Ali in prison and pictures of Nasser removed from the streets of Baghdad, with those Arab nationalists suspected of working for Nasser under arrest or surveillance, a counter-challenge had come within Iraq which Nasser was not prepared to ignore. But Iraq bordered on Syria and not on Egypt, and it was from Syria that any moves towards supporting dissident elements in Iraq would have to come.

At that time Colonel Abdul Hamid al-Sarraj, Chief of the Executive Council and head of the *Deuxième Bureau,* was concerned in Syria with underground activities and from him the dissident groups received promises of military support as well as of a broadcasting station. Nasser was in Damascus at the time of the Mosul revolt and remained to 'watch' events.[11] It will be for future historians, with access to information at present undisclosed, to determine the respective roles of Nasser, al-Sarraj, and others in the underground activities of the UAR with respect to Iraq at this time. As elsewhere in this period the intervention took the form of measures to encourage and assist dissident local elements.

The immediate local focus of the revolt was a group of Mosuli 'free officers' who had come out in support of Qassim and Arif when they marched on Baghdad. These men had welcomed Arif's speeches in favour of union with Egypt and Syria and were distressed by his downfall. Qassim had sent one of the original Free Officers, Colonel Abdul Wahhab al-Shawwaf, to Mosul to command the armed forces there, an assignment which did not please the colonel, who had hoped for a cabinet post and in any case had preferred to remain in Baghdad. Al-Shawwaf was in contact with two other groups of disaffected Free Officers, who also resented Qassim's personal assumption of power and his failure to establish a military Revolutionary Council, and who disliked his unwillingness to seek *rapprochement* with Nasser and his toleration of communist activities. One of these was a nationalist group in Baghdad headed by Colonel Mustafa Rifaat al-Haj Sirri, Qassim's Chief of Military Intelligence, the other was led by Brigadier Nazim al-Tabaqchali, the Commander of the Army Second Division in Kirkuk. Al-Shawwaf and these men laid their plot against Qassim.

Early in 1959 a group calling itself the Peace Partisans and widely believed to be a communist front organization, decided to hold a big rally in the north as part of its activities against imperialism and in favour of 'peace and socialism'. Qassim did not appear to object. Although al-Shawwaf was already plotting against Qassim, he came twice to Baghdad to warn Qassim against allowing a communist demonstration in Mosul and urged him to prohibit the meeting of the Partisans, which he felt would be a provocation to traditional conservative elements of the city and would incite the disaffected people from the poorer sections.

Qassim and his security services were aware that plots against him were being formed, but did not take seriously the warnings from left-wing circles in view of their past predilection to issue such warnings somewhat indiscriminately. For many, however, the planned rally was an indication of Qassim's sympathy for the communists, and al-Shawwaf prepared to act, for he saw in the rally an action which would attract popular support for a revolt centred in Mosul.

The rally was called for 6 March 1959. It of course attracted the students from Baghdad. A number of our students had informed us ten days earlier that the meeting in Mosul would be so important that they felt they must attend it: the enemies of the Revolution were continuing to plot against the new order and 'Things are going to happen'. The government encouraged student attendance by granting reduced train fares, of which many took advantage.

To Baghdad residents in general what followed was only known incompletely at the time, and from a one-sided point of view. Few people outside the leading figures in government and some in left-wing circles were aware that arms were flowing in from Syria to support a rising. The intemperate propaganda of the left wing, and at times their vicious behaviour, had created an atmosphere of distrust of their activities; the belief prevailed among the middle classes and among the conservative Arab nationalist section of the students that the disturbances and affrays in Mosul were started by the aggressive actions of the Peace Partisans, who were said to be under communist direction. In fact, however, the mass rally of the Partisans passed off without disturbance in spite of the great numbers coming from Baghdad who took part in it. Most of the students returned by the special train on the same night and the accounts that they gave us the next day made no reference to any abnormal developments. Some of the Peace Partisans stayed on for the next two days, in some cases because it was not easy for all of them to find places on the trains immediately.

But Colonel al-Shawwaf, without consulting other collaborators, decided to start the planned uprising on the morning of 8 March. He proclaimed a revolt, which was also broadcast to Iraq from Damascus, and immediately attacks were made on the remaining elements of the Peace Partisans, particularly against persons accused of being communists. A number of suspected communists were shot, one of the most prominent of whom, Kamil Qazanchi,[12] a Mosuli lawyer, was murdered in prison. Others were marked for the same fate, but the whole city fell into a state of chaos when the Shammar tribesmen were summoned in accordance with the plans for the rising. Kurdish forces also entered the city. Confused reports reached Baghdad. A radio transmitter had been supplied to the conspirators from Syria and continued to broadcast fabricated stories of the alleged victory of al-Shawwaf's forces, even after the rising had collapsed.

Al-Shawwaf had on his side the higher officers in his command, but inadequate attention had been paid to the non-commissioned officers and the rank and file. Al-Shawwaf soon found, when it was too late, that he could not rely on the latter. In addition, co-ordination with his co-conspirators was poor: the Kirkuk forces did not move and Colonel Sirri, the chief of the conspirators in Baghdad, who, according to the original plans, was supposed to carry out a similar *coup* there as soon as the Mosul rising had achieved the initial expected success, also remained inactive. The army and air force in Baghdad remained loyal to Qassim. When two of al-Shawwaf's pilots flew towards Baghdad on a bombing mission, they were quickly blocked and planes from near Baghdad bombed al-Shawwaf's headquarters with some success. Al-Shawwaf was wounded in the bombing; later he was shot in hospital by one of his soldiers loyal to Qassim.

Then followed a day of fighting in which local groups of left-wing partisans were joined by Kurdish forces. The bombing had dispersed the Shammar tribesmen and the city soon fell into the hands of the forces opposing al-Shawwaf. Revenge was then taken for the earlier murders of Kamil Qazanchi and other opponents of al-Shawwaf's uprising. These mixed forces dominated Mosul for a few days, during which the great families of the city, who were believed—in a number of cases with reason—to have collaborated with the plotters, were the object of persecution and in many cases the victims of brutal personal attacks with considerable loss of life and property. Vivid accounts were given to us privately soon afterwards by some of our students whose homes were in Mosul. The extent of the casualties cannot be estimated with accuracy, but it far exceeded those in the Iraqi Revolution itself.[13]

The Significance of the Revolt

The clash in Mosul remains as an event of outstanding interest to the historian: it brought a variety of smouldering grievances and antagonisms, ancient and modern, into the open. It was the product of external as well as internal forces, and without the aid and the weapons supplied by Nasser through Syria the rising could hardly have taken place. The passions which it aroused were of composite origin derived from historic rivalries across the Great Syrian Desert and between Baghdad and Cairo, between semi-nomadic tribes and settled townsmen, between Kurds and Arabs, between ideological antagonisms of 'left-wings' and 'right-wings', between 'Arab nationalists' and in effect—though not in explicitly avowed terms—Iraqi nationalists.

The violent campaign carried on by the Cairo Radio and press before, during, and after the Mosul clashes seized on every incident that could be exploited to create the impression that Qassim and his associates were betraying the sacred *credo* of Arab nationalism, interpreted as Cairo interpreted it, and led by Egypt during and since her victorious struggle to eliminate foreign bases from her soil and to resist uncompromisingly the foreign invaders of 1956. The denunciations were intensified when the government of Iraq—here with the concurrence of the moderates as well as of the extreme left and even of some former qualified supporters of the old regime—established relations with the Eastern European countries as well as with the Soviet Union and China.

Economic negotiations were conducted with these countries and agreements were reached for the exchange of goods and for the establishment of cultural relations.[14] Ibrahim Kubba, Minister of Economy, led the Iraqi negotiators. A former teacher in the College of Commerce in Baghdad whose approach to economics was Marxist, he established good relations with the Russians and Eastern Europeans and used 'left-wing' phraseology. In Egyptian propaganda and by the more conservative sections of the bourgeoisie he was attacked as a 'communist'. We found, however, that the communists themselves did not regard him as such, although he was in good standing with them as a negotiator and later supported their demand to be admitted to the Cabinet. However, the coincidence in time of the Mosul conspiracy and the radical change in Iraq's policy toward Eastern Europe and the Soviet Union ensured that Kubba's activities would be in the forefront of controversy.

The international atmosphere of conflict at the time encouraged simplified interpretations based on the fashionable doctrines of the day expounded by Dulles, and echoed in substance by an unexpected temporary ally, Nasser. Qassim was, in this view, an ally of 'communism'. The Soviet Union was engaged in a deep plot, in co-operation with the communist parties in Iraq and Syria, to advance Russian interests and to establish Soviet hegemony in the Middle East; the communists appeared to many observers, both within and outside Iraq, to be exerting strong and growing influence on Iraqi affairs.

But as we have tried to show, the disturbed conditions in the spring of 1959 cannot be interpreted simply as an unprovoked attempt by the 'communists' to take over in Iraq. They surrounded a struggle led by the more fanatical wing of the Arab nationalists supported by Nasser against a heterogeneous collection of elements which included the communists, who were well organized and played a leading role, but also included others who, while accepting the existence of a special relationship among the Arab peoples, were not ready to merge into the United Arab Republic, surrendering the independence of Iraq to Egyptian control.

From an early stage the role that Qassim chose was that of maintaining a balance among the contending forces, thus nullifying the extremes on both sides. The effort to accomplish this primary aim, the realization of which alone could save the country from civil war with attempts at intervention from outside, occupied his efforts fully, and at no time more than during the aftermath of the Mosul hostilities. But because of these hostilities the restraints which Qassim had begun to exercise on the communists[15] and on the less well-organized extreme 'left' from early in the year were lessened, and for a time the activities of these groups were intensified.[16]

Thus the civil war in the Mosul area in spring 1959 was a major setback to hopes of establishing a stable government in succession to the Hashemite regime. Its aftermath was prolonged, in Baghdad and central Iraq as well as in the north. The breakdown of justice, the spread of civil disorder which characterized it were carried over into the succeeding weeks, when the search for culprits and the arbitrary attempts to provide safeguards against a repetition far exceeded the bounds of law.

More than anything else the Mosul affair set back Qassim's efforts to effect a more even balance among the contending forces inside Iraq. This central aim was now subjected to its greatest strain since the Revolution. The left-wing groups had supported him and some of the right-wing had taken action to overthrow him. It was therefore natural that he should lean towards the left for a time. Those involved in the Shawwaf revolt were tried in the People's Court and for the first time the death sentences on four of the officers condemned were carried out with Qassim's approval. Although the court had by this time become discredited because of the behaviour of Col. al-Mahdawi and served little useful political purpose, the accused, in this instance guilty of the offences charged, were given full opportunity to defend themselves.

Within the left the Communist party now adopted an increasingly militant attitude, seeking to take over the left-wing forces and eliminate all potential opposition from other directions. The 'nationalists' were in a state of anxiety, particularly those whose homes were in Mosul. Some of the absentees in the college classes were Mosulis and the spirit of the times may be judged from the characterization of these students by the left wing as 'traitors'. Affrays broke out in the grounds from time to time, but the main body of students showed restraint and during such affairs rushed in quickly to force the combatants to desist. There were reports of sporadic street-fighting at night, especially in districts dominated by very conservative Arab nationalists who resented the intrusion of individuals who were supposed to be communists. Particularly in Mosul, but also elsewhere, strife was aggravated and complicated by religious cleavages, with attacks on Christians suspected of being communists.

Demonstrations in Baghdad

As we had done earlier in the autumn of 1958 on the occasion of large-scale street demonstrations in support of Qassim and the Revolution, we now made a close examination on three successive days of the demonstrations that had been called in Baghdad following the Mosul rising. They were organized on such a large scale that it was difficult to estimate the total numbers, which, however, must have exceeded 100,000 people. Massed groups of manual workers, students, employees of the 'white-collar' classes, nondescript groups drawn from all over the city and especially from the *sarifa* camps outside, marched one after another through the streets, their organizers slipping along their ranks and occasionally jumping on a pile of bricks or other raised object to deliver fluent, short harangues to the groups. High over their heads as they passed the tallest new concrete business building near the North Gate of Rashid Street, dangled long ropes lowered by demonstrators from the roofs to illustrate the demand of the communist groups among them that all the prisoners sentenced to death by the People's Court should be hanged at once.

When the foremost sections of the immensely long procession arrived in front of the Ministry of Defence, in which Qassim lived, he suddenly appeared on the roof of a building adjoining the road. A great cheer arose from the crowd which stampeded in his direction, those behind pressing on those in front to a dangerous extent: fainting persons had to be lifted out and carried aside with great difficulty. Qassim was at the height of his popularity with the crowd. Not a natural orator, he yet cherished a deeply sincere feeling for the poor and dispossessed and they, in their turn, sensed this and believed in him to the end. When later he lost support, it was not among the very poor classes but among doctrinaire political groups and among sections of the middle classes.

Observing the second day of demonstrations, we found that Qassim did not appear: instead, when we arrived in front of the Ministry of Defence, we found a speaker's stand set up in the street, from which a succession of speakers harangued the sections of the crowd within hearing, to which the stock resolutions of the times were put and 'passed'. These demanded the immediate execution of the political prisoners, the distribution of arms to the people, immediate withdrawal from the Baghdad Pact,[17] and a purge of the army and the civil service of reactionaries.

A large part of the crowd paid little attention to the speakers, but there were some among it, especially students, who could understand, partially at least, the significance of the 'meeting' and the resolutions. In a sense these could be interpreted as a challenge to Qassim himself, or at least as a means of bringing pressure to bear on him to adopt a policy closer to that of the communists.

The procession on the third day was given over to commemoration of Kamil Qazanchi, the victim of a cold-blooded murder in Mosul (alleged to have been committed personally by Colonel al-Shawwaf). It was the most thoroughly prepared of all the demonstrations, with a lavish supply of banners of various colours. Schoolchildren, elementary and secondary, university students, manual workers, government employees—all formed a longer line than the eye could encompass, perhaps covering 5 kilometres. The slogans on the banners may be represented roughly as follows:

> Shame Nasser; death to traitors; glory to you Kamil; long live our sole leader; death to traitors and plotters; death to all enemies of the people. Death to the warmongers; leave the Baghdad Pact at once; hang the traitors.

A Kurdish onlooker whom we knew told us that Qazanchi had been his teacher in a Baghdad school in 1943. He was a Chaldean Christian and not then, it seemed, a communist and was constantly telling the students that they must treat each other as brothers. Later he joined the communists, impressed with their emphasis on the equality of all peoples. The Mosul affair certainly appeared to accentuate for a time the religious differences in the area.

Only a very small proportion of the demonstrators were communists. But the slogans on the banners and the resolutions 'passed' at the 'meeting' in front of the Ministry of Defence certainly infringed on the policies of the government, which, early in January 1959, had warned against arbitrary acts. Yet after the Mosul fighting there were, as we have seen, widespread acts of violence against individuals. The smashing of the offices of two newspapers representing moderate views which were operating under official licences was perhaps the most glaring case of defiance of the government. It was a genuine case of mob action. Other cases of violence were sometimes mixed with vicious personal feuds. We knew of one liberal Arab nationalist, but opposed to Nasser's ambitions and to Egyptian domination, who was suddenly carried off to a distant prison at the instigation of colleagues who entertained a personal grudge against him and who persuaded acquaintances in the Popular Resistance Force that he, with others similarly 'arrested', was a reactionary plotter against the Revolution.

These arbitrary actions were neither desired nor sanctioned by Qassim. The attempt in Mosul to overthrow the regime brought a sharp recurrence of violence on the initiative of the Communist party and of other less-organized elements on the extreme left. In the aftermath of the Shawwaf revolt they consciously attempted to prod the regime by taking actions that went far beyond anything that it desired; members of the Popular Resistance Force continued to stop private cars to examine their interiors and question their occupants, all in flat contradiction to the orders of the Military Governor.

Indiscriminate acts in violation of the ordinary rights of citizens continued for several weeks. Abroad the radios of Cairo and Damascus thundered and fulminated. Nasser's rivalry with Qassim had temporarily brought him out of neutrality and on to the American side of the Cold War. It was an uneasy position, especially when President Eisenhower hailed Nasser as leader of the 'anti-communist' forces in the Middle East, an appellation which embarrassed Nasser in his relations with the Bandoeng countries. An American–Egyptian hue and cry against Iraq on the ground that she was 'going communist' was hardly calculated to inspire confidence in Egypt within much of the Third World.

Much was made of the monster demonstrations in Baghdad, but in fact a close scrutiny of them from the inside might well justify very different inferences from those drawn in the alarmist press abroad. The crowds were very different from those that had rushed into the streets in response to Abdul Salam Arif's broadcast effusions on 14 and 15 July 1958 at the time of the seizure of power. Those formed genuine 'mobs' in the worst sense of the term, which responded to Arif's open incitements to violence and destruction with murder and 'dragging'. They had soon been suppressed by the military, and subsequent demonstrations in the autumn were thoroughly organized and controlled. The three described above might, from some points of view, be said to resemble fêtes. On their way to Rashid Street could be seen a succession of lorries and other vehicles packed with shouting demonstrators, including a large number of young people and children, all provided with various types of colourful banners. The drivers were given free petrol and half a dinar a day to drive the vehicles around. They picked up organized groups, but also cruised the streets, finding volunteers who would jump on, and join in the singing and shouting.

The Decline of Communist Influence

The high tide reached in this period by the communists and the more extreme non-communist left soon began to recede. These groups had overestimated their strength and had underestimated the political shrewdness of Qassim. The reprisals provoked by the abortive Mosul plot and uprising were carried too far. The disturbances and the encroachments on the liberties of the moderate as well as the extreme Arab nationalists which followed al-Shawwaf's collapse soon began to turn the tide of sentiment against the extreme left-wing elements. The issue was brought to a head by a new conflict that broke out in and around the northern oil city of Kirkuk among Turkoman, Kurdish, and Arab sections of the population.

The indigenous Kurdish population of Kirkuk had been augmented over the years by a migration of large numbers of Kurds who had come from the surrounding countryside to work in the oil industry. These formed a low-paid proletariat in a city dominated socially, culturally, and economically by a minority of great Turkoman families who had been settled in the area for three or four hundred years. Many of the Kurds had joined the Kurdish Democratic party which had been organized before the Revolution in response to an increasing radicalization of the Kurds, especially of the younger people, as a result of intensifying dissatisfaction with the treatment of Kurdish interests by the Arab-dominated central government in Baghdad. The KDP was affiliated with the Iraqi Communist party.

The situation was explosive, and an explosion occurred on 14 July 1959, the first anniversary of the Revolution, when local communist groups, reinforced by groups from Baghdad, decided to purge the 'reactionary' elements of the city. The conflict was far more than one of political doctrines: it was a clash also of ethnic groups and an explosion of ancient animosities. But the communists behaved even more ruthlessly than they had done in the Mosul fighting, and a vicious massacre occurred.

This time greater attention was drawn to communist excesses than previously, particularly after the discovery of the mutilated bodies of some of the victims. By this time also the public and the authorities had been influenced by the lawlessness and arbitrary acts of the Resistance Force and their informal allies, which had created a mood conducive to a sharp reaction against those responsible for the crimes in the Kirkuk area. A turning-point had come. The plotting and scheming of the right-wing Arab nationalists had led Qassim to use left-wing elements, including the communists, against the real dangers they posed, for a time tolerating excesses on the other flank as the less dangerous to the stability of the state and the continuance of the regime. Now, however, the extreme left had exceeded a tolerable limit. At the same time the immediate dangers of former plots had been removed. Nasser had experienced a setback. The older leaders of Arab nationalism, like Rashid Ali, were outdated and had little appeal for the young. The fanatical Baathists were an underground danger, but had not gained mass support and were comparatively small in numbers.

Qassim was therefore no longer so dependent on the left wing, in its more extreme forms at least, and humanitarian instincts were particularly aroused by the outrages in the Kirkuk area, including outrages against women.

Still overestimating their strength and influence the communists in Iraq nevertheless intensified their campaign, in particular their demand to participate directly in the government. Their propaganda was designed to maintain an atmosphere of suspicion and of apprehension of further plots and conspiracies from the 'imperialists' and their domestic accomplices. After the decisive defeat of the real plots of the autumn and of March this was unfounded and untimely and drew severe public censure from Qassim. He began publicly to criticize the communists and they were quickly placed on the defensive. The Central Committee of the party engaged in a bout of self-criticism, admitting and condemning their excesses.

The communists found themselves in a difficult position. It was of little use to turn against Qassim. They were not strong enough by themselves to gain control of the state. Nor was any other party willing to associate with them. The National Democratic party, which had done so to a limited extent in the past, had been in serious conflict with the communists in several parts of the country subsequently. Within its own ranks differences of opinion had arisen over the appropriate attitude to adopt towards the Communist party. A left-wing section held that while the excesses of the communists must be criticized, nevertheless only reactionaries would gain by a total refusal of the NDP to co-operate. Kamil Chadirchi, the leader of the party, while also fundamentally at odds with the undemocratic and anti-democratic aspects of communist structure and policy, was so strong an adherent on principle of complete freedom of association and of speech that he consistently urged Qassim to establish representative parliamentary government immediately.[18] This brought him into conflict with Qassim and also with other members of his own party.

These issues were not resolved and the National Democratic party split. Muhammed Hadid headed the section of the party, later forming it as a separate party, which, while disagreeing on many matters with Qassim, held that for a time the conditions in the country were such that it was preferable to continue a 'transition period' with Qassim as a non-party head of state, rather than licence all parties freely at once, as Chadirchi desired, and open the way to the violent extremes of the Communist, the Baath, and other far right parties.

From the time of the Kirkuk affair, Qassim resumed the process of curbing the activities of the Iraqi Communist party and of left-wing extremists in general which he had begun on Army Day in January 1959. In carefully chosen stages, the policy of reducing the influence of the Communist party was carried out with thoroughness. The circulation of the party newspaper, *Ittihad al-Shaab,* was restricted in the latter part of 1960 in the southern provinces. The communist delegates and officers in the peasants' organizations and in the trade unions were removed, not by direct expulsion but during new elections of officers in which the former manipulation by communist ingenuity was replaced, with the help in some areas of local governors, by equally astute devices to win victories for non-communist competitors. Similar measures, though under different auspices, were taken to change the political complexion of the students' associations and the Lawyers' Association.

In the removal of communists from positions of leadership in these organizations, Brigadier Abdi, in co-operation with provincial governors and other local officers as well as with officers in the organizations who were opponents of the communists, played a leading role, at times using arbitrary tactics. During the turbulent earlier periods Abdi had himself suffered much from the deliberate disregard by militant communists of his public orders as Military Governor. But an important supplementary factor in the rapid decline of communist influence was the widespread resentment felt by a large part of the Iraqi people over the excesses of the communists and other elements of the extreme left who often acted with them. Consequently much co-operation and approval was forthcoming when the authorities began to remove them.

Attempted Assassination of Qassim

Qassim's moves to curb the activities of the communists in the autumn of 1959 were not strong enough to satisfy the Pan Arab and especially the Baathist groups. The latter, led by Fuad al-Rikabi, an ardent Pan Arab, who had been dropped from the

Cabinet by Qassim in February 1959, at the time of the break with Arif, had for some time been plotting against Qassim and had decided to kill him as the only way to stem the tide of communism, for which the Baath held Qassim personally responsible. When in September 1959 Qassim ordered the execution of some of the officers implicated in the Mosul uprising together with a Kurd, Said Qazzaz, who was Minister of the Interior under Nuri al-Said and had been condemned to death by the People's Court at the end of 1958, the Baath plotters decided to act. There was no doubt that the officers, particularly Brigadier al-Tabaqchali and Colonel Sirri, were participants in the plan to overthrow the government, kill Qassim, and seize power. The case of Qazzaz was very different: it was an obvious gesture to the extreme left—in the balancing tradition. The courage and outspokenness of Qazzaz drew much admiration, and his Islamic convictions much respect, even from many of those who had been strong opponents of the previous regime.

These executions and other developments convinced the Baath group that Qassim was not going to turn seriously against the communists and they decided to kill him as he drove through Rashid Street on his way to the Ministry of Defence. Such an attack seemed easy: we had ourselves been within a few metres of Qassim several times as his car passed through Rashid Street and anyone could place himself in a similar position.

The attempt failed. Qassim escaped death through confusion among his would-be murderers, but was wounded and confined to hospital for nearly two months.[19] Rikabi fled to Cairo, Abdi, continuing to act as the guardian of public order, maintained the administration in working order and the country in comparative tranquillity throughout the period of Qassim's absence. That he could do this throws light on the state of public opinion. As far as we could judge, it was only in the early stages of the Revolution that the unorganized public showed satisfaction and enthusiasm over the change that had taken place. The attempt of the groups inspired by political ideologies to maintain a high tempo of political fervour began to meet increasing apathy and distaste after a time.

Thus the stability of the period in which Qassim lay helplessly in hospital while Abdi controlled the government and maintained public order can be readily accounted for when it is realized that a public, tired of unprofitable political turbulence, welcomed a quieter political tempo which corresponded to its mood. Nor did the attempt of the extremely fanatical, very young Baathists to murder Qassim deflect him from his resolve to curb the communists, as the plotting and uprising earlier in the year had done. The youth and fanaticism of the would-be murderers led him to look on them as misguided, inexperienced victims of illusions who, by lenient treatment, could be brought to see the error of their ways, and he refused to carry out the death sentences subsequently imposed on them.[20]

During the later part of 1958 and throughout 1959 Nasser had adopted as one of his major aims of external policy the isolation of Iraq in Middle Eastern and wider international affairs.[21] In the Middle East, however, Egypt was in an unfavourable position to influence the more conservative Arab countries. Both Saudi Arabia and Jordan, although distrusting developments seemingly towards the left in Iraq, distrusted Nasser even more. Saudi Arabia was especially distrustful of the secularizing tendencies in Egyptian politics and of Nasser's close association with Russia over the Aswan Dam. The monarchical regimes in both countries were prominent targets of Cairo propaganda.

When the Shawwaf plot and the Baathist attempt on Qassim's life failed, Nasser intensified his efforts to isolate Iraq, for the challenge to his claim to Arab leadership remained, perhaps stronger than before. After all, the UAR was widely known to have given material support to, and Cairo Radio had publicly espoused, the defeated side in Iraq. But Nasser now attempted to exploit the renewed outburst of left-wing, including communist, activity which followed the Shawwaf rising by approaching Iraq's conservative neighbours, King Hussain of Jordan and King Saud of Saudi Arabia, inviting the latter to visit Cairo.

The violent attacks on Qassim by Cairo Radio and occasionally by Nasser himself, which continued during the period of his convalescence, had up to this time generally failed to draw Qassim into direct responses, though they sometimes brought sharp comments from his associates. This refusal to engage in verbal warfare with Nasser favourably impressed a large part of the public in the Arab world, especially outside Iraq and Egypt. The spectacle of public quarrels between Arab leaders was unpopular: many realized that the only beneficiaries were certain foreign circles unfriendly to the Arab countries. But in the summer of 1959 there were already signs that Qassim was modifying this attitude, and after the Baathist attempt on his life in October it was not long before he began to issue sharp statements from the hospital replying to hostile Egyptian criticism. He now took up the challenge of Nasser's attempts to isolate him.

Qassim's response to Nasser's approach to Jordan was to recall the ineffectiveness of the Egyptian army against Israel in 1947 and 1956 in the protection of Palestine and to claim that Iraq was the more reliable ally. He went further and advocated the establishment of a Palestine state in face of Nasser's aim at unification of Arab states without regard for the special circumstances of each of them. He challenged Nasser's conception of Arab nationalism, representing it as a cover for Egyptian domination.[22] Arab unity could not be achieved on a basis of Egyptian hegemony, he maintained, and he went on to substitute the conception of Arab nationalism as unified action by the Arab states which would safeguard their freedom and their independence from imperialism without encroaching on each other's independence. Turning to the United Arab Republic, he effectively exploited the growing discontents and rifts in Syria, where it was more and more realized that the union had in practice amounted to a 'take-over' of Syria by Nasser, at the expense of almost all vestiges of representative government and of Syria's traditions.

These were telling points which, in substance, were for the most part in harmony with the viewpoints of governing circles in Amman and Riyadh. Thus, while Jordan and Saudi Arabia welcomed the change of attitude which brought an end to, or at least a respite from, the attacks on them by the Cairo press and radio, they had little incentive to join Nasser in condemning Iraq for not following Nasser. However strongly King Hussain might feel towards the Baghdad regime which had been responsible for the death of his kinsman, he could not fail to see that an Iraq brought into the UAR would leave him isolated and nearly surrounded by a union of countries completely under Nasser's control. Nor did Saudi Arabia welcome Nasser in control of a bordering country. By this time disillusionment was spreading rapidly in Syria, and Baghdad's charges of Egyptian domination found sympathetic listeners. Nasser had never realized how great were the reservations where Egypt was concerned, of large numbers of Arabs in the Fertile Crescent and North Africa and how very limited were the knowledge and experience that Egyptians had of other Arab countries. The insensitivity and occasional arrogance of Egyptian administrators who were sent to Syria in considerable numbers, and who often initiated changes without an adequate understanding of Syrian conditions and Syrian history, were widely resented.

Notes

1 For a brief outline of the immediate actions of the Qassim regime and of the terms of the provisional constitution see Majid Khadduri, *Republican Iraq* (London, 1969), pp. 62–6, and Uriel Dann, *Iraq Under Qassem* (London, 1969).

2 Abdul Salam Arif was a 42-year old officer from Baghdad. He came from a poor family who had recently migrated from a tribal area in the Middle

Euphrates region. He was a mediocre student at the Military College in Baghdad and served in the army after graduation, where he met and became a friend of Abdul Karim Qassim.

3 BBC, *Summary of World Broadcasts,* Second Series, Part IV, No. 796 (1 March 1959).

4 See Khadduri, op. cit., pp. 92–8 for a description of Arif's fall. The proceedings of the trial were subsequently published in Volume V of the *Proceedings of the Special Military Court* (in Arabic), Baghdad. For a useful analysis see Simon Jargy, 'Une page d'histoire de la révolution irakienne: le procès Abd al-Salam Aref', *Orient* (1959), no. 12. See also accounts of Dann, op. cit., pp. 81 ff.

5 See Patrick Seale, *The Struggle for Syria* (London, 1965), esp. pp. 322–3.

6 Hashim Jawad, the Foreign Minister of Iraq during most of the Qassim period, informed us privately that Qassim specifically gave him a completely free hand in the selection of staff in the Foreign Ministry and the Foreign Service, with an understanding that communists would be quietly excluded from entry.

7 As we were in a position to study conditions directly, including the state of the 'street', from September 1958 through the first year of the Revolution, and from time to time in later periods, we have drawn on our own direct experiences as well as on 'documentary' sources in the following discussion of internal conditions.

8 *Proceedings of the Special Military Court,* Baghdad.

9 See above, Ch. 4.

10 Dann, op. cit., p. 132.

11 Khadduri, op. cit., p. 111.

12 Kamil Qazanchi was a Chaldean Christian born in Mosul and educated at the American University of Beirut and the Law College in Baghdad. In 1955 he was deported to Turkey as a communist by Nuri al-Said, but was arrested by the Turks and imprisoned until 1958 when he returned to Baghdad after the Revolution. He went to Mosul in March 1959 to take part in the demonstrations and was killed by Shawwaf's supporters.

13 See Khadduri, op. cit., for a brief description of the Mosul uprising. We have no reason to question his description but, as the reader will note, our interpretation differs from his in a number of respects.

14 The relations established with China are discussed in Bernard Vernier, *L'Irak d'aujourd'hui* (Paris, 1963), pp. 266–7. See also below, Chapter 10.

15 In January, for example, Qassim had attempted to curb the activities of the Popular Resistance Force and of the Students' Union, which was under extreme left-wing control.

16 After the rising, it was indeed claimed in some circles that Qassim had deliberately encouraged the Peace Partisans in order to bring the conspirators into the open. But this view has little to commend it. There was no reason to believe that the meeting would have achieved this object and the evidence is that the Partisans maintained good order and avoided provocation on the way to, during, and immediately after the demonstration. The idea that the Mosul clash was a planned incident in a bid for power by the Communist party of Iraq cannot, we think, be sustained. It represented a conflict of external as well as internal forces.

17 Qassim did not withdraw Iraq from the Baghdad Pact until December 1959.

18 The late Kingsley Martin, long-time Editor of the London weekly the *New Statesman*, after coming from an interview with Chadirchi in Baghdad which we had arranged in early 1962, remarked to us 'I have been talking with the last of the pure nineteenth-century type of radical!'. Chadirchi

was then virtually under house arrest. We made the appointment for Martin directly with Chadirchi by telephone, fearing that official channels might attempt to bar it. Later when we informed the Foreign Minister, Hashim Jawad, of the editor's visit, he immediately made him an official guest of the Foreign Office. Its protocol section at first objected to the interview with Chadirchi, but were finally persuaded that the news of any ban would find its way into the columns of the *New Statesman,* which would prejudice international opinion against Iraq. The objections of course had been due to fear of offending Qassim. Later the latter gave Kingsley Martin a long midnight interview.

19 See Khadduri, op. cit., pp. 129–30 for a description of the attack. One of those prominently involved in the plot was a young student in our classes in the College of Arts. He had been absent from the college for some time earlier in the year and we had met him accidentally at a café in a distant part of Baghdad. He expressed doubts about the prospect of an early return to the college. We did not known then, what came out later in the trials, that he was a citizen of the UAR.

20 They remained in prison until after the fall of Qassim in 1963.

21 On the external relations see particularly Marcel Colombe, *Orient arabe et le non-engagement* (Paris, 1973), Tome II, pp. 112–16, 175–82.

22 Qassim's attacks on Nasser tended to be indirectly phrased, but everyone knew what he meant. For example, in a speech in August 1960 at a ceremony to lay the foundation stone of the new East Baghdad Railway Station, Qassim spoke of 'imperialism' attempting to divide the Arab 'front', whereas he had tried to unite it. He called on the people to slam the door on 'imperialism, traitors, and greedy ones'. He noted that the army was now strong enough to smash any of these 'intruders'. His policy was not to interfere with the internal affairs of any Arab or Muslim country and he was surprised and amused when listening to some broadcasts and to hear their unholy attacks on Iraq. The references to 'imperialism', 'traitors', 'greedy ones', 'intruders', did not refer to the older imperialist powers, but were, in effect, 'code words' recognized by all to refer to Nasser and to Egypt, an Arab and Muslim country clearly making 'unholy' attacks on Iraq. See the report in *Al-Hurriyah* (Baghdad), 4 August 1960.

10 Social, Economic, and Oil Policy under Qassim

Against a disturbed and almost chaotic political background, the new regime attempted to implement the economic and social reforms which had been promised, the expectation of which had kindled much of the enthusiasm for the Revolution among the people. Changes were expected in many directions: in international economic relations, in education and housing policies, in the relationships with the oil companies, and above all in the relation between landlord and tenant in agriculture. Different groups in the country had very different expectations, but none of the politicians and few if any of the remaining civil servants had any clear conception of the real nature of the agrarian problem.

Agrarian Reform

As we have seen, the system of land tenure was politically extremely unpopular, had grave economic defects, and was often socially vicious, particularly in the south of the country. Extensive reform was required, but so intense had been the concentration of attention on the evils of the existing system that there had grown up a general conviction that any action—any reform—could only improve the situation and could not adversely affect output. The complexities of the organization of Iraqi agriculture were ignored and, apart from a clear distinction between irrigated and non-irrigated areas, the differing conditions in different parts of the country and the different needs of different crops were forgotten. The advice of foreign experts, and especially of the Food and Agriculture Organization, bordered on the irresponsible; it displayed a naive confidence in the administrative resources available to the government, a deplorable lack of understanding of the attitudes of and the skills available to the peasants, and an ill-founded faith in the possibilities of a rapid and extensive organization of co-operatives in the Iraqi environment.[1] It must be said, however, that the advice of foreign (or any other) experts had little to do with the urgency with which the revolutionary government viewed the necessity of land reform and with the speed with which it acted. The conservative elements in the old regime had been powerfully supported by the great landed shaikhs who were able much of the time to manipulate affairs in their own interests. The political power of the landlords represented a potential danger to the new government. They acted quickly to remove it.

Hence, before three months had elapsed, the government promulgated its land reform law (Law No. 30, 1958). The law was modelled on that of Egypt in spite of the fact that agriculture in the two countries had little in common. It provided for the expropriation of 75 per cent of the privately owned arable area of Iraq (over nine times the area that had been expropriated in Egypt). Except for differences in the maximum holding of irrigated and non-irrigated land, the law took no account whatsoever of the great regional differences in Iraq, the wide variety in the conditions of tenure, in the role of landlords, and in the circumstances affecting different crops. The area of agricultural land that could be owned by a single owner was reduced to 1,000 *mesharas* (250 hectares) of irrigated land and 2,000 *mesharas* of rain-fed land. Lists of landowners coming under the law were to be prepared and their land in excess of these amounts expropriated against compensation in government bonds. This land was to be redistributed to small owners to provide each recipient with not less than 30 and not more than 60 *mesharas* of irrigated land and double that for rain-fed land, payment to be spread over 20 years. Other provisions regarding the share of the landowner in the crops, wages, etc., were also included.

The continuance of agricultural activity during the 'transition period' between expropriation and the actual distribution of the land to individual farmers (which was set at three years and has not yet been completed 20 years later) was to be ensured by the landlords, who were to manage the land and supply agricultural requisites to the cultivators, as they always had. The landlord was to receive a modest management fee, but his share in the crop was to be reduced. The law provided for the establishment of co-operative societies, which recipients of land were required to join and which would function under the supervision of officials of the Ministry of Agriculture.[2]

In the most favourable of circumstances, a reasonably smooth implementation of such extensive changes in the framework of Iraqi agriculture would have been almost impossible. Dispossessed landlords, even 'good' ones, subject to continuous and vitriolic abuse, had to be persuaded to continue to manage their lands and to provide the necessary agricultural requisites and guidance to the peasants at reduced remuneration and in conditions of the utmost insecurity, as if nothing had happened; alternatively the state would have to organize the supply of seeds, fertilizers, credits, and agricultural machinery (where used), the control of water, the maintenance of pumps, the marketing of crops, the managements of rotations, and the creation of co-operatives, all without any established administrative machinery or even a minimum of trained personnel. All this had to be done in addition to the actual expropriation and redistribution of land. To carry out effectively any one of these functions on a scale adequate to prevent a fall in agricultural output would have absorbed all the relevant resources available to the government. And it was unrealistic in the extreme to expect the landlords to continue as before.

Unfortunately, an already impossible task had to be undertaken in the least favourable of circumstances. Nature combined with politics to compound disaster. The Agricultural Bank reported:

> The general agricultural situation in Iraq during the year 1958–59 was very unfavourable. In most areas agriculture was exposed to various natural disasters and pests and injurious insects. Each of these factors contributed substantially to the poor harvests in general. Unfortunately, drought was a striking feature in most of the important agricultural areas, for there was lack of rain in the Liwas (provinces) of Mosul, Erbil, Sulaimaniya and Kirkuk (which are the most important grain-producing areas), as well as in the Liwas of Baghdad, Kut, Ramadi and Nasiriya. Moreover, crops which were fated to grow and ripen in certain areas did not escape considerable damage, having been attacked by pests, such as the sunna, or devoured by swarms of locusts. Other crops were to a large extent damaged by hail. The date crop suffered some damage due to rain falling on it before it had ripened, as was the case in Kerbela Liwa, or by reason of dust storms, as happened in Nasiriya Liwa; apart from all that, the dullness of the markets and the decline of date prices in that season were also marked, with the result that the date-growers in the central Euphrates area were compelled to sell their products to date merchants before the Date Association started to buy the dates of that area.[3]

The Director General of the Bank also reported that the bank was '. . . flooded with applications from cultivators, particularly after all ways of borrowing from individuals had been blocked to them'. Loans on implements fell heavily because expropriated landlords postponed purchases, dealers stopped importing, especially when some customers did not pay their debts, and city-dwellers who used to purchase and install pumps against a share of the produce agreed with the cultivators, ceased doing so.[4]

In addition to the serious drought, which was to last for three years, and the other natural disasters, some of which, such as locusts and other pests, were not unusual, came political disturbances. These had two sources. First was the natural reaction of peasants, especially in areas where the landlords had been particularly oppressive and were genuinely hated. Peasants impatient for land and drunk with the heady wine of revolutionary rhetoric, took direct action and occupied the land they felt was now theirs without waiting for the administrative process of distribution. Second was the attempt of the communists in the central ministry and in the countryside to gain control of the agrarian reform programme and administration and establish a political base among the peasants through the promotion of peasant associations. The communist groups encouraged the peasants to occupy the land and to refuse to accept the management of existing landlords, and they promoted mob action to intimidate the landlords.

In the first six months or so, when the communist attempts to gain a leading position in the government were at their height, and their influence in the administration of land reform was strongest, some government officials, themselves communists, took the lead in setting up local peasant political committees in the rural areas and attempted to use these committees to encourage the peasants to take over the property of the landlords, including their private dwellings, and to engage in intimidation generally. Thus, the conflict between the communists and others in the central ministry created confusion in the administration of land reform, while the disorder in the rural areas intensified the problems facing the authorities. The fundamental aim of the communists was to organize the peasants and obtain their political allegiance in the struggle to gain political power in Baghdad.

In this political confusion and under adverse natural conditions, the land-reform programme was launched. Expropriation of landlords continued rapidly and haphazardly, but next to nothing was done to maintain the services previously rendered by them. Apart from the great public works programmes—dams, barrages, large irrigation projects, and settlement schemes on government land—almost all investment in agriculture had in the past been made by the landlords, or, especially in pumps, by town merchants. Many of the landlords, particularly those with medium-sized and small holdings, lived on the land and themselves supervised operations, while the large ones employed agents or foremen (*sirkals*) who were responsible for the management of the water supplies, the provision of seeds, the granting of credit, the supervision of agricultural operations generally, and the marketing of crops. The peasant sharecroppers, illiterate and used to the simplest techniques, were heavily dependent on their landlords, who were frequently their tribal chiefs. There were enormous variations in the relationships between landlord and tenant in the different parts of the country, but nowhere could the landlord be summarily removed without creating great hardship for the peasants unless arrangements were made to maintain the services he had provided.

Although the government authorities had no clear realization of the scale and complexity of the problem, they did of course recognize that the peasant farmers, on their own land, and unused to running their own affairs, would need much help and that for a number of functions, such as maintenance of canals and use of water, the supply and maintenance of machinery, and the organization of credit and marketing, a collective organization would be required. In its interim report on Iraq for the Mediterranean Development Project the FAO had put very great emphasis on the role of co-operatives in providing the services previously provided by the landlords and in the reorganizing of agriculture generally.

Unfortunately, under the conditions prevailing in Iraq there was no chance that co-operatives as proposed by the FAO and envisaged in the law could be organized to replace landlords. Iraq had little experience in forming co-operatives and lacked even the minimum personnel. The Iraqi government had been strongly influenced by the land reform law in Egypt where conditions were very different. Egypt's agricultural activities, and in particular the large estates to which the reform had been applied, were well organized and efficient. There was no problem of settling titles or boundaries; transportation and marketing systems were highly developed and supervisors were available to impose compulsory co-operatives which could maintain production with different ownership relations.[5] In Iraq even a cadastral survey had not been completed, the system for the registration of titles was inadequate, marketing was primitive, and local transportation often hopelessly defective. There were pitifully few people capable of effective farm management, organizing marketing or credit, or even of giving advice to farmers,[6] and in some areas peasants were still dependent on tribal ties. The peasants themselves did not understand the meaning and functions of co-operatives and feared the collectivization and political organization that the militant communists were attempting to promote. As elsewhere, the farmer wanted an independent holding of his own and not land controlled by a collective. There was simply no hope of an effective organization of co-operatives throughout the rural areas. It was estimated by the

FAO that some 2,000 co-operatives would be needed; by 1961, 17 had been organized, by 1963 there were 25.

There was equally little hope that the landlords, especially in the more disturbed areas, would continue as usual; the incentives were very weak, intimidation was too great, and many estates had been forcibly occupied by peasants, who often simply used them for grazing. Failure to integrate expropriation and distribution involved much waste of resources—even water already laid on for irrigation was left unused as irrigated land was expropriated but not allocated for use. In these circumstances it was inevitable that agrarian reform should immediately be followed by a heavy fall in the output of the main crops and also a sharp fall in the area planted.

The agriculture statistics of Iraq are notoriously poor. They have frequently been revised and are probably better now than earlier (although reports persist that a poor performance is often concealed for political reasons). It is almost true to say that the only reason for citing figures is often that 'any statistic is better than no statistic'—a proposition of doubtful validity. Khair al-Din Haseeb, in his careful study of Iraqi national income, found it necessary to discard entirely the results of the 1952–53 agricultural census, so unreliable did he find the methods of collecting data as well as the data.[7] He did use the 1958–59 census because procedures for collection were much better and the data were clearly an improvement over those of the Ministry of Agriculture. In this census the reported area cultivated under the three major winter crops—wheat, barley, and rice—was some 36 per cent higher than the estimates of the ministry, though output figures were only 3 per cent higher. After making the best adjustments he could, Haseeb presented figures for the cultivated area and the output of field crops for the years 1953–61. Table I reproduces these for 1958–61.

Table I Area and Output of Field Crops, 1958–1961

Crop	*Cultivated Area* (000 *donums*)				*Output* (000 *tons*)			
	1958	1959	1960	1961	1958	1959	1960	1961
Winter	14,373	13,773	12,385	12,798	1,675	1,278	1,367	1,760
Summer	1,360	939	1,083	977	331	235	275	186
Total	15,733	14,712	13,468	13,775	2,006	1,513	1,642	1,946

Source: K. Haseeb, *The National Income of Iraq, 1953–61,* Tables 20 and 21, pp. 42, 43. 1 donum = .25 ha.

Regardless of disruption and uncertainty, however, the peasants had to do their best to plant and harvest, for their survival depended on it. Some grain land, and even irrigated land, was used for grazing and food crops were planted on cotton land, for the cultivation of cotton was often beyond the technical means of the unguided peasant. The demand from the Agricultural Bank for credit was very heavy, and its capital was increased in an attempt to meet the need. The total number of loans rose rapidly, especially very small loans (in 1959–60 loans of between 10 and 500 dinars reached 95 per cent of the total number). Special arrangements were made to advance both cash and seed. The farmers tended to treat these loans as grants and the Bank had great trouble in collecting its debts. This increased the Bank's financial difficulties and led to wasteful use of funds by the farmers. In 1961 the farmers were exempted from paying for the land distributed to them as originally envisaged in the land reform law, and this, together with the lack of control over the use of loans, according to one FAO observer, corrupted the farmers and led to neglect and irresponsible use of land.

Land was expropriated rapidly, but distribution was extremely slow. Around 1.5 million hectares had been sequestrated up to 1963, but less than 363,000 hectares had been distributed to slightly under 29,000 beneficiaries. Difficulties arose over compensation arrangements for buildings, pumps, trees, and other investment on the land (as many as twenty people, for example, might have an interest in a single tree[8]). The process by which the former landowners selected the lands they wished to keep, the frequent lack of documentary evidence to title, the expropriation of land not yet even settled, the fact that past land sales were not always properly registered, all meant that far more surveyors, engineers, and experienced legal officers were required than were available. Even transport was inadequate to enable officials in the rural areas to do their jobs.

In consequence, most of the land so quickly expropriated still remained in 1976 under the direct administration of the Ministry of Agrarian Reform and farmers had to cultivate it under agreement with the ministry. Because the ministry was in no position to give the direction previously given by the landlord, or to provide the services given by the landlords or their agents, private arrangements were often made between the farmers and their former landlords. This gave rise to charges, especially from the reform authorities in Baghdad, that the 'old regime' was reappearing. In fact, no one really knew what was going on in the countryside. The need of the peasants, and of the smaller and medium-sized landlords, to maintain production as far as possible, led to all sorts of special arrangements and improvisations. The somewhat romantic notion dear to the 'intellectuals' and administrators that a new class of small farmer with managerial responsibilities, strong incentives to improve productivity, and extensive help from efficient co-operatives would quickly rise from the ruins of the old system was soon seen to be hopelessly impracticable in the conditions of Iraqi agriculture. The old system was destroyed and very little could be done to build a new one.

The confusion in the ministry in Baghdad grew steadily worse as the communists struggled to impose their views. The communists wanted in effect to collectivize agriculture through the establishment of compulsory co-operatives linked with the political Peasant Union which they were attempting to create and which was designed to control the whole structure. They pressed to lower the amount of land the landlord could retain to 400 donums in rain-fed areas and its equivalent in productivity in other areas. The communists opposed the provision of the law that the landlords should continue to manage the land until it was distributed and to receive management fees. They held that the land should be turned over to the Peasant Union who could manage it better.[9]

The communists also encouraged the peasants to take direct action and to withhold repayment of their loans. During the first half of 1959 communist influence in the ministry was gradually eliminated, but much damage had been done to the reform programme, partly through the general confusion engendered and partly because of the increased suspicion on the part of the peasants of co-operative societies in general.

Iraqi agriculture had not fully recovered from the disastrous effects of the agrarian disruption before a new and even more drastic 'reform' was imposed in 1970.[10] In the early 1970s the area cultivated was little greater on average than it had been in the late 1950s and fluctuations in output and yields were as great as ever, even in the irrigated areas. The country had become a net importer of food grains. To be sure, the motivation for the agrarian reform was more political and social than economic in that the paramount considerations were the elimination of the political power of landlords and the removal of the oppression of the peasants, notably in the south, for Qassim was genuinely concerned to help the ordinary people of the country. Improvement of productivity and the protection of the land from abuse were almost neglected considerations. But without at least the maintenance of production, let alone increases in productivity, improvement in the standard of living of the majority of the farmers was not possible. Migration to the cities continued at a rapid rate.

The agrarian reform, in eliminating the control of the landlords over the peasants, removed an important barrier to migration. But since the cultivators had been promised land and government assistance they

> ... welcomed the new policy and waited for the promises to come true. In the meantime they had to resist blackmail by the landlords, the bureaucracy in the government offices handling the application of the new law and the uncertainty of the future. The political instability, the delay in the application of the new law and the disturbed social order in the rural areas made the cultivators sceptical about the future and the migration waves started again, but this time more freely for the risks the migrants used to face before did not exist any more, and furthermore the promises given by the government to the residents of the shanty towns in the outskirts of the cities [to improve conditions for them] were equally appealing to the potential migrants in the rural areas.[11]

Thus, Baghdad received an estimated 210,000 people in the eight years 1957–65, or 13,000 more than in the previous decade, and the drain from the southern *liwas* continued with Kut, Diwaniya, and Basra taking the place of Amara and Nasiriya as the chief losers.[12]

Welfare and Standards of Living

A number of surveys carried out in 1961 and 1962 indicated that the standard of living of the people, particularly around Baghdad, continued to improve slowly. A team from the Institute of Nutrition in Baghdad made a number of useful dietary surveys in areas around the city in 1961 and 1962. One study was of workers in the brick industry, which employed about 20 per cent of those working in large industries in the area. Most of the workers were migrants from the southern *liwas* and received wages averaging 429 fils a day, the unskilled receiving 300 fils (1,000 fils = £1). Pure drinking-water was not available and at certain seasons of the year the river water was so bitter that the workers bought water for drinking at 10 fils for a 4-gallon tin from passing pedlars, but the food intake was reasonably adequate although calcium, vitamins A, B1, and C were low. Consumption of animal protein was below the average in Baghdad, but the immigrants from the southern marshlands who 'were accustomed to eating fish frequently' had more protein in their diets.[13] (This is an illustration of the fact that poor diets are often more the result of taste and habit than of inability to obtain adequate food, for river fish was available and comparatively cheap.)

In another survey in rural areas around Baghdad, the team from the Institute found that in apparently very poor areas where water was collected by women in tins carried on their heads from streams, firewood, similarly carried, was cut from kilometres around, food was prepared in the open near the simple reed and mud huts and with few bits of cooking equipment, nevertheless diets were adequate. The families ate three meals a day: tea, bread, milk or yoghourt for breakfast; bread, dates, leban, vegetables and raw fruits, onions, cucumbers, tomatoes, watermelons in season at noon; and in the evening bread, *marga* (a tomato paste soup with onions and fat), tea and sugar, sometimes rice but seldom meat. There was, however, some anaemia, which may have been due to blood loss resulting from parasitic infestation of the intestinal tract.[14]

A 1962 Household Budget Inquiry in the city of Baghdad and its environs reported a considerably higher average monthly expenditure per household both for the families living in 'houses' as well as those living in *sarifa* areas. The percentage of income going on food was somewhat lower than in the survey of 1954 (usually taken as an indication of rising standards of living) and the proportion of food expenditures going on meat and fish rose at the expense of cereals. The two surveys are difficult to compare because of differences in the way they were carried out and the results presented, but the impression of a substantial improvement since 1954 is inescapable.

The new government's concern for the welfare of the working classes and the poorer sections of the population was reflected in measures affecting education, health, conditions of work, and particularly housing. In all these directions, however, the authorities soon found that even with the best of intentions social policies hastily conceived and incautiously implemented raised at least as many, if not more, problems than they solved and sometimes created situations worse than those they were designed to ameliorate, at least in the short run.

Concern with education and the students was immediate and a very rapid expansion of educational facilities was effected. Between 1957–58 and 1962–63 the number of students at all levels nearly tripled, although the increase in the number of teachers lagged behind. Even in universities the number of students increased nearly three times, but the number of teachers less than doubled. The budget of the Ministry of Education was increased in similar proportions and school-building boomed. Such an expansion inevitably brought with it a substantial fall in standards, especially since it was announced as a general policy that all candidates would be admitted to all schools including the university—the so-called 'open door' policy.[15] This was particularly serious in the colleges as admission became easier. The University of Baghdad was never considered one of the best universities in the Arab world, but in a number of fields its international reputation, the standing of its staff, and the quality of its better graduates were good. Hasty expansion and the fall in academic standards soon much reduced any reputation the university had acquired abroad—at least in the social sciences.

The nationalist attitudes accompanying the Revolution led to the elimination of teaching in any foreign language and to a sharp fall in the mastery of foreign languages by the students. In some fields, where little of the important literature existed in Arabic and where good students were expected to acquire higher qualifications abroad, the narrow training at the undergraduate level imposed by short-sighted policies seriously handicapped them in the acquisition of higher degrees, thus raising costs and reducing their potential contribution to their country.

As in other fields, education also suffered from the political confusion and conflicts in the early years of the Qassim regime which were discussed in the last chapter. Students in both the secondary schools and the university were encouraged to be active politically and a substantial minority gave more attention to politics than to their studies. Communist groups made the same attempts to gain influence in teachers' and students' organizations in the educational system, including the university, as elsewhere and with similar early successes. Many were the complaints in the press of discrimination against 'nationalists' and in favour of communists in appointments and missions abroad. As elsewhere, too, there was a sharp change in the autumn of 1960.

The old regime had attempted to keep students and the schools and colleges out of politics through the exercise of considerable censorship, at times dismissing teachers and students who had become engaged in 'left-wing' political activity. In the university radical political or economic doctrines were not included in the courses of study, the result of which was illustrated by one of our students whom we met in the college grounds after the Revolution, prominently carrying a large volume of Marx's *Capital* in English. He was proud to carry it, but when we asked him if he understood it, his face fell, and he confessed he could not. We offered to help by recommending a simplified interpretation! The newly-found freedom was clearly intoxicating to many students, but the active involvement of students and staff in politics led to much conflict in the colleges, including victimization of both staff and students who were not considered sufficiently 'left-wing'. Partly as a result of the intense political divisions in the colleges, partly because of the less selective admissions policy which reduced the average quality of new entrants, and partly because of the policy of passing students without examinations (which was not long continued), standards of instruction fell markedly. University education received a setback from which it has not yet recovered, although the role of political indoctrination was not formally given the dominant position that it has attained since.

Health facilities and other social services were also expanded rapidly as increasing amounts of funds were allocated to them. New hospitals were built and the number of beds increased some 55 per cent between 1958 and 1963. Great efforts were made to increase the number of doctors and nurses, although the rate of expansion, especially for doctors, was necessarily slow given the period of training required.

New labour laws were passed designed to raise wages, reduce hours of work, increase accident and unemployment compensation, encourage trade unions, and in general improve working conditions. Although the government had been empowered to fix minimum wages since 1936, it did not attempt to do so until 1953 and enforcement was minimal. In 1958 provision was made for wage-fixing boards for different industries, including agriculture (as provided in the agrarian reform law). It is doubtful that this accomplished much for the mass of workers. Progress was slow and enforcement was probably not better than earlier except in government and in the modern organized sectors of industry. There was very little collective bargaining in Iraq and there was often political intervention in the settlement of disputes. In any case, wage-rates were often much above the minimum set by law, especially for skilled workers. As was to be expected, fringe benefits such as pensions and annual and sick leave were generally much better in the public than in the private sector.

The most important and enduring of Qassim's social policies, however, lay in the field of low-income housing. Not only were workers provided with land and cheap loans to enable them to build their own houses, but extensive public housing projects were undertaken in many parts of the country, and particularly in Baghdad, to rehouse the *sarifa* dwellers. The new housing projects, spreading in various parts of the city, and notably around the new Army Canal to the west, made a spectacular and permanent change in the environment. The attachment to Qassim of the old *sarifa* dwellers thus rehoused in modern buildings approached idolization.[16] But, as usual, there was an unexpected adverse side-effect: the good fortune of the old migrants attracted new ones who proceeded to build new *sarifa* camps. Added to the pressures to migrate from the rural areas was this new attraction to come to Baghdad. An expensive programme of public works in Baghdad was also initiated: main streets were widened and modernized, imposing public buildings and monuments were erected, and elaborate plans for new buildings for the university were made.

Industry and Planning

Among the more prominent criticisms of the economic policy of the old regime had been its alleged failure vigorously to promote the rapid industrialization of the country and a tendency to devote too great a proportion of resources to infrastructure and agriculture. There were also those among the younger economists and engineers who wanted to see a more comprehensive and controlled planning of the economic development of the country. The idea that economic progress generally, and the economic development of underdeveloped countries in particular, required not only effective government intervention, but comprehensive and integrated planning as well, spread rapidly after the Second World War. At the same time disillusion was also spreading with relatively liberal *laissez-faire* policies, both because they did not produce the desired results with the hoped-for speed and because they seemed to permit the rich to gain a disproportionate share of the fruits of increased output.

Moreover, the development of national income statistics and of other statistical measures of economic performance and structure (regardless of their quality), together with the growing body of macro-economic and 'development' theory (which is concerned with the analysis of the factors affecting the level of activity in the economy as a whole and of the process of economic development in poor countries) encouraged economists to believe that the information and analytical knowledge were finally at hand which would permit the state effectively to plan economic development. The younger politicians and civil servants, with little knowledge of the extraordinary complexity of men and the affairs of men, were not difficult to convince, especially since the 'centrally planned' socialist economies of the world seemed to be reasonably successful without the guidance of market principles and the trappings of 'capitalist democracy'. Also, and perhaps of more weight in the Iraq of the time, a National Planning Committee had been set up in Egypt after the 1952 revolution to work out a comprehensive economic plan for social and economic development, and a National Planning Act had been promulgated in 1957.[17]

It was not surprising, therefore, that among the first acts of the new revolutionary government was the disbanding of the Development Board and its replacement with a Planning Board and a Ministry of Planning (Law 74, 1959). The Board was chaired by the

Prime Minister and composed of other ministers concerned with economic and financial affairs. At the same time a Ministry of Industry was created to undertake activities concerned with the industrialization of the country and to supervise both public and private industrial affairs. While the Planning Board, of which the Ministry of Planning was to be the technical secretariat, was charged with the task of formulating plans, the ministries were to execute them. Thus the concentration in a single body of both formulation and implementation of plans, which had characterized the old Development Board and was the subject of much criticism, was eliminated. But the reorganization was not successful and the operations of the new agencies were surrounded by increasingly serious administrative confusion. Members of the Planning Board were made responsible for much purely administrative detail and decentralization and delegation were very difficult; the civil servants were poorly paid and often had to supplement their salaries in other ways 'including dishonesty', promotion was not based on merit, turnover was high, and it behoved a senior civil servant to cultivate the more successful politicians. Clerical staff was poorly trained and even the most routine tasks of filing and record-keeping were often inadequately performed.[18]

Ferhang Jalal sums up the state of affairs: 'After the reorganization of the government's development administration in 1959, the industrial planning and implementation agencies became so numerous that one can hardly think of any aspect of industrial development which lacked a specific department to deal with it' except—he notes—the improvement of administration itself, which seemed to have been nobody's business.[19] But, as has often been pointed out and as frequently ignored, if a country had the administrative and technological capacity efficiently to organize a rapid development and expansion of its economic activities, it would not be an underdeveloped country.

The administration quickly promulgated a 'Provisional Economic Plan' for the period 1959-60–1962-63 which, admittedly, had to be improvised very rapidly. It had the declared aim of changing radically the direction of the previous regime.[20] Although the plan declared that oil revenues had been wasted by the previous regime and had not been spent in the interest of the Iraqi people, the percentage of oil revenues to be devoted to the development programme was reduced from 70 per cent to 50 per cent.[21] The significant change in the pattern of expenditure envisaged under the provisional plan was a reduction in the proportion of expenditure allocated to agriculture from the 39 per cent on average under the Development Board investment programme to 12 per cent, and an increase from the 9 per cent previously allocated for building and housing to 49 per cent.

In addition to the industrial projects covered by the plan itself were the projects to be included under a 1959 loan agreement with the Soviet Union. With two exceptions (an electric-bulb factory and an electrical equipment plant) all of the projects had been included in previous studies and plans.[22]

The provisional plan was soon dropped and superseded by a 'Detailed Economic Plan' for the period 1961-62–1965-66. This plan was better balanced in that it increased the allocations to agriculture and reduced those to building and housing. It continued to give first place to industry, but again included nothing new to speak of. In other words, the new regime continued the industrial programme of the older one and with a smaller proportion of oil revenues devoted to development. The 'plans' were primarily a collection of investment projects. The Prime Minister and other politicians opened numerous new projects with great ceremony, claiming credit for the 'Revolution'; in the nature of the case the credit should have been shared with the past regime—but revolutions prefer to ignore the continuity of history.

The value of gross industrial output as estimated by Haseeb at constant prices (excluding oil-refining) rose at an average annual rate of 17 per cent between 1958 and 1961 as the fruits of past investment bore fruit and new investment was undertaken.[23] This is a respectable record, but was not much more than the 15 per cent increase between 1953 and 1958. To be sure, planned targets were not reached, the funds allocated were, for a number of reasons, not fully spent, and inefficiencies were very great. Nevertheless, capital investment in the public sector nearly doubled between 1957 and 1960, reaching ID 47 million; that of the major privately owned industries—excluding the very small-scale operations for which no data are available—rose only 21 per cent, to ID 23 million. Altogether industry contributed something in the region of 10 per cent to Iraq's national income by 1963.

International Economic Relations: Trade and Foreign Exchange Policies

Very quickly the new government initiated far-reaching measures to change the direction of Iraq's international trade, to protect the home market for Iraqi industry, to reserve the conduct of commercial operations for Iraqi agencies, and to bring about the 'liberation of Iraqi money from the restrictions imposed by its subservience to sterling'.[24] As we have seen, Nuri al-Said's identification of Iraq's political interests with those of Britain and the United States and his antipathy towards and fear of communism had prevented the establishment of political and economic relations with the Soviet Union and other communist countries. Such a restriction on trading relationships had been widely criticized in Iraq, together with the restraints imposed on the country, especially in the few years following the end of the war, by its inclusion in the sterling area. Hence that steps to remedy the one-sided nature of Iraq's international relationships would be taken was widely expected.

Within the first year of the Revolution, trade and economic agreements were signed with eleven communist countries: Yugoslavia, Russia, the German Democratic Republic, Czechoslovakia, Romania, Poland, Hungary, North Korea, North Vietnam, Bulgaria, and Albania; and talks were opened with China, with whom an agreement was signed in 1960. In subsequent years, the drive to expand exports and to diversify the direction of Iraq's trade through trade agreements continued, and a number of special agreements were made with Arab countries and most other countries in Asia, Africa, and Europe.

Many of the agreements involved the 'principle of proportional trade exchange' according to which the partner country agreed to import from Iraq goods of a value equal to a specified percentage (commonly 25, 30, or 50 per cent) of the value of its exports to Iraq. Some of the agreements specified the value of Iraqi goods that were to be purchased, which often related to quantities or values of dates, the chief Iraqi export after oil.[25] Provisions for the exchange of experts, technical information, and students were often included and sometimes specific commitments to help in Iraq's development programme. An extensive economic aid agreement was signed with the Soviet Union in March 1959, followed in 1960 by an economic and technical agreement which provided *inter alia* for the building of a broad-gauge railway between Baghdad and Basra.[26]

As a result of these policies, Iraq's non-oil exports to the socialist countries rose from nothing in 1957 to over a quarter of the total in 1963. The Soviet Union became the second largest importer of Iraqi goods (excluding oil) after Lebanon (whose trade was largely entrepôt trade in any case). Exports to the United Kingdom and the EEC fell drastically. However, if oil is included in the export figures, then Europe and the United Kingdom regain their predominant position, over half of total exports still going to EEC countries in 1963. Although imports from the socialist countries rose from nothing to a high of 21 per cent of the total in 1963, the United Kingdom, the United States, and Europe continued to be by far the most important suppliers to the Iraqi market, though with a somewhat diminished share.[27] In general, however, the drive to diversify Iraq's international trade (apart from oil, the exports of which were in the hands of the oil companies and not the government) succeeded in establishing extensive and continuing economic relationships with the socialist countries, even if it did not significantly displace Europe and the United States as the chief source of imports.

The other important facet of Iraq's trade policy under Qassim was the attempt to protect the home market by prohibiting the import of goods that could be produced at home and also to reduce the import of luxuries and semi-luxuries. Import licensing was at first rather stringently introduced; some items that competed with local industry were prohibited entirely, others were admitted subject to quotas, but some were admitted freely. The restrictions proved to be too severe, creating shortages and rising prices of some essential commodities. Consequently in 1960 the policy was 're-studied' and the restrictions relaxed. But licensing of imports was reimposed in 1961 when the dispute with the IPC and the fall in oil revenues put pressure on exchange reserves. However, the actual value of goods imported fell considerably short of the total value of licences granted and it is not clear what effect the licensing programme actually had.

Laws were also passed to restrict the handling of foreign trade to Iraqi agencies; foreign agencies (commercial agencies, commission agencies, transport agencies, distributors, and commercial representatives) were required to register as Iraqi companies and had to arrange for 50 per cent of their capital to be owned by Iraqi nationals. With the rise of government expenditures, and therefore of imports, as oil revenues rose, increasing numbers of agencies of foreign firms supplying the Iraqi market were established. Even before the Revolution there had been demands that such agencies in the hands of foreigners caused an unnecessary outflow of 'national wealth' and should be placed in the hands of Iraqis. A bill had even been introduced into the Chamber of Deputies early in 1958 to ensure this.[28]

At the end of June 1959 Iraq formally left the sterling area. After 1952, as oil revenues rose, Iraq had been building up her own dollar balances in agreement with the United Kingdom. With the growing strength of her currency, her expanding exports of oil, and the increasing diversification of her trading partners, continued membership of the sterling area served little useful purpose and certainly did not bring benefits sufficient to offset the nationalist resentment of a compulsory and automatic link between the value of sterling and the value of the dinar.[29] In practice, however, the withdrawal made little difference. The government diversified its foreign-exchange holdings and, in particular, increased the gold component. But since the sterling area continued to account for around one-third of Iraq's imports and one-fifth of her exports (including oil), the departure from the sterling area was not of much significance so far as trade was concerned. It can be argued that the country gained greater control over its internal money supply, but, again, this seems not to have had much practical significance since the government did not use monetary policy as an important means of economic control. The move was, therefore, primarily a political symbol of the country's newly won economic independence from the power with which the previous regime had maintained such close economic and political links. In any case the break with sterling would have come about within a few years as a natural corollary of the development of the financial position of a major oil-exporting country.

International Economic Relations: Oil Policy

Before the Revolution, as we have seen, relations between the government and the Iraq Petroleum Company, though occasionally strained, were reasonably amicable in spite of the fact that the government was always under considerable pressure from various sections of the public and from opposition politicians to take a more aggressive attitude towards the company. The critics included powerful and moderate members of the Chamber of Deputies, such as Muhammed Hadid, vice president of the National Democratic party, who had long advocated modifications in the concession agreement. (Hadid was later Qassim's Minister of Finance and chief architect of his oil policy.) Because of such criticism Nadim al-Pachachi, Minister of National Economy from 1954 to December 1957, felt it necessary to publish an account, which included documents and exchanges of letters between the government and the company, of the benefits and concessions obtained by Iraq from the company before the Revolution during his time in office.[30] Some of the issues in dispute were important and it is clear that the government had doggedly pressed its point of view. Nevertheless, at no time did the bargaining create any serious threat to the company's position in the country.

Although foreign 'imperialism' in the shape of the IPC was second only to 'feudalism' as a rallying cry in popular demonstrations, the Qassim government was cautious and loath to take any action that would risk a diminution of its revenues. The fate of Mossadeq in Iran was still remembered; the 'power' of the oil company was still feared; and the government needed money. Qassim had no intention of attempting to nationalize it or, in the beginning, of antagonizing it to the extent of impairing production. On the contrary, his first public statement on oil assured the company that existing agreements would be honoured and obligations respected.[31] As the government's need for revenues grew, demands, which had been made by earlier governments that the oil company should increase output, were intensified. The company readily agreed, pointing out that it had already laid the groundwork through exploration and investment for substantial increases. Output from the Kirkuk field alone rose from under 12 million tons in 1957 to over 27 million tons in 1959, an increase which could not have been accomplished without a considerable amount of previous investment over a long period. And at the beginning of 1959 the company announced investment plans totalling £100 million to raise production capacity from the existing 34 million tons to 57 million by the early 1960s and to 70 million tons in 1962.

Negotiations with the new regime opened in the spring of 1959. The company representatives were encouraged by the apparently pacific atmosphere. After an adjournment, talks continued in the autumn, only to be interrupted by the attempted assassination of Qassim in October 1959. When meetings were resumed in the autumn of 1960, the government attitude had clearly hardened and Qassim, who had taken personal charge of the negotiations, behaved with a bitterness and belligerence not previously displayed. Some have explained this by the allegation that he suspected the oil companies of being involved in the attempt on his life.[32] Be that as it may, however, two other events that had occurred between the autumn of 1959 and the resumption of negotiations a year later go far to explain the change in Iraqi attitudes.

The first related to the companies' reaction to an increase imposed by the government in port dues at Basra. The Iraqi port authority wanted to raise additional funds to finance improvements of the harbour and a special investigation had been made of the dues charged by neighbouring countries in Gulf ports. It was found that Iraqi dues were exceptionally low, and in July 1960 a very large increase from 23.4 fils a ton to 280 fils (1,000 fils = 1 dinar) was announced. The Basra affiliate of the IPC group (the BPC) argued that such a large increase made Iraqi oil non-competitive with other oil from the Gulf and immediately announced that output would be reduced to 8 million tons a year (the minimum required under the concession agreement)—a reduction of over 4 million tons. The Iraqis were incensed and considered the reduction in exports to be not only an unacceptable attempt on the part of the company to bring pressure on the government, but also an interference with the sovereign right of the government to impose taxes (a subject on which the Iraqis had always been particularly sensitive). In the face of veiled threats to take 'measures' from Qassim and protests from the government, the company agreed to raise production again and the question of port dues was placed on the agenda of the negotiations. Iraqi resentment remained.

The second act of the international companies that upset the Iraqis, along with all other producers in the Middle East, was the reduction of posted prices in August 1960 following an earlier reduction in February 1959. As already explained, posted prices were the prices used by the companies to calculate profits to be shared with the governments of the producing countries. Posted prices thus determined the revenues of the governments on the one hand, and the tax payments of the companies on the other. They were not necessarily the prices at which crude oil was actually sold in international markets, nor did they necessarily reflect the imputed value of crude to the integrated companies which produced refined products from their own crude oil.

As the effects of the Iranian nationalization of 1951 and the 1956 Suez crisis receded, the rapidly increasing output of crude oil in the Middle East began to outstrip the increase in demand, and competition among international sellers began to depress prices both of oil products and crude oil. A decline in the prices actually realized from sales of oil and products in international markets reduced the unit receipts of the international companies, but the proportion of these receipts taken in taxes by the oil-exporting countries naturally rose so long as the posted prices which determined their taxes remained unchanged. For this reason the companies, led by Esso, unilaterally announced a reduction in Middle East posted prices in August 1960. Although this action was not related to the Iraqi negotiations, it reinforced the Iraqi government's determination to increase its share of the oil revenues, and also led Iraq to take the initiative in calling the conference of oil-producers for which Venezuela had long pressed and which resulted in the formation of the Organization of Petroleum Exporting Countries (OPEC) in September 1960.

These two events—the attempt to reduce output because of the increased port dues and the unilateral reduction of posted prices—no matter how justified they may have seemed to the companies in the light of market conditions, indicated an unbelievable insensitivity, and lack of understanding, or simply plain ignorance, of Iraqi circumstances on the part of the major oil companies. One is tempted to give credence to the charge subsequently made that, in the face of an emerging oil surplus on world markets, the big companies had little intention of increasing Iraqi output or revenues any more than could be helped and indeed would actually have welcomed a reduction in output. They had to respect their obligations to the government and would have had to expand production as promised, but they would have faced difficulties, as H. W. Page of EXXON testified in the United States Senate hearings:

> . . . suppose we hadn't had the trouble in Iraq and we had to dispose of that crude oil too . . . I admit we would have been in one tough problem, and we would have had to lower our liftings from the consortium [in Iran] down to the minimum that we could possibly take there and meet the agreement . . . we were taking an equal amount, though, from Saudi Arabia, we would have had to cut back on both of those and we would have had to slow down on our development of Libya, which nobody wanted to do, but this was discussed at a time when people came to me and said, 'Can you swallow this amount of oil?' and 'Of course, with Iraq down', the answer was, 'Yes, I am going to have a lot of problems and some tough problems, but I will undertake to do it.' . . . But if Iraq had come on, it would have been that much harder but we would have done it because we weren't going to lose any concessions because of this.[33]

This then was the immediate context of the resumption of negotiations between the oil companies and the Iraqi government, led by Qassim, in August 1960. In addition to the issues already under negotiation—the treatment of dead rents and exploration and drilling expenditures, the discounts on sales, the currency in which revenues were paid, a unilateral reduction of posted prices by the companies, and the position of the Iraqi directors of the IPC—the government insisted on the resolution of long-festering and fundamental grievances; it more than once extended its earlier demands in the process of negotiation. The Iraqis insisted not only that a large part of the unexploited concession territory should be given back, but that the government should itself choose the areas to be relinquished; they asked for more government participation in the investment decisions of the IPC; they demanded 20 per cent of the ownership of the company as well as an increase in the percentage of profit accruing to the government; and they extended their claims relating to natural gas to the demand that the company either pay for the surplus gas then being flared—burnt off—in the oilfields or else give it to the government with the right to export it. They also proposed that the company should give priority in the shipment of oil to the new Iraqi tanker fleet then in prospect.

The companies had reached the point at which they were willing to give way on all minor issues and to offer limited compromises on some of the major ones, but they were still unwilling to concede fundamental changes in the concession arrangements, especially those changes which would certainly give rise to similar demands from other oil-exporting countries. Already part of the Iraqi case regarding profit-sharing and relinquishment rested on the fact that elsewhere in the Middle East the 'fifty-fifty' principle had been breached and favourable provisions for the relinquishment of unexploited territory agreed to. The companies pointed out, however, that they had agreed to reconsider Iraqi profit-sharing arrangements only if any of the neighbouring countries received higher revenues per ton of oil. No oil had as yet been produced under the new agreements in Iran, Kuwait, or Saudi Arabia and the companies argued that in view of the higher cost to be expected in some of them, it was unlikely that government revenues would be higher than in the older concessions. Hence, the conditions which would have permitted Iraq to ask for a greater share of IPC profits had not arisen and the companies could not accept the Iraqi request. 'Fifty-fifty' was still staunchly defended by the major companies, who expressed grave doubts that the new ventures offering a higher share to the governments elsewhere would be commercially successful.

Nor could the companies see their way to granting the demand for 20 per cent of the equity of the IPC, quite apart from the fact that the government had offered to pay no more than book value. Similarly, on the question of relinquishment, the companies were prepared to compromise but would not agree that the government should choose the areas to be given up. This would not only have set a precedent dangerous for them but could well have left the companies entirely at the mercy of the government. Posted prices, the IPC negotiators insisted, were outside the control of the IPC as an operating company, but were determined by the parent companies who were the sellers of oil. It was true that posted prices in Iraq were determined by the parents and could not be set independently of those prevailing elsewhere in the Middle East and therefore could not be controlled by the national company. But this argument from the IPC negotiators was disingenuous to say the least since they were acting on behalf of the parent companies with whom they had continually to consult. Nevertheless, the issue did raise considerations affecting the position of the international oil companies throughout the Middle East. It was soon to be the subject of OPEC's first and most successful major action.

The negotiations broke down completely in October 1961, both sides having reached the limit of compromises they were prepared to make. In addition to an immediate relinquishment of 75 per cent of their concession, the companies had offered to relinquish an additional 15 per cent after seven years. Although they continued to reject Iraq's demand for equity participation outright, relying on the terms of the concession agreement and pointing out that no shares had ever been issued to the public, they did make an effort to appease Iraq in this respect by offering to set up a new company, in which the government would have a share, to exploit the 15 per cent of the territory they were prepared to relinquish after 15 years. Not surprisingly this late offer of partnership in the least desirable of the relinquished areas (it could be presumed that the companies, who insisted on choosing the areas, would not give up the most desirable areas first) did not appeal to Qassim and the proposal was rejected.

On natural gas, the companies suggested that either the IPC or the governments should be entitled to take the surplus, depending on which first found markets for it, including export markets, but they insisted on the inequity of having to pay for gas being flared in view of the technical impossibility of avoiding flaring in the conditions at the time.[34]

Qassim's final offer included a willingness to modify his demand for 20 per cent participation on condition that the companies relinquished 90 per cent of the concession area immediately and accept government participation in the remaining 10 per cent with new principles for the sharing of profit. The IPC negotiators could not agree to this 'sudden proposal' and the final meeting on 11 October 1961, after three years of intermittent negotiations, broke up with the announcement by Qassim that legislation had been prepared to take over all areas other than those containing existing wells, which the companies could continue to operate.

In December, the government enacted their famous (or notorious) Law 80, which expropriated the IPC's rights to just over 99.5 per cent of their original area without compensation, and thus introduced over a decade of acrimonious controversy between the international companies and the government. The companies protested and demanded arbitration as provided for in their agreement, a demand which the government ignored. The law did leave the door open, however, for the future restoration of some territories to the companies if the government saw fit to do so. In passing Law 80 the government went as far as it dared; it could not risk the complete nationalization of the operating companies since it relied on them for markets, and the oil revenues were of vital importance for the country's economy.[35]

The increasing internal and external difficulties facing Qassim as time wore on undoubtedly influenced his attitude during the oil negotiations. After the attempted assassination in October 1960, his statements became increasingly aggressive and he displayed a growing tendency to make public pronouncements designed to arouse the Iraqi people against the companies and also to use the press for the same purpose. At the same time, the Iraqis were clearly becoming increasingly impatient with what they saw as the delaying tactics of the companies, whose negotiators would come for a short time and then request an adjournment of the talks while they went home for further instructions. The government representatives frequently expressed their inability to understand why the companies did not send negotiators of sufficient authority to make decisions on the government proposals without having to return home for instructions.

In the spring of 1961, when the negotiations, adjourned the previous December to permit the IPC negotiators to return for consultations with their principals, were resumed, Qassim was particularly impatient and inflexible. He demanded full compliance with the government's demands and when this was not forthcoming on one of the less important issues, he broke off negotiations and informed the IPC group that it would have to stop all exploration and drilling in areas outside those in which they were actually producing until an agreement was reached. Talks were not started again until August, but even though the companies had sent a much stronger and authoritative team, including not only the managing director of the IPC, but a director of Standard Oil of New Jersey and the chairman of Shell Transport and Trading, the talks had once again to be adjourned when the government's demands exceeded the brief given to the negotiators. To the Iraqis this looked like simple procrastination and they did not like it. Qassim, faced with a Kurdish revolt in the north and other disturbances at home, and having committed himself publicly to a complete 'wresting of Iraq's rights' from the oil companies, either through negotiations or through cancellation of the concession, needed a resounding victory and was unprepared to permit the negotiations, which had already been spread over nearly three years, to drag on longer. He had threatened unilateral action and was unwilling to compromise.

It is not difficult to understand the Iraqi suspicion of and frustration with the oil companies. We have already seen that at one time they had been promised a 20 per cent share in the IPC only to lose it during negotiations over the concession agreement at a time when the country was not fully independent. Some of the minor positions of the IPC are difficult to defend, in particular its insistence on recovering 'dead rents' and on receiving a discount from the posted price for the cost of selling, even though the parent companies themselves lifted the oil and, in all conscience, should themselves bear the cost of selling it. These discounts were simply a way of reducing tax payments. It is also understandable that the Iraqi government would feel strongly that the IPC had been unreasonably using its monopoly power when it refused to make natural gas available to the government for export even though the company was burning it off because it had no use for it.

Certainly the oil companies adequately appreciated neither the mood of the Iraqis nor the needs of the revolutionary government and they overestimated Qassim's perception of the dangers inherent in an open breach; equally the Iraqi government for its part did not fully grasp the problem of the companies. It did of course realize that any gains it obtained from the companies would immediately be demanded by other countries in the Middle East and that the IPC group would always have to bear this in mind. But the complications arising from the fact that the IPC group was owned by several oil companies whose interests by no means coincided did not seem to be fully understood.

It was not, for example, so much because the men sent to negotiate were insufficiently 'high up' that they had continually to return for instructions, but more because the individual companies making up the IPC consortium had to agree on each issue. Having agreed, they could instruct their negotiators, but when these negotiators, no matter how authoritative within their respective enterprises, were faced with demands that went beyond their brief, there was no alternative than to ask the owning groups to negotiate among themselves and agree on new instructions.

It is clear from the text of minutes of the negotiations that Qassim understood that the IPC operating companies did not produce crude oil for sale in independent markets, but it is not clear that he realized the extent to which these companies were an integrated part of the international groups who owned them. He continually complained that the parent companies kept introducing considerations into the negotiations which concerned difficulties met only after the oil had left Iraq and which he therefore insisted had nothing to do with Iraq.[36] The companies' negotiators tried to explain the relationship between costs and profits at different stages of operations. But Qassim would have none of this.

The IPC was only one of many dozens of crude-oil producing companies in an intricate international network involving eight multinational corporations, five of which owned the Iraq company. None of these five was primarily in the business of selling crude oil. Only one of them—British Petroleum—produced significant amounts of crude oil in excess of the needs of its own refineries and its commitments under long-term contracts with other major companies and which it wanted to sell on the open market. The revenue of the oil companies came primarily from the sale of refined products produced from their own crude. Posted prices of crude were set relatively high in relation to the prices of products, which resulted in the attribution of a large proportion of the total profits of the companies to crude-oil production.[37] But, as noted earlier, when product prices fell and crude prices did not, profits attributed to downstream operations also fell, bringing losses to a number of refining subsidiaries. This created difficulties with the host governments in some consuming countries which refused to accept the loss of tax revenue; for some companies it also caused tax liabilities to their host governments to exceed the tax credits granted by home governments with the result that net integrated income was reduced not only by falling prices but also by higher taxes on lower profits.

How were the companies to explain this kind of problem to Qassim, let alone convince him that such a situation provided acceptable reasons for the companies' inability to give Iraq a higher percentage of crude-oil profits? The minutes of the last three sessions in the negotiations, which were published by the Iraqi government, clearly reveal the difficulties.[38] H. W. Fisher, a director of Standard Oil of New Jersey and a member of the negotiating team for the IPC, stated that 'the fifty-fifty profit-sharing formula cannot possibly be altered' and tried to explain that the Iraqi government's share of the profits from the production operations was in any case greater than that of the companies because posted prices were above 'real' sales prices and the companies had to bear the costs of refining and selling. Qassim replied:

> I do not know why the companies add the costs of transport, refining, and marketing to the costs of production, then deduce that the Government's royalties are bigger than their royalties.... It may be that the companies' share would appear smaller because the costs of other operations include high wages being paid to the workers and so forth. This does not mean that the Iraqi Republic should bear the amounts paid to workers in England and other places.

Qassim's questions were shrewd, for when Fisher emphasized that 'profits from the operations that follow production are scanty and probably nil', Qassim enquired 'If you are losing, then why do you not spare us the time which is consumed by negotiations and share with us all operations?' Qassim refused to see why Iraq should be concerned with the difficulties of the companies 'after the shipment of oil from Iraq' and asked with respect to allegations that the companies were making losses, 'If you [i.e., the IPC] were an oil-producing company would you still have losses?'

Fisher: That is something different.

Qassim: If you separated the companies into oil producing companies and others to carry out the other functions, then you would avoid losses. That is something which concerns you. I mean to say that if you were a separate company then the profits arising from oil production would have become clear. But you are complicating matters by participating in a number of companies.

Fisher: The question is a complicated one.

Again, when F. J. Stephens, chairman of Shell Transport and Trading, tried to explain that although Shell International made profits, the British subsidiary of Shell made losses, Qassim could only comment that the matter appeared to be 'a question of trade secrets'. As Jean Duroc Danner, the CFP representative on the company team, ruefully observed afterwards, 'It is difficult to explain that a subsidiary is making losses while we continue to pour in money to expand the business'.[39]

The Iraqis were understandably not impressed by Fisher's insistence that the agreement between the government and the companies was a 'commercial' agreement, and that the companies were willing to work in accordance with it, but that both sides 'should . . . adhere to the commercial basis'. They not only felt that in some important respects the companies were not living up to the agreement, but they also insisted that in any case the agreements of the past had been extracted from them under conditions unfair to the Iraqi side and were accepted by men not entirely loyal to the Iraqi people. There is no question that at the time of the 1952 agreement the Iraqis had not appreciated the role of posted prices in the integrated oil industry and it was therefore understandable that they should assume that the company's inability to observe even the spirit, let alone the letter, of that agreement with respect to the procedure for setting such prices, was simply an unwillingness to do so and thus an act of bad faith. Similarly, they had good grounds to suspect the company's goodwill over the issues of dead rents, sales discounts, and treatment of natural gas, even though the company negotiators eventually gave way.

Qassim may have been erratic, unreasonable, and at times brutal in the negotiations, but the Iraqi grievances were genuine, many of them were justified and had been strongly felt for a long time. After years of stonewalling, the IPC had finally reached the point at which it would make the necessary concessions on the accounting issues, natural gas, some aspects of relinquishment, etc., but it still was considerably less than straightforward with its host government. Nevertheless, the time had not yet come when the profit-sharing and other fundamental aspects of the concession arrangements could be changed, and in this respect the companies were correctly protecting their own interests. To accept government participation in the ownership of their major crude-oil subsidiaries would have required them to make extensive changes in the organization of the international industry, including the methods of pricing crude oil and of planning the amount and distribution of total output among themselves. This they were not as yet prepared to contemplate.

It may have been realized that at some time in the future the oil-producing subsidiary companies would either be taken over by, or would have to be operated in partnership with, the governments, but there seemed little reason for the companies to think then that that time had come. Although the companies were not of one mind, they could not openly divide on such fundamental issues. That they would hold out as long as they possibly could against granting any ownership interest to governments in their major concessions was later amply demonstrated by the events of the early 1970s. The owners of the IPC certainly saw no reason to start the process in 1960 with Iraq, the least important of the major Middle Eastern producers. Hence it was out of the question at that time that the companies would meet Qassim's demand for an ownership share in the existing producing operations. On the other hand, the development in partnership with the government of new areas which could not possibly become as important a source of oil as the existing fields for a long time to come and for which appropriate financial arrangements and methods of planning output, offtake, and prices could be developed as circumstances warranted, was (reluctantly) acceptable to the oil companies, with the exception of Standard Oil of New Jersey.

This type of arrangement was part of Qassim's final offer, but it was linked with the demand for an increased share of profits for the government in the existing operations. Again, such an increased share might have been (reluctantly) acceptable to the companies for new operations, for it was clear that the pattern of new concessions in the future would provide for more than 50 per cent of the profits to the government; but they did not want to grant it for their largest sources of crude oil—and anything given to Iraq would have to be given to all. Moreover, the companies were correct in their assertion that the high posted price for tax purposes operated to give the governments more than an equal share of the profits which would be attributable to crude-oil production if crude were valued at market prices, and they believed, with reason at that time, that the government's share would continue automatically to increase as market prices continued to fall. So long as the calculations of profits were made with reference to posted prices which not only were no longer under the control of the companies as a result of OPEC action, but also were likely to remain considerably higher than market prices, the companies could hardly be expected to grant an increased share of profit to the government. As the negotiations which were later to lead to government participation in ownership in other major Middle Eastern producing countries were to make clear, participation, profit-sharing, and the valuation of crude oil all have to be considered together, for changes in any one of these had important consequences for the others.

Finally, the companies remained unyielding in their insistence that they must have the right to choose the areas to be given up under any relinquishment programme. Both the government and the companies believed that the North Rumaila field in southern Iraq had very large reserves. The companies wanted very badly to retain their hold on this area while the government was anxious, at the very least, to share in its development. It seemed very probable that the North Rumaila field would be the only really important new source of Iraqi oil for a long time to come, and certainly if the companies had had to relinquish it while retaining other areas in which they were under an obligation to maintain a reasonable rate of exploration, much of the value of their concession could be in jeopardy.

It seems clear that one of Iraq's major objectives was to break the existing pattern of profit-sharing and ownership in the major concessions in the Middle East. In this she failed, for she obtained neither an increased share of the profits nor a share in ownership. The pattern was not to be broken for ten years and Iraq paid a stiff price for being ahead of her time, since the companies, though continuing to produce, failed to expand Iraqi output significantly for the next two years with, of course, a commensurate effect on revenues. When they did start increasing output, the increase was well below that of other exporting countries in the Middle East. Ten years later other countries were still receiving substantially greater per barrel revenues from oil and Iraq was still locked in serious conflict with the companies, while Iraqi national production from the expropriated areas was only just beginning.

Nor did Iraq's action hasten the coming changes in the Middle East generally. In spite of the fact that OPEC had been formed in Baghdad at a meeting called on the initiative of Iraq,[40] when the Iraqi government appealed to the organization in the dispute with the IPC, it received only formal support in a guarded resolution which left the government dissatisfied; the other major oil-producers were not sympathetic to Iraq's precipitate action.[41] Iraq did not attend the Third Conference of OPEC, opened on 28 October 1961 in Teheran, at which this resolution supporting Iraq's position was passed, and she took almost no part in the organization's work for the next fifteen months. During the period when Iraqi oil output was held back, the output of other countries in the Middle East rose; in Iraq's eyes other members were benefiting at her expense. In other respects, also, Qassim's policies had alienated the Iraqi government from most of the Arab countries. By this time, for example, Iraq had left the Arab League because the League had affirmed its support for the independence of Kuwait, to which Qassim laid claim in June 1961.[42]

Law 80, the final act of Qassim's regime with respect to oil, was, however, an irreversible achievement. No subsequent government would dare to attempt to rescind it; its political popularity with the Iraqi people was never in doubt in spite of the cost to the country of confrontation with the IPC. Oil continued to flow, but for the two years 1961 and 1962 Iraqi output remained unchanged while that of other countries rose rapidly. Stagnation of output meant also stagnation of revenues; the country had some incentive to come to a more satisfactory arrangement with the IPC if possible, but it would have to be within the terms of Law 80.

Article 3 of Law 80 was designed to permit some future accommodation with the companies, for it permitted the government to allocate additional lands to the companies equal to the area left to them under the law. In principle this would permit the recovery of the northern extension of the great Rumaila field which, quite apart from their distress at the loss of large potential low-cost reserves, the companies did not want to fall into competitive hands. One of their primary objectives became to recover North Rumaila, which Law 80 permitted at the government's discretion.

Notes

1 The Food and Agriculture Organization reported: 'There can be no doubt that the legislation on rural relationships and its long run corollary land reform *by itself* will bring immediate benefits to the peasants and will create the conditions for the modernisation of Iraq agriculture'. FAO, *Mediterranean Development Project, Country Study: Iraq* (Rome, 1959), Part V, p. 15 (italics added).

2 For a useful discussion of the land reform see Doreen Warriner, *Land Reform in Principle and Practice* (Oxford, 1969), Ch. IV.

3 *The Annual Report on the Operations of the Agricultural Bank for the Financial Years 1959, 1960 and 1961* (Baghdad, 1961). The bank reported that the agrarian reform threw its affairs into extreme confusion and it had a hard

time disentangling them for the years 1959–61. It therefore had to issue a single report for those years. (The financial year is from 1 April to 31 March.)

4 ibid.

5 This was true only of areas in Egypt which were dominated by large estates. When the attempt to introduce co-operative organization as a means of land reform was extended to smallholdings, there was a marked slowing-down of the co-operative programme and much difficulty.

6 Although there were a considerable number of graduates from the Agricultural College in Iraq, few of them actually entered agriculture. The government departments tended to absorb them for desk jobs in Baghdad, which most of them eagerly preferred over jobs in extension work in the rural areas where officers were badly needed, but where they would have to live far from the amenities of cities. Those who did go were often loath to leave their desks in town to visit the dusty (or muddy) villages and fields.

7 See K. Haseeb, *The National Income of Iraq, 1953–61* (London, 1964), pp. 37–9. The discrepancies between the figures reported by the Ministry of Agriculture and the census data were very serious. Areas under particular crops as reported in the census ranged from 62 to 197 per cent of the areas reported by the ministry. Yet one still sees both sets of figures quoted without adjustment. See also below, Chapter 18.

8 See, for example, the discussion of the problems of tree-growers and the land reform in *Ittihad al-Shaab* (an organ of the Communist party), 8 February 1960.

9 See the article by Zeki Khairi, 'Problems of Agrarian Reform', in *Iraqi Review* (31 August 1960). This was the weekly English supplement of the communist newspaper *Ittihad al-Shaab*.

10 See below Ch. 18 and Charts I–IV.

11 Atheel al-Jomard, in an unpublished working paper presented at the Development Seminar of the School of Oriental and African Studies, December 1976, mimeo.

12 Estimates of al-Jomard.

13 Demarchi, M., Mohanty, M., Ali, M., al-Azzawee, M., as-Saidi, S., and Isa, A., 'Family Food Consumption Survey of Workers Belonging to the Brick Industry', *Journal of the Faculty of Medicine* (*Baghdad*), Vol. 5 (New Series), No. 4, October 1963.

14 Demarchi, M., *et al.*, 'A Dietary Survey in Rural Areas of Baghdad', *Journal of the Faculty of Medicine* (*Baghdad*), Vol. 4 (New Series), No. 4, October 1962. A 1961 haemoglobin survey showed considerable deficiency in iron among the children in Baghdad province. But 20 per cent of the sample suffered from ankylostomiasis, 35 per cent from a sort of intestinal parasitic infestation, and 18.5 per cent from urinary bilharziasis. The authors also criticized the government subsidy in the big cities of low-extraction flour; the adequate thiamine and niacin content of the diet of the farmers in the rural areas was entirely due to their use of whole-wheat flour.

15 See Higher Committee for the Celebration of the 14th July Revolution, *The Iraqi Revolution in its Second Year,* Section on Ministry of Education.

16 Although the following report is typical of the government propaganda common in Iraq, it does illustrate a behaviour typical of Qassim, who would prowl around at all hours of the day and night to see for himself what was going on. It also is a faithful reflection of his relationship with ordinary people: 'It was a great surprise to the passengers, driver and collector of Bus No. 385 when H.E. the Faithful Leader, Prime Minister and Commander-in-Chief of the Armed Forces, got into the bus as any ordinary passenger of the people, took his seat among the passengers, paid for his ticket like any

other citizen and began talking to his fellow passengers listening to their remarks concerning the transport and communications inside the Capital. When H.E. knew about the discounts allowed in bus fares, the difference between that allowed for the students and that for other people, he expressed his feeling for the necessity of effecting equality among all the people whether they were students or not.

'In accordance with the Faithful Leader's wish implying the lowering of the passenger bus books by 25 per cent of their real rates, the Service has effected this as from 15.2.62.

'This gracious gesture of the Faithful Leader had its deep affection in the hearts of the people as it facilitates their transport and saves their money in such a way that they were ever thankful'. Iraq, Higher Committee for the Celebration of the 14th July Revolution, 1962, *The Iraqi Revolution in its Fourth Year* (Baghdad, 1962), pp. 221–2.

17 See Robert Mabro, *The Egyptian Economy, 1951–1972* (Oxford, 1974), pp. 113 ff.

18 For a graphic description of near administrative chaos see Jalal, op. cit., Ch. 11.

19 ibid.

20 See Explanatory Note for Law No. 181 of 1959 for the Provisional Economic Plan, pp. 81 f.

21 The change in the use of oil revenues was widely criticized, but it is clear that the Iraqi economy and administration was not capable of investing productively even the amounts it received and in these circumstances it is not necessarily inappropriate to increase consumption expenditures, particularly on health, education, and housing. Unfortunately, the defence budget received the additional funds in view of the demands imposed by the conflict with Israel and the Kurdish war in the north.

22 The plan envisaged a small sugar and a small cement factory in Mosul, a large sugar factory in Sulaimaniya, a small date-syrup plant, a small rayon factory, a small shoe factory, a large paper plant, a cigarette factory, a natural-gas pipeline, and electricity projects. Under the Soviet agreement, planned projects included a steel mill, and plants to produce fertilizers, sulphur, wool and cotton textiles, clothing, agricultural machinery, knitted goods, electric bulbs, canned goods, glassware, pharmaceutical and electrical equipment.

23 Haseeb, op. cit., p. 101.

24 *Report of the Central Bank of Iraq* (June-December 1959), p. 7.

25 Iraq is an important exporter of dates to the world market, accounting for about 76 per cent of world exports in 1960–63.

26 There was an open and acrimonious debate in the press over this agreement, with *Ittihad al-Shaab* and *Al-Hurriyah* attacking each other over their different views of the agreement. With hindsight it looks as if many of the criticisms were justified: that the projects were ill-studied, that the Soviet Union did not have adequate experience for some of them, that costs were too high, and that no adequate provision was made for ensuring that factories, having been constructed, functioned properly. Of course, many such criticisms could be made of projects under any aid agreement, but it does seem as if the haste with which Iraq attempted to absorb Soviet aid in this period was exceptionally wasteful. It was alleged that Iraqi officials at times insisted that the Soviet Union undertake specific projects even at higher costs than alternative bids and against the objections of the Soviet officials themselves. (See for example the discussion of the difficulties over a telephone-exchange project as reported in *Al-Hurriyah*, 21 September 1960.)

27 See United Nations, *Studies on Development Problems of Selected Countries of the Middle East, 1972,* 'Planning the Foreign Trade Sector of Iraq', for a comprehensive discussion of Iraq's trade in the period 1956 to 1969.

28 See report in *Iraq Times,* 26 February 1958.

29 See F. Shehab, *Iraq* in the *Bulletin of the Oxford University Institute of Statistics* (Vol. 21, No. 4, 1959).

30 See Nadim al-Pachachi, *Iraqi Oil Policy, August 1954–December 1957* (mimeo) (Baghdad, 1958).

31 The announcement was broadcast as follows: 'In view of the importance of oil to world economy, the Government of the Iraqi Republic wishes to declare its anxiety to see the continuation of the production and flow of oil to the markets where it is sold, because of its importance to national wealth and the national and international economic and industrial interests. The Government of the Iraqi Republic respects its commitments with the parties concerned. It has taken all necessary steps to protect the oil wells, pumping stations, pipelines and all other installations within the borders of the Iraqi Republic. The government of the Iraqi Republic will, at the same time, work for the preservation of its sublime national interests, and hopes that those concerned will respond to its desire to see the continual existence of this vital resource for the good of the national economy as well as the international economy'. British Broadcasting Company, *Summary of World Broadcasts,* Part IV, No. 605 (19 July 1958), p. 13.

32 There are still many knowledgeable and moderate Iraqis capable of taking a balanced view of the period and of the relation between the IPC and the government, who are firmly convinced that the intelligence arms of foreign governments, particularly the American CIA but also, in the belief of some, British Intelligence, had a hand in the attempted assassination. Only with the opening-up of historical records is this issue likely to be resolved—if it ever is.

33 *Multinational Corporations and United States Foreign Policy* (Hearings before the Sub committee on Multinational Corporations of the Committee on Foreign Relations of the United States Senate, 93rd Cong., 2nd Sess.), Part 7, p. 309.

34 Some 17 years later, in June 1977, most of Iraq's gas was still being flared. There were gas-gathering systems and LPG plants planned or under construction, but at least 20 years will have elapsed between the time when the Iraqi government demanded that the IPC stop flaring gas and when it could do something about it, even though it had had the right to do so for nearly a decade. See *Middle East Economic Digest,* 3 June 1977. *Special Report on Iraq.*

35 Some Iraqis, believing that the IPC and the 'foreign interests' backing it had a powerful influence in Iraq, hold that Qassim took, and knew he took, great political risks in moving against the IPC as he did. As we shall see, he also laid claim to Kuwait at the same time—against which he had been warned by many. Instead of strengthening his position, he further weakened it on this reading because the IPC and 'foreign interests' could be expected to work even more assiduously for his overthrow. The people who accept this interpretation also believe that the same 'interests' had a hand in his assassination in 1963. We know of no way of appraising the degree of truth in these arguments.

36 If one looks back over the history of the negotiations between the international oil companies and their host governments up to this time, it will be noted that the companies were not consistent on the question of how far the governments of the crude-oil producing countries should concern them-

selves with the profits made by the companies outside these countries. Whenever such host governments demanded a share of *all* profits made on their oil, including those attributed to its refining and distribution, the companies (with few early exceptions) insisted that they had no right to do so. On the other hand, when losses were made in these activities, as was argued in the Iraqi negotiations, then the companies expected the government to take account of this fact.

37 See Edith Penrose, *The Large International Firm in Developing Countries,* Chs. II and III. This state of affairs was profitable for those companies that could claim depletion allowances against their tax liabilities to their home country on the profits made on crude-oil production. Because of the availability of such allowances, the companies could obtain greater tax deductions on profits attributable to crude-oil production than on the same profits had they been attributed to refining or distribution. Moreover, at that time income taxes of 50 per cent imposed by the host countries on profits attributed to crude oil could in most cases be entirely offset against a company's income-tax liability to the home country.

38 'Minutes of negotiations in Baghdad on the IPC Agreement, meetings of 28 September, 8 October and 11 October, 1961'. Published in translation by *Platts Oilgram News Service,* Special Supplement (24 Nov. 1961), Vol. 39, No. 228-A. The following quotations are from this source. The minutes have also been published in a variety of other sources, including the *Middle East Economic Survey*. For a useful account see George Stocking, *Middle East Oil* (London, 1970), Ch. 9.

39 In a discussion with Edith Penrose when she met the company negotiating team, Messrs Stephens, Fisher, Danner, and Stockwell (BP), on 12 October 1961 in Baghdad just after the final negotiating session.

40 See below, Chapter 19 for a discussion of Iraq and OPEC.

41 In this resolution the conference expressed 'its concern and, while reiterating its full support of Iraq's position in safeguarding its legitimate interests, once more urges the foreign companies operating in the territories of its Member Countries to realize that a spirit of true understanding between them and the Member Countries is indispensable to securing those healthy conditions in the world oil industry which the furtherance of social justice and international co-operation demands' (Resolution III, 18). In little over five years OPEC resolutions were to move from such mild 'urgings' to strong demands with threats of effective sanctions that the oil companies had to take seriously. In 1961, however, the companies wanted to appease, but did not feel the necessity of satisfying, OPEC, and the OPEC countries were still pressing nervously against the companies.

42 See below, Chapter 11.

11 The Later Qassim Period: 1961–63

The difficulties of the Qassim regime changed in character in the second half of its period of power. The break-up of the United Arab Republic reduced the pressure from Nasser and al-Sarraj. The Iraqi Communist party, as we have seen, was brought sharply under control. Quiet was restored in the streets of Baghdad, and the public, weary of ideological tumult, resumed its daily activities in a generally peaceful environment.

New conflicts arose. Two of them concerned external affairs, the status of the oil companies (discussed in the last chapter) and the status of Kuwait. The third, the outbreak of serious conflict with the Kurds over their movement for autonomy in local affairs, threatened internal order and economic activities in the north.

The Kuwait Affair

In the nineteenth century Kuwait was a small and insignificant province of the Ottoman Empire under the administration of the governor of the Basra *vilayet*. Towards the end of the century the Ruler, Shaikh Mubarak al-Sabah (known as Mubarak the Great), began to assert the kingdom's independence of Constantinople and turned to Britain for support and protection. This was granted in a treaty between Kuwait and Britain in 1899. Britain recognized Kuwait as an independent state under British protection, and negotiations were begun with Constantinople over her status. In 1914 a British Political Agency was established and Kuwait's foreign relations were conducted by the Political Agent.[1] After the First World War, Kuwait's disputed boundaries with Saudi Arabia were settled and Neutral Zones were created. Kuwait was not included in the territories of the Ottoman Empire which were taken into the state of Iraq.

Oil was discovered in Kuwait before the Second World War. After the war Kuwait became one of the world's leading petroleum producers. She was, however, devoid of other resources. Her population, which in 1960 was less than a quarter of a million, had reached nearly a million by 1976. Having the prospect of immense future revenues, she was looked upon in many circles, in the Arab world and outside it, as an anomaly in her existing form. She ought, these critics argued, to be included in a wider federation or confederation, or, as the aggressive circles in Iraq held, to be absorbed by Iraq, where, they argued, her revenues could be used to greater advantage. King Ghazi had laid claims to Kuwait before the war and on the eve of the Revolution Nuri al-Said had proposed that she should be included in the union between Iraq and Jordan.

On 19 June 1961 the agreement with Britain of 1899 was ended and the independence of Kuwait was declared. In an exchange of letters Britain undertook to come to Kuwait's assistance if she requested it. On 25 June Qassim demanded the reintegration of Kuwait, which, he stated, had been 'arbitrarily held by imperialism', into Iraq and announced that he was appointing the Ruler of Kuwait as the governor of the district under the province of Basra. Reports of preparations for moving Iraqi troops to the south reached the British embassy. The British ambassador advised postponement of any decision to place British troops in Kuwait until Qassim made an overt move, for otherwise charges of imperialist action would be made by Arab countries. But the British government acted on a War Office assessment of the military position and dispatched troops from Kenya to Kuwait.[2] The Arab League was informed. Britain and Kuwait requested that a meeting of the United Nations Security Council should be called. Britain aimed to protect her interests and to protest at the threat to Kuwait's independence; Iraq complained about Britain's 'threat to the independence and security of Iraq'.[3]

In the circumstances, however, the Arab League, which Kuwait had asked to join, was in a much better position to deal with the problem than the United Nations, particularly since there was no support for Iraq's move among the member governments of the League. On 20 July, at a meeting which Iraq did not attend, the Council of the League admitted Kuwait to membership, supported her application to join the United Nations, undertook to give effective assistance to safeguard her independence, and asked the Kuwaiti government to request withdrawal of British troops as soon as possible, while also asking the Iraqi government to undertake not to use force to annex the country (which Qassim had never threatened to do in any case). The Secretary General of the League was entrusted with the task of ensuring the implementation of the resolution. In August British forces were evacuated and replaced by an Arab force.[4]

Iraq withdrew her representatives from the Arab League and her ambassadors from those countries which recognized Kuwait.

Presumably, with the announcement of Kuwait's independence, and, according to some,[5] because of rumours that Kuwait might join the British Commonwealth, Qassim felt that the time had come for Iraq to assert herself. He may have thought that it would be politically impossible for Kuwait to call on the British for support and, since he never threatened force and apparently never intended to use it,[6] it is improbable that he anticipated the landing of British troops, which forced Kuwait to take the issue to the Arab League. He thus gave Britain an opportunity to recover some credit in the Arab world by her restrained though prompt action in response to the Ruler's request, and her equally prompt response to the Arab League in accepting the replacement of British troops by Arab troops. Qassim's actions were tactically inept; they isolated Iraq in a political sense from other countries in the Middle East and created an unfortunate impression in the world outside it. Although his claim to Kuwait only represented a continuation of longstanding Iraqi, and previously Ottoman, claims, in its timing and manner of approach, it represented a serious error of judgement.

The Revolt of the Kurds

The habit of ascribing the ills of the past in Iraq to the shortcomings of the Hashemite regime and of Nuri al-Said influenced early attitudes towards Kurdish questions after the Revolution. A wave of optimism spread for a time in circles concerned with Kurdish affairs. The large-scale rejoicing in Baghdad when Mulla Mustafa of Barzan returned on 8 October 1958 seemed to many to mark a new era in Arab–Kurdish relations within the state of Iraq.

The Kurdish consciousness of separate identity goes back far in history. The loose structure of the Ottoman Empire, the primitive forms of transport and communication, and the deficiency of public revenues, limited outside interference. This comparative isolation was interrupted by the development of petroleum extraction in Mesopotamia. New ideas and modern ways began to infiltrate unevenly among the Kurdish people after the First World War. Though the centre of the Kurdish population was in the mountainous regions, there was much coming and going between these areas and the towns to the south and west, where many Kurds settled, especially in Baghdad.

Since the new influences were spread unevenly among the Kurdish population, it is not surprising that the leaders in the developing movement for autonomy in domestic affairs should be divided over the best means of organizing, and the best strategy for guiding, the movement. The traditional tribal leadership was still strong in the north. The Barzanis were clearly the most influential of the tribes and Mulla Mustafa Barzani held a distinguished record of armed combat and revolt over several years against temporary British administration, against the early Iraqi government under the Mandate, and against the government in office on the eve of the Revolution, some of whose spokesmen had eulogized the Baghdad Pact on the ground that it facilitated the special relations that Iraq must maintain with Iran and Turkey in order to meet the threat of civil war in the north which, it was alleged, Russian communists had instructed Barzani to wage.[7] After the Revolution, Barzani's record was in his favour amongst most sections of opinion. But another feature of his past career had a more mixed reception.

Several years of his exile had been spent within the Soviet Union and this led the extreme right-wing groups to assume that he was an additional and dangerous element added to the communist forces in the country, while the left wing assumed that he would have returned either as a communist or at least as a supporter of the 'Eastern' side in the Cold War, and an opponent of Great Britain. To conservative Iraqis his experiences in the Soviet Union were an additional reason for opposing his Kurdish claims, but they remained quiet during the period of revolutionary fervour.

Both of these viewpoints were erroneous. Barzani has been a consistent undeviating Kurdish nationalist throughout his life. His opposition to Great Britain over a number of years was based on British policy and actions after the downfall of the Ottoman Empire which had led to the extension of the borders of Iraq in the north to cover an area in which Kurds constituted the majority of the population, without provisions to safeguard their autonomy or at least without the will to make such provisions effective even if they were accepted in principle. But this was past history, and Barzani was too shrewd to waste time on recriminations over it when the Kurdish cause had every interest in establishing or maintaining good relations with other countries, including Britain, in order to gain international sympathy and, where practicable, direct or indirect support. We had witnessed the arrival of Barzani in 1958 and the tumultuous reception he received at Baghdad Airport, and were reliably informed later that he repudiated the demands of a left-wing delegation for a break with Britain.

Similar considerations applied to the extreme left-wing attempts to draw Barzani into taking a position in the Cold War on the Russian side. Such attempts were inspired, not by the desire to advance the cause of Kurdish nationalism, but in the hope of gaining additional support for the aims of the extreme left, to intensify class conflict at home, and to align Iraq in the Cold War abroad. The clamour and strife over these issues diverted public attention from the central issues concerning the position of Kurds within the state of Iraq.

The Kurdish leaders had quickly realized that the draft constitution which the revolutionary government had adopted near the end of July 1958 had, for the first time in the history of the constitutions of Iraq, recognized the Kurds as associated with the Arabs in the society of Iraq, and as being entitled to equal rights. But not only did the constitution fail to recognize Kurdish nationalism, it also emphasized that Iraq was an integral part of the 'Arab nation'. Inevitably this aroused Kurdish distrust; the Kurds were a minority in the state of Iraq, and in a wider union with other Arab states they would be a still smaller minority and would thus experience still greater difficulty in safeguarding their interests. Qassim, it is true, soon demonstrated that, as long as his regime lasted, Iraq's independence would be preserved and that any wider union including Iraq would take the form of co-operation rather than fusion. But even so, such co-operation might, like that associated with the Baghdad Pact, be prejudicial to Kurdish interests.

In the earlier part of the Qassim period, however, these questions were overshadowed by emergencies in which the Kurdish movement and the Qassim regime shared a common interest. Kurdish support in 1959 was of great value to Qassim in combating attempts by the extreme Arab nationalists to displace him. In this cause the Kurdish leaders found themselves side by side with left-wing forces, including communists. Their opponents attempted to make capital out of this by identifying them with the communists. The Kurds, like other groups, included a left-wing element, and, in a sense, Kurdistan was undergoing a social revolution, but the majority, including their leaders, were not adherents of the far left-wing ideologies: communism and Kurdish nationalism did not mix well, since communist ideologies traditionally gave precedence to class rather than to national emancipation.[8] This was shown from 1959 onwards when the communist party organizations in the north attempted to 'integrate' Kurds along with non-Kurds in various institutions, directing their attention to the class struggle to be pursued in common, rather than to the struggle for national recognition.

From some points of view, Qassim was a man of simple ideas, though he was capable of subtle strategy in giving effect to them. On the Kurdish question he shared the prejudices and preconceptions of the majority of his politically conscious countrymen and was unwilling to recognize an active Kurdish nationalism even within Iraq. He was thus unequal to the task of dealing with what was an immensely complicated external as well as internal question, which extended into both political and administrative fields. It was a legacy left by the British to the Iraqis when, for reasons discussed earlier, they put forward all their diplomatic skill to bring the northern areas inhabited by Kurds into the new state of Iraq. In this they were supported by the Hashemite rulers and their associates, and would probably have been supported by any alternative Arab rulers. No provision had been made for the protection of minority rights, either of the Kurds or of the Assyrians—who had also been brought into Iraq by British initiative.

Qassim was usually discreet in his public utterances and when he spoke on Kurdish matters, he carefully avoided giving encouragement to the main aims of the Kurdish leaders and confined himself to the alleged benefits of the Revolution in freeing Kurds, like Arabs, from earlier repression. He assumed at first that the Kurdish leaders would be grateful, but he showed no signs and, as far as we are aware, gave no public expression of understanding or supporting the special regional measures of autonomy which alone could satisfy Kurdish aims. Nevertheless, he valued the help of the Kurds in the earlier months of 1959 and during this period the central issues were set aside.

At this time some attempts were made in the Ministry of Education to improve the position of the Kurdish language and literature. In the College of Arts we received notice of a new course to be established on these subjects. But, as happened so often, transition between the announcement of a policy and its practical application was so slow as to raise doubts of the good faith of the authorities.

Kurdish publications were released from some of the restrictions which had been placed on them under the preceding regime; a number of new journals in Kurdish appeared and the principal Kurdish newspaper was able to discuss political news and political questions. The relatively freer press which Qassim permitted in the earlier period was active in the formulation of demands for the development of Kurdish institutions, the spread of the Kurdish language, and the wider publication and diffusion of Kurdish literature.

In practice, the cultural demands presupposed political demands. Here, as we have seen, the organized Kurdish movement was concerned above all to safeguard its position against the drive to include Iraq in a unified wider Arab state. As to the other relationship, that of federation between Arab states, which the moderate Arab nationalists proposed, the Kurdish position was that in such circumstances they would demand the right to constitute an autonomous unit to be included in the federation.

With the defeat of the early plots against Qassim, these central issues re-emerged and relations deteriorated. In 1960 and 1961 an accumulation of grievances, some of them common to the whole country, and others specific to Kurdish areas, led eventually to war, which only required the spark of a trivial clash with Iraqi police to set it off.

The final break of the Kurds with the regime was the outcome of a variety of incidents all of which, however, were mere aggravations of a fundamental difference of viewpoint based on the unwillingness of the regime—including both Qassim and many of his associates—to recognize that Iraq was a bi-national state and to adjust both the constitution and the internal structure and policies of government to this fact. Qassim's central policy of balancing the contending forces was disconcerting to the Kurds when it led to puzzling fluctuations in policy towards any given group. The more general question of the recognition of political parties and the legalization of their activities impinged on the Kurdish Democratic party as well as on the communists and other groups, and when Qassim imposed restrictions on publications as well as on party political activities, their impact in the north provoked strong reactions.

Qassim had also followed other Iraqi regimes in attempting undercover activities to incite other groups or clans against Barzani, particularly among the neighbouring clans of Zibar and Lolan. At the same time Barzani was working to expand his own political influence in the north and numerous tribal clashes occurred when he moved against his tribal enemies. Returning from a visit to Moscow in 1961, reportedly in an unsuccessful attempt to enlist Russian support, he found that Qassim had taken steps to weaken his position, and he left Baghdad. The lines were drawn for an armed clash. From then to the fall of Qassim war continued.

Looking back on the period in the light of subsequent events, the conflict appears to have been less ruthless and more subdued than those that some of the later regimes conducted. Unfortunately the comparative moderation in the conduct of the war was not accompanied by any constructive efforts capable of achieving reconciliation. The Iraqi army was intent on a military victory and so was Qassim himself. In addition to the withdrawal of Iraqi troops to their pre-war lines and the disbandment of the forces of mercenaries recruited from groups other than the Barzani and their allies, the Kurds were demanding the establishment of democratic freedoms, statutory recognition of measures of domestic autonomy, and modification of the agricultural reform to suit Kurdish conditions. The demands were not precisely formulated, but in any case an autocratic government in Baghdad faced demands which overlapped demands that it had not yet been willing to accept for Iraqi Arabs and so could hardly then grant to Kurds.

The Kurdish question should take an important place in any analysis of the decline and fall of the Qassim regime. Minority questions are always embarrassing to autocratic rulers. A minority characterized by such marked ethnic, linguistic, and historic differences as those that divided the Kurds from the Arabs in Iraq could only be satisfied by concessions granting them even greater liberty than that enjoyed under existing rule by the majority. But if an area of greater liberty were established with a view to reconciling its inhabitants to life within a larger state in which they would constitute only a minority, it could hardly be expected that the principal group, constituting a large majority of the population, would rest content with a continuation of the authoritarian rule which had been modified for a minority. And if we assume, as we may safely do with respect to Iraq under Qassim, that in any case the majority were by no means content with the existing authoritarian rule, it may be assumed that concessions to a minority would intensify the existing discontent in the capital and perhaps endanger the survival of the regime.

In this respect Qassim was in an even more unfavourable position than Nuri al-Said had been. For the latter, in spite of all the abuse that had been levelled against him, could hardly be described as a dictator. He was indeed responsible for the dissolution of political parties, a backward step in Iraqi political history that made it all the easier for revolutionary successors to go back on their promises made in opposition. But a parliament still met and speakers in its debates could criticize Nuri and his policies. Moreover, the responsibility for the failure of his regime to make progress towards a Kurdish settlement did not lie with Nuri himself, but with army officers and right-wing politicians. His own ideas on the subject were more flexible than those around him and, left alone, he would have moved towards an accommodation.

Both Nuri and Qassim, however, faced opposition from highly placed army officers who, when Kurdish resistance arose, favoured a military solution and believed that they could attain it. Part of this opposition was sincere, although some of it seems to have arisen out of the opportunities for personal gain by army officers who were not obliged to render accounts for the secret funds which they handled when they met rival Kurdish groups in secret attempts to bribe them to fight the Barzanis. And Qassim could not ignore sentiment within the army.

The prolonged Kurdish war played a part in the declining popularity of the Qassim regime. The appreciable number of Kurds living in Baghdad, the many connections between Arabs and Kurds, the disruption of trade with the north, the disturbed conditions in

Sulaimaniya, Arbil, and smaller towns of which news was brought to Baghdad, added to the social and political unrest in the capital.

The Overthrow and Murder of Qassim

Thus the ill-conceived pressures which Qassim applied to Kuwait, and his inability to rise above his predecessors in dealing with the legacy of Iraqi Kurdistan bequeathed to Iraq by Britain, threw long shadows over the later part of his reign. The first of these misadventures had no great domestic effects, but the second brought the brave and hardy non-Arab nationalists of the north into active opposition to his regime.

Nevertheless, the discontents arising from these and from other domestic issues, such as the failure to restore or to progress beyond the very limited elements of representative government in the preceding regime, would not have displaced Qassim if public opinion had been the determining factor. It is easy to overlook the limits of active political consciousness in Iraq, the preference of the great majority of people for sufficient stability to carry on their daily avocations in peace, the weariness following the turbulence in the earlier months of the Revolution when mass demonstrations, noisy broadcasts of ranting political orators, and street affrays at night, created a general atmosphere of insecurity. Disillusionment with all these disruptions of political life and with the meagre practical achievements of revolutionary fervour had certainly spread widely in Baghdad, while in the country the disorganization resulting from a maladministered land reform act was creating severe difficulties for the cultivators and was disrupting economic life.

On the other hand, the experience of the aftermath of a revolution which had been greeted with delirious fervour did not dispose the public to favour another revolution. To most people the comparative outward calm of the later period of the Qassim regime, except in the north and a few regions where revenge was sought for the events of 1959, was a welcome development which enabled them to go about their business in normal conditions. This viewpoint was widely expressed by small shopkeepers, caretakers, employees in businesses, and among those students who had realized that their qualifications, and consequently their future prospects of earning a living, had been prejudiced by the effects of political uproar on the regularity and continuity of instruction and studies. These things may appear obvious, but their importance in political analysis is too often forgotten by students of politics who concentrate primarily on the conflicting doctrines or ideologies. Bewildered and disillusioned as the people were, popular opinion did not favour the overthrow of Qassim.

The stability and calm of 1961 and 1962 in Baghdad and in a large part of the country apart from the north was, however, deceptive. If Iraq had been isolated from her neighbours, such conditions might have continued longer, but the small Baath party in Iraq made up in persistence and intrigue for its lack of numbers and, with allies in the army, was working secretly in collaboration with allied groups in Syria to get rid of Qassim. As we have seen, they had determined to murder him and, after a number of abortive plots, they had almost done so in October 1959. Qassim had restored to liberty his would-be murderers and this clemency had encouraged the leadership of the Baath party, which had been disorganized after the failure of their attempted assassination. They maintained contacts with the Syrian Baath party.

Unrest in Syria had markedly increased since the earlier period of the revolutionary regime in Iraq. By the end of the 1950s the civilian Baathists had experienced the danger of attempting to use military officers as instruments of, but subordinate to, the party in order to outflank democratic processes and seize power. They soon found themselves under the control of a group of army officers, on whom they had to rely if they were to attain power and, having attained it, to hold it against the opposition which inevitably follows the seizure of government by a minority. The Syrian Baathist army officers had been even more naive than the civilian leaders, and it was their hasty action in February 1958 that had made Syria almost a colony of Egypt. The action of the Syrian Baathists who had precipitated the formation of the United Arab Republic had led to results contrary to those which they desired.

The civilian party leaders and the intellectuals associated with them had imagined that they would serve as the philosophers of the UAR, developing its 'ideology' and having a formative influence on its policies; they had not demurred at the necessity of dissolving the Baath party itself, giving way to a single state party—the National Union—which, even though it would have its headquarters and its leaders in Cairo, they expected to be able to shape. But they failed to make any impact at all on Nasser and his associates. Equally important, the Syrian Baathist army officers themselves began to realize that they had been deceived in imagining that they would have positions of power in the UAR; they had now become ready to join with the civilian leaders against it.

Nevertheless, it was difficult for the Syrian Baathists to take the lead in dissolving the union which they had taken the initiative in creating. After proclaiming Arab unity as a sweeping, unqualified dogma, after denouncing Qassim in Iraq for standing in the way of a larger union, how could they acknowledge the correctness of the latter's retort to Nasser in the forcible exchanges of compliments between Cairo and Baghdad in 1959 and 1960?

It was in the midst of this dilemma that the much-despised bourgeoisie came to their rescue in 1961. Syria had experienced a more active political life than Iraq since the Second World War. The Baath was only one of several political parties. In economic affairs Syria had been noted for her active merchant class, which reacted against the less flexible ideas of trading which Egypt was introducing under the guise of 'Arab Socialism'. In agriculture the land-reform measures also raised controversy and complicated the problems of administration. The sudden nationalization of a number of industries raised further opposition to the wholesale importation of Egyptian economic policies and models. Thus, it was not the Baathists who liquidated the United Arab Republic. The resentment of Egyptian dictatorship in Syria was much more widespread, particularly among the middle classes, the better-paid workers, and the leaders and followers of the other parliamentary parties, as well as among the army officers. The parliamentary political groups, and the merchant, industrial, and financial classes joined with army officers in resenting the imposition of Egyptian economic and political forms of organization in Syria.

The UAR was dismantled in a sudden *coup* in September 1961 when a group of Syrian army officers arrested and sent back to Cairo Field Marshal Amr, who had been appointed by Nasser as a kind of overlord in the hope that he would be able to reduce the growing resentment against the union. The secession of Syria from the UAR was announced, and a civilian government was formed which proceeded to call elections, which returned a conservative government to power and led to the repeal of most of the socialist measures of the previous regime and the modification of the land reform law. Political parties were re-established, except the Communist party, and parliamentary government was renewed under the suspicious gaze of the military officers who, as in Iraq, were reluctant to abandon political power after having held it.

At first sight these developments would appear to have been favourable to Iraq. They removed fear of invasion by an independent Syria, or of further active interventions on behalf of a pro-Nasser domestic opposition in Iraq. Moreover, Nasser's prestige had been lowered by the ease with which the break was accomplished, which in turn exposed the flimsiness of the geographical connections between the two large areas of a supposedly united state.

On the other hand, the doctrinal regroupings that followed were less favourable to the Qassim regime. The severance between Syria and Egypt, which had seemed to open the way to the establishment of closer relations between Iraq and Syria, had been effected by what was popularly characterized, with pejorative intent, as 'the bourgeoisie'. Although both the Nasser regime and the Baathists had also sprung from the middle classes, and the Arab nationalist movement was above all a middle-class movement, the adoption in principle of the idea of 'Arab socialism' by both of these movements, the first from the late 1950s and the second from its inception, was presumed to have placed them on the *progressiste* side, and in opposition to the 'reactionary' bourgeoisie.

Nasser and Cairo Radio were quick to attack the 'reactionary' and 'secessionist' regime in Syria and a stream of denunciation was directed against it as an offence not only against Arab socialism but also against Arab nationalism. Thus Syria was exposed, metaphorically, to firing from two directions although, in rejecting socialism, she was vulnerable to one of them only. It now became in the general interest of both Iraq and Syria to co-operate in face of a common danger and to effect a reshuffling of the triangular Egyptian–Syrian–Iraqi interrelations. But these underlying considerations of the balance of power were subject to limitations when doctrinal or ideological factors were taken into account. Iraq under Qassim was widely regarded, up to that time at least, as one of the few *progressiste* countries in the Middle East, having curtailed the power of the landlord and to some extent the merchant and capitalist classes. An open and intimate *rapprochement* with Syria would have exposed her to a barrage of propaganda charging her with a betrayal of Arab socialism in addition to Arab nationalism.

These difficulties did not stifle all negotiations between Iraq and the new and independent Syrian regime. Rather they influenced the form and scope of the agreements that were reached. In January 1962 Hashim Jawad, Qassim's Foreign Minister, visited Damascus with a delegation of military officers and civil servants. Preparations were made for a meeting between the heads of state, which took place in March at the little Iraqi frontier town of Rutba, in the middle of the desert. Qassim and President Qudsi of Syria agreed on proposals to be made to the other Arab states that a joint military command and a joint economic council should be established and that the Arab states should by treaty assume the obligation to pursue a common foreign policy. The aims were formulated in general terms to avoid antagonizing certain groups inside the two countries and to minimize opportunities for hostile propaganda in other Arab states. While rejecting union in the form which Nasser had imposed on Syria, many Syrians were strongly attached to the idea of Arab unity, and would have supported some form of unity with Egypt if Iraq were also included. A triangular 'federal' union would, they believed, be a safeguard against the sort of domination that they felt had existed from 1958 to 1961.

The *rapprochement* at Rutba was not developed further during the rest of the Qassim period. Qassim's subsequent actions in Kuwait drew on Iraq the disapproval of other Middle Eastern countries and, even though Syrian Arab nationalists were unsympathetic, if not opposed, to Kurdish aspirations, the existence of civil war in Iraq, then as later, weakened the country in the eyes of its neighbours.

Nonetheless, the collapse of the United Arab Republic through the initiative of the 'bourgeoisie' profoundly affected the subsequent course of events in the Middle East, including Iraq. It threw into clear light the marked differences between the Syrian and Egyptian peoples and their traditions and the superficiality of the uncritical conceptions of 'Arab unity' which, stimulated by temporary exigencies arising out of local political manoeuvres in Syria, had given birth to the union. By restoring independence to Syria it reopened on an intra-regional and an international scale the divergencies of interests, and of the means of giving expression to them, which had been marked throughout history during and since ancient times. It also opened the way for the revival of the Baath party in Syria and for the full re-establishment of relations between it and the small but aggressive Iraqi Baath party which, though it had no legal position, was active behind the scenes in Baghdad.

Always engaged in conspiracies against non-Baathist regimes, the leaders of the parties in both countries now began to plot against their governments. Early in 1963 members of the Iraqi and Syrian Baath parties discussed in Beirut ways of overturning both the Qassim and the Syrian regimes. The active engagement of military officers who had linked, or would link, themselves with the Baath parties was of course essential to the success of any such scheme, and a secret committee of Baath representatives and members of the former Free Officers' Association brought the two groups together in a plot to overthrow Qassim. Of the officers who later became prominent in Iraqi Baathist governments it does not appear that any, with the possible exception of Lt-Gen. Hardan al-Takriti, was a member of the party, although some of them have been described as 'sympathetic' to it, particularly because of its uncompromising antagonism towards Qassim. More than a year before the *coup* which displaced Qassim, Colonels Saleh Mahdi Ammash, still on the active army list, Tahir Yahya, and Ahmed Hasan al-Bakr had joined in the committee's secret conspiracy.

Just as the elements which composed the forces arrayed against the Hashemite regime had been united only in a desire to destroy the regime, so the elements which composed the forces secretly arrayed against Qassim were held together by a single negative aim. The conspirators from Iraq and Syria who formed their plans in west Beirut aimed at a single concerted plan of attack in Damascus and Baghdad, to be executed at as nearly the same time as possible. In spite of the party façade which was placed over the proceedings, the *coups* were essentially the work of military officers determined to create, maintain, or strengthen what were at bottom military regimes in spite of the ideologies offered to the public.

The plots encountered serious obstacles in Baghdad. Qassim became aware of the dangers from some, though not all, of the conspirators. He arrested a few and warned others. Alarmed at these disclosures, the army officers allied with the Baath decided to move promptly, even though the Syrian conspirators were not yet ready to strike.

Evidence of serious popular discontent on a scale dangerous for the regime was lacking, but a boycott of classes by university students which began in December 1962 and was supported, if not instigated, by Baathist groups among them, provided the occasion the plotters were seeking. The student protest was creating considerable feeling within the capital and Qassim showed no disposition to deal with it. It was directed particularly against the intervention by Fadhil al-Mahdawi, president of the Special Supreme Military Court, on behalf of his son in a student affray. The strike was still in process and arousing much bitterness in the capital, when on 8 February 1963, a military *coup* was attempted, starting with a movement from the Abu Ghurayb army camp in the west of Baghdad. At the same time the Commander of the Air Force, an officer of outstanding ability, was murdered in his home by a group of Baathists. But the rising met no popular response: the issue was in doubt for a time and stiff popular resistance was met. Only by repeated bombing from a section of the air force was the Ministry of Defence taken. On 9 February 1963, Qassim was murdered in the Ministry of Defence by members of the Baath party. It has been argued since that if Qassim, instead of remaining in the Ministry of Defence, had gone out on the street to rally the forces favourable to him, the rising could probably have been suppressed.[9] It was two days before the conspirators were able to take control, after much street-fighting with considerable loss of life.

The street-fighting had scarcely ended when a murderous campaign of terror began, directed against real and supposed communists. The loss of life was many times greater than that which occurred during the 1958 Revolution. The communists whom Qassim had held in detention since the disturbances in Mosul and Kirkuk were dragged out of prison and shot without a hearing. The orgy of revenge against known and suspected opponents of the Baath knew no bounds or restraints and was accompanied by a breakdown of law and order on a scale not seen since the short-lived episode immediately after the seizure of power by Abdul Salam Arif which had been quickly suppressed by Qassim. Qassim claimed later that only 19 people had died then.

Well-informed Iraqi officials, including Baathists, have stated to us that the United States Central Intelligence Agency collaborated in the overthrow of Qassim. Our own view at the time, which we have seen no reason to change since, was that the United States ambassadors in this period, Waldemar Gallman and John Jernigan, were experienced envoys of good judgement, who were well aware that the accusations of 'communism' against Qassim were absurd. Over this whole period, however, the same cannot be said of the judgement of the CIA, which, under Allen Dulles, was dedicated to the pursuit of the Cold War. Hashim Jawad, the Iraqi Foreign Minister, told us later that the Iraqi Foreign Ministry had information of complicity between the Baath and the CIA. In many cases the CIA supplied the Baath with the names of individual communists, some of whom were then taken from their homes and murdered.

The prolonged resistance on the street, which the instigators of the *coup* had not expected, demonstrated the popularity of Qassim among the poorer classes. The resistance disturbed the Baath and some of the military officers who were associated with them. Violent methods of revenge followed and many rank and file soldiers who carried out their duty in resisting the *coup* were summarily shot.

The massacre of the communists and other opponents of the Baath was partly in revenge for the support given in the earlier stages to the Qassim regime and partly an attempt to eliminate a rival doctrine regarded as directly contrary to the sort of Arab nationalism that the Baath sponsored.

Conclusion

Whether or not Qassim, if he had lived, would have attempted to introduce representative government can never be known. A week before his death, in an interview with Edouard Saab, correspondent of *Le Monde,* he insisted that it was his intention to do so. By that time he had been left in a lonely situation. His earlier aptitude for balancing conflicting groups against one another in ways that blocked each from attaining a dominating position had been lost. Just as he had allowed, at an earlier stage, extreme elements of the political left wing to override the law, so, at a later stage, he allowed the political right wing to override the law in seeking revenge. He had alienated some of his best-qualified ministers who had formerly co-operated with him, although they had no desire to replace him by the Baath. He had failed to seize the opportunity to re-establish parliament, and to re-establish it on a new and more representative basis.

These criticisms must be placed in the context of the times, the place, and the alternatives. As soon as the disorders early in his regime had been suppressed by firm action, conspiracies were formed both within and without, aiming at the establishment of regimes corresponding to the political ideas of the conspirators, diverse and contradictory though these were. The central motive which the Baath and nationalists professed was that of displacing Qassim to make way for union between Iraq and Egypt. The restless Rashid Ali was behind one of them and the *haute bourgeoisie* of the north behind another. In contrast to their aims, which appear in retrospect to have been impracticable, Qassim's view may be summarized in the following extract from one of his speeches.

> Communists, Arab nationalists, democrats and others, I beg you to remember that you are sons of the same country. You have an imperative duty to defend the Republic. Stop your futile quarrelling and address yourselves above all to the task of making Iraq a modern and prosperous country. The Iraq Republic is an independent and democratic state, determined to defend its neutrality and to establish good relations with all countries.[10]

These sentiments were repeatedly expressed in Qassim's speeches. In the light of what had gone before and what followed it can hardly be denied that they were more appropriate to the circumstances of Iraq than those of his Nasserite and Baathist opponents, whose incessant claims to sponsor 'unity' masked attempts to impose their own viewpoints on those who did not share them. The outcome was the reverse of that which they professed to be seeking.

In appealing to the Iraqi people to restrain their political and sectarian quarrels in the interests of the whole country, Qassim's instincts were sounder than those of his opponents who called for a merger with Egypt in a union in which the latter would inevitably dominate, even if Syria were also included. It did not follow that Qassim was opposed in principle to Arab nationalism: rather he reflected the views of many Iraqis in favouring the gradual construction of wider Arab unity in a form of union in which local interests would be protected.

In internal affairs Qassim showed a more liberal spirit than most of his predecessors and successors by drawing a greater proportion of Shia into prominent positions. His views were no doubt influenced by the circumstances of his early life, and his actions were in harmony with his incessant emphasis on the necessity of internal unity within Iraq.

He was deeply concerned to raise the standard of life of the lower economic classes, particularly to replace the *sarifa* dwellings by houses with running water and electricity. Advances were made in certain aspects of education and health. But a wider and more carefully organized framework of responsible government would have been necessary if the possibilities of social reform within the available means were to be realized.

These shortcomings must be assessed against a background of intense preoccupation with political conflicts, internal and external. A succession of conspiracies, a stream of hostile radio propaganda from without, reflecting divergent ideological currents from various directions, created an atmosphere of unrest and uncertainty which diverted attention too often from constructive efforts at internal development. Two of Qassim's early ministers, themselves undeviating supporters of constitutional government, later emphasized in private conversations the disastrous effects of these early conspiracies in frustrating their efforts and those of others to influence Qassim in the direction of constitutional government. Qassim shared the tenacious opposition of military officers to any notion that they should give up their hard-won power to civilians. His comment on a request from Kamil Chadirchi, a genuine liberal, for an elected civilian government is illustrative: if, Qassim said, 'anything had gone wrong with our plans and I had failed, I should have been hanged while he took no risks and remained in perfect safety. Does he think I am going to hand over government to him and his friends?' Whether Qassim would have differed from the majority of other army officers who, once they had experienced political power, were reluctant to relinquish it, remains an unanswerable question.

In continuing the legal prohibition on parties which had been a fatal weakness of pre-revolutionary regimes from 1954, Qassim had merely followed in the footsteps of Nuri. There was considerable resemblance between the motives which led both these leaders to adopt the view that the quarrels between parties hindered national unity and made it difficult for any government to follow a consistent policy of development. Neither Nuri nor Qassim accepted that party disputes were mainly a reflection of wider national divisions of opinion and sentiment which, if parties were suppressed, would reappear through other channels which might require greater violence to block. The attempt to ban organized expression of differences through parties tended to produce instead highly explosive outbursts which threatened the stability of the state more seriously than the controversies among parties had ever done, but which Qassim was not ruthless enough to suppress. Qassim's approaches towards the re-establishment of political parties were ambiguous in their timing, in their selection, and in their scope. Above all, they were not accompanied by the establishment or re-establishment of a legislature, nor by the representation of the parties in the government. The activities of parties are insufficient when they are not linked to the executive machinery of government by direct participation of the party leaders in legislative and policy matters. This deficiency rendered futile the gestures which Qassim made towards the parties by 'licensing' a number of them. Parties divorced from the machinery of government and never meeting in debate in representative organs of government are of little avail.

The demand for freedom of political parties encountered serious obstacles in practice. It was particularly forcefully expressed by the Communist party in their press and in their pamphlets. That it should come most obtrusively from this quarter was a hindrance rather than a help to its attainment, for the public had not forgotten the disturbances of the earlier years and the role particularly of the least disciplined section of the party, along with outsiders, in them. The special meanings which communist orthodoxy attached to the conceptions of democracy and liberty raised suspicions that, if general freedom were given to establish political parties, the Communist party of Iraq would either obtain too dominating a position among the parties or, if it failed to do so, would obstruct the operation of legislative and executive machinery of government by taking advantage of administrative loopholes and ambiguities. Thus, while the power and the importance of the Communist party were often exaggerated, it remained true that their influence was in practice unfavourable—if only because of the fears which it aroused—to the establishment of political freedom and representative government.

There is, however, one important feature of Qassim's regime that is sometimes overlooked. Although the regime was never democratic and it promulgated laws and regulations by decrees, yet there was more freedom of discussion in that period than in many later periods. We often heard the regime freely criticized in ordinary discussion in daily life. It was only when Qassim suspected individuals of plotting against him directly that he took repressive measures. Scope was given, in varying degrees at different times, for the expression of contrasting and conflicting viewpoints in the press. Newspapers of different political orientations were permitted at times, and in the period of maximum freedom there were such violent altercations between the newspapers of different factions, especially in inquests over excesses of the recent past, that restrictions were reintroduced. The records of the People's Court were published, containing useful evidence from the prosecution, from the statements of some of the accused, and from witnesses, several of whom spoke freely.

The clash of ideas was almost always related to external as well as internal politics. At no point in the history of the Qassim regime can domestic developments in Iraq be interpreted without reference to intra-regional and to international affairs. No judgement of Qassim and of his regime is possible without taking into consideration the external conditions which he faced and which were always a threat to domestic stability and a source of actual or potential internal divisions of allegiance in affairs which had both internal and external (at least intra-regional) ramifications. Much has been made, often with reason, of the internal divisions inherent in the composition of the Iraqi population. The ethnic divisions in the north, the sectarian divisions in the central and southern regions embodying social and class, as well as religious or theological, distinctions, have all grown from deep historical roots and have made the task of building a modern state very difficult and complicated. But superimposed on them are other sources of division which largely affect all Arab countries and give rise to conflicts of interest, short-run and long-run, and particularly of interpretation. Some of these are shaped by geography and all are aggravated by history.

The principal influences which transcended the divisions within any single Arab country were those surrounding the idea of Arab nationalism and its implications in practice on the one hand, and those which were bound up with the rivalry between the United States and the Soviet Union on the other.

Each of these disrupting forces was at work during the Qassim period and an Iraqi government of any complexion would have been in great difficulties during those years. Others might have acted more wisely than Qassim did, but at least he saved Iraq from becoming a largely passive instrument in the hands of external powers and, in a fitful way, he sometimes left a larger—though still limited—scope for freedom of expression than most of his successors have done. Notwithstanding all the shortcomings of the Qassim regime, in subsequent years Iraqis were increasingly heard comparing it with later regimes—to their disadvantage.

Notes

1 It will be recalled that in this period Britain, Germany, and Russia were all manoeuvring for position in southern Mesopotamia and the Gulf. Hence Britain had a strong imperial interest in establishing a special position in Kuwait at the head of the Gulf. (See above, Chapter 2.)

2 Humphrey Trevelyan, *The Middle East in Revolution* (London, 1970).

3 Nothing came of these requests to the United Nations. Later, at the end of November, the Soviet Union vetoed Kuwait's application to join the United Nations on the ground that she had remained a British colony.

4 For a useful brief account of the Kuwait incident see Khadduri, op. cit., pp. 166–73, and Dann, op. cit., pp. 349–53, whose account is somewhat different.

5 Khadduri, op. cit., p. 169.

6 We were later privately informed by the Iraqi Foreign Minister that Qassim had had no intention of using military force to enforce Iraq's claim, but this view was not shared by the British embassy in Iraq nor by the Foreign Office.

7 Ismet Chériff Vanly, *Le Kurdistan Irakien. Entité nationale: Étude de la Révolution de 1961* (Neuchatel, 1970), p. 78, citing a brochure published in Baghdad containing the text of Nuri's speech.

8 The increasing diversification of communist doctrines—itself a sign of the strength of national sentiment on the left—since the Second World War and following the encroachment on the independence of many small powers by the two largest imperialist systems, the United States and the Soviet Union, has greatly modified the traditional communist doctrine on the role of nationalism.

9 Brief accounts of the *coup* are given in both Dann, op. cit., ch. 30, and Khadduri, op. cit., pp. 189–96. This *coup* is sometimes referred to as the '14 Ramadan' *coup* as contrasted to the '14 July' *coup* of 1958, since it took place on 14 Ramadan 1382, which corresponds to 8 February 1963 in the Roman calendar.

Misconceptions about the circumstances of Qassim's death were widespread at the time in some circles and have re-appeared in the otherwise outstanding study by Uriel Dann. Fearing that Qassim's prolonged resistance might lead to hero-worship after his death, the Baath spread a story that he broke down and begged for mercy and that he was given a formal trial and then 'executed' in due form. This was always an absurdity against the background of disorder and lawlessness among the Baathists. We discussed the matter privately with a number of individual Baathists during 1963 and all agreed that Qassim's courage was never in question and that he was shot in his room in the Ministry of Defence, the notion of a 'trial' being fictitious. That he reminded Arif on the telephone of his own clemency to him is possible, but Arif was quite powerless in any case at that time.

10 In a speech on 30 March 1960, quoted in Vernier, op. cit., p. 196.

Part Four

Post-Revolutionary Iraq: Political Developments after February 1963

12 The First Baath Government

At the opening of 1963 Qassim had held office four and a half years, a long period for any head of government in Iraq. As we have seen, his central aim was to maintain a balance of power among contending groups in Iraqi society, to induce them to observe a truce among themselves and work together in the national interest. He had failed, however, to establish the basis of a representative government which might have restored the lost sense of legitimacy, never strong, which had been attached to the constitution adopted under the Hashemite regime and its parliaments.

Revolutionary sentiment had almost died in the country. The public was weary of turbulence that led to no constructive results. Even the Iraqi Communist party no longer called for it, although many of its members had been treated with severity. Not long before, a prominent left-wing intellectual, who had also been a leading civil servant for a time, remarked to us in Baghdad that the country was settling down and that he hoped there would be no more *coups* to reopen disturbances that merely set back economic recovery.

The exception was in the north, where the Kurdish war continued and where the fall of Qassim was greeted with satisfaction and even rejoicing. This was easy to understand, but it was based on faulty judgement. A regime under military and Baathist domination held little prospect of a sustained improvement in the outlook for Kurdish local autonomy. First appearances were deceptive. Michel Aflaq's philosophy of Arab nationalism was directed in principle to a reconciliation of Arab minorities, Christian as well as Muslim, and presumably Arab agnostics as well, within a greater unity comprising the Arab nation. This approach was more comprehensive than that of conservative Islamic circles, particularly in eastern Muslim countries. But it did not admit a non-Arab minority like the Kurds to a separate and legitimate place in a recognized bi-national or multinational state.

Beyond these considerations of doctrine, it quickly became clear in 1963 that the small political group constituting the Iraqi Baath party that attached itself to the military in Iraq in 1963 was in no sense even in its own ranks a group united under principles enunciated by the Baath philosophers. Their age distribution was extremely unbalanced: the young age-groups so predominated that little practical experience was to be found in their ranks. They lacked economic understanding.[1] In this they reflected a general weakness in the Baath philosophy. In both economic and political matters, the youthful inexperience of the rank and file was combined with an incompetence of their leaders in the art of government. These shortcomings were aggravated by fundamental divergencies within their ranks which were quickly revealed.

The Prime Minister was a soldier, comparatively popular among the officers, but inferior to Qassim in ability, and occupying his position because of his acceptability to contending colleagues rather than through his intrinsic abilities. The army officers who had associated themselves with the Baath had been undistinguished in their profession. The deputy Prime Minister, Ali Salih al-Saadi, secretary of the Iraqi Baath party, was destined to become a central figure in the conflicts of the year. For him there were no nuances calling for discretion in the application of Baathist principles and slogans. He was above all a man of action devoid of capacity for political analysis. Loose in his personal life in ways abhorrent to strict Muslims, but influential with the younger rank and file, he became the leader of the 'left wing' in the government. The prominent role which he was destined to play during the year was based on his consummate skill in organizing plots and conspiracies, which contrasted sharply with his lack of political ability directed to constructive ends.

On the other side a 'moderate' group formed itself which reacted from time to time against Ali Salih al-Saadi and his followers. The new Minister of the Interior, Hazim Jawad, and the new Foreign Minister, Talib Shabib, represented a point of view close in many respects to that of Michel Aflaq and Salah al-Din al-Bitar in Damascus, which recognized that the application of Baathist principles and the adoption of Baathist policies would require numerous adjustments that could not be made overnight. A similar controversy arose among the Syrian Baath after the *coup* in March and at certain points the respective opposing wings in Iraq and in Syria sought reinforcement from one another during the struggles within the two Baathist countries. This represented a continuation of the co-operation between Aflaq and the Iraqi Baath in the plotting against the previous regimes. Aflaq had approved the date of the Iraqi *coup,* even though Syria was not yet ready for her own.

The new regime, unlike that of Qassim, decided to appoint a President. Their choice fell on Colonel Abdul Salam Arif, formerly the collaborator and later the enemy of Qassim, who, it was thought, might be a more acceptable spokesman than any of the Baathist leaders in negotiations with President Nasser, at a time when Bitar, one of the two leading Syrian Baathists, was in disfavour in Cairo because of his approval of the non-Baathist *coup* which ended the United Arab Republic.

A 'National Council for the Revolutionary Command' was appointed, on which army officers predominated. The massacre of communists immediately after the *coup* had subsequently created a fear among some of the more moderate Baathists of counter-assassinations organized by relatives of the communists and it was not intended to give prominence to the role of the Baath in the *coup*. But the publicity given to a congratulatory telegram from Michel Aflaq left no choice, and the rapidly growing unpopularity of the regime during 1963 fell more on the Baath party than on the military elements in the regime.

Ali Salih al-Saadi used Aflaq's telegram as a justification for pursuing a militant advocacy of the immediate and thorough application of 'Arab socialism'. Aflaq, however, had expounded his views on Arab socialism since 1944[2] in a very different sense from al-Saadi's crude interpretation. He had distinguished them from Marxist socialism, which he regarded as incompatible with Arab nationalism, and had advocated, with al-Bitar, prudence in their application to current conditions. In attempting later to correct al-Saadi's interpretation of his message, he urged that socialism should be postponed until progress had been made towards unity. This advice was rejected by al-Saadi and his associates.

The *Coup d'État* in Damascus

On 8 March the postponed military *coup* was carried out in Damascus, displacing the parliamentary regime which had been re-established in September 1961, and which had been attacked as a 'separatist regime' by both Nasserites and Baathists, although the majority of the latter had privately approved the dissolution of a union in which their identity and influence had been lost. (Al-Bitar had openly approved but later retracted.) Syria had been the birthplace of the Baathist movement. The Arab Baath Socialist party was established in 1963 by the union of the Arab Baath party with the Arab Socialist party led by Akram Hourani, a member of the Syrian parliament, whose connections with Syrian officers had led the Baath, contrary to their philosophy, to seek short cuts to power through military means.

A special feature of the Damascus *coup* was the part played by a secret 'Military Committee' organized by three officers of the Alawi sect, a heretical sub-group of the Shia,[3] who included Hafiz al-Assad and Salah Jedid, both destined to play leading roles in Middle East politics later. They may be described as 'Baathist' in a less equivocal sense than is given to the term when it is applied to some of the Iraqi officers in the government of 1963. But they were a small minority, and the *coup* in Damascus was mainly by independent officers with some of whom the Baathist leaders were in communication.[4] There were among them, however, and among other officers who did not directly participate in the rising, a number who leaned towards the Nasserite position.

The new government thus established by force was therefore in effect a kind of coalition in which the Baathists were only one element. Here as in previous and later cases, the Baathists gained power, as it were, on the shoulders of others, who naturally demanded a subsequent place in the counsels of the new regime. Since the majority of the Baathists had joined the Nasserites in denouncing the 'separatists' while profiting from their actions, they found themselves in an embarrassing position in face of coming negotiations with Egypt and Iraq.

It was at this point that the limited information on the composition of the group which organized the seizure of power by force became important. The Alawi officers who took part in the *coup* appear to have adopted Baathist principles and were thus a valuable aid to the Syrian Baath leaders who worked to achieve Baathist domination of the new government. They influenced the appointment of Salah al-Bitar as Prime Minister. Later they acted as a counterweight to the Nasserite officers. When stationed in Cairo, they had felt frustrated and deprived of opportunities and had formed an unfavourable estimate of Nasser. Nevertheless, they were ready now to demand that both Iraq and Syria should join with Egypt in the formation of a new and wider unity among the Arab countries.

In practice it was much easier to break up the old United Arab Republic than to form a new one. First, on the Syrian side no slogans could disguise the fact that many in the Syrian Baath party, including Salah al-Bitar and Akram Hourani's socialist wing, had approved of the departure of Syria from the UAR in 1961. And the majority of the Baathists had been as dissatisfied with the treatment of their leaders by Nasser as had the 'secessionists'.

On the Iraqi side, equally, there was in fact, in spite of all slogans and public professions of Arab unity, little disposition to accept Egypt as the arbiter and the dominant influence in a united Arab state. The Iraqi Baathists, like the Syrian, considered the Baath party to be a leader in the movement for an interdependent Arab nationalism and Arab socialism distinguishable from earlier Arab nationalisms by its provision for the social and economic side of Arab unity. They all expected that the party would make a leading contribution to, and play at least one of the leading parts in, a unified Arab Nation.

As we have seen, they deceived themselves if they supposed that the Egypt of President Nasser would accept them on their terms, but they had become prisoners of their own ideologies. At the same time the positions of the older politicians in the Baath movement had been weakened by the rise of aggressive and militant younger groups of a more radical turn of mind, such as Ali Salih al-Saadi. The movement was split within, and the consequences were to be seen during the rest of the decade. 'Arab unity' was becoming increasingly compromised at source among its most aggressive advocates. Serious contradictions were developing rapidly within the whole Baath movement. Always the fundamental difficulties were concerned, not with the idea of unity in the abstract, but with the terms on which, and the means by which, it was to be pursued.

The new Syrian government was at first, like the Iraqi government that succeeded Qassim, a coalition in which Arab nationalists not of the Baath party were represented. It included more or less independent army officers, some of whom tended to lean further towards the nationalists than towards the Baath; they were correct in thinking the former were much more favourable to Nasser than the latter. Al-Bitar, who did not share the ideas of the militant wing of the movement, became Prime Minister.

The Iraqi Baath groups also formed an uneasy coalition, but their structure differed from the Syrian in some respects. It contained no orthodox senior figures of prominence in the Baathist world. It had at that time a far more aggressive avant-garde than the Syrian party contained. The 'moderate' elements were led, not by mature thinkers of the movement, but by young men who had little experience in the application of general ideas to the circumstances of real life. The party did not have within its ranks the makings of a stable government. In intra-regional affairs and in wider international affairs it was no better equipped. Thus, in both domestic and external affairs the structure of the new government was so confused and ill-conceived that no clear organization existed to formulate a policy and to devise adequate measures to deal with the pressing tasks facing the country.

The Cairo Discussions

While the senior Baath leaders in Syria wished primarily to avoid continued clashes with Egypt, which they regarded as dangerous to their position at home, the young militants of the Baath party in Iraq rushed in to take the lead and to press for an immediate tripartite meeting with Egypt to create a union among the three countries with additions from other *progressiste* Arab countries.

In Egypt the news of the *coups* in Iraq and Syria had been received with mixed feelings. The overthrow of the preceding regimes evoked unqualified approval. Beyond this, however, Nasser entertained important reservations. He was not impressed by the new leaders in Iraq, except to a limited extent by Abdul Salam Arif. Still less was he pleased by the return of Aflaq and al-Bitar to prominent positions in Syria. From Nasser's own character and his attitude from 1958 to 1961 it would have appeared to any discerning observer that no union except under Egyptian domination would be possible in 1963.

It was this form of union that both Baghdad and Damascus were resolved to reject. The more cautious senior leaders in Syria desired if possible to avoid any sharp and direct clash with Nasser. But the militant leaders in both countries, with considerable support from the rank and file, were much more outspoken in their determination that the Baath parties should play an important role in any union government, and that there should be no return to the structure of the United Arab Republic. With this firmly held viewpoint on the one side and Nasser's unchanged resolve to maintain Egyptian leadership on the other, it might appear strange that either side should think it worthwhile to undertake discussions on union.

But this would be to overlook important realities of political life. Nasser's appeal in Syria was by no means negligible, especially among the comparatively low income groups and among some, but not the majority, of army officers. The existence of this body of opinion forced the Baath in Syria to show some enthusiasm for a movement towards union, if only to forestall criticism that they were indifferent. After all, unity combined with socialism had always been the central plank of the party.

Nasser stood in a somewhat analogous position. He could not afford to appear in the eyes of Arab opinion generally to be less anxious for union than his chief ideological competitor in the Arab nationalist movement. In the circumstances this would be to give the impression that Egypt wished only to dominate, not to co-operate.

Consequently neither side could evade the discussions, though neither felt confident that anything constructive would come out of them. They took place from 14 to 20 March and from 6 to 14 April 1963.[5] Sharp controversy arose early, for the discussions brought together heterogeneous groups in which a variety of cross-currents appeared, and still others ran in subterreanean streams, so to speak, below the levels that came to the surface in public utterances. Nasser's attitude was aggressive, notably against the Syrian Baath leaders, and particularly towards al-Bitar. Aflaq and al-Bitar were more restrained, but were confused and out-manoeuvred by Nasser's tactics. Realizing the strength of Nasser's following among 'small men' and many in the lower-income groups in Syria, they did not want to lose the political advantages that association with Nasser would bring, nor did they want to increase tensions and embitter relations within the Arab world. But they insisted on collective rather than individual leadership in a renewed union, for they remained unwilling to accept domination by Nasser.

The results of these discussions and wrangles were as extensive in print as they were meagre in application. The Iraqi group had joined the Syrian group in pressing for collective leadership and Nasser was adept at manipulating and embarrassing them in negotiations, but he eventually realized that if he responded with a formal refusal, he would appear in an unfavourable light in the rest of the Middle East. He therefore accepted the idea of a 'federal' union in which there would be an assembly with representatives from all three countries and other tripartite bodies, all, however, subject in the last resort to a President who held the final executive power and appointed ministers to a Cabinet. The façade of the structure represented the concessions to Iraq and Syria, but the conditions of the presidential office in reality turned the tripartite institutions into advisory bodies whose decisions could be overruled and whose ministers were subject to appointment and dismissal at the will of the central executive power. Thus Nasser attained his chief aim, even if the procedures which had been adopted gave an appearance to superficial observers of participation in the government by Iraqis and Syrians. And at least the parties in these two countries were not to be formally dissolved.

On 17 April the text of an agreement was published which envisaged union after a transition period and outlined its general form. The agreement was known as the 'Cairo Charter' or 'Cairo Manifesto'. A long 'transition period' before formal union was deemed necessary by the Syrians and Iraqis to consolidate their respective 'revolutions'. None of the countries was satisfied with the outcome, and a number of important points of substance were left unresolved.[6]

Underground conspiracies against the Syrian Baath regime continued in Syria among the elements which still supported Nasser, particularly in the army. Some of these elements had gained in the army reorganizations dictated by Nasser to reduce Baathist and 'bourgeois' influences. When an unsuccessful *coup* was attempted in Damascus in July by Syrian forces which favoured the restoration of the UAR, heated recriminations broke out again and the 'constitution' was soon abandoned and allowed to die a natural death in accordance with the concealed desires of the parties concerned.

The rival forces which proclaimed the cause, and aspired to be the leaders, of Arab unity had reached an impasse once more. There was indeed an inherent and straightforward contradiction when two political communities separated by geography and by historical experience, each claiming to be the authentic and unique leader of a movement for unification, attempted to reach an agreement on their respective roles in a single, unified state. In the original merger of Syria and Egypt in the United Arab Republic, Nasser had sought a solution by the elimination of the Baath party and, paradoxically, the way seemed then to have been opened for this solution by the demonstrated unpopularity of the Baath in elections held in July 1959, a little over a year after the union had taken place. The Baath members resigned from the UAR government in December. Believing that his rivals had thus been disposed of, Nasser had then installed Marshal Amr and a large group of Egyptian advisers, administrators, and technicians to reshape drastically the economic life of Syria in harmony with that of Egypt. The tightening of Egyptian domination and the severe discontent of the Syrian army officers in the UAR who had been demoted or whose position had been prejudiced, aggravated the underlying resentment felt from an early stage and caused the final collapse of the UAR.

The 'Radicals' Bid for Power

The radical elements among the Iraqi Baathists intensified their activities during the summer and autumn of 1963, and again there were parallel developments in Syria. The Sixth National Congress of the Baath[7] party took place in October 1963 when the Iraqi and Syrian parties were in power in both countries and deeply divided within by personal rivalries and on doctrinal grounds. A report approved by the congress indicated important changes in Baathist ideas.[8] Both the conservative and the radical wings, if we may use these terms loosely, had clearly moved towards greater authoritarianism than had been accepted in the earlier period of the Baath movement. The Sixth National Congress revealed the clash between the originators and earlier guides of the movement and the dynamic, often reckless, young recruits who apparently were prepared to attempt to outflank the non-Baathist left-wing radicals, including the communists, by adopting many of their policies.[9] After this conference, party membership increased and it seems probable that the majority of the new members sympathized with the more radical and militant position, rather than with the more cautious views of the older leaders.

The left-wing ideas of a number of the younger Baathists went so far as sometimes to claim affinity with 'Marxist–Leninist' (while rejecting 'Stalinist') doctrines, in radical contradiction to the viewpoint of Aflaq and al-Bitar who had set themselves aggressively against communism on the ground that it was openly and irreconcilably the enemy of nationalism; that it saw the modern world as divided, not by struggles among nations, but by a struggle between two broad classes common to all developed societies; and that it saw religion not as in harmony with, and an inspiration to, Arab nationalism but as an 'opiate' designed to dull the sensibilities of the masses and divert their attention from the supreme issue of the class war and the unfolding of historical materialism. But Aflaq's earlier writings preceded the changes of the early 1960s in the attitudes of the communist parties towards 'national liberation movements' and his view that 'Marxism' placed emphasis solely on the class struggle at the expense of the struggle for national independence, was not necessarily still applicable without qualification. The 'national bourgeoisie' were given a place in revised Russian communist theories.[10]

In addition, during 1963 the Baathist regimes in both Iraq and Syria, when faced with the responsibilities of office, departed in other ways from the doctrines earlier preached by Aflaq and al-Bitar. There was no concerted reappraisal by the party as a whole. Rather, the older doctrines were challenged by younger new elements in the party and a severe contest ensued between the moderate elements which broadly accepted the older ideas and the *progressiste* groups which considered them outmoded.

Marxism, and communism based on it, claim to be universal. Baathism claims to be general only within one linguistic and partially ethnic group. Both communism and Baathism face within their respective frameworks the problem expressed in the phrase 'socialism in one country'. As soon as revolutionary groups inspired by these ideologies seized power in actual states, they were forced to come to terms with nationalism. Communists could do no other than first recognize socialism 'in one country' and then recognize socialism 'in several countries' without even attempting to unite them in one country. Communist countries proved to be as jealous of their independence as other countries.

Similarly, Baathism starts on a localized scale with a refusal to recognize as legitimate any 'national' or even state lines of division among the Arab peoples. But when faced with the responsibilities of office, its leaders were forced to recognize that even if the Arabs were 'one nation', a union of existing Arab states of uneven size and physical power would raise difficult questions concerning the comparative positions in the new enlarged Arab state of those who directed the original states. This problem was raised in its most acute form when the Baath attempted to find a common ground for unity with the Egypt of Gamal Abdul Nasser. In addition, Baathist ideas of the indissoluble relationship between 'socialism' and Arab nationalism introduced a further difficulty in the path of unity among Arab states which were not of identical political persuasion—even the socialist states among them might have different conceptions of 'socialism'.

Furthermore, a combination of Arab nationalism and socialism raised particular difficulties for Iraq—a state not wholly Arab.

Kurdish Nationalism and the Baath

For a time after the military seizure of power in 1963 even the Baath ministers desired at least a respite in the north, and Hazim Jawad, Minister of State, speaking for the government, declared that the Kurdish problem would be dealt with by peaceful means as soon as Kurdish demands and Kurdish opinions were known.

On the Kurdish side the overthrow of Qassim was welcomed and a unilateral cease-fire was proclaimed. Meanwhile the massacre of the Iraqi communists continued and the new Iraqi government declared its intention of extirpating the Iraqi Communist party. Although the Kurdish position was that the communists had not supported them, the wholesale murder of communists disturbed the Kurdish leaders, who had consistently held that constitutional government should be established as the only means of maintaining liberties.

The new Iraqi government seemed to speak with a number of divergent voices in subsequent exchanges. Tahir Yahya, who had engaged in secret conversations with Barzani in 1962, apologized on one of his visits for the failure by the Baath to live up to an engagement they made during the Qassim regime to recognize Kurdish autonomy when they had overthrown Qassim. He explained this on the ground that subsequently other groups had joined them who would not consent to autonomy, believing that it compromised Arab nationalism. The familiar proposal of 'decentralization of regions' was put forward.

The Baathist doctrine expounded by Michel Aflaq made Arab nationalism and Arab socialism interdependent. As Marcel Colombe wrote in the course of an exposition of Aflaq's doctrine, to the founder of Baathism

> . . . le socialisme est une fin en soi, il est la condition même de la formation de la nation; seule son application peut permettre de faire disparaître sur le sol de la patrie les différends confessionnels ou raciaux réduits d'une façon peut-être arbitraire à des antagonismes de classes.[11]

Thus, though giving a special cultural place to Islam, he broadened Baathist philosophy to embrace a union of all sects and religions in a common Arab nationalism. But the Baathist philosophy failed to adjust itself to the conditions of what, in fact, was a bi-national state. Iraq as a whole—all the territories within the boundaries approved of in the mandatory period—was for them essentially a part of the Arab nation, one and indivisible. This claim appeared inadmissible to the Kurds. They felt as intensely about, and would hold as tenaciously to, the idea of Kurdish nationalism as any Baathist would to Arab nationalism, and they were a more cohesive community. To them, Iraq must be a bi-national state if she was to endure within the boundaries drawn up after the Second World War. The more vehemently Arab nationalism was proclaimed, the greater the reservations of the Kurds. The wider the scope of 'Arab unity', in the sense of the coalescence of Arab states, the greater would be the superiority of the Arabs over the Kurds and the less would be the chances of safeguarding Kurdish national rights.

After the military seizure of power and the return of the Syrian Baathists, Aflaq and al-Bitar became an influence in Baghdad for a time and put their weight against autonomy in any region. The Iraqi Foreign Minister had already publicly declared against Kurdish autonomy. Thus the 'moderate' members of the party were as great an obstacle to concessions to Kurdistan as the radical groups were. Applied in this context the Baathist dogma of 'unity' went beyond the scope of reason. Whatever tactical and practical qualifications might be made from time to time, Baathist sentiment tended to ignore the existence of any other national groups in the community, and to assume that the peoples composing them were Arabs, or at least should consider themselves as part of the Arab world. Occasionally the claim was made that Kurds were in reality of semitic or Arabic origin. For a time, such self-deceptions screened those who held them from reality, but they could not last indefinitely. Even Nasser and President Ben Bella, replying informally to Jalal Talabani, a Kurd who on occasion represented Mulla Mustafa Barzani when he visited Cairo and Algiers in company with Iraqi government representatives, were sympathetic to the claims of the Kurds to a position of autonomy within the state of Iraq on the ground that they constituted a separate nationality.[12]

The new government of Iraq, while some of its members admitted privately the claim to Kurdish autonomy within Iraq, would not agree to announce this in a public statement. Soon they went back even on this admission and the Kurdish leaders began to lose patience. Talib Shabib, the young civilian Baathist Foreign Minister, was particularly hostile and threatening, and on the military side some of the officers maintained that they could have disposed of the Kurdish forces if Qassim had allowed them a free hand and had given them the equipment that they demanded.

As if this were not enough, an additional obstacle stood in the way of a settlement. The Kurdish leaders firmly held to a demand that had been almost general before, and in the early stages after, the 1958 Revolution. This consisted of a return—this time in a genuine sense—to constitutional, parliamentary government in Iraq, in which all parties and all minorities could find representation. Barzani and his associates, with good reason, had little faith in the promises of a dictatorial, military regime, responsible to no representative body, and one which had stifled freedom of speech and freedom of the press.

In this demand the Kurdish leaders were consistent. Their own proposals provided at the outset for the administration of the Kurdish area—which they envisaged as comprising Sulaimaniya, Arbil, Kirkuk, and those districts in the *liwas* of Mosul and Diala which contained a Kurdish majority—by an executive council responsible to a legislative assembly. It was incorrect to assert, as Iraqi propagandists did, that Barzani aspired to become a dictator over the Kurdish people. Such a role was common in military regimes but not in traditional tribal society, nor would it be acceptable to the younger, more modernized Kurds who had been attracted to Barzani notwithstanding his tribal affiliations. His capacity to gain the confidence of both these groups gave him a unique position among the Kurds of Iraq: he was able to control extremes among his followers, whether ideological or political or military.

The Kurdish proposals were explicit on the question of secession, which opponents alleged to be their goal: the area enjoying regional autonomy was to be part of the state of Iraq. Foreign affairs, national defence, economic and financial affairs, transport and communication, and a number of additional smaller fields, belonged to the central government. Clearly these were key areas of government.[13]

There remained, however, one question which was to become increasingly important in succeeding years: the Kirkuk area and the sharing of oil revenues.

A Breakdown of Law

In the summer and autumn of 1963 Baghdad and the surrounding areas were in as great a state of agitation and turbulence as they had ever been during the early days of the Qassim regime. Among the Baath rank and file, which had expanded rapidly in numbers after the Baath governments had come to power, the influence of the new militants both in Iraq and in Syria appeared to be increasing, and that of the veteran Baath leaders, Aflaq and al-Bitar in Syria and the moderate group in Iraq (which numbered Talib Shabib and Hazim Jawad among its young members and Tahir Yahya and Hardan al-Takriti among its military members), to be declining.

The outstanding feature of the autumn crisis lay in the breakdown of law and order in the Iraqi capital. The Iraqi Baath party was torn apart by internal dissension and the nominal central government had lost its monopoly of armed force. The police were displaced from the enforcement of the laws against personal violence and abduction by the National Guard, originally designed as a civil militia to protect the new Baath government against its enemies. The National Guard had been taken over from an early stage by the party militants and under Ali Salih al-Saadi it had become a private army of the militant Baathists over which even its own leaders had imperfect control.

In a cabinet reshuffle in May the 'right wing' in the Cabinet, led by Talib Shabib and Hazim Jawad, had succeeded in shifting al-Saadi from the Ministry of the Interior to the Ministry of Guidance in the hope of reducing his influence, but without success. He still continued to use the National Guard for his purposes. Up to a point the Guard bore some resemblance to the Popular Resistance Force of the Qassim period, and one could hear cynical remarks that the Popular Resistance Force, which had been suppressed in the later stages of the Qassim government, was back again. But a fundamental distinction soon appeared. Qassim and the Military Governor of Baghdad had always kept the supplies of small-arms and ammunition under army control. The Force could draw arms for their daily periods of military training, but after the activities of the day they were obliged to give up their arms to the regular army officers for storage. Qassim was too shrewd to permit a second army to grow up outside the regular army. The Baathist militia, however, quickly acquired arms of their own, which became a danger to the community. Voices were soon heard comparing Qassim favourably with those responsible for the chaos in 1963.

During the discussions at the Sixth National Congress of the Baath party the radical group in the Iraqi party had been prominent and a resolution calling for the strengthening of the National Guard in

Iraq and Syria had been passed in spite of the fact that the Guard was responsible for the chaos in Iraq. At this congress al-Saadi had prevailed over Hazim Jawad (by then Minister of the Interior) and Talib Shabib, who were dropped from the National Command. But public opinion was at last aroused. The activities of the Guard impinged on the life of the community at a number of points. In some of the principal areas of Baghdad the streets had become dangerous at night. The police no longer gave protection and the bands of young armed men and boys of the National Guard roamed the streets in the darkness, stopping cars and searching their occupants, kidnapping suspected opponents and carrying them off to an unknown fate. The National Guard, which was neither 'national' nor a 'guard' but a menace to all the legal forces of order, brought Baghdad to a state approaching anarchy.[14] The non-Baathist members of the government, together with the army officers who had recently joined the party from expediency rather than from doctrinal conviction, were increasingly disturbed by the challenge to public order, which was also resented by the police services.

The End of the Baath Regime

Notwithstanding the apparent success of the extreme wing of the Baath party at the Sixth National Congress, the days of the Iraqi National Guard were already numbered. The army officers in Iraq, Baathist and non-Baathist, were about to be joined by the moderate civilian Baathist leaders, who were on the side of Aflaq and al-Bitar in the political struggle in Syria. The role of the National Command was soon to be put to the test: the militants were not disposed to soften their demands.

The first move was made by the moderate civilian ministers with the prearranged collaboration of a group of army officers. A meeting of the Regional Command was summoned for 11 November at which they ensured that their supporters would be present. Ali Salih al-Saadi and his associates were taken by surprise. They were called on to face charges that they had taken unauthorized actions contrary to the policies of the government and the party. The charges were upheld by a majority vote and al-Saadi and his associates were at once escorted to a waiting aeroplane which flew to Barcelona and left them there without passports.

But the Regional Command had to reckon with the National Command. Aflaq, al-Bitar, and their associates were likely to gain from the removal of the extreme group in Baghdad: they had their own troubles with an extreme left wing in Damascus, and Aflaq's position on the Regional Command in Syria had weakened, while it remained much stronger on the National Command. He and his associates therefore had a strong interest in maintaining the predominant place ascribed to the National Command. From this point of view the action taken by the Iraqi Regional Command was irregular and set a dangerous precedent. The National Command therefore decided to dispatch a delegation led by Aflaq to Baghdad to re-examine and correct the decisions and actions of the Iraqi Regional Command.

Meanwhile the followers of the evicted members of the latter organized a quick riposte in Baghdad, which began early in the morning before the arrival later in the day of the members of the National Command from Damascus. During the day we were able to observe each step on the streets. The National Guard, led by associates of al-Saadi, came out on the streets and took up positions in the early morning. Some sporadic firing broke out, and a spectacular dive-bombing attack was made on the Presidential Palace by a fanatical member of the Baath party within the air force, Captain Windawi. The attack missed its mark, the best plane the Iraqi air force possessed was wrecked beyond repair, and Windawi fled to Damascus. The National Guard, ill-equipped and poorly trained, formed into groups to occupy the streets.

The government reacted quickly by sending tanks and armoured cars to occupy all strategic points—the Post Office, the Broadcasting Station, the main government buildings, and the entrances to all bridges across the Tigris. A curfew was imposed, and all students were sent home, while traffic disappeared from the streets.

Observing the quality of the National Guard during part of the day, we concluded that in a full-scale combat they would have no chance against a disciplined army. But the army leaders correctly estimated that to press matters to a conclusion that day would cause considerable loss of life and at the end of the day stalemate prevailed, with the army in firm control of strategic centres.[15]

In the meantime, on 13 November a group of Syrian members of the National Command of the Baath party arrived in Baghdad to attend a meeting with their Iraqi counterparts at which the decisions and actions taken by the Regional Command on 11 November were to be debated. The discussions continued on the next day. Sharp criticisms were to be heard of the National Command, which struck at the basis of Baath doctrine and revealed unmistakably the existence of an Iraqi nationalism, however unacknowledged the term might be. What, it was asked in the bazaars and coffee shops, were the Syrians doing in Baghdad? Were they attempting to interfere in Iraqi affairs? To this was added religious feeling: Aflaq was the target which drew fire in conservative Islamic circles. By what right did a

Syrian Christian come from Damascus to tell Iraqi people how to manage their affairs?

These criticisms, already heard on 13 November, were redoubled when the results of the meetings on the 13th and 14th were announced on the 15th. The National Command condemned the actions which the Iraqi Regional Command had taken on 11 November. It decreed the immediate expulsion of Hazim Jawad and Talib Shabib to offset the removal of al-Saadi and his associates on the Regional Command, and as an assertion of the supremacy of the National over the Regional Command.

The National Command went further and declared that it would temporarily assume the direction of affairs in Iraq until the legitimate working of the Regional Command and the government was restored.

This action was a turning-point. It not only enraged what there was of public opinion in the country; it also finally alienated the leading military officers, Baathist as well as non-Baathist. Their patience had already been stretched to the limit by the National Guard's open challenge to the army and to the forces of public order. Officers as well as others asked whether the country was to be taken over by a youth movement.

The riposte was swift. It was the work in the main of army officers who were now aware that they would be backed by public opinion. The leading senior Baathist officers, Ahmed Hasan al-Bakr, the Prime Minister, General Salih Mahdi Ammash, Minister of Defence, General Tahir Yahya, Chief of Staff, and his deputy, General Hardan al-Takriti, Commander of the Air Force, acting in agreement with the President, Abdul Salam Arif, called in the commanders of divisions on 16 and 17 November and organized a plan of action.

The army's tactic on 13 November had been to secure strategic points but to avoid a direct clash in conditions that would have led to much bloodshed. On the 18th the army used first the tactic of surprise in the early morning and, second, the deployment of overwhelming force to create in the first place the maximum effect on morale while minimizing casualties. An intense bombardment and a deafening noise were directed to this end and very quickly the National Guard was decisively defeated. Well before noon Baghdad was quiet. So far as we are aware no official estimates of casualties were made public. In presenting a number of guesses to Iraqi friends who had acquaintances among the military and the police, we found the most acceptable estimate of the number killed was somewhere near fifty.

In the next few days a deep and widespread feeling of relief was evident among the public. For many months the outrages committed by the National Guard, the connivance of police officers in giving them access to a store of police weapons, the collapse of the machinery of law and order, had made the Baath party, and the government based largely on it, the most hated regime in Iraq since the Second World War.

For several nights occasional shots could be heard, followed by bursts of fire from automatic weapons. But resistance was at an end. Many of the members of the National Guard disposed of their soiled semi-military clothing and abandoned or hid their weapons. Their leaders had fled at an early stage, leaving to their fate the inexperienced youths whom they had used as instruments of their ambitions. The collapse was complete.

But the Baathist movement, even the 'radical' section, had not collapsed as the National Guard had done and the last had not been heard of them.

Reactions in Egypt and Syria

The fall of the Baathist left wing was hailed by President Nasser. Desiring for tactical reasons to obscure the role of Baathist officers who initiated and executed the measures to suppress the National Guard, he gave exclusive credit to Abdul Salam Arif. Nasser was delighted that the risk of united action by Baath regimes in Baghdad and Damascus against his interests had been removed and both he and a number of Iraqis expected that Iraq would draw closer to Egypt. He seized the opportunity to increase his verbal attacks on the Baath.

The Baath government in Syria now followed a more moderate line towards Nasser in the hope of reducing Egyptian hostility. Aflaq and al-Bitar had always desired to follow this course, but in attempting it they invariably exposed themselves to violent attacks from the al-Saadi group within the movement, and from other militant elements outside it. Nasser would have no compromise and gave no heed to any of his advisers who thought it wiser to reduce internal tension in the Arab world in order to face external difficulties with greater confidence. The fact was that Nasser's feud with the Baath party was irreparable in the sense that under no conditions was he willing to share power.

In Syria the party was torn with internal strife between those who followed the philosophy of its early leaders and those who aimed at a more radical approach to politics. The presence and the activities of the movement's leading founders and thinkers had been a restraining influence not present in Iraq. The collapse of the Baath government in Iraq had served as a warning against pushing differences too far. But the differences were acute and those who pressed for more vigorous action towards socialism, among the military as well as among the civilian party members, were gaining. The condemnation of al-Saadi heard in Damascus[16] in late November hardly lasted into the New Year, and soon al-Bitar's sharp attack on al-Saadi would be held against him. For it was not easy to dispose of al-Saadi. Quickly he moved from Spain to Syria. Imbued with vague, confused, and ill-digested political ideas, lacking in political judgement, he was still a master of the art of political intrigues and in the organization of conspiracies. Nevertheless, political life, in spite of its instability, was less immature in Syria than in Iraq. The level of discussion and debate was higher. Moreover, Damascus was not the only political centre in Syria which counted, as Baghdad tended to be in Iraq.

A Turning-Point for the Baath Party

The events of 1963 marked a decisive stage in the history of the Baath party. The priority given to 'Arab unity' by its founders, the idea that 'Arab socialism' was a means in the service of unity and not simply an end in itself, ceased to be the main preoccupation of the leaders of the movement. The National Command had been overshadowed in practice by the Regional Commands, even though, in Syria, it attempted to intervene up to 1966. From a Syrian point of view the question of 'Baathism in one country' arose in an acute form; the non-Syrian representatives on the National Command were backed by no government mandate; the governments of their countries regarded them with suspicion. For a considerable period the Syrian Baath stood alone as the only 'regional' Baath party in power. Internally it was divided on what until a short time before had been unquestioned dogma. Aflaq and al-Bitar had placed first importance on uniting the Arab peoples in a single state. This might also be described as almost a religious as well as a political doctrine. To advance this aim they were prepared to minimize other political differences with Nasser and with Iraq. The radicals were now placing greater stress on 'socialism', and even 'Marxism', and demanding sweeping economic changes immediately, all of which, as Aflaq and al-Bitar clearly saw, would alienate many in Syria and Iraq as well as in a number of other Arab states favourable to the cause of Arab nationalism. Thus, it would set back their primary aim as founders of the Baath movement. To give a priority to socialism and Marxism at the expense of Arab unity, as al-Saadi and his Syrian supporters did, would change the character of the Baath party, and intensify the Cold War among the Arab countries. The violence of the left-wing Baathists had also alienated Islamic sentiment and opinion, especially in Saudi Arabia and Iran (with her Arab religious connections through the Shia) and the Gulf States. To the external observer it appeared to aim at unity of the revolutionary left rather than at Arab unity.

Notes

1 See E. F. Penrose, 'Une année de coups d'état', *Orient*, No. 28 (1963), p. 27.

2 For a convenient exposition for the European reader, see the translation by the late Jean-Pierre Viennot of a number of Aflaq's statements of doctrine in 'L'idéologie du parti socialiste de la résurrection arabe', *Orient,* No. 29, 1964, pp. 151–72. See also Seale, op. cit., ch. 14; I. Rabinovitch, *Syria under the Baath, 1963–66* (Jerusalem, 1972), pp. 6–11; Tabitha Petran, *Syria* (London, 1972), pp. 90–2; and Simon Jargy, 'Le declin d'un parti', *Orient,* No. 11, 1959, pp. 21–39.

3 See J. Weulersse, *Le Pays des Alaouites* (Tours, 1940).

4 On the secret military committee see especially Rabinovitch, op. cit., pp. 42–6, 57–66.

5 For a useful summary and analysis of these discussions, see M. H. Kerr, *The Arab Cold War* (London, 1965), Ch. 3.

6 ibid., pp. 68–76.

7 The European reader is required to reverse his usage of the terms 'regional' and 'national' to interpret Baathist ideas. The latter term must be taken to mean a *group* of politically sovereign states, the former a single state. 'National' refers to the 'Arab Nation'; 'Regional' to an Arab state therein.

8 Arab Ba'th Socialist Party, *Some Theoretical Principles Approved by the Six* [*sic*] *National Congress, October 1963* (Beirut, n.d.).

9 The *Report* referred to above begins by making a distinction between a 'theory of struggle' formed in an 'ivory tower' of intellectuals and one 'formed as a result of confrontation of and involvement in the state of affairs through a series of violent conflicts between the masses and their enemies and those who oppose their progress' (p. 5). The appropriate theory of struggle is held to grow with struggle.

10 J. P. Viennot, 'Le Ba'th entre la théorie et la pratique', *Orient*, No. 30, 1964.

11 M. Colombe, 'Le monde arabe au seuil de l'année nouvelle', *Orient,* No. 28, 1963, p. 9.

12 Vanly, however, suggests that Nasser's attitude changed in accordance with his relations with the Iraqi government and was in any case feeble and equivocal: op. cit., p. 283.

13 Of course there were, and still are, numerous Kurdish groups which present wider claims and draw larger maps for Kurdistan, but there is little reason to confuse these with those of the responsible Kurdish leaders.

14 It is essential to an understanding of the events of 1963 that an adequate place should be given to the position in 'the street' and the way in which daily life was affected toward the end of this Baathist period. From direct observation and discussion with numerous individuals one of us wrote an account of this very quickly after the downfall of the 1963 Baathist regime. Although we have since learned much from later accounts of the political

manoeuvring behind the scenes among the leaders of the groups concerned, we have not found it necessary to correct what we then wrote on the events of the time. See, E. F. Penrose, 'Une année de coups d'état', *Orient,* No. 28, 1963.

15 E. F. Penrose was residing in Baghdad during the later months of the Baath regime and was on the streets when the National Guard occupied them and Windawi attacked the Presidential Palace. The text above is based on his account of events on 13, 17, and 18 November, written at the time. See also ibid.

16 On a visit to Damascus in November we discussed the Syrian attitude towards Ali Salih al-Saadi in the offices of *Al-Baath*, the official organ of the party. They approved the action taken against him and against the National Guard.

13 Moderate Arab Nationalism

The Iraqi Baath party, some of whose leaders were suspicious of al-Saadi's bid for power through the National Guard, had removed him from office. The moderate, but predominantly military, groups had then joined with President Arif in suppressing the subsequent violence, thus bringing down the Baath government. Chief among the officers with little or no commitment to Baathism, however, was Lt-Gen. Tahir Yahya, whom Arif then asked to form a new government. Over one-third of his government consisted of army officers, who were given the most important posts; a few prominent Nasserites were also included, two Baathist officers, and representatives of other groups; a number of ministries were held by technocrats. Arif appointed Ahmed Hasan al-Bakr as Vice-President.

The new government was well advised in the first instance to include leading Baathist officers. This provided some safeguard against Baathist plotting and checked any tendency for the Baath party to unite against it. From the beginning, of course, the radical wing of the Baath party bitterly opposed the government, and especially Abdul Salam Arif.

The officers, even those who were of, or inclined towards, the Baath, such as al-Bakr, had acted primarily because of the challenge that the National Guard had posed to the army. Once this challenge was disposed of, further co-operation between Baathists and non-Baathist officers was unstable. The non-Baathist Arab nationalist officers, and the non-political elements in the army, now led by President Arif, whose political stature had risen, were irreconcilably opposed to the Baath party and all its works. In some directions they leaned towards Nasser, though the extent of their leanings was exaggerated by outside observers.[1] The ambitions of the Baath party, embedded deeply in Baath doctrines, likewise rendered impossible a lasting coalition between it and the Arab nationalist officers and civilians around Abdul Salam Arif. The officers more or less seriously attached to the Baath movement, particularly al-Bakr, and perhaps Hardan al-Takriti, would have exposed themselves to virulent attack from the radicals of the Syrian party and from al-Saadi and his group now sheltering in Damascus. They would also have faced less violent but even more effective criticism from Aflaq and al-Bitar and other moderate Baathists who, while observing prudence and remaining open to compromise on particular measures, were averse to the sacrifice of Baath principles in a coalition in which they were not the dominant party.[2]

In view of the Baath record in 1963 it was not surprising that most of the public was ready and anxious to see all Baathist ministers excluded from the new government. Hence, the first concern of non-Baathist officers was to shed the leading Baathists. This was accomplished within a few months. In January 1964 the post of Vice-President was abolished and al-Bakr appointed to the Foreign Ministry with the rank of ambassador. According to press reports he refused the appointment and announced that he would leave politics. In March Hardan al-Takriti was removed as Minister of Defence. Only Tahir Yahya remained, and he had apparently cut most of his ties with the Baath.

With the removal of most of the Baathist ministers the new government represented a moderate Arab nationalism. Outside observers expected it to take on a pronounced Nasserite appearance. In many respects Abdul Salam Arif had outgrown some of his earlier immaturity and impetuosity, but he still showed the limitations of the army officer as well as of his own character and education when he had to deal with the complex economic and political issues before the modern world.

The Arab nationalist government had the advantage as well as the disadvantages of following an almost universally detested regime under which the ordinary citizen had lost the protection of the law. It hastened to confirm the return to normal working of the laws and institutions and the personnel responsible for their operation. Nevertheless, it was pointed out that political parties still had no legal status, including the Baath. Arif announced that the government would seek 'Arab unity'; at the end of December Prime Minister Yahya stated that a provisional constitution would shortly be announced which would ensure freedom of opinion and belief.

A great opportunity was open to the new regime. The civilian groups which supported the 1958 Revolution, and some of the military officers who executed the *coup*, had correctly charged the regime they displaced with crippling parliament by prohibiting political parties and the electoral system. One of their declared aims was to return to representative government. But from the beginning military officers dominated succeeding governments: no elections were held and the fine new building which had been completed for parliament had not been brought into its intended use. Rather it was turned into luxurious quarters for the new dominant governing class.

Arif claimed that the replacement of the Baath regime marked a return of the country to the true principles of the 1958 Revolution from which first Qassim and then the Baath had diverted it. But he and the members of his government were not equal to the occasion: moreover, by this time the military officers had been confirmed in their taste for the exercise of political power.

The regimes during the presidencies of Abdul Salam Arif and, later, his brother, Abdul Rahman Arif, may be loosely described as Arab nationalist, but they differed from the Baathist regimes in having no such organized party as the Baath. The abortive attempt to set up an Iraqi Socialist Union was aimed at establishing a monopolistic association. The regime was composed of military officers in the political posts with civilians in a number of departments requiring specialized knowledge and experience. In this respect it resembled the Egyptian regime, but Nasserism had less appeal in Iraq than in Egypt. In Egypt Nasser was a symbol of Egyptian, as well as Arab, dignity and independence, whereas in Iraq there were many who, while appreciating Nasser's importance to the Arab world and admiring his ability to stand up to imperialist encroachments,[3] nevertheless resented the prospect of Egyptian dominance in Iraq of the kind they had seen in Syria. Moreover, many Shia feared that Nasserism would strengthen the Sunni dominance in Iraq, while the Kurds feared that their position would be even more restricted in a larger Arab union.[4] To these reservations must be added those of the groups which, as in Egypt itself, did not like the kind of 'socialism' that Nasser had introduced.

Refusing the extremes of Baathism and Nasserism, the new regime was unable to formulate a coherent political programme, and its uncertain political course disillusioned those who had greeted it enthusiastically at the outset. Like the preceding governments it failed to reopen the political life of the country on a representative basis, although there was some hope in one brief period within the years 1965–66 when Abdul Rahman al-Bazzaz clearly wanted to move in that direction. It was, however, much more civilized than its predecessor had been.

Nationalism and Unity

A month after forming his government Prime Minister Yahya announced its general policies. They stressed the unity of the Arab nation and referred to the Cairo discussions of March and April 1963 and to the 'Cairo Charter' as the starting-point of the advance toward Arab unity.[5] It was clear that the government had no intention of permitting political parties, but would move to establish a single national organization—reminiscent of Egypt's Socialist Union. In the economic sphere, however, only passing mention was made of socialism, and reliance on Islamic tradition and law was declared to be a sufficient basis for Iraq's social and economic system. Government encouragement for the private sector was promised. The early promulgation of a provisional constitution was announced.

A high degree of uncertainty had clouded economic prospects under the preceding regime. The violent menaces directed at the business community by Ali Salih al-Saadi and his associates had raised fears of wholesale nationalizations. In such conditions the private sector had little disposition to invest or to proceed with projects that carried appreciable risk. Consequently Abdul Salam Arif and the new government made special efforts to give verbal reassurance to private business in the hope of stimulating investment and faster economic growth.

It was generally supposed in the first half of 1964 that the government would follow a comparatively conservative economic policy, more favourable than that of the Baath party to private enterprise and to the middle classes, and this was borne out by its announced programme. But the business community, whether engaged in private or in public enterprise, were influenced, not merely by the proclaimed policies of particular governments, but even more by the prospects of political stability, and for this reason it probably did not make very much difference what the government said: business would wait to see what it did. Indeed, ever since the 1958 Revolution business confidence had been low, and capital had been leaving the country. As we shall see, this was one of the factors influencing the government later to embark on extensive nationalizations.

The provisional constitution, duly promulgated in May 1964, was not entirely discouraging from this point of view in spite of the fact that it proclaimed the aim of 'comprehensive Arab unity', commencing with unity with the UAR, and stressed comprehensive planning. For at the same time it emphasized the 'inviolability' of private property. Those who, correctly as events proved, were sceptical of Arif's commitment to union with Egypt, could find comfort in the document. Public ownership of the means of production was not part of the Iraqi provisional constitution as it was in the constitution of Egypt. On the other hand, the political structure was modelled on that of Egypt: political parties were not to be permitted and a kind of 'national front' was envisaged, which in practice left great power in the hands of the President.

In drawing up the constitution there had been no consultation outside government circles with leading Iraqi political figures and the announcement was coolly received by these, although it was recognized that the publication of any constitution, provisional or otherwise, was already an advance for Iraq.[6]

With the fall of the Baath government, relations between Iraq and Egypt changed dramatically. Arif's Arab nationalist regime drew approval from Egypt and criticism from Syria, thus reversing the position of 1963. But the new alignments were more complicated than might have appeared at first sight. The popular expectation at the time that Egypt and Iraq would unite, now that the new Iraqi regime followed an Arab nationalist line closer to Egyptian than to Baathist ideas, was based on misunderstanding. Nasser and Abdul Salam Arif were not as close as appeared outwardly. From earlier experience, Nasser's estimate of Arif's abilities was far from high. Arif had also lost some of his earlier enthusiasm for Nasser. But each had his own political reasons for concealing these differences from the public and Nasser praised Arif extravagantly at the time of the suppression of the National Guard. Arif on the other hand was gaining political experience and recognized that any form of close union with Egypt would leave Iraq at a disadvantage. He also recognized that he himself would be a distinctly junior partner.

Nevertheless, Nasser was quick to take advantage of the bitter relations that now existed between Syria and Iraq to co-operate with the latter and intensify attacks on the former. Agreement was reached with Iraq to co-ordinate policies. This was followed by frequent visits of officials and economists between Cairo and Baghdad for economic consultations. In May a preliminary agreement was signed by Nasser and Arif envisaging union, and in June the Iraqi Cabinet was changed to strengthen the Nasserite component. Then came an announcement that a conference to organize and prepare the Charter of the Iraqi Arab Socialist Union would be held which, it was stated, would give civilian elements a chance to raise their voices on political affairs. A list of candidates for the Union was published and included the leaders of the former Iraqi political parties.

The proposal to imitate Egypt in this matter made little appeal to these leaders. It contradicted their own demand for freedom to restore political parties, and, except for the Communist party and a few politicians, they did not respond to the appeal to attend the conference on 4 July 1964 to construct an organization which, from their knowledge of Egypt, they believed to be only a 'front' designed to serve the interests of those who held the central power. The scheme languished from lack of appeal or even of interest, partly because the Arif government itself was ineffective in supporting it. Similarly, the project for a 'Unified Political Command' led to little more than a series of meetings between Egyptian and Iraqi specialists on economic and military affairs. It is difficult to detect any important political results from all these efforts, but the agreement and the resulting publicity intensified the impression in the Arab world of the isolation of the Syrian Baath regime and the *rapprochement* between Iraq and Egypt. In addition it may have contributed, along with other influences, to the sudden and unexpected change in Iraq's domestic economic policy in the middle of 1964.

Socialism and Unity

Early in 1964, the removal or resignation of the Baathist ministers in Iraq, with the exception of Tahir Yahya, widened the split between the governments of Syria and Iraq. At the same time government spokesmen vigorously called for more investment in private industry, assuring industrialists that private enterprise would be fostered under the new regime. Abdul Salam Arif was known to have always favoured such a policy.

There were, however, underlying contradictions—as dialectical thinkers would have called them—in these declared general policies. On the political side, when Syria withdrew from the UAR and repealed the economic measures Egypt had imposed, Nasser's denunciation was echoed by the Syrian and one section of the Iraqi Baath parties, which decried the alleged 'bourgeois reaction'. In March 1963 when another section of the Syrian army overthrew the government and established a military–Baath hegemony, an economic policy closer to Nasser's was established, at least in principle. But this could not be admitted in Cairo, for behind the façade of economic doctrines lay the political rivalry for the leadership of Arab nationalism.

Although President Arif and most of the ministers had been anxious to induce the business community to invest, they also professed support for Egypt, and the government benefited from Nasser's approval. One of their economic advisers was Khair al-Din Haseeb, an intelligent young Nasserite who was on good personal terms with Nasser and made frequent visits to Cairo. He had taken a doctorate at Cambridge some five years earlier and worked closely on economic matters with the Prime Minister, Tahir Yahya. Thus he was a private link between the Egyptian and the Iraqi governments. Haseeb thought that nationalization of industry in Iraq, as in Egypt, was desirable to ensure an adequate rate of investment and an industrial structure that would best serve the development of the country.

In Iraq, as in Egypt, socialism appealed not only to the left wing, but widely to intellectuals and others, especially students and the young, to whom idealism came easily and who longed for a more just economic order than they saw around them. The undoubted exploitation of the peasants by agrarian landlords, the ostentatious consumption of the rich urban property speculators and financiers, and the high profits of some industrialists, contrasted starkly with the poverty of the urban proletariat and rural workers. For Egypt, socialism meant the state ownership of the means of production combined with social welfare legislation to improve the lot of the ordinary people. The principles had a widespread appeal and their practicability was apparently demonstrated by the economic strength of the socialist bloc in Eastern Europe. Nasser's rejection of communism implied to many that the economic advantages of socialism could be obtained without the political disadvantages of communism. There is truth in this, and the appeal is thoroughly understandable, especially in countries where parliamentary democracy has appeared far too often to be a system by which the high-born and well-placed, the owners of land and industry, were enabled to manipulate politics to support their exploitation of the peasants and workers. The practical problem lay in the necessity of constructing an efficient, just, and non-political bureaucracy, on the one hand, and of keeping the government out of the hands of the military and subject to democratic processes on the other. Unless these conditions can be met, the sequel to revolution may be worse than its precursor. Neither the Egyptians under Nasser nor the Iraqis under the Baath were able to meet them.

After the dissolution of the UAR, Nasser seems to have intensified his propaganda on behalf of Arab socialism for internal as well as external reasons. His considerable success in dissociating Arab socialism from anti-religious secularism contrasted with the failure of the radical Baath to remove the impression in the Islamic world that its aim was an atheistic form of secularist socialism, in spite of the statements of Aflaq and other intellectual leaders.

It followed that the Arab nationalist Iraqi government that succeeded the Baath in 1963 was in a position to make socialism appear respectable to Islamic groups in a way which its predecessor could not have done. Its closer, though incomplete, affinity to Nasserism rendered some of its leaders sympathetic to the establishment in Iraq of an economic structure closer to that of Egypt. This would arouse less resistance from the general body of opinion, particularly Islamic opinion, than measures taken by the Baath would have done, even if in substance there was little economic difference between the actions that might be taken.

But in this area the reaction of the business community will not correspond to the reaction of the public. Here the new government faced a difficult choice. It desired to allay economic discontent by promoting economic expansion. But political instability had deterred investment. Ministers of the new government had repeatedly reassured businessmen that they had no intention of nationalizing industry. But, as noted earlier, assurances would not be sufficient to meet the doubts of businessmen suspicious of the government. Haseeb put this argument strongly to the Prime Minister, who decided to accept his nationalization proposals. On the morning of 14 July 1964, the anniversary of the 1958 Revolution and of the inauguration of the first assembly of the Arab Socialist Union, Iraqi businessmen awoke to find locks placed on the doors of the banks, and on the offices of insurance, cement, edible oil, asbestos, cigarette, and other large companies—14 in all. A list of the nationalized firms was announced. Haseeb was appointed to head the newly established economic organization to supervise the nationalized industries.[7]

Only the communists, some socialists, and militant Nasserites applauded this sudden reversal of policy. Some Iraqis attributed it to pressure from Egypt. It had certainly been influenced by the example of Egypt, but it is unlikely that pressure had actually been put on the Iraqi government by Nasser; nevertheless, Nasser had consistently made it clear that in his view the adoption of socialism in the Arab countries was a prerequisite to Arab unity.

Since the fall of Qassim political difficulties had been aggravated by an increased emphasis on the economic aspects of the political doctrines or ideologies of the rival groups struggling for ascendancy. Only a small group among the population understood or cared about these hotly debated matters. From 1954 rival political parties no longer had legal existence and from 1958 no election had been held and no parliament had met. The population received no education on the questions on which decisions had to be made. The army officers who held a monopoly of political power were in little better position, but the adoption of some form of Arab socialism in Egypt, Iraq, and Syria in the early 1960s was associated with intra-regional rivalries and with the intra-regional circulation of advisers and of ideas. It illustrates once more the impracticability of interpreting either the political or the economic history of any single Middle Eastern country without close reference to parallel events in neighbouring countries.

In Iraq, the nationalization measures, extensive government monopolization of the import trade, and the imposition of other economic restrictions, created economic dislocation, adversely affected production, and encouraged a flight of capital as well as of business and technical personnel.[8] In addition to the economic problems, there remained considerable political repression. The elimination of Baathist tyranny restored law and order in daily life for the ordinary people, but the government continued to act against its left-wing critics, particularly communists and suspected communists, although in a less open manner than had the Baathists.

The nationalizations were looked upon by the Nasserites as part of a package which was to include fulfilment of the unity agreement with Egypt and also constitutional reform. A new Cabinet was formed in November 1964, again under Prime Minister Yahya, which strengthened the Nasserite representation. Arif thus pre-empted the extreme nationalist position. In December a unified political command was established as agreed, and in June 1965 Iraq adopted as her national emblem the 'Arab eagle' of the UAR. With such harmless symbols did the Arif regime attempt to walk the tightrope.

The new set of policies came to nothing; they gained the support neither of the politically conscious Iraqi public, who looked for a permanent constitution and a more representative way of establishing the consultative council, nor of the Nasserites, who considered that Arif was not as zealous as he ought to be in the pursuit of their version of Arab socialism. In these circumstances they resisted his attempts to control the army; they also opposed the direction which the oil negotiations seemed to be taking.[9]

Nasser himself was disturbed by the developments in Iraq and in some Iraqi circles fears were expressed that there might be intervention from the small contingent of Egyptian troops which had been sent earlier to assist the Iraqi government in case of a counter-attack from the Baath after the overthrow of the al-Saadi faction. But Nasser did not want to push Arif further than he was willing to go; he did not want to get directly embroiled in Iraq's domestic controversies. He therefore exercised a restraining influence on the Iraqi Nasserites.

But inter-Arab conflicts were not the only source of political conflict for the Iraqi government: there remained the constant problem of how to deal with the brave, hardy, and proud men of the north.

The Kurdish War

The Arif government had followed the pattern of its two predecessors in proclaiming that the war in the north was the consequence of the misdeeds of the regime that it had displaced. As this claim implied that the unpopular war would cease with the disappearance of the offending regime, each new government was obliged at least to make an appearance of seeking, or at least accepting, a truce and to make an attempt at a peaceful settlement. Negotiations were opened on 10 February 1964, just under three months after the fall of the Baath government, and President Arif and Mulla Mustafa each issued a communiqué announcing a cease-fire in the Kurdish war. Arif followed with a statement in more detail expressing recognition of Kurdish national rights to be included in a constitution. He announced the release of political prisoners, the lifting of the economic blockade, the return of confiscated property, the reinstatement of Kurdish officials suspended from their posts, and the adoption of measures to reconstruct the northern regions and to compensate those whose lands had been submerged by the construction of the barrages of Dokan and Darbendi Khan.

Then came, however, a clause providing for the 're-establishment of security and stability in the north' which was taken by the Kurdish Democratic party (KDP) officers to imply that the army under the Baghdad government would be the instrument used to effect it. This was represented in some quarters as a scheme to reassert Arab domination. Certainly the clause had been unwisely drawn from a diplomatic point of view.

But the issues that led to the subsequent breakdown in negotiations were complicated by differences within both parties to them. We have already noted the cross-currents in the Kurdish national movement arising from the mixture of tribal affiliations and 'modern' political ideas which at times created strains between the military fighting men led by Mulla Mustafa Barzani and the Kurdish Democratic party, with its 'intellectual' approach to the Kurdish national problem. Barzani did combine some aspects of a reasonably modern outlook with his traditional attachments and he had been able to attract a large number of the younger educated Kurds to his camp. At the same time, however, a section of these younger men was influenced by a range of political ideas derived from Europe and Russia loosely characterized as 'Marxist'. These included conceptions of how to organize 'liberation movements' which differed widely from the traditional tribal forms and, if adopted, would have raised questions of 'collective leadership' that were not easily reconcilable with the tactics used in the struggles of the past, including the very recent past, by Barzani.

These conflicting tendencies were a grave handicap to the Kurdish cause at a critical stage in 1964. They provided useful propaganda material for the intransigent elements in the Iraqi army and among the political groups in Iraq, as well as for the Syrian Baath party. First, a number of leading figures in the Kurdish Democratic party openly criticized Barzani for his part in the truce, arranged from 10

February 1964, between himself and Arif. Barzani's right to conclude any such agreement with the Iraqi government except with the consent of the KDP was called in question.[10] The majority of the officers of the party, while accepting Barzani as commander-in-chief, held that political issues should be decided collectively through procedures laid down by the party, which in turn was dominated, so far as questions of policy were concerned, by its Political Bureau, situated in the south of the area.

Each side in the dispute was able to advance weighty arguments, but Barzani was in a position to carry the strongest tribal elements with him. His long experience of warfare and his ability to estimate the strength and limitations of the forces engaged in the conflict were indispensable. His judgement that the Kurdish forces needed a respite for reprovisioning and regrouping had influenced him to accept the truce of 10 February. The Political Bureau of the party, distant from the scene of action, was ill-suited to direct the course of a military campaign.

On the other hand, there were disadvantages in appearing to present the world outside with the spectacle of an independence movement led by a tribal leader. Though in fact such an unqualified representation was misleading, nevertheless the propagandists in anti-Kurdish circles in Baghdad could make much play with it by picturing Barzani as an old-fashioned tribal leader who represented only his tribe, and there were, of course, many tribal rivalries and affiliations in the Kurdish movement to which they could point. It was argued that the KDP fulfilled an essential function by uniting Kurds of different tribal and other groupings and by giving a more modern appearance to the movement.

There was some force in this argument for leadership by the KDP. Unfortunately, it was weakened by the wider claims of the party. A criticism similar to the one that the party brought against Barzani could be directed against it. If Barzani appeared to be adopting an authoritarian position, independent of the party, so also, in its turn, the party appeared to a number of Kurds to be advancing claims to an exclusive position as the sole authority representing the Kurds. Its reply to this criticism was that independent Kurds could find a place in its ranks. But this defence was unconvincing. Authority, according to the party, rested in its officers and officials. Often these were young men, placed in authority over more experienced and qualified Kurds outside the party machinery. The familiar tendency of young left-wing intellectuals to insist on centralizing political control in their own hands was apparent.

The dispute in the spring of 1963 led to attempts by the Political Bureau to detach some elements from Barzani. The attempt was unsuccessful. Barzani enjoyed the confidence of most of the units.

This raised the question from what source did the Political Bureau derive the authority which it claimed the right to exercise? Attempts were made by the Political Bureau to meet this issue by summoning a congress of the KDP in Mawat, the headquarters of the party. Here a resolution was passed calling on Barzani only to issue orders approved by the organizations of the party. This was conveyed to Barzani's headquarters by a delegation, but was met by a counter-proposal to call a congress at Kalat Diza, in Barzani's territory. It met at the beginning of July with 900 delegates; the Political Bureau did not appear. Later a conflict broke out between the two groups which threatened the whole movement. In the event, the Political Bureau failed to gain the support of the KDP members, but Barzani recognized the importance of the KDP, which was reconstituted with the addition of a Revolutionary Command Council on lines similar to those he desired. The earlier conceptions of the members of the Political Bureau were widely recognized as impracticable in the conduct of military operations. Some members of the previous central committee were expelled.

In Baghdad there was again evidence of the unpopularity of the war in the north. Casualties could not long be concealed from the public. The new government which had brought such a sense of relief to the people by ending the terrorist regime of the National Guard was losing much of its earlier popularity. To the war in the north were added the dissensions within the government on a wider range of questions. As we have seen, almost all of these originated in external, particularly intra-regional, differences.

The Resignation of the Nasserites

The new regime, though freed from Baathist influence, remained divided over other forms of Arab nationalism, chiefly between Nasserites and other Arab nationalists who, while supporting the idea of Arab nationalism, with its corollary of closer approaches to unity among Arab peoples, feared Egyptian domination and disliked some of the forms of socialism that Nasser had introduced in Egypt. It is, however, impossible to determine how much of the dissension within the government was over genuinely held beliefs and how much was related to personal animosities and struggles for position.

In July 1965 both types of tension had reached an acute stage and the Nasserite ministers in the Cabinet resigned. Their departure not only failed to restore a sense of unity in ministerial ranks, but weakened the Prime Minister: this organized group was now firmly outside the government. A variety of measures had been taken by Arif and Yahya designed to appeal to the public, including the abolition of military tribunals, the end of martial law, the release of a large number of political prisoners, the relaxation of restrictions on other elements of opposition to the regime, and the inauguration of an extensive five-year development plan. But the public was not to be reconciled to military rule, the conflicts within the Cabinet were not to cease, nor were the Kurds to accept the less-than-genuine efforts to meet their own nationalist needs. Yahya's standing declined for a variety of personal and political reasons and his relations with President Arif deteriorated.

In his attempts to control the army Arif followed Qassim's example in transferring army officers between different posts in accordance with their presumed loyalty to him. He began to make arrangements to secure Yahya's resignation and, in an attempt to reduce the Nasserite opposition within the army, he manoeuvred to persuade Brigadier Arif Abdul Razzaq, Commander of the Air Force, to accept the premiership.[11] Razzaq considered himself to be a Nasserite and was part of a Nasserite organization in the army. He was very critical of Arif's slow progress towards both union and socialism. Hence his appointment as Prime Minister and Minister of Defence on the resignation of Yahya at the beginning of September 1965 was a surprise to most observers. At the same time, however, Abdul Rahman al-Bazzaz, former Secretary General of OPEC, was moved from his position as Iraqi ambassador in London to take the posts of deputy Prime Minister, Foreign Minister, and Minister of Oil. Al-Bazzaz was a distinguished Professor of Law and Dean of the Faculty of Law in the University of Baghdad. He had been one of the pioneers in the development of the idea of Arab nationalism and had been the object of attack from the extreme left wing in the winter of 1958–59. He had faced his opponents courageously. He was a personal friend of Colonel Arif and had been regarded with suspicion by Qassim.

A Prime Minister's Abortive *Coup*

The doubts about the new Prime Minister were justified. He had been invited to form a Cabinet on 6 September; on the 12th President Arif, along with al-Bazzaz, left for Casablanca to attend an Arab summit meeting. Razzaq, supported by a number of the chief officers of the air force and some units in the army, promptly moved to effect a *coup* with the intention of requesting immediate unity with Egypt. The *coup* was blocked by other groups in the army and President Arif was informed. Arif flew to Cairo, where he changed planes and returned to Baghdad accompanied by Nasser's brother. Razzaq, reportedly assisted by Arif's friends in the army who wanted the affair to be kept quiet, escaped to Cairo.[12] Nasser had not been informed of Razzaq's attempt and he did not support it, although he granted Razzaq and his accomplices political asylum. The bizarre Razzaq episode could not be kept quiet and it added to the discredit into which the armed forces had fallen in the eyes of public opinion in Iraq. Razzaq was widely ridiculed as the man who staged a *coup* against himself.

Arif then turned to Abdul Rahman al-Bazzaz, who on 21 September was invited to form a government. The following eleven months were to be a notable, if short, period in post-war Iraqi history which clearly demonstrated the superiority of civilian over military rule. It was the first, and so far has been the only, break in the succession of military autocracies which, in setting aside constitutional law for government by decree, and in substituting *coups d'état* and armoured vehicles for elections, had deceived the civilian political groups which had expected to be among the main beneficiaries of the 1958 Revolution.

Notes

1 At the same time the enmity between Nasser and the Baath which had been brought to a head by events in Syria could not fail to influence the position of many. In July the Nasserites in Syria had attempted a *coup* against the ruling Baath regime in Damascus which had been suppressed with violence and a number of the Nasserite rebels were summarily shot. This led to an open break with Nasser and bitter verbal attacks from each side. After this the Syrian and Iraqi Baath governments began negotiations envisaging union, and agreements relating to union on economic and military affairs were signed. The Sixth National Congress of the Baath party held in Damascus in October called for full federal union. Nasser, of course, was not only at odds with the Baath party but was also irreconcilably opposed to any union between Syria and Iraq, which would have scuttled the foundation of his own Arab policy. A useful account of this can be found in Kerr, op. cit., Chapter 4.

2 See especially Edouard Saab, *La Syrie ou la révolution dans la rancour* (Paris, 1968), pp. 219–23, for an illuminating interview with the Secretary General of the Baath party, Mounif al-Razzaz, who with Aflaq and al-Bitar constituted the moderate section of the leaders who maintained the orthodox doctrines from their origin and steadily opposed the extreme groups of al-Saadi and others.

3 Admiration of this aspect of Nasser's activities was almost universal in the Arab world. One of the biggest demonstrations Baghdad had ever seen took place at the time of Nasser's resignation following the Six-Day War of June 1967, with the Iraqi public, along with the Egyptian public, hailing

Nasser and demanding that he remain in office. To some, and perhaps to Nasser himself, this demonstration was taken as evidence of his popularity in Iraq. But enthusiasm for Nasser's attempt to stand up to Israel, even when disastrously ineffectual, could not properly be taken as enthusiasm for 'Nasserism' in inter-Arab politics.

4 It should be noted, however, that Nasser himself generally recognized that the Kurds were a separate people and believed that a degree of autonomy should be recognized within the state of Iraq.

5 See above, Chapter 12.

6 See the report of a memorandum by Kamil Chadirchi to President Arif in Khadduri, op. cit., pp. 227–8.

7 The announcement of the nationalizations was the subject of considerable confusion. The Prime Minister's speech on the occasion of the celebrations had been drawn up in the Ministry of Planning and included a statement assuring the business community that there would not be nationalizations. However, the Prime Minister had been finally convinced by the arguments of Haseeb and others that such an action should be taken after all. He accordingly deleted the assurance from his speech as actually delivered. Unfortunately, it was not deleted from the published version and this led to widespread accusations of deception and bad faith.

8 See below, Chapter 18 for a discussion of the nationalization, and the consequences of the economic policies adopted.

9 See below, Chapter 16 for a discussion of the oil negotiations and the position of the Nasserites. In the Cabinet, the Nasser group was headed by Col. Subhi Abdul Hamid and Col. Abdul Karim Farhan. The group included an ardent Arab nationalist, Fuad al-Rikabi, originally a Baathist who served Qassim briefly, and who conspired with the Baathists to kill Qassim, but when the Baath clashed with Nasser, he left the Baath and went to Cairo to become a Nasserite. He returned to Iraq when the Baath government collapsed in November 1963 and in November 1964 became Minister of Rural Affairs in Yahya's Cabinet.

10 A detailed discussion of these issues is contained in the remarkably informed work of Ismet Chériff Vanly, *Le Kurdistan irakien: entité nationale* (Neuchâtel, 1970), especially pp. 220–7. He characterizes the difference between the approach of Barzani and the Political Bureau as follows: 'Pour Barzani, le peuple est réel et ses problèmes sont concrets; pour les doctrinaires du Bureau, cette réalité existe, certes, mais on la voit à travers le voile transparent de considérations théoriques' (p. 221). Most helpful on the background too is Serge Gantner, 'Le Mouvement national kurde', *Orient,* Nos. 32–3, 1964–65, pp. 29–120.

11 Khadduri, op. cit., pp. 242–4 discusses some of the manoeuvres and intrigues associated with the removal of Yahya. He does not give any sources for his discussion of the events he reports, but generally much of his information is based on personal interviews with the people involved. He suggests that Arif was preparing to introduce civilian rule. While Arif showed no disposition to restore free political parties, he does seem in his later days to have aimed at reducing military influence and increasing the civilian role in moves towards a position more consistent with his criticism of Qassim, even if his underlying motive was to retain a deciding voice in his own hands; after all, he was an army officer. His appointment of al-Bazzaz as Prime Minister may perhaps be taken as evidence for Khadduri's suggestion. It has also been stated to us by a high official close to Arif that Arif was merely using Bazzaz to help get rid of the Nasserites, after which he intended to dispense with him, a policy which began to become clear after al-Bazzaz's

attack on the army. This, however, is speculation. It is easy to exaggerate the consistency with which political aims were pursued by army officers often out of their depth. In the event, Arif was killed before any such policy could be carried out.

12 An account of this was given by Mohammed Hasanain Haykal (*Al Ahram*, 24 September 1965). An English version is given in BBC ME/1970/A/45, 27 September 1965. See also Khadduri, op. cit., pp. 245–6.

14 Civilian Interlude

The change of atmosphere was remarkable. No one with direct experience of Iraq could fail to be impressed by the freedom of expression and the sense of relief from past tension which accompanied it. In the year before the 1958 Revolution, and during part of the Qassim period, some freedom of expression had existed; it disappeared in the Baathist period and had returned in the first part of the Arab nationalist regime. But there were always limits; some subjects were not spoken of freely in public. With the coming of Abdul Rahman al-Bazzaz there was a brief psychological transformation: full discussion was publicly invited and even Abdul Salam Arif lent himself to a movement towards a form of government that would be at once more representative and more civilian—in the view of al-Bazzaz wholly civilian.[1]

The open expression of the public's critical attitude towards the military class was an outstanding feature of the Bazzaz period. The Iraqi Revolution and the changes in Syria in the later 1950s and the early 1960s had brought into power armies whose officers had become the new privileged class, eclipsing the merchant class and the great landowners. Air-conditioned barracks contrasted with nearby slum conditions; the special arrangements in both Damascus and Baghdad by which officers could buy products in daily use for their families as well as for themselves at specially reduced rates, contrasted with the position of the civilian professions as well as that of the masses. These contrasts were observed daily by the public and were freely discussed even in front of the officers themselves. Those of our former students who in preceding years had entered other professions than the army were not slow to remind their friends in officer's uniform of their privileges at public expense. (To escape these attentions the latter often changed into civilian clothes before going out in the evening.)

But it was not simply among the professional classes that the change of regime was welcomed. Enquiries about opinion in the *suq* and among the poorer classes brought responses wholly favourable to the change. And here the radio and television contributed to the public impressions formed. It was obvious to viewers and listeners that the new premier was a man of high culture, with an excellent command of Arabic, who could marshal his thoughts in logical sequence and present reasoned arguments with moderation, in contrast to the army officers whose tanks and guns had brought them to power without the qualifications needed to deal competently with affairs of state. The privileges of the military class and the frequently inferior level of their intellectual attainments in comparison with those of entrants into the other professions were now openly discussed in Baghdad. The takeover of government by military officers had contributed to a lowering of the prestige in which they had earlier been held. Outstanding officers like General Ghazi al-Daghistani, commander of the Army Third Division before the 1958 Revolution, had been greatly respected;[2] he had created an excellent impression when he appeared in the People's Court. But this type of officer had been displaced when the high command became selected in accord with political and personal rather than professional military criteria.

During this period public opinion played an important role for a time. The politically minded officers resented al-Bazzaz from an early stage. By 1965 the army had begun to take for granted that it had the right to govern the country and was not subject to higher authority. President Abdul Salam Arif, in appointing al-Bazzaz, had made a breach in this system of power and the prompt expressions of public approval made al-Bazzaz's military opponents hesitate before taking steps against him. In addition, Arif, up to the time of his death, remained a powerful influence behind al-Bazzaz.[3]

General Government Policy

Al-Bazzaz, whose term of office was to last from 21 September 1965 to 6 August 1966, faced three main problems at the outset: domestic economy questions; the war in the north, which Brigadier Abdul Aziz al-Uqaili, the Defence Minister, had renewed early in the year; and the question of the re-establishment of representative government.

On the economic side he had to deal with the aftermath of what, at the time, had been unexpected changes in government policy towards industry. The contrast between what industry and commerce had been led to expect by the early declarations of the new government in 1964 and the measures suddenly announced six months later had created dissatisfaction and restraint in business circles both great and small.

The second problem facing Iraq at the time of al-Bazzaz's appointment was also domestic in a territorial sense, but not in an Arab context. The truce of February 1964 in Kurdistan had given way to a Baghdad offensive in the spring of 1965, organized and led by al-Uqaili, an intransigent anti-Kurdish officer who, in the face of events, denied that Mustafa Barzani represented an important part of the Kurdish people. The offensive which he planned had failed. The public in Baghdad was weary of the war and sceptical of the good faith of some of the officers conducting it who, they suspected from some examples of conspicuous consumption in Baghdad, were enriching themselves from funds received for operations in the north on which they were not required to render a detailed accounting.

The third problem was the improvement of administration and the extension of the area of civilian control in government. His bold approach to the problem of militarism disconcerted some of his friends and annoyed his enemies. We heard two contrasting opinions on the wisdom of his outspokenness. The first was that it would cause his downfall. But the second, which was vigorously argued in other quarters, was that in any case al-Bazzaz could not expect to last long against the vested military interests and that in the circumstances it was best to make as great an immediate impact as possible. 'Bazzaz has debunked the military', we heard an experienced observer remark at a social gathering. Several weeks later we mentioned these two general viewpoints to the Prime Minister. He was aware of them and gave a strong impression that he had acted deliberately and not on impulse.

As long as al-Bazzaz was associated with Abdul Salam Arif it was difficult to make progress towards a Kurdish peace. Although Arif had concluded the cease-fire agreement of February 1964 when his new government had to establish itself firmly in the difficult conditions left by the Baathist anarchy of 1963, he had taken no effective steps to follow the truce with constructive measures to settle relations between Kurds and Arabs. The new Arab nationalist government was reputed to seek wider unity, especially with Nasser, of which the Kurds had always been apprehensive. Only in politically experienced circles was it realized that the outward appearance of closer approach to unity with Egypt under Arif's leadership was deceptive.

But even without wider Arab unity, Arif and a number of army officers and a few ministers were hostile to any attempt to meet Kurdish aspirations. A disastrously provocative speech had been made early in 1965 by the Nasserite Minister of the Interior, Subhi Abdul Hamid, flatly rejecting the idea of any form of Kurdish autonomy within a single state, 'now or in the future'. Such a declaration was bound to complicate the task of future negotiators. Nor did it seem to represent the general sentiment in Iraq, however pleasing it may have been to some of the Arabs of Mosul.

Thus, in the early stages of his ministerial period al-Bazzaz was unable to take effective measures to deal with the war in the north. He turned to questions of economic policy and civilian administration: 'The time is ripe', he said, 'for the country to restore normal conditions of life in which there will be no more room for military courts, military rulers, emergency situations, tanks in the street or anything that may give the citizens a feeling of a lack of stability in the country'.[4]

Such outspoken statements made a profound impression on the public and placed military officers on the defensive. They expressed the aspirations of large numbers of civilians and of many of the military themselves, for whom stability and freedom to go about their business without menace from armed men, whether soldiers or unofficial groups, represented their deepest wishes after years of frustration. The military revolutionaries had eliminated a defective old order without producing a convincing new order. As al-Bazzaz said in the course of an interview with us: 'I have told the military that they have only been carrying out a series of *coups,* not a revolution'.

Such was the preliminary message of al-Bazzaz, clear and challenging in its central theme, but inevitably couched in general terms. His plea that all citizens should take part in choosing their political heads and in determining the nature of the regimes under which they lived drew general support except among the partisans of authoritarian rule. When al-Bazzaz at the outset spoke of 'union' with Egypt as one of Iraq's aims, the Nasserites were prepared to claim that Egypt fulfilled the requirements of representative government. Al-Bazzaz certainly did not share this opinion, but out of political discretion avoided direct public criticism of Nasser. But al-Bazzaz maintained publicly that co-operation with Egypt ought to take account of the nature of Iraq and her special circumstances. More directly he spoke freely of the shortcomings of the Arab Socialist Union, which had made little or no headway in Iraq. He was in a better position than others to do this; his well-known lectures in Cairo, published in a book later, constituted one of the pioneer formulations and classic expressions of the doctrine of Arab nationalism.[5]

The checks to the army in Kurdistan and the rising list of casualties, which provoked unfavourable comment in Baghdad, brought the Kurdish war increasingly into public attention, competing with the problem of the future form of government in Iraq. Although the Prime Minister was now a civilian, the Minister of Defence was not.

Al-Uqaili, who had prepared the spring offensive against the Kurds, opposed the least concession to Kurdish nationalism, which to him did not exist. Friction arose between him and al-Bazzaz, who did not believe that Iraq could be unified without concessions to regional demands. But as long as both the President and the Minister of Defence took an intransigent view of the issue, he had to postpone action until circumstances were more favourable. The spring offensive continued. Barzani now possessed artillery and the prognostications of al-Uqaili were in contradiction to the few authentic reports from the field of battle. At this point a wholly unexpected event changed the outlook for peace in the north.

The Death of Abdul Salam Arif: the Succession of his Brother

The differences among Arab nationalists, related as they were to the schisms and controversies between Nasser and the different brands of Baathism, had reduced the popularity of Abdul Salam Arif and of some of the other political officers. Arif undertook political tours to attract support in the country and it was on one of these that he met his death in a surprising accident to a helicopter that was to carry him from Qurna to Basra after dark. The exact circumstances of the crash remain obscure. During that night (13–14 April 1966) we happened to be travelling across the desert from Damascus to Baghdad soon after the *coup* in Damascus that, with much bloodshed, replaced one Baathist military faction by another. On arrival at Baghdad we found that a curfew had been imposed: everyone we met during the morning assumed that the death of Arif, which had been announced a short time earlier, was the result of political assassination. In spite of the absence of any concrete evidence this belief continued to be widely held. Prompt and discreet action by al-Bazzaz again proved his competence.

The choice of a new President reopened the military–civilian struggle. The National Defence Council and the Cabinet, meeting jointly, were to elect the new President, but a two-thirds majority was required. The army officers pressed for another military officer to succeed Abdul Salam. Al-Bazzaz, then acting President, insisted on the principle that the office was open to civilians. The army, unable to agree on a single candidate, presented both al-Uqaili and Brigadier Abdul Rahman Arif, Abdul Salam's brother. No candidate could obtain a two-thirds majority on the first vote. On the second, the civilians turned their votes to Abdul Rahman, who had gained a reputation for greater moderation than his late brother, particularly on the war in the north.[6] Having formally established the principle that a civilian had as much claim to the presidency as a military officer, al-Bazzaz did not press his own claim, fully realizing the risks of a riposte in the form of another military *coup*.

Al-Uqaili was omitted from the new Cabinet and the way was clear for peaceful moves in the north. Although al-Uqaili professed support for a civilian representative government, he attached primary importance to the liquidation of Kurdish resistance. The new President was a military officer of milder disposition, greater moderation in making judgements, fewer prejudices and animosities—indeed fewer genuine convictions—than his predecessor had been, and was widely believed to be even more limited intellectually. For the first time al-Bazzaz could attempt to end the war and effect a settlement in the north. Abdul Rahman did not share the emotional antagonisms of his brother towards Kurdish claims.

Towards a Kurdish Settlement

The premier was thus in a position to move both on the question of restoring representative government and also on the war against the Kurds. Although these questions were not formally linked, in practice the type of political organization for the country could not be discussed without facing the fact that the population of Iraq consisted of two nationalities, whose relations could only be harmonized by clear acceptance of and mutual respect for each other.

Early declarations by the new President and by the Prime Minister foreshadowed a sharp change of policy. The President was moderate and conciliatory; the premier held out prospects of satisfying Kurdish aspirations so long as the unity of Iraq was maintained. Private exploratory discussions were held secretly.

Al-Uqaili's spring offensive had failed: the political judgement and military expectations on which it had been based were erroneous. The accounts given to the outside world by the Iraqi military through Baghdad radio described imaginary rather than real military operations. They claimed that the results they hoped to achieve had actually been achieved. The army, it was said, had been victorious, the rebellion had been crushed, several of Barzani's sons had been killed, and an ultimatum had been delivered to the survivors to surrender themselves and their arms.

In reality, the Iraqi army was in flight towards Ruwanduz. An independent witness was present at Barzani's headquarters in the remote mountain region in which the decisive battle had been fought. His account of personalities and events is an indispensable contribution to the history of the conflict.[7]

A favourable moment had come for a cease-fire in Iraqi Kurdistan. Not all army officers shared al-Uqaili's diehard emotions, and some realized that the involvement of a large part of the Iraqi army in a civil war weakened the country in its external relations within and beyond the Middle East. Many even of the military politicians realized that the war was extremely unpopular. The greatest opposition to a settlement was to be found largely among the Mosuli Arabs, both officers and civilians.[8]

On 16 May 1966 we had a long interview with al-Bazzaz during which we discussed the Kurdish question in considerable detail. Although a leading Arab nationalist, he was far too intelligent to accept the view of some Baathists that Iraq was an exclusively Arab state and that the Kurds were either Arab in origin or that they must assimilate themselves completely to the Arabs and their language; nor could he accept the equally naive view of al-Uqaili that Kurdish dissent was only due to unrepresentative agitators and would collapse completely if strong military measures were taken against them. Al-Bazzaz first referred to the law on administrative decentralization, then in preparation. But he did not contest strongly our suggestion that this approach was inadequate in face of the reality of a separate Kurdish nationalism that went far beyond such sectarian differences as those between the populations of Baghdad and Basra.

Commenting on the suggestion that in any measures to satisfy Kurdish aspirations within a single Iraqi state a necessary preliminary step would be to delimit an area within which the population was mainly Kurdish, the Prime Minister at first objected that this would attract claims for similar concessions from other areas. He then agreed that local autonomy might be granted to the Kurds in respect to special services, education, and some other types of administrative services, and in the end agreed that some delimitation of geographical areas would be needed for these purposes.

Within Iraqi government circles, within Kurdish circles, and in discussions between them, the scope and depth of analysis of the issues had been inadequate. Sometimes the discussions followed a cease-fire proposed and accepted for tactical reasons to give time for a regrouping of forces. They had never been preceded or accompanied by careful preparation based on a study of the geography and demography of the areas in question and of the precise administrative structures that would be involved in measures of devolution. Military officers were wholly unsuited to deal with such questions, and even civilian political leaders needed the detailed help of a number of persons with special knowledge of particular aspects of the issues concerned. The coming of al-Bazzaz into government provided an opportunity for a competent examination of the question on the basis of which alone a workable plan of reconciliation might be accomplished.

The discussions between the Kurdish representatives and those of the Iraqi government led to the comprehensive agreement in principle of 29 June 1966. The main part of it had been reached in Haji Omran, in Kurdistan, in discussions with Barzani in person.

In the preamble the Iraqi government undertook to conform to the measures outlined.[9] A full acknowledgement of Kurdish nationality in unambiguous terms came in the first of the twelve points. It was followed by an undertaking to make the necessary adjustments in the law dealing with the decentralization of regional administration then in preparation. Next came acceptance of the Kurdish language as an official language along with Arabic in the provinces that were predominantly Kurdish. The civil servants in these regions would also be Kurds. The government also declared its determination to hold parliamentary elections within the period fixed in the provisional constitution. The Kurdish population was to be represented in an elected National Council in proportion to its numbers, and was to share in public posts whenever qualified candidates were available. Parliamentary life was to be reorganized and revived and certain political organizations were to be established in which Kurds would take part. A general amnesty was to be proclaimed; all Kurdish civil servants and employees were to return to their posts and Kurds would rejoin the armed forces after two months. The government was to make every effort to resettle those who had been displaced and to compensate those who had suffered material losses in the conflict.

Three additional clauses remained secret: first an agreement to create a new governorate, Dohuk, composed of the Kurdish parts of Mosul governorate; second, an agreement to liberate all political prisoners in Iraq; and third, legalization of the Kurdish Democratic party.

Such is a bare outline of the most constructive effort yet made to deal with the most dangerous threat to internal peace in Iraq, and to end the fratricidal conflict into which the army had drawn Iraq from time to time in the northern region, much of which, with obvious injustice to the population, had been included in the state of Iraq without safeguards for its people.

Much remained to be done before the well-conceived twelve-point agreement could be followed by a detailed plan of application. On the Kurdish side the chief difficulty arose from the doctrinaire criticisms by the more ideologically minded members of the Kurdish Democratic party who were simultaneously striving to gain complete control of political policy for the party. This controversy remained a source of weakness on the Kurdish side, but if al-Bazzaz had continued in office, there is no reason to suppose that, given a reasonably free hand, he could not have reached a firm settlement of outstanding issues.

Representative Government

The statesmanlike efforts of al-Bazzaz to end the war in the north went hand-in-hand with efforts to prepare the way for genuine representative government. Here again the heritage of the past impeded progress at critical points. This was illustrated during our discussions with al-Bazzaz in connection with the war in Kurdistan. Al-Bazzaz spoke of the resumption of elections as the next step to be taken towards representative government and of the need for debate and criticism among the elected representatives. But when we asked him how nominations of the candidates would be made, he replied that he saw the objective we had in mind and that he would have to say frankly that an immediate return to general freedom for all parties would mean that the Communist party would be recognized and carry on its activities openly. This he could never agree to; 'I am not', he said firmly, 'going to let the Communist party enter again'.

Thus the fear of the Iraqi Communist party played a leading role in hindering the supporters of genuine representative government from pushing their advocacy of it to its logical conclusion. For this the ineptitude of local communist leaders was partly responsible. Their violent abuse of al-Bazzaz and a number of others whom they denounced as 'reactionaries' and 'imperialists', merely directed attention away from the real sources of Iraq's troubles. Although Qassim had effectively dismantled the IPC, and the Baathists had murdered numerous communists in a series of atrocities that made communist misdeeds appear small by contrast, the fear of communism continued to haunt the middle classes in the Fertile Crescent, not only in Iraq but also in Syria and Jordan.

Bazzaz went on to say that he looked forward to the creation of a political organization that would hold parliamentary discussions open to free criticism of the government of the day. He avoided the term 'Arab Socialist Union'. Undoubtedly he intended to move beyond a mere front designed to support the government, but he had seriously restricted the choices before him by his excessive fears of the Iraqi Communist party.

The Prime Minister's ideas of economic policy and his attitude towards Arab socialism were consistent with his political policy. He was a sincere democrat who desired to see Iraq governed by constitutional and representative institutions. The extension of nationalization might be desirable on economic grounds, but this would not, in his eyes, justify its imposition by a few individuals in key places without public discussion and examination in representative bodies.[10] Many interests and the livelihood of many people were affected by it and it seemed to him, with his legal and democratic approach, wrong that such changes should be suddenly made by dictatorial *fiat*. This point seems to have been overlooked by commentators on the Iraqi nationalizations and socialist policy. Some of those who carried through the changes sought to justify their actions by the plea that if they had not done so swiftly and without warning, the measures would have been defeated by powerful reactionary groups. For them the end took precedence over the means. But if the end was an economic one, the means were political; they raised fundamental questions respecting the nature of government.

Foreign Policy

From the beginning al-Bazzaz held the view that it was in the interests of Iraq to maintain friendly relations with her neighbours, including non-Arab neighbours. With the passing of the older generation, which at the time of the foundation of Iraq had had certain links with Turkey surviving from the past, relations between Turkey and Iraq had diminished, especially following the settlement of the controversy between Britain and Turkey over the northern border of Iraq which had been carried to the League of Nations in the 1920s.

On the east Iran, the other non-Arab state which bordered Iraq, was equally important. Between her and Iraq an unresolved territorial issue remained. Like Turkey, Iran was larger than Iraq in population, in the extent of fertile territory, and in some economic resources.

The visits of al-Bazzaz to Ankara and Teheran, the impression made by his moderation, the friendliness of his manner of approach, and the high quality of his intellect, contributed towards a long-needed improvement in relations, which had suffered from the conflicting, unstable, and unpredictable attitudes of a succession of military regimes. Moreover, the most important of his domestic achievements bore directly on Iraq's relations with Turkey and Iran, for from time to time the war against the Kurds had been a source of friction between Iraq and her neighbours. On the Iranian frontier other longstanding difficulties existed which al-Bazzaz was anxious to resolve.

In spite of his stern opposition to the Iraqi Communist party, al-Bazzaz was also eager to improve Iraq's relations, especially her economic relations, with the Soviet Union. A mission to Moscow undertaken in August 1966 made a favourable impression there. It appeared that the leading political figures in Moscow had little previous knowledge of al-Bazzaz and were not seriously influenced by the ideological fulminations of the Iraqi Communist party, which had not kept up with the developments and fluctuations in Russian thought since the Twentieth Party Congress, particularly concerning attitudes towards the varieties of national bourgeoisie. Al-Bazzaz would be classified as one of the national bourgeoisie of liberal tendency with whom at certain stages local communists should collaborate if possible. This the Iraqi communists evidently had not realized.

Thus the first civilian Prime Minister since the 1958 Revolution had within a few months opened the way towards a Kurdish settlement, taken steps towards the beginning of representative government, and moved to establish normal relations between Iraq and her neighbours. In these directions he had done more than all the military governments in the eight preceding years. Popular sentiment was on his side, but the time given him was too short to permit him to carry through any of his policies or to make effective moves in the direction of a restoration of democracy.

If the people of Iraq had been given an opportunity to express themselves collectively a verdict in favour of the Arif–Bazzaz regime could hardly have been in doubt. But ultimately, the disposition of governments now was in the hands of those who could put tanks on the streets and fighter and bomber airplanes in the sky. The widespread approval of the regime and of its actions which represented only the beginnings of a much needed transformation had united the military politicians, the extreme nationalists, and the anti-Kurdish elements, who now feared that the changes initiated and in prospect might become firmly established.

Displacement of al-Bazzaz by the Army

The political–military class watched developments with a jealous eye. They had come to regard political leadership as their preserve. Enjoying greater privileges than any class since the foundation of Iraq, with the exception of, for over three decades, a limited group of large landowners, they resented the intrusion of an outstanding civilian who had gained greater public approval than any leading political figure since Qassim in his early 'honeymoon' period. Still more resented was his outspokenness concerning the proper role of the army. At most, however, this had added a little fuel to the fire. Their opposition would have grown in any case out of reluctance to lose their monopoly.

Not only was al-Bazzaz resented by the military politicians, however; he was also opposed by the extreme left wing, which denounced him as a tool of capitalist interests, and by the Nasserites. At first sight it may appear strange that the latter should oppose one who had stood out as a leading philosopher of Arab nationalism. But the naive and somewhat primitive ideas of some who regarded 'union' as a simple and straightforward question were intermingled with the downright insincerity of others who, though they would never themselves have been ready to accept an arrangement making President Nasser supreme in Iraq as well as in Egypt, were ready to exploit the issue to gain political power. The second of these two attitudes was to be found in both Syria and Iraq. It was almost universal among the Baathists, and widespread among professed Arab nationalists calling for union with Egypt.

To this unacknowledged combination of the militarists and extreme nationalists and communists against the civilian premier must be added the Baathists, still smarting under their failure in 1963 and still conspiring to return to power. Since leaving the post-Baathist government in January 1964 Colonel Ahmed Hasan al-Bakr had been a centre of Baathist intrigue in his home, watched by the two Arifs in turn. But his Arab nationalist successors were less ruthless than he himself would have been, and subsequently was, in eliminating opposition.

Clearly the groups opposing al-Bazzaz—communists, Nasserites, military politicians, and Baathists—constituted the active and organized (whether open or clandestine) political groups. In the absence of political parties, politics in Iraq consisted of the intrigues and personal rivalries within and among these groups. The failure of parties to develop in Iraq with some degree of cohesiveness among the members based on a common objective and loyalty to each other intensified personal power struggles and in some ways gave personal relationships a more decisive role in politics. Equally, the absence of 'cabinet responsibility' and some sense of loyalty among members of the government to a common objective again enhanced the role of individual rivalries.

Abdul Rahman al-Bazzaz was a man of strong personality, firm convictions, and a high standard of integrity. He did not 'suffer fools gladly' and was sometimes abrupt in his individual dealings. His critics have made much of his allegedly indiscreet outspokenness. They have in some cases maintained that he might have gained more support in certain directions if he had spoken more softly. It is extremely doubtful, however, whether the support of these critics would have weighed against the vested interest of the military who had more far-reaching motives for displacing a civilian who, by his example and his achievements, was exposing their limitations. Moreover, his outspokenness had brought him much support in other directions. He showed us in his bureau a sheaf of letters received from young army officers expressing appreciation of his work.

They realized that they would have a more assured career if the army confined itself to its proper function.

Towards the end of June 1966 the Nasserites among the military, or rather air force, attempted a *coup* which coincided in time with the agreement al-Bazzaz had made with the Kurds. Brigadier Arif Abdul Razzaq, already having failed, as we have seen, in one attempt at a *coup* against the government which he headed, decided to try again. The Iraqi Nasserites were becoming increasingly restive at the caution with which al-Bazzaz approached the question of unity with Egypt, and at his insistence on Iraq's independence and right to deal with her own special difficulties in her own way. Abdul Razzaq returned to Iraq from Cairo in June 1966 and plotted with other Nasserites to overthrow the government by force. An air attack was made on Baghdad, but Arif had been forewarned of the plot and the rebels were easily defeated by forces led by the commander of the Presidential Guard and other loyal military units.

Razzaq's second bizarre attack on the government again involved Nasser's relation to Iraqi politics and to al-Bazzaz in particular. The tension between them was related to the intra-regional cold war over the Yemen, which had divided the Arab states into 'conservative' and *progressiste* groups, corresponding very roughly to an East–West division. Al-Bazzaz's policy to maintain good relations with neighbours, setting aside doctrinal questions, ran directly counter to this cold war. Late in 1965 it appeared that an accord might be reached between Nasser and King Faisal after their meeting at Jeddah on 23 November. But Egypt's internal difficulties and Faisal's preoccupation with an Islamic conference were unfavourable to it and the propaganda as well as the Yemen war continued. Both Egypt and Syria represented the cold war as a conflict between liberated revolutionary and feudal reactionary states, and the Alawi regime under Salah Jedid in Syria made particularly violent attacks on al-Bazzaz. It was in this psychological atmosphere that Razzaq left Egypt and attempted his second *coup*. The widespread charges that Egypt had instigated it led Hasanain Haykal to declare that Razzaq had been in Cairo as a guest and not as a prisoner—a far from reassuring explanation. Al-Bazzaz's diplomacy was as discreet as it was well conceived.[11]

From this time relations between al-Bazzaz and Arif appear to have deteriorated as the officers increased their pressure on the President to remove al-Bazzaz. Abdul Salam Arif might well have responded to this pressure in time if he had lived: having tasted political power, he had lost enthusiasm in 1964 for a union with Egypt that would overshadow his role in Iraq and a similar change of attitude towards al-Bazzaz might have been expected. But Abdul

Rahman Arif was much less ambitious and would have fitted well into a society in which the army played its proper role. In the conditions of Iraqi society in the 1960s this implied that his influence among the political officers was weak.

For some time he resisted the officers demanding that he should dismiss his popular Prime Minister. 'Who', he asked, 'do you propose that I should put in his place?' For several months this question struck a vulnerable spot. The officers were divided. Al-Uqaili had already put himself forward as a candidate for the Presidency, but in addition to his violent hatred of the Kurdish leader, which would undoubtedly have opened a new war in the north, he was cold to Arab nationalism and would have been resented by Nasserites. The army was as divided among factions as the civilians.[12] The only real source of unity among them was limited to the determination to maintain government in the hands of themselves and their class.

By August, however, their opposition to al-Bazzaz had reached a point at which their divergencies over the choice of successor were at last overcome and they agreed on a candidate of compromise: Brigadier Naji Talib, a Shia, who had been one of the Free Officer group that overthrew the monarchy, and was Minister of Social Affairs under Qassim. He was known as a moderate Pan Arab, having friendly personal relations with men of widely different views.

Having made their choice after much controversy, the militarist group redoubled their pressures on Abdul Rahman Arif. In the view of some observers, however, he had become more self-confident since the failure of Razzaq's attempt to displace him and more susceptible to the insinuations of military politicians that he should assert authority over the civilian premier. He was hardly a man of strong character. On 6 August 1966 President Arif requested and received the resignation of al-Bazzaz and invited Brigadier Talib to form a new government.

Both Arif and the officers who sought the removal of al-Bazzaz realized that such an action would not meet with public approval. In surrendering to the pressures of the military groups Arif at the most only put off the day when he would himself be expelled from political life. To the public also it was a confession of weakness. He lost the regard of the civilian public without gaining military support. He laid the foundations for the renewal of the war in the north. There were to be no further moves towards representative government, and Iraq was to be under military rule for an indefinite period.

Disunity Among the Military

The period of office (6 August 1966–10 May 1967) of Naji Talib was marked by one achievement only—a patient and effective handling of a dispute between Syria and the IPC which could have had explosive political consequences but which in the event was peacefully solved. The dispute is discussed in Chapter 16. The Baath Syrian government tried to turn the affair into a test of Arab solidarity, but Talib's moderate and skilful conduct of negotiations kept the temperature down and prevented any political group from being able to transform the dispute into a major domestic political issue. On other matters he did little; he did nothing to follow up al-Bazzaz's agreement with the Kurds, nor did he take a lead in constitutional reform.

Al-Bazzaz, with his keen sense of the primacy of law, had given a strong impetus to the movement to replace the haphazard political machinery which the 1958 Revolution and subsequent *coups* had erected. The desire for legitimacy was reasserting itself. Amendments to the provisional constitution had succeeded one another without meeting the constitutional needs of the country. Three years had passed since the provisional constitution had been drafted and no action had been taken on the provision it contained that within three years a permanent constitution should be enacted by a National Assembly. No electoral laws had been adopted; Abdul Rahman Arif had been elected by an *ad hoc* procedure for only one year. Since no constitutional provisions had been agreed, it was decided by the Cabinet and the National Defence Council to extend Arif's term for another year and to grant legislative powers to the Cabinet until a National Assembly was elected.

The disunity among the groups which had schemed to replace al-Bazzaz by a military officer now led on 10 May 1967 to the displacement of Naji Talib himself. The absence of any political leader of influence to resolve the disputes, and the inability of the rival factions to reach any agreement, led Abdul Rahman Arif to assume the posts of both President and Prime Minister. The new Cabinet drew its members widely from the different ethnic and religious sections of the community. It contained no less than four vice premiers, two of whom were Sunni officers, one a Shia civilian, and one a Kurdish follower of Barzani.

Before a month had passed, however, the Cabinet was faced with the problem posed by the Israeli attack on Egypt, Syria, and Jordan on 5 June 1967. Unlike Syria and Jordan, Iraq had no common boundary with Israel. The great Syrian desert protected her from the type of military attack which Israel launched against these countries. It was possible, however, for Iraq to send military forces to Jordan and Syria by the road which had been constructed to build a petroleum pipeline which, because its outlet to the sea was in Israeli-held territory, had never been brought into operation. The provisional agreement for union between Iraq and Egypt, which had been signed in May 1964, seemed to carry an obligation on the part of Iraq to aid Egypt in the war, and the government despatched what was in effect a 'token' force that played no role in the fighting. We observed elements of the Iraqi army during an earlier journey in the desert bus, Damascus–Mafraq–Baghdad. At the points where the bus stopped in this military area, the conductor had invariably to throw off the bus Iraqi soldiers who had boarded it in a most undisciplined manner to obtain free rides and enjoy a weekend leave in Baghdad! There was little evidence that the forces were preparing for combat.

The war affected all the Middle Eastern countries, whether or not they were in the combat area or took part in the battles. Egypt and Jordan almost alone fully engaged their forces and suffered heavy losses. The traditional regime in Jordan was loyal to the cause of Arab unity while the 'revolutionary' regimes of Syria and Iraq made little more than token gestures. The Syrian government dominated by Salah Jedid, whose Alawi faction of the Syrian Baath had seized power in February 1966 in savage street-fighting in Damascus, lost important territory almost without resistance. Its Alawi leaders, unpopular and representing only a minority, retained the main Syrian forces around Damascus, fearing that if the army left the area, the way would be open for other elements to organize a *coup* against the government; alternatively, the officers of some of the units, if sent on an offensive and out of reach of the secret 'security' service, might organize a plot to overthrow the Alawi regime, or at least the faction dominated by Salah Jedid, whether or not the outcome of the intervention against the enemy was successful. Following the Israeli surprise attack which destroyed the Egyptian air force on the ground, the swift defeat of the Egyptian forces and the failure of the Syrian army to fight destroyed any incentive Iraq might have had to intervene.

But the disastrous effects of the war of 1967 were as far-reaching in a political as they had proved to be in a military sense. They affected the internal political life not only of the countries directly involved, but also of some of those more distant. In the prolonged debates in the Security Council and the Assembly the spokesmen of almost all Arab countries were brought into a broadly common position concerning the Israeli attack, even if there remained certain differences among them about Resolution 242, or the interpretation of the resolution, which after much debate was adopted on 22 November 1967.

In the aftermath of this war, Abdul Rahman Arif realized that it was not practicable for him to continue as both Head of State and Prime Minister. The Cabinet was reorganized and Tahir Yahya once again became Prime Minister, the functions of which office he had in fact largely taken over during the war. The government immediately became involved in the debate over oil policy. Political conditions in the country were deteriorating, and to meet some of the criticism the Cabinet introduced proposals for an appointed temporary Legislative Council. But a non-elected body of this kind could no more obtain widespread support among the divided opposition groups than could the 'front' represented by the Arab Socialist Union. Disharmony in the Cabinet grew and there were three resignations (one of them a Kurd).

Whatever criticisms may be made of the Arab nationalist ministries between November 1963 and July 1968, it must be said that much free political discussion was carried on and heads of governments were obliged to enter into debate. It was not supposed in principle that they were established for life or for an indefinitely prolonged period. As the radio stations in Eastern Europe showed, extra-legal penalties, including occasionally the death penalty, were sometimes inflicted on 'communists', though not on the scale of the Baathist massacres in 1963. Such measures against communists were all too common in the Arab world, particularly in Egypt under Nasser.[13] In other ways, however, political life and political discussion were much freer than they became later, and the disputes grew between the Arab nationalists, who called for unity within the Arab world, and others, who were in reality more concerned with Iraqi interests or with the application of Islamic ethics in political life.

In the drafting of a new law relating to elections, the shadow of Egypt fell across the discussions. In the Arab nationalist view the idea prevailed that Egypt was the model for any Arab nationalist revolutionary system. But other important voices were raised in favour of a political system of competing parties. Nuri al-Said's law prohibiting parties had not been repealed after the 1958 Revolution, but parties continued to exist and to hold meetings without legal recognition. Here again nothing had been done to remove a grievance which the revolutionary forces had exploited against Nuri, but which they themselves had no intention of removing.

The demand that free political parties be permitted clashed sharply with the idea of a single Arab Socialist Union. The supporters of each of these two incompatible systems faced a serious obstacle. For the first, the question of the recognition of the Communist party arose. For the second, it was certain that the Kurdish Democratic party would never be absorbed into an Arab Socialist Union. An attempt in that direction would probably have reopened the war in the north.

Criticism of the regime was particularly widespread on the ground of alleged corruption among new civil servants introduced to deal with the wider government tasks associated with extended government responsibilities in economic, especially industrial, affairs, that the nationalizations had imposed. Just as the old merchant class and their friends in government had been widely criticized by the public for alleged corruption, so now some of the leading ministers and administrators of government industrial and financial enterprises were the objects of comparable accusations and insinuations. It was difficult to confirm or refute these charges, but there was no doubt that they were widely believed, and that Baathist intrigue endeavoured to make the most of them, especially with a view to discrediting Tahir Yahya, who was felt by many Baathists to have betrayed their cause.

In Baathist propaganda the internal difficulties in Iraq at the time of the Baath military *coup* in July 1968 have been greatly exaggerated. They were trifling in comparison with those during the Baath regime in 1963. In both periods we were able to observe conditions in Baghdad closely. Civil order was not threatened in 1968. The ordinary citizen went about his work free from menace. There was certainly no public desire to see the Baath return, then or, in our opinion, at any later time. There were of course severe disagreements within civilian government ranks and, more decisively, in the ranks of the military. It is true, however, that the public was disturbed by the deterioration in economic conditions and the increased taxation imposed by the government, partly as a result of the heightening of the dispute with the IPC.

Once an army has taken government as its proper preserve, any period of disharmony in government ranks tempts the politically minded officers to form plots and to seize power on the pretext that the security of the state requires prompt action. And, in Iraq the unpopularity of the Baath had not deterred it from pursuing its underground activities, seeking also the support of military officers without whom it could not hope to gain power.

After its defeat on 18 November 1963, it was long before the Baath could recover sufficiently to enlarge its support in the army and to plot another *coup*. But al-Bakr and a small group around him, aided by the toleration shown by the Arab nationalist regimes under the Arif brothers, were able to continue the plotting and intrigue against the existing regime. The memory of 1963 had not died in the public mind, and for several years the Iraqi Baath leaders judged that conditions were unripe for an attempt to seize power.[14] In Iraq the

Baath party had received even less support than in Syria, where it was never able to gain more than 15 per cent in a free vote. There was no evidence that by 1968 it had gained ground appreciably outside its own committed members.

The dissensions within the Arab nationalist government, however, and the weak and ambiguous behaviour of Iraq during and immediately after the war of 1967, had inspired more than one source of opposition to seek a change. The Baath was above all a conspiratorial party, and other sources of opposition had no comparable organization behind them. But the *coup*, when it came, was not led by, nor was it the work of, the Baath.

Notes

1 For a discussion of the Bazzaz period written at the time, see E. F. Penrose, 'Une tentative de gouvernement civil en Irak', *Orient,* No. 39, 1966, pp. 7, 34.

2 General Ghazi al-Daghistani was the son of 'National Hero' Muhammed Pasha Daghistani who at the age of 80 went as a volunteer to fight against the British during the First World War and was killed. Ghazi was educated at the American University of Beirut, the Military Academy, Baghdad, the Woolwich Military College, England, and the Staff College in Quetta, India. He was an officer of the Engineering Corps and Chief of Military Public Works. In the early 1950s he was Military Attaché at the Iraqi embassy in London. When the 1958 Revolution broke out, he was Commander of the Third Division in Baghdad. He was arrested and sentenced to death, but was set free in the early 1960s and died in London in 1966.

3 But see note 11, Chapter 16.

4 Quoted from BBC Summary of World Broadcasts, 2nd Series, Part 4, *The Middle East,* 25 September 1965.

5 Abdul Rahman al-Bazzaz, *On Arab Nationalism* (London, 1965).

6 For an account of the choice of a new President see Khadduri, op. cit., p. 265.

7 René Mauriès, *Le Kurdistan ou la Mort* (Paris, 1967). In the present context. see especially pp. 178–208. M. Mauriès was editor of *La Dépêche du Midi.*

8 The Mosuli Arabs felt that any autonomy for the Kurds would be to some extent at their expense. In so far as responsibility for a variety of social economic and cultural matters of special concern to Kurds was transferred to Kurdish from Arab hands, the influence of the Mosuli Arabs would, of course, be reduced.

9 The agreement was broadcast by al-Bazzaz on 29 June 1966 over Baghdad Radio. For text see Khadduri, op. cit., pp. 274–6; and BBC, Summary of World Broadcasts, 2nd Series, *Middle East,* 1 July 1966.

10 In a lecture delivered in Baghdad in May 1955 al-Bazzaz declared: '. . . it is far better for the nation to err in the exercise of its democratic rights until it reaches, though after a time, the right path, than that one individual or a group of individuals should monopolize power and push it into wild and dangerous paths on the pretence that they are an "elite" alone capable of

knowing what is good for it'. Published in Cairo (1963) in *From the Inspiration of Arabism,* pp. 139–64 and republished by the Iraqi embassy in a pamphlet *Al-Bazzaz on Arab Nationalism* (London, 1965). The quotation is taken from p. 26 of this pamphlet.

11 For a detailed analysis of the intra-regional situation which al-Bazzaz had to face during this period see E. F. Penrose, 'Une tentative de gouvernement civil en Irak', especially pp. 25–31.

12 See Khadduri, op. cit., pp. 284–5, for a summary of the divisions among the factions.

13 See, for example, Jean Lacouture, *Nasser* (Paris, 1971).

14 The party itself had long and seriously examined the reasons for its failure in 1963, putting it down essentially to poor leadership and a failure to achieve a 'balance between the ideal and the possible'. See *Revolutionary Iraq, 1968–1973. Political Report* adopted by the Eighth Regional Congress of the Arab Baath Socialist Party–Iraq (Baghdad, January 1974), p. 60.

15 The Return of the Baath

The authors of the *coup* of 17 July 1968, al-Naif and al-Daoud, had held views in harmony with a number of officers and civilians—some of them associated with the government—who under the preceding regime had wished to replace the existing system with a more representative form of government.[1] In economic policy they felt that nationalization had been carried too far and they would have left more scope for private enterprise; on foreign policy they wished to avoid entanglement in inter-Arab controversies on the one hand and a drift into an isolated position for Iraq on the other. Seeking in advance organized support for the immediate steps which they proposed to take, they approached other political groups, including the Baath. Al-Bakr considered that the time was not ripe for displacing the government: the public had not yet forgotten the Baathist experience in 1963.

The two officers decided that if the political organizations were not yet ready to join, they would themselves act alone, believing that the decline in popularity of the existing regime would bring public opinion over to their side.[2]

The *Coup* and the 'Mini-*Coup*'

On 17 July 1968, al-Naif and al-Daoud notified their military supporters and took action to remove the President. The defection of the Presidential Guard was decisive. Abdul Rahman Arif, who had in fact often listened to their criticisms and taken note of their advice in the past, agreed to leave the country and make way for a successor. He had been placed in his position more by accident than by design, and had never been a strong or confident head of state.

Al-Bakr then took the Presidency. He recognized that the two officers who had carried out the *coup* would, at least for a time, have to be given leading places in the government. Al-Naif became the new Prime Minister and al-Daoud Minister of Defence

According to the Baath account of the *coup*, presented later to the eighth National Congress of the party, these appointments created a difficult problem for the leadership:

> An extremely delicate and sensitive situation arose in the ranks of the Party and the masses when the first cabinet was announced with Abdul Razzaq al-Nayef at its head. Party members had not yet been informed of the last minute developments and considerations taken into account by the leadership. They had not yet been told of the decision to liquidate him. It was impossible to explain. For the circumstances dictated that the leadership should pretend to have no reservations about al-Nayef so that the second part of the plan be implemented.
>
> The Party was under unprecedented stress. For reasons of security the leadership could not explain matters to Party members and had to depend mainly on their confidence and discipline during the thirteen tough days that followed . . . On July 30th 1968, the liquidation plan was to be implemented . . . At 6 p.m. the Regional Secretary of the Party made the historic announcement over the radio . . .[3]

Under the 'liquidation plan', President al-Bakr's cousin, Colonel Hammad Shihab, brought his armoured brigade into Baghdad and, taking advantage of the absence of al-Daoud in Jordan on a tour of inspection of the Iraqi contingent which had remained there since the Israeli attack on Egypt, encircled the Presidential Palace. A 'mini *coup'* followed. Al-Naif was arrested and quickly sent abroad. With this act, as Kelidar states, the Baath 'alienated the politicised ranks of the armed forces and society which did not support the Baathists. The dissidents had to be systematically purged and suppressed, a process which has continued ever since'.[4]

At the outset the new premier, with an eye on outside opinion, had appointed as Foreign Minister Nasir al-Hani, a scholar and a distinguished member of the Iraqi Foreign Ministry, who at the time of the *coup* was ambassador to Lebanon. In 1963 he had been a mainstay of the Foreign Minister, Talib Shabib, a young Baathist of intelligence and moderation but, like the rest of his party, little versed in diplomacy. Al-Hani was well educated,[5] with a good knowledge of international affairs. He promptly issued a reassuring public statement which was relayed to Iraqi embassies abroad and was designed to allay apprehension in other countries about the intentions of the new government and for several days he worked energetically to improve external relations.

The al-Naif ministry was quickly dismissed. But al-Hani did not remain silent. We had known him over a decade as a fearless man of high integrity and genuine convictions, and he acted in character to the end. After leaving the Foreign Ministry, he was openly critical on a number of points. This aroused the anger of the Baath Revolutionary Command Council. It was decided that he must be silenced. One night in November 1968, a group of young Baathists called at his house and informed him that al-Bakr urgently wished to see him and that he must accompany them. He entered the car with them.

He was never again seen alive. On 12 November Baghdad radio reported that he had been assassinated.

Such a well-known public figure could not disappear without comment at this stage, for the military–Baath regime had only just been established. Persistent enquiries were made. Baathist circles claimed that the murder was the work of ordinary criminals. But the dead man's widow recognized in a picture on television the man who had called at their house on the night of his disappearance. This agent of others was later killed in an 'accident'. The Baathist regime had not fundamentally changed since 1963.

Search for Legitimacy

It would be an error to suppose that the *coup* of 30 July marked a complete break in the elements of continuity in Iraqi history. The reinstatement of the military officers who had formed the Baath government in 1963 and who had then lost control to another faction in the Baath party, was in no sense the result of a popular rising, nor did it produce any spontaneous rejoicing as the Revolution of 1958 had done. The consolidation of the Baath regime which had been re-established by an opportunism that, as in 1963, took advantage of the work of non-Baathists, could not be accomplished without attention to the developments in the intervening years. Notwithstanding their weaknesses and divisions, the Arab nationalist ministries had shown recognition in principle of the illegitimacy in the long run of regimes not based on representative government. Discussions in leading government circles on the proper form of representative government to adopt had been proceeding up to the time of the *coup* with a view to the fulfilment of an undertaking, given in the provisional constitution accepted in May 1964 under the Arab nationalist ministry of Abdul Salam Arif, to adopt a definitive constitution within five years. Moreover, some political officers had joined in declarations and petitions on the subject. In one case they included al-Bakr himself.

The constitution of 3 May 1964 was, therefore, the starting-point.[6] It had been adopted in the first flush of enthusiasm for restoring relations with Egypt, which had deteriorated during the 1963 Baath regime. In these conditions the constitution had been inspired largely by the 'organic law' of the UAR; 73 out of 106 articles were identical with the latter. This was supposed to facilitate the establishment of uniform institutions in the two countries, with a view to their union. It presupposed a single party, the Arab Socialist Union, in Iraq as in Egypt. As we have seen, this appealed neither to Iraqi political leaders nor to many of their followers in the Arif regime. Although lip-service to it remained, it was no more than an outward show designed to avoid any clash with Egypt; for it is probable that most Iraqi Arab nationalists were neither confirmed Baathists nor confirmed Nasserites. At the same time, neither they nor their governments wished to reawaken controversy with Egypt, or to provide openings for opponents of either the Iraqi or Egyptian regime to exploit. Nevertheless, in Iraq under the presidencies of the Arif brothers, open support was given to the recognition of a number of political parties, for opposition to an exclusive Arab Socialist party was strong. By implication, however, this applied also to an exclusive Baath party, which of course had also been denounced on other grounds after 1963.

How then was the regime to proceed to provide some sort of constitutional framework for its rule? Unable to evade the issue completely, faced with political groups and with a public that shared no enthusiasm for the events of 30 July, the new regime produced the Provisional Constitution of 21 September 1968. This was not a document agreed on by a representative group, but a promulgation signed by five military officers who had been associated with the Baath regime of 1963 and who now designated themselves as the 'Revolutionary Command Council'. This body reserved to itself the right (Article 92) to amend the constitution 'in case of necessity', the criteria of 'necessity' being determined by them. The President was to exercise the functions of Head of Government, Commander-in-Chief of the Army, and President of the Council of the Revolutionary Command. On Kurdistan the 'constitution' took a backward step in omitting recognition of Kurdish nationality. It was sufficient commentary on its declaration of 'freedoms' that the press joined in a chorus of uncritical approval except for the one independent Arab–Kurdish paper *Al-Taakhi,* which engaged in pointed comments on the failure to consult the people before characterizing the constitution as 'democratic and popular', and on its 'provisional' character, which seemed to indicate an indefinite period. This was a significant characterization, since the hostility of the Baathists to democratic institutions was well-known. On 12 November the government suspended the newspaper.

The Suppression of Internal and External Opposition

Having attained power on the shoulders of non-Baathist military officers who had aimed at constructing a less totalitarian state than theirs, the Baathist military leaders, after nearly five years in the political wilderness, set out with the aim of preventing a recurrence of the split in the Baath party that led to anarchy in 1963. From the beginning al-Bakr and his associates were determined at all costs to prevent a repetition of the events of 1963. The Baath leadership had tried to analyse the causes of that débâcle and concluded that the leadership must move cautiously, keeping its real objectives secret even from the party members, dissimulating at every turn and purging the country of enemies as carefully and unobtrusively as possible.[7] But they were ready, if necessary, to use the most ruthless methods to suppress any challenge to their hegemony, whether from outside or from within. The organized murder of Nasir al-Hani was directed against an outsider, but in the next few years the most important struggles took place within the Revolutionary Command Council itself—among the rival officers, together with a civilian, Saddam Hussain al-Takriti, linked with al-Bakr and within the Baath party, and originating in the same geographical area as the dominant military leaders.

These conflicts cannot, however, be attributed purely to the desire to exercise power for its own sake. There were of course always the individual fears of being 'liquidated' when leaders did not trust each other. But beyond this lay differences over the way in which power should be exercised, and how far compromises were acceptable. Moreover, the new military element was not exempt from the division which had beset civilian politicians, and the five senior officers who had issued the 'Provisional Constitution of the Iraqi Republic' were quickly at odds among themselves.

The dissensions within the Baathist regime since 1968 have been of a different character from those of 1963, where Ali Salih al-Saadi had been the spearhead of a drive within the Baath to make a radical change in its philosophy, accepting a Marxist as well as an Arab nationalist approach, and drawing industrial development almost exclusively into the public sector. He was now living in Cairo, having made peace with Nasser on the latter's terms. He had been one of the murderers of Qassim: now he admitted that it was all an 'error of judgement'.

It is doubtful whether any lesson was drawn from the experience of 1963, beyond the necessity of controlling internal dissension and of suppressing all opposition if the leaders were to remain permanently in power. This meant the suppression of movements within as well as movements outside the Baath party. But what was to be the criterion of legitimacy *within* the Baath party? In ideological terms what was to be suppressed could only be decided in the light of what was accepted as the true faith and doctrine; yet ideological purity was hardly the chief objective of the Iraqi military–Baath leaders.

The regime was largely in the hands of a group of army officers and a few civilians coming from the town of Takrit on the Euphrates and from the region around it, lying on a route on which the British generals were planning a drive to the north after they had taken Baghdad in the First World War. This region is a Sunni stronghold,[8] and the group reflected a Sunni interest which had aimed to restore Sunni dominance after Qassim had opened public posts much more widely than they had ever been open before to Shia. The incongruity between this sectarianism and the professed universalism within the Arab world which Aflaq preached was particularly glaring.

That many of the civilians, most of them very young, who had been drawn into the Baath party were genuinely influenced by its doctrines can hardly be doubted. That the leaders, militarists as well as Baathists, were equally, if not more, influenced by a mere determination to maintain a dominating position over the government of Iraq at all costs and never to permit a repetition of the humiliating turn of events of November 1963 is equally clear. But this left ambiguities and inconsistencies which have remained ever since. The split *within* the Baath in 1963, both in Syria and in Iraq, was sharp and genuine,[9] and memories of it persisted under the new regime in 1968. The co-operation of the moderate Baathist officers with Arab nationalist officers at that time to rescue the country from anarchy was still an embarrassment to the party. The unpopularity in extremist Baathist circles which it brought on General Hardan al-Takriti, who had then been Minister of Defence, and who, in that position, had issued the orders for the disposition of the forces to suppress the National Guard, was exploited both by his enemies in the internal personal feuds characteristic of the party's history, and by the extremists among the civilian Baathists.

Traces of the tension between the moderate and extreme groups reappeared when the policy to be followed towards opposition was debated. Outside knowledge of these discussions is limited. The young civilian Baathists seem in the main to have urged drastic measures to exterminate all opposition. The officers seem to have been a little more divided, but the 'hawks' prevailed. 'Plots' were discovered and sentences of death by public hanging were imposed freely in the next few years. From Damascus it was reported that

Saddam was at the head of a network of special agents responsible for acts of terrorism and torture.[10]

Bursts of hangings took place from time to time. Geoffrey Somner reported from Baghdad on 28 February 1970:

> For 8 hours on the day of the hangings the police virtually handed over central Baghdad to the youths. Directed by Baath Party Commissars they erected the gibbets in flower beds, patrolling the approach roads, controlled the tens of thousands of watchers, and chanted for more executions. Each of the three soldiers among the executed had a bandage on an ankle or wrist; the joints were so clearly misshapen that they had clearly been broken.[11]

On 29 January Baghdad radio broadcast a sharp attack on other Arab countries which, in harmony with the press throughout the world, had expressed horror and condemnation of these doings. The strong criticism in the Lebanese press drew an order from Baghdad to Iraqi residents in Lebanon to return to Iraq. It was ignored by Iraqi refugees. The Secretary General of the United Nations publicly deplored the hangings. Again the Baath, in association with the army, had isolated Iraq from the outside world.

Thus the return of the Baath had brought a return of the terrorism which, to the general relief, had been ended on 18 November 1963. But this time it was no longer a terrorism exercised by an undisciplined wing of the government, of which the President, perhaps the Prime Minister, and certainly the Ministers of the Interior and of Foreign Affairs, disapproved. This time the tortures, the hangings, the organized murders through agents, were official acts, the work of the Baathist government and party. Qassim's People's Court now seemed in retrospect an approach to a respectable judicial tribunal by comparison with the summary disposal of the victims of the Baath regime set up in 1968.

In 1963, following the massacre of 'communists' immediately after the *coup* of 8 February, the practice of terrorism and murder (sometimes described as 'executions') was confined to one wing of the Baath—that led by al-Saadi. From the latter part of 1968, however, the Baathist political leaders have used organized terrorism from the top against any form of active, serious political opposition.

The pretext of alleged collusion of the victims with foreign 'spies' can hardly explain the atrocities.[12] The chief motive must be sought in domestic affairs. First, the freer discussion, public and private, of a return to a more representative form of government in the period between 1963 and 1968 had created expectations of greater freedom for parties and a wider and more variable distribution of power within a peaceful political framework. Second, the unpopularity of the Baath, and the memory of the anarchy which it had brought in 1963, remained. Third, the new military–Baath regime, feeling its unpopularity, made approaches to other groups in the hope of securing co-operation of a kind. But other political circles, for the reasons stated above, were not disposed to accept the only terms on which the Baath would ever 'co-operate'—a basis which left them always dominant. Hence the resort to a reign of terror specifically designed to intimidate all forms of political opposition.

Attempts to Obtain Co-operation

On the other hand, the still-remembered example of the al-Bazzaz regime, hardly three years earlier, and the subsequent discussion of ways of returning to civil government, had created a public atmosphere which even so autocratic a party as the Baath could not ignore. Al-Bakr had therefore selected Saddam Hussain al-Takriti, a young member of the party coming from the Takrit area, as a deputy who could be regarded as a civilian. The selection was arbitrary, favouring the region, the religious group, and the religious party to which the selector belonged. His character was very different from that of Ali Salih al-Saadi. He aimed to increase the proportion of civilians not only in the Regional Command but also, after the *coup,* in the Revolutionary Command Council. In this he was supported by al-Bakr, without whose backing he could not have accomplished it. In November 1969 the RCC was enlarged from 5 to 14 members, and Saddam was appointed Vice-President; in December the post of deputy Prime Minister was abolished and cabinet meetings made subject to the call of the Prime Minister instead of weekly as previously.

Conscious of the unpopularity of the regime among the people and of the dangers which they faced in the north, al-Bakr and Saddam made advances in the middle of 1969 to other political groups. But neither wing of the Communist party, nor the Kurdish Democratic party, nor the Arab nationalist and the Nasserite groups, responded favourably to the idea of co-operation within a framework of Baathist hegemony. Only a fraction of dissident Kurds from the KDP were willing, for a time, to co-operate with Baghdad. The regime retorted with an intensification of the witch-hunt and by renewed hangings. In effect the policy of the Iraqi Baath under al-Bakr and Saddam was then, and has been since, to offer a choice between entry into a national front under military–Baath hegemony and total cessation of political activity. Iraq then desired arms not so much to meet external threats as to use in her civil war in the north.

The Kurds were too firmly entrenched to be intimidated in this way, and the Communist party had constructed an organization that remained active underground when it was banned from public activities. The military–Baath were divided on both questions, which were entangled in intra-regional and wider international developments. The moderate elements in the Baath included officers and civilians who, as in 1963, were intransigent rather than moderate on the Kurdish question. But other elements in the regime, led by al-Bakr and Saddam, pursued wider aims, related to a continuation and extension of the petroleum policies of the preceding regime, the realization of which required closer relations with the Soviet Union and an improvement of conditions in the north of the country.[13]

Faced with rejection of their advances to other political groups and with continued unpopularity, al-Bakr and Saddam Hussain al-Takriti decided to halt the war in the north. They suspended the customary practice of bribing tribal elements opposed to Barzani and of supporting a breakaway minority of the KDP led by Talabani, and they turned instead to direct negotiations with Barzani and the KDP itself. Although the latter were sceptical of the ultimate intentions of the military–Baath regime, particularly about the Kirkuk area, they felt that a truce would give time for recuperation.

On 11 March 1970 al-Bakr announced the conclusion of an agreement, confirmed two days later by Barzani, which provided for autonomy on local affairs for the northern regions inhabited by a majority of Kurds. Foreign affairs, including customs, as well as control over national resources, including petroleum, remained with the central government. There would be a Kurdish Vice-President of the Republic, and Kurds would take part in proportion to their numbers in the government and in the Revolutionary Command Council during the interim period until a new legislative body would be elected.[14]

Such were the broad outlines of the scheme. If in some respects it merely repeated proposals which had gained formal acceptance in the past during short-lived periods of respite or attempts at settlement, in another respect it was novel. For the first time the Iraqi Baath, including some of their military officers, acknowledged in principle the justice of Kurdish autonomy in a considerable range of internal affairs.

The outcome depended wholly on the willingness of the Baghdad government to follow the verbal and written agreements with actions designed genuinely to give practical effect to the agreement. This in turn required agreement on principles and efficient and impartial means of putting them into practice. The principle that the measures of devolution should be applied to the areas containing a majority of

Kurdish peoples conformed to ideas of natural justice. Four years earlier Bazzaz, the only premier trusted by the Kurdish leaders, had considered the suggestion that the first task in implementation should be to appoint a committee of experts to delimit this area. The same issue had to be faced in 1970 by his successors, who were distrusted on all sides. Unable to refuse assent to the general principle that must lie behind all schemes of devolution, they were determined in practice to violate it in respect to the Kirkuk area, the centre of Iraq's oil production. Having accepted the general principle in question, they could only evade it for this area by falsifying the statistics or by hurriedly trying to change the composition of the population. They decided to attempt both methods, by the use of an early census in the first case and by bringing in more Arabs from another area in the second. It was not in the interest of either side to denounce the 'agreement' immediately, but its eventual collapse could hardly be avoided. Within the military–Baath group it ran counter to the views of a number of officers and civilians who were unwilling to recognize any nationalism but Arab nationalism or to consider any solution other than a military solution.

Moreover, the agreement was made in a period when the military–Baath were persisting in their campaign of terrorism with a view to establishing totalitarian rule and suppressing all opposition. This excluded in principle one of the indispensable general conditions of success which Mulla Mustafa Barzani had specified several times: the adoption of democracy in Iraq.

Continued Suppression Through Terror

The instability within the Baath regime continued with fluctuating intensity in spite of purges and violent repression. Michel Aflaq and Salah al-Bitar had followed a comparatively conservative policy in their later period in Syria, favouring compromises and slower progress in the adoption of socialistic measures during economic difficulties, when abrupt 'confrontations' with private enterprise led to disorganization which in turn increased public discontent. In principle this prudent attitude clashed with the slogans adopted by the Iraqi Baathists and with the reckless attitude of the younger civilian rank and file of the party.

But the Iraqi leaders, uneasily conscious of their lack of mandate from the people, were glad to secure in Aflaq, as one of the two founders of the Baath, an appearance of legitimacy. Aflaq himself, who, from some points of view, might be regarded as more suited to a contemplative life than to the rough and tumble of Arab politics, nevertheless saw an opportunity to maintain himself as the source of legitimacy under Baathist rule. He served as a useful 'front' for the Iraqi regime. About a decade earlier he had welcomed Saddam to Damascus as one of the youthful refugees from Baghdad who had attempted to murder Qassim in Rashid Street because, among other offences in Baathist eyes, Qassim had failed to form an immediate union with Egypt. Aflaq had been regarded as a 'moderate' among the Syrian Baath, and later a 'reactionary' after the Alawi regime established itself. To Saddam in Baghdad his well-known opposition to military domination within the Baath was useful. Finding a refuge in Iraq, he became a party to the actions of the Takriti group, however much he may have privately disapproved of some of them. A sad outcome of the idealistic dreams of the two Damascus schoolteachers who founded the movement!

The feuds and rivalries within the regime were actively pursued in the next few years. Hardan al-Takriti and Salah Ammash were appointed Vice-Presidents in April 1970 as a means of removing them from the control of government departments. General Aziz al-Uqaili, who, though a diehard opponent of any concession to the Kurds, was also a man of integrity and an advocate of genuine representative government, was sentenced to death. He, however, was an outsider, and the main aims of al-Bakr and Saddam Hussain al-Takriti were to establish their supremacy in the army, the party, and the state. Hardan al-Takriti resented the growing domination exercised by al-Bakr and Saddam. Ammash was at odds with both Hardan and al-Bakr. The Baath was living up to its reputation of being, above all, a conspiratorial organization. At the same time it was rent apart internally by bitter feuds. There seemed this time to be no moderate wing of the party: at most, among the leaders there were different degrees of intransigence.

The pursuit of political opponents by the dominant leaders of the regime extended far outside Iraq. Hardan al-Takriti was murdered in Kuwait in February 1970 when leaving the Iraqi embassy in a car with the Iraqi ambassador, who was untouched by the bullets of the murderers. The Iraqi Baath regime was now openly admitting in some of its party reports that it judged in secret, and passed sentences of death on, opponents in their absence. In many cases assassins were then dispatched to carry out the sentences. We have reason to believe that al-Bazzaz would have been disposed of in Baghdad but for widespread publicity in other countries. Fuad al-Rikabi, who had oscillated between Baathism and Nasserism, was murdered in prison in November 1971.[15] Abdul Karim Moustafa Nasrat, former minister who was in sympathy with the Syrian faction of the Baath, was stabbed to death in his home in August 1971.[16]

Colonel Abdul Razzak al-Naif, one of the two officers who displaced the preceding regime, was aware that attempts might be made on his life. Knowing the standard techniques followed by assassins dispatched to carry out the 'executions' decreed by the Revolutionary Command Council in secret he was on his guard at his residence in London when he was asked about his movements by an Iraqi named Yahya Qassim who was living in London. When he went outdoors did he walk or go by car? He evaded the questions. Later Qassim asked by telephone for an appointment and proposed that the Colonel should meet him at the door. He refused, but at the appointed time Qassim rang the bell and when the door was opened, three young men of dark, Mediterranean complexion were standing behind him and immediately opened fire with automatic pistols. But al-Naif ran into another room. Madame al-Naif was hit in the shoulder. All four men disappeared. Qassim was apprehended. The Crown Prosecutor at the trial charged him with complicity in the attempted murder. When asked why he ran away, he replied, 'He was sentenced to death in his absence, so what could I do about it? My country is not like yours'. He admitted that in Baghdad he printed the Communist *People's Press,* and the newspaper supported by the Baath government.

The Crown asked for conviction; the jury voted for acquittal.[17]

In 1973 internal Baathist conflicts were more violent than ever, and the regime was itself in danger. In February renewed shootings or hangings were announced which included 'military officials'. Al-Bakr and Saddam were looking for support from other groups. But soon they were absorbed in problems related to their own survival. The quarrel among the Takritis which had led to the murder of Hardan al-Takriti was superseded by a plot on the part of the director of the Internal Security Services, Kazzar, a Baathist of Shia origin who resented both Sunni and Takriti domination of the Iraqi Baath party. He had joined the Baath party in his student days in the 1950s, and had soon become one of its most fanatical members. He had taken a prominent part in organizing the massacre of communists in the anarchy that followed the seizure of power by the military in February 1963. The moral law had no meaning for him. Opposition must be rooted out and its leaders exterminated.

Kazzar, as chief of Security, had acquired a sinister reputation. Torture was not introduced as a novelty by him into the Baath party's political apparatus. It had been practised extensively by Ali Salah al-Saadi and his associates in 1963. But Kazzar specialized in it to an inexpressibly horrifying extent. The old palace which he had taken over as the headquarters of these operations was known as 'Qasr al-Nihaya', 'the Palace of the End'. Few who entered ever came out, nor did their bodies receive civilized burial. Political prisoners of the Baath often simply disappeared so far as their relatives or friends were concerned.

Resenting the domination of the regime by al-Bakr, Saddam, and the Takriti group, Kazzar planned their destruction. As Eric Rouleau wrote in Baghdad: '. . . l'intrigue, même s'il été exposé d'une manière incomplète, n'a rien à envier à la fiction'.[18]

The plot and its outcome were not part of an attempt to restore the rule of law, as the measures taken on 11 and 18 November 1963 had been: they merely represented a single-handed revolt against Sunni–Takriti domination. Kazzar seized an occasion when al-Bakr had gone on an official visit to Bulgaria to plan his assassination at the airport on his return. Meanwhile he induced Colonels Shihab and Ghaidan, who were also from Takrit, to visit him on the same morning. The airplane was delayed two hours and plans miscarried. Kazzar fled towards the Iranian border, forcing the two colonels to go with him. Near the border he shot Shihab dead, but was himself seized before he could cross. Shortly afterwards he met the same end.[19]

This episode was followed by a tightening of military control through the vesting of powers in al-Bakr, who also assumed the functions of Minister of Defence, left vacant by the death of Shihab. The Department of Internal Security of which Kazzar had been Director was reorganized, as Kelidar reported:

> A new Department of General Intelligence (*al-Makhabarat*) was set up incorporating the Special Security Section of the Baath which commands the party's private militia, under another young Takriti, Saadun Shakir, a member of the Iraqi Regional Command, who is assisted by Saddam's younger brother. The party militia is organized on a cell basis, and for security reasons, individual units are separate and independent, which makes them susceptible to personal and regional influences. Kazzar's abortive coup caused confusion among the militia and the authorities because no-one could ascertain whether the commanders of the different units were loyal to Kazzar, their political boss, or to the government. Consequently they had to be disarmed. Their organization under a centralized control may ensure consistency but not complete loyalty.[20]

This picture of confused loyalties, ideologies, and opportunism reveals elements of long standing. Among them attitudes concerning Iraqi Kurdistan played a role. In general, the army officers supported a military solution, while civilians were more divided. Kazzar, although he was military only in name, like Saddam more recently, had been violently opposed to Kurdish autonomy, but, as events have shown, Saddam followed opportunist policies. Even during the period of the Kazzar episode this issue was coming to a head. At the same time it was entangled in international and intra-regional rivalries among the powers.

Some writers have given much attention to the adoption of a number of measures of independent local administration in Iraqi Kurdistan as the main cause of the deterioration in relations between Baghdad and the Kurds since the accord in 1970. We cannot accept this view. The fact is that Baghdad, not for the first time after reaching formal agreement in negotiations, failed to follow it up by initiating further discussions about the means of implementing the accord in detail. Second, the basis and the structure of government in Iraq are inimical to local or regional measures of autonomy. Mustafa Barzani was correct in consistently maintaining that the one-party supremacy insisted on by the Baath was incompatible with a genuine settlement. From the beginning there was no mutual trust between the military–Baath government and the Kurds. It could not be expected that the Kurdish leaders would disarm and dismantle the internal organization which had grown up under conditions of war, without any sign of concrete moves towards implementation of the general terms of the accord of 1970. The final break, which was to come in 1974, however, was preceded by far-reaching changes in the structure of the intra-regional relations among the Middle Eastern countries.

Iraq and the Fourth Arab–Israeli War

The war with Israel in 1967 and the death of President Nasser in September 1970 profoundly affected the structure of intra-regional relations in the Middle East and the positions of the great powers outside it in their relations with the individual countries of the region. It had given an opportunity to those Israeli leaders whose ultimate aim was the realization of Eretz–Israel to push nearer to their goal, at least temporarily, if not, as they hoped, permanently. The death of President Nasser had opened the way towards ending the East–West Cold War within the Arab world, with a view to creating unity and developing effective resistance to Israeli expansion.

Iraq had been well represented at the United Nations under the Arif regime by Adnan al-Pachachi, one of the ablest members of the Foreign Ministry. After the murder of al-Hani, and when the direction of the new regime's policies became clear, he resigned, openly stating his disagreements.

President Sadat's new policies in Egypt, following President Nasser's withdrawal from the Yemen, soon began to prepare the way for healing the rupture between Egypt and Saudi Arabia, which was an essential condition for effective resistance to Israel. Although the change in policy did not end all the divisions among the Arab countries, it reduced the rifts between those countries whose co-operation was essential if the territories overrun by the expansionist drive of the leaders in Israel were to be recovered. The Iraqi leaders after 1968 subordinated their external to their internal policies, but they were obliged at the same time to make the former appear to harmonize with the ideological pretensions of the latter.

The changes in Egypt, which led to a restoration of relations with Saudi Arabia, modified the alignments in the Arab Cold War which later were to affect the civil conflict within Iraq. From 1967 the Soviet Union had a strong interest in the reopening of the Suez Canal, which was of great importance to Russian commerce. But Israel rejected her own leader, Levi Eshkol, when, in March 1968, he authorized acceptance of the Security Council resolution of 22 November 1967 and was ready to evacuate the invaded territories. He was outmanoeuvred by the future Prime Minister Golda Meir and General Moshe Dayan. A great opportunity was lost and another war was provoked.

Under their new rulers both Egypt and Saudi Arabia were re-shaping East–West policies within the Middle East in such a way that, with Syrian co-operation, they were able for the first time to combine effectively Egyptian and Syrian military power and the Saudi Arabian economic power derived from her position as a supplier of crude oil to world markets.

In the October 1973 war Iraq made a larger military contribution than before, sending some two divisions which, along with forces from Algeria, took an active part in the fighting. But this brief military co-operation was not accompanied by political, diplomatic, or even economic,[21] co-operation. The Egyptian operation had been carefully planned to achieve a limited objective. It had demonstrated that Egyptian soldiers were not inferior to Israeli soldiers, even under modern conditions. It revealed a capacity to conduct a combined operation to cross the Canal and establish a position on the east side. The Egyptian victory was only checked in extent by extensive military supplies hurriedly flown from the United States.[22]

It was an outstanding though rare example of Arab unity among the countries that were in a position to affect the outcome. But unity was partially broken when Egypt accepted a cease-fire on 22 October while some countries more distant from Israel maintained that the struggle should have been continued until all occupied territories had been liberated. The military–Baath government of Iraq was among them. Its leaders, conscious of their lack of internal support, persisted in a policy of extirpating political opposition or silencing it through a 'National Front' which they dominated. In these circumstances, it was almost inevitable that they would see even a question so important both to the Middle East and to the international community as peace in the Middle East largely from the point of view of domestic politics. But domestic politics can rarely be isolated from intra-regional or international affairs and the eventual Syrian acceptance of the truce widened the ideological gap between the Syrian Baath and the Iraqi Baath, although the differences on this question are partly explicable on geographical grounds.[23]

The Iraqi government's policy was stated in ideological terms which concealed underlying contradictions. Fadil al-Jamali has well expressed the dilemma facing the Arabs in their conflict with Israel:

> . . . et l'on sait que la force militaire arabe, quelque degré qu'elle était atteint, ne peut resoudre le problème palestinien dans la situation internationale actuelle. Tout accroissement de la force militaire arabe est contrebalancé par un accroissement de la force zioniste. Et si les Sovietiques appuie les Arabes les Zionistes sont aidés par le front occidental.[24]

A decade later the only change in the situation is that the European powers, particularly Britain and France, no longer supply Israel, but the United States is still ready to do so, not from considerations of justice but for internal political reasons. Consequently the predominantly Arab countries have had to rely on a combination of political, diplomatic, economic, and limited military measures. In 1973 this brought considerable success. But large territories remained to be liberated and the success of further measures depended on the maintenance of the co-operation realized in 1973. Iraq was among those Arab states which, taking advantage of their geographical positions, turned away from the three states adjoining Israel which had borne, and would continue to bear, the brunt of the military combats with Israel.

Calling for what, in economic and military terms, was an impossible feat of arms at one remove, the Iraqi leaders found allies in a wing of the Palestinian organizations, the Popular Front for the Liberation of Palestine, led by George Habash, a Palestinian physician whose family had been driven out of their home during the invasion by Ben Gurion's forces. His organization had broken with the main body of Palestinians by rejecting all compromise and proclaiming the goals of the liberation of all Palestine and the defeat of 'imperialism and reaction' in the Gulf. In February 1974, the formation by Iraq and this group of the 'Rejection Front' was proclaimed. It was directed particularly against Saudi Arabia and Kuwait, but in joining it the Iraqi regime also set itself against Egypt, Jordan, and Syria. The policy of restoring good relations with neighbours, which al-Bazzaz followed in his period of office, was set aside, to the detriment of a much-needed Arab unity in face of Israeli expansion. If, later, Iraq set out to restore relations with Iran, one of her most powerful neighbours, it was not out of a 'good-neighbour policy' but from motives of expediency concerned with the suppression of Iraq's most important minority.

The Betrayal of the Kurds

The faltering accord of 1970 with Mustafa Barzani and the main body of the KDP, which Baghdad had made no serious moves to put into practice, was already falling apart at the time of the fourth combat between Israel and the Arab countries. It was evident from an early stage that the regime had acted in bad faith in accepting the principle that the Kurdish region should consist of those areas in which Kurds were in a majority. Soon it became clear that the government was determined to exclude Kirkuk, with its petroleum riches. At the opening of 1971 Barzani charged Baghdad with transferring a number of Kurds from the area. Actually, the Kurds did not claim all the oil revenues derived from production in the region; they demanded only that a share proportionate to the Kurdish population should be applied to the area of partial autonomy. But there was never a chance that Baghdad would agree. We do not know what went on in inner government counsels, but the army officers appear to have been opposed to a political settlement and it seems possible that Saddam in any case may have feared to alienate them further.

On other issues the rift widened in 1973. Saddam and his associates returned to their earlier attempt to constitute a National Front of the Baath, the Communist party, and the Kurdish Democratic party. From the Kurdish point of view the same objections applied as in 1970. They were even reinforced by what had happened and by what had not happened since that time. In their eyes both the sins committed and the sins of omission had deepened the grounds for distrust. Hence in July 1973 Barzani declined to enter the proposed National Front, pointing to the undemocratic nature of the regime and emphasizing that Kirkuk contained a majority of Kurds.[25]

In the same month the Communist party was legalized. Its secretary at the time had spent ten years in prison. He had escaped the massacre of 1963 which Ali Salih al-Saadi and Saddam Hussain al-Takriti had played a part in organizing. But in 1973 he took the Communist party into a Front with the Baath. Such an extraordinary reversal in relationships seems to be more characteristic of totalitarian than of democratic groups. The leaders were concerned above all with the problem of gaining or maintaining power. Their followers were more prone to accept directions from above than a democratic rank and file would have been. Even so, the memories of torture and massacre had not died among Iraqi communists. The action of the secretary in accepting Baathist terms for a Front led to a split in the party.

These moves cannot be interpreted in terms of Iraqi politics alone. Both intra-regional and wider international affairs lay behind them. Relations between Egypt and the Soviet Union having deteriorated, the Russian leaders sought compensation in closer relations with Iraq, who, in turn, could supply them with oil in exchange for arms. Though the Soviet Union had been responsible along with the United States for the success of Ben Gurion's invasion of Palestine, its new leaders realized that the motives behind Russian actions in 1947–48 were no longer relevant, if indeed they ever had been. While still recognizing Israel's right to exist, they had supported the demand for evacuation of the occupied territories ever since the war of 1967.

There appeared, then, to be enough in common between the Soviet Union and Iraq to justify an accord. But a closer analysis reveals contradictions in detail. The war party had gained the upper hand on the Kurdish question and Iraq's desire for more Russian arms was related to the war in the north rather than the conflict with Israel. But the Soviet Union's policy had long been to support the Kurds and its leaders had no particular desire to see them suppressed. During the war they appear to have made representations to Baghdad in favour of a political rather than a military settlement. But Moscow obviously considered this question to be less important at the moment than the broader question of increasing Soviet influence in Iraq to offset the decline in Soviet influence in Egypt.

A second reason for seeking closer relations with Iraq seems to have been a desire to counterbalance to some extent the growing power of Iran. Although relations between the Soviet Union and Iran had greatly improved in the preceding years, the ambitions of the Shah to command the Arab/Persian Gulf could impinge on Russian interests there and in the Indian Ocean. However, both countries moved prudently. Iran had endeavoured to extricate herself from the Cold War as far as possible by removing American bases. She now regretted the negotiation of a United States lease of naval facilities in the newly independent state of Bahrain, which quickly brought a riposte from the Soviet Union in the form of naval visits to the Gulf. She was determined to preserve her position after the departure of Britain from the area. For a time she had claimed Bahrain, but this issue was happily settled when, for once, the United Nations was able to play a part without a usurpation of its functions by a few great powers. But a dispute over the two islands of Tumbs and Abu Musa was not brought within the scope of its impartial findings and Iranian troops had seized the islands in 1971. This had led to a sharp protest from Iraq and Libya. The former withdrew her ambassadors from Britain and Iran, and expelled a large number of Iranians. Relations between the two countries continued to deteriorate and the Shah continued not only to give extensive help to the Kurds but to encourage them in their resistance to Baghdad.

Thus the course of the conflict between the military–Baath government and the Kurds was largely determined by outside powers, each of which gave priority to what it conceived to be its own interests, with little regard to the merits of the case or to the fate of the individuals concerned.

The decision had been taken in Baghdad early in 1974 to promulgate unilaterally a 'Draft Law of the Progressive National Front for Autonomy of the Kurdish Region'. It laid down that the 1957 census of population should be followed in the delimitation of the area deemed to contain a majority of Kurds. On education it specified both Arab and Kurdish as the official languages of the region. Kurdish was to be the language of instruction for Kurds and Arabic for Arabs, but the alternative language was to be a compulsory subject for each group.

Unlike the document of 1970 the new law contained no recognition of the existence of two separate nationalities. It declared at the outset that 'The Region is an inseparable part of the land of Iraq and its people shall be an inseparable part of the people of Iraq'. This was not in itself unacceptable to the Kurds, who were not asking for separation, but whatever the detailed provisions might have been, the document would have been rendered unacceptable to the Kurdish authorities by its sweeping provision that the president of the Council to be set up for the region was to be appointed by the President of the Republic and could be dismissed by him, all other members automatically going with him. This reassertion of the complete hegemony, not only of Baghdad, but implicitly also of the small group from the Takriti area which dominated the government, ensured the rejection of the scheme by the Kurds. It was clear that in any case the Kirkuk area would not be included in any autonomous region.

Saddam and al-Bakr had reverted to the idea of a military solution. But they decided to respond forcibly to the Kurdish rejection of the 'Draft Law for the autonomy of the Kurdish Region'. The army, equipped with more Russian planes and armour, started a full-scale offensive in October 1974. Casualties were heavy on both sides, including civilians of all ages and both sexes on the Kurdish side. Baathist commissars were distributed among the armed forces, in some sections of which there was discontent. The bulk of the rank-and-file soldiers were Shia from southern and central Iraq. Orders were issued for ruthless advances, with Baathist officers in the rear to shoot soldiers who tried to retreat. In the Kirkuk area there were a number of executions of Kurds. Phosphorus shells were used by the Iraqi army.[26]

Wide publicity in the world press attracted protests from outside Iraq. The Liberal spokesman for Foreign Affairs in the House of Commons protested against the British government's silence and inaction in view of British responsibility for the inclusion of this part of Kurdistan in Iraq. Even the Russians, who had made it possible for Baghdad to undertake the offensive, now urged a 'political solution'. Two French lawyers, representing the Fédération internationale des droits de l'homme, reported that the methods of 'total war', with complete economic blockade, were being used.[27] The majority of the Iraqi Communist party had surrendered completely to the government, no doubt at Moscow's urging, and had accepted military–Baath domination of the Front. A member of the party, in an article in the London *Morning Star,* defended Saddam and attacked Barzani.[28] The leaders of the Soviet Union, faced with President Sadat's reversal of policy, had decided to support fully the military–Baath regimes of Syria[29] and Iraq. Iraqi communists were divided, but the majority accepted the Moscow position. It was the same party whose central committee had earlier described the regime of 1963 as 'a nightmare of fascist rule'.

The Kurdish army counter-attacked and for a time recovered ground. The war continued through the winter and the new Russian supplies gave an advantage to the Iraqi army.

Meanwhile, the strained relations between Iraq and Iran had become a matter of concern to the oil-exporting countries and at the 'summit' meeting of OPEC Heads of State in Algiers, 6–17 March 1975, President Boumediene initiated efforts, supported by the Tunisians, to bring together the Shah and Saddam. This gave a good opportunity to both to revise their positions in the light of the immediate difficulties facing them. For the Shah it opened a prospect of strengthening the Iranian hold on the Gulf and safeguarding the single large-scale outlet for Iranian oil exports. On the Iraqi side it brought reconciliation between the war party among the Iraqi officers and the two dominant figures in the government.

The agreement provided for the demarcation of the land borders in line with the Protocol of Constantinople of 1913 and the findings of the Frontier Committee of 1914. It settled the maritime frontiers in the Shatt al-Arab at the Thalweg (median) line, which had been resisted by Iraq for certain parts of the waterway. The two parties then agreed to 're-establish security and reciprocal confidence along the length of their common borders' and they undertook to 'exercise strict and effective supervision . . . with the aim of putting a final end to all infiltration of a subversive character from either side'.[30] As *MEES* commented: 'In plain words this translates into an Iraqi concession over the Shatt al-Arab border problem . . . in return for an Iranian undertaking to close the Iranian border to the Kurdish insurgents from Iraq and suspend military aid to them'.[31]

The Shah abandoned his support of the Kurds, who were left facing an Iraqi army part of which had returned from the war areas in Syria and Jordan and which was reinforced with Russian arms. The Soviet Union had not only ceased aiding the Kurds but had also, in pursuit of its own rivalries with the United States, given armaments to the Iraqi government, knowing that they would be used against the Kurds. In the Russian case this was a matter of priority among aims; nevertheless it was a reversal of a long-continued Russian policy. In the Iranian case it was a particularly cynical reversal of attitude, since it followed a policy of encouraging Kurdish resistance. Here the Shah considered it justifiable in terms of so-called *Realpolitik* because of the gains to Iran in the Gulf. In addition, however, he may also have been influenced to some extent by fears of contagion among Persian Kurds from successes of Iraqi Kurds in their claims on Baghdad.

Thus, the tragic events of the autumn, winter, and spring of 1974–75 in Iraq were largely a consequence of the actions of two outside powers to the east of Iraq, both of them pursuing objectives which they believed to be in their international political interests, without regard to the effects on Iraqi internal developments.[32] The consequences were to strengthen the hands of those elements in Iraq, military and civil, which preferred a 'solution' by brute force to a solution by patient negotiation and conciliation. They have left behind a trail of suffering and bitterness, of destruction and disorganization, which will last far into the future.

The total censorship in Iraq and control of all imported publications concealed the knowledge of subsequent events from the Iraqi public which was reported in the world press: particularly the ruthless acts of the Iraqi military, executions in the Kirkuk area, and the extent of Iraqi casualties. But the last could not be completely concealed from the public: funerals were numerous of the Shia soldiers and there was evidence of wide discontent in areas south of Baghdad, especially in the sacred Shia cities. Representations were made by some of the Shia divines and complaints were raised in discussions in the mosques. The Baath leaders retorted by seizing and hanging a number of prominent Shia divines in 1975. There had been several demonstrations which had frightened the military–Baath leaders and led them to return to their terrorizing methods.

The attempts to apply some parts at least of the Law for the Autonomous Region had no marked effect in pacifying Kurdish areas, although some Kurds were drawn to collaborate with Baghdad. Visitors to the area reported continuing guerilla activities. One characteristic of the Kurdish war was the 'clean' methods used on the Kurdish side. Unlike the Palestinians and a number of other minorities which engaged in struggles for liberation in several parts of the world, the Kurds did not attack non-combatant civilians, or resort to kidnapping, seizure, and sometimes murder of hostages, or to the use of booby traps and bombs in civilian areas. In these ways the Kurdish movement was a model. But the world took little note of this respect for humanity, and in consequence one of the guerilla groups began later to resort to kidnapping and holding hostages.

The Baath regime, faced with this continued resistance, retaliated with mass deportations from some areas, especially from Kirkuk to parts of the south where agricultural colonies were to be established. According to some reports this had unexpected results: it was said that the Kurdish immigrants were able to gain local sympathy when they explained to their new neighbours the circumstances in which they had been forcibly removed from their homes. All publicity on these measures was banned in Iraq, but news quickly reached the outside world.

The Iraqi leaders, conscious of world disapproval, invited a number of writers to visit the Kurdish areas. Among these was Ismet Sharif Vanly, a Swiss citizen of Kurdish origin on the staff of the University of Lausanne, who had written a standard history of the Iraqi Kurds. After his return he was interviewed by the distinguished French scholar of the Middle East Pierre Rondot.[33] He pointed out that only in three provinces of Kurdistan did Baghdad's decentralized system of administration apply—and that by unilateral edict. Some economic measures had been introduced and the Kurdish language was used in schools along with Arabic, but this was not entirely new in the region. The administrative organs had in practice no power to make financial and administrative decisions. The barrages which had been constructed by preceding regimes had been designed largely to be used by the populations established on the lower courses of the rivers descending from Kurdistan.

The refugees who had escaped into Iran had been given the choice of settling there or of later repatriation. Those who chose the former were dispersed in small groups over the country with a view to their assimilation into the Iranian people. Many others who had been influenced by Iraqi promises of repatriation had found on their return that they were moved out of Kurdistan to the lower Euphrates region. Vanly estimated that some 93,000 refugees were still in Iran.

The Kurds were divided after these events. Some remained faithful to Barzani,[34] others were critical of him for trusting Iran and for adopting frontal military tactics rather than guerilla operations. Some sought refuge in Syria. As to the future, Vanly considered, 'L'éffort de libération des Kurdes ne peut être jugé au jour le jour: c'est un combat de longue haleine'.[35]

The publication of Ismet Sharif Vanly's findings on the north of Iraq was resented in government circles. We have no knowledge of the discussions which took place over them in secret, but there followed an attempt on Vanly's life in Lausanne which, like the attempts in London against al-Naif, met with routine denials from Baath-appointed diplomats in the capitals concerned.

The military successes against the Iraqi Kurds were applauded widely in Iraq. They pleased not only the Baath but many other groups which had refused to recognize Kurdish nationalism, although the communists split on the issue. Other aspects of the 'deal' with the Shah of Iran were, however, much less acceptable to some Baathist circles. The sacrifice of Iraq's claims in the Gulf, which had been tenaciously held over a long period, went contrary to the ideological position of the party and drew criticism from other quarters in the Arab world.

The continued guerilla activities in the north brought disillusionment, even in some Baathist circles, and the resentment among the southern Shia over the disproportionate losses of their young men in the northern fighting led to demonstrations in Najf and Kerbela and reprisals in the form of the execution of religious leaders after a secret and summary 'trial'. This caused the resignation in March 1977 of Izzat Mustafa, Minister of Municipalities and a veteran member of the Baath party, who, as head of the Special Tribunal set up to try the holy men, was unwilling to rush them to their deaths without any genuine trial.

Even the Soviet–Iraq treaty of 1972 was interpreted by the Iraqi leaders in a sense not wholly in harmony with Russian desires and expectations. Iraq tended to seek European rather than Russian economic assistance in her development programme.[36] Notwithstanding the presence of the Iraqi Communist party in the National Front, the leaders of the regime were far removed from Soviet political doctrines. Pierre Rondot quotes from the Iranian journal *Keylan* the following criticism of Arab communists by Saddam Hussain: 'Les communistes sont hostiles à l'unité arabe, déclare-t-il, et le monde arabe ne sera jamais marxiste; le monde arabe est en faveur de la révolution et du nationalisme'.[37]

As this statement was reported on 26 April 1975, shortly after the Algiers agreement, it was no doubt intended to reassure the Shah and his advisers, but it may be presumed to represent the views of the Takriti group and many, but not all, elements in the Baath. There appears, however, to be a more radical wing among the younger groups; certainly many of them would not reject the term Marxist, even though they would oppose assimilation with the communist parties.

With the guerilla activities in the north, the serious unrest in the religious centres, and the evidence of splits and rivalries within the Baath party itself, the present regime can hardly be described as having reached stability.

Notes

1 *Revolutionary Iraq, 1968–1973. Political Report,* p. 42.

2 We have been told by a reliable authority that Arif had been informed of the planned *coup* and had summoned both al-Naif and al-Daoud to see him the night before. Both denied their complicity and tearfully kissed his hands assuring him of their undying loyalty. He believed them.

3 *Political Report,* pp. 43–4.

4 Abbas Kelidar, *Iraq: the Search for Stability* (London, July 1975), p. 8.

5 Nasir al-Hani had studied at the Universities of Baghdad, Cairo, and London. He had been Assistant Professor at the University of Baghdad, Director of Education Missions in the Ministry of Education, and Cultural Attaché at the Iraqi embassy in Washington. In the Ministry of Foreign Affairs he had been Director of Public Relations and had held the posts of ambassador to Syria and to Lebanon. He was also a Lecturer at the School of Oriental and African Studies, London, for a time and had published a number of works of literary criticism.

6 For an analysis of the constitution and the full text see 'La Constitution provisoire de la République irakienne du 21 Septembre, 1968', *Orient,* 1968, pp. 325–36.

7 *Political Report,* esp. Ch. 3.

8 For a good discussion of the Takrit group see Kelidar, op. cit., esp. pp. 6–7, 9–10. In 1976 the Takrit area was made into a separate governorate, Salah-

addin, with the administrative centre at Takrit. It included the administrative subdivisions (*qadhas*) of Takrit, Samarra, Balad, and Touz. If one moves a little further west to the Euphrates to take in the areas of Haditha, Ana, and Rawa, one finds that this triangle produces an extraordinary concentration of Iraq's rulers, including army commanders as well as a large number of the Baghdad and Basra garrisons. Because of the predominance of names from these areas in the Baath ruling group, the government has issued an instruction forbidding the use of names with a regional or tribal identification in any public document.

9 See Chapter 12.

10 *Al-Thawra* (Damascus), 5 April 1969.

11 *Sunday Times* (London), 28 February 1969.

12 Former Prime Minister Abdul Rahman al-Bazzaz was sentenced to prison for 15 years in October 1969 on the charge of 'spying for Israel'.

13 A group under Jalal Talabani was apparently under the impression that the new regime in 1968 was *progressiste* and would make real concessions to the Kurdish collaborators. See Vanly, op. cit., p. 277.

14 ibid., p. 341.

15 *Le Monde,* 8 November 1971.

16 Jean Gueyras, *Le Monde,* 27 August 1971.

17 See *The Times,* 15 June 1972 and trial records.

18 *Le Monde,* 19 July 1973.

19 For discussion of the history of the Qazzar plot and its outcome see especially Eric Rouleau's three illuminating articles 'L'Irak à l'ombre des intrigues', *Le Monde* 19, 20, 21 July 1973, and Jean Gueyras in *Le Monde*, 3, 4 July 1973 for the events of the climax.

20 Kelidar, op. cit., p. 9.

21 Even on oil matters Iraq refused to co-operate with her fellow members in OAPEC, as we shall see in Chapter 19. She refused to co-operate in the reduction of oil supplies and made no effort to ensure that Iraqi oil did not reach boycotted countries.

22 See the excellent military appraisal by the outstanding French military strategist, the late General André Beaufre, in *Forces Armées françaises* (Paris), April 1968.

23 This point is discussed by Hamid al-Shawi, 'L'Irak et le dernier conflit Israelo–Arabe', in *Maghreb-Machrek,* juillet-août, 1975, pp. 19–23. See especially the section 'L'eloignement de l'Irak du théâtre des opérations militaires', pp. 20–1.

24 Muhammad Fadil-Djamali, 'Retour sur le passé', translation by Marcel Colombe, *Orient,* Nos. 45–6, 47, 48, 49–50 (1969).

25 There were of course other minorities in Kirkuk. The Turkomans were generally hostile to the Kurds but the majority of the Assyrians supported their claims.

26 *The Times,* 13 December 1974. See especially the reports of the Special Correspondent of the *Financial Times* (London), 1 November 1974.

27 *Le Monde,* 27 December 1974.

28 *Morning Star*, 27 December 1974.

29 The Syrian regime was now being described as 'neo-Baath' in some quarters. For a discussion of the neo-Baathist idea, see Petran, op. cit., pp. 172–3.

30 For a convenient summary and analysis of the accord from the points of view of Iraq and Iran, though not of the Kurds, see Hamid al-Shawi in *Maghreb-Machrek,* No. 63, 1974.

It should be noted that in some discussions on this subject the Kurdish position is described as 'separatist'. This description is inaccurate. The position of Barzani and the Kurdish Democratic party had been repeatedly defined as one calling for regional autonomy within a single state of Iraq. It was so defined in the accord of 1970, in which the Iraqi regime accepted the definition of the region in terms of a majority of Kurds only to break faith on the area of Kirkuk, for which the Kurdish claims were only that a proportion of the oil revenues should be used for the development of the region.

31 *MEES*, 7 March 1975.

32 For an excellent analysis of the Soviet Union's policy at the time, see Carrère d'Encausse, op. cit., pp. 231–44; see pp. 207–30 for the wider setting in which Russian relations with Iraq should be viewed. For Iran's actions see R. M. Burrell, 'Iranian Foreign Policy During the Last Decade', *Asian Affairs,* February 1964, pp. 7–15. For a longer-range view see also Ronhollah K. Ramazani, *Iran's Foreign Policy* (Charlottesville, 1975).

33 Pierre Rondot, 'Pour les Kurds d'Iraq, le temps de l'épreuve n'est pas fini', *Revue française d'études politiques mediterranéenes,* February 1976, pp. 57–60.

34 Barzani took refuge in Iran and then in the United States.

35 Rondot, op. cit., p. 60.

36 See below, Chapter 18.

37 Pierre Rondot, 'Iraq: données constantes et modalités actuelles du jeu politique', *Revue française d'études politiques mediterranéenes,* February 1976, pp. 61–77.

Part Five

Economic Policy after 1963

16 Iraq and the IPC: the End of an Era

The expropriation of the greater part of the concession territory of the IPC group by Law 80 of 1961 was irreversible; the company could not expect ever to regain its former position. This much was clear—but nothing else. It would take another decade before a firm resolution of the dilemmas facing both government and company appeared.

The government had taken control over all the potential oil-producing areas of the country, but in 1961 it had no plan for their further development. The creation of a national oil company was envisaged, but none was in being and there was no clear policy respecting the scope of the operations of the company to be established. Before such a company could be created as an effective operating organization its precise functions had to be clarified and policies had to be worked out for the acquisition of the finance, of the skilled help and technical assistance required to explore for oil, to drill wells, and to obtain and install the capital equipment necessary to produce oil and get it to the ports, and then to market it. In the meantime, the government remained dependent on the oil revenues generated by the operations of the IPC, which would continue to produce and market almost all of the country's oil for many years to come.

The Problem of Law 80

The company, for its part, did not 'accept' Law 80 since the law violated the clause of the concession agreement which provided for arbitration. It hoped therefore to obtain some alleviation of the full severity of the effects of the law and it pressed for negotiations. Moreover, there were a number of urgent practical issues outstanding, notably the question of port and cargo charges at Basra, for which temporary annual agreements had to be made. During 1962 Iraqi oil output did not rise—and neither did government oil revenues.

The Minister of Oil in the government that succeeded Qassim was a young American-trained refinery engineer, Abdul Aziz al-Wattari, an intelligent non-political technocrat and a sincere but peaceable Iraqi nationalist with experience in the administration of the Iraqi oil industry. Here, at least, was a man the companies could talk to, one who had some understanding of the industry and of their problems, a moderate negotiator who sincerely believed that Iraq would gain more from partnership with the foreign companies than if she tried to 'go it alone', at least in the near future. Al-Wattari was to remain in office from February 1963 to September 1965.

Negotiations were therefore quickly resumed with the new government and the companies started with high hopes of a reasonably favourable agreement. The leaders of the new government had disapproved of Qassim's methods of conducting negotiations, and especially of his use of press campaigns to put pressure on the companies, and they believed that a settlement with the IPC would be desirable. By June 1963 an interim compromise agreement had been reached to take the heat out of the controversy over the port dues at Basra and the cargo charges imposed at the new deep-sea terminal. The company agreed to raise output and the government agreed to suspend the increased charges on shipments over 8 million tons.[1]

But the major problem related to the application of Law 80, on which the companies were completely unyielding in their attitude; no progress towards an improvement in the relations between company and government could be made until one side or the other was ready to compromise. The real difficulty for the oil companies of accepting Law 80 related less to their interests in Iraq than to the implications for their position in other countries. Once expropriation without compensation of concession territory was accepted anywhere, a precedent would have been set which would make it more difficult for them to resist similar action by other governments elsewhere. Above all, the American parents in the IPC feared any precedent that might prejudice their position in the great Saudi Arabian concession of Aramco.

At the same time, a basis for compromise existed in the self-interest of the parties. So long as the dispute with the IPC group continued, other international companies would hesitate to bid for exploration rights in the expropriated areas of Iraq in view of the near certainty that the IPC parents would take legal action. The Iraqi government had neither created the institutional framework within which it could move to develop the area nor had it the expertise to do so without outside assistance. These deficiencies could, of course, be made good in time, but most Iraqis who favoured an agreement probably did so primarily because of the difficulty of marketing oil without the help of the companies. They were aware that even if Eastern European countries took Iraqi oil, they could not supply the goods Iraq wanted in return (the last thing useful to Iraq would have been unconvertible roubles).[2]

For their part, the companies, though still in possession of their producing fields, nevertheless wanted to get back North Rumaila. But they were not of one mind. The companies most opposed to compromise with the Iraqis were Standard Oil of New Jersey (SONJ—now EXXON) and British Petroleum, both of which had very large supplies of oil elsewhere and had most cause to worry about the precedent that would be set. The most eager to maintain and expand access to Iraqi oil were Shell and CFP. Both of these companies were short of oil. For the French economy and for CFP as a company, Iraqi crude was very important. The French government was attempting to reduce the country's dependence on the American majors and to strengthen the position of French companies and French sources of oil, of which Algeria was the only other major producer.

As we have seen, Iraqi politics in this period were unusually unstable even by Iraqi standards, and in some ways this gave al-Wattari greater freedom of action than he might have had if the Cabinet had been less concerned with its own internal conflicts and able to give more attention to the activities of the Oil Minister. Al-Wattari wanted a resolution of the conflict with the companies, but he knew that he could not seek the abrogation of Law 80 even if he wanted to. He, after all, shared the view that the companies had not treated Iraq fairly in the past, that relinquishment and improved profit-sharing were necessary, and that ownership participation was desirable if it could be had. The companies had to be brought around to the acceptance of Law 80 and they had to recognize that the oil-exporting countries in general, and Iraq in particular, were irrevocably committed to bringing about changes in their concessionary relationships. This was brought home to them in two separate directions.

In the first place, al-Wattari took a strong position on OPEC's demands that royalties be expensed and marketing allowances eliminated; secondly, he pressed forward with the establishment of the Iraq National Oil Company.

Expensing of Royalties

OPEC had not succeeded in its original aim of raising posted prices to the level existing before the price reductions by the companies in 1959–60, but it had prevented any further decreases as market prices continued to slide. Unable to raise tax prices, OPEC had turned its attention to the ways in which the companies calculated the net revenues paid to the governments. As we have seen, in the Middle East concession agreements after 1950–51, royalties, which in principle are payments to resource-owners for the depletion of their reserves, were included in the 50 per cent of the profits received by the government in the form of income taxes. Thus, they were in effect treated as part of the tax and not as a payment for depletion of reserves and therefore as a cost, which is the normal treatment of royalties by mining enterprises. In June 1962 at the Second Session of its Fourth Conference in Resolution IV.33, OPEC recommended that each member country should approach the companies 'with a view to working out a formula whereunder royalty payments . . . shall not be treated as a credit against income tax liability'. Under a fifty-fifty profit-sharing arrangement the expensing of royalties as a cost of production would increase the revenues of the governments by 50 per cent of the royalties payable. In addition, OPEC called for the elimination of marketing allowances which, as we have seen, had already been greatly reduced in Iraq.

After the controversy over Qassim's claim to Kuwait in 1961 and the refusal of the Arab states to support it, Iraq had declined to attend OPEC meetings. She returned to OPEC in February 1963, and at the Fifth Conference in December 1963, Abdul Rahman al-Bazzaz was appointed Chairman of the Board of Governors and Secretary General. The Iraqis in OPEC took a leading role in pressing for action on the expensing of royalties and the elimination of marketing allowances. The companies, though reluctantly agreeing to discuss the issues, refused to recognize OPEC as a collective negotiating body and insisted on negotiating with each government separately.[3] At this point Iraq made an important contribution to the establishment of OPEC as a collective bargaining agency. The Iraqi government asked the IPC to appoint a negotiator and it then authorized the first Secretary General of OPEC, Fuad Rouhani of Iran, to negotiate on Iraq's behalf. Kuwait and Qatar immediately took the same action and others followed. In consequence the companies found that in practice they were negotiating with OPEC countries as a collective group.

Iraq was the most radical country in OPEC at the time. Moreover, Law 80 was the most extreme action that had been taken in the Middle East against the oil companies since the Iranian nationalization of the consortium in 1951. Iraq, like Iran, had acted alone and was suffering the consequences, for the other more cautious governments saw no advantage in following Iraq's example. Iraq therefore was anxious that OPEC should take radical action on other issues and thus reduce her own isolation. Apart from the ineffective demand that posted prices be raised, the expensing of royalties was the first substantive issue on which the member governments could act in concert. Consequently, Iraq pressed OPEC, not merely to negotiate with the companies, but to recommend that the individual governments pass legislation unilaterally imposing by law the expensing of royalties. Iraq argued that negotiation implied equality between governments and companies and was thus a derogation of state sovereignty, which was especially unacceptable on tax issues. Venezuela strongly supported the demand for action through legislation, as did Indonesia (which had been admitted to OPEC in 1962).[4]

Although the companies accepted the principle of expensing royalties, they were unwilling to base the calculation of royalties on oil valued at posted prices since market prices were considerably lower. They therefore offered to expense royalties on condition that the OPEC governments permitted discounts off posted prices in calculating the value of oil for the purpose of determining royalties. The initial offers of the companies were unacceptable and negotiations became tense, with Iraq and Venezuela leading the demand for unilateral action by OPEC governments and Iran leading the more conciliatory members. Iraq threatened to act alone if necessary and to introduce unilateral legislation if the companies did not produce a suitable offer.

Towards the end of 1964, the companies made an offer that was acceptable to the majority of OPEC members, but Iraq, Venezuela, and Indonesia dissented. In view of the strongly held differences of opinion, OPEC decided to leave it up to the individual governments whether or not to accept the companies' offer. Iran, Qatar, and Saudi Arabia ratified the agreement and it was approved by the Kuwaiti Finance Minister.

The agreement provided for the expensing of royalties, but government revenues were to be calculated with reference to discounted posted prices, discounts to be 8.5 per cent in 1964, 7.5 per cent in 1965, and 6.5 per cent in 1966. A formula for price differentials was agreed that would take account of the gravity differences among crude oils. The agreement also contained a 'quit claim' clause to the effect that it constituted a full and final settlement of all outstanding financial claims governments might have against their concessionaires. Arbitration of any disputes would take place under the auspices of the International Court at The Hague. It also contained a 'most-favoured-company' clause, which provided that the signatory concessionaire should receive fiscal treatment as favourable as that given any other present or future concessionaire.[5]

Iraq objected to all four aspects of the agreement. The government held that all royalties should be fully expensed against full posted prices. But even if partial expensing was to be accepted, there was a special difficulty in Iraq because government revenues were calculated with reference to the 'border value' of oil, which differed from the posted prices at Mediterranean seaboard terminals by the cost of transportation from the Iraqi–Syrian border to the sea. The IPC was prepared to expense royalties using border values as the basis of calculation. This, Iraq held, violated the 1952 agreement which stipulated that royalties were to be calculated at posted prices, and would substantially reduce the value of royalty expensing to the government. Like the Kuwaiti Assembly, Iraq held that the arbitration provision was unacceptable, casting doubt on the sovereignty of the state, and that the 'most-favoured-company' clause prevented the government from offering oil land to new entrants on more favourable terms. In addition, Iraq had long contested the pricing of Basra oil and the 'quit-claim' clause would prevent her from pursuing this issue. But even more compelling from Iraq's point of view was the fact that the IPC would consider the question of royalty expensing only as part of a settlement with the government over the effects of Law 80. This issue alone was to prevent any application of royalty expensing in Iraq until the matter became irrelevant following the nationalization of the IPC.

Iraq's isolation from the general evolution of relationships between companies and governments in the Middle East was intensified by this first attempt at common action by the OPEC countries, and her relations with the IPC were further embittered by the insistence of the company that any royalty-expensing settlement be related to the whole set of problems raised by Law 80.

Within Iraq, al-Wattari went ahead with the legal and administrative arrangements for the establishment of an Iraq National Oil Company (INOC). In February, Law 11 of 1964 was announced, under which the company was created, and al-Wattari expressed the hope that the IPC would co-operate with it. He denied that the creation of INOC was a step to pave the way for the nationalization of the IPC, for there was a provision in the law which permitted INOC to associate with other companies, including foreign companies then operating in Iraq. But the fact that the government had gone ahead to organize a body with power to bid on the expropriated area—and North Rumaila, being the choicest acreage, would be the obvious first choice—gave the IPC companies pause. Once such bids were made, even the companies would have to realize that retreat would be politically impossible for the government.

Shell and CFP had been working hard among their partners to

persuade them to abandon their obdurate insistence on arbitration over Law 80 and to find a way to co-operate with the government. INOC was to select its areas and make bids by September. This made it necessary that the companies should urgently attempt to take advantage of the provision in the law which permitted association between INOC and themselves. INOC would have to work with some outside body, for it lacked the ability to develop oil production without assistance, and it would be better for the companies, while it might still be possible, that they should take on this role in some capacity rather than that other companies (or governments) should do so. Unpublicized negotiations began, with the IPC endeavouring to obtain the additional territory permitted under the law (including North Rumaila) and the government proposing arrangements within the terms of Law 80 which implied not only acceptance of the law by the companies but also an entirely new type of association with them in the development of Iraqi oil resources.

The 1965 Draft Agreement with the IPC

From August 1964 to June 1965 negotiations continued on three sets of issues. In addition to the position of the IPC and North Rumaila under Law 80, and the terms on which the constituent companies would associate with INOC in the development of other areas, remained the unsettled issues relating to IPC accounting, which the Iraqis insisted had cost the government over $100 million since 1955. Throughout the negotiations the French representative of CFP, Jean Duroc Danner, aided by Shell, played a crucial role in promoting conciliation. SONJ was the most recalcitrant of the companies, unable to shed its fears of setting a precedent if the expropriation effected by Law 80 were to be recognized by the companies. It was also unwilling to accept the cost of developing oil under the Iraqi proposals for the joint enterprise, especially in view of the large reserves of lower-cost oil it had at its disposal elsewhere.

A draft settlement, consisting of two agreements, was initialled in June 1965. One agreement provided for the establishment of a joint venture, the Baghdad Oil Company (BOCO), to be jointly owned by four of the IPC oil company shareholders—CFP, BP, Shell, and Mobil—Gulbenkian interests, and INOC. The second agreement, which was to be signed at the same time as the first, dealt with the points at issue between government and IPC. The two together comprised what became known as the '1965 draft (or Wattari) agreement'. Each of the companies was to have 15 5/6 of the shares, Gulbenkian, 3.33 per cent, and INOC, 33.33 per cent. The four companies and Gulbenkian were each to appoint a director to the board, INOC would appoint three, and the government would have one. This gave the companies collectively a controlling voice. An INOC director would serve as chairman of the board, and the general manager would be appointed by the board from outside. Minimum expenditures for exploration were laid down, the exploration risk being borne entirely by the companies who would also buy back from INOC the oil it could not dispose of at a price between cost and posted prices. There were provisions for relinquishment. In these respects the agreement was in line with the recent developments in other new Middle East agreements. SONJ declined to participate, arguing the cost of oil won would be too high.[6] Taxation was to be 50 per cent of profits. Royalty payments of 12 per cent would be expensed. Full agreement on the OPEC expensing formula was left for later discussion. The new company could determine its own selling prices.[7]

North Rumaila and other proved areas were restored to the IPC under the provision of the law which permitted the government to give back to the company an area equal to that left to it by Law 80. The IPC thus obtained access to all of the important producing areas of Iraq together with the most promising areas yet to be developed. The new position established by the draft agreement would have been much the same as that which would have resulted under the final IPC offer rejected by Qassim. A lump sum of £20 million was to be paid to the government by the IPC in settlement of the accounting issues. The IPC raised its minimum production obligations and agreed to attempt a large increase in output in 1966 and 1967.

The 1965 draft agreement, had it been able to survive the maelstrom of Iraqi politics, not only would have brought a sharp increase in oil output but would also probably have accelerated a movement for revision of the older concession terms in the Middle East. Undoubtedly there would have been pressures on the companies to move in the same direction elsewhere, and this the companies feared above all else. But in Iraq they had little choice than to accept new terms even for expropriated areas if they wanted to ensure that the large amounts of oil still to be discovered and developed there would not fall into the hands of their competitors. This could be as damaging to the long-run position of the major companies as revisions in their concession agreements, which eventually they would have to accept in any case.

The agreement gave the IPC parents a very strong position in the future developments of Iraqi oil, and thus reopened very sensitive political issues in Iraq. Al-Wattari was naturally aware of these, but did not expect quite such a severe reaction as in fact occurred; a cabinet committee had been set up under Tahir Yahya, after Arif had pushed out the Baath in November 1963. The committee included Muhammed al-Obousy, Minister of Finance, and Abdul Aziz al-Hafiz, the Nasserite Minister of Economy. It had regularly discussed the course of the negotiations, although it had not approved the agreement.

The pro-Nasser Arab nationalists were especially critical of the agreement and when it was presented to the Cabinet in July 1965, they made a heated attack on it. This brought to a head the deep differences within the Cabinet on a number of issues other than oil and the six Nasserite members resigned the next day. A violent press campaign against the agreement followed. But before any decisions were taken, a general dissatisfaction with the Yahya government, together with political intrigues, led to the resignation of Tahir Yahya and the appointment of Arif Abdul Razzaq as Prime Minister. Wattari was dropped from this Cabinet and Abdul Rahman al-Bazzaz, the deputy Prime Minister, took over both the oil portfolio and foreign affairs. The oil agreement then became overshadowed by other matters. There followed the abortive Razzaq *coup* and the appointment of al-Bazzaz as Prime Minister. The al-Bazzaz government lasted but eleven months, during which President Abdul Salam Arif was killed and his brother, Abdul Rahman Arif, succeeded to the Presidency.[8]

The new President promised to throw the whole question of the agreement open to full public discussion after it had been reconsidered by the Cabinet, for one of the complaints of its opponents was that it had been secretly negotiated and that inadequate information had been given to the public. But al-Bazzaz had more urgent matters on his agenda, including an attempt to find a solution to the Kurdish problem, and before any serious moves to deal with the oil question could be taken, his government was removed (6 August 1966) and Naji Talib came in as Prime Minister.

Naji Talib, though reportedly not himself opposed to the agreement, was unwilling to take a strong position, and he appointed an advisory committee which represented a wide range of opinion to consider it. The committee included strong advocates of co-operation with the IPC, such as Ghanem al-Uqaili, as well as Nasserites who opposed it, such as Adib al-Jadir. Talks were opened with the IPC, but once again events were to overtake the ill-fated agreement. Any chance of settlement receded further in 1966 when the crisis (discussed below) in the relations between the IPC and the Syrian government over pipeline payments erupted. This dispute was not settled until March 1967 and in the accompanying controversy demands for the complete nationalization of the IPC were strongly pressed. Relations between the IPC and the government became increasingly strained, for the closure of the pipeline through Syria prevented exports from the Kirkuk fields for nearly three months. Moreover, as soon as the dispute was settled with Syria, a bitter controversy arose between the Iraqi government and the IPC over the payment of revenues to Iraq for oil which had not in fact been exported. The atmosphere was not at all conducive to the acceptance of a conciliatory agreement. Finally, even if there would still have been a chance of saving something out of the wreckage of the results of al-Wattari's efforts, the door firmly closed with the outbreak of war between Egypt and Israel in June 1967.

The Syrian Pipeline Controversy

The dues and other payments from the IPC to the Syrian government in consideration of the pipeline transit of oil through Syria to the Mediterranean had long been a subject of dispute. The bargaining position of the countries through which oil had to pass was, of course, very strong, especially after the pipelines had actually been built, and these countries wanted to get as much as they could from the oil companies for the right of transit. The original agreements made by the IPC with Syria and the three other transit countries (Lebanon, Palestine, and Transjordan) in 1931, which were signed to last for 70 years, did not provide for transit payments but only for loading fees at the terminals.[9]

Between 1947 and 1950 additional annual payments were made by the IPC and agreements were negotiated which provided for annual transit dues, payments for protection of the line, and for specified amounts of crude oil for domestic consumption to be supplied to the transit countries at world prices. The pipeline companies, which were subsidiaries of the oil companies, were exempt from all other taxes, fees, and customs duties. The transit fees were based on the amount of oil transported.

In 1952, after the introduction of the profit-sharing agreements in the producing countries, both Lebanon and Syria tried to get a similar sharing formula applied to pipeline 'profits'. Profits attributable to the pipeline operations were to be equivalent to the difference between the posted price of oil at the Mediterranean port and the posted price of equivalent oil at the Gulf. The principle was accepted by the IPC and substantial increases in payments were obtained, more than quadrupling the receipts of each of the two countries under agreements in 1955 for Syria and 1959 for Lebanon. The 1955 agreement in Syria provided for a lump-sum settlement of past claims of £8.5 million, £250,000 annually as payment for protection, and increased transit and loading fees which rose from £414,000 in 1955 to £4.9 million in 1956.

In form the 1955 agreement was not a profit-sharing arrangement. Transit fees per ton mile were calculated by the IPC on the basis of the difference in the value of the oil at the Syrian terminal of Banias and its value at Basra, the alternative loading port for IPC oil, less the costs of pipeline transportation. Fifty per cent of the 'national profit' thus attributed to the pipeline was then allocated to the transit countries of Syria and Lebanon (which implied the adoption of the 50 per cent profit-sharing principle), divided between the two on the basis of the pipeline mileage within each and reduced to shillings per ton mile. Similarly profits were attributed to the terminal operations at Banias and a loading fee of 50 per cent of these profits was agreed on.[10] Both the IPC and the government agreed that the intent of the agreement was to share pipeline and terminal profits equally between them. By 1965 the transit and loading fees exceeded £9.6 million.

In August 1966 (the same month when Naji Talib became Prime Minister in Iraq) the Syrian government under Prime Minister Yusuf Zuayin, who had come to power in February through a violent *coup* led by Colonel Salah Jedid and represented an extreme wing of the Syrian Baath party, demanded that the IPC enter negotiations with a view to increasing oil transit payments. The purpose of the Syrian government in challenging the IPC was wider than simply to increase pipeline revenues. The government had earlier decided that it would exploit its own oil directly without the intervention of the international oil companies. The Baath party, long an advocate of the nationalization of oil, the 'freeing' of all Arab lands from the foreign companies, and the development of a Pan Arab oil organization to establish a unified Arab policy, would have liked to see Iraq nationalize the IPC. A successful confrontation with the IPC in Syria would enable the Syrian Baath government to augment its prestige in Arab eyes and would perhaps push Iraq nearer to nationalization.

In demanding an increase in transit payments, the Syrian government did not contest the 1955 agreement as such, but contended that the IPC calculations of profit and its accounting had been incorrect. In particular, it argued that the costs per ton used in the calculation of profits were too high because the large increase in throughput which had risen from the base of 26 million tons in 1955 to over 40 million 10 years later, must have reduced average costs. The IPC accepted that some increase was in order, although it pointed out that it had had to incur heavy expenditures because of the destruction of Syrian segments of the pipeline in 1956, which had raised its total costs. It also pointed out that its labour costs in Syria were excessive because it was forced by the government to keep on full pay some 3,500 workers who had been temporarily hired for construction when the line was built, but for whom the company had had no work for several years.

The company's offer of increased current payments did not fall very far short of the demands of the Syrian government, but the government also insisted on retroactive payments for alleged deficiencies in accounting, which would have cost the company an additional £40 million. The dispute became increasingly acrimonious and the company pressed without success for the arbitration provided for in its agreement with the government. In November 1966, with no agreement in sight, the government officially broke off negotiations and on 1 December issued a decree raising transit fees from 4*s*. to 5*s*. 10*d*. for each ton of oil moving through Syrian pipelines, raising loading fees and imposing an extra 3*s*. a ton for the company's alleged underpayments for the past ten years, to continue until all accounts were settled. The government then issued a writ of attachment on all IPC properties in Syria and informed the company to stop sending oil to Banias until it paid the amounts claimed. Pumping stopped in the middle of December; Iraq was deprived of two-thirds of her oil exports for the next three months.

The whole affair put the Iraqi government in a political dilemma. The Syrian action against the IPC was popular in many Iraqi political circles, and the hints of the Syrian government that it would not insist on the same level of fees if Iraq decided to sell her own oil was a thinly disguised suggestion that Iraq ought to nationalize the company—also popular in many circles. An extensive propaganda campaign was mounted by Syria to gain support in the Arab world; it met with considerable success—the 'Arab nation' was struggling with Zionism, imperialism, and the monopolistic oil companies, and the Syrian action could be portrayed as part of this wider struggle—as in some ways it was. Clearly it was politically difficult for the Iraqi government to support the oil company in such a struggle, but there were a number of Iraqi politicians of moderate persuasion and opposed to the existing Iraqi government who nevertheless urged it to take steps that would undermine the Syrian position and eliminate the country's dependence on Syrian goodwill, such as the construction of a pipeline from Kirkuk to Basra in the south.

The loss of revenues, if prolonged, would have very serious economic consequences for Iraq. The government was well aware that the nationalization of the IPC would not solve the problem in view of the difficulties Iraq would undoubtedly have in attempting to sell not only the 40 million tons of oil a year from Kirkuk, but the 20 million from Basra as well, against the opposition of all the major oil companies. Officially, the government remained neutral and informed the IPC that it considered the dispute to be between the company and Syria to which Iraq was not a party, and that it expected to continue to receive revenues based on normal exports. It also intervened privately with the Syrian government to make its situation and attitude clear and urge a solution.

Except for CFP the IPC shareholders had, as we have seen, adequate alternative sources of oil, and in view of the growing amounts of oil seeking markets throughout the world, the loss of Iraqi oil was not entirely unwelcome from a marketing point of view, although it did bring an unwelcome exacerbation of relations with the Iraqi government. The IPC was willing to increase the transit and loading fees, but it was adamantly unwilling to make the retroactive payments demanded; its bargaining position was strong in view of its ability to do without Iraqi oil for the time being. In these circumstances, and faced with Iraqi unwillingness to take the losses which nationalization would clearly have inflicted, the Syrian government began to modify its position, and in March 1967 a new agreement was reached. The Syrian government cancelled its decrees imposing a new schedule of fees and impounding the IPC properties; the IPC thus won acceptance of the principle of agreement as contrasted with unilateral legislation. The company agreed then to pay the fees which had been laid out in the rescinded legislation; the face and sovereignty of the Syrian government were both protected. The fees imposed by the government on account of retroactive charges were rescinded, but the company agreed to review its past accounts with the government. Thus all of the important matters of principle from the IPC point of view were also protected, including refusal to accept unilaterally imposed retroactive charges. On the other hand, the Syrian government could claim a victory because the company accepted the higher fees it had earlier decreed and thus recognized its 'sovereignty'. The prestige of the Iraqi government suffered, and the prospect for the IPC shareholders of expanding their activities as provided for by the Wattari agreement receded, as, of course, did the prospects for Iraq of getting a rapid development of her North Rumaila field. But most of the opposition to the Wattari agreement arose precisely because of the provision permitting the IPC to regain North Rumaila instead of providing for its exploitation by the INOC.[11]

The settlement of the conflict with Syria and the resumption of oil shipments immediately brought to a head the question of the Iraqi government's claim to revenues for the exports lost. The government demanded full payment equal to the revenues of the first quarter of the previous year, arguing that the loss was due to a commercial dispute with Syria. The IPC pleaded *force majeure*. A compromise was reached with an advance by the IPC to the government of £14 million to be repaid out of future revenues. Although this dispute was amicably settled, relations between the company and the government remained uneasy; the issues of Law 80, of the future of North Rumaila, and of the association between INOC and the IPC, were still hanging fire.

There were substantial divisions of opinion within the government and among Iraqi oil experts and politicians, but it seemed fairly clear that the politics of the matter would force the government to give INOC a greater role in the development of North Rumaila than the Wattari agreement had envisaged. Before a clear decision was announced, however, the conflict between Israel and the Arabs, which erupted in the Israeli invasion of June 1967, dominated all policy. Two laws were passed in quick succession which enlarged the role of the INOC and closed the door to any further concessions to foreign companies. The Minister of Economy in Tahir Yahya's new Cabinet, which had been formed in July, was Adib al-Jadir, a strong opponent of the 1965 draft agreement who had resigned from the government oil committee in 1966. He had long advocated that a national oil company should take over the development of the country's oil.

The End of Concessions: the Primacy of INOC

Law 97 of 16 August 1967 gave exclusive rights to INOC to develop the expropriated territories and specifically prohibited the restoration to the IPC of North Rumaila. Any further oil concessions were also prohibited, but INOC was permitted to associate with others in developing oil territories. The IPC protested formally, calling Law 97 a further breach of international law by the Iraqi government and stating that the IPC shareholders would take all possible steps to prevent other parties from exercising the rights legally belonging to the IPC. The British government, which had no diplomatic relations with Iraq at the time, also sent a note of protest along similar lines, stating that it would assist the British companies in reaffirming their rights.

Association with the IPC was not specifically barred, but the political opposition to any association was clearly decisive. The supporters of the Wattari approach to a co-operative development of Iraqi oil had lost the argument. A new law was passed (Law No. 123 of 1967) to reorganize INOC. It abolished the post of managing director, reconstructed the board, and strengthened the power of the chairman, who was to be appointed by Presidential decree and would have the rank of cabinet minister. Adib al-Jadir was appointed president of INOC and chairman of the board. The previous managing director, Ghanem al-Uqaili, and his co-director Tariq Shafiq, both leading 'moderate' technocrats who had hoped to use the resources of the IPC in association with INOC to bring about a rapid increase in Iraq's oil output with the effective development of North Rumaila, were dropped.

The reorganization of INOC under the new laws was designed to bring the company firmly under direct political control and remove all vestiges of the earlier hints of collaboration with the IPC. The new direction in oil policy was taken against the background of ongoing discussions with the Soviet Union and with the French and Italian state companies over the kinds of assistance and co-operation that might be provided to INOC. Although INOC could take responsibility for the further development of Iraqi oil resources, it was not capable of their actual exploitation without extensive technical, managerial, and other assistance from industrial countries. Fears that any resort to the IPC group would lead to a reassertion of its dominance over INOC, grievances over IPC's unwillingness to accept Law 80, and political resentment over the attitudes of both the United States and Britain in the Arab–Israeli conflict, ruled out the most experienced companies and countries. Hence the Iraqi government was very much concerned to interest other countries in committing themselves in some form to the development of Iraqi oil. Clearly countries against whom it would be politically difficult for the IPC parents and their home governments to enforce sanctions would be especially welcome. North Rumaila was of course the biggest and most important bone of contention and France and the Soviet Union were the most important of the likely partners, although in addition to Italy, both Spain and Japan had evinced interest.

The political cloud that had hung over Iraqi–French relationships during the Algerian struggle and at the time of the Anglo–French–Israeli attack on Suez had been dispelled, both by the settlement with Algeria and by de Gaulle's attitude towards the Arabs in their conflict with Israel. CFP recognized that with the passage of Law 97, the IPC had no chance of regaining North Rumaila or any other territories; it thus felt free to enter the lists independently of the IPC. In October 1967 the CFP put in its own bid to get into North Rumaila, but at the same time it informed its IPC partners that should its bid be successful, they would be given proportionate access to the oil. The CFP initiative was not favourably received by the IPC which also bid on its own account, offering financial terms a little better than those of the 1965 agreement. The only attraction of this offer to the Iraqis was the prospect of greater output, for the IPC offered to expand production elsewhere in Iraq as part of the deal. The proposal was rejected by the government as simply another move to regain North Rumaila in contravention of Law 97.

The CFP offer, which was slightly better financially than that of the IPC, envisaged a service contract between INOC and the French company, but CFP wanted to purchase all of the output and wanted to operate in North Rumaila. This appealed less to Iraq than the type of service contract another French company, ERAP, had made with the Iranian National Oil Company, and serious negotiations were carried on with ERAP for a similar contract in Iraq—but not including North Rumaila.

While continuing negotiations with the CFP, however, Iraq was also discussing with the Soviet Union the plans for the development of North Rumaila.[12] A Soviet delegation visited Baghdad in December 1967 and a 'letter of intent' was signed by Adib al-Jadir and the leader of the Soviet delegation. This envisaged Soviet assistance for INOC as it engaged in exploration, production, and marketing in North Rumaila and elsewhere.

Not only was government policy now clear about the scope and functions of INOC and the type of foreign relations it could enter into, but the prospect of assistance from other countries opened the way for the new management to take practical action. A distinction was made between areas where oil reserves had not been proved, for which service contracts could be made with foreign companies, and areas with proved reserves, such as North Rumaila, where there was no exploration risk and which INOC would develop itself. Accordingly, on 10 April 1968, in what was termed a 'dramatic declaration', Adib al-Jadir announced the intention of INOC to reject all offers for North Rumaila and to proceed to develop the area on its own account.[13]

This action was indeed a major turning-point in Iraqi oil policy and represented the final triumph of those opposing the IPC group and all its works. The announcement was widely acclaimed, for 'direct exploitation' was seen as the only way for the state to 'safeguard its full rights to oil' and also to maximize its financial return; the establishment of an independent oil sector was believed to be the only road to the eventual removal of the 'imperialist monopolies', an object of obsessive fixation in Iraq. At the same time it was made clear that foreign companies would be welcome as contractors to INOC in exploration and development in other areas of Iraq where oil had not been discovered. Experienced older hands, such as Muhammed Hadid, erstwhile oil adviser to Abdul Karim Qassim, though not disapproving of the new policy, warned that it might be difficult for Iraq to sell her oil without reducing prices and thus reducing revenues per barrel, in view of the world surplus of oil at that time. But this was a risk it seemed necessary to take. (No one could foresee in 1968 that within three years the market would turn around, the 'surplus' turn to 'scarcity', removing this cause of concern for the oil-exporting countries.)

It was also now clear to the IPC that nothing was to be gained by continuing to insist that its claim to regain the territories lost under Law 80 be included in any discussion of the government's financial claims on the company, although it did not intend to drop its own claims for compensation. Negotiations between the company and the government now began and covered not only the longstanding accounting disputes, but also the disputes over the basis of pricing oil shipped from the Mediterranean, and the losses Iraq sustained because agreement had not been reached on royalty expensing. Altogether, the government claims came to around $200 million. In June 1968 after some six weeks of negotiations on Iraq's demand for increased prices for her Mediterranean oil (the price of oil delivered directly to the Mediterranean had risen substantially after the closure of the Suez Canal), the companies agreed to pay a lump sum of £10 million ($24m.) to take account of the increased value of oil for the period June 1967 to May 1968, and, in addition, to pay 7 cents a barrel from June 1968 so long as the 'extraordinary circumstances' (i.e., the closure of the Suez Canal) continued.

Although after many years of hesitating government attitudes Iraqi oil policy was now set on a defined and decisive course from which there would be no retreat, the triumph of those who had been largely responsible for the new policy, Abdul Sattar Ali al-Husain, the Minister of Oil, and Adib al-Jadir and Khair al-Din Haseeb of INOC, was short-lived. They were swept away by the military *coup* of 17 July 1968 which overthrew the government of President Arif and Prime Minister Yahya. Accused of corruption along with other prominent members of the former administration, they were arrested and their properties impounded while the press hinted that they would be put on trial.[14]

Communiqué Number 1 of the new Revolutionary Command Council (RCC) attacked the old regime in the usual flamboyant language of Iraqi politics as a 'clique of ignoramuses, illiterates, opportunists, thieves, spies, Zionists, suspects, and agents', accusing it of the most heinous crimes and of deliberate disloyalty in every respect to the Iraqi people. At the same time, there were no specific attacks on oil policy; indeed, it seemed clear that the new regime would continue the policy much as before, including the association under the ERAP agreement. On 30 July, two weeks after this *coup,* the Baath members of the new Cabinet, in a second *coup* of their own, succeeded in pushing out the two officers who had affected the original *coup.*[15]

In spite of the extreme nationalist attitude of the Baath party, it was in no better position decisively to break with the IPC group and finally to nationalize it than the previous governments had been. Above all, Iraq needed the oil revenues, and in 1968 the international oil market was still weak, and was still dominated by the major companies. The IPC group produced and marketed Iraq's oil, and it was by no means obvious to the government that it could successfully sell enough to maintain its revenues, especially since the IPC parents made it clear that legal action would be taken against buyers. Consequently the new regime declared its intention of negotiating with the IPC over outstanding issues while at the same time insisting that there would be no compromise whatsoever over the provisions of Law 80 (1961) and Laws 97 and 123 (1967), which were so strongly challenged by the foreign companies. The Oil Minister, Rashid al-Rifa'i, also stated the government's intention to put the issue of government participation in the ownership of the IPC on the OPEC agenda and, consistent with Baath Pan Arab nationalism, he affirmed the government's intention to press for a union of Arab national oil companies.

Again in January 1969 the minister issued public warnings to the companies that there was to be no compromise over Iraq's decision to exploit the expropriated lands herself. A year later, in February 1970, the government cancelled the one remaining provision of Law 80 which permitted the allocation of further territory to the IPC group. This was the article under which the 1965 Wattari agreement had been negotiated. Law 97 of 1967 had in any case effectively removed its significance, but the new Oil Minister, Saadoon Hammadi,[16] explained that the purpose of the formal cancellation was to make absolutely firm the government's intention to prohibit any further concessions and to exploit its resources without further dependence on the 'international monopolies'. Evidently, the Iraqis could not believe that they had actually defeated the powerful IPC, and were desperately insuring that there was no chink through which its ghost could emerge again to haunt them.

Renewed Negotiations

In spite of an impressive flurry of Iraqi activity on the international scene in order to line up effective assistance for INOC's work after 1969, and of the hectic construction activity within Iraq in order to explore the country's natural resources and establish the production and export of nationally owned oil,[17] the major proportion of Iraq's oil continued to be produced from the fields that had been discovered and developed by the international oil companies. In 1972 INOC was producing only 2.3 million out of a total production of 71.2 million tons, and almost all of the country's foreign-exchange earnings came from the revenues paid by the IPC group of companies.

New IPC investment had been drastically reduced after the passage of Law 80 and production stagnated for three years, but between 1963 and 1968 output rose steadily (except for a steep drop in 1967 as a result of the controversy with Syria over pipeline charges and of the war with Israel). During 1969 the conflict with the government over the port charges imposed at Basra, which had been simmering ever since 1960, and which the company insisted made Basra oil 'uncompetitive', became acute, but was settled, at least temporarily. In the spring of 1969, also, the Shah of Iran was putting very heavy pressures on the consortium companies operating in Iran to increase his government's revenues in view of the heavy financial requirements of the Iranian development plans. There was considerable concern among the Arab oil-exporting countries that the companies would meet the Shah's demands, in part at least, by raising Iranian output at their expense. Iraq, along with other Arab governments, warned the companies not to do this.

Except for these instances, however, there was little pressure on the IPC group until the middle of 1970. The new regime was busy consolidating its internal political position (which included the problem of the continuing struggle with the Kurds in the north), strengthening its international economic and political relationships, and attempting to lay the foundations for a rapid expansion not only of the national oil industry but also of industrial investment generally. Nevertheless, the government was dissatisfied with the level of oil output, particularly from Basra, where production was below the export capacity of the port facilities. It was also becoming increasingly restive over the companies' refusal to give Iraq the benefit of the royalty-expensing agreement negotiated by OPEC and given effect in the other exporting countries.[18]

A vigorous offensive was opened in July 1970 on the occasion of two ceremonies, one inaugurating the beginning of drilling in the North Rumaila field under INOC auspices and the other celebrating the second anniversary of the Baath *coup*. Strong speeches from President al-Bakr, Vice-President Ammash, and Oil Minister Hammadi attacked the companies and warned the Basra Petroleum Company that if it did not increase output to the capacity of the export facilities, which was around 36 million tons from Fao and the new deep-water terminal at Khor al-Amaya taken together (as against the current output of around 16 million tons), the government would take over the spare capacity and use it to export its own oil. The government also demanded that expensing of royalties be accepted without delay and the appropriate payments be made to the government.

At the same time, OPEC had been becoming increasingly militant in its attitude towards the oil companies. In June 1968 at its Sixteenth Conference a general 'Declaratory Statement of Petroleum Policy in Member Countries' had been adopted in which it laid out its long-run objectives.[19] This statement did not seem to worry the companies at the time, for such general statements are taken seriously only when those issuing them seem likely to have the power to enforce their demands. Iraqi officials had taken a leading part in the drafting of this declaration, and it contained most of the objectives for which Iraq had been pressing. The programme as set out in the Declaratory Statement included direct exploitation of their hydrocarbon resources by the member countries themselves, or, failing this, the greatest possible measure of participation in and control over operations; revision of concession contracts as justified by changing circumstances; progressive relinquishment of areas under contract to the companies, with the government participating in the choice of area to be relinquished; tax reference (or posted) prices to be determined by the government[20] and set so as to sustain the terms of trade between oil and manufactured goods; net earnings considered excessive were to be paid to the government by the companies.

Some of these objectives had been, or could reasonably be, met by the companies in some degree, but those regarding prices, taxation, and participation, if any more than a statement of long-run intentions, would, of course, threaten the basis of existing concessions. However, the companies were on good terms with most of their host governments and did not seem very concerned, although Aramco officials had displayed some nervousness at a talk by Zeki Yamani, the Saudi Arabian Oil Minister, to a seminar at the American University of Beirut, also in June, in which he declared: 'Partnership with the host governments is a must; any delay will be paid for by the oil companies concerned'.[21]

After the successful negotiations over royalty expensing and the acceptance of progressive relinquishment arrangements in most of the concessions, the next major issue to be taken up by OPEC related not to participation but to prices—the original *raison d'être* of OPEC. All governments wanted improved prices, but Iraq, along with Venezuela, had been the most active in advocating strong measures to achieve them. As early as 1964 at the International Trade Conference in Geneva, Iraq had presented a paper calling for a more equitable distribution of earnings from crude-oil sales and arguing that sooner or later the consuming countries would have to deal directly with OPEC. Later Iraq urged unilateral legislation to increase the rate of income tax and again raised her longstanding demand for production controls.

Iraq was particularly incensed by the fact that the rate of increase of her oil production was far below that of other major Middle East exporting countries.[22] The government believed that the companies were deliberately holding back production in retaliation for the policies which affected their interests adversely, and as a means of bringing pressure on it to compromise, but the BPC still argued that because of Iraqi policies the cost of Basra crude was too high to compete on world markets.

Iraq had also presented a memorandum to the OPEC conference held in June 1970 at Algiers requesting the support of the organization in its dispute with the companies. A resolution pledging support for Iraq in any measures she took to 'safeguard her legitimate interests' was adopted, but some members indicated that they did not feel bound by the general OPEC policy of maintaining the 'solidarity' of members in the face of sanctions imposed by oil companies because in this case Iraq had refused to state what measures she intended to take. Iraq was disappointed with the OPEC response.

In 1970, however, the bargaining position of the oil companies was rapidly being eroded by the changes taking place in the international oil market. Demand for oil delivered in the Mediterranean was rising rapidly because of the closure of the Suez Canal following the 1967 war with Israel, while at the same time where had been a number of interruptions of supply. Colonel Qadhaffi was engaged in a full-scale confrontation with the oil companies in Libya, his position strengthened by the tightening market position, and he was able to bring severe pressure on the independent companies operating there.[23] Algeria took over a number of foreign oil companies and unilaterally raised the tax prices of her oil. United States demand for imported oil was increasing and adding to market pressures in the Mediterranean. As prices and freight rates rose (the supertankers had not yet taken over), there was increasing talk of an impending 'oil crisis'.

OPEC was solidly behind the Libyans and Algerians and it was clear that gains for these countries would have to be extended to all OPEC members. Moreover, pressures on the international companies to concede a measure of participation in the ownership of their oil-producing subsidiaries were speedily intensifying, with Saudi Arabia taking the lead. Changes in the international oil market and in the position of the companies *vis-à-vis* their host countries were clearly working in favour of Iraq in her own struggle with the IPC and were improving the long-run prospects of successful marketing for INOC. The time had come when the companies would have to meet at least some of the Iraqi demands or the government would legislate to obtain them. But nevertheless both the government and the companies still insisted that they wanted a negotiated settlement of the issues between them.

As always, the companies had to consider the effect of any concessions made to Iraq on their position in the other crude-oil exporting countries. This very much limited their scope for action, since above all they wanted to avoid weakening their negotiating position elsewhere. But in September 1970 most of the oil companies operating in Libya had reached agreement with the Libyan government on an increase in posted prices and in the rate of income tax. Hence the companies could now grant similar terms to Iraq without prejudice to negotiations in Libya. The way was open to conciliation by the IPC group, although the BPC still continued to threaten legal action when INOC invited bids for service contracts from other oil companies to explore and develop areas that had been expropriated from the BPC.

At the end of September when Esso and BP announced increases in posted prices for Libyan crudes of 30 cents a barrel with effect from 1 September, they also announced increases of 20 cents a barrel for Iraqi and Saudi crudes at Mediterranean ports, and other companies soon followed suit. Although the increase did not fully meet the Iraqi government's demand (which was for the same increase as Libya had received), it nevertheless accepted, at least temporarily, the company's prices.

In addition, the IPC group decided that it would be desirable to go some way to meet Iraq on the royalty expensing issue. Without explicitly adopting the OPEC formula for royalty expensing, the companies offered increased payments to Iraq in lieu of royalty expensing, which gave the same financial result. These payments also fell short of Iraq's demands since they were to be effective only from 1 January 1971, and Iraq had wanted retroactive payments to 1964 when royalty expensing had been put into effect for other countries. However, BPC agreed to raise output to an annual rate of 21 million tons immediately and 28 million tons in 1971, and throughput from the northern pipeline by 4.5 million tons a year (by about 8 per cent). In October the IPC group also agreed to lend £20 million to Iraq without interest, with repayments to begin in July 1971.

Following the 1970 negotiations in Libya, OPEC moved to open negotiations to obtain increased payments for the other oil-exporting countries, and it also expressed support for Libya, Algeria, and Iraq in their own conflict with the companies. Intricate negotiations followed at Teheran and then at Tripoli in 1971 in order not only to find a formula for the application in the Gulf countries of the price and tax arrangements obtained by Libya, but also to attempt to ensure that the prices and other terms applicable to oil shipped from Gulf ports bore an appropriate and stable relationship to those applicable to oil shipped from Mediterranean ports. Here, again, Iraq and Libya insisted on separate negotiations for Mediterranean crude oil and their joint pressure was effective in protecting their special interest.

After one month of hard and often bitter bargaining, which at times seemed on the brink of collapse, a five-year price agreement applicable to oil exported from the Gulf was signed in Teheran in February 1971.[24] Iraq signed the Teheran agreement and accepted its terms for her Basra oil. At the same time the Iraqi Oil Minister signed a protocol with the companies, reserving Iraq's rights with respect to her outstanding financial claims on the IPC group, which were estimated to be around $200 million and included back payments on account of royalty expensing and alleged underpricing of Basra crude, as well as lesser matters. Iraq also reserved her position with respect to her oil exports from the Mediterranean, the financial arrangements for which were to be separately negotiated between the companies and the Mediterranean exporters represented by Libya.

The negotiations with the Mediterranean exporters and Libya over the financial terms to be applied in the Mediterranean opened in February 1971 in Tripoli and were even more difficult than those for the Gulf and lasted much longer. The companies were determined to get an agreement for the full five-year period. Libya was very critical of the Teheran settlement, believing that the price accepted was too low and the period of the agreement too long. The companies had obtained assurances in Teheran from the Gulf countries that there would be no 'leapfrogging' on their part if better terms were obtained elsewhere—in other words if Libya succeeded in getting more from the companies, the Gulf states agreed not to use this as an argument for trying to improve even further the terms of the Teheran agreement. Nevertheless, the companies knew that it would be unwise to agree to any Libyan terms that strained the tolerance of these countries. In the event, they did have to concede more to Libya and the Mediterranean exporters than they had to those in the Gulf, but they did get a five-year agreement, signed in Tripoli on 2 April. Unfortunately, their troubles were still not over; when they attempted to apply the agreement to Iraqi oil exported from Mediterranean terminals, the Iraqi government refused to accept the proposed posted prices.

Under the Tripoli agreement Libya's high-quality, low-sulphur crude was given a premium of 10 cents a barrel to reflect its greater value. This premium was not included in the price offered to either the Iraqis or the Saudis for their high-sulphur oil exported from the Mediterranean. The Saudis did not contest the matter, but the Iraqis argued that although Iraqi crude had more sulphur, it had other good qualities which more than offset the sulphur disadvantage. They therefore refused to accept the lower price for Iraqi crude attributable to its sulphur content. The companies might have been willing to agree to the Iraqi demand had it not been for the risk that Libya would use any such concession for Iraqi (and Saudi) oil as an argument for demanding a still higher price for her oil in order to restore the differential thus eroded. This was the 'leapfrogging' between Gulf and Mediterranean that the companies were determined to avoid. The Iraqi and Saudi Oil Ministers tried to persuade Libya to give guarantees against such leapfrogging, but without success. Once again, the companies' scope for manoeuvre in Iraq was limited by their position elsewhere.

Negotiations dragged on, but in June a settlement was finally reached. The government gave way on its claim to higher prices, but the companies, in addition to applying all of the Teheran and Tripoli terms,[25] accepted a number of the government's longstanding demands and offered associated financial arrangements. The former included minor questions that had been a source of friction between company and government since 1955: the method of calculating costs of production for tax purposes, the accounting treatment of dead rents and intangible exploration and drilling expenditures, the allocation of head office expenses, the interest on loans, company donations, and of the cost of Iraqi students studying in Britain, and the government's demand for an adjustment of the price of Basra crude.

Agreement was reached on procedures for the treatment of the cost items; a lump sum of £20.2 million (less £6.2 million to cover the cost of oil supplied to government refineries in the past but not paid for by the government) was paid over by the company, which also granted a four-year loan of £10 million free of interest and agreed to defer repayment of the £20 million loan of October 1970, for which repayments were scheduled to begin in July 1971. Finally, the BPC agreed to use its 'best endeavours' to raise output to 29 million tons in 1971 and to the full productive capacity of 35 million tons in 1974, providing the port capacity of Khor al-Amaya could be enlarged to take the very large tankers of over 100,000 tons. Government revenues resulting from these arrangements (excluding the loans and lump sum payment) were expected to rise from ID 183 million ($512.4 m.) to ID 330 million ($924 m.) in 1971.

Apparently the government, and certainly the companies, looked on this agreement as the beginning of the road to a comprehensive settlement of the issues between them. The demands of the government had by no means been fully met, especially with regard to back payments for royalty expensing, and the government reservations were noted in the agreement; nor was the issue of compensation for the companies as a result of Law 80 touched on. Nevertheless a good start had been made and it was agreed that talks should be resumed in October. But events were once again to conspire against a settlement.

Nationalization of the IPC

OPEC was becoming increasingly militant over the participation issue and impatient over the failure of the companies to take adequate account of the effect of the continuing depreciation of the United States dollar on their oil revenues (oil prices were expressed in dollars). Soon after the Teheran and Tripoli price settlements were completed, OPEC had turned its attention to its other major demand—the right of the producing countries to participate in the ownership of the oil companies operating in their territories. Algeria, with which Iraq had close associations, had already acted unilaterally by nationalizing a number of foreign companies and taking over 51 per cent of the assets of the major French oil companies in the country. The Oil Minister of Saudi Arabia, Zeki Yamani, made some very strong speeches, and at an OPEC conference in July 1971 it was resolved that member countries should take immediate steps to implement the 'principle of Participation in the existing oil concessions' (Res. XXIII. 133). The pressure was on; less than three months later the companies were to accept the principle of participation.

The actions of the other radical Arab governments, Algeria and Libya, together with the growing militancy even of the conservatives in OPEC, naturally encouraged those in Iraq who were pressing for extreme action against the IPC group. Participation was an issue on which Iraq felt particularly strongly in view of the never-forgotten bitterness over the 20 per cent participation promised under the San Remo agreement of 1920 but never realized. Moreover, in the draft agreement of 1965 the major companies had accepted participation in a joint company which was to operate in areas expropriated from them under Law 80. The Iraqi Oil Minister had believed that this would set a precedent for future developments in concession contracts, and Yamani and others did cite it in the OPEC arguments for participation in spite of the subsequent failure of the Iraqi draft agreement as a whole. When OPEC took up the demand for participation in earnest, the Iraqis saw it as a continuation of a trend which they had initiated and long advocated.

As we have seen, Iraq frequently accused the companies of using reductions in offtake as a means of bringing pressure on the government in negotiations. In the autumn of 1971 a very sharp drop in freight rates reduced the delivered cost of oil from the Gulf in relation to that from the Mediterranean and buyers therefore began to take more oil from the Gulf. This, together with the normal summer fall in consumption, led to a drop in shipments from Iraq's Banias and Tripoli terminals in the Mediterranean. The fall in exports angered the Iraqis, who demanded that offtake be restored as a precondition for the opening of further talks.

These developments ensured that talks, when they did begin, would not take place in the most favourable of atmospheres. And as if this were not enough, Iraqi politics again erupted. At the end of September there was a shake-up in the leadership of the government and in the Revolutionary Command Council of the Baath party. The losers were Lt-Gen. Salih Mahdi Ammash, Vice President, and Abdul Karim al-Shaikhly, Minister of Foreign Affairs, who were dismissed from their government and party posts. Saddam Hussain al-Takriti took over as Vice President and emerged as the 'strong man' of the government and party.

Ammash had been chairman of a special ministerial committee and was 'understood to have initiated the strategy of limited reconciliation with IPC'.[26] Whatever the interpretation of the rivalries of men and policies within the government and party (and they were various), the Iraqi government's attitude towards the IPC distinctly hardened after this change, as did its attitude in talks with ERAP, which were in process at the same time.[27] In November 1971 a 'National Action Charter' was promulgated which declared that 'the total liberation of the country's oil resources from foreign exploitation and control and their subjugation to national sovereignty in every respect is a natural aim of the revolution'.[28] At the end of December Saddam Hussain announced that the oil companies had been asked to prepare for 'decisive negotiations' during the first half of January 1972. Iraq was in no mood to compromise and 'leniency' with the companies was no longer possible.

Iraq was insisting on effective participation in ownership, the removal of IPC headquarters from London to Baghdad, continuous audit of accounts, agreement on a 'cost procedure manual', payments with respect to expensed royalties since 1964, and agreement on an oil development programme. Saddam warned that Iraq must prepare herself, both psychologically and economically, for confrontation with the companies; people would have to accustom themselves to doing without the non-essentials of life.

The talks started on 15 January 1972 and were adjourned five days later with the return of the IPC team to London for consultations.[29] Opening again on 1 February, they remained deadlocked. According to the *Middle East Economic Survey*[30] the companies offered to increase BPC production and export capacity in 1976 by two-thirds (from around 600,000 b/d to a million b/d in 1976 and 1.5 million b/d in 1980); to purchase 8,000 million barrels from INOC over 20 years for $1.62 a barrel (more than 20¢ below the then current market price); to make payments on account of royalty expensing and marketing allowances back to 1 January 1968; and to pay a lump sum of £10 million in settlement of a variety of other financial issues. They also agreed to make oil available to the government for certain of its barter deals with Eastern Bloc countries. In return, the companies asked to receive 12.5 per cent of oil produced by INOC delivered free of royalties, taxes, and costs at seaboard in recognition of the losses suffered through the deprivation of the fruits of their discoveries before 1961 and of the loss of their rights. In other words, the companies demanded compensation for the effects of Law 80.

These proposals were offered as a package deal to the government. They were rejected out of hand on several grounds, but primarily because the Iraqi government would not entertain any suggestions of compensation for Law 80. *MEES* reported the Iraqi view:

> Compensation to the companies for the effects of Law 80 of 1961—apart from the book value of any prior installations and exploration work on the acreage taken over by the government in 1961—would be absolutely unthinkable. If anything it was Iraq that should receive compensation for the discriminatory production and other policies followed by the companies since 1961, as a result of which the government sustained financial losses estimated at ID 550 million.[31]

Accordingly the Iraqis announced that the companies' offer provided no suitable basis for negotiation.

Thereafter events moved rapidly, with Iraq clearly preparing for direct action against the IPC. Saddam Hussain, Saadoon Hammadi, and the Foreign Minister, Murtadha Said Abdul Baqi (chief of the team negotiating with the IPC), and Fakhri al-Qadduri, a member of the Economic Affairs Bureau of the RCC, immediately made an official trip to the Soviet Union which, predictably, expressed its support for Iraq's stand but, according to a reliable source close to Hammadi, advised privately against nationalization (as did the Communist party of Iraq).

In January 1972 Zeki Yamani, representing the OPEC countries, entered into preliminary negotiations on the participation issue. The Saudi minister had assumed the leading role in the drive for participation largely because he saw it as an alternative to nationalization, demands for which were vociferous and growing under the prodding of the radicals in the area, of whom Shaikh Abdulla al-Tariki, a former Saudi Oil Minister, was among the most prominent. Zeki Yamani saw no advantage to Saudi Arabia in nationalizing the industry, and many disadvantages. He recognized that control of the market by the international companies was important for the maintenance of prices at that time. On the other hand, the radicals like Iraq continually stressed the political desirability of the Arabs controlling their own industry and escaping from the clutches of 'monopolists and imperialists'. The nationalist political argument had great popular appeal, but Yamani believed that it could be outflanked by effective participation.

Very intense pressure was put on the companies and by March 1972 they had accepted the principle of 20 per cent participation for the host governments. The parents of the IPC and the BPC also accepted it—indeed, OPEC had declared that unless the IPC made an offer to the Iraqi government similar to the Aramco offer to Saudi Arabia, OPEC negotiations would be called off. Consequently, the IPC group informed Iraq in March that it accepted the principle of 20 per cent government participation in the Iraqi concessions.

During March and April deliveries of oil from the Mediterranean ports again fell drastically to about half the production capacity. The Iraqis were outraged. They regarded this as another high-handed attempt to bring pressure on them. The companies repeated that Mediterranean oil was simply too costly compared to that from the Gulf, given current freight rates. In May, however, the companies told the government that they would raise Mediterranean throughput from the current 600,000 b/d to a million b/d if the government would agree to reduce the taxes on the oil exported. This offer further outraged the Iraqis, who saw it as an attempt to get around the Teheran price agreement, and in this they were supported by OPEC.

The Oil Ministry then proposed that the companies should: (1) Raise production from the 600,000 b/d to one million b/d and hand the difference over to the government at cost to market on its own account; or (2) Relinquish excess production and pipeline capacity to the government; or (3) Give up the northern fields and concentrate on production in the south.

The RCC then gave the companies an ultimatum: within two weeks (by 31 May) they should respond to the government's demand to raise production and take steps to do so; draw up a definite long-term production programme; and submit a positive offer in response to the government's outstanding demands.

At the same time, the government prepared for its confrontation with the IPC group. The government had no way of knowing exactly what steps the oil companies or their host governments would take in retaliation, and felt it necessary to prepare for the worst. Nor was the government entirely sure how far it would receive effective support from OPEC, which was itself deeply involved in working out the participation agreements, even though the IPC's efforts to secure a reduction in tax prices in the Mediterranean had aroused the ire of other OPEC members. In preparation for the expected struggle, which could have brought a very severe and prolonged fall in the country's revenues, the government announced that work on public sector projects under the country's investment programme would cease except for maintenance and work already underway, and it imposed 'total austerity' on the use of foreign-exchange earnings. (INOC, which had just started production, was exempt from restrictions.) In May it put on a vigorous campaign to arouse popular support and took two leading communists into the Cabinet as 'a necessary political requirement for the confrontation' with the companies.[32]

On the international front efforts continued to secure as much support as possible from 'friendly' countries and from OPEC. Close contact remained with the French, for the Iraqis attempted to exploit their 'special relation' with France and the differences between the French and the Anglo–American viewpoints in the Middle East, in order to enlist French help in negotiations with the IPC. The government withdrew its deposits from the banks of those countries which it feared might impound them in the event of nationalization of the IPC.

On 31 May the companies submitted another proposal which went some way towards meeting the Iraqi objections to the earlier one, but, although the compensation demanded was reduced to 7 per cent of INOC output (from 12.5 per cent), the new proposal firmly reiterated the demand for compensation under Law 80. The Iraqis rejected the company offer out of hand. They objected to a number of the terms proposed—most of which were clearly negotiable—but above all they would have no mention whatsoever of compensation for lost oil rights. No offer from the companies would be treated as serious that included this issue.

There was nothing more to be said. On 1 June 1972 the RCC issued Law 69 of 1972 nationalizing the IPC (but not the BPC) and setting up the Iraqi Company for Oil Operations (ICOO) to take over the IPC facilities in the north. Syria immediately issued her own

Legislative Decree No. 46 which nationalized the IPC pipelines and other IPC property in Syria, including the Banias terminal and the IPC share of the oil stocks therein.

Saddam Hussain declared later that the IPC did not believe the government would actually take the drastic step of nationalizing the company in spite of French efforts to convince the company's negotiators that the government was serious. This may be true, but the government had very early taken a position with respect to the status of Law 80 from which retreat was clearly politically impossible—and the IPC must surely have realized this.

In addition, any concession to the company's demand for compensation for oil reserves it had lost would have been flatly inconsistent with the position of the OPEC negotiators in the participation discussions that were going on at the same time. Zeki Yamani, leading the OPEC negotiations, was insisting that compensation for the government's equity share in the companies should be the book value of net fixed assets; the value of potential production was not to be considered. Iraq was willing to concede compensation equal to the book value of work undertaken by the IPC group before the 1961 expropriation, but could hardly go further even if she wanted to (and this is not to imply that she did) without creating a precedent which would prejudice the OPEC negotiations. It is clear that the IPC negotiators knew this; and therefore they must have known that so long as they maintained their position on compensation, agreement would be impossible.

On the other hand, and by the same token, the company could not accept Iraq's proposals without undermining the position of the international companies in the OPEC negotiations. Geoffrey Stockwell, managing director of the IPC, who conducted the Iraqi negotiations, stated the point clearly:

> We could have done a deal, but only by complete capitulation. We would have sold the pass on the current industry talks on participation. Equally if the Iraqis had met our terms they would have sold the pass on the OPEC side. The question of participation and compensation in Law 80 were obviously intermingled. Both sides had their hands tied by the attitudes of OPEC and the oil industry.[33]

On the other hand, if Iraq unilaterally nationalized the IPC and decreed the terms, there would be little effect on the OPEC discussions, particularly since neither Saudi Arabia nor Kuwait wanted at that time to nationalize their oil companies (i.e., enforce '100 per cent participation').

A similar question, though of lesser direct impact, also existed with regard to the other major point at issue in the negotiations—the amount of oil that the IPC or its parents would be entitled to buy from INOC and the price to be paid. One of the primary aims of the companies in the OPEC participation negotiations was to ensure that they would have access to crude oil on better terms than were available to their competitors in the market. Until this issue was settled, it would be difficult for an OPEC member to make separate arrangement with its own concessionaires.[34]

In such circumstances one can only conclude that the 'cliff-hanging' negotiations in Iraq were, on the one hand, a method whereby each side manoeuvred for position in negotiations over settlement terms that would inevitably follow nationalization, and on the other, a means of gaining time while the OPEC discussions were going on. Both of these considerations were important for both sides, but the last was probably most important for the IPC. Both sides wanted to establish as good a public relations image as possible. That Iraq was anxious for the support of outside opinion is clear from the fact that shortly after the negotiations, the government sent emissaries to a number of countries, including Italy, France, Britain, and Eastern European countries, to explain the government's position. After all, having nationalized the IPC, Iraq would herself soon face the problem of selling the oil, and she could not afford excessive international antagonism even in a tight oil market.

By and large, therefore, we can conclude that during the first six months of 1972 both sides were sparring and neither wanted decisive action. Each side knew that the outcome of the negotiations would probably be the nationalization of the IPC before very long, and each was determined to mark out its territory for the struggle that would follow. The eventual outcome of the post-nationalization discussions would be much influenced by the outcome of the OPEC negotiations, but none knew how long these would take. From the IPC point of view the loss of Iraqi oil at that time, particularly from the south, would have been extremely inconvenient, while from the Iraqis' point of view the loss of revenues would have brought considerable hardship. In this respect, the continued operation of BPC was a pawn in the hands of both; so long as it continued producing, the government would receive revenues and the company would receive oil.

The skirmishing for position began immediately after nationalization. The Iraqi government announced its willingness to enter into negotiations to settle the issues between them, but it insisted that neither Law 80 nor the nationalization could be discussed. A spokesman for the IPC stated that the company would take legal action against anyone buying the nationalized oil; Nadim al-Pachachi, Secretary General of OPEC, issued a statement in support of Iraq's action and condemned the IPC for reducing production of its northern oil as a '. . . deliberate and premeditated measure . . . aimed at punishing Iraq . . . and exerting pressure'.[35] He warned against any attempts to bypass the OPEC price agreements. The French quickly accepted Iraq's right to nationalize and indicated their desire to discuss ways of protecting the French interest and French oil supplies. OPEC at an Extraordinary Conference held on 9 June 1972 in Beirut approved Iraq's nationalization and agreed that no member country would permit increases in its own output which were designed to replace reductions in Iraqi output. More important, it delegated its Secretary General to mediate between the government and the companies.

The IPC had itself proposed mediation under the auspices of OPEC and had agreed to the two conditions OPEC had laid down—that the mediation should be conducted within the framework of Iraq's nationalization law, and that during the mediation period the company should take no legal action which would hamper Iraq's exports from the northern fields. In agreeing to these, the company implicitly recognized Iraq's right to nationalize and accepted the action; it also abjured the use of the one weapon which in similar circumstances in the past had been a reasonably effective means of bringing pressure—a legal threat against buyers of expropriated oil. ICOO at once invited offers from prospective purchasers.

Nadim al-Pachachi of OPEC and Geoffrey Stockwell of IPC began immediately to work out arrangements for the mediation proceedings. In a letter to the president of the OPEC Conference to be held in Vienna on 26 June, the IPC proposed that the period of mediation should be 90 days and that Jean Duroc Danner of CFP should act as co-mediator with al-Pachachi. These proposals were taken under consideration in Baghdad, but decisions were not quickly forthcoming.

Iraq was moving in many directions. Negotiations were being conducted with the French over CFP's entitlement to Iraqi oil. Saddam Hussain made an official visit to Paris from 14 to 18 June 1972 and a general agreement was concluded on the 18th. Negotiations were continuing with Syria about the transit arrangements for ICOO crude across Syria to the port of Banias and over the disposition of the oil stocks at Banias. (Syria wanted a large increase in transit fees. She also laid claim to half the Banias stocks and had not permitted the French to lift the oil.)[36] Many countries were being approached to find markets for ICOO crude and contracts were being negotiated. Internally, the government continued to prepare for the confrontation with the IPC that it still half expected, and for the reduction in revenues that the country was facing. Travel of Iraqis abroad was further restricted and those already abroad were urged to return. Civil servants were required to purchase government savings bonds equal to between 7 and 25 per cent of their basic pay depending on their salary level. (This was a compulsory loan to be repaid when the RCC decreed an end to the period of austerity.) The government was also involved in arranging for loans from OAPEC countries, following up an OAPEC resolution supporting Iraq (and Syria) and offering financial help. The negotiations between OPEC and the companies on the application of the principle of participation were at a very critical stage, with the OPEC countries becoming increasingly impatient and issuing threatening warnings to the companies.

In the midst of all this the Iraqi government was attempting to decide how it should proceed in negotiating a settlement with the IPC. The arrangements already made with the French raised the possibility, supported by some, that bilateral negotiations should be conducted with each of the IPC parent companies. There was some preference in Baghdad for direct negotiations of this sort, or with the IPC as a whole, instead of accepting mediation. Moreover, the limit of 90 days proposed by the IPC during which it would suspend any legal action was resented.

In view of the Iraqi objections to the 90-day time limit, the IPC issued a statement on 14 July reiterating its position that the government's actions were a breach of the company's agreements and of international law and reserving its rights, but announcing that in view of the mediation

> it will, without prejudice to its rights, abstain from commencing legal proceedings . . . prior to any declaration by one or both of the mediators regarding the status of the mediation. . . . A declaration will be made not later than the 12th October, 1972. If this or any other declaration states that the mediation has failed, the Company will be free to exercise its full legal rights.[37]

In other words, the company withdrew the rigid 90-day limit for the mediation and substituted a more flexible procedure.

The announcement nevertheless angered the Iraqis, who issued an announcement of their own, choosing to interpret the IPC statement as an attempt to 'initiate a publicity campaign' and to claim title to the crude being produced and exported by ICOO. The government reserved the right to claim compensation for any damage the publicity campaign might cause.[38]

The mediators nevertheless continued at work, and since they were able to report progress in their efforts, the IPC extended its 'deadline' twice, first to the end of January 1973 and then to the end of February. In the meantime, a general agreement was reached between OPEC and the oil companies on the arrangements for participation, and negotiations had begun over the application of the arrangements to individual countries. The time had now come when external conditions favoured an Iraqi settlement. On 28 February 1973 the terms of an overall agreement between the Iraqi government and the IPC group were finally accepted. The government conceded no matters of principle; the agreement was 'in conformity with the laws and regulations prevailing in Iraq; particularly Law No. 80 for 1961 . . . and Law No. 69 for 1972 . . .'; thus the companies implicitly recognized Iraq's sovereign rights to expropriate and nationalize. The word 'compensation' was not mentioned, but the Iraqi government agreed to provide 15 million tons of Kirkuk crude free of all cost and charges in final settlement of all claims of the companies on the government at the rate of a million tons a month or faster if agreed.[39] On prevailing price expectations this crude was estimated to be worth over $300 million.[40]

For their part the companies were to pay the government £141 million (at $2.45=£1 this would equal $345 million, or nearly the estimated value of the oil) in settlement of all the government's claims against the companies. Since the companies had never doubted their liability eventually to pay for accumulated royalty expensing, which alone was estimated by the Iraqis to have reached some $200 million between 1964 and 1969, it can be concluded that the financial settlement was not a bad deal for the IPC.

The companies retained their rights in the BPC, which agreed to expand output from an average of 35 million tons in 1973 to 80 million tons in 1976 and the government agreed to provide all reasonable facilities to enable it to do so. No mention was made in the agreement of the implementation of the OPEC participation arrangements for the BPC, although negotiations on government participation in it were taking place; nor was the prospect of the IPC companies obtaining long-term contracts for Iraqi crude at preferential prices included, although, again, rumours were that such an agreement had in fact been made. (CFP already had such an arrangement.) Nevertheless, the way now seemed open for the emergence of a better relationship between the IPC group and the national oil company. Moreover, with the nationalization of the IPC over and done with and a final settlement effected, Iraq had greater scope to decrease her dependence on the communist countries for capital goods, technology, and skilled services.

Following the October 1973 war, however, the American interests

(Near East Development Corporation) and the 60 per cent Dutch interest in the Shell Petroleum shareholding of BPC were nationalized in retaliation for the failure of these governments to back the Arab cause; in December Gulbenkian's interest (Participations and Explorations Corporation, owned by the Gulbenkian Foundation in Portugal) was nationalized because of Portugal's attitude.[41] This left CFP, BP, and the British 40 per cent of Shell as the foreign partners in the company. In December 1975, having rejected the companies' proposal for a participation agreement, Iraq decided to nationalize these interests in order to bring all of the industry into government hands. With this act the half-century—1925–75—relationship between the IPC group and the Iraqi government drew to a close.

Even before the nationalization of the remaining foreign interest in the BPC, the Iraqi government felt that it had freed its country from the 'foreign monopolies' and had eliminated the strongest base of imperialism in the country (although this would not, of course, prevent it from continuing to blame 'imperialism' when internal difficulties arose). But regardless of the view taken of the history of imperialism in Iraq, which is certain to change as perspective on the period is gained with the passage of time, a new era had clearly begun for the country. It was more a product of developments throughout the Middle East—and indeed throughout the world—than of the specific actions of the Iraqi government. Iraq's action in promulgating Law 80 was premature and cost her dear, for it achieved nothing for Iraq that a decade later her OPEC colleagues had not achieved, but without having to pay the heavy price in foregone revenues and perhaps less efficient development of resources.

Many Iraqis believe that the extra costs to the country merely represented the price always paid by trail-blazers and pioneers and that it was Iraq's boldness which opened the way for others to follow. The government had taken earlier and more severe action against the oil companies than had other governments in the Middle East, with the exception of Iran. But just as others had not followed Iran in 1951, so others did not follow Iraq in 1961, and a country can hardly be considered to have led the way if it is not followed. The fact that others took a similar path to that of Iran and Iraq one or two decades later was due more to the evolution of general economic and political conditions affecting oil and the Middle East generally, which permitted the oil-exporting countries to adopt new policies. Iraq played a role in the adoption of such policies, but not the leading role. And although Iraq's actions were later cited as precedents for similar actions that others wanted to take, this was simply an application of normal bargaining tactics in which any argument that comes handy is used.

In practice, when the other countries, even including for the most part Libya and Algeria, decided to take radical action to force the oil companies to concede their demands, they chose a time when success was possible. No matter how severe the threats, or how heavy the pressure on the companies, a negotiated settlement as contrasted to unilateral action more often than not brought results without sanctions. Unilateral action by political decree may successfully impose the sovereign will and delight militant nationalists, but the economic cost can easily far outweigh any economic gain, particularly for an individual country which acts alone and fails to attract followers. One cannot judge how far the Iraqi public understood the issues and appreciated the cost, but there is no doubt that they were delighted by the political assertion of sovereignty through Law 80 and subsequent laws, and many felt it well worth almost any cost. It is clear that both politicians and officials were divided. An outsider can only note the actions of successive Iraqi governments and observe that everything Iraq gained, other countries were subsequently able to obtain with nothing like the cost suffered by Iraq.

A number of Arabs, even economists, have insisted that it is incorrect to treat the revenues foregone by Iraq because of reduced production as a net loss to the country. It is argued that the oil not produced was saved to be sold later when prices would be higher, and therefore that the country in fact gained. This is, of course, simply a statement that the optimum rate of depletion for Iraq was lower than the government had thought in the 1960s (especially if hindsight is brought into the argument). However, any argument that it was in Iraq's interest that the rate of depletion should have been reduced requires an analysis of the uses of current revenues and the optimum pattern of revenue receipts over time. This kind of analysis has not been done, and we can only conclude that those who insist that Iraq gained from the reduced rate of depletion must take their position on emotional and intuitive grounds. One cannot on this account condemn the judgement as wrong, but Iraq is likely to be able to produce at current rates for well over 30 years, and a barrel of oil not produced until 30 years or more hence has, at any reasonable rate of discount, a negligible present value. Nor was the prospect in the 1960s of Iraq using additional oil revenues productively as limited as it is today, for the flow of revenues had not reached such high levels as it since has.

It has often been said that the oil companies in the Middle East and their host governments existed in a 'symbiotic relationship', where each was dependent on the other for its survival. This was not true for

Iraq. In the crucial years of the 1960s the oil companies, except for CFP, could easily accept a reduction in their offtake. Therein lay the bargaining weakness of the country.

Notes

1 Exports from the port of Basra between 1958 and 1965 were as follows in millions of long tons:

1958	10.9	1962	8.6	
1959	12.0	1963	12.4	
1960	11.1	1964	17.2	
1961	9.6	1965	17.8	(Source: British Petroleum)

This agreement was widely criticized by al-Wattari's opponents as being less favourable to Iraq than the one reached earlier with the Basra Petroleum Company, since it reduced cargo dues. The validity of such criticism, however, depends on how far one accepts that lower dues did lead to an increased offtake which increased total revenue.

2 The advocates of a strongly nationalist oil policy for Iraq were extremely critical of the Qassim regime for failing to push the establishment of an Iraq National Oil Company after the promulgation of Law 80. A draft law had been drawn up in 1962, but nothing was done to implement it. The critics accused the moderates of stalling and of being stooges of the 'imperialists'. The reason for the delay was the division of opinion in government circles over the desirability of the 'go-it-alone' policy, and there was much uncertainty over the degree of co-operation that should be permitted between the IPC and the national oil company. Many of the 'oil militants' saw the sinister hand of the IPC and of the international oil companies and their parent governments behind the delay. In the nature of the case, the evidence is not available to judge how much foreign interference of this kind was involved.

3 Apart from their reluctance to strengthen the position of OPEC, the companies, and especially the American companies, had to consider the legal implications of negotiating as a group in the light of the American anti-trust laws.

4 Neither Venezuela nor Indonesia was directly affected by the question of royalty expensing since their contracts with the companies already provided for it. Nevertheless, royalty expensing in the Middle East would increase the cost of Middle East oil to the companies, and would therefore improve the competitive position of their oil. This was of particular importance to Venezuela.

5 The Kuwaiti Assembly refused to ratify the agreement on the grounds that the 'quit claim' clause prevented Kuwait from demanding compensation for the earlier reduction in prices; that the arbitration clause was inconsistent with state sovereignty; and that the 'most-favoured-company' clause would prevent the government from giving special treatment to its own national oil company. Kuwait did not ratify the agreement until 1967 when a new election changed the complexion of the National Assembly. OPEC issued a number of pamphlets explaining its point of view. For a useful discussion of the issues see Stocking, op. cit., pp. 359–73.

6 The high cost that was reported to have worried SONJ related to the fact that the companies would have to buy back from INOC the oil that it did not need at a price half-way between cost and posted prices. However, Khair al-Din Haseeb, one of the vigorous opponents of al-Wattari's policy, calculated that this price would yield the same revenue to the government (and therefore the same cost to the companies) as that obtained from the IPC concession after the OPEC amendments.

7 The draft agreement was never published, but as it seemed more and more likely that agreement would be reached, *Petroleum Intelligence Weekly,* which had secured a copy, prepared an analysis which it set up in proof to be published as soon as the agreement was released. In the event, of course, the story in *PIW* never appeared, but the publisher kindly lent us a copy, since, as past history, there was no longer need to keep the matter confidential.

8 See above, Chapters 13 and 14.

9 A useful brief summary of the arrangement made between the companies and the transit countries can be found in Charles Issawi and Mohammed Yeganeh, *The Economics of Middle Eastern Oil* (New York, 1962), pp. 137–40 and George Lenczowski, *Oil and State in the Middle East* (New York, 1960), Chapter IX.

10 The details of the calculations based on the mimeographed statements of the IPC are presented in Stocking, op. cit., p. 273.

11 President Arif accused the IPC of using the Syrian dispute to bring pressure on the Iraqi government, presumably to persuade it to sign the draft agreement which would permit the IPC to develop North Rumaila. It was argued by many that the IPC hoped that the fear of a prolonged loss of revenues because of the stoppage of Kirkuk exports would induce the government to favour a very rapid development of North Rumaila as an alternative source of oil to be exported from the Gulf.

12 See the following chapter for a discussion of the ERAP agreement and of the arrangements with the Soviet Union.

13 *MEES,* 12 April 1968.

14 Some were arrested and after rough treatment (amounting in some cases to physical torture) were released without trial (including those mentioned in the text). Other prominent Iraqi officials, including Ghanem al-Uqaili, were still in prison at the time of writing. So much for human rights in Iraq.

15 See above, Ch. 13.

16 On 31 December 1969 there had been a cabinet change and Saadoon Hammadi had assumed the oil portfolio.

17 See discussion of INOC in the following chapter.

18 After the increase in tax rates from 50 to 55 per cent as a result of the Libyan settlement in 1970, the treatment of royalties as a cost instead of as part of the government's 55 per cent of the profits would have raised government revenues by 55 per cent of the royalties payable. The IPC made provisions in its own accounting for the liabilities arising, but was unwilling to settle this question with the government separately from a settlement of other financial questions at issue between the government and the company which had risen since the passage of Law 80.

19 Resolution XVI.90 adopted 24–25 June 1968.

20 Since posted prices had long had little relation to market prices and were used primarily to determine taxes for the host governments, the term 'tax-reference prices' gradually came to be used interchangeably with the term 'posted prices'.

21 See *MEES*, 7 June 1968 for an approved report of the talk.

22 Between 1969 and 1970 Iraqi output increased by only 4 per cent compared

to 19 per cent in Saudi Arabia, 14 per cent in Iran, and 6 per cent in Kuwait.

23 The so-called 'independent' or non-major companies in Libya were companies that had very little, if any, oil available from other countries in the Middle East, and had to rely almost entirely on Libyan oil to meet their European marketing requirements. They were, therefore, extremely vulnerable to government restrictions on their Libyan production. Most observers of the events in Libya in 1970 tend to attribute the bargaining weakness of the oil companies to the entry of 'newcomers'. The weakness did not arise primarily because the independents were newcomers to Libya, but because they did not have alternative sources of oil with which to supply their downstream operations. For a discussion of the role of Libya in this period see Edith Penrose, 'The Development of Crisis', in R. Vernon (ed.), *The Oil Crisis in Perspective* (New York, 1976).

24 The negotiating team for the Gulf states consisted of representatives of Iraq (Saadoon Hammadi), Saudi Arabia (Zeki Yamani), and Iran (Jamshid Amouzegar). For discussion of the OPEC negotiations and of the role played by Iraq in these see below, Chapter 19. The Teheran and Tripoli negotiations and agreements were very intricate and it is impossible to present a clear picture of the complicated manoeuvres and cross-currents in a short space. Not all of the details are of much importance for an exposition of developments as they affected Iraq. But see the discussion in the reference cited in note 23.

25 These included an increase in tax rates from 50 per cent to 55 per cent, annual increases in posted prices on account of inflation, payments equivalent to full royalty expensing, payment of taxes and royalties monthly instead of quarterly, and a new scale of payments relating to gravity differentials. For details of these and of the rest of the agreement with Iraq see the statement of the Iraqi Minister of Oil and Minerals reproduced in *MEES*, 11 June 1971.

26 *MEES*, 1 October 1971. In commenting on the changes in the party's leadership, Saddam Hussain denied rumours that the dismissal of Ammash and others was the result of a struggle for power in which he had emerged as the strong 'number one' man, insisting that President Ahmed Hasan al-Bakr was still the primary leader. In a press interview with the Kuwait newspaper *Al-Siyasah* (reported in *MEES*, 22 October 1971) he argued that it was a matter of party democracy and in 'accordance with the principles of self-criticism practised by the party'.

27 *MEES*, 27 October 1971. The participation discussions being conducted on behalf of OPEC by Yamani were scheduled to open in January 1972. It is possible therefore that the Iraqi government wanted to anticipate events and pre-empt Yamani's initiative since it prided itself on being a radical leader in oil matters.

28 See *MEES*, 19 and 26 November 1971, which reproduces translations of the relevant text of the press conference and of the National Action Charter.

29 The information for the account in the text has been obtained from a number of sources, including personal discussions with Iraqi and other Arab officials, journalists, officials in oil companies, and the usual newspaper and other published accounts, chief among which is the *Middle East Economic Survey* (which we have cited most frequently because of its relatively easy accessibility). In the nature of the case it is not possible to be sure of one's judgement when the evidence is conflicting, nor is it possible to reveal the sources of information obtained from individuals.

30 *MEES*, 16 June 1972. Supplement.

31 ibid.

32 *Revolutionary Iraq, 1968–1973. Political Report* adopted by the Eighth

Regional Congress of the Arab Baath Socialist Party–Iraq (Baghdad, 1974), p. 91.

33 In an interview with *Platt's Oilgram,* 1 June 1972 as reported in *MEES*, 16 June 1972. Supplement.

34 Iran, for example, was not concerned with the participation negotiations since she had nationalized her industry in 1951. But in view of the changes taking place in the relationship between the companies and the governments in the Arab oil-exporting countries, the Shah had reopened negotiations with the oil companies after the Teheran agreement. He refused to accept final arrangements until the outcome of the participation discussions was clear, especially on the prices and volumes of oil to be delivered to the companies.

35 Quoted in *MEES*, 2 June 1972.

36 Iraqi relations with Syria after the nationalization of the IPC are discussed below in Chapter 17.

37 Text of statement reproduced in *MEES*, 21 July 1972.

38 See *MEES*, 4 August 1972 for the text of the official announcement.

39 For text see *MEES*, 2 March 1973. Supplement. The crude deliveries were to cover the acquisition by the Iraqis of the transit and terminal facilities in Lebanon if the Lebanese government agreed. In the event, the Lebanese government decided to acquire the facilities itself and Iraq thereupon deducted their value from the compensation due the IPC.

40 The value of net fixed assets of the IPC Group at the end of 1970 had been estimated by *Petroleum Industry Trends* (London: Parra Ramos and Parra) at only $104 million. *MEES*, 19 May 1972.

41 See discussion on the 'oil weapon', below, Ch. 19.

17 Iraq's Independent Oil Policy

Law 80 of 1961 expropriating most of the concession territory of the IPC group was a major assertion of Iraq's sovereignty over her oil industry, but because of the confusion in policy and political uncertainties there was little clear direction in oil affairs, and activity in the industry was stultified. The emergence of an unambiguous national oil policy and a defined role for the state and its oil company can fairly be attributed to the decisions underlying Laws 97 and 123 of 1967 and the subsequent arrangements leading to the announcement by the Arif government in the spring of 1968 of Iraq's decision to entrust the development of North Rumaila to the Iraq National Oil Company.

An 'independent' oil policy for Iraq does not of course imply that it could proceed with the development of her industry without outside assistance, but it does imply that operational as well as financial decisions could be taken into the hands of the relevant Iraqi authorities. It was not until 1973 following the settlement with the IPC after its nationalization in 1972 that all of Iraq's oil industry could be said to be clearly under the control of its government. Accordingly, the development of the country's 'independent' policy, so far as it relates to the control of domestic production, went through a preliminary formative period between 1967 and June 1972, when the scope for local control was limited by the dominance of the IPC in production and export, and a 'transition' period between June 1972 and February 1973. Since then the Iraqi government, through its relevant agencies and contractual relationships, has had full control of decisions not only over exploration and production but also over export sales. It must be remembered, however, that 'independence' and 'control' in this sense cannot confer complete freedom of action, especially in an industry dependent on exports to international markets and on access to international technology and skills, and where the decisions of individual exporters are constrained by the policies of an international organization to which they belong.

On the other hand, Iraq has always taken an independent line in the deliberations of international and Arab organizations. The dominance of the IPC in her oil production and export never inhibited the government in its formulation and advocacy of international policies—on the contrary, this very dominance undoubtedly enhanced Iraq's militancy in such councils. But the coincidence between the significant dates in the progressive assumption by Iraq of control over her own oil industry and the significant dates in the general evolution of events affecting oil in the Middle East is no chance coincidence. Law 80 of 1961 followed close on the formation of OPEC in 1960; Laws 97 and 123 of 1967 were passed in an atmosphere conditioned by the Israeli war and OPEC militancy which culminated in the OPEC 'Declaratory Statement' in 1968; the nationalization of the IPC in June 1972 followed the successful OPEC discussions on participation in March, and the conclusion of the OPEC participation agreement at the end of 1972 paved the way for the IPC settlement in February 1973; finally the timing of the large increases in prices for Iraqi oil and the consequent increase in revenues in 1973 and 1974 was determined by the October war of 1973. In other words, for the most part the practical success of actions by Iraq was determined by events outside Iraq—events in which Iraq had a hand but in which this hand was not decisive.

In the formulation and implementation of its domestic policies between 1968 and 1972 the government's primary preoccupation was to develop an appropriate organization for the national oil company, to begin exploration and production operations, and to find markets for its expected production. To these ends, arrangements had to be made for the necessary international assistance and co-operation.

The nature and scope of the government's responsibilities and operations were very much changed by the nationalization of the IPC. New administrative arrangements had then to be made for the continued production, transport, and sale of oil previously handled by the IPC, for continuing exploration, and for the development of new oil production. Moreover, Iraq almost at once found herself in conflict with Syria over transit rights in much the same way as had the IPC and she had to find alternative ways of getting her oil to ports. Finally, there were far-reaching changes in Iraq's policies both with respect to production and export and to the nature of her international arrangements, as a result of the large increases in oil revenues and in the amount of crude oil that became available to the government for sale in the market. These changes were complicated by the rapid changes in the oil market itself, which were the result partly of the increased oil prices imposed by the oil-exporting countries, partly of the changed expectations held by the importing countries about future supplies, and partly of the increased power of OPEC over prices and output.

The Formulation of an Independent Policy

The road which was to lead to the fulfilment of Iraq's dream of owning and controlling her own oil resources (though neither markets nor rate of development) had been opened, as we have seen, by the promulgation of Law 80. The operating agency of the government for this purpose was to be a national oil company such as had already been established by Iran, Indonesia, Venezuela, and Kuwait. A draft law prepared in 1962 was unacceptable to the regimes that followed Qassim, but in 1964 under Law 11 of that year the Iraq National Oil Company was established.

The new company was authorized to engage in all aspects of the petroleum industry except refining and distribution for the local market (which was reserved to existing government bodies). It could form subsidiaries and could associate with other companies (including foreign companies then operating in Iraq) for the purpose, but subject to the approval of the Cabinet. INOC was directed to select areas in Iraq where it wished to work and to submit within six months for the approval of the Minister of Oil and the Cabinet an application for the areas selected. Capital was provided and it was granted the right to borrow within limits, also subject to the approval of the Cabinet. Its profits were exempt from taxation for five years, but it was required to pay 50 per cent of its net profits to the government. A board of directors was established, one-third of which were to be government officials; six full-time directors were to be technical specialists, but they were to be appointed by the Cabinet who would also select the chairman of the board and the managing director of the company. INOC was attached to the Ministry of Oil, but the Cabinet had to approve the budget and would settle disputes between the company and the Minister of Oil. Clearly, INOC was not granted much autonomy; it was not to be operated as a commercial company but as an instrument of government policy; oil production and export was very much a question of high political policy.

For the first four years of its existence INOC was given very little money or personnel and its organization remained rudimentary. Nor was it given much of a job to do, for, as we have seen, successive governments failed to establish a clear and consistent policy respecting it, largely because of the political differences of view over how development of the country's oil industry should be organized and the role of the IPC in it. Once it was decided that INOC should work as an operating organization without close co-operation with the

IPC group, and a firm decision had been taken to permit it to go ahead with a programme for the development of North Rumaila, the company found itself in a position to begin building up an organization and a set of policies designed to fulfil definite and long-range objectives.

In September 1967 the government had provided for the reorganization of INOC and its board, had attached the company to the office of the President of the Republic, and had given the chairman of the board greater authority both within the company and in the government. The administration was expanded, new departments were organized, and managerial and vocational training programmes taken in hand. The French were already available to help in the immediate training of personnel for these functions and both Egypt and Algeria were consulted for their experience. At the same time, detailed plans for the development of North Rumaila had to be drawn up and practical means established for using foreign assistance.

The ERAP Agreement

Discussions were continued with both the French and the Russians. Although CFP had made a bid to get a contract for North Rumaila, in the end it failed and Iraq made a service contract with the French state oil company, ERAP, similar to the one that had been made in Iran.

The Iranian arrangement took the form of a contract under which ERAP would explore over specified areas (to be reduced as exploration progressed) and would bear the full cost of exploration if no oil was discovered; the cost would be repaid (without interest) by the National Iranian Oil Company (NIOC) only if oil was discovered in commercial quantities. ERAP would also finance the cost of development, loans for this being repaid (with interest) after production was established. Fifty per cent of the discovered reserves could be set aside by NIOC as a 'national reserve' and ERAP would be entitled to purchase a large proportion of the oil produced from the remaining reserves and would pay 50 per cent income tax on the profits, calculated with reference to market prices as agreed. It also undertook to market oil for NIOC for a commission.

The NIOC/ERAP agreement was a sharp break from the old concession system and was widely heralded as a 'revolutionary' advance for the exporting countries. Although the foreign company bore the loss if exploration was unsuccessful, and was only repaid in the event of commercial discoveries, the Iranian company bore the capital cost of developing the oil production. The nominal share of profits received by the government was 75 per cent overall, but since these were calculated on *market prices,* it was not clear whether actual revenues would exceed those yielded by the 50 per cent share based on *tax prices* provided for in the older concession agreements. The official Iranian view, and later the official Iraqi view, was that the commercial advantages to the host country were very great compared to those of the older agreements, especially if the provision for a national oil reserve was taken into account, but this conclusion was hotly disputed by others. The primary appeal of this type of agreement to the Iraqis, however, was the *de facto* recognition of Law 80 and the role provided for the national oil company. For the first time the host country would have a full and active part to play in decision-making; the foreign company would act under contract and could no longer be looked on by anybody as master in the host company's house, so to speak.

Thus, a precedent had been set which the Iraqis found well suited to their immediate needs. But they wanted to extract somewhat more favourable terms from the French company in view of the criticisms that had been made of the Iranian contract and because the prospects of discovering large quantities of oil in the territory Iraq had to offer were considered to be far superior to those in Iran. Negotiations were pushed ahead speedily and at the end of November 1967 a contract was initialled by ERAP and INOC covering nearly 11,000 $km.^2$ in four separate blocks in southern Iraq north of the Rumaila field.[1] The terms were perhaps somewhat better for the host country than those of the ERAP/NIOC agreement, but many thought that they were still far too favourable to ERAP in view of the greater promise of the area granted. The agreement was bitterly assailed by a number of Iraqi experts, including two of the former directors of INOC who had strongly supported the 1965 agreement with the IPC and felt that Iraq would gain more if she obtained the co-operation of the IPC companies in the development of her oil. In part the opposition to the agreement reflected political opposition to the Yahya government and its general oil policy, but the specific argument against it was that ERAP had obtained some of the best oil land in Iraq at a very cheap price and would make enormous profits.

The group fiercely defending the agreement were variously called 'nationalists', 'Nasserites', 'leftists', and 'the popular forces'. Their chief spokesmen on oil were Adib al-Jadir and Khair al-Din Haseeb (chairman and member of the board of INOC respectively). This group had been associated with the formulation of the agreement and saw it not only as a profitable arrangement for INOC but as a forerunner to the eventual assertion of state sovereignty over the oil industry. In addition to the technical arguments, much was made of the political aspects, specifically linking the oil arrangements with the struggle against imperialism, in which American 'military aggression' and 'political manoeuvres' were active, as contrasted to the understanding policy of France under General de Gaulle.[2]

The agreement with ERAP in November 1967 was the first step in the establishment of the wider channels for foreign assistance necessary if INOC was to fulfil the tasks expected of it, and it was looked on in Iraq as an important political step in that an established Western company undertook to operate in an area in dispute with the IPC. In addition, the government stressed that it was a kind of 'reward' for sympathetic French political attitudes towards the Arabs in their conflict with Israel.

A month later a more far-reaching association was initiated with the Soviet Union following the visit at the invitation of the Iraqi government of a Soviet delegation headed by the Chairman of the Committee for Foreign Economic Relations of the Soviet Council of Ministers.

Co-operation with the Russians

At the end of December 1967 a 'Letter of Intent' was signed by the Chairman of the Soviet Committee and the chairman of INOC, and approved by the Iraqi Cabinet, which envisaged Soviet assistance in the development of the Iraqi oil industry.[3] The letter read as follows:

> The Government of the Union of Soviet Socialist Republics has agreed to provide assistance to the Government of the Republic of Iraq in the direct development of its oil industry. Such assistance can be provided by Soviet organizations in the following fields: drilling producing wells in southern Iraq, and supplying the equipment and services required for this purpose; carrying out geological and exploratory surveys in connection with the search for oil in the northern areas of Iraq; and determining well locations in areas with proven reserves in southern Iraq, as well as in the areas where geological surveys and exploration operations are to be carried out in northern Iraq.
>
> The scope, terms and conditions of the assistance to be made available in the above-mentioned fields will all be determined in the course of subsequent negotiations between the delegated representatives of the two parties. It is understood that the expenses incurred by the Soviet organizations in the supply of the equipment and provision of technical assistance for geological surveys and exploration and development drilling, together with expenditure on other operations connected with assistance required for the

direct development of Iraq's national oil industry, will be reimbursed by the Iraqi side in the form of deliveries to the Soviet Union of crude oil produced by the Iraq National Oil Company. The terms and conditions applicable to such deliveries will be determined at the same time as those governing the provision of assistance mentioned earlier.[4]

Thus the framework was established for a series of agreements and contracts to be made between Iraqi and Soviet agencies not only in the field of oil but also in many other fields.

In the meantime, INOC secured a loan of ID 5 million from the state owned Rafidain Bank to help finance its initial operations. Bids were invited from other foreign firms in efforts to secure plant and equipment, tankers, and other goods and services in exchange for crude oil, and offers were sought from refiners for long-term sales contracts for crude oil.

By April 1968 small exploration and drilling departments had been established and training programmes had begun in earnest with the help of the ERAP group. The broad outline of a two-stage development programme was disclosed. Drilling was to begin immediately to bring the field into production at a rate of 5 million tons a year (100,000 b/d) by the end of two years from the start of work,[5] exporting from the port of Fao (where capacity was limited to relatively small tankers). The cost was estimated at some 6 million dinars, including the cost of pipelines, field installations, storage facilities, and improvements of the port. The second stage, which was planned to take another two years, required the construction of a new deep-water terminal for large tankers for a planned output of 18 million tons a year (360,000 b/d). Foreign firms were invited to bid on specific projects on a 'turn-key' basis.

There was a marked drop in momentum and a long period of relative inactivity following the Baath *coup* in July 1968 which brought in a new Oil Minister and changes in the top officials of INOC. But there was no substantial change in policy, for the new Baath government had no specific oil policy of its own; it merely proclaimed in general terms that it would pursue a less hesitating, more radical, Pan Arab policy. Negotiations continued with the Soviet Union, but it was a year before agreements were drawn up pursuant to the Letter of Intent of 1967 to arrange for assistance in specific terms in the development of the national oil sector.

In June 1969, a general agreement was signed between INOC and the Soviet firm Machinoexport, providing for a loan valued at ID 25 million ($72 million), under which contracts for the provision of drilling rigs, survey teams, oilfield equipment, the services of

Soviet experts to assist in preparing designs and specifications, and training facilities of all kinds would be negotiated. The agreement was to be administered by a permanent Joint Committee of the two parties. The value of the goods and services supplied would be calculated in dollars at 'competitive world market prices' and interest was to be charged as provided for in the 1959 agreement at 2.5 per cent. Two contracts were also signed in accordance with the general agreement, one for $9.5 million worth of exploration and drilling equipment and the other for the supply of experts and technical services and for training facilities in the Soviet Union for INOC technicians.

In July 1969 an additional loan of $70 million was agreed, payment to be made entirely in crude oil over seven years, and in April 1971 loans of $222 million were provided for, to be paid entirely in crude oil, although should crude not be available, payment would be made in convertible currency.

With these agreements Iraq was guaranteed that the completion of the first stage of her announced programme, which was set for the second quarter of 1975, would be on time. Soviet equipment and technical services began to flow into the country for the development of the southern fields and large-scale training programmes were put in motion, including a programme for training abroad. By 1970 the first seismic teams had started work and drilling operations had commenced in a small way with equipment supplied by the Soviet Union. The Iraqis announced that their own efficiency improved rapidly:

> INOC's first drilling, in mid-1970, was on a small scale. The first well was drilled by 4 Iraqis previously employed by the IPC, assisted by some Hungarian experts. The second well was drilled by the Iraqis alone. Since then, by intensive training, 4 INOC teams have been organised to set up and dismantle the drilling installations. According to INOC there has been a remarkable increase in the efficiency of these operations, as each team, at end 1974, sets up a rig in 18 days, compared with 82 days when the work was first started, even with the assistance of expatriate experts.[6]

Resources for INOC

In December 1971 the RCC allocated nearly ID 500 million (nearly $1.5 thousand million) for a ten-year programme for the development of the oil industry. Exploration and production were to be accelerated, pipeline facilities and new export facilities, including a deep-water terminal on the Gulf which would take the large tankers, were to be built,[7] a tanker fleet was to be established,[8] and the exploitation of natural gas and the building of oil-processing facilities pushed forward. All to be matched by the necessary programme for training Iraqis for the tasks. INOC's production was projected to rise from 2.5 million tons in 1972 to 39.5 million in 1976 and 74.5 million in 1981 (excluding the estimated production under the ERAP agreement). The company was expected to become self-financing.

Activities expanded rapidly and there was a constant stream of foreign delegations visiting Iraq to discuss all sorts of contracts and ventures, and of INOC teams visiting abroad to arrange for the supply of equipment, technicians, and training facilities. The search for markets was also in full swing. INOC was using crude-oil supply contracts to finance the equipment and services it required, but some buyers at least were hesitant in view of the (decreasingly effective) legal threats from the IPC parents directed at purchasers of North Rumaila oil, which were backed up by an official protest to Iraq from the British government.

It is difficult to appraise from the outside the operational effectiveness of the organization, but in spite of the priority given to it by the government, most reports indicate that its efficiency, at least for several years, suffered in some degree from the same problem as those of Iraqi state enterprises generally: poorly organized bureaucracy, excessive paper, and rudimentary and inexpert accounting. Technically competent people too often became discouraged with the use made of them, while others were politically unacceptable to the Baath party and hence to the government. Moreover, there were a number of reorganizations and shifts in the top political management as time went on, from which the company must have suffered.

Oil was, of course, the most politically sensitive industry in the economy and it was inevitable that the national oil company would be kept on a tight rein. At the same time it was given many privileges and exempt from many restrictions. Moreover, it was necessary to negotiate large numbers of economic and technical co-operation agreements, including barter agreements, with foreign, primarily East European, countries to obtain the foreign help required. Many of the agreements had a strong political content and included wide-ranging provisions for political and cultural co-operation. Consequently they necessarily had to be negotiated at the highest political level. In addition to all this, the government had to recognize that sales on world markets of oil produced from the areas expropriated from the IPC group remained under a legal cloud. Until a final settlement was made with the IPC, buyers of INOC oil ran the risk of court actions against them as the IPC pursued its claims. Thus, the government's foreign policy was tied up with oil sales.

In March 1970 a special committee of ministers, directly responsible to the RCC, was established to supervise commercial contracts and foreign agreements, and particularly oil matters affecting INOC. The chairman of INOC and his relation to the Minister of Oil, to the ministerial committee, and to the Cabinet changed several times in the following years. The most important change occurred in September 1971, when after an extensive shake-up in the party's top leadership, Salih Mahdi Ammash was replaced as chairman of the ministerial committee by Saddam Hussain, Vice-President of the Republic. In November, the ministerial committee became the 'Follow-up Committee of Oil Affairs and Implementation of Agreements' and took direct control of the marketing policy of INOC.

Iraq, however, had not been entirely satisfied with the pace at which Soviet assistance arrived, with the equipment supplied, and with the way in which commitments were being met. For example, the Soviets did not supply the necessary pipelines and Iraq had to buy them from Europe. After discussions in Moscow and Baghdad, additional protocols were signed in September 1971 under which the Soviet government agreed to urge the various Soviet organizations involved to speed up the supply of equipment, the provision of experts and of technical services, and the training of Iraqis. The Soviet Union assured the Iraqi government that the plans for the development of the North Rumaila field would be completed by the prescribed time. It also agreed to supply the necessary tankers to export the oil and committed itself to assist in the construction of the projected pipeline from Rumaila to the Mediterranean.

The Iraqi government needed assurances that commitments would be met, and on time, for it was extremely important politically to the government that its plans for the production of its own oil be carried through successfully in this crucial initial period.

In addition to the continuing large credits and extensive assistance obtained from the Soviet Union within the framework of the various agreements, Iraq made technical, trade, or barter agreements involving INOC crude oil with many other countries between 1969 and 1972, including seven Eastern European countries and countries from the Third World, but also including Spain, Italy, and France in Europe. After the nationalization of the IPC the number of countries associated with Iraqi oil developments increased very rapidly.[9]

The purposes, terms, and scope of the agreements and contracts varied widely; some were wide-ranging technical and co-operation agreements; some were specifically related to identified projects or to trade in particular commodities; some were simply credits supplied in return for guaranteed supplies of crude oil or were primarily related to Iraq's efforts to find markets for her crude. In many, the foreign partner was to provide 'turn-key' plants and factories. Most of the earlier loan agreements were to be repaid in crude oil, some taking the form of an 'oil-for-goods' barter agreement, while others simply committed Iraq to supply oil in specified quantities or to some specified value. Not all of them were directly related to the development of the Iraqi oil industry, for some committed the foreign partner to participate in the implementation of specified agricultural or industrial projects or to supply certain kinds of technical services or capital goods or both. It is not possible to estimate the total value of the credit agreements since some were barter arrangements and the value depended on the prices attached to the exchanges under the contracts, some were in currencies the exchange rate for which would be uncertain. Furthermore, interest rates were not always published.

France and Italy[10] (and later Japan) were the important non-communist industrialized countries participating in the development of Iraq's oil industry. As we have seen, France was very early on the scene with the ERAP agreement of 1968, widely hailed as a great step forward for Iraq at the time. But in spite of the special political relationship that the Iraqi government proclaimed for France, Iraq's relations with ERAP quickly ran into difficulties after the company discovered oil in commercial quantities. The original contract had been ratified in February 1968. After the July *coup* there were widespread rumours that the new government intended to demand a renegotiation of the agreement, but this was denied and the government reaffirmed Iraq's adherence to her commitments and her friendship with France. In January 1969 ERAP announced 'interesting shows' from its first wildcat well and in January 1970, the Buzurgan field was declared to be commercial, although the oil was of disappointing quality.

Friction with ERAP

Almost from the beginning there had been considerable friction between the Iraqis and the company. The Iraqis attempted to insist on the use of Iraqi contractors and the employment of Iraqi engineers whom the company considered to be inadequately qualified. ERAP was not unwilling to use qualified Iraqis, but there were considerable differences of opinion over the level of qualifications required. ERAP wanted to get on with the job and difficulties arose over what the company considered to be excessive Iraqi interference. When commercial oil was discovered, however, additional and more serious differences emerged over the interpretation of the original agreement, and especially of the provision requiring that half of the recoverable reserves should be turned over to INOC as a 'national reserve' when production reached 75,000 b/d. The provision was loosely drawn and in any case there is no objective way of unambiguously determining the amount of 'recoverable reserves' at any time, and therefore no unambiguous way of evaluating the 'national reserve'. Thus there were difficulties in determining the financial arrangements for its production and the sharing of output between ERAP and INOC. Moreover, the agreement had provided that ERAP could recover its exploration costs from INOC free of interest once commercial production was established. INOC wanted to go back on this aspect of the agreement on the ground that exploration costs were low and were they to be repaid, the company would make excessive profits. Talks were opened in March 1971 to resolve the problem and further development of the ERAP discoveries was held up.

In the meantime, the Teheran agreement of February 1971 had substantially raised the posted prices of oil, and this exacerbated the dispute, for now the Iraqis demanded a substantial improvement of the financial terms of the contract in the light of the changed conditions. The company refused Iraq's demands, but the government was adamant, and in an interview with the Beirut paper *L'Orient-Le Jour*, Abdullah al-Sayyab, technical adviser to INOC, indicated that Iraq would cancel the contract unless ERAP agreed to a modification of the financial provisions of the agreement. He argued that the rise in tax prices after the Teheran agreement gave a higher return to the government per barrel of oil produced from the IPC than it received from ERAP, which could not be tolerated. He referred to the 'principle of the equivalence of contractual advantage' as a justification for Iraq's desire to change the terms of the agreement. The rise in prices simply made the ERAP margin of profit too high to be acceptable to Iraq. Moreover, as an additional consideration, he referred to '. . . the non-oil considerations of an emotional and psychological nature which influenced the conclusion of our agreement with ERAP, in that General de Gaulle had just come out in support of the Arab cause against the Israeli aggression of June 1967'.[11]

Elf/ERAP,[12] on the other hand, insisted that had it not been for the rise in prices after Teheran, its Iraqi discoveries would not have been commercial in view of the high costs of development and production and of the poor characteristics of the oil discovered. The attempts of the Iraqis to impose higher costs on the company by changing the financial provisions for the production of the 'national reserve', and by increasing the cost to the company of the oil it lifted, would make the whole project unattractive commercially.

In spite of the growling, however, the political relationship between Iraq and France was not seriously affected, for neither country wanted a rupture. In the Iraqi struggle with the IPC, which was reaching a climax, Iraq wanted French goodwill, for the government was preparing for a long and painful confrontation which it thought might include the British and American governments as well as the IPC parents. For their part, the French were much interested in retaining privileged access to Iraqi oil. Both sides had strong reasons for desiring a mutually acceptable solution. Accordingly, in January 1972 it was announced that Saddam Hussain would make an official visit to Paris, and in an interview with *Le Monde* Saddam stressed the special nature of Iraq's friendly feelings towards France. He softened the obduracy of Iraq's position, indicating that all Iraq wanted was a modification of the price terms of the agreement in line with the decisions at Teheran and that a solution should not be difficult to find.

Production Begins and a Soviet Treaty is Signed

In the meantime, INOC was preparing its inaugural programme. Its own operations were on a very small scale, but it was proud of its accomplishments: in April 1972 production and export from the North Rumaila field were officially commenced. Exports began with the departure of a Soviet tanker under charter to INOC loaded with 21,000 tons of crude oil for the Soviet Union. In the second quarter of 1972 INOC exported 388,183 tons, half of which went to the Soviet Union and another quarter to East Germany. The company had in 1972 8 rigs in operation, 3 seismic teams, and owned 5 tankers. With this beginning and the North Rumaila field in production, an independent Iraqi oil policy had met its first test.

Alexei Kosygin, Chairman of the Council of Ministers of the Soviet Union, headed a Soviet delegation to the inaugural ceremonies in Baghdad on 7 April. On 9 April a 15-year Treaty of Friendship and Co-operation was signed between Iraq and the Soviet Union (just two months before the nationalization of the IPC). In February 1972, less than five months after the signature of the protocols tightening up the Soviet commitments, Saddam Hussain had visited Moscow, where the prospects of concluding a formal treaty between the two countries were discussed. This very comprehensive treaty provided for full co-operation in political, economic, commercial, technical, cultural, and other fields, including regular consultations between the two countries, defence support, and military co-operation in the interest of security. The *Middle East Economic Survey* commented: '. . . the treaty's significance lies in the fact that it consecrates the economic and political presence of the Soviet Union in the Gulf area'.[13] Libya protested strongly against the treaty.

Iraq had for some time been pressing the Soviet Union to permit the repayment of its loans in crude oil. In August 1970 the Soviet Union agreed to increase its purchases of Iraqi crude, but reserved the right to export it if it so wished; in the April 1971 agreement it finally agreed to accept payment in crude oil, but the price at which the crude was to be valued was almost 30 per cent below the posted price.[14] In September 1972, after the nationalization of the IPC presented INOC with very large amounts of crude to dispose of, a more general agreement was signed which permitted all utilized credits to be repaid in crude oil and provided for a schedule of deliveries through 1980.

In June 1973 a joint Iraqi–Soviet planning committee was created in order to improve Iraqi economic planning and this was followed in November by a new economic and technical agreement which provided for a loan of 150 million roubles ($210 million at the official rate of $1.40 to the rouble). Total credits from the Soviet Union had thus reached nearly $600 million.

Expanding Relations with France

Since CFP was one of the companies affected by the nationalization, the government had immediately offered to discuss with France the future of her oil interests in Iraq. Within two weeks Saddam Hussain began his official visit to Paris, accompanied by a powerful team of ministers and officials. On 18 June, a ten-year agreement was announced under which CFP would be able to contract to buy 23.75 per cent of the production of the former IPC fields (its percentage shareholding in the IPC) on the terms prevailing before the nationalization (which was tax-paid cost) plus any further increases in fiscal revenues that the OPEC countries might obtain, and also to buy additional crude at market prices.

In not contesting the nationalization and immediately agreeing to buy nationalized oil, the French nevertheless made it clear that the implementation of the agreement was subject to the conclusion of satisfactory compensation arrangements for the IPC shareholders. France also promised to increase technical and financial assistance for oil and other projects in Iraq, and later agreed to guarantee bank loans direct to Iraqi importers for the finance of Iraqi industrial projects.

The communiqué issued by the two governments following Saddam Hussain's visit reaffirmed continuing Iraqi–French friendship and co-operation over a wide area, including cultural co-operation and 'the diffusion of the French language in Iraq and the Arabic language in France', but there was no mention of the INOC dispute with ERAP. Later, in an interview with Eric Rouleau of *Le Monde*, Saddam Hussain stated that he wanted to see Iraq's relations with France raised to the level of those with the Soviet Union.[15] In the meantime, the negotiations about an IPC settlement were continuing and a few weeks before the final settlement was reached at the end of February 1973, a formal contract was drawn up providing for the lifting of CFP's entitlement to Kirkuk crude.

In March, talks on the ERAP dispute were resumed and in May an agreement was reached. Regarded as a supplementary agreement to the 1968 Elf/ERAP service contract with INOC, it substantially changed the terms, dropping the provision for separate treatment of a 'national reserve' and providing for the discovered fields to be produced as one unit. The financial provisions were brought into line with the Teheran price agreement, but Elf/ERAP was given approval for the assignment of 40 per cent of its interest to a Japanese group. Many Iraqis were critical of the revised agreement, regretting the dropping of the provision for a 'national reserve', but such a provision was bound to raise difficulties from a purely technical point of view since estimates of reserves are notoriously difficult. There would inevitably be continuing disputes over the appropriate size of this reserve as time went on and knowledge of the characteristics of the discovered field changed.[16] The agreement was not ratified by the RCC until February 1974, just before an extensive economic and technical agreement was signed with France. The way was then open for Elf/ERAP to develop the fields under the agreement, which envisaged production of 8 million tons a year (160,000 b/d) as soon as Iraq completed the construction of the projected deep-sea terminal at Khor-al-Khafji (now Mina-al-Bakr) in the Gulf and to continue exploration in its other areas. By the third quarter of 1976 production from the two fields began. The oil is a heavy, high-sulphur crude. But in December that year Iraq once again sought to renegotiate the price agreement on the ground that at the existing prices the French profit margin was too high. In July 1977 Iraq decided to take over the operation and management of the fields in order to obtain full state control of all oil production. A new directorate, Misan Oilfields Directorate, was established to manage the operations, but Elf/ERAP's supplies were not affected.[17]

The economic and technical co-operation agreement was signed in March and under it France agreed to extend credit valued at $500 million to Iraq for specified projects to be implemented by French firms in many sectors of the economy, including oil. At the end of the year, during a visit of the French Prime Minister to Iraq, even larger agreements for the supply of French plant and technology were entered into in the context of discussions covering many aspects of political, economic, and cultural relations, including an expression of Iraqi support for the French proposal for a multinational energy conference embracing both producing and consuming countries. Economic relations between France and Iraq continued to expand, French firms gaining a number of oil and industrial contracts (notably for the expansion of the pipeline and export capacity from the Kirkuk fields and for the construction of the first stage of an iron and steel complex in the south, for which France would supply the machinery, equipment, and technical services). But on oil matters, it was not at all clear that the 'special relation' established because of France's greater understanding of the Iraqi position and sympathy towards the 'Arab cause' would yield much material or financial advantage for the French. In 1974 the price that CFP had to pay for the oil lifted from Kirkuk, for example, was again increased, leaving little margin over the cost to others.[18]

Other Major International Economic Relations

Italy's early 'oil-for-goods' contract was followed up in 1973 when Italian companies obtained major contracts for the construction of the pipeline to run between Haditha, where one of the main pumping stations of the Kirkuk–Mediterranean pipeline was located, and Fao, Iraq's southern port. ENI's subsidiary, Snam-Progetti, made the initial studies for the pipeline and was responsible for the overall supervision of the project. This pipeline was to permit the export of Kirkuk oil from the Gulf and of Rumaila oil from the Mediterranean, giving Iraq greater flexibility in disposing of her oil and reducing her dependence on Syria.[19]

In May 1974 Iraq and Italy signed a general economic co-operation agreement which was followed in July by a specific agreement covering a variety of major projects in agriculture, construction, and industry, including petro-chemicals, and in housing, public works, and training programmes. The value of the agreement was reported to be over $3,000 million, and Italy was to receive an additional 10 million tons of oil a year for ten years over and above the 20 million tons contracted for in March 1972. In April 1977 the Italian Minister of Industry announced that Iraq was planning to award contracts worth $600 million to Italian firms, which would pay for 40 per cent of Italian oil imports from Iraq.

The other major consuming country offering substantial loans and economic assistance to Iraq in this period in return for oil was Japan. As early as August 1973 the Mitsubishi corporation had signed a 15-year agreement with INOC for the purchase of liquid petroleum gas (LPG) to begin as soon as INOC's LPG plant was in production. Mitsubishi was also participating in the Japanese consortium which in 1973 acquired the 40 per cent interest in the Elf/ERAP contract. At the beginning of 1974 an economic and technical co-operation agreement was negotiated between the Japanese Minister of Trade and Industry and the Iraqi Minister of Industry, under which Japan would lend Iraq $1,000 million to be used to finance a variety of projects in the industrial field including chemicals, gas liquefaction, an export refinery, and other plants. The usual provisions were included for the supply of expert assistance and for the training of Iraqis. The loan was to be for 15 years, a quarter of which to be provided by the Japanese government and three-quarters by private Japanese firms. In return Japan would receive crude oil, refined oil products, and liquefied petroleum gas. Prolonged negotiations over the details of the contracts followed because Iraq demanded the full posted price for Basra crude, which the Japanese refiners considered too high. The agreement was formally signed in August and arrangements were made for large bank loans. The price of crude was settled in September. The first big industrial contract within the framework of the agreement was in September 1975 for the construction by Mitsubishi Heavy Industries Ltd of a chemical fertilizer plant. This was followed in October by the award of a contract to construct a natural-gas pipeline linking the South Rumaila fields with Khor al-Zubair, a large industrial complex being built in the south.

The original estimates of the costs of the projects planned under the 1974 agreement soon became unrealistic in view of the rapid rise in costs. At the beginning of 1976, Iraq asked the Japanese to double the original loan commitment, bringing it to around $2,000 million, and additional projects were envisaged under the agreement.[20] Japan also built tankers for the Iraq Oil Tankers company.

In her widespread search throughout the world for assistance and markets from countries able and willing to provide the goods and services needed to develop her oil industry and her economy generally in return for supplies of crude oil, Iraq did not neglect the less-industrialized countries of Europe and the Third World. In addition to Italy among the former, Spain was early approached.[21]

In her drive to establish her independence from the international companies Iraq had placed great importance on the development of a nationally owned tanker fleet, for the government feared that the companies could and would frustrate Iraq's attempts to export because of their alleged control over the world tanker industry. Iraq first turned to Spain for help in this direction. At the end of 1969 a $50 million loan agreement was negotiated with the Spanish company Compañía Financiera de Exportaciones Industriales (COFEI) for the provision of tankers as well as other industrial plant, and in 1971 an additional credit of $20 million was obtained. Altogether Spain built and delivered seven tankers to Iraq, which formed the nucleus of an Iraqi tanker fleet. In 1972, and again in 1974, economic and technical co-operation agreements were concluded under which Spain continued to supply industrial goods and to participate in industrial projects in Iraq in return for crude oil. In June 1974, the Iraqi government, in appreciation of Spain's friendship for the Arabs, made a gift to the Spanish government of 35,000 tons of crude (worth some $3 million by that time).

As to the Third World, agreements were made with a large number of countries, including Ceylon, Morocco, Bangladesh, China, India, Brazil, and others. Of these Brazil and India were the two most important countries with which Iraq established close economic relations. Between April 1968, when Iraq formally abandoned the policy of granting oil concessions and embarked on the exploitation of her oil through service contracts with foreign firms (of which the 1968 ERAP agreement was the first), and June 1974, when she abandoned the general contract in favour of what were called direct work contracts, both the Brazilian oil company, Petrobras, and the India Oil and National Gas Corporation (ONGC) were granted acreage in which they were to operate under service contracts with INOC. The Petrobras contract, signed in August 1972, in some respects was similar to the 1968 ERAP contract, although there was no provision for a 'national reserve'. In return for its services Petrobras was entitled to buy oil on special terms.

The Indian contract, which was signed a year later, was for exploration and development operations in the south of Iraq, and operations began in March 1974, the first well being spudded in August 1975. After spending $9 million without finding commercial oil, ONGC relinquished its rights early in 1977. This contract, however, was only one of a series of agreements dealing with oil and economic relationships stretching back to an Iraqi–Indian trade agreement of 1962, which was substantially extended in 1970 and again in 1971. In addition to increased purchases by India of oil and other Iraqi products (notably dates), provision was made for the construction of a refinery in northern India which Iraq would finance and supply with crude, and the construction of a steel mill in Iraq to process Indian ore. In October 1972 deliveries of INOC crude from North Rumaila were begun under a contract with the Indian

Oil Corporation in spite of legal action taken by the Basra Petroleum Company in Bombay courts in an attempt to prevent the shipments. The price was reported to have been substantially lower than prevailing market prices.

The August 1973 service contract for ONGC operations in Iraq was itself foreshadowed in a series of economic agreements between the two countries negotiated the previous April during a visit to India by the Iraqi Minister of Oil and Minerals. These agreements provided the framework for extensive economic and technical co-operation through the establishment of a joint ministerial committee, provision for an oil exploration contract and a development contract, for Indian assistance to Iraq in the implementation of industrial and agricultural contracts, for an Iraqi credit of $50 million in the form of crude-oil supplies to help finance a new state oil refinery in India, and for arrangements for further oil supplies. In March 1974 Iraq made a further soft loan to India of $110 million to finance oil imports. And in May a contract was signed for India to establish technical institutes in Iraq and to train Iraqis in India. Iraq also recruited Indian technicians and engineers for work on Iraqi projects.

In addition to the general loan, co-operation, and technical agreements such as those we have been describing, there were large numbers of trade agreements, some of which included oil, some not; hundreds of contracts and subcontracts connected with the general investment programmes of the country; as well as specific consulting and training arrangements involving all of the large industrial countries and many small ones. The total value of these foreign commitments is of course impossible to estimate; nor can one easily discover from the published material—and very likely even the Iraqis do not know—just how many of the projects planned, agreements signed, and contracts let, were actually completed as envisaged, for a large number of announced arrangements sooner or later fell by the wayside.

The Marketing of Iraqi Crude Oil

There were two main considerations underlying the wide variety of agreements, contracts, and other arrangements made with foreign groups of all kinds by the Iraqi government in this period. One, of course, was political—to extend general 'friendship and co-operation' arrangements. The other was economic—to find markets for oil in return for the supplies of goods and services it wanted in order to develop its economy or to increase its military strength. As Iraq moved away from dependence on her IPC shareholders for the disposal of her oil, she moved into an area in which she had no experience and no organization. Before INOC production was established, bids were invited for long-term oil contracts on either cash or barter terms. This attracted speculative brokers and middlemen of all kinds, many of whom were foreign, but most of whom were Iraqis who had set up offices in Baghdad to represent foreign firms which wanted to sell their products in Iraq and were willing in return to take oil (which they would then resell). Thus pharmaceutical firms, tea traders, and engineering firms, among others, all entered the lists. When INOC was faced with the prospect of selling large quantities of nationalized oil (perhaps in the teeth of IPC opposition), it again appealed to middlemen to help in the disposal of it:

> This 'national' appeal brought to the doors of INOC a flood of all sorts of persons, firms, and organisations (solicitors, teachers, chemists, merchants, retired men, in fact people from many walks of life), which only added to an already confused picture. The inappropriateness of such a procedure to tackle a trade as complex as oil was soon realised by both the government and INOC, upon which the former declared that it would be illegal for such people to continue their enquiries with INOC's marketing department...[22]

During the period between the nationalization of, and the settlement with, the IPC, INOC had to dispose of its oil through the type of barter arrangement discussed above, mostly to Eastern European countries (except for the CFP entitlement, which was paid for in cash). As we have seen, the Soviet Union had agreed in September 1972 to take payment for its credits in crude oil. But barter has many disadvantages, as Iraq quickly found: the terms of trade were a constant source of friction, partly because it was extremely difficult to test how far prices of goods received were appropriate, and partly because of difficulties over the price to be charged for crude oil. Many were the complaints that goods supplied on barter terms were overpriced, of poor quality, or of inappropriate specifications in other ways. As oil prices improved and the market strengthened, Iraq was eager to establish a more straightforward market relationship in the sales of her oil.

As soon as the settlement with the IPC was accomplished, the government announced that 'cash not barter' would be the terms of its sales, and it moved to shorter-term contracts with provisions for renegotiating prices as conditions changed. It preferred to market directly to customers and to state oil companies, but as the oil policies and international relationships of the country settled down, its range of customers broadened.[23] Barter agreements, except for a continuation of the obligations of the past or when special conditions or needs warranted it, became a thing of the past, but in phasing them out, Iraq had some difficulty in persuading some Eastern European countries to move to cash terms.

Syria Refuses Transit Settlement

The nationalization of the IPC brought another burst of tension between Iraq and Syria, once more over transit payments. It will be recalled that in 1966 the Syrian government had demanded increased dues from the IPC to be paid retroactively. Failing to enforce its demands, it stopped the transit of oil to Banias and put pressure on the Iraqi government to nationalize the IPC. The dispute ended with the defeat of the Syrian attempt unilaterally to impose terms on the IPC, although a new agreement for substantially increased fees was reached in March 1967.

In February 1971, just before the Teheran price agreement was signed, but presumably partly in anticipation of the increase in oil prices, a new transit agreement was made between the Syrian government and the Trans-Arabian Pipeline Company (Tapline) covering the charges applicable to the transportation of Aramco oil across Syria. It was estimated that the new charges would nearly double Syria's revenues from Tapline at full capacity. Syria then approached the IPC for a revision of the agreement covering the IPC pipeline fees and in July 1971 a revised agreement substantially raised the fees.

In the meantime, Iraq had decided to build a 48-inch crude-oil pipeline from North Rumaila to a Syrian port on the Mediterranean, capable of carrying a million barrels a day (50 million tons a year), a distance of some 1,250 km. This would supplement the port capacity of the Gulf, where export facilities were limited and would facilitate deliveries to Eastern European markets. In addition, discussions with Turkey on the feasibility of building pipelines to carry gas and crude oil to (or through) Turkey were also under consideration.

In June 1970 Syria and Iraq agreed in general terms to co-operate in the implementation of the pipeline project to Tartus, the Syrian Mediterranean port, and on the construction of a jointly-owned refinery on the coast. Snam-Progetti, a subsidiary of the Italian ENI group, was awarded a contract in March 1971 for the preliminary surveys and technical work required while talks continued between the two governments to work out a formal agreement. Snam-Progetti completed the preliminary work on the Iraqi side by September 1971 and, still in the absence of agreement between the two governments, obtained permission to survey the Syrian side. But the Iraqi–

Syrian discussions did not progress smoothly. The two governments represented two wings of the Baath party and each was wary of taking any action which would benefit the other, in spite of the Pan Arab protestations of both. Syria wanted a half-ownership in the proposed pipeline as well as in a refinery at the proposed terminal. Iraq, though willing to grant Syrian equity participation, wanted to retain majority control.

In January 1971, while talks with Syria were still continuing, Salih Mahdi Ammash, the Iraqi Vice President, headed a delegation to Turkey to discuss economic relations, including feasibility studies for a gas pipeline from Kirkuk to south-east Turkey. It was agreed that the two countries would go ahead with the construction of the gas pipeline and also consider the building of a crude-oil pipeline from Mosul to Iskanderun. Clearly, a pipeline to a Mediterranean (or Black Sea) port in Turkey could provide an alternative to a pipeline through Syria,[24] a point well emphasized by hints dropped in the Baghdad press for the benefit of the Syrians.

Before any firm arrangements could be worked out for the Syrian pipeline, Iraq was involved in the nationalization of the IPC. Syria immediately nationalized the company's facilities there and this made necessary a new transit agreement between the two governments. Iraq also wanted agreement on the transport of Iraqi sulphur across Syria (for the Mishraq fields developed by Poland's Centrozup were coming into full production) and, even more important, on the use of water from the Euphrates river. Early in July the Iraqi Foreign Minister, Murtadha Said Abdul Baqi, took an official delegation to Damascus to discuss the outstanding issues between the two countries. The communiqué following the visit reported amicable discussions and general agreement that Syria would facilitate the transport and storage of Iraqi sulphur, ensure the continued flow of Iraqi oil across Syria, and enter into a formal agreement on the subject, and continue to work on the formulation of a joint approach to the development of the Euphrates water. It was also agreed to increase the value of trade between the two countries.

In spite of the apparent willingness of the Syrians to co-operate with Iraq, however, in subsequent discussions they asked a very high price for doing so—a near doubling of the transit fees. Iraq had offered to guarantee the same revenue and fees as Syria had obtained from the IPC plus a fixed percentage of the profits made on the sale of nationalized oil passing through Syria, or to apply, as a basis for Syrian revenues, any other formula used anywhere else in similar cases. Iraq urged Syria to co-operate to make nationalization a success in the face of 'the attempts of world imperialism and monopoly' to cast doubt on her ability to do so. The Syrians, for their part, argued that since Iraq doubled her revenues in nationalizing the IPC, increasing her share of revenues from 50 to 100 per cent, so should Syria be granted a doubling of the transit revenues based on posted prices. In any case, Syria argued that she deserved the money because of the heavy and disproportionate burden she had carried in fighting Zionism and, moreover, that she needed it to continue the fight.

Iraq invited two well-known Arab consultants, Nicolas Sarkis and Shaikh Abdulla al-Tariki, to give their views. Sarkis reported that the only practical basis for calculating transit fees was with reference to the profits of the pipeline, which should be calculated as the difference between the realized prices less costs at the Mediterranean, and realized prices less costs at the Gulf, for the same crude.[25] The difference should be shared equally between the two countries. This would give Syria slightly over 2¢ a barrel more than she received before nationalization.[26] Although Syria accepted profit-sharing and the Sarkis formula in principle, she disagreed with the Iraqis on the level of realized prices and wanted more than the formula produced.

Talks were adjourned without agreement in September, and in January 1973 the Syrians publicly threatened to adopt legislation that would raise their transit fees to 50¢ a barrel. The Iraqis bitterly attacked the Syrian attitude, maintaining that transit dues of this magnitude would take all of the profit for Iraq out of the nationalization of the IPC.[27]

Iraq was, of course, in a very weak bargaining position and Syria was determined to exact as much as possible. In the end, the compromise reached in January 1973 gave Syria most of the gain over the taxes previously received from the IPC that Iraq had hoped to obtain from nationalizing the company. Syria modified her demand to 41¢ a barrel for Iraqi oil going to Banias (or to the Homs refinery) and 30¢ a barrel for oil going on through Lebanon to Tripoli. The agreement was to continue to 31 December 1975, although the obligation to use the pipeline and installations was to last for 15 years, during which Syria agreed to guarantee passage for Iraqi oil and Iraq agreed to transport crude at the rate of 12 million tons a year, or, in the event of *force majeure*, to pay Syria $13 million a year. Oil for the Homs refinery was to be supplied at stated prices which were less than those earlier paid to the IPC. Transit dues were to be paid retroactively to 1 June when the IPC was nationalized. All in all, the agreement was very favourable to Syria; there remained much bitterness in Iraq at the extent to which Syria had taken advantage of the situation.

For the moment, at least, relations between the two countries were calm, and in June, in order to finance an expansion of the pipeline,

Iraq lent Syria ID 6.5 million without interest to be repaid from transit dues. But talks continued between Iraq and Turkey on the construction of the proposed crude-oil and natural-gas pipelines to Turkish terminals. A protocol was signed on 1 May 1973 for the construction of a 40-inch crude-oil pipeline with an initial capacity of 25 million tons a year (500,000 b/d) from Kirkuk to Dortyol, on the Mediterranean near Iskanderun, a distance of a thousand kilometres. A 20-year agreement provided for the payment by Iraq to Turkey of a flat transit fee of 35¢ a barrel. In the meantime, discussions continued on the gas pipeline project.

The agreement to construct the crude-oil pipeline provoked a strong outburst from the Damascus newspaper *Al-Baath,* the organ of the Syrian Baath party, which accused the Iraqis of delivering Arab oil into the hands of imperialists and Zionists. The reply of the Iraqi Baath newspaper, *Al-Thawra,* also invoked the ritual reference to imperialism, noting that Iraq needed to diversify her outlets for crude instead of depending on a single outlet which might be blocked for one reason or another by imperialism and its agents.[28] The newspaper stressed the importance to Iraq of flexibility in the choice of export outlets for her oil and referred to the way in which Syria had taken advantage of Iraq after the nationalization of the IPC when such flexibility did not exist. With the construction of the Turkish pipeline and of the planned 'strategic' pipeline from Haditha on the Kirkuk–Mediterranean pipeline to Fao in the south, which would be able to carry oil either north or south, Iraq would have not only flexibility of outlets but could also export a greater quantity of oil since total transport capacity would be increased.

Although oil prices rose dramatically after the October 1973 war, the Syrians did not immediately ask for an increase in transit dues since the transit agreement held until 1975. On the surface relations were friendly. In February 1973 Iraq gave Syria a grant of $50 million to help repair the damage of the war and as an 'expression of the national bonds between the two countries'. In October they signed a protocol providing for co-operation in industrial projects, including textile, mechanical, and electrical industries, joint electric power networks, a railway between Baghdad and north-east Syria, and an Iraqi free zone on the Mediterranean coast. Before long, however, in mid-1975, a serious dispute broke out over the division of water from the Euphrates river which runs through Syria on its way to Iraq.

In 1966 the Soviet Union had agreed to provide a large part of the finance to build a dam on the Euphrates at Lake Assad, the construction of which began in 1968. This dam, together with the newly built Kaban Dam in Turkey, also on the Euphrates, severely reduced the flow of the river into Iraqi territory. Attempts to obtain agreement over the use of the water were unsuccessful in spite of mediation by Saudi Arabia, and Iraqi agriculture along the Euphrates was severely affected. According to Iraqi official sources the area under irrigation along the Euphrates valley dropped from the normal 136,000 hectares to 10,000 hectares in the 1974–75 crop season.[29]

Iraq therefore had strong incentives to reduce her dependence on Syrian goodwill for her oil export terminals. The new 'strategic' pipeline from Haditha (a pumping station on the Kirkuk–Mediterranean line) south to Rumaila and thence to the port of Fao, was opened in December 1975. The line was designed to take Kirkuk oil south to the Gulf terminals or Rumaila oil north to Haditha and thence to the Mediterranean. Alongside it ran a gas pipeline to take gas to the pumping stations along the line from Rumaila. The initial capacity of the line was 15–20 million tons a year (300,000–400,000 b/d), less than one-third of the capacity of the Mediterranean system, but was expected to reach 48–50 million tons a year (1,000,000 b/d) going south, or 44 million tons a year (880,000 b/d) going north. In his speech inaugurating the project, Saddam Hussain referred to the 'unequal conditions' that had forced Iraq to accept the Syrian (and Lebanese) terms for the transit of oil, stating that in addition to a loss to Iraq of $700 million from the time of the agreement (and of $500 million which would have been incurred in 1976 had the agreement remained applicable) the Syrian attitude had left 'deep psychological scars' on the Iraqi people.

In spite of the completion of the strategic line and the work urgently under way to expand its capacity, Syria pressed for even higher transit dues in renegotiations in 1975, insisting that the transit fees should reflect the increased price of oil. At the same time Syria wanted oil supplied to her own refineries at prices much lower than market prices. The talks between the two countries failed to bring agreement and in March 1976 Iraq began advising her customers to make plans to lift their crude from Basra instead of from the East Mediterranean terminals. Apart from the dispute with Syria, the very low level of freight rates continued to decrease the cost disadvantage of crude lifted from the Gulf. The higher transit fees demanded by Syria would make Mediterranean liftings of Iraqi oil completely uneconomic.

Syria's net income in 1975 from transit fees was around $100 million, and the difference between a market price of over $11 a barrel and the $3.055 a barrel paid by Syria for Iraqi oil for the Homs refinery yielded a benefit of around $88 million. Hence Syria stood to lose substantially should Iraq switch her oil exports entirely to the Gulf. Syria nevertheless persisted in her demands and, unable to reach agreement in another set of talks, Iraq finally stopped oil shipments through the Mediterranean line. The full capacity of the 'strategic' north–south line, on which Iraq would have to rely for exports from Kirkuk until the Turkish line was completed, was some 60 per cent below that of the Mediterranean line (only about 40–42 million tons per year) when it was opened, and thus exports were restricted by the capacity of the line.

The construction of the line to Dortyol in Turkey was pushed rapidly and in January 1977 Iraq announced the inauguration of the line. Stretching nearly a thousand kilometres from the Kirkuk fields of Iraq to the Mediterranean port, 40 inches in diameter, and reported to have a capacity of 35 million tons a year by the end of 1977, this pipeline, together with the new north–south line to the Gulf, would remove any constraint on Iraq's ability to export her Kirkuk production. In addition to transit and loading fees Turkey was entitled to lift some 10 million tons from the line for her own domestic consumption. The line began filling up in March with deliveries expected to begin in April; its opening was delayed as a result of a dispute between Iraq and Turkey over the price the Iraqis wanted to charge Turkey for the oil she took, but the first crude was finally loaded on 25 May.[30]

Domestic Developments

The role and activity of Iraq's national oil company were inevitably shaped by the overwhelming importance of external affairs in the development of the country's oil industry. The negotiation of foreign technical and co-operation agreements and of specific contracts under them for domestic operations and marketing, the nationalization of foreign interests and the negotiation of the subsequent settlements, the management of conflicts with neighbours over transit rights and prices—all not only required the close attention of the central government, but made it necessary that all important decisions be taken by central government. INOC could in the nature of the case have very little autonomous power of decision, nor could it act as a commercial enterprise since the decisions were essentially political, even including decisions as to where equipment would be bought, to whom contracts would be given, and where and at what prices sales would be made.

After the nationalization of the IPC, the two major Iraqi oil agencies were INOC and the Iraq Company for Oil Operations (ICOO), the latter having responsibility for the northern operations taken over from the IPC. We have seen that the organization of INOC changed frequently as Iraqi oil policy developed. For the first few years of its existence it had little to do, and its organization was rudimentary, with most of the effective authority lying with the managing director. After 1967 with the clarification of policy, power moved to the hands of a chairman who had a much closer association with the government. The effective direction of the company changed hands several times after the Baath *coup*, the Minister of Oil twice heading the company, except for a short period when a non-ministerial chairman was appointed. As operations in North Rumaila got underway, the organization of the company became more differentiated with the establishment of appropriate operating departments and the appointment of directors-general to run them.

In March 1970 a ministerial oil affairs committee was created to oversee the activities of INOC. In September 1971, this became the powerful 'Follow-up Committee of Oil Affairs and Implementation of Agreements', with the Vice President as chairman, and the company suffered a further reorganization, with marketing coming under the direct control of the committee. Later the marketing department was for all practical purposes detached from the company and placed under the direct instructions of the Follow-up Committee. In January 1973 the committee took over full responsibility for INOC from the office of the President and the chairman of the Follow-up Committee was given all the prerogatives of the President. This reflected the importance of international agreements for all aspects of INOC's operations.[31]

The nationalization of the remaining foreign interests in the Basra Petroleum Company in December 1975 put the entire oil industry directly into government hands. In considering the appropriate organization for the management of the national industry, the so-called 'Western model' of a group of reasonably independent and autonomous enterprises operating on commercial lines was rejected in view of the extent to which decision-making for the entire Iraqi economy was centralized in the hands of the government, and also of the government's desire to use the oil industry as an instrument for 'integrating' the Iraqi economy.[32] Hence the Iraqis looked to what they called the 'Soviet model'—a variety of state companies to be set up on a functional basis. That is to say, general companies for construction, marketing, exploration, petrochemicals, etc., all to be co-ordinated through some central administration or 'follow-up' committee at the ministerial level.

This type of organization was provided for by legislation in September 1976 (Law 101 of 1976). A central administration of the Ministry of Oil was established to prepare plans and supervise their implementation for the oil sector generally. INOC, together with the general organizations associated with it, were attached to the Ministry of Oil. These included a general organization replacing ICOO for production of oil and gas in the northern area and in the Khanaqin oilfields, and another for production in the southern area; the existing directorates within INOC for exploration and drilling were grouped in still another general organization, and the directorates for marketing and oil tankers in a fourth. In addition to these organizations associated with INOC there were other general organizations attached directly to the ministry for refining and gas processing, for product distribution, and for oil projects. Thus, there was a rationalization of oil activities in an administrative framework which remained highly centralized and under the direct control of the Ministry of Oil.

One of the primary functions of the Ministry of Oil had been to evaluate the productive potential of the country and establish a large production capacity; the rate at which capacity should be produced remained an unsettled question. In the event, the world market determined exports, subject to pipeline capacity. For a while the government stopped publishing statistics of production and exports, but publication was resumed in 1977 when it was clear that both were rising. There was a sharp drop in production in 1972 and a slight drop in 1974, but by 1976 output had reached 2.4 million b/d, which was well above the average of the early 1970s.[33] Output by area is not officially published, but in 1975 OAPEC reported production by ICOO from the northern fields of 1.1 million b/d (1974 output was estimated at 875,000 b/d). The Basra Petroleum Company was reported to have produced 998,100 b/d, while INOC produced only 163,600 b/d from the southern fields. INOC was therefore nowhere near the production targets that it had earlier set for itself for North Rumaila; but these targets had been heavily revised as market conditions changed, and after INOC had assumed responsibility for selling the oil of the old IPC. Work continued on the expansion of capacity at Kirkuk and a products pipeline from Baghdad to Basra was completed in early 1977. Although the importance of the major companies as customers declined after nationalization (by how much is not clear since Iraq does not publish the relevant statistics), it was reported in 1976 that all except EXXON were lifting Iraqi crude.[34] INOC had developed a flexible type of renewable oil contract which was said to be very well received by customers. Considerable progress was also made in acquiring a nationally owned tanker fleet. By April 1977 the Iraqi General Establishment for Oil Tankers had a fleet of 12 vessels representing 949,000 dwt, with another 3 vessels on order, which would provide an additional 144,000 dwt.

Notes

1 The text of the agreement was published in *MEES*, 22 March 1968, Supplement. It was signed and ratified on 3 February 1968, the eve of President Arif's visit to France.
2 In a supplement to the 5 January 1968 issue of *MEES*, Ian Seymour presents a useful analysis of the Iraqi oil discussions of the time. As we shall see later, the fears of the critics that the ERAP contract would provide a windfall to ERAP proved unfounded in view of the quantity and quality of oil actually found. At the same time, Iraq twice insisted on renegotiating the agreement as conditions changed.
3 It will be remembered that in March 1959, a week before the Qassim government withdrew Iraq from the Baghdad Pact, an economic and technical aid agreement had been signed with the Soviet Union. Hence the oil understanding was not an entirely new development in Iraq's relations with the Soviet Union.
4 Quoted from *MEES*, 29 December 1967.
5 The Basra Petroleum Company (an IPC affiliate) was producing around 22 million tons a year from the southern part of the Rumaila field.
6 al-Haidari, op. cit., p. 375 (footnote omitted).
7 At the beginning of September 1970 the IPC had handed over to the Iraqi Ports Administration its export facilities at Fao which had been unused since 1968, and had not been needed after the deep-water terminal at Khor al-Amaya had come into use in 1964. The facilities at Fao could only handle small tankers up to 50,000 tons and needed continual dredging to clear the silt. With a capacity of some 10 million tons a year it would be large enough to enable INOC to begin exporting on the planned scale of 5 million tons, and plans had already been made for the pipeline to connect the port to the North Rumaila field.
8 As early as 1969 a contract had been made with Spain to build tankers for Iraq.
9 For a summary of the agreements between 1969 and 1974 see al-Haidari, op. cit., pp. 289 ff.
10 Italy had early taken the legal risk of contracting for Rumaila crude through her state oil company, Ente Nazionale Idrocarburi (ENI). After protracted and intermittent negotiations, a contract was finally signed in March 1972 which provided for 20 million tons of INOC crude to be delivered over ten years in return for capital equipment and technical services to be supplied by ENI or by other Italian firms.
11 Quoted in *MEES*, 26 November 1971.
12 The two French state oil companies Elf and ERAP had merged to form Elf/ERAP.
13 *MEES*, 14 April 1972. This treaty took place at the time when relations between Egypt and the Soviet Union were rapidly deteriorating. Sadat had also visited Moscow in February to explain Egypt's economic difficulties and her need for additional supplies of arms. His talks with the Soviet Union having been unsatisfactory, he announced on 18 July 1972 his request that all Soviet military advisers be withdrawn. Clearly a treaty similar to that which the Soviet Union had with Egypt was, in these circumstances, particularly advantageous to the Soviet Union.
14 We were told by an 'authoritative' source that the price was $1.70 a barrel.
15 *Le Monde*, 20 June 1972. A useful summary of the discussions, communiqué,

and agreement can be found in *MEES*, 16 and 28 June 1972. The text of the CFP agreement is published in the issue of 30 June 1972.

16 *MEES*, 18 May 1973, summarizes the agreement. Elf/ERAP became entitled to lift 30 per cent of half the output at a guaranteed preferential price and received an option to buy 60 per cent of half the output (the so-called 'national reserve' half) at market prices. The company was also obligated to help INOC market up to 200,000 b/d, but would receive a commission for its services. See also ERAP's *Bulletin Mensuel d'Informations*, 25 October 1976.

17 *MEES*, 11 July 1977.

18 *PIW*, 19 August 1974.

19 See below for a discussion of the renewed pipeline dispute with Syria after the nationalization of the IPC.

20 For further details see *MEES*, 31 January 1977.

21 Agreements were also made with other countries. Among the earlier ones was an oil-supply contract with Austria in May 1973 in return for economic assistance in the implementation of projects. In November of that year a general economic and technical co-operation agreement was also signed.

22 Al-Haidari, op. cit., p. 398. We have relied on the account of al-Haidari, who served with INOC's marketing department in the period, for the discussion of the changing marketing arrangements for Iraqi oil.

23 See below, and note 33.

24 This was not the first time such a pipeline had been considered. Longrigg reports that in November 1956 a force of the Syrian army 'in a moment of anti-Western political excitement' destroyed some pumping stations on the Syrian pipeline. The position was restored, but 'A plan conceived at this period, as an alternative or addition to transit through Syria, was that of a large diameter pipeline to run from northern Iraq across southern Turkey to a Mediterranean port, Mersin or Alexandretta . . . The Plan commended itself to the Turks and was taken seriously by conferences of oil-men in Europe; but the Iraq government, from reasons of Arab solidarity, vetoed the project . . .' S. Longrigg, *Oil in the Middle East*, p. 271.

25 The prices used for the purpose of calculating the Syrian transit fees by the IPC were the 'posted prices' of the company at the Mediterranean terminal, which, as we have seen, were above the prices at which oil actually moved (realized prices). In consequence, profits attributed to crude oil calculated with reference to posted prices were higher than on the basis of realized prices. So long as the oil-exporting countries were sharing in profits, they insisted that posted prices be used to calculate them. When, however, it became necessary to share profits with someone else, they naturally changed their position and insisted on realized prices as the basis for calculations.

26 Syria had received about 22¢ a barrel from the IPC before nationalization. The payments she demanded from Iraq would have come to around 44¢ a barrel at maximum throughput (Syria was asking for a minimum guaranteed throughput about this level). The Sarkis proposal on existing prices would have given Syria nearly 25¢ a barrel.

27 The Syrian proposal included the costs of operating the pipeline, while the 22¢ a barrel fee paid to the IPC had been net of operating costs. Hence a 50¢ transit fee implied an increase of the order of 17–22¢ a barrel, depending on the estimate of operating costs. The Iraqis offered a fee of 30¢ a barrel including operating costs. Moreover, Syria demanded hard currency in payment, while much of Iraq's nationalized oil was sold on a barter basis for the time being.

28 *Al-Baath*, 27 September 1973; *Al-Thawra*, 30 September 1973, both cited in *MEES*, 5 October 1973.

29 As reported by K. S. McLachlan, *The Developing Agriculture of the Middle East*, K. S. McLachlan and M. Donovan, eds. (London, 1976), p. 49. It seems likely, however, that the Iraqis exaggerated their losses.

30 See *MEES*, 13 June 1977. The construction of the pipeline provides a good example of the multinational nature of Iraqi projects: the principal contractor was a West German firm, pipelaying was by a British firm with pipe supplied under a contract from the Japanese, construction of marine facilities was by Dutch and Turkish firms, with a French company doing the tank farm.

31 For a detailed discussion of the evolution of the organization of INOC up to 1974, see al-Haidari, op. cit., pp. 428 ff.

32 The Iraqi economists and politicians put great emphasis on the notion of 'integrating' the economy on the basis of oil, which, they held, was not possible unless the industry was taken out of foreign hands. It was never very clear exactly what they had in mind other than the obvious policy of developing industries using oil as a raw material and industries supplying inputs to the oil industry. To the extent that such 'integration' required central planning, one can see why they felt that plans for the oil industry had to be co-ordinated with the plans for industry generally. The difficulty, as we shall see in Chapter 18, lay in the inability of the government effectively to implement a co-ordinated central plan.

33 *Annual Abstract of Statistics, 1976*, Table 5/2.

34 According to *MEES* (28 January 1977) contracts by the end of 1976 included: Shell (200,000 b/d); BP (80,000 b/d); Mobil (50,000 b/d); CFP (150,000 b/d); Gulf (50,000–100,000 b/d); Amoco (50,000–100,000 b/d); Elf/ERAP (40,000–50,000 b/d); Petrobras (200,000 b/d); Japanese group (125,000 b/d); ENI (80,000–90,000 b/d); Coastal States (80,000 b/d); Montecatini Edison (40,000 b/d).

18 Economic Development: Agriculture, Industry, and Planning

In spite of large investments resulting from the growing oil revenues, productivity in both the agricultural and industrial sectors of Iraq remains extremely low. Fluctuations in agricultural output are as severe as ever; there is a slight trend towards increasing yields, but the cultivated area has been declining. The statistics of industrial output showed steady advance at moderate rates with a substantial spurt in the middle 1970s as the government rapidly pushed public investment in new industrial projects, especially in the construction of factories by foreign contractors on a 'turn-key' basis and in the capital-intensive industries such as oil refining and petrochemicals which have accounted for the bulk of the increase of industrial output since 1970. Factories have been operated much below capacity and productivity of workers is low. Little progress has been made towards the desired reshaping of the 'structure' of the economy through a substantial increase in the proportion of the national income contributed by commodity production (other than oil), as contrasted to that contributed by services. In this chapter we discuss all three aspects of Iraq's economy, beginning with agriculture, which remains by far the weakest sector and a continuing drag on the country's development.

Agricultural Policy and Performance

Although generous with water and good alluvial soils, nature herself created difficult conditions for the development of a flourishing agriculture in the climatic extremes, locusts and other pests, and the perverse flooding of the rivers. Man could not control the first of these conditions, but he could go a long way in controlling the others and, as we have seen, great progress had been made in this respect in the four decades after the creation of the state, and especially in the 1950s, as oil revenues put greater resources into the hands of the government.

From 1913, when the Hindiya Barrage on the Euphrates was constructed to raise the level of the river and divert water for irrigation purposes, up to the present time, Iraq has been engaged in building dams, barrages, regulators, weirs, canals, and reservoirs, ranging from networks of small irrigation systems and the great new dams of Dokan and Derbendi Khan and their associated reservoirs, to the great storage area of the Wadi Tharthar depression, from which by 1972 nearly 200,000 hectares could be irrigated. The devastating floods were largely under control by the late 1950s and the provision of a smoother flow of irrigation water throughout the year had been largely accomplished.[1] The use of the water in efficient irrigation and especially in drainage systems has not, however, kept pace with its provision. In particular, the integration of the large canal and drainage systems with the small systems required to link them to the individual fields of farmers has lagged badly.

Efficient agriculture requires skilled management, and this is especially true of irrigated agriculture under conditions such as those imposed by nature on Iraq. But man has been as perverse in his field of administration and organization as nature has been in hers. Almost from the beginning, the organization of agriculture has been such as to minimize the commitment of the cultivator of the soil to the maintenance of its long-run productivity. As we have seen, the well-meant efforts of the British authorities to settle the ownership titles to land, partly for administrative convenience and partly in the belief that clear-cut rights of ownership would ensure the direct interest of the owner in the revenue from his farm and therefore in the maintenance of its productivity, led to widespread absentee landlordism over very large areas and to landlords who far too often had no direct knowledge of or interest in their land, leaving its management to agents who dealt with sharecropping tenants. Large holdings, and a relatively small population, permitted a fallow system under which half the land was left uncultivated every year, and in the dry-farming zone reflected the rotational requirements of cereal monoculture. An absence of interest in the long-run fertility of the land combined with this system to give rise to a kind of shifting cultivation as more and more land went out of cultivation every year, largely because of poor drainage and the consequent salinization of the soil.

The land reform of 1958 substituted a government department for landlords. Such a department had less direct interest in the cultivation of the land than had even the bad landlord and, at the same time, through ignorance, incompetence, technical inadequacy, and political confusion, it could not fulfil the function of the landlords whose places the bureaucracy now occupied. As we have seen, distribution of land into private ownership was slow and in 1963 out of 2.125

million hectares to be expropriated some 62 per cent had been sequestrated by the state, of which only 316,000 ha. had been distributed to the farmers.

The situation remained substantially unchanged throughout the following decade. According to the 1971 Agricultural Census total agricultural holdings comprised 5,732,000 hectares. Of this amount, 2,273,000 hectares were 'directed temporarily' by the Ministry of Agrarian Reform.[2] Between 1970 and 1975 there was a very large increase in the area sequestrated as a result of a new agrarian reform law (No. 117 of 1970) which reduced the maximum holding of irrigated land from between 10 hectares and 150 hectares depending on the type of irrigation, crop, and type of land, and of non-irrigated land to 250–500 hectares depending on the average rainfall of the region. Land held above the new limit was expropriated without compensation, which was paid only for trees, structures, pumps, implements, etc. Even the permitted holdings could in certain circumstances be further reduced and the landowners could be completely dispossessed if the agrarian reform found it desirable to do so. Until the expropriation was effected, landowners were required to farm the land as usual. Farmers to whom land was distributed could lose their land if they failed to obey the orders of the Agrarian Reform and to farm in accordance with the instruction of the High Agricultural Council set up to administer the law. They were required to join a co-operative. Fines and imprisonment were to be imposed for violation of the law and there was no recourse to the courts.

The purpose of the law was to reduce the area open to private ownership in accordance with the general policy of the Baath regime to bring agriculture as well as industry largely into government hands. Thus, whereas up to 1970 1.1 million hectares had been sequestrated, between 1970 and 1975 an additional 1.5 million hectares were taken, making a total of 2.6 million sequestrated by the end of 1975 under the agrarian reform laws, or approximately 46 per cent of the agricultural area. An additional 759,000 hectares were held by the state in full ownership (*miri sirf*), bringing total state acquisition over the period 1959–75 of agricultural land to about 60 per cent of the country's agricultural area.

In this period a total of 1.6 million hectares was distributed, of which 780,000 were in irrigated land and 777,000 in non-irrigated land. Of the sequestrated land about one-third had been distributed by the end of 1975, and an additional 66,850 hectares of *miri* land.[3] From 1971 there was a substantial increase in the rate at which land was distributed to cultivating units. During 1964–69 around 58,000 hectares per year were distributed; this rose to 139,000 per year in the five years 1971–75. But the number of hectares distributed per family fell from an average of 11.6 in 1964–68 to 6.9 in 1970–75. This substantial increase in the number of beneficiaries per unit of land distributed implied smaller private farms. On the other hand, there was a large increase in collective farms, the number rising from 6 in 1972 to 35 in 1973 and then to 78 in 1975, in which year collective farms accounted for 144,000 hectares and 10,543 farmers. In addition, there were 8 state farms with a total area of 9,408 hectares.

With the ending of the war (at least temporarily) in Kurdistan, an agrarian reform law was passed in April 1975 (No. 90 of 1975) to regulate landownership there. The law was designed to break up the estates of the tribal landowners. It was quickly implemented and an additional 200,000 hectares of such land were sequestrated during 1976.

Because of the increased rate at which land was distributed after 1973 the land managed temporarily by the Agrarian Reform and hired out to farmers had dropped to 1.3 million hectares by 1975. Nevertheless, over one-third of the country's agricultural land was still cultivated by farmers who were on very short-term contracts (one crop year usually) and who therefore had no direct interest in its long-run improvement or even its preservation, and who received little help from a government which preferred to put its efforts into co-operative farms. Land is still going out of cultivation through inadequate drainage and improvident farming; even the necessary rotation of crops is at times neglected according to reports. The agricultural census of 1952–53 reported 6.4 million hectares in agricultural holdings; the 1958–59 census, 5.8 million; and the 1971–72 census 5.7 million, a loss of 600,000 hectares in 10 years. Reported agricultural holdings include uncultivated and some uncultivable land, but they do not include land which has reverted to the state through lack of cultivation. Hence, they undoubtedly understate the rate at which land has gone out of cultivation.

As we have noted, the plans for agrarian reform originally included the rapid establishment of co-operatives. But progress has been slow. Although between 1964 and 1969 the number of co-operatives went up 170 per cent and the membership 158 per cent, there were still only 608 societies in 1969 and a membership of less than 76,000. The number of societies established continued to rise, exceeding 1,800 by 1976; with nearly 300,000 members. After 1970 the official emphasis shifted to the establishment of collective farms. In any case, it is difficult to interpret the statistics relating to the growth of co-operatives in view of the wide variety of loosely organized groups that can be enumerated in this category. However, loans by the Agricultural Bank to co-operatives for seeds, fertilizers, insecticides, and machinery, as well as for general purposes, have risen very fast.

The efforts of the government to spend money and invest in agricultural development must be appraised against this background of confusion and uncertainty affecting the position of the Iraqi farmers and the lands they cultivated, which was aggravated by the new law of 1971. Between 1953 and 1963, when especially heavy expenditures were incurred for very large water-control projects, expenditures on the agricultural sector totalled ID 108 million; over the next decade ID 134 million was spent. Between 1971 and 1973 expenditures were not only considerably greater than in earlier years but the ratio of actual expenditure to planned allocations was very much greater.[4] Moreover, in the 1970–75 Plan only 15 per cent of agricultural allocations was for dams and large storage projects and over 42 per cent for irrigation and drainage. But in spite of all this investment there has been very little improvement in agricultural production.

In Charts I to IV are shown the estimated production and yields for the major crops: wheat, barley, rice, and cotton for the 23 years 1953–75. Fluctuations from year to year are great, indicating how completely the major crops depend on the weather, and Chart II shows a clear four-year cycle in production. Output has also been affected by pests of various kinds and in the north by the conflict with the Kurds. Some of the series shown in the charts display a slight upward trend, but the figures are unreliable, especially for the earlier years.[5] It was not until 1965 that pilot surveys were made with the assistance of experts from the Food and Agriculture Organization to estimate production of the principal crops by field sampling. The traditional method of estimating production relied on the judgement of local officials (who often had special reasons of their own for reporting a high, low, or unchanged crop). This was supplemented by the judgement of central government officials, personal observation by miscellaneous agricultural officials, and direct enquiry from farmers (who had every incentive to minimize the size of the crop reported to officials). In the north only speculative estimates could be made in those areas where there was trouble with the Kurds. Hence the picture shown in the Charts is very rough and may well seriously underestimate output in earlier years, but it does in broad outline demonstrate the nature of the fluctuation in Iraqi agriculture and the lack of clear progress since the early 1950s.

Because of the magnitude of the annual fluctuations, any statistical presentation of trends or of periodical averages is likely to be misleading. The Charts show that 1972 was a really freak year with a bumper harvest, due largely to record yields; by contrast there was an unusually long drought between 1958 and 1960, which equally distorts summary statistical measurement for that period. It is also difficult to find genuine improvement in the long-run output of rice, an irrigated crop, which seemed to make considerable progress between 1965 and 1969, but fell off in later years.

It has been widely reported that the production of vegetables, especially in market gardens around Baghdad and other major cities, has grown rapidly; the statistics produced by the Department of Agricultural Statistics of the Central Statistical Organization also showed a large increase in the area under cultivation and in total production of most vegetables over the period 1961 to 1974. But in 1971 the figures of area planted under vegetables given by the department are on the average more than twice those reported in the 1971 Agricultural Census. Since the census attempted as complete an enumeration of all the 591,178 holdings in Iraqi agriculture as possible, it ought to be more reliable than the Department of Agriculture estimates. The area under the principal vegetable crops was found by the census to be 88,245 ha.; that reported by the CSO in the regular annual series for the same year was 182,682 ha. We can only conclude that the data available do not permit a judgement relating to changes in the production of vegetables over any period and that indexes of production presented in the *Statistical Abstract* must be ignored.

In general, there has been rising disquiet over the low level of productivity in agriculture. The increased expenditures by the government in other sectors of the economy and a rising population have resulted in a growing demand for food and other agricultural products; since domestic output has not substantially increased, imports have soared, grain imports alone averaging ID 2–3 million during the 1960s, reaching ID 40 million in 1971 (a poor crop year) and ID 56 million in 1975—in a country that could well be an exporter of food grains.

The government's attempts to raise agricultural output have given insufficient attention to the general experience elsewhere indicating that the productivity of the individual farmer is not only a matter of skills possessed and the services provided, but also of his attitudes and incentives. It would be well for the authorities to heed the advice of one of the most experienced of the international students of land reform, who strongly advocated agrarian reform in Iraq, as in many other countries, but who pointed out in a comment on Russian agriculture:

> . . . what the Soviet experience shows is that though tractors and combines can increase the area cultivated, the advantages of large-

> scale farming will not offset lack of incentive. *No farming system is efficient if people will not work under it;* this is a principle worth remembering.[6]

In the 1971 'follow-up report' on the 1964–69 Iraqi Plan, it was noted that the

> Low level of agricultural productivity . . . is due to faint propagation of modern technological methods of agricultural production owing to weakness of the agricultural guidance agencies, weakness of the agricultural cooperative agencies, presence of salinity in many agricultural lands, absence of field drainage, ineffectiveness of the agencies responsible for the fight against plant and animal pests and diseases and non-pursuance of a wise fertilization policy that would help to propagate the use of fertilizers and to raise the level of productivity per meshara in the various regions.[7]

This type of diagnosis poses the problem as essentially one of 'weakness of agencies'. The government response is clear: expand state control and create a more effective bureaucracy. Thus the activities of all sorts of organizations dealing with drainage, land reclamation, mechanization, credit, etc., are to be expanded. More co-operatives are to be registered, including increased numbers on private land not under the agrarian reform, and 'advanced' co-operatives will be turned into collectives, while more collectives and state farms will be formed. It is recognized that a prerequisite for any substantial improvement in Iraq's agricultural productivity is the direct provision of assistance to and the instruction of farmers in order to improve agricultural techniques. Schools and training institutes are being expanded: in 1966–67 there were 9 agricultural schools with 219 teachers and 2,124 students; eight years later in 1974–75, there were 15 schools with 371 teachers and 4,112 students. The rural population aged 15–30 is, however, nearly 2 million. Nevertheless, there is still difficulty in persuading graduates to go to the rural areas to live, and if they are forced to go, in persuading them to leave their desks to visit the fields.

Drainage and irrigation projects absorb the greater part of plan allocations for agriculture—and this is the correct priority. Sales of agricultural machinery and equipment are rising rapidly, especially of pumps and water machines, but many have remained unused and have become unusable because of the administrative difficulties of distribution. Government plans for providing services include field drains and feeder roads, but these are primarily associated with very large state projects where farmers are more or less forced to join co-operatives, in turn to be transformed into collectives.

The original aim of the Iraqi Revolution was to expropriate the large landowner and promote the development of small-scale agriculture on the basis of owner-operated holdings supplemented by co-operatives. Progress towards this objective has been abysmally slow, as we have seen; for a quarter-century little or no improvement has been brought to the land in this potentially rich region by a succession of military governments. Under the present Baath regime, this aim has been finally abandoned and the intention proclaimed of developing a very capital-intensive collectivized agriculture; with the farmers to become workers on state land and employed by the state. One of the chief Baath measures towards this end was Law No. 117 of 1970, which in reducing the maximum permissible private holding brought 75 per cent of all tenancy arrangements under the agrarian reform law, thus paving the way for the spread of collective farming.

The type of agricultural organization on which the government has now embarked is among the most difficult to implement efficiently, especially when the farmers want their own land, as the Iraqi farmers clearly demonstrated they did when they vigorously resisted the communist attempts to collectivize agriculture under the land reform administration in 1958. It remains to be seen whether the efficiency with which the state can control and manage agriculture will be superior to that with which they manage industry, for inept bureaucratic control is a heavy weight retarding industrial productivity and stifling innovation. It is improbable that the state will be able to do better in agriculture, where the problems are very much more difficult. Already by 1975 reports were growing that agricultural conditions were deteriorating. Migration to the cities continued and labour shortages were reported in some areas.[8] Even the drive towards collective farming seemed to have lost momentum; only 7 new farms were set up between 1973–74 and 1975–76 and total reported membership decreased by 1,396. Half of the increase in agricultural co-operatives between 1973 and 1975 was accounted for by new co-operatives in the so-called autonomous area of Kurdistan, where under a 1975 law the big estates of the Kurdish tribal leaders had been forcibly broken up. An additional one-third of the co-operatives were in Nineveh and Kirkuk, also in the north. Thus, well over half of the new co-operatives were founded in an area where the local inhabitants had recently been defeated, at least temporarily, in a civil war, while only 113 new co-operatives had been established in all the rest of the country in the two-year period. If predictions are based on past experience, even the very recent past, the omens are not favourable for the present policy.

The various kinds of large-scale organization of agriculture which the Iraqi government is attempting to create—whether they be state farms, collectives, or some reasonably centralized form of co-operative, all tend to be capital intensive. Given the growing shortages of labour as industrialization proceeds in the cities, the migration of people from the rural to the urban areas, and the difficulties of holding workers on the land, together with the desire to establish a state-run 'socialist' agriculture, it might seem as first sight to be appropriate policy for the government to encourage highly mechanized capital-intensive agriculture. But this type of agriculture requires highly skilled workers—just the type of worker who tends to migrate to the city where not only are his opportunities greater but where social status and amenities are also more attractive. Iraq may therefore in the near future find herself in an even more difficult position than at present: increasing food imports; continued emphasis on industrialization; failure to keep independent farmers on the land because farmers will leave if they cannot have their own private land; and difficulties in attracting enough skilled workers against competition with industry for the capital-intensive agriculture which cannot depend on the unskilled—all leading to an unwelcome, and perhaps in some degree irreversible, deterioration in agriculture.

Industrial Policy and Performance

The 1958 Revolution and the policies pursued by Abdul Karim Qassim had a much smaller impact on the industrial sector of the Iraqi economy than on the agriculture and oil sectors. In both oil and agriculture Qassim had initiated fundamental and irreversible changes in policy and the immediate result was a disruption and stagnation that could only be remedied by further far-reaching changes. The country has still not been able to escape from agricultural stagnation and it had to await the conclusion of agreements between the oil companies and the governments of other Middle East countries before it could effectively solve its problem with its own oil companies. But in the industrial sector few important changes had been made by Qassim's government.

Qassim shifted the emphasis in the *allocation* of expenditures in government development plans to favour housing, health, education, and industry over agriculture (but the *implementation* of the plans, as measured by the percentage of allocations actually spent, was low, and lowest of all in industry). Government-controlled industry was expanded at the expense of the private sector, which was thus faced with increasing uncertainty. The Detailed Economic Plan for the period 1961–62 to 1965–66 did not run its full course because of the Baath *coup* of 1963, and annual 'transitional plans' were adopted for the three years 1963–65. But before the new Five-Year Plan of 1963–69 was announced, the major part of large industry was nationalized by the government of Abdul Salam Arif. This brought over one-third of the net national income originating in manufacturing under government control, created a complete state monopoly in some industries, and severely restricted the role of the private sector in a number of others.

Abdul Salam Arif, like the military regimes before him, announced that his government endorsed 'socialism', but he did not include the nationalization of private industry in his original version of the doctrine. Arif was finally persuaded by the Nasserites, notably the governor of the Central Bank, Khair al-Din Haseeb, that nationalization was an appropriate action for the protection of the public and the advancement of Arab unity as well as for the more rapid development of the economy. Haseeb, after examining the position and the accounts of the major industrial companies, became convinced that they had been making excessive profits and inadequate investment; the solution in his view was to nationalize them, as had been done in Egypt. The nationalization decrees included 30 large industries, all of the banks and insurance companies, and were accompanied by other decrees allocating 25 per cent of corporate profits to workers, providing for worker representation on boards of directors, a limitation on the size of individual shareholdings in larger companies, and the formation of an Economic Organization to own and operate the nationalized establishment in the public sector. All of this was on the Egyptian pattern.

In announcing the nationalization decrees the Prime Minister, Tahir Yahya, stressed their connection with the question of Arab unity:

> After implementing our national policy by proclaiming the 26th May agreement as a first step towards unity with the UAR, today we implement the confirmation in the provisional constitution that Iraq will become a socialist state. We have decided to transfer to the public sector the banks, insurance companies, principal industries, and economic establishments listed in the Law prepared for this purpose. We have also decided to promulgate the necessary laws guaranteeing the interests of the Iraqi working class and the workers' share in the profits and administration of the economic establishments.[9]

The nationalized enterprises included four cement companies, five milling companies, three cigarette companies, three trading companies (one of which was Baghdad's largest department store), two detergent companies, two shoe companies, two spinning and weaving companies, and a jute, a cotton seed, a carpet, a building materials, an asbestos, a paper, a match, a vegetable oil, and an estate company. In some of these industries, such as cement, milling, detergents, and cigarettes, among others, there are considerable economies of scale and individual firms may well have had a strong monopoly position in spite of the fact that there were several firms in each industry. Others, for example asbestos, supplied almost the entire home market. Most of the industries had been growing rapidly in the previous few years, some of them were relatively new to Iraq (asbestos), some were heavily protected against imports, in some there were already large government plants (cigarettes, shoes, cement) competing with the private sector which could 'monitor prices and quality'; in others (some textiles) the role of government factories effectively limited private expansion, and therefore private investment.

Just as the agrarian reform in the late 1950s introduced a sharp discontinuity in the development of Iraqi agriculture, disrupting the existing productive relationships and necessitating the introduction of entirely new forms of organization, so the nationalization laws of 1964 created a similar discontinuity in the development of Iraqi industry and necessitated the creation of new forms of management and control. Twenty years have passed since the agrarian reform law, and the organizational problems are by no means solved; similarly the new organization required for the development of an efficient and dynamic industry in Iraq has not yet materialized after thirteen years, and there is no sign that it will do so in the near future. The primary motive for both the agrarian reform and the industrial nationalizations was political, but in both cases it was also confidently assumed that an improved economic performance would result. Industry did not suffer as badly as agriculture, but the rate of growth of industrial output has been commensurate neither with the amount of investment poured into it nor with the rate of growth of demand. The reasons for the unsatisfactory results are much the same in industry as in agriculture: the heavy hand of bureaucracy and the lack of co-operation from a dissatisfied population.

So far as industry is concerned, it is not at all clear, at least from the public record, that investment in the firms nationalized had been low nor that excessive profits, where they existed, could not easily have been removed by less drastic means, such as removal of tariff protection, taxation, or even price control. According to a report issued by the Ministry of Industry in 1964, domestic production of cotton and woollen and artificial textiles grew between 1957 and 1961 at 19 per cent per year.[10] Of the six private plants in the industry only one showed losses, while of the three government plants only one made a profit.[11] The rayon industry (private) enjoyed a 52 per cent duty protection. The government was establishing, under its Five-Year Plan, rayon, textile, and cotton plants at the time of the report. Similarly in footwear the report states that 'Private industry is doing a good job in meeting the demands of the country'.[12] A government shoe factory already in production was designed to ensure adequate supplies for the growing market for cheaper shoes.

The production of vegetable oil, the nationalization of which was considered very important, also grew rapidly and the value of imports dropped from nearly ID 314,000 to less than ID 50,000 between 1957 and 1961.[13] As to soaps and detergents, imports began increasing very rapidly after 1958, but began to fall in 1960; between 1957 and 1961 they fell by more than half while domestic production rose over 100 per cent, supplying 85 per cent of total consumption. This does not seem a performance which urgently calls for nationalization to ensure increases in investment and output.

In asbestos there was only one factory, which produced 92 per cent of domestic demand in 1960, displacing imports. Profits were high and since it had a domestic monopoly, either import competition or government price regulation might well have been called for. The industry was new and capacity utilization was low, hence with further expansion (and if tariff protection was not required) there might have been some export potential created. The case for nationalization of cement on grounds of excess profits or inadequate expansion also seems unconvincing in that production increased between 1957 and 1961 by an annual rate of 15.8 per cent and exports by 19 per cent from 5 plants, while the average rate of return was only 13.6 per cent. A new government factory had been built and around 57 per cent of total output was absorbed in government projects, which would presumably give the government considerable bargaining power over prices.

To be sure, the above figures must not be taken too seriously, for the accounting procedures in Iraq were extremely poor. Few firms had any real record of their invested capital, this term often referring simply to paid-up share capital. The 'capital' reported for many enterprises at the time of their nationalization was apparently largely arbitrary since further investment in companies after their formation was often not recorded at all; reported profits were often little more than the difference between expenses and receipts in a given period. In an industry where demand was growing rapidly this could well lead to the reporting of rather large profits. Most companies lacked book-keepers trained in modern methods and some lacked even the simplest ideas of keeping accounts. Machines were often expensed, and sometimes even whole factories. When a factory was handed over in finished form, especially by an Eastern European contractor, the government often had no idea of the capital value to put on it. Commonly, depreciation accounting was primitive or entirely ignored. In these circumstances, any figures, even those derived from a study of company accounts, must be suspect. When a figure purporting to represent a company's 'return' or profit rate—e.g., 25 per cent—was quoted, it was often impossible to find out what it really meant.[14]

Clearly these accounting and statistical difficulties not only cast much doubt on the reported profits (or lack of them) for individual enterprises, but also on all figures of costs and value added in industry and therefore on the national income accounts themselves. Such problems are, of course, common among less-developed countries and for small business in almost all countries, but one has no choice but to use the statistics generated. In this study we have presented few financial and accounting data because we fear that they are often more misleading than helpful; but at the same time, even when errors are absolutely large, the broad picture is not always much affected relative to much larger magnitudes such as national income. The description we have just given of accounting in industrial enterprises refers to the situation as it appeared in 1968. There is reason to accept the claim that statistics have much improved since then, even at the level of the enterprise, since much effort has been put into the statistical service and into the training of statisticians and accountants. As statistics improve, however, it becomes even more difficult to make comparisons over time since differences due to real changes are confused with differences due only to improvements in the quality of the statistics.

By the same token, it is not possible to feel confidence in appraisals of the economic results of the nationalizations. Not only are the statistical data unreliable but reports are contradictory. A 1969 World Bank report stated that

> The 1964 nationalization has, to some extent, discouraged private investors although compensation was agreed to in all instances . . . But the takeover by the Government had no detrimental effects on the efficiency of operations, and output and profits actually increased in most of the plants concerned.

It went on to report that few changes had been made in management and that former owners were even asked to stay in some cases.[15] Our own enquiries in Baghdad indicated that many of the old managers of nationalized industries left their posts, especially Christians and Shia, and that many had been replaced, at least in the first instance, by army officers.

Output in the affected industries does not seem to have fallen after the nationalizations, but a recent careful non-governmental attempt to construct indices of the volume of output in manufacturing shows that there was a fall in the rate of growth of all manufacturing in the period 1964–69 compared to the period 1960–64, and that in twelve industries where nationalization had been extensive, the growth-rate also declined in all but four, in some instances severely (see Table II). Official statistics also indicate a decline in the annual rate of growth of manufacturing output in constant prices after 1963, and in the period 1964–69 compared with 1958–62. Over the ten years 1953–63, manufacturing output (including oil refining) grew at an annual compound rate of 11.5 per cent, but between 1964 and 1971 output grew at only 6.7 per cent.[16] Similarly between 1958 and 1962 manufacturing output (including oil refining) grew at a

Table II Growth in Volume of Output of Selected Industries 1960–64 and 1964–69
1965 prices

	1960–64 Annual Increase per cent	*1964–69 Annual Increase per cent*
Grain milling	8.8	7.7
Vegetable oil	11.9	9.1
Cotton textiles	2.9	4.1
Wool textiles	5.0	8.6
Jute and rope	20.5	8.2
Footwear	8.6	2.3
Soaps and detergents	40.9	19.0
Matches	6.0	8.3
Asbestos	25.1	9.6
Cement	8.0	7.5
Paper and paper products	17.7	6.5
Cigarettes and tobacco products	0.6	8.8
All manufacturing	7.3	6.6

Source: Calculated from the indices constructed by Zeki M. Fattah, *Production, Capital Stock, Productivity and Growth in the Industrial Sector of an Oil Economy: Iraq 1960–1970* (unpublished Ph.D thesis in the University of Oxford, 1976). Includes establishments employing 10 or more persons in each industry.

compound annual rate of 15.7 per cent (1956 prices) and between 1965 and 1969 at 5.7 per cent (1969 prices).[17] (See Chart v.) In the short period, however, such figures can be seriously distorted by a variety of factors which affect the end years. But in this period only 1963 seems to be an unusually poor year, due probably to the political uncertainties.[18] One can in general expect growth-rates to decline after a point since market demand will not grow indefinitely and imports will be increasingly displaced. But in Iraq, where oil revenues and money incomes were rising and imports increasing, there is every reason to expect that the market for domestic manufactures would also have been expanding. Gross capital formation increased by 9.7 per cent at constant prices 1964–69, or at about the same rate as in the period 1958–62.[19]

The main point to be made is that the evidence does not support the contention that the nationalization of large industry in Iraq brought about any improvements in output or productivity or investment; rather it indicates a slowing-down in the growth of output. But it must also be noted that the expansion of the public sector at the expense of the private sector and in competition with it, the official policies of 'socialism', and the economic uncertainty generally which the 1958 Revolution and its *sequelae* created for private industry, necessarily had an adverse effect on the private willingness to invest. In other words, while it is true that the rate of growth of output apparently declined after the nationalizations, it might well have declined at an even more rapid rate in the absence of such government intervention in view of the political confusion and generally unfavourable investment climate. At the same time, there is no doubt that the absorption of the large industrial firms into the Iraqi bureaucratic machine did not lead to an efficient organization of industry. In our judgement the policy cannot be considered to have been a success from this point of view. A different judgement can, of course, be arrived at from the point of view of ideological principle or the political necessity to seize economic power.

In the follow-up discussions of the 1965–69 Five-Year Economic Plan it was noted that only 40 per cent of the planned target had actually been met, which was in part due to

> . . . under-utilization of a part of the productive capacities in many factories belonging to the public or private sector. Although no accurate data exist as regards the magnitude of idle capacities, or reasons for under-utilization thereof, some indicators point to the fact that idle capacities in certain productive units within some activities of the manufacturing sector constitute a noticeable

percentage of the productive capacities in many factories. This can be attributed to more than one factor, e.g., lack of spare parts, raw materials, or intermediate goods, or lack of technicians or transport difficulties, or decreased demand for goods.[20]

In a study for the United Nations, Haseeb himself discussed the kinds of inefficiencies characteristic of the economic controls of the government.[21] At the top there were frequent changes of Ministers. (Between 1964 and 1968 there were 8 Ministers of Industry and Transport, 7 Ministers of Public Works, 6 Ministers of Agrarian Reform, and 6 Ministers of Planning.) This led to changes in programmes and plans and often of the subordinate personnel. Political changes in countries without a secure, professional, and stable civil service are always disruptive. More generally, government consultants and committees often paid close attention to technical aspects of industrial projects but little to economic aspects, including marketing—a persistence of the engineering 'bricks and mortar' bias. There were also long delays due to the need for import permits, labour permits, residence permits; deliveries would be made with no one to take them. Delays in periods of inflation led to increased costs at a later date, which could thus cause cancellation of projects and the need for subsequent retendering. Installation of imported equipment might take over two or three times longer than had been expected, or be delayed indefinitely. Personnel difficulties arose because of inflexible government regulations (e.g., personnel on government projects were required to be government employees, but there was a regulation which prevented storekeepers from being classed as government employees: there was no way around the impasse). Another example of poor planning: a factory designed to employ 220 college graduates and 130 foreign experts was put in a town with less than ten modern houses—more delay, greater costs.

By contrast the private and mixed sector, although at times severely handicapped by government regulations and discriminated against in a variety of ways, was nevertheless more efficient than the state sector. It was promoted by the State Organization for Industrial Development, which was created at the end of 1973 within the Ministry of Industry. To it was attached the Industrial Bank and the Directorates General of Research and Control and of Industrial Promotion which dealt with licensing and import permits. The chairman of the State Organization for Industrial Development and the director general of the Industrial Bank, which had branches in Mosul, Hilla, Basra, Kirkuk, Najf, and Sulaimaniya, was an enterprising Iraqi economist, Farhang Jalal, whose study of industrial development in Iraq we have often had occasion to cite. The bank's equity investment at the end of 1975 exceeded ID 7 million at cost valuation in spite of the fact that over ID 2 million had been lost by the bank in 1964 when a number of companies in which it had holdings were nationalized. In the same year the bank had loan assets of nearly ID 7 million and issued nearly ID 25 million in documentary letters of credit, of which 74 per cent went to companies in the private sector. Some of the companies were very small, with a nominal capital of only ID 200,000, while the capital of others reached ID 1,500,000.[22]

The government has made special efforts to persuade Iraqis to repatriate capital held abroad. In anticipation of the nationalization measures in 1964 heavy penalties were imposed to prevent capital flight, but they were not entirely successful in their objective. In 1970 the penalties were lifted for anyone repatriating his capital during a specified period. In addition, it was decreed that businessmen with foreign exchange would be permitted to hold accounts in foreign currency in Iraqi banks and to use the exchange to import raw materials and industrial products, partly to encourage them to invest in the private sector. But large new industrial investments were reserved primarily for the state. For example, between July and September 1974 nearly a hundred licences were issued for projects in the private sector, but these averaged only about ID 30,000 each, whereas the four public-sector licences issued were for projects totalling ID 22 million. Even if permitted, however, it is not surprising that private investors would be loath to make really large industrial investments. The private and mixed sector nevertheless produced some 30 per cent of the industrial output of Iraq in 1976. There were fifteen companies in the portfolio of the Industrial Bank, nine of which were in production and all but two of which were profitable. The bank had little difficulty in selling shares to the private investors. The group of private and mixed companies was small but vigorous, and made a substantial contribution to Iraqi industry.

The 1970–75 Development Plan introduced by the new Baath government was designed to promote an even faster rate of industrial investment, yielding a 75 per cent increase in value added in manufacturing between 1969 and 1974, or a 12 per cent annual rate of growth. Financial implementation was rapid and between 1971 and 1975, 85 per cent of the allocations for industry had in fact been spent.[23] Before this plan had been completed, however, the rise in oil prices and the nationalization of the oil industry made large additional funds available to the economy and the financial allocations to the plan were greatly increased. The structure of imports reflected the rapid rate of capital formation: imports of machinery, equipment, and other capital goods increasing from nearly ID 100 million in 1971 to over ID 725 million two years later as the investment effort intensified. And the import of food more than doubled between 1973 and 1975. But import prices increased by some 84 per cent during the period.

In the type of project (and even the rhetoric) the new plan for industry was not qualitatively very different from those of the past quarter-century;[24] the scale, of course, was much larger not only because of increased oil revenues and planning resources but also because prices were very much higher and correspondingly greater expenditures were required to obtain the same goods and services. Projects comprised petrochemicals (including fertilizer), pulp and paper, vehicles and assembly of vehicles, electrical appliances, intermediate and finished synthetic textiles, paints, and plastics. The contracts for the construction of the factories were made with foreign firms from a wide variety of countries in Europe (both East and West) and from Japan and the United States. New factories for electronics (radios, calculators, television sets) were opened in 1976. Iron and steel projects and a glass factory were also put in hand. A preference for 'turn-key' projects persisted. Altogether the revised plan after the rise in oil revenues allocated ID 391 million for the manufacturing sector.

After the settlement with the IPC following nationalization, the uncertainty over how the oil companies and their parent governments would react, and the effect any reaction might have on Iraq's revenues, was removed and the government moved ahead very rapidly. The volume of contracts with foreign firms and governments increased very fast for the construction of factories, the importation of goods, the design and execution of transportation, electricity, port, and other infrastructural projects. Moreover, there was a marked shift in the proportion of contracts granted to countries other than those of Eastern Europe. A rough analysis of published information indicates that whereas in the early 1970s somewhat more than half of the development contracts went to the Eastern European countries, from 1974–75 well over two-thirds were going to other countries. But the Minister of Industry and Minerals, Taha al-Jazrawi, denied that this implied any shift of political orientation: he noted that 'it would be a mistake to interpret Iraq's awarding of major development contracts to Western Governments or firms as a sign of Iraq's re-orientation towards the West. The fact that Iraq is turning to the Western companies is not a sign of change but of the speed and volume of development'.[25]

The results of the new 'big push' to create very rapidly a modern and large manufacturing sector with an export potential will not be clear for at least ten years from the time of writing. The Iraqi planners were naturally aware that they would continually run into serious 'bottlenecks', as indeed they have, and there is little point here in going into the details of the various problems encountered in the attempt to force the pace of industrial development. The general outlines are well known and afflict in varying degrees all the oil-exporting countries making similar efforts. Common to all is the problem of shortages and rising prices as local expenditures create an excess demand for local resources which cannot easily be fully substituted for by imports. Land prices rise, housing becomes very short, and there is often difficulty in importing construction materials rapidly enough. Transport and port facilities become congested. And labour, especially skilled labour, becomes very scarce. Such problems became particularly intractable in Iraq as oil revenues and expenditures rose with the increase in oil prices. Foreigners brought in their own resources to build factories and even their own labour on occasion. By 1977 some of the bottlenecks were substantially eased (for example, port congestion) but others continued to tighten (for example, labour shortages).

In addition to these 'normal' difficulties, however, Iraq faced special problems arising from her government's commitment to a type of socialism which required that all of the larger new enterprises should not only be owned by the state but also run by, in effect, government departments. This created problems of appropriate organization for which by 1977 no solution was even in sight, and compounded the strains on management and workers. The Iraqi government shows no sign of being able to produce a reasonably efficient and stable organization for the control and operation of its state enterprises.

Organization and Efficiency

In 1964 the newly nationalized banks, insurance companies, trading companies, and industrial firms had been grouped under four public organizations: the General Organization for Banking, the General Insurance Organization, the General Trade Organization, and the General Industrial Organization, the last three of which were placed under the umbrella of the Economic Organization. The governor of the Central Bank, Khair al-Din Haseeb, who was also one of the chief architects of the system, was appointed acting chairman of this new giant organization in addition to his post as governor of the Central Bank.

Predictably the structure was unwieldy and was reorganized in the following year when a General Organization for Industry, which took over insurance companies, manufacturing establishments, and general industrial services was created and some regional rationalization of industries was attempted. This new and similarly unwieldy organization was again reorganized in 1970 with the abolition of the General Organization and the establishment of six State Organizations, one each for Spinning and Weaving Industries; Clothing, Leather and Cigarettes; Chemical and Food Industries; Construction Industries; Engineering Industries; and Planning and Industrial Construction. Further organizations and reorganizations have taken place, but none has overcome the bureaucratic inefficiency of the state industrial sector. There are now ten state organizations covering the industrial sector, including the State Organization for Industrial Development for the private and mixed sectors.

In 1973 a paper presented to a conference of an expert group of the United Nations Economic and Social Office in Beirut described the chief characteristics of the management of public industrial enterprises in Iraq and analysed the problems.[26] It showed that industrial enterprises were, in effect, organized as part of the state bureaucracy and were given very little autonomous power of decision. There were several levels of authority over the enterprise, including not only the state organization to which it belonged but also up to at least four ministries (Industry, Economy, Finance, Planning) and a variety of sub-ministerial agencies. Nearly all decisions had to go through several layers; many of them had to go high up in the relevant ministries. The planning, evaluation, and implementation of investment decisions required approval from a number of sources, and even the implementation might be undertaken by an agency outside the enterprise. Pricing decisions were made by the state organization, and were subject to ministerial approval, giving the enterprise very little flexibility to meet market conditions. Even to sell off obsolete inventories, surplus raw materials, etc., managers of enterprises had to obtain authorization from higher authority and then sell at public auctions according to procedures laid down. Full-cost pricing was common, leading to excess capacity and unwanted stocks. Distribution and marketing were often separated from the productive enterprise; procurement of materials was subject to lengthy procedures and to numerous approvals regardless of the value of the material. In the larger enterprises compensation of personnel was regulated and transfers of workers between enterprises had to be approved by the state organizations. (In general resignations from the public sector to transfer to the private sector are not permitted without special authorization; layoffs are illegal.)

The disposal of profits is regulated by law, but enterprises are allowed to retain some of their profits and depreciation reserves for expansion. The forms of finance available to the enterprises are regulated and procedures must be followed with long advance notice. In practice, there is a reluctance on the part of individuals in the hierarchy to make decisions even if empowered to do so and in consequence decisions are commonly passed to a level higher than necessary.

Thus, not only are there many levels of decision-making, but the process is highly centralized; delays are long, and are made longer by the reluctance of officials to assume authority. Moreover, there is generally little weight given to the value of time. This is characteristic of any bureaucracy which is not under some sort of external pressure, and is notoriously common in state bureaucracies: it is especially damaging when extended to 'business' enterprises.

The United Nations report drew attention to a number of consequences of the methods of organization adopted in Iraq: long lags between proposals and final decisions which were especially serious in the procurement of goods, including imports (it should be remembered that the prompt availability of imports is about the only way in which Iraq can keep the rate of inflation down in present circumstances); inflexibility in using labour, even including restrictions on overtime arrangements; undue interference and overruling of decisions by higher authorities and even reversal of the normal direction of the lines of authority; the very low premium attached to the value of time 'so that it does not matter how long it would take between the initiation of a decision and its implementation'[27] causes great losses while unnecessary routine procedures are carried through. This last consequence is made worse by the fact that the costs of administration and control have no direct economic consequence for individuals or enterprises. Thus, an evaluation of the results of the operation of state enterprises has no important role in the system. The cost of capital is largely ignored, and there is no effective provision against the misuse of fixed assets. There are large holdings of inventories because of the time-consuming purchasing system and there is excess involvement of high-level managerial staff in routine decisions. As might be expected from this brief description of the inefficiencies inherent in the methods of control, state enterprises frequently find themselves at a competitive disadvantage *vis-à-vis* the private sector.

All of this is reminiscent of the problems of the Egyptian industrial structure on which the Iraqis originally modelled their state organizations. It is now widely recognized in Egypt that the bureaucracy and the methods of managing the public sector have been among the most serious obstacles to the country's industrial revival. In Egypt, the public sector accounts for an overwhelming proportion of gross value added in industrial establishments employing 10 persons or more (90 per cent in 1966–67 and not much changed in the succeeding decade) and observers report very similar difficulties: the pricing system tends to insulate state firms from the market and capacity utilization tends therefore to be inefficient; lack of direct access to foreign markets entails economic losses; import delays lead to emergence of idle capacity and costly excess inventories; overmanning is serious in plants and offices; and incentives are inadequate. The heavy burden of administrative controls creates obstacles to efficient and dynamic performance.[28]

Iraqi labour policies are also similar to those in Egypt and give rise to the same inadequacy of incentives, overmanning, and poor deployment of the labour force. Many graduates are not employed in the areas of their specializations and their jobs are not necessarily consistent with their qualifications. Yet they cannot easily be moved without their consent.[29] In the autumn of 1976 the low productivity in Iraqi industry was the subject of a number of officially sponsored discussions and 'seminars' in the country. *Al-Thawra* (the Baath official organ) reported the proceedings of a 'seminar' in September 1976 at which members of the Revolutionary Command Council, members of the Regional (Iraqi) Baath party, ministers, heads of institutions, and trade union heads, were among those present. The group considered a working paper on the causes of the fall in productivity which had been prepared by representatives of labour and government.[30]

The working paper listed factors which adversely affected productivity: emphasis was placed first on the labour laws, which prevented management from giving a worker a job different from that mentioned in his contract and hence made it difficult or impossible to teach new skills or to train workers for other kinds of work according to the demands of industry; second, the administrative machinery, especially in the productive sector, which was considered to be of low standard because of ignorance and lack of specialization on the part of those responsible, inability of administrators to control and supervise inefficient workers, and unproductive efforts of management and small administrators to please workers, who were too often resentful, bitter, and indifferent. The 'umbrellas' of the state organizations which were used to protect top administrators and trade unionists were criticized. Inappropriate wage policies, inadequate incentives, competition for workers without regard to productivity, and the shortage of primary products, especially evident in food industries, were all brought up.

In general, the impression was of poor co-ordination, tension between workers and managers, particularly tension between 'inspectors' and the private sector, and an underlying tone of political discontent. Saddam Hussain addressed the seminar and insisted that 'there should be no increase in wages if there is no increase in productivity. The quantity and quality of Iraqi productivity needed to be improved in industry, agriculture, and services'. He pointed to the disorder at the airport, in the telephone, water, and electricity systems and asked who was responsible. He then denounced all who did not work and all who did not criticize those they found at fault, whether they were managers, workers, or directors.

In the discussion on the report, representatives of the workers defended the labour law as necessary to safeguard their position against management and they cited many instances of managerial 'maladministration', shortages of materials for production, excessive inventories with inadequate storage space, inadequate supplies of spare parts, etc. In short, very many of the same problems as those outlined in the 1973 United Nations report. On entering the airport in Baghdad passengers were greeted with posters announcing 'Those who do not work shall not eat'; 'He who does not work well at all times, is a thief stealing time'; 'Your work is your honour; those who do not work have no honour', etc.

When attempts to control markets, including labour markets, are inefficient, they usually create at least two problems for every one solved; the Iraqi attempts seem to provide no exception. Wage restraint has not been very successful, especially in large industries where the pressure of demand is very heavy (like brick-making), and in the private sector where higher wages naturally cause difficulty for the public sector in a variety of ways. Badly administered controls, badly designed administrative structures, ineffective incentives, inadequate provisions for training and retraining, etc., adversely affect the morale of workers and create conflicts between the individual interests of workers and industrial productivity.

The labour laws give a worker almost complete security in his existing job and thus provide no immediate personal incentive for him to exert himself unduly or to accept change which would increase the effort demanded of him. The government now offers financial inducements and bonuses to increase productivity, but also relies heavily on slogans, and on exhortation, which are evidently not convincing to a sufficient number of workers. The 'seminars' referred to above are part of the propaganda drive. It is also likely that the unpopularity of the regime with large sections of the population, especially the Kurds and the Shia (which form the majority of the working class), increases workers' resistance to government attempts to persuade them to work harder and to accept personal inconvenience in the interests of the Iraqi state, the 'broad masses', or even of the 'Arab Nation' which, according to the Baath government's 'National Action Charter', was 'the frame of reference' for Iraq's planners and 'not the limited aim of developing only Iraq'.

On the negative side, the continued attempt to trace the country's difficulties to the machinations of imperialists seems to have been having a somewhat diminished impact after nearly 20 years of 'revolutionary' government. There is little evidence that the government and people feel united in a genuine common effort at economic and political development. The tensions between management and worker seem to be less in the private sector, where firms are small, than in the large state firms where workers blame management for most of the inefficiencies that the system of control imposes, as well as for remoteness. The government invites criticism, but tales are common of people, mentioned by name, whose criticisms reached too close to the top or to the nature of the system and quickly found themselves in prison or otherwise punished. The regime is ruthless in acting against or even eliminating any critic it considers dangerous[31] and in these circumstances there is considerable scope for victimization resulting from personal feuds. Administrators are safer if they can avoid taking decisions and are cautious over those they do take. Few have much to gain by exerting special effort; many do not do so, although, as usual, there are always those who work very hard at anything they undertake. Iraq is as abundantly endowed as are other countries with those whose nature pushes them to work hard at anything they do.

The very high degree of job security given to workers is a severe obstacle to the kind of change required in the process of economic development. The workers see their interest in zealously defending the security and privileges given them by the labour laws, while these very privileges are often among the greatest obstacles to the increase in productivity and standards of living that they also want. Thus, the rhetoric of Baath socialism leaves the regime little scope to deal with one of the major sources of severe inefficiency in the economic system. Individual workers gain more in the short run from resisting change, and they have little incentive to put forth their best efforts unless the system of productivity bonuses can be made successful. That the government is concerned about the problem is evident from the widespread use of exhortation—a notoriously difficult method of motivating workers, for any positive effects wear off quickly. But the growing labour shortages are pushing up wages in all sectors where the widespread use of exhortation—a notoriously ineffective method of motivating workers, for any positive effects wear off quickly. But the growing labour shortages are pushing up wages in all sectors where control is absent or difficult to enforce, and especially in the services sector. Here wages are rising very rapidly and it often becomes necessary to make special side payments to retain a driver or hire a taxi, etc.

As we have noted, migrants from rural areas often go first into the services sector, where entry is easy, special skills are not needed, and where relatives and friends who have come from the same areas in the past are likely to be found. Moreover, in many service occupations the reach of the government is likely to be easily evaded. The large organized industries are not supposed, for example, to hire a worker whose occupation is listed as 'farmer' on his identity card, but the application of this type of control to—say—drivers may be very difficult to enforce. As labour scarcity spreads and the wages or other forms of remuneration in the service industries rise, the differential between incomes in the rural areas and those in the cities widens further, especially in view of the stagnation of agriculture. Migration is therefore further encouraged, and labour shortages become greater in rural areas as well as urban.

Planned Growth and Structural Change

At the end of the 1970–75 Development Plan, Iraq completed nearly 25 years of development planning. Although her plans had steadily grown in scope and in technical proficiency, very few of them had been allowed to complete their full course. Uncompleted plan succeeded uncompleted plan as changes in government policy (often because of unexpected increases in oil revenues) or successful *coups* intervened.

As we have seen, planning began with the four investment programmes of the Development Board between 1951 and 1959 which overlapped each other and took the form of investment budgets separate from the ordinary budgets. The programmes were amended as revenues grew, and the last, which was to have covered the period 1955–56 to 1960–61, was cut short by the 1958 Revolution. In the earlier years these programmes consisted primarily of large infrastructural projects—flood control, irrigation works, roads, hospitals, schools, and other buildings, electricity generation, etc. After the Salter Report in 1956 more attention was paid to the immediate needs of the people.

With the formation of a Ministry of Planning in 1958 after the Revolution two further plans were introduced successively, the second cutting short the first and designed to cover the period

1961–62—1965–66. These picked up most of their projects from the previous plans and proposals, but put more emphasis on housing, education, and health services. During the earlier period, expenditures of this type were left in the hands of the relevant ministries, but as time went on, social policy became incorporated in the Development Plans themselves. It was considered, correctly, not only that such expenditures were important aspects of a country's development but also that they should be 'integrated' into the industrial and agricultural plans.

The 1962–66 Plan was itself cut short by the 1963 *coup* and was followed by annual 'transitional' plans until the introduction of the 1965–66—1969–70 Five-Year Plan, which ran its full course. This was succeeded by the 1970–75 Development Plan, the allocations for which began at ID 1,169 million, but were increased eventually to reach ID 1,932 million as oil revenues exceeded expectations with rising oil prices.

From 1951 through 1964 a total of about ID 1,250 million had been allocated for expenditure on development, but only about 46 per cent of it was actually spent; over the next decade through 1974–75, ID 2,556 million was allocated and 60 per cent spent, over three-quarters of the expenditures taking place in the five years 1970–75.[32] In part, this increase reflects not only the very substantial rise in oil prices and revenues but also the general rise in the prices of goods and services purchased.

As might be expected, Iraqi expertise in planning grew with experience. The techniques used became more complicated and sophisticated as more and more students studied economic theory and econometric methods in their postgraduate work at foreign universities. Each successive group of planners roundly criticized its predecessors for their simplified approach and inadequate technique. The objectives of all the plans were very similar: industrialization and diversification of the economy; reduction of dependence on oil, and development of alternative exports; greater processing of the country's raw materials, including oil; the local manufacture of increasing amounts of local-consumption needs; the improvement of productivity in agriculture; and a large expansion of education, health services, water supplies, urban amenities, rural electrification, and other social needs. As noted, the more urgent capital investments in the control of the rivers and the use of water in the development of irrigation, and in the improvement of communications and roads, early had the highest priorities, but the relative distribution of funds among the major sectors—agriculture, industry, and construction—changed without obvious reason from plan to plan, although there was a steadily increasing emphasis on education and health expenditures. There was extensive carry-over of projects from one plan to another since actual expenditures always fell far short of allocations.[33] Although investment grew rapidly (and the number of civil servants employed in the Ministry of Planning grew even more rapidly, the numbers rising from 639 in 1968 to 2,932 in 1976), the 'over-all, integrated, and balanced' approach that planning was designed to ensure never materialized.

As the Baath government consolidated its power after 1968, considerable effort was put into the elaboration and articulation of economic development policy and the 1970–75 Plan was the most ambitious and the most advanced of all the plans. The broad approach was outlined by Jawad Hashim, Minister of Planning during 1968–71 and during 1972–74, in a series of lectures published in April 1975. Hashim claimed that under the 'third stage' of comprehensive planning, which began with the new Baath regime, a 'clearer understanding of the meaning of development' had been obtained. 'The meaning of reducing dependence on crude oil exports is more clearly understood now', he wrote. Economic independence, it was now understood, required 'a very fast rate of growth, laying down the foundations of a strong industrial society and an industrial programme which would use the available raw material and energy resources to the utmost benefit of the country'. Moreover, it was also now understood that dependence on oil could only be reduced by the development of exports based on Iraqi resources and substitutes for imports of consumer goods.[34]

By this time Iraq had accumulated a large number of economists, statisticians, planners, and engineers, many of whom had been trained in some of the best institutions of Europe, including Eastern Europe, and the United States; in addition the government imported, often under United Nations auspices and on the United Nations payroll, some good foreigners, prominent among whom were a number of experienced Egyptians. This group expounded with great expertise the theory and practice of 'scientific' and 'comprehensive' planning and outlined a 'stage theory' of industrial development. The rhetoric was impressive and the general approach was technically unexceptionable. Iraq's past development efforts were considered to be defective because the problem had not been approached in a 'scientific', 'comprehensive', and 'integrated way'; this was now to be changed.

The 1970–75 Plan was hailed as an example of 'scientific planning', its feasibility studies, its estimates of demand and supply, its input–output calculations and commodity balances all used modern econometric and computer techniques; the crude capital-output estimates and 'rule-of-thumb' judgements of earlier plans were gone for ever.

The euphoria induced by the nationalization of the Iraq Petroleum Company and the end of the austerity programme which preceded it, encouraged very expansive development policies. After 1973 the plan was much enlarged, but still in the belief that the country was safely embarked on scientific planning—on a scientific road to development through planning. Iraqi and foreign observers were much impressed; the planners appeared to grasp the important economic issues and to know how to deal with them; the government appeared to be very firmly established in power.[35] Political stability, economic expertise, and rising oil revenues appeared to many to be exactly the combination required to transform the Iraqi economy rapidly into that of a modern industrialized economy.

In spite of the planners' expertise, however, nothing effective was done to grapple with the really important problems: how to implement *any* plan, given the real shortages of effective managers, supervisors, office workers, and skilled factory workers; how to overcome the social, organizational, and other institutional barriers in the way of rapid increases in productivity; and how to mobilize an enthusiastic commitment of the people. These fundamental weaknesses remained. The gap between the ability to plan and the ability to implement was still wide—indeed, the rising oil revenues, leading to larger plans, may well have widened it. And the plan itself was built on the same shifting base as the preceding ones—the expected availability of foreign exchange. Thus, in spite of official statements to the contrary, the constraint on the size of the plan was clearly the money expected to be available, rather than the rate at which available real resources could be efficiently organized in production. But in spite of the rise in the prices of goods and services, including a very sharp rise in contracting services, less than two-thirds of the allocations could in fact be spent and inflation (or shortages) accelerated in the economy as it became increasingly 'overheated'.

The then Minister of Planning noted that the plan integrated '. . . investments, consumption, production, employment, exports, imports and other economic activities so as to achieve the defined economic and social targets. For the first time, this plan included a set of coordinated monetary, fiscal and trade policies'.[36] Certainly the plan attempted this, but the planners soon found that the binding constraint was not the availability of oil revenues and finance, but rather the supply in the short period of real resources, including adequate supplies of the local resources that were required in combination with the imports of foreign goods to establish and maintain efficient production.

Oil revenues are nothing more nor less than the power to purchase foreign goods and services; they cannot buy 'development' like a commodity. 'Turn-key' factories can be purchased from foreigners, but not the ability and experience to run them efficiently with local management; workers can be imported but not all the skills required, and in any case large-scale importation of labour creates social problems; accommodation and housing can rarely be expanded fast enough. The heavy reliance on foreigners has encouraged a large expansion of what might be called an Iraqi 'quasi-private' sector—the contractor-intermediary. Foreign firms that want to secure contracts for projects in Iraq need to be associated with and have the co-operation of domestic Iraqi contractors, or agents. These provide many services, ranging from guidance around the ministries and through the regulations, to the organization of supplies of domestic materials and labour and the securing of the goodwill of local politicians and administrators necessary to facilitate their work. All such contractors must be registered with the Planning Board and are classified into groups according to the value and type of their resources. Major contractors use subcontractors and the value of contracts can be considerable at every level.

The larger contractors are naturally close to the high officials in government and in the ministries, since they perform the role of intermediaries for firms seeking or executing government and public-sector contracts. The 'conspicuous consumption' of some of the contractors, which is taken as evidence that their incomes are considerable, is a matter of widespread comment among Iraqis. Obviously there is much scope for the corruption of officials and politicians, which is again widely rumoured to have spread far, but which in any case has become serious enough to have led the government to issue draconian decrees in an attempt to deal with it. Penalties for illegal activity are severe (including death and life imprisonment)—which implies that the problem is serious.

One of the major difficulties of planning in Iraq, as in other parts of the less-developed world, is absence of adequate information about the economy. Iraqi efforts to provide sound data on which to base economic analysis and build economic policies have had considerable success. Large numbers of students have been sent to foreign universities for postgraduate study and the development of local training in statistics and quantitative economic analysis advanced rapidly as the students returned home to pass on to others their own expertise. Foreign experts from United Nations organizations and from individual countries have been extensively employed, with the result that the collection of statistical data has made remarkable advances both in quantity and in quality. As the state took control over—or at least responsibility for—more and more aspects of economic life, the need for better information grew increasingly urgent and accordingly the collection of statistical information was accelerated.

But solid statistical series from which reasonably firm conclusions can be drawn can only be established over considerable time. As late as 1968 the United Nations experts could write:

> In the absence of detailed relevant information, it is difficult to measure the degree of improvement or otherwise in the standard of living of the Iraqi population. The most commonly used indicators of per capita consumption/spending, or of individual wealth/properties, of educational and cultural factors, etc., are not being compiled.[37]

Hence all estimates of trends over time in the major sectors of the economy are of necessity very rough. And, as noted earlier, much of the basic accounting data from which statistics relating to the productive units in the economy can be compiled are not available because there have been so few qualified book-keepers and accountants. The collection of statistics requires extensive organization and large numbers of skilled enumerators, estimators, and reporters. This kind of service is not provided by people with Ph.Ds in statistics, and to meet this need there has been a large expansion of vocational training in commerce. In 1969 Iraq had 5 schools of commerce, 64 teachers, and 1,246 students; five years later these figures had risen to 21, 368 and 7,782 respectively. Although a rate of increase of this magnitude cannot have produced very well trained people, especially in accounting and statistics, it is evidence that the problem has been taken seriously.

The absence of adequate statistical data about the economy implies, of course, that the planning of an integrated investment programme was necessarily built on a very shaky empirical basis. In consequence, the impressive technical and conceptual advances in planning, and the elaborate planning mechanisms and procedures with their numerous logically connected stages, were to a great extent irrelevant. That industrial projects in the obvious directions—processing of petroleum, including petrochemicals, and of other raw materials, expansion of investment in consumer goods and in the more suitable capital goods—would be pressed, could have been predicted without regard to 'comprehensive planning'. Similarly the expansion of schools, health facilities, and housing were obvious necessities. 'Planning' was expected by Iraqi economic planners to provide integrated approaches which would avoid bottlenecks and excessive calls on resources, and lead to co-ordinated changes in the structure of the economy. These it has not produced. Not so much because the planning as a technical exercise was either incompetent or incomplete: it was simply unrealistic, and, given its technical targets and methods, was unavoidably so in the absence of better information about the economy.

For example, Kamal Hameed, an International Labour Office consultant, reported in 1974 that very few reliable studies of labour requirements had been made in spite of the large expansions planned, and that there was a severe shortage of training capacity. Migration from agriculture was not, and could not be, controlled, so that there were severe seasonal labour shortages in agriculture, although agriculture contained half the work-force of the economy.[38] It was also difficult to control the movement of labour within the industrial sector. It is common knowledge that the regulation which forbids private firms from employing anyone who has resigned from the public sector has not stopped the practice, especially in the less-organized sectors of activity.

Overall, actual employment fell far short of the planning targets up to 1973. A 22 per cent increase in agricultural employment between 1969 and 1974 was planned; the actual increase by 1973 (the latest figure available at the time of writing) was 13 per cent. Similarly, for industry an increase of 40.5 per cent was projected; by 1973 the increase over 1969 was only 15 per cent. And so on for every sector, with the result that by the end of 1973 the total increase in employment was only 15 per cent instead of the 24 per cent planned; unemployment had increased by 26 per cent.[39] It follows that the planned change in economic structure was equally unobtainable. Industrial employment, in particular, fell further below the target than that of any other sector. This reflects in part the capital intensity of Iraqi investment. No statistics were available to us for later years, but all reports were of a severe labour shortage by 1976–77.

In spite of its 'sophistication', therefore, Iraq's planning, and even more the execution of the plans, not only tended to favour the obvious investments, but also the easier ones—easier because, being capital intensive, they minimized the number of workers who had to be organized and trained quickly. It is always simpler and quicker to make large capital investments where relatively little labour is required and to hire foreign contractors to install turn-key plants than to invest in industries which require the recruitment, training, and organization of a large labour force. That Iraq should go in for the obvious projects is not a criticism; equally, much large capital-intensive investment was unavoidable, given the fact that the industries which process oil are of this type—especially petrochemicals. But a similar preference is displayed in other industries as well. Large capital-intensive plants require highly skilled labour, where the shortages are greatest. Training programmes are being developed rapidly, but to the extent that one of the major objectives of planning was to co-ordinate the rate and type of investment in Iraq with the size, composition, and rate of development of the skills of the labour force, it has not been notably effective.

Iraq can expect a rapid rate of growth of the urban labour force as population expands, as an increasing proportion of the population, notably women, enter the labour force, and as migration continues from the rural areas. After the nationalization of industry in 1964 the role of the public sector became of central importance from the point of view of national planning and of the implementation of national plans. But in spite of the rapid expansion that took place in the public sector, it had absorbed only about one-quarter of the employed labour force by 1974.[40] A survey of manpower in the state organizations undertaken in 1972 showed that about 42 per cent of all public-sector employees were recruited between December 1968 and May 1972; in 1974 all unemployed university graduates were taken into the public service. The failure to provide employment on an adequate scale in the directly productive sectors of agriculture and industry reflected the failure of these sectors to grow at the planned rate, as well as the capital intensity of production. As industrial demand grew, the services of many of the skilled and educated people who had been absorbed into government service were needed in industry, but it was often difficult to squeeze them out of government.

Iraq has for decades had an extensive programme for the training of students abroad on government scholarships. All government-supported students are bonded and they or their guarantors have to repay the government for money received if they do not return. Nevertheless, many who could find alternative employment abroad often preferred to remain abroad, some because they did not like the political regime in Iraq, others because they feared that if they returned, they would not be permitted to travel out again, and still others because they found more remunerative or congenial employment elsewhere. Often too, a student with a foreign wife hesitated to bring her to Iraq. In order to induce students with foreign degrees to return, the government for a short period permitted them to import goods free of duty, including television and Hi-Fi sets, refrigerators, freezers, etc., as well as an automobile. They were guaranteed employment, although it might not have any relation to their training. Returning students were thus almost as privileged as army officers in society. Although the special inducements reportedly had some success, the policy was abandoned after a short while, partly because others who had taken the relevant foreign degrees in the past demanded similar treatment on grounds of equity, and partly because the results in attracting students to return were disappointing.

During their course of study students were also required to return periodically to Iraq for brief periods. The government stated that it wanted to ensure that they did not lose touch with their own country since many were abroad for several years.

Planning was also intended to bring about a co-ordination of monetary, fiscal, and trading policies, one of the effects of which should have been to control inflation. Again there is no evidence that Iraqi planning has been effective in this respect. Although the plans made ample provision for the expansion of the transportation, ports, and other infrastructure required to handle the high level of imports, shortages were bound to develop. The enormous pressure on resources that resulted from the very large expenditures seriously strained the internal transportation facilities and thus even large imports could not prevent the inflation of prices; the prices of goods were heavily protected by import tariffs, and prices of goods which could not easily be imported, like bricks, rose substantially more than the planners had counted on. For this reason special efforts have been made to increase production of items like bricks.[41]

The official indexes of prices do not reflect the underlying pressures, partly because of their statistical deficiencies and partly because of the extensive subsidization of food. Iraq could not, of course, escape the general world inflation of prices in the period after the middle 1960s, but her attempts to control food prices led to severe shortages of a number of foodstuffs, especially vegetables, dairy products, and meat. The prices of construction materials nearly doubled between 1969 and 1975, and those of some locally produced materials increased even more. In 1974 there was an especially rapid increase of prices and complaints of shortages of fruits, vegetables, meat, and other consumer goods seemed to rise in volume. The price of bricks increased nearly three times between 1973 and 1975; exports of cements had ceased under pressure of local demand and wages rose rapidly.

The broad targets of the long-heralded 1976–80 Plan had just been announced at the time when this book went to press in mid-1977. After the end of the 1970–75 Plan, development expenditures had been incorporated into annual budgets, in which the largest expenditures were allocated for industry. There had been reports of considerable disagreement over the appropriate scope of the 1976–80 Plan within the Iraqi establishment, which presumably accounts for the delay in announcing it. The investments envisaged are very large, reaching a total of $49,000 million, and few among the Iraqi economists would have considered that the growth-rates announced by the RCC could be attained in real terms; only very high rates of inflation can ensure the achievement of such rates. Table III below shows the growth-rates at constant prices which are officially reported as having been achieved by the Iraqi economy between 1969 and 1975, together with the rates envisaged in the 1976–80 Plan. As can readily be seen, the plan targets must assume a very high rate of price inflation, but no other details of the plan had been reported.

Table III Annual Growth-Rates of Gross Domestic Product by Economic Sectors

	1969–74 Constant prices 1969=100	*1976–80 Planned*
Oil and Mining	5.5	15.5
Manufacturing	8.3	32.9
Agriculture (incl. forestry and fishing)	0.06	7.1
Distribution	6.4	16.9
Services	12.9	10.4

Sources: The rates for 1969–74 have been calculated from the data presented in the *Annual Abstract of Statistics,* 1975, Table 6/8. The rates for the 1976–80 Plan are taken from the report of the RCC announcement in *MEES,* 11 July 1977. The prices used were not stated.

Clearly the government intends to push ahead with industrial and other investment even more rapidly than before. Larger oil revenues are naturally expected and these have presumably tempted the authorities to disregard the strains that existing rates of spending have placed on the economy. Productivity will have to be increased at truly unprecedented rates if the country is to avoid increasing shortages of goods and services of all kinds.

The considerations behind the disappointing past performance of the 'directly productive sectors' of the economy—agriculture and industry—and in particular the difficulties in effecting planned expenditures, were less prominent in the services sectors, including especially social services. The number of educational institutions of all kinds and of hospitals and clinics continued to increase very rapidly. Free medical services spread and became more widely available outside the major cities and the numbers at all levels of education almost exploded. Pupils in secondary-education institutions rose nearly two and a half times between 1963–64 and 1974–75, while the numbers of students in universities, colleges, and technical institutes rose three times.

The expansion of the universities and colleges was especially rapid after 1969–70, with a near doubling of numbers in five years. There was every evidence that this rapid increase was accompanied by an even more serious fall in standards than in the Qassim period, and it became increasingly difficult for Iraqi graduates to find places in good institutions abroad for postgraduate study, at least in some disciplines. In other words, if 'productivity' in education could be measured in terms of quality as well as of numbers, it, too, fell with such a very rapid rate of expansion. The number of universities rose from 2 to 5 as new ones were established in the provinces (Mosul, Basra, and Sulaimaniya) and the proportion of total students in Baghdad fell from nearly complete dominance to 60 per cent in 1969–70 and to 40 per cent in 1974–75.

In secondary education the percentage of women students rose from around 21 per cent in 1963–64 to a peak of 29 per cent in 1970–71, where it has remained. (The pass-rate of females in both arts (78 per cent) and sciences (75 per cent) was very much higher than that of the males (49 per cent and 60 per cent respectively).) The total allocations for education in the ordinary budget doubled between 1970–71 and 1974–75, that for health rose two and a half times, while that for 'youth and social affairs' went up nearly three times.

There remained wide disparities among the different provinces. Income *per capita* had always been much higher in the central provinces than in those of the south and north, and Baghdad had always dominated all others in this respect. There are no good data available, but the preliminary findings of a study by Shakir Moosa Issa being carried out in the University of London, but still uncompleted at the time of writing, indicate that the traditional pattern had not changed much by 1971. Basing his work on the 1971 Household Budget Survey and the 1971 Agricultural Survey, he found that the value added in agriculture in the Baghdad province accounted for 21 per cent of the national total and 41 per cent of the value added in the six central provinces; the five southern provinces, by contrast, produced less than one-third of the national total. Baghdad province alone produced some 50 per cent of the meat and more than 11 per cent of the milk of the country. He also found that inequality in the distribution of land had not changed very much as a result of agrarian reform, especially for the smallholders, and argued that the unequal distribution of land was still a primary cause of rural income inequality.[42] The spread of industry, however, into other areas probably has reduced the predominance of Baghdad in this respect. Mineral projects in the north, petrochemical projects in the south, processing plants in other areas have all been major parts of the government's industrial programmes.

The steep rise in the price of oil defeated Iraq's attempts to reduce her dependence on oil, but was hardly unwelcome to the country.

The Iraqi government has always claimed that it wanted to become more independent of the crude-oil industry by reducing the proportion of the national income, the proportion of export receipts, and the proportion of government revenues attributable to crude oil. What was wanted, of course, was simply a growing and substantial increase in the production of other commodities for domestic consumption and for export, and of other sources of revenue for the government. As we have seen, there has been a considerable increase in industrial output even though it has been low in relation to the increase in investment; total manufacturing output at constant prices rose by 25 per cent between 1971 and 1974, as recorded in the accounts, and reached 10 per cent of the gross domestic product in 1972 before the rise in oil revenues reduced it to less than 5 per cent.[43] But since agricultural output lagged badly and food imports increased, while dates and petroleum products were the only remaining exports of note, together accounting for over three-quarters of the total non-oil exports, any significant reduction of dependence on crude oil was not yet in sight.

But efforts in this direction must inevitably struggle against perverse economic forces. Large oil revenues from the export of oil imply a strong currency on the foreign-exchange markets. A strong currency is by definition expensive for the importers, who must buy it in order to buy the country's exports. This discourages exports. The development of export industries capable of competing on world markets is, in consequence, handicapped by the very strength of the country in other directions. An economist might argue that in principle the value of a country's currency should reflect its strength in export markets, for this enables the people to gain the benefit of their exports in the form of cheap imports. But if the chief export commodity is an exhaustible resource which must eventually be replaced by the development of other export industries, then it behoves the country to take especial care to ensure that its domestic cost structure does not become inordinately inflated and that the prospects of achieving international competitiveness by its newer industries are favourable when eventually helped by falling exchange-rates. This Iraq shows no signs of doing.

Students of the Iraqi economy have on occasion tried to treat its development as an example of the model of 'export-led' growth that has been prominent among the theories of growth of less-developed countries. In such a model, economic growth is stimulated by productive activity in the export industry through its links with other industries as a purchaser of output, and because the income received by its workers and employers stimulates demand for the goods and services of other industries. But the direct economic stimulus to an economy from crude-oil production is extremely limited. Except for short periods when construction activity is high, wages are a very small proportion of value added, and in non-industrial countries much of the equipment and other inputs required by the industry have to be imported. The bulk of the revenue generated goes to the government and the stimulus to the economy depends largely on how the government chooses to spend its funds. Oil revenues permit the imports which make possible high levels of domestic investment without excessive inflation, but the production of crude oil does not in itself strongly stimulate development.

Notes

1 See W. B. Fisher, *The Middle East,* 6th edn. (London, 1971), pp. 362–5, for a summary of the water-control and irrigation projects in Iraq.

2 See *Abstract of Statistics,* 1975. Tables 28 and 65. See below, Basic Data, pp. 546–8, for a summary of important statistical information for Iraqi agriculture.

3 These figures are mostly taken from the 1975 issue of the *Annual Abstract of Statistics.* They have been converted from the Iraqi unit of measurement, the donum (=.25 hectares), for ease of international understanding. However, other issues of the *Abstract* and other official sources do not necessarily present exactly the same figures. This state of affairs is not uncommon in the compilation of Iraqi statistics.

4 Jawad Hashim, *Development Planning in Iraq* (Baghdad, 1975), mimeo, pp. 72 and 75.

5 In 1963, for example, the Agricultural Bank (*Annual Report,* 1963), commented: '. . . we have no accurate statistics of the areas cultivated in those [earlier] years and in the year under review to compare the rate of increase and assess the quantities of crops . . .' Moreover, it is necessary to be very careful to check all published data to ensure as far as possible that they are on a consistent basis. For example, between 1968 and 1970 there is considerable confusion over whether the reported figures for the area under wheat and barley refer to the total cultivated area or to the area actually harvested. If the figures given for the years 1970–71 and 1971–72 in the 1973 *Abstract of Statistics* for the cultivated area are checked with the figures in the 1975 *Abstract,* it appears that the former in fact refer to the harvested area only. The 1975 *Abstract* presents figures for the 'gross cultivated area' and the 'net harvested area' separately, but reported yields are based on the *harvested* area. Since this is often very much less than the cultivated area, it probably explains some of the increase in yields as reported in the statistics as compared with earlier years. In the Charts presented below, pp. 492–6 yields are expressed in relation to cultivated area, since this indicates the productivity of the area actually devoted to the crop and not merely of the area that in the event turned out to be sufficiently productive to harvest. If, however, some land was not harvested because of civil war, it would be appropriate to ignore the area so affected. There is no explanation of why the Statistical Office chose their method of presentation.

6 Doreen Warriner, *Land Reform in Principle and Practice* (Oxford, 1969), p. 43 (italics added).

7 Ministry of Planning, *National Development Plan*, 1970–74 (Baghdad, 1971), p. 110.

8 Iraq has arranged for Egyptian agricultural families to settle in Iraq because of the shortage of Iraqi farmers in some areas. Between 100 and 500 families are reported to have arrived in the country, but we were not able to find much solid information about the scheme to encourage Egyptian immigrants, nor about how the new farmers were settling down. Some of the problems that arise with the importation of single workers (as contrasted to migrant families) have been discussed by Rushdi Abdul Hassan in an Egyptian journal *Sabah el Khair* (2 December 1976). He reported instances where Iraqi and Egyptian contractors promised jobs to and took money from Egyptian workers attracted by the promise of work and good wages. On arrival in Baghdad, the workers were taken to 'the middle of Iraq in the middle of summer', which was designated as 'hell'. They were shocked at the low wages, which left them with very little after paying the advances and expenses. The author added: 'I was told in Baghdad that many workers were roaming around seeking jobs by themselves with nowhere to go'. This type of situation is of course common wherever contract labour is employed.

9 Broadcast of the Prime Minister on 14 July 1974, published by the Iraqi embassy, London.

10 Directorate General of Industrial Planning, *The Industrial Sector of the Economy of Iraq* (Baghdad, June 1964). Table B, p. 82.

11 ibid., Table C, p. 87. According to this report the net return of some of the other industries was as follows: three large flour-milling plants, 27.5 per cent; the cotton textile plant, 29.2 per cent; a woollen-textile plant, 26.1 per cent; and a rayon plant, 28.9 per cent. The private return on five cement plants averaged 13.6 per cent and that on asbestos reached 29 per cent. These figures were compared with an average return of 24.2 per cent in 27 miscellaneous industries (pp. 68 and 87). (But see above, pp. 463–4 for a discussion of this type of Iraqi statistic.)

12 ibid, p. 110.

13 ibid.

14 The observations on the state of Iraqi accounting procedures are based on discussions we held in Baghdad in 1968 with officials of the State Organization of Industries and foreign expert consultants. We were given many examples of the inefficiency of government-run plants and were told that there was a great deal of unplanned excess capacity in them. One Iraqi study indicating a 70 to 80 per cent utilization of capacity very much overestimated the true situation, which was nearer 30 to 40 per cent according to some foreign experts. One foreign engineer reported that the Iraqis who were making the estimates had no training in how to estimate the capacity of a plant. Moreover, overmanning was almost endemic; one spinning and weaving factory which required some 700 workers, employed nearly 1,200; the management in some factories was extremely weak and the factories were virtually run by the workers, with appalling productivity, while for other new ones the estimates of local demand far exceeded any possible rate of increase in the foreseeable future.

15 IBRD/IDA, *Current Economic Position and Prospects of Iraq*. Report on a Mission in May/June 1968 (January 1969, mimeo), p. 13.

16 The 1953 to 1963 figures are the estimates of Khair al-Din Haseeb widely published in Iraqi official series; those for the later period are those of the Central Statistical Office of Iraq.

17 Calculated from the figures given in United Nations, Economic Commission for Western Asia, *National Account Studies, Bulletin No. 1. Economic Growth of the ECWA Countries throughout the period 1960–1975.* (May 1977, mimeo), pp. 72–7.
18 GDP at 1966 factor cost prices for 1962–65 were as follows in million ID: 1962, 145.2; 1963, 109.2; 1964, 145.1; 1965, 169.3. Source: ibid.
19 Jawad Hashim, *Gross Fixed Capital Formation in Iraq, 1957–1970* (Baghdad, Oct. 1972), mimeo. In Arabic. The capital formation figures, especially in the earlier period, are probably even less reliable than those of output.
20 Republic of Iraq, Planning Board and Ministry of Planning, *The National Development Plan, 1970–74* (Baghdad, 1971), p. 110.
21 See the report to the United Nations by Khair al-Din Haseeb, 'Plan Implementation in Iraq, 1951–67', in *Studies on Selected Development Problems in Various Countries in the Middle East, 1969* (United Nations, 1969).
22 Min stry of Industry, Industrial Bank of Iraq, Report.
23 Jawad Hashim, *Development Planning in Iraq: Historical Perspective and New Directions.* Six Lectures (Baghdad, April 1975, mimeo), and the *Abstract of Statistics 1975.*
24 See, for example, the discussion of industrial plans in K. Langley, *The Industrialization of Iraq* (Cambridge, Mass., 1961) and Jalal, op. cit. See also above, Chapter 8, note 18.
25 Quoted in *Middle East Economic Digest,* 25 July 1975. Vol. 19:30, p. 16.
26 United Nations Economic and Social Office in Beirut, *Review and Appraisal of the Process of Decision-making and Management in the Public Industrial Enterprises in Iraq* (Beirut, October 1973), mimeo.
27 ibid., p. 29.
28 See Robert Mabro and Samir Radwan, *The Industrialization of Egypt, 1939–1973* (Oxford, 1976), p. 96.
29 See the Report of K. A. Hameed, *Manpower and Employment Planning* (Beirut, United Nations, 1975), mimeo.
30 *Al-Thawra,* 8, 9, 10 September 1976.
31 The following story, for the truth of which we cannot vouch but which we have heard from a number of different sources, at least illustrates the type of fear that exists among the people. A university teacher was reported to have quoted in his class the remark attributed to Saddam Hussain himself, to the effect that those who do not work shall not eat. The teacher then pointed out that a universal application of the principle would be wrong because there were sick, handicapped, and old people in the economy who could not work. It was reported that the lecturer was brought before the authorities for criticism of Saddam, together with his students. His students were asked whether or not he had made the remark. Those who said he did were freed; those who said that he did not were deprived of their work permits, detained in custody, and otherwise punished.
32 Calculated from the *Abstract of Statistics,* 1975, p. 257.
33 This aspect of the planning of development in Iraq has been discussed in a number of studies listed in our Bibliography. See especially the works of F. Jalal, A. Alnasrawi, and J. Hashim.
34 Hashim, op. cit., pp. 60 ff. Jawad Hashim is a good example of the young Baathist technocrat. He obtained his Ph.D in statistics from the London School of Economics in 1966, and in 1968 became Minister of Planning in Iraq. His Ph.D thesis produced estimates of capital formation in Iraq and ever since then his estimates of capital formation have figured prominently in Iraqi statistical publications. He was removed from his ministerial post for a short period in 1971–72 and then again in 1974, becoming an adviser

to the Office of Economic Affairs of the Revolutionary Command Council, but remaining a Member of the Planning Board.

35 See, for example, Yusif Sayigh, an experienced Arab economist, who after a critical appraisal of Iraq's economic performance was nevertheless impressed by the Baath government's grasp of the problems. See his *Economics of the Arab World* (London, 1977).

36 Hashim, op. cit., p. 62.

37 United Nations Special Fund Project, *The Economic Status of Iraq*. Report prepared under Assistance in Development Planning and Execution (Baghdad, April 1968), p. 8.

38 Hameed, op. cit.

39 Compare the employment targets as presented in the *National Development Plan, 1970–74*, p. 157 with the employment statistics, 1964–73, given in the *Annual Abstract of Statistics,* 1974, Table 208. The data are based on the United Nations Report on Manpower in Iraq by Nils Storm. The 1975 *Abstract* did not give employment figures.

40 Hameed, op. cit.

41 The brick industry in Iraq is a very old one with many small, old, and labour-intensive factories. These are being replaced by large capital-intensive factories using the newest technology. It was reported in May 1977 that the old factories were being closed as new ones, 10 of which were planned or coming into production in 1977, were built to replace them. See *MEES*, 6 May 1977.

42 Shakir Issa's preliminary findings were presented in a Working Paper at a Development Seminar in the School of Oriental and African Studies, University of London, 'The Distribution of Income in Iraq 1971' (June 1977, mimeo).

43 *Annual Abstract of Statistics,* 1975, pp. 162 and 163.

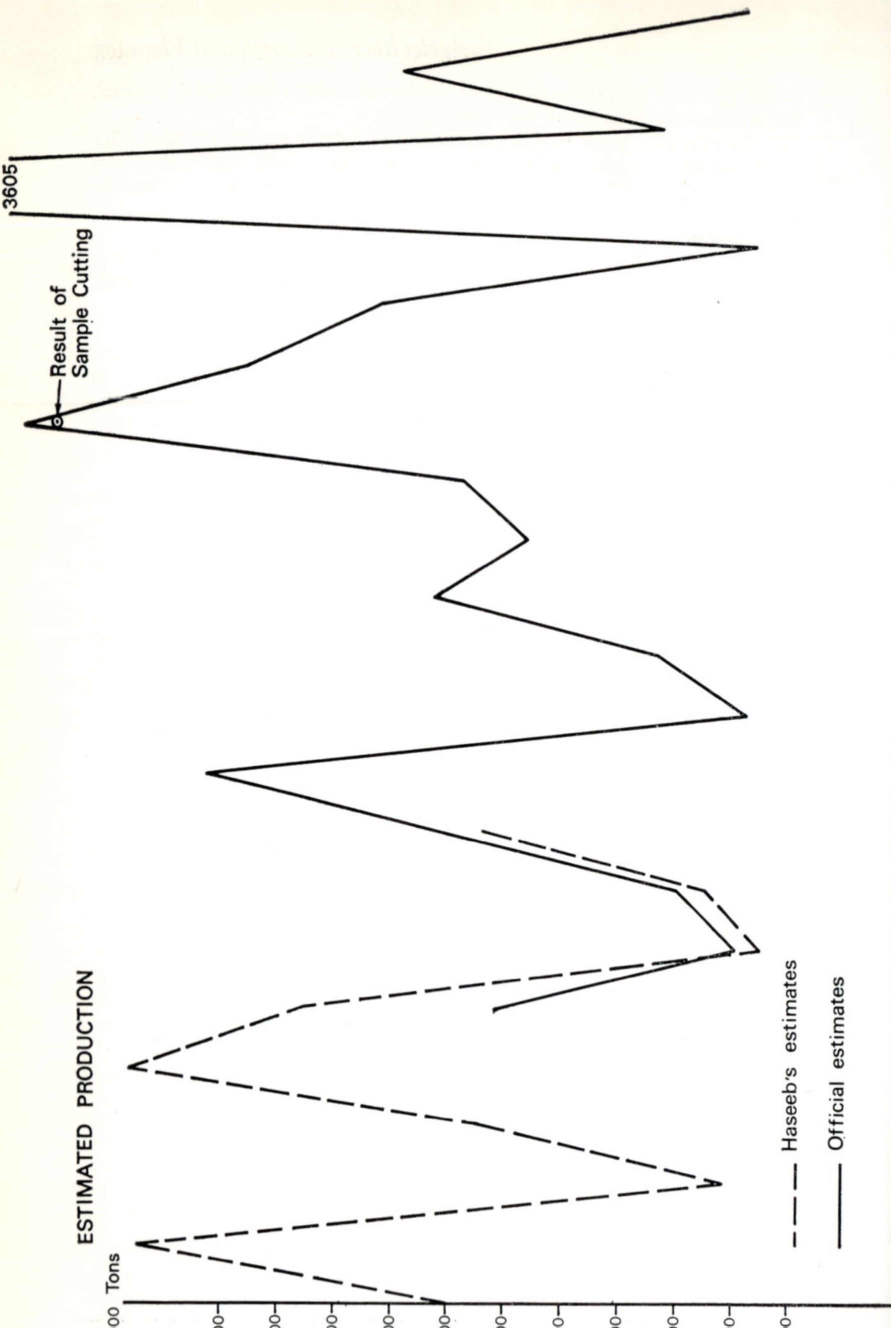

I Wheat and Barley, Estimated Production, 1953–75. Sources: 1953–61 K. Haseeb, *National Income of Iraq*; 1958–75 Central Statistical Office, *Annual Abstract of Statistics*

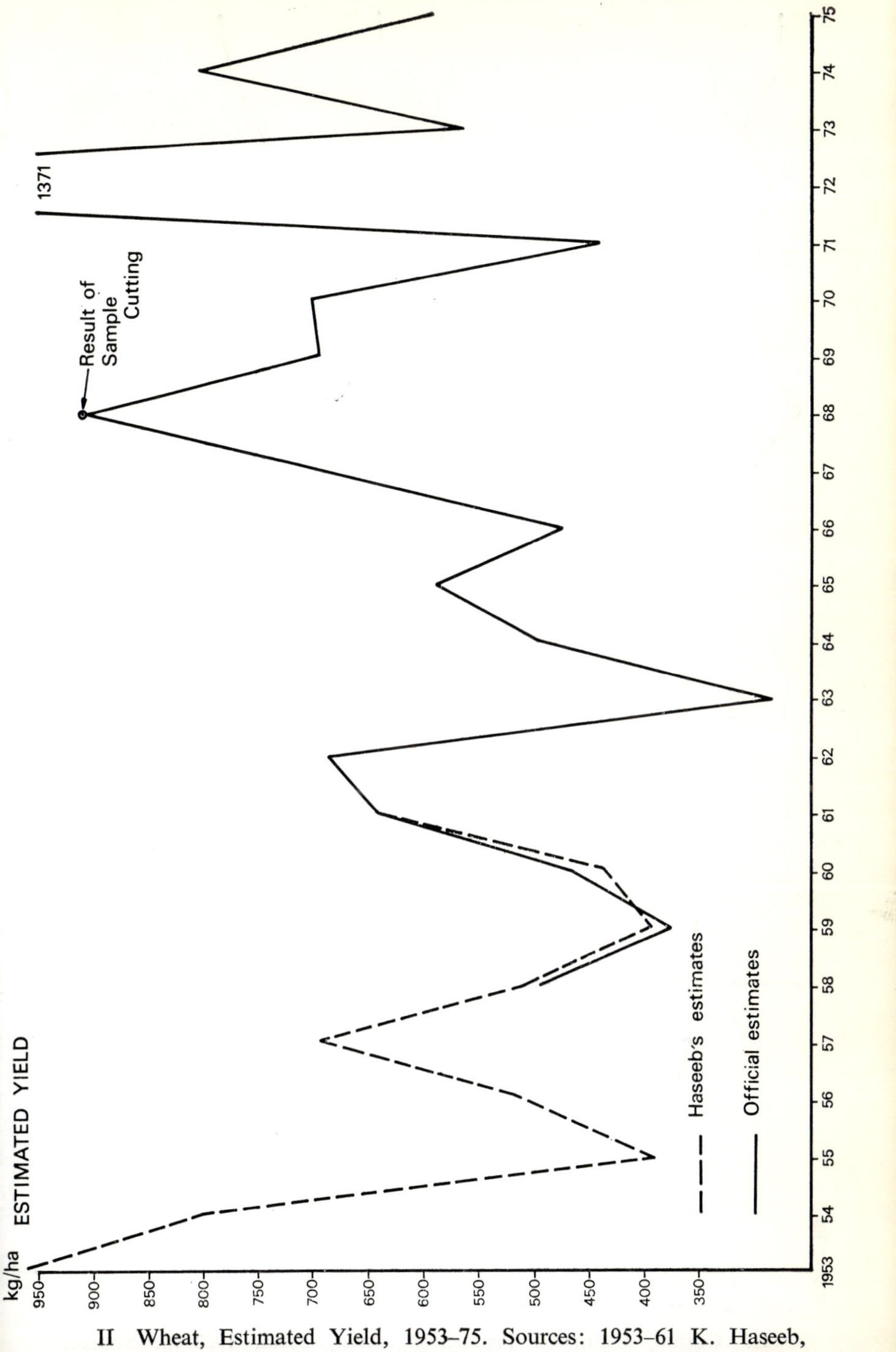

II Wheat, Estimated Yield, 1953–75. Sources: 1953–61 K. Haseeb, *National Income of Iraq*; 1958–75 Central Statistical Office, *Annual Abstract of Statistics*

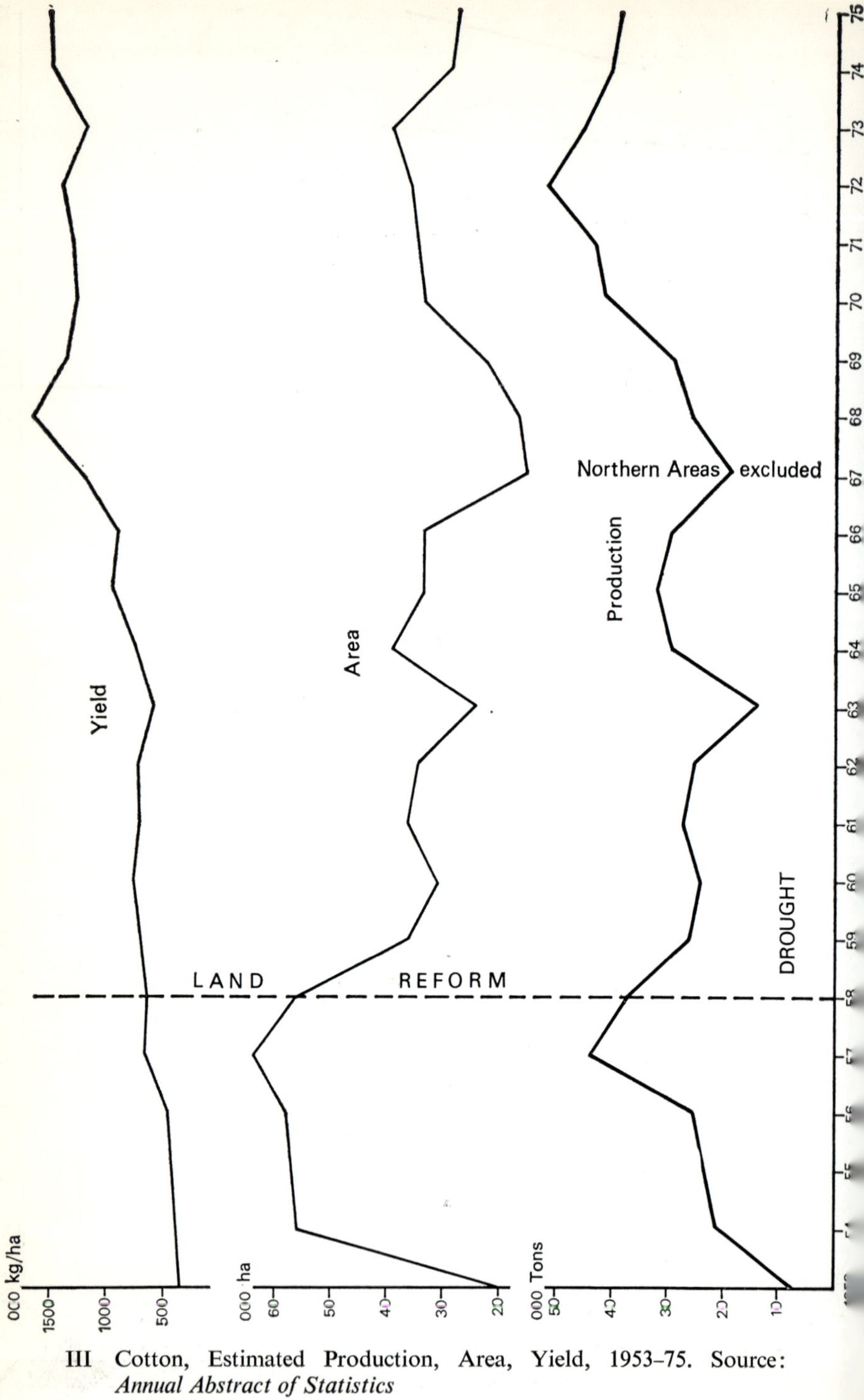

III Cotton, Estimated Production, Area, Yield, 1953–75. Source: *Annual Abstract of Statistics*

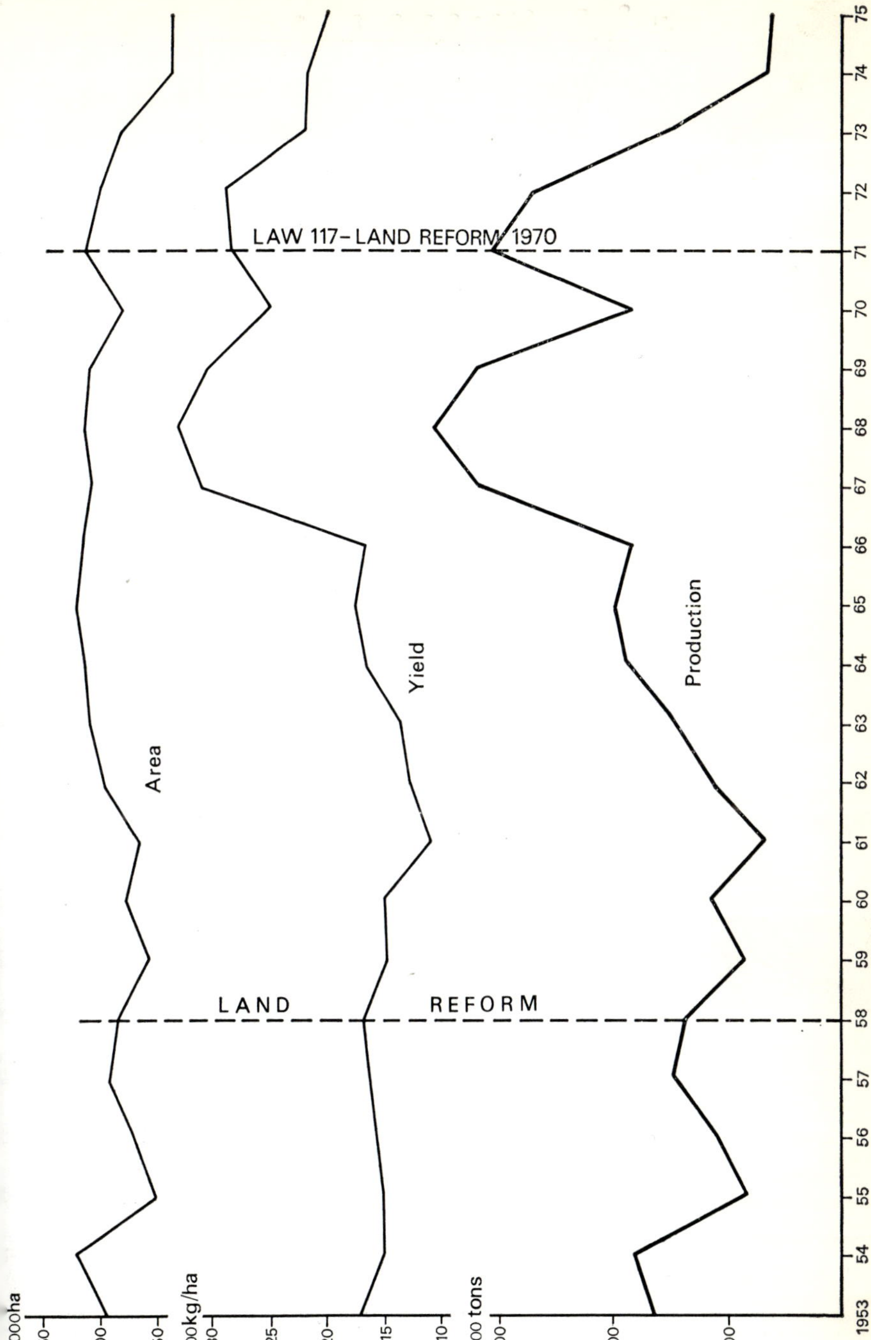

IV Rice, Estimated Production, Area, Yield, 1953–75. Source: *Annual Abstract of Statistics*

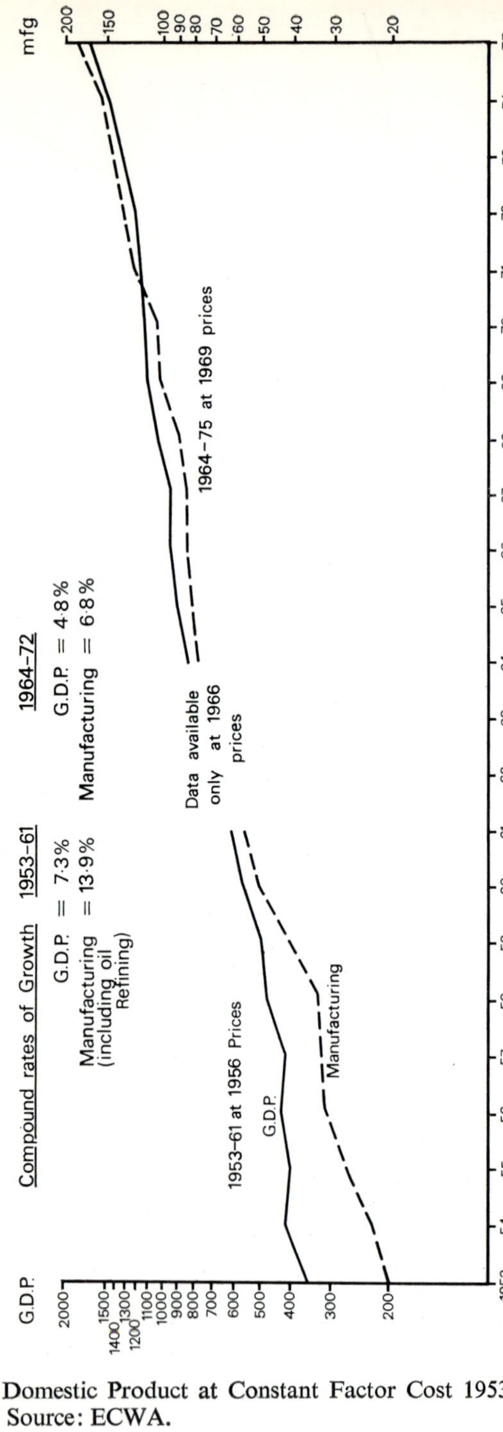

V Gross Domestic Product at Constant Factor Cost 1953–75 (million dinar). Source: ECWA.

19 Iraq in OPEC and OAPEC

It is necessary briefly to recapitulate the salient aspects of Iraq's early relations with OPEC. Although Venezuela had been in the forefront of those proposing some sort of organization which would encompass all of the major oil-exporting countries, Iraq had taken the initiative in calling the conference which set it up. But Iraq's relationship with OPEC has always been uneasy and frequently severely strained. The actions of the oil companies in reducing tax prices in 1959–60 provided the immediate occasion for the formation of OPEC and exacerbated the tensions in the negotiations between Qassim and the IPC which led to the passage of Law 80. Iraq was extremely disappointed with OPEC over its lukewarm support in the controversy with the IPC following Law 80 and she felt that other countries gained from the subsequent restrictions of Iraqi oil exports. The success of OPEC in persuading the companies to expense royalties did not benefit Iraq since the concessionaires insisted on linking the application of royalty-expensing in Iraq with a settlement of the problems raised by Law 80. Iraq had also been, along with Venezuela, the country pressing most strongly for physical controls over production as the only effective means of maintaining prices, and for the policy of forcing the companies to relinquish to the host governments the unexploited areas held under their concession agreements. The attempt to control production through the voluntary observance of production quotas by the member countries failed, primarily because other OPEC members would not give effect to it, but the companies did agree to schedules for progressive relinquishments of concession areas.

Both the Libyan Petroleum Law of 1955 and the Iranian Petroleum Act of 1957 contained provisions for relinquishment, and the IPC companies had offered to relinquish a large proportion of their territory during the negotiations with Qassim in 1960. Many Iraqis believed that the passage of Law 80 had frightened the companies and had emboldened the governments to press harder for relinquishment, permitting them to use the Iraqi precedent of 'forced relinquishment' which they believed Law 80 had established. How far the

Iraqi legislation had this effect is difficult to determine, but it seems more likely that by the early 1960s, and with the growing effectiveness of OPEC, the companies had realized that it was no longer possible to hold large areas under concession which they were either unwilling or unable to exploit in a reasonable period of time. OPEC was rapidly gaining confidence and pressures on the companies were intensifying in several directions.

The Formation of OAPEC

During the 1960s Iraq was becoming increasingly dissatisfied with OPEC, partly because of OPEC's inadequate support of her policies and partly because of a generally conservative and cautious approach adopted under the influence of Saudi Arabia and especially, in Iraq's view, of Iran. Iraq's relations with Iran were not of the best in this period, and the government felt that Iran too often dominated OPEC policies; many Iraqi leaders believed that the Shah used OPEC when he thought it was to his advantage, but he went his own way at the expense of other members when he did not. Iraq therefore persistently pressed that the Arab League should establish a co-ordinated Arab oil policy.

The Arab League's interest in oil matters, and its recognition that control over oil supplies could be used in the Arab struggle with Israel, was longstanding. It was in response to a request from the Arab League that Iraq suspended shipments to Haifa during the first war with Israel in 1948. Shortly thereafter, in 1951, the League established an Oil Experts Committee and a permanent Petroleum Department, of which Muhammed Salman (later Qassim's Minister of Oil) was the first director. This department organized the first Arab Petroleum Congresses in 1959 and 1961 and sponsored a variety of inter-Arab economic projects, including an Arab Oil Tanker Company for which an agreement was signed in 1964 between Iraq, Kuwait, Jordan, and Syria.

A draft agreement for the co-ordination of oil policies was proposed by Iraq to the Arab Oil Experts Committee in 1958. It included a comprehensive set of measures designed to ensure uniform regulations governing oil, price maintenance, Arabization of personnel in the foreign oil companies, the establishment of Arab oil companies, consultation over prices, and relinquishment of unexploited concession territory. Although approved by the Arab Economic Council in 1960, nothing came of it, partly because of general political differences among Arab countries at the time, and partly because the formation of OPEC on a wider international basis superseded it, at least for the time being.

In 1966 Iraq again renewed her efforts to promote the formation of an Arab petroleum organization under the auspices of the Arab League, and there were rumours that she intended to leave OPEC for such an Arab organization. These were quickly denied, but it was clear that there was widespread support in the more radical and nationalist Iraqi circles for such an Arab organization.

The differences of view over oil policy were sharply illustrated in 1967 as the Arab governments attempted to work out appropriate strategy in connection with the 1967 Six-Day War with Israel. In a conference called in Baghdad on 4 and 5 June attended by eleven Arab states, including all the major oil-exporting countries, Iraq took the lead in demanding a total ban on oil exports. It was unanimously agreed to enforce an embargo on deliveries of oil to any country directly or indirectly taking part in aggression against any Arab state, although a number of countries, notably Saudi Arabia, showed considerable reluctance to do so. Nevertheless, Saudi Arabia, along with others, did prohibit exports entirely for a few days; however, the Saudi government was the first to decide that a total ban was inappropriate, and on 13 June replaced it by a limited embargo forbidding shipments only to the United Kingdom and the United States. Others soon followed, except for Iraq which maintained her embargo until 19 June, when she, too, authorized shipments to all countries except the United States, West Germany, Rhodesia, and South Africa.

There had always been a fear on the part of many of the Arab exporting countries that a ban on oil shipments (which automatically entails a reduction in, if not the elimination of, oil revenues) would do more harm to the producing countries than to the consuming countries, especially since the Arab exporters did not have a complete monopoly over oil supplies. The limited embargo was not effective and oil exports soon equalled or exceeded their pre-war level for most countries.

Iraq continued her efforts to persuade the Arab governments to take measures of considerable severity against the 'imperialist' countries. At the Arab summit conference in Khartoum in August 1967, Iraq put forward proposals which had been discussed by Arab finance and economic ministers at a conference two weeks earlier in Baghdad. The proposals included a total embargo on shipments, with closure of pipelines and of the Suez Canal for a period long enough to deplete Europe's oil stocks, followed by a selective embargo. In addition, Western oil interests were to be nationalized. None of Iraq's proposals was accepted and the conference voted for what it called a 'positive' use of the oil revenues to help strengthen Arab economies; as an example it agreed to contribute $378 million a year to Jordan and the UAR, the countries which had borne the brunt of the war.

In many ways OPEC was clearly proving its effectiveness and had achieved considerable success, not only in such matters as the expensing of royalties and relinquishment, but also as a technical and economic advisory body and a focus for co-operative exchanges. But it was not oriented to serve the special interests of the Arab oil-exporting countries. During the abortive embargo, for example, oil shipments from Iran and Venezuela had increased. It was clear, especially after the 1967 conflict with Israel, that the long-pressed demand for an Arab oil body would have to be met.

On the other hand, some countries, and Saudi Arabia in particular, feared the political militancy of Iraq and Algeria in oil policies, and were worried that an organization in which these two countries took the lead, or even one established under the auspices of the Arab League in Cairo and heavily influenced by Egypt, would be too prone to take rash action damaging to the interests of the major oil-exporting countries. Very largely as a means of forestalling the latter type of development, Saudi Arabia, Kuwait, and Libya, on the initiative of Saudi Arabia, formed the Organization of Arab Petroleum Exporting Countries in January 1968. It was not designed as a rival to OPEC, nor has it turned out to be one, and there was a strong emphasis on the economic and commercial aspects of its proposed activities, but the tension between the 'militants' and the 'conservatives' in Arab oil affairs, and the struggle among them for influence in the politics of the Arab world generally, provided the immediate background for its establishment.

Any Arab state for which oil was the 'principal and basic source of its national income' was entitled to join. Iraq barely fulfilled this condition, for in 1968 the net contribution of crude-oil production to the Iraqi national income was only around 20 per cent. Iraq was nevertheless invited to become a founding member of the organization. It is not surprising that she refused; among other reasons was the fact that neither Egypt nor Algeria was eligible and Iraq feared that she would be a lone voice in an essentially conservative organization, dominated by Saudi Arabia.

The obvious move for Iraq was to establish closer formal links with Algeria and Egypt as a counterweight to OAPEC. On 1 February 1968, therefore, INOC signed an agreement with Algeria's state oil company, Sonatrach, for the co-ordination of the oil policies of the national companies and specifically to promote co-operation against the major international oil companies. In the communiqué announcing the agreement, other national companies were invited to join provided that their policies were independent of the 'international monopolies'. A few weeks later, the national companies of both the UAR and Syria were officially invited to join the agreement because of their 'revolutionary tendencies' and 'independent policies'. In March, an INOC delegation visited Algeria and Egypt to consolidate their relationship, and in June a Sonatrach delegation visited Iraq and Syria to investigate prospects for technical co-operation. These developments were well under way when the Baath seized power in 1968. The change of regime made little difference to this type of policy.

With the revolution in Libya in September 1969, in which the monarchy was overthrown and a group of young military men headed by Colonel Muammar Qadhaffi seized power, the so-called radical coalition of Arab countries was strengthened. In January 1970 Iraq invited the national oil companies of Algeria, Libya, the UAR, and Syria to Baghdad. Agreement on strengthened co-operation and co-ordination of policies was reached, which included provisions for exchanges of technicians and information, co-ordination of marketing policies, the establishment of joint projects, mutual support in conflicts with the foreign oil companies, and continuation of regular meetings. Iraq, Algeria, and Libya continued to support each other as a special group within the main body of OPEC in the Teheran and Tripoli price negotiations, in spite of occasional conflicts of interest, and in the various actions, including nationalization, which each took from time to time against its concessionaires. Iraq looked on the co-operation of the three countries as a 'consolidated petroleum front', the establishment of which she had initiated.

The Libyan revolution also changed the complexion of OAPEC. At a meeting of the Council of Ministers of the three OAPEC countries on 26–27 January 1970, Suhail Sadawi of Libya was appointed to succeed Zeki Yamani as Secretary General of the organization. In May, Algeria, Abu Dhabi, Qatar, Bahrain, and Dubai were admitted as members. In June, Iraq applied for membership, but the application created much controversy; the Gulf states led by Saudi Arabia opposed Iraq's admission, while Libya and Algeria strongly supported it with Kuwait's tacit compliance. The controversy held up the work of the organization for nearly eighteen months, and for a time it looked as if OAPEC might break up over the issue. However, in October 1971 Abu Dhabi announced that she would support the admission of Iraq, and in December Saudi Arabia proposed a change in the charter regulations governing admission to permit any Arab country exporting oil to become a member. This opened the way for Syria and Egypt as well as for Iraq, all of which were duly admitted upon the acceptance of the amendment to the charter in March 1972. From then on Iraq took an active part in OAPEC's work and co-operated in most of its policies until the October 1973 war. After the nationalization of the IPC, Iraq called on the Council of Ministers of OAPEC to consider giving her and Syria financial aid. The OAPEC ministers agreed to offer £53.9 million to Iraq and £6.8 million to Syria for three months from 1 June 1972.

The OPEC Price Agreement Under Attack

Although the initiative slipped from Saudi Arabia's hands in OAPEC, it was firmly maintained in those hands in OPEC. Nevertheless, even there concessions clearly had to be made to the more radical points of view. At the same time, pressure from 'militants' often strengthens the position of 'moderates' in collective negotiations with outsiders. Thus the companies had to realize that if concessions to the demands of the moderates were not made, more radical demands would be pressed even harder.

The Teheran and Tripoli price agreements, which were discussed above in relation to Iraq's relations with the IPC, had made allowance for a moderate inflation in world prices, but they had not taken into account the problems that might arise from instability in foreign-exchange markets, and in particular from the devaluation of the United States dollar.[1] Iraq, Libya, and Algeria[2] joined to lead a demand for revision of the Teheran agreement after August 1971 when the United States suspended the convertibility of the dollar into gold. At Geneva in January 1972 an agreement was reached with the companies for an increase in posted prices on account of the dollar devaluation of December 1971, but Iraqi officials thought that the formula adopted did not fully adjust prices for the fall in the dollar. When a second devaluation occurred in February 1973, the three countries again joined to press the issue. A ministerial committee consisting of representatives of Iraq, Libya, and Kuwait was established to negotiate. Iraq let it be known that she intended unilaterally to declare higher tax reference prices if the companies did not give satisfaction. In June 1973 a second agreement was reached, but only after the original negotiating committee had been enlarged by the addition of Saudi Arabia and Iran.

Iraq led a major attack on the Teheran agreement in the closing days of June 1973 at the Thirty-fourth Conference of OPEC and proposed that the agreement be scrapped entirely and that tax reference prices be determined unilaterally by OPEC countries acting together. This effort attracted as little support as had a similar attack by Algeria at an OPEC meeting in Vienna the previous March. But inflation was continuing to reduce the real price of oil and OPEC made it clear that something must be done to revise the relevant terms of the Teheran agreements. OPEC was pressing forward all the time, but the pace was moderated and controlled by the judgement of the conservative members, especially Saudi Arabia and Iran.[3]

The economic and political judgements of these countries had to take into account a wide variety of considerations: pressure from the more militant members of OPEC, political relations with Western countries, especially the United States, political rivalries within the Middle East as well as political co-operation, especially with respect to the problem of Israel, relations with the oil companies, and changes in market and other circumstances affecting the appropriateness of the agreements negotiated with the companies. It was the continued change in the oil market, together with continued general inflation, that in the first instance brought Saudi Arabia and Iran to accept that the time had come when radical revision of the price terms of the Teheran agreement was necessary. The October war brought them to agree that the time was ripe for the assumption by host governments of the power unilaterally to determine prices.

Nevertheless, although one must be careful not to place excessive weight on the effectiveness of Iraqi pressure for revision of the price agreements and for assertion of the host governments' right to set prices, the Iraqis, led by Saadoon Hammadi, Minister of Oil and Minerals, tirelessly exerted every bit of influence they had. When in July and August 1973 market prices steadily approached and then overtook posted prices, Iraq sent delegations to Saudi Arabia and Kuwait to press the issue. The Saudis conferred with the Iranians. The OAPEC Council of Ministers discussed the problem.

By September it was clear that revision of the price agreements would be proposed at the OPEC meeting in the middle of the month. Shaikh Yamani stated that the Teheran agreement was now 'dead' in view of the 'dramatic change in circumstances': surging market demand had produced a 'fierce upward pressure on prices'. He indicated the types of revisions to be proposed: an increase in tax reference prices sufficient to raise them substantially above the prices realized in the market, provision for a mechanism to ensure that they stayed above market prices, and a more realistic provision for annual price increases to take account of inflation. If a satisfactory agreement was not reached with the companies, the governments might exercise the right asserted in the 1968 'Declaratory Statement' of OPEC and themselves set prices to prevent any deterioration in the terms of trade between oil and manufactured goods.[4]

The September OPEC meeting duly called for a revision of the agreements and for the opening of negotiations between the companies and a ministerial committee of the member countries bordering the Gulf which was appointed for the purpose. Negotiations began on 8 October. The OPEC counter-proposal in response to a company offer of a modest increase asked for more than the companies were prepared to consider, and on 12 October the companies asked for an adjournment of the negotiations. Since by then the Arab–Israeli war had been going on for six days, it was inevitable that the governments a few days later should decide to dispense with negotiations and to announce the new prices. Thus the long-pressed demand of Iraq that governments alone set prices was at last satisfied, but the final decision was unrelated to Iraqi pressure.

OPEC Negotiates Participation Arrangements

The price agreements effectively gave the OPEC countries a right to participate in the setting of tax reference prices for crude oil, and thus met their immediate primary objective. The other major item left on OPEC's agenda for collective negotiation with the companies was the question of government participation in the ownership of the oil-producing companies. Directly after the conclusion of the monetary agreement in Geneva in January 1972, Zeki Yamani opened negotiations with the companies that were to lead eventually to the assumption of control over their industries by the governments of the oil-exporting countries. We have already seen how these negotiations influenced those between Iraq and the IPC.

As the pressure on the companies to negotiate acceptable participation terms grew, the prospect that in the absence of agreement the individual governments might nationalize was increasingly threatening, usually implicitly but sometimes explicitly, particularly after the IPC nationalization. By then, however, the companies had accepted participation in principle and the negotiations were primarily concerned with compensation, the terms on which the companies would be able to acquire the oil to which the governments would become entitled, and the rate at which the equity of the host governments would grow over time. Nevertheless, the negotiations were very difficult, and before a satisfactory agreement could be reached with the companies King Faisal of Saudi Arabia had himself to intervene, warning the companies of serious consequences and even hinting at a government takeover of operations if the issue were not settled satisfactorily.

The agreement that was finally worked out in New York in October 1972 between Yamani and the companies laid down general principles within which each of the governments would negotiate its individual agreement with its own concessionaires. It provided for an initial participation of 25 per cent rising gradually to 51 per cent on 1 January 1983. Compensation would be the net book value of assets adjusted upward for inflation ('updated book value'). Arrangements were made for the companies to purchase some of the government share of oil in order to enable them to meet their sales commitments and refining needs, the prices to be determined in individual negotiations according to certain principles outlined in the general agreement.

The outcome of the participation negotiations directly affected Iraq with respect to the Basra Petroleum Company and, of greater importance, with respect to the compensation that still remained to be settled with the IPC. The Iraqis did not like 'updated book value' as the basis of compensation, preferring net (or written-down) book value, which would be much lower, especially in Iraq where there had not been much investment in the oil industry for a number of years. Iraq also had reservations about the fact that compensation was payable in dollars to be converted into sterling at the rate current at the time, since Iraq's revenues were normally paid directly in sterling. Also, from a political point of view, Iraq preferred to await the decision of Kuwait. The Kuwaiti government had approved the agreement, but it seemed likely that the Assembly might cause difficulties. Moreover, Iraq did not want to sign any agreements with the companies until all outstanding issues with them were settled. With the IPC settlement in February 1973, there was some discussion of the possibility that Iraq might accept a participation agreement with the BPC. Nothing came of this before the outbreak of the October war, which brought changed conditions on all fronts.

Oil as a 'Political Weapon'

In spite of the failure of the oil embargo during the 1967 war, the possibilities of exercising the political control of Arab governments over a large proportion of world oil supplies in a way which would advance the Arab cause in the struggle against Israel remained a subject of intense discussion in the Arab world. All agreed that in some sense oil resources could be so used, but there were wide differences of view about appropriate strategy.

During 1972 the Arabs were becoming increasingly restless at the lack of progress in persuading Israel to take seriously their insistence that the United Nations Resolutions be complied with. Demands that the oil-exporting countries should use their control over oil to force a solution were rising in intensity in the Arab world. The Kuwaitis and the Saudis argued that the flow of oil revenues should not be prejudiced by a curtailment of oil supplies because the revenues were needed and should be used to strengthen the Arab economies for the final struggle. The Cairo-based Arab Economic Council approved a report of a committee of experts which recommended, among other things, that increased pressure should be exerted on the United States and others through a reduction in production and an increase in prices. The Iraqis again proposed to the Arab Defence Council that the interests of countries supporting Israel should be nationalized, but if a government preferred not to nationalize, it should reduce supplies to the United States and threaten to reduce them to other countries supporting Israel. The proposal also called for the withdrawal of financial reserves from the banks of such countries.

During 1973 the Arabs intensified their efforts to bring home to the Western world the injustice of the Israeli treatment of the Palestinians and of the Israeli occupation of Arab lands. Attention was focussed particularly on the United States in order to persuade her government to modify its almost complete and uncritical support of Israel and Israeli policies. The Palestinians, supported by large sections of the Arab press, by militant Arab groups, and by the left wing in many other countries as well as by the Iraqi, Libyan, and Algerian governments, continually pressed for the direct use of oil as a political weapon in the struggle; but the country that really counted, especially with the United States, was Saudi Arabia.

On this issue, as on others, the Saudis were cautious, although their commitment to the struggle against Israel was no less firm. They preferred to hold their fire until they saw a good chance of success; they lacked the flamboyant and precipitate emotionalism of the Iraqis and the desperation of the Palestinians. But by 1973 the 'energy crisis' and the rapidly growing dependence of the United States on imports from the Middle East were opening the way to successful action, and the Saudis began to take advantage of the emerging situation. Presumably also they were aware that war might be near. Saudi Arabia had always had especially close links with the United States, both economically (Aramco is entirely composed of American companies) and politically, but in April 1973 Zeki Yamani warned the United States government that any expansion of Saudi oil production would be linked to United States attitudes towards Israel and that Saudi Arabia would not continue to supply increasing amounts of oil if the United States did not change her policy.

In May Kuwait joined Iraq, Algeria, and Libya in a short symbolic cessation of oil production on the occasion of the 25th anniversary of the foundation of the Israeli state. Also in May, Nadim al-Pachachi, an Iraqi former Secretary General of OPEC and an oil consultant of considerable weight, called on the Arab oil-producing countries to freeze production at existing levels until Israel agreed to withdraw from the occupied territories. In June, the Saudis again stated that the Arabs were ready to refrain from expanding exports to countries supporting Israel. In July, President al-Bakr reiterated Iraq's earlier call on the Arabs to adopt the policy advocated by Iraq at the meeting of the Arab Defence Council the previous year. And at the end of August King Faisal himself stated on American television:

> We do not want to place any restrictions on our oil exports to the United States, but America's complete support of Zionism against Arabs makes it extremely difficult for us to continue to supply United States petroleum needs and even to maintain our friendly relations with the United States.[5]

When the war broke out, the OPEC countries were engaged in renegotiating the price terms of the Teheran agreement with the companies, but, as we have already seen, they did not use these negotiations to impose penal prices in connection with the war. It was the companies who suspended the negotiations, requesting an adjournment, and only then did the OPEC governments decide to impose without further discussion the prices they had already proposed to the companies. In other words, prices were not used as a 'political weapon'.

Iraq was the first country to bring oil into the arena for political purposes when on 7 October she decided to retaliate against the United States for her support of Israel by nationalizing (with compensation) the American interests in the Basra Petroleum Company; she also called on other Arab countries to nationalize American interests and to suspend exports to the United States and other countries supporting Israel. Ten days later the oil ministers of the ten OAPEC countries agreed on a plan to cut production progressively until Israel withdrew from the territories occupied in 1967 and until Palestinian rights were restored. Saudi Arabia was unwilling to embargo exports to the United States immediately, still hoping that the United States government would modify its policy in response to Arab appeals and pressure and that a flexible approach would give the United States time to reconsider her position. Other countries were free to impose an embargo, and most did so.

Shipments of oil from Banias were suspended on 8 October for security reasons and on 11 October the Banias storage tanks were damaged by an Israeli raid. Tartus was also bombed and liftings were suspended, but Tripoli continued to operate. The Arab governments embargoed oil first to the United States and later to the

Netherlands and introduced a series of graduated cutbacks in production. But Iraq did not observe the embargo, did not cut back production, and continued exports without any control over their destination. Exports from Tripoli reportedly reached some 700,000 b/d, or 40 per cent above rated capacity; Banias remained out of action.

With the United Nations call for a cease-fire and its acceptance by Israel and Egypt, Iraq announced that she was consulting the Soviet Union and the Arab states which were parties to the cease-fire, and reserved her position. When the Arab states intensified their production cuts, Iraq publicly dissociated herself from their actions.

That a country which had been one of the leading advocates of a ruthless use of oil in the Israeli struggle should take such little action aroused much criticism in other Arab countries. The Iraqi government's official, and extremely disingenuous, explanation issued at the beginning of November presented the following argument:[6] United States 'imperialism' had plans to persuade friendly countries that only a United States–Zionist victory could ensure stable oil supplies to the world and was attempting to form a consumer bloc to reassert its control over world oil. Arabs should be careful to differentiate between friend and foe in using oil as a weapon and should help the friendly and punish the hostile. Otherwise their policy would give credence to the United States argument. Therefore Iraq was opposed to the decision taken in Kuwait by OAPEC countries on 17 October to cut back oil production 'because it will lead to the fulfillment of the objectives of US policy in that it lumps the states of Western and Eastern Europe together with American in one trench for the purpose of confronting them with the same crisis . . .' Friendly countries would feel that the Arabs were harming them in spite of their moderate attitudes.

Iraq held that the appropriate actions for the use of oil as a weapon were nationalization of American and other hostile interests, denial of oil to supporters of Israel but full supplies to friendly countries, and the withdrawal of Arab funds from the banks of hostile countries. Iraqi shipments from Banias were resumed at the beginning of November and by the middle of the month Iraq's oil shipments were back to the pre-war level of some 2 million barrels a day; all cutbacks imposed by OAPEC were ignored. It did not seem that Iraq would be inconvenienced by her use of the 'oil weapon', especially since she was merely pursuing her long-run policy of nationalizing the foreign interests in her oil industry.

Along with Libya, Iraq refused to attend the sixth Arab Summit Conference in Algiers (26–28 November), where the Arab heads of state agreed to continue the embargo and production cutbacks and reaffirmed the Arab objectives in the struggle. Just before the conference the Iraqi press published a statement from an 'official spokesman' of the Follow-up Committee on Oil Affairs and Implementation of Agreements of the RCC which again demanded that harder blows be struck directly at the United States, while friendly countries should be treated favourably. In administering their oil policies, the Arab countries were in fact attempting to give favourable treatment to such countries, but since they were not able in practice to control the distribution of world oil supplies, and could do no more than prevent their concessionaires from shipping Arab oil to the embargoed countries, attempts of this kind had little effect.[7]

In November Saadoon Hammadi again explained at length Iraq's oil policy in extensive interviews with the Beirut newspaper *Al-Anwar* and the Paris *Le Monde*.[8] The interviews added little to earlier statements. Hammadi stressed that oil exports should be linked directly to development assistance, and that revenues should be put to the 'service of the Arab cause in Palestine'. Emphasizing that the real battle was with the United States and that nationalization of the oil companies was the only way to wipe out United States interests and 'liberate' oil wealth, he nevertheless was careful to state that other American companies which wanted to work with Iraq and serve her interests in promoting economic development would be welcome. In the *Al-Anwar* interview the minister admitted that Iraqi oil production was much higher in 1973 than it had been in 1972, but in reply to the question how he reconciled the increase in production with Iraq's stated policy that oil should be used in the struggle against Israel, Hammadi stated:

> Iraq as part of the Arab nation certainly uses its oil production and the revenues from it in the service of the Arab cause in Palestine. This was dictated to us by previous considerations, the condition of our oil policy, the direction of our exports and our trade links. For these reasons there is no connection between our use of oil as a weapon and our increase in production.

As if aware of the vague and unconvincing nature of this reply, Hammadi added, irrelevantly, that the increase in oil production is 'not as large as it appears' and is 'only partial compensation' for the failure of the IPC companies to increase output earlier.

Hammadi repeated the call for the withdrawal of funds from United States banks and their employment in the development of Arab countries or their deposit in the banks of 'friendly countries'. It is not clear that Iraqi leaders realized how ineffective their financial proposals would be at that time before the distribution of oil funds could seriously disrupt financial markets. To withdraw funds from dollar accounts, for example, would require Iraq to buy some other foreign currency, either from the United States itself or from another country. Thus, the action would merely redistribute Iraq's holdings of foreign exchange, and if this were seen to be an action designed to upset currency markets for political reasons, the Central Banks of the world could easily (and probably would) have offset it through operations of their own, unless, of course, the dollars were sold to the Eastern European countries. It is difficult to believe that Iraq wanted to put her foreign-exchange reserves in roubles or zlotys, yet by 'friendly countries' Iraq usually referred primarily (though not exclusively) to Eastern Europe.

The demand that withdrawn funds should be used to develop Arab or African countries could only increase, directly or indirectly, exports from the United States, since oil revenues in foreign exchange can be spent only on *foreign* goods and services; dollar funds can be used to buy American goods or to pay other foreigners for their goods which, in turn, permits the foreigners to purchase American goods in their turn. Thus, demands often heard from Iraqis (as well as other Arabs) that revenues should be 'brought back' to Arab countries are simply demands that they be spent on imports. This in itself solves few problems of development. It is therefore possible that such demands were made largely for propaganda purposes, but Iraqi leaders have in other contexts often showed little understanding of international financial markets, foreign-exchange revenues, and the relation between foreign and domestic transactions.

Iraq, having refused to accept the Arab policy, was barred from attending meetings of the Arab oil ministers and complained that some Arab countries aimed at isolating her. The government may really have believed that the Arab policy was self-defeating, but it was difficult for critics to understand how a government which had been so insistent on the importance of the unity of OPEC in its successful negotiations with the companies could so blatantly refuse to act in unity with its fellow Arab governments in OAPEC in time of war.[9] To do so would not have prevented Iraq from nationalizing the companies if she chose to do so, nor from continuing to press her point of view about the treatment of friendly countries. It seemed likely to Iraq's critics that the Baath government was attempting to score an ideological point against the other members of OAPEC which it thought would embarrass them, and at the same time to remain free to expand its own exports without restraint. In taking the action it did the Iraqi government may have believed that the cutbacks would not bring about the results desired and therefore that Iraq was not doing any damage to the Arab cause by refusing to co-operate,[10] but it is also likely that the government's obligations to the Soviet Union and Eastern Europe under the barter agreements were an important consideration as well as her need for arms.

In the interviews with *Al-Anwar* and *Le Monde,* Hammadi referred to the demand for large increases in prices as a way of using the 'oil weapon'. He stated that he did not think a large increase was desirable, although he insisted that the price of oil should bear a stable relation to the price of other commodities in order to protect the purchasing power of oil revenues. He stressed particularly the effect of higher prices on the currency reserves of 'friendly' countries, and on the developing countries of Asia and Africa. He also discussed the possible repercussions from the industrialized countries whose economies could be put in 'real jeopardy'. These included the possibility that they might search for sources of energy other than oil and attempt to confront the exporting countries with economic sanctions; high prices might also lead to economic instability in the industrialized world. In any of these circumstances the economic damage suffered by the producing countries might exceed the benefits of 'unlimited price increases'.

Saddam Hussain, the Iraqi Vice-President, made an even more strongly worded statement a few days later in which he accused 'reactionary ruling circles well-known for their links with America and American monopolistic interests' of rejecting all of Iraq's 'serious proposals' to use oil as a weapon and of only taking action when Iraq's nationalization, public opinion, and the course of the war forced them to. While approving the embargo, Saddam again deplored the production cutbacks as a dangerous policy because it encouraged friends to distrust the Arabs while strengthening the position of the United States and harmonizing with American policy. The increase in prices made the Arabs appear extortionate, increased the profits of American companies, and gave 'imperialism and Zionism the excuse it had been looking for to commit hideous crimes against the rights of the Arab people under the pretext of defending the world and human civilization'. Nationalization was the weapon which would 'really force America to stop supporting the enemy'.[11] Within a month, however, Iraq was to be found in the camp of those countries opposing any negotiations on prices; demands for lower prices were not again to be heard from her, although she was later to be accused of shading her own oil prices to increase sales at the expense of other OPEC members.

Iraq's Policy Towards Oil-Pricing

Iraq was present at the OPEC meeting on 22–23 December 1973

when the posted price of oil was raised from $3.036 a barrel to $11.651 for the 'marker crude' (Arabian Light, 34° API), thus increasing government 'take' from $2.998 to $7.008 and tax-paid cost to the companies from $3.098 to $7.108 a barrel. Increases of this magnitude were opposed by Saudi Arabia, but the Shah of Iran wanted even larger increases. Some sales in the open market had at one time exceeded $17.00 a barrel, and the Shah insisted that the market must set the price. Moreover, he argued that the minimum cost of developing alternative sources of energy, notably coal and shale, was equivalent to about $7.00 a barrel, which was therefore an appropriate government 'take' from oil.

Saudi Arabia publicly denounced the price of $11.651 as too high and several times called for a reduction; Iraq did not support the Saudi position, and in the discussions in OPEC on 7–8 January, Iraq, along with Libya, vigorously opposed a reduction in prices in accordance with the Geneva agreement of June 1973 on currency fluctuations, in the negotiation of which she had participated. The agreement had provided that posted prices should be adjusted every month according to an index which reflected the change in the value of the United States dollar relative to that of eleven other currencies. Because of the appreciation of the dollar, the application of this index would have brought a fall of around 6 per cent in posted prices. This did not meet with the approval of Iraq.

Although refusing to accept the agreed Geneva formula, OPEC decided not to raise the price of oil during the first quarter of 1974. In March it took a similar decision for the second quarter. Iraq accepted both of these decisions, but Saadoon Hammadi felt it necessary to explain why he had done so instead of demanding the increase which market conditions warranted. Hammadi expressed Iraq's concern for a 'healthy, balanced and sustained growth' of the world economy, and particularly of the less-developed countries, which further increases in the price of oil might jeopardize. For this reason, he said, Iraq had agreed to a 'freeze' of oil prices in spite of the fact that increases were justified by the market and by the needs of the oil-exporting countries, for which oil revenues were the chief source of foreign exchange and oil their chief resource.

By the opening of the third quarter of the year, when OPEC again took up the question whether to raise prices, Iraq had joined other members of OPEC in a strong and at times bitter attack on the Saudi Arabian insistence that the prices should not go up. Only the threat by Saudi Arabia that she would unilaterally cut prices and increase production if OPEC members attempted to raise prices brought agreement to increase government revenues by increasing royalty payments (from 12.5 per cent to 14.5 per cent for most countries) instead of prices, which remained for another quarter at the same level as before.

Saudi Arabia as the dominant force in OPEC was firmly established; her very large oil reserves gave her such power over total market supply that prices could not easily be increased without Saudi consent. At the beginning of the last quarter of 1974, she won the day again, but with greater difficulty; posted prices were maintained at the existing level, but once again the cost to the companies of lifting oil was increased. While agreeing with other members of OPEC that company profits were too high because the margin between the cost of oil to them and market prices was too great, the Saudis maintained that the consumers and the importing countries could not afford an increase. (Pressure from the industrialized countries for a reduction in oil prices was very intense at this time and the United States was leading an attempt to organize co-operation among the consuming countries both to co-ordinate their energy policies and to induce OPEC to reduce prices.) The Saudis therefore wanted a reduction in both posted and government sales prices, but would accept an increase in tax and royalty rates, thus increasing the cost of oil to the companies.[12] Royalties went up from 14.5 per cent for most countries to 16.75 per cent.

Once again Iraq went along with the OPEC decision, but again voiced strong objections. In the Iraqi view, not only were prices too low but the pricing system favoured the major international companies over the national oil companies, especially in times of surplus when there were pressures of supply on prices. Iraq insisted that there should be a single price applicable both to government sales and to all oil received by the companies. Production programming should be introduced to control total supply.

The pricing system was becoming increasingly complicated and it did intentionally favour the large international companies. Posted prices were still used for tax-reference purposes; they were also used as a reference for the determination of prices for the sale of government-owned oil. The governments (or national oil companies) sold their own 'participation crude' (about 60 per cent of total output obtained by virtue of their 60 per cent ownership in the producing companies under the revised participation agreements) partly in the open market but mostly to their foreign partners under 'buy-back' arrangements. Some countries, notably Iraq, also had oil of their own apart from the participation agreements. Government-owned oil did not move at posted prices but at government sales prices (at that time between 93 and 95 per cent of posted prices). The companies disposed of their own 'equity' oil, and that which they bought back from the governments, in the normal fashion: in their own refineries, to fulfil their contracts, or in the open market at market prices.

Government revenues consisted of a combination of receipts from direct sales in the market, sales to foreign partners, and taxes and royalties paid by the foreign partners on their own share of the output. The cost of crude to the companies was an amalgam of the cost of production plus taxes and royalties on their equity crude (tax-paid cost), and the cost of buying crude from the governments. It was not possible to calculate the average cost of a barrel of crude to the companies or to estimate the average revenues from a barrel of crude to a government unless one knew the weight of each of these various elements in the purchases and sales.[13] Company oil supplies included a large element (mostly around 40 per cent) of their own equity crude which they obtained at tax-paid cost and thus well below government sales prices, and the Iraqis pointed out that this put the companies in a position to compete with the national oil companies by cutting prices below government sales prices in the market.

The Iraqi government argued that the most important objective of the oil-exporting countries was to obtain control over their own oil by strengthening the position of their national oil companies in world oil markets. The fact that the major companies had access to supplies at a cost below the government sales price could push market prices down in periods of oil surplus and force the national oil companies to lower their own prices or lose their markets. The increases in taxes and royalties decided on by OPEC in September had helped to raise the cost of oil to the companies, but it did not go far enough to eliminate entirely the companies' margin over government-owned oil, and Iraq believed that this margin should be entirely eliminated.

Iraq's views, though soundly argued and to a large extent correct, did not get widespread support in OPEC. Most governments were willing to give their former concessionaires (now their foreign partners) preferential access to crude oil. They valued the companies' expertise in production and recognized their usefulness in disposing of the government's share of the oil. Few were as yet ready to attempt to build up their own companies as independent international marketers on a large scale and most were prepared to make use of the companies for the time being. Since the foreign companies were still partners with the governments in oil operations, it was appropriate that they should receive oil at tax-paid cost. At the same time, there was a consensus that the profit margin for the companies on their crude-oil purchases and sales should be strictly controlled to prevent their earning excess profits.

This approach was very different from that of Iraq, who had

ambitious plans for her own oil company. The government now controlled 68 per cent of Iraq's oil and sold most of it. Buy-back arrangements for the companies had not been adopted and INOC intended to sell as much of its own oil as it possibly could. The whole thrust of Iraq's internal policy towards her concessionaires, and in OPEC, was towards the 'liberation' of Arab oil, and for Iraq this meant the use of foreign companies as contractors only, without special privileges in their access to oil. This view was not shared by all the members of OPEC, and especially by the most powerful ones, Iran and Saudi Arabia.

On the other hand, the difficulties posed by the decline in oil consumption were also recognized. By the middle of 1974 the oil shortage, which had led to rising market prices as companies competed for supplies, was disappearing. In the summer oil-product prices in Europe began to sag. Oil output from the Middle East began to fall in June and continued to be depressed, falling in January 1975 to a level below that of January 1974 when the embargo and cutbacks were still in force. A number of countries, notably Venezuela, had long strongly supported Iraq's demand for production control. Most others accepted that it would be too difficult to enforce, and in any case it had no chance against Saudi and Iranian opposition. Moreover, OPEC was still searching for an efficient method of pricing oil.

An important aspect of Iraq's demand for production control was the problem posed by the fact that crude oil is not a homogeneous commodity. Crudes differ in quality, which makes some of them more, and some of them less, valuable to refiners. Hence their prices differ. At the same time, a refiner can, at a cost, substitute one crude for another to achieve the combination of refined end products most appropriate for the market in which he sells. If he has to incur extra costs in order to use a less suitable crude oil, its net value to him is, of course, reduced. Whenever the relative prices of different crudes become out of line with their relative net value to refiners, demand for the underpriced crudes will rise relative to that for overpriced crudes. Such changes in refiners' demands will not be reflected in corrective price changes if the factors determining the relative prices of crude oil are not sensitive to market changes. Thus, underpriced crudes would get more than their 'fair' share in a market governed by an administered pricing system, and overpriced crudes less.

OPEC had continued the traditional posted-price system which had been established by the international companies decades earlier, under which the posted prices of different crudes were related to each other by a formula which took account of the differences in their quality, primarily with respect to specific gravity and sulphur content. The higher the specific gravity of a crude, the higher the price, because when refined, it yielded a larger proportion of the lighter products, such as gasoline or naphtha, which were more valuable than the heavier products, such as fuel oil. The higher the sulphur content, the lower the price because of consumer preference for low sulphur products and the cost of removing the sulphur.

OPEC had adopted a medium-quality crude oil (34°, 1.7 per cent sulphur) called Arabian Light, as the 'marker crude'. The prices of all other crudes were related to the price of the marker crude and carried discounts or premiums according to quality. Crude oils delivered to Mediterranean terminals also carried a 'freight premium' over crudes at the Gulf in accordance with the OPEC price agreements in order that the exporting countries should reap the advantage of the fact that freight costs from the Mediterranean were lower than those from the Gulf, especially after the closure of the Suez Canal. When freight-rates fell, an insufficiently flexible premium would tend to overprice Mediterranean crude oils.

The composition of the demand for oil products is by no means stable; it differs in different markets, changes according to the seasons of the year, is affected by changes in industrial activity, technology, and many other factors. Such changes are reflected in the demands of the refiners for the different crude oils. It is very difficult, if not impossible, for a system of administered prices to maintain the relative prices of crude oils in appropriate relation to market demand at all times. This is the notorious problem of 'price differentials' which in this period caused persistent strains in OPEC.

The Iraqi government had been very much annoyed when in 1971 it had not been able to claim under the Tripoli agreement a premium for the quality of its Mediterranean oil equivalent to that of Libyan low-sulphur oil. It had been long at loggerheads with the IPC over the price of Basra oil, which the company insisted was too high. After the nationalizations and the development of INOC's production the government became responsible for selling more and more of the country's oil. It naturally became very much more directly concerned with the level of market prices for its oil than it had been when the companies had to pay taxes on posted prices which they could not reduce even though they had to reduce sales prices to maintain offtake.

Early in 1974 exports of Kirkuk oil were stagnating and in May exports fell to only 600,000 b/d or about half the capacity of the pipeline and export system. The steep drop in May was accounted for partly by the cessation in the middle of the month of the delivery of about 241,000 b/d to the IPC as compensation for the nationalized assets, and partly by the depression in European demand. The latter was aggravated for Kirkuk crude by the fall in freight-rates, which had improved the relative position of the Gulf crudes. There was evidence that Kirkuk crude was overpriced. In July Iraq reduced the price of Kirkuk oil at Mediterranean ports from $12.20 to $11.50 a barrel.[14] In January 1975 there was a further reduction to $11.20; later Iraq was accused of secret price-cutting.

That 'market forces' should govern the distribution of demand among OPEC countries was no more acceptable to Iraq than that they should determine either prices or the total output of oil, for the Iraqi government believed firmly in a 'planned' system. The development of an agreed programme not only to decide the level of total production but also to allocate it among the member countries of OPEC was, to the Iraqis, the only sensible procedure and they never ceased to press this point of view. Quotas should be allocated to different countries according to equitable criteria which would take into account such things as a country's oil reserves, its development needs, and its historical position. In this last respect Iraq believed she would have a strong case for special consideration. Even before the dispute with the IPC and the expropriation under Law 80 of most of her concession, Iraq had complained, as we have seen, of the slow rate at which the companies had developed her oil relative to that of the other countries, and the passage of Law 80 aggravated the situation. Iraq was therefore eager to expand her oil production as fast as possible and believed that the discrimination she had suffered at the hands of the companies in the past was a good reason for especially favourable treatment in the future.

All OPEC members recognized that the problem of appropriate price differentials was a serious one and was complicated by the emergence of surplus capacity as consumption remained depressed, but they saw no way of obtaining an agreed solution to it. In the meantime, the level of prices was the more immediate problem since inflation was seriously eroding unit revenues; the least that should be done was to increase prices enough to offset the increase in the prices of imported goods.[15] But Saudi Arabia, perhaps wanting to retain influence in the United States, remained determined to prevent any increase in the posted prices of oil and to bring about a reduction if possible.

Agreement on the level of prices was to prove intractable for a considerable time to come, with Saudi Arabia refusing the strong pressure of most of the other producers for ever-higher prices. The Saudis have very large reserves of oil and probably have more to lose from an acceleration of the rate of substitution of other energy for oil than any other country; moreover, they cannot invest in the development of the country at the rate at which revenues are already accruing. Thus, their own interest coincided with the interests not only of the major consuming countries, but perhaps even more of the poor developing countries, as well as with that of the international monetary system which, though adjusting more effectively than had been feared in 1974, nevertheless continued to be upset by the large surplus oil revenues. There is reason to believe that the Saudis were genuinely concerned about the effect of further heavy increases in oil prices on the world economy (and also on its politics), which could have undesired incidental repercussions on themselves.

Iraq was in a different position from the other countries at this time since she had nationalized her concessionaires, except for the residual interest in the BPC, and her revenues therefore came from sales of oil.[16] The revenues of most of the other countries were still derived from a combination of government market sales, sales to the companies under the participation agreements, and taxes paid by the companies. Together these constituted what was called the 'government take' per barrel of oil. In order to meet in some degree the insistent demand for an increase in revenues while avoiding an increase in prices, OPEC decided in December 1974 to fix the average government take instead of prices. This was to average $10.12 a barrel on the marker crude, effective from 1 January 1975 to 31 September 1975. Thus government sales prices were to remain unchanged for nine months. Posted prices lost their traditional function as tax-reference prices. The construction of a new system of oil pricing was beginning.

As a result of the OPEC decisions, Iraq reduced the prices of her oil from both Basra and Kirkuk, with 60 days credit in both cases, effective on 1 January 1975. The new prices still left Kirkuk oil overpriced relative to oil from the Gulf, and for the second quarter of 1975 prices were again reduced, the reductions being much more for Kirkuk than for Basra. Iraq was accused in the trade press of cutting prices even below those announced in order to sell Kirkuk oil, and of moving much of it under barter, which made the price difficult to discern in any case. Both accusations were of course denied by Iraq, but the suspicion that prices were being cut persisted as Iraq's output continued to rise at a higher rate than that of the rest of the Middle East. Price differentials were becoming an increasingly difficult problem for OPEC members as oil consumption continued to be depressed and the existing relative prices became increasingly out of line with the market, especially for heavy crudes. While defending herself against charges of price-cutting and insisting that the fall in consumption was deliberately engineered by 'United States imperialism', Iraq, along with most other members of OPEC, demanded more and more loudly an increase in oil prices.

At the September 1975 meeting of OPEC a 10 per cent increase was agreed, but only, according to the *Middle East Economic Survey,* after the 'worst bout of international tension the Organisation had experienced since the royalty expensing drama of 1964' and a threat by Saudi Arabia that she would freeze her own prices and let her output rise to the limit of capacity if the demands for a 15–20 per cent increase by the 'hard-liners' led by Iran and Iraq were accepted.[17] Such action by Saudi Arabia would have been disastrous for OPEC at that time and at such a prospect the members agreed on a compromise put forward by Kuwait with the assistance of Algeria and Venezuela and the discreet help of Iraq.

The decision was to increase the price of marker crude by 10 per cent effective from 1 October and to hold it until 30 June 1976, when it would be reviewed. There was no mention of posted prices nor of the earlier method of attempting to fix the average government take, and so another step was taken towards the simplification of the pricing system. Exactly how prices of other crudes would be related to the marker remained unclear, however, since these were traditionally set as a percentage of posted prices. In other words, no definitive action was taken on the problem of price differentials. A certain amount of informal agreement had been worked out in OPEC's Economic Commission on the discounts and premiums relating to sulphur and gravity differentials on crude delivered to the Gulf. Similar agreement did not exist for Mediterranean crudes, and both Algeria and Saudi Arabia charged that Iraqi oil was underpriced by 30¢ a barrel (and Libyan oil by 50–60¢ a barrel).

The market for the heavier crudes with high fuel-oil yields continued weak and prices were depressed. The Saudis and Kuwaitis concluded that the differential for the heavy crudes with a high sulphur content was too small and they therefore cancelled the increased prices for these crudes that they had announced earlier in accordance with the 10 per cent increase agreed by OPEC, and substituted increases ranging from 8.4 to 9.6 per cent depending on the crude. The widened differential between the marker and the heavier crudes immediately provoked a sharp and intemperate attack from Iraq, who accused Kuwait of making unilateral price reductions threatening the unity of OPEC, and also of serving the interests of the monopolies and the International Energy Agency. In a dignified reply, Kuwait argued that her crude had been overpriced, and that she had made the adjustments in the light of adjustments by other producers and of economic studies of the positions of other member countries of OPEC. Kuwait undertook not to allow any buyer of Iraqi crude to shift to Kuwaiti crude or to allow her own output to rise beyond the average of the first nine months of the year unless and until an agreement on differentials was reached for OPEC crudes.

To other members of OPEC, Iraq's attack on Kuwait for underpricing her crude had ironic overtones since most believed that Iraq was not only underpricing Kirkuk crude by as much as 10–20 cents a barrel, but also even selling at below the announced price. When the December conference of OPEC opened, Iraq was severely criticized, particularly by the Algerian delegate, for underpricing and for not conforming to OPEC's rules of the game. Iraq denied price-cutting, but also argued that in any case she should be permitted to do it—the others did worse in granting discounts to the international companies with equity in the producing operations. Since the margin allowed the companies was supposed to be insufficient to allow them to compete with government sales, the Iraqi argument implied that the Iraqis should be allowed to undercut the sales price of other governments. It was noted, however, that difficulties in arriving at appropriate differentials were part of Iraq's case for her own proposals for straightforward price-fixing across the board and for production controls; few wondered that Iraq made such difficulties.

In the midst of the debate on these issues the OPEC headquarters in Vienna where the conference was being held was attacked by terrorists and some of the leading officials, including ministers, were kidnapped. Attempts were subsequently made, particularly by Iraq, to get an OPEC Ministerial Conference convened to discuss differentials, but without success. It was reported that Algeria at one time refused to attend such a meeting unless Iraq first reduced the price of her oil. Clearly other countries feared that in any such meeting Iraq would want to use the 'overpricing' of her crude not only to push prices up all around, but also to provide a basis for a pattern of prices and controls which would favour her own position.

The Iraqis were particularly caustic about Saudi Arabian opposition to any policy for programming production. The Iraqi Oil Minister attacked the 'big producers' whose policies were linked to those of foreign countries and who could not even absorb their revenues in their own development and exported them abroad, while at the same time other countries, like Iraq, were in great need of funds.[18] Iraq wanted an allocation of production quotas among OPEC countries which took into account a country's need for funds. This kind of policy was, in effect, a proposal for the allocation of oil revenues according to need. Clearly countries with great financial surpluses, notably Saudi Arabia, Abu Dhabi, and Kuwait, would come off less well than some other countries, were revenue needs to become a criterion for allocating oil-production quotas. It is not surprising that Iraq's proposals found little support, and it is doubtful that the 'unity of OPEC' could easily have survived such an exercise.

At Saudi Arabian insistence, prices remained stable all during 1976, although the same type of conflict occurred in every OPEC session. But some progress was made in dealing with the problem of differentials. The OPEC oil ministers, apart from Iraq, agreed that a procedure similar to that adopted by Algeria should be accepted. Under the 'Algerian formula' relative prices were determined for crudes of differing qualities with reference to product yields and values in major world markets, using the marker crude as a reference base. If adopted by OPEC, a weighted average price with a range of permissible variation could be established for each crude, and the price actually set by member governments would be reviewed periodically by OPEC. Although OPEC governments were unable to reach full agreement on prices for all their crudes, the general notion of a 'price band' seemed acceptable and broad agreement was reached on a temporary basis, with studies still to continue. Only Iraq remained recalcitrant, demanding that all discounts to ex-concessionaires be eliminated (although Iraq was granting concessionary terms to CFP, which Algeria claimed were excessive).

The controversy over Iraqi price-cutting continued, with the Abu Dhabi Oil Minister stating: 'We cannot understand the position of some OPEC member countries which reduce their own market prices while often simultaneously calling for a general OPEC increase. This does nothing to help maintain either OPEC solidarity or the present reasonable level of prices'.[19] And the Saudi minister complained: 'Iraq is dumping its oil at cheap prices. It is the only OPEC country which raised production, while other members cut output'.[20] After the June 1976 meeting of OPEC, which reaffirmed the decision not to raise prices, the prices of most medium and heavy crudes were reduced from 5–10 cents a barrel, although Iraq raised slightly the official price of Basra crude. The Iraqi Oil Minister complained about the failure to increase prices and, commenting on the reductions made for the medium and heavy crudes, he charged that 'the reduction of crude oil prices by certain Arab states is part of the efforts made by various parties to prevent the marketing of nationalized oil'.[21]

In the middle of 1976 demand for oil strengthened as recovery in the industrialized countries seemed to get underway. With the increase in demand there was some hope that competitive pressures on OPEC members would diminish, alleviating the bitterness over the problem of differentials. Moreover, the issue was most acute in the Mediterranean and centred around prices for Kirkuk crude. The completion of the 'strategic pipeline' and the switching of Kirkuk exports from the Mediterranean meant that Iraq was no longer so concerned over Mediterranean prices, at least temporarily. The Saudi Oil Minister maintained strongly that an increase in prices might check the incipient industrial recovery abroad and adversely affect demand which, in turn, might bring further competitive pressures among OPEC members, such as Iraq:

> Saudi Arabia's views are based on the clear economic interests of OPEC, which is to say that oil prices should not be raised in a way which would reduce demand for oil and as a consequence weaken OPEC's position. In fact demand for oil did fall to a point where OPEC members began to compete with each other. Some countries, such as Iraq, lowered their oil prices substantially and entered into competition with other exporting countries, which resulted in a weakening of OPEC's position on the international plane. But when demand for oil increases, we can then raise the price of oil.[22]

It is not easy to evaluate with any precision the extent to which Iraq did cut the prices of her crude as charged by her colleagues in OPEC and in the press. The government consistently denied price-cutting, but at the same time it argued that Iraq had a right to do so in view of the discounts or fees that the international companies received from some other members. Moreover, Iraq did not publish her prices as fully as did other countries, which in itself gave rise to suspicion that there was something to conceal. Iraq was the most insistent of all OPEC countries that the allocation of production through price differentials was not acceptable and threatened the unity of OPEC; she may have deliberately chosen to demonstrate this by her own behaviour.

But the most compelling evidence that Iraq was cutting prices lies in the fact that during the period when complaints from other OPEC members were most intense, Iraqi output was rising much faster than that of other countries of the Middle East. From January to September 1975 Iraqi output rose 28 per cent as contrasted to 16 per cent for the Middle East as a whole. Output from the northern fields alone rose 53 per cent. Average output for 1975 was 17 per cent above that of 1974, while output in the Middle East as a whole was down by 10 per cent. Iraq's output remained high during the first three months of 1976, especially from the northern fields (Kirkuk production in March was nearly 48 per cent above that of January 1974 contrasted to 6 per cent for the Middle East generally), but was falling rapidly from the high peaks of August, September, and October 1975. Output from the southern fields declined from a high of nearly 1.4m. b/d in September 1975 to little over three-quarters of a million in January 1976 as a result of the fall in output of the BPC, 100 per cent of which was nationalized in December. By July, BPC output had climbed back to its early levels, while that of the northern fields had fallen drastically following the cessation of exports to the Mediterranean in April as Kirkuk oil was sent southwards through the new 'strategic' pipeline. The strained relations between Iraq and Syria over transit dues (as well as other questions) cost both countries dearly.

OPEC Divides and Survives

The longstanding strains among OPEC members over the pricing of crude oil finally erupted in open and acrimonious disagreement in December 1976 at the Forty-eighth OPEC Conference in Doha. The Economic Commission Board of OPEC had reported that since the last oil price increase on 1 October 1975, the prices of goods imported by OPEC countries had gone up by 26 per cent. Iraq and Qatar both pressed for increases of this amount in oil prices. Some member countries wanted 15 per cent and others would have accepted 10 per cent. But Saudi Arabia again argued that in view of the weakness of the international economy the price of oil should remain unchanged for another six months. The United Arab Emirates agreed to follow Saudi Arabia's lead, although preferring a 10 per cent rise. No agreement was reached, and 11 members decided to increase prices by 10 per cent as of 1 January 1977, with a further 5 per cent to take effect in July. The Saudis and UAE decided to raise their prices by only 5 per cent for all of 1977. This created a so-called 'two-tier' level of oil prices. Saudi Arabia announced that she would increase output in order to support her position.

The Iraqi Minister of Oil strongly attacked Saudi Arabia and defended the Iraqi insistence that oil prices should have been raised even further with the argument that such an increase would have advanced the prospects of achieving a more equitable world economic system: Iraq consistently argued in both Arab and international forums that her own position, whatever it was, would advance the welfare of the Arab world, the Third World, or even, on occasion, the consumers of oil. She had little weight in OPEC, not only because of the dominance of Iran and particularly of Saudi Arabia in oil supplies, but also because her intransigence on so many issues, her territorial demands on Iran and Kuwait, both OPEC colleagues, and her unrestrained public attacks on others, such as Saudi Arabia, had left her with few allies. The *Middle East Economic Survey* reported Tayeh Abdul Karim, the Oil Minister, as stating:

> Saudi Arabia wanted to impose on OPEC a freeze in oil prices as a guarantee for the implementation of plans for a Middle East settlement. But the world liberation forces and Arab public opinion are well aware that this stand is no more than a means of neutralizing the Arab oil weapon, as well as being a threat to weaken OPEC by breaking the price structure.[23]

In replying to a question about the relationship between OPEC's price decision and the North–South dialogue, he said:

> We believe that the idea of the North–South Dialogue attracted the consumers when oil prices were rising—then, after that, they just lost interest. In our opinion, an increase in prices now will help the Paris Conference to succeed by rekindling interest on the part of consumers. . . . We were one of the first to call for such a conference because we believe such forums are the best means of attaining a more equitable world economic system. Once we see that such an objective might be feasible, we would be prepared to negotiate all sorts of things—including oil prices.[24]

In subsequent months there was considerable confusion in world oil markets while the companies attempted to adjust to the dual system. The Saudis insisted that the companies lifting cheaper Saudi oil should not be permitted to make higher profits as a result, but they had difficulty working out an appropriate mechanism to ensure it. Sales of some other countries, notably Iraq and Iran, fell temporarily as companies moved to lift cheaper oil. Nevertheless, the companies could not antagonize their normal suppliers by shifting too openly and quickly their purchases, since all knew that the two-tier system could not last very long. Moreover, the Saudi effort to expand output to keep down prices was hampered by a severe winter which increased demand, by gales in the Gulf which prevented tanker loadings, and by a serious fire in the oilfields which disrupted production for a while. Nevertheless, the countries charging the higher prices found their own offtake unacceptably reduced.[25]

OPEC suffered for these few months the most serious strains in its sixteen-year history; feelings among some of the member countries ran strong and bitter. But the common interest in the end prevailed, for all could see clearly that they stood to lose a great deal if OPEC failed. The two countries of greatest importance in this respect are Iran and Saudi Arabia; they are undoubtedly rivals for leadership, but both are pragmatic and realistic. In this case the trial of strength was a draw; both governments had made their point and a compromise was reached, with the help of the mediation of the Venezuelan President, Carlos Andrés Pérez, who visited Saudi Arabia, the Gulf countries, Iraq, and Iran during May. The Saudis agreed to raise prices by 5 per cent in July, and Iran along with the other countries agreed to abandon their intention to add a further 5 per cent to the previous level. Iraq strongly objected to this compromise, but eventually agreed to accept it, having little choice in the face of the seasonal weakening of demand that could be expected, the re-emergence of oil surpluses, and the concurrence of other OPEC countries. Saudi Arabia had not expanded her output to full capacity and a number of countries were genuinely worried that if she did so, their exports would be hit even further.

The Saudis had long stated that if no progress was made towards meeting the demands of the developing countries at the Paris Conference on International Economic Co-operation ('North–South dialogue'), which had been dragging on for some time, the world could expect an increase in the price of oil. In the event, no progress was made for a variety of reasons, and this was widely believed to have been a factor in the Saudi decision to increase prices. Although Saudi Arabia, because of her predominance in world oil supplies, was undoubtedly in a position to make her wishes felt, not everyone, and in particular the United States State Department,[26] believed that her insistence on a link between oil prices and the outcome of the CIEC Conference need be taken seriously. Of greater potential importance is the suggestion, frequently made by the Saudis but not so far followed up, that they would take a harder line over the price of oil if effective steps to meet the Arab position in the conflict with Israel were not taken.

Iraq and International Financial Aid

The 'oil crisis' consisted primarily of a sudden necessity for all countries importing oil to pay very much more for their imports. In consequence they faced the alternative of reducing oil consumption or of sending a greater part of their national product abroad to maintain imports (or of incurring large foreign debts in the short run). This not only created economic difficulties for all countries, and very serious difficulties for some, but also made necessary appropriate adjustments in the world's economic and financial system. Nor did the 'oil crisis' erupt in otherwise peaceful waters, for inflation had already taken hold and incipient industrial recession was clearly under way.

The diversion of income to the oil-exporting countries not only had in itself serious recessionary implications for the oil-importing countries, but made necessary a reorganization of international financial flows (so-called 'recycling') and of 'real' flows (an increased import of goods and services by the oil-exporting countries). The general issues associated with these changes are outside the scope of this study, but a specific issue for the oil-exporting countries, including Iraq, was the need to consider how far new riches should be used to aid other countries. They had now the means to give aid and, within limits, they accepted an obligation to do so.

Iraq participates in Arab aid programmes, such as the Arab Fund for Economic and Social Development, and the OAPEC facility for Arab oil-importing countries; she has her own development fund, the Iraq Fund for External Development, established in 1974, which gives aid for development projects in Arab and other developing countries. She has contributed fairly substantially to the so-called 'front-line' countries in the struggle with Israel—Egypt, Jordan, and Syria. She co-operates in OAPEC, the Arab League, and other joint Arab development projects; she invests in joint projects with other governments in Asia and Africa, occasionally contributes supplies of crude oil to the poorer countries, or makes grants or low-interest loans (she has been especially generous to India). We have no reasonably accurate or up-to-date statistics which would enable us to present an estimate of the amounts of concessionary and non-concessionary aid contributed by Iraq in comparison with other oil-exporting countries. What figures appear suggest that Iraq's contribution is relatively modest;[27] she has pressed investment in her own development to the limit—and beyond—and insists on her own needs. She has herself received aid from Kuwait and has borrowed abroad, although such borrowing is probably largely precautionary or a means of ensuring the commitment of foreign countries to the projects for which the loan was intended.[28] In giving assistance, and in her external investment projects, Iraq has demonstrated clear priorities: first for Arab countries, then Islamic countries, other developing countries, and last international agencies.

For most aid-givers the world over, motives for offering assistance to other countries are mixed, but prominent among them is the self-interest of the donor. Iraqi aid to 'front-line' countries to enable them to sustain the military and economic burden and to reconstruct their economies after defeat needs no explanation; aid to other Arab countries is consistent both with Baath insistence on the unity of the Arab world and with Iraq's efforts to win friends in and to influence the governments of other Arab countries; it is a means not only of encouraging them to sympathize with Baath ideology but also of asserting Iraq's leadership, especially against the conservative 'reactionary' countries. Iraq was making increasing efforts in the late 1970s to improve her image abroad, for she had gained a reputation for militant, doctrinaire, and extremely repressive and brutal radicalism, leaning heavily on the Soviet Union, intolerant of her Arab neighbours, and in practice unconstructive in the councils of the Third World.

Iraq opposed multilateral aid through international institutions, notably the International Monetary Fund. Aid contributed in this form is not so closely connected with the donor in the minds of the recipients as is aid directly disbursed; moreover, Iraq, deeply suspicious of the United States, has regarded the IMF as a tool of this big capitalist power and has consistently warned the Arab world against co-operating with it. In May 1977, for example, *Al-Thawra* attacked the effort of the IMF to get the oil-exporting countries to make more of their surplus funds available to the new (Witteveen) IMF aid facility. *Al-Thawra* saw this as primarily an attempt by the United States to get control of Arab funds.[29]

All of the Arab oil-exporting countries have consistently resented the insistence of the rich Western countries that they ought to contribute more to world aid funds in view of the very large revenues they receive. They have pointed out that in spite of the size of these revenues, their people are still poor and their countries still undeveloped; their funds are needed at home now, or will be needed in the future, since oil is a diminishing resource and, for some of them, is almost their only resource. The real standard of living of the rich countries is high and, it can be argued, has been obtained in part by the exploitation of the resources of the Third World, including those of the oil-producers. Hence, the Iraqis (amongst others) insisted that at most the oil-exporters might match the aid offered from the rich countries—they should not be asked to exceed it. The latest OECD figures available at the time of writing show the following contributions in the years 1973–76.

Table IV Financial Flows to Less-Developed Countries
Iraq and OPEC, 1973–76 ($US millions)

	OPEC	*IRAQ*		
	Total net flow	*Total net flow*	*(of which concessional)*	*Total net flow as per cent of GNP*
1973	1,722.4	10.6	10.6	0.19
1974	5,809.3	440.3	423.0	4.17
1975	8,071.6	251.4	251.4	1.9
1976	7,491.7	119.3	96.3	0.75

Source: Unpublished figures of OECD

Among the most favoured countries for bilateral aid were India, Bangladesh, Lebanon, Egypt, Jordan, Somalia, and Sri Lanka.

Notes

1 See above, Chapter 16 and the discussion by Edith Penrose in *The Oil Crisis* (R. Vernon, ed.).

2 Algeria was not a signatory to either agreement, but since the agreements governed oil prices delivered by other countries, Algerian prices would inevitably be affected by them.

3 'Cautious' is perhaps a better word than 'conservative' in this context, especially as applied to Iran. In general, Iran tended to delay arranging her affairs with the oil companies until the Arab countries had settled theirs; and it was only in December 1973, when it was clear it could have an effect, that the Shah took a militantly hard attitude on pricing.

4 See interview with Shaikh Zeki Yamani in *MEES*, 7 September 1973, Supplement.

5 Quoted in *MEES*, 7 September 1973.

6 For the full statement as put out by the Iraqi News Agency see *MEES*, 9 November 1973.

7 For a discussion of the way in which the international companies distributed oil supplies while observing the terms of the embargo, see Robert Stobaugh, 'The Oil Companies in the Crisis' in R. Vernon (ed.), *The Oil Crisis*.

8 The translation of the text of the *Al-Anwar* interview (18 December 1973) is presented in *MEES*, 21 December 1973. The *Le Monde* interview appears in the 19 December 1973 issue of *Le Monde*.

9 Even the Algerians, who were generally among Iraq's strongest defenders, had no sympathy with her wartime position. The Algerian newspaper usually representing government views, *Al-Moudjahid,* wrote on 27 December: 'Baghdad's position is very dogmatic and ineffective, because the Arab cause is at a point where actions speak louder than words. The Iraqi Oil Minister himself has revealed that Iraqi oil production has never been so high; it is approaching three million barrels a day. Where is all this oil going? It is quite simply injected into the world system and by this very fact considerably improves the supply situation. If the Iraqi Minister calls this an effective contribution to the Arab cause and to the rights of the Palestinians we, for our part, think it no such thing. We regret deeply writing these words, but by pushing its production to the maximum Baghdad is allowing the companies to use the flexibility of their supply systems . . .' Quoted in *MEES*, 28 December 1973.

10 Iraq was probably wrong in believing that a collective embargo on the United States together with nationalization of the American companies would have been as effective as the policies actually adopted; even if the latter had only limited influence on the American attitude, they did have some. Although the Arab governments did not nationalize the companies, they had considerable power over them. Without this power the governments would have had no way of enforcing their embargo. Once oil had left their shores, it would have been impossible for them even to trace it to its final destination, let alone to control it. They had to rely on the companies for

this and the evidence is that the companies did observe the embargo. See Stobaugh, op. cit.

11 Quoted in *MEES*, 28 December 1973. At no time, however, did the Iraqis explain why the United States would stop supporting Israel once the American companies were nationalized.

12 Saudi Arabia did not agree to apply the new tax and royalty rates to Aramco, for the government was still discussing the arrangements for its participation in the company, and in these discussions the cost of oil to the parent companies was a major consideration.

13 *MEES* attempted such estimates and in September 1974 published interesting tables giving estimates of prices, average revenues, and costs to the companies for the first half of 1974 and as a result of the September decisions of OPEC. *MEES*, 20 September 1974.

14 The prices were 'cash terms'—but it soon became clear that buyers could bargain successfully, especially over credit. The granting of credit for from 30 to 90 days was one of the chief forms of competition among sellers. Each 30 days credit was worth around 6¢–8¢ a barrel at the prices and interest rates prevailing at the time. For a discussion of OPEC's pricing policy at this time see especially R. Mabro, 'OPEC After the Oil Revolution', *Millennium,* Vol. 4, No. 3 (1975–76).

15 Calculations by the Economic Research Institute for the Middle East (Tokyo) indicated that the average rate of inflation of import prices for Iraq in 1974 had reached 28.3 per cent (average for OPEC countries 28.6 per cent). In the fourth quarter of 1974 import prices had risen 40.8 per cent over the first quarter of 1972. Reproduced in *MEES*, 14 November 1975. Supplement.

16 Kuwait took 100 per cent of the equity in the KPC in December 1975, and Qatar took over the QPC in September 1976. In November 1975 Aramco agreed to 100 per cent participation, but final arrangements had not been completed at the time of writing.

17 *MEES*, 19 and 26 September 1976.

18 See *MEES*, 5 March 1976 for a summary of an article by Tayih Abdel-Karim, the Iraqi Oil Minister.

19 *MEES*, 31 May 1976.

20 ibid.

21 Remarks of Tayih Abdel-Karim quoted from the *Baghdad Observer* by *MEES*, 26 July 1976.

22 Interview with *Al-Nadwa* (Mecca daily newspaper) quoted in *MEES*, 27 September 1976.

23 *MEES*, 10 January 1977. Supplement.

24 ibid.

25 See *MEES*, 16 May 1977.

26 In November 1976 the Dutch press published a cable alleged to have been sent by the United States State Department to the United States Delegation to the Paris Conference, which stated: 'In our view, the connection which some OPEC officials have made between CIEC and OPEC is more rhetorical than actual. While lack of satisfaction with CIEC's outcome—a highly subjective judgment—could be used by OPEC to justify an oil price increase, it is unlikely that OPEC countries view CIEC as a major factor in a decision on an oil price increase'. Published in *MEES*, 20 December 1976.

27 Askari and Cummings calculated that only Algeria, Libya, and Nigeria among the OPEC countries committed a smaller percentage of their oil revenues for assistance than Iraq in 1974, and only these three plus Iran disbursed a smaller percentage. See Hossein Askari and John Cummings, *Middle East Economies in the 1970s: a Comparative Approach* (New York, 1976), p. 487.

28 The Iraqi government frequently announces that its financial resources are strained by its development needs (one could add, also, by its very high defence expenditures). The government may have trimmed budgetary allocations because estimated revenues were thought to be inadequate for all desired expenditures, but the funds allocated in the development budgets have rarely been spent. Iraq has for a long time demonstrated a fearful and curious uncertainty that she will not have enough money to meet all contingencies. This was especially marked during her various clashes with the Iraq Petroleum Company, when the government was always quick to impose 'austerity measures', prohibit imports, and generally tighten up in anticipation of trouble even when its foreign reserves were high. It provided for foreign borrowing in its 1977 budget and, as we have seen, it has borrowed some $2,000 million from the Japanese for a project to be implemented by them. This kind of borrowing is probably at least partly designed to attempt to ensure a Japanese vested interest in the project, just as the Saudis and others often insist on some foreign equity interests in projects undertaken by foreigners. In general, one cannot take seriously the assertion that Iraqi foreign borrowing demonstrates financial stringency.

29 Quoted in *MEES*, 23 May 1977.

Part Six

The Summing-up

20 The Summing-up

The emergence and the early history of a new state reflect in some degree the social and political heritage of the larger area from which it had been severed. At the same time, whatever its heritage may be, the course of its political and economic development will be shaped partly by its endowment of natural resources, by natural obstacles, and by its location in the world. The sum of its heritage and its geographical endowment constitute the initial assets of the new state.

But this is not all. The course of its subsequent development will also be affected by contemporary conditions in the wider world into which it is drawn as an independent political unit. A large well-endowed new state may itself be in a position to exert considerable influence on those conditions, but the ability of a small state like Iraq to do so is severely limited.

For Iraq in the first half-century of her existence as an independent state, conditions in the outside world, both near and far, were of leading importance. Emerging as a political unit out of the collapse of an empire in the greatest war which the world had yet known, the shape of her territory, and with it the composition of her population, was determined partly by bargaining among the great powers and partly by adjudication based on the findings of an investigation conducted by smaller powers through the League of Nations. Later, after another troubled period in Europe and the Far East, she was drawn by her geographical position into an even greater war between powers to the east of her and powers to the west.

The Second World War was followed by the Cold War between the two largest powers that emerged from it with a long lead in destructive weapons over other great powers. This provoked a dangerous rivalry between them in which each endeavoured to draw into its orbit the smaller powers, including, with some success, Egypt and the countries of the Fertile Crescent.

It appears ironical, however, that the first grave conflict leading to war in the area should have been the result of American and Russian actions in the same direction, inspired by the same objective, and culminating in the forcible intrusion in the Arab world of a new state, directed and partially populated by Eastern Europeans. United States actions were determined by internal political influences and Russian by out-of-date conceptions of political balance in the Middle East. Iraq sent a force to join other Arab forces to resist the Eastern European invasion and the establishment of the state of Israel on Arab lands, but disunity led to failure, followed by recriminations among the Arab states. Iraqi political leaders had shown particular concern from an early period with the Palestine question. But all the efforts of Iraq and of the other Arab countries failed in face of the intransigence of political Zionists.

While these external forces have worked against the chances of harmonious development in the new states that replaced the Ottoman Empire, other forces within Iraq were shaping her forms of government and domestic political development. The Ottoman inheritance was directly felt in the earlier stages, for some of Iraq's political leaders and military officers had themselves grown up within the Empire and a few had even held posts in its service. In the early twentieth century political development was still seen largely as a struggle to replace old autocracies by representative democracy. But the dilution of democracy by militarist elements in Hohenzollern Germany impressed some young Turkish officers and later led the Ottoman Empire into a war which destroyed it. The ultimate victory of Britain and France restored faith in parliamentary democracy for a time, and the establishment of the Mandate for Iraq under Britain favoured the introduction of such a system into Iraq. The success of Turkish nationalism under Mustafa Kemal, the political wisdom and prestige of İnönü, and the restraint of General Gursel kept Turkey, if at times falteringly, among parliamentary governments.

In face of these external conditions Iraq adopted a constitution, and institutions for parliamentary rule under a limited monarchy were set up. But Iraq's social and political heritage and the nature of her population strained the system from an early stage. The hopes of King Faisal and his advisers that the army would be a unifying influence were quickly frustrated. The massacre of the Assyrians and the early appearance of *coups d'état* that violated the constitution and emasculated the parliamentary institutions, showed the army in a very different role. These institutions themselves were the only hope of forging a genuine unity in terms of a national interest.

In spite of military interference, the parliamentary institutions threw up a number of able Iraqis, some of whom had studied abroad and tried to introduce Western European ideas of social democracy. The difficulty then and up to the time of the 14 July Revolution lay not merely in the opposition of conservative and traditional elements in society, but also in the competition of the superficial and over-simplified ideas spread by some of the Arab nationalists, by the communists, and by the Baathists after the Second World War. For each Iraqi who had engaged in serious studies in Western Europe or North America, there were dozens who had absorbed the slogans rather than studied the doctrines of the political thinkers. During the first decade of the new state, the communism which the Russian Revolution had introduced was followed by the rise of right-wing movements loosely characterized as 'fascist', of which the German Nazi movement was the most developed. A communist party had been formed in Iraq. But on the eve of the war, communists outside the Soviet Union were thrown into disarray by the Soviet-German Treaty. The German attack on Russia in 1941, however, was followed by a reversal of the position of communist parties outside Russia.

By this time the politically conscious public was thinking no longer in terms of a competition between democracy and autocracy. There were instead a number of competing autocracies on both the right and the left. And, as in the Ottoman Empire before 1915, so in Iraq on the eve of and during the Second World War, Germany attracted a section of the army officers, and Iraqi politics was dominated by the army. During the Anglo–Iraqi war resentment against Britain reached a new height. The politically conscious class had increased in numbers: the doctrine of Arab nationalism had found a home in Baghdad while Syria was under French rule.

The interpretation of Arab nationalism raised serious obstacles in the way of consolidating Iraq as a sovereign state. The charge against Britain and France was that they had been responsible for preventing the emergence of a single unified Arab state covering the whole area in which Arabs had been a majority in the Ottoman Empire. Although Iraq and Syria in most of their present boundaries were the product of competitive Anglo–French imperialisms, it does not follow that but for Britain and France no boundaries would have existed in the Arab world to the east of Egypt. Judging from the failure of the limited attempts at unity since then, this outcome seems most unlikely. But such was the assumption of Arab nationalist and Baathist doctrines, and the resulting dogma created an element of serious instability in the independent Arab states. It led also to intrigues by one Arab country in the affairs of others with a view to the displacement of governments believed to be unfaithful to Arab nationalism.

Thus, from the time when the Iraqi state was founded, but especially since the Second World War, there have been wide divergencies between the world of facts and events and the world of doctrines and ideas. These very divergencies have themselves led to further events in the form of actions producing results contrary to those desired by the actors. And behind these contradictions and disharmonies there often appeared the use of words as unanalysed slogans which are calculated to arouse emotions by repetition and to create expectations beyond any reasonable chance of fulfilment. So it was with the idea of Arab unity in the short run.

The Iraqi government with Nuri al-Said in a prominent place, whether in or out of office, had proved to be correct in forecasting the downfall of the Nazi and Fascist regimes in the Second World War. But the assets of the Hashemite regime were limited, and were further diminished when Iraq was brought into the scope of the Cold War, and when the Regent and Nuri, not content with the defeat of the officers who had led Iraq into war with Britain in 1941, pursued their enemies in the vengeful spirit characteristic of the Ottoman period. Once again, however, external developments exerted an influence. The split among the wartime allies tended to divide opinion inside other countries and the Turkish heritage of some members of the Iraqi regime predisposed them against the Soviet Union. 'Anti-communism', intense in the United States and spreading to other conservative circles, led them to disregard the changes in Russian policy towards Iran and Turkey, notably after Khrushchev had succeeded Stalin.

The Revolution and its Sequel

In the Iraqi Revolution the contrast between the world of events and the world of doctrines and ideas reached a high-water mark. There was no doubt of its popularity. Though the seizure of power was conducted by the military, it was immediately greeted with approval in conservative, radical, and communist circles. It is the only seizure of power in Iraqi history that can be called a 'revolution'.

It followed, however, from the extent of the poverty and the problems of development in the country, that the gap between expectations and early results would be wide and disillusioning. The disillusionment extended from economic to political affairs and the experience was an important step in political education for Iraq. Never again were Iraqis to pitch their expectations from political change so high. The preceding regime had been criticized for manipulating elections and for restricting political parties: the new regime, except during a brief period when a certain number of parties were licensed, continued the same restrictions. From then onwards no elections were held at all and parliament ceased to function. Compared with its successors, however, the Qassim regime was moderate and far from totalitarian, and it did move towards a genuine unity within Iraq, opening official posts more equally to Sunni and Shia. But from 1958 to the autumn of 1959 it passed through a stormy period in the Arab world as a whole. Nasser was at the height of his popularity and aspired to be the leader of the Arab world. The Baath movement, which was small in Iraq, was active as a conspiratorial body, which regarded Qassim as a traitor for not immediately effecting a union with the United Arab Republic.

The military *coup* and the murder of Qassim, followed by a military-Baath government, was the sharpest retardation in political development experienced since the foundation of the state. The regime failed at home and abroad. It was torn with dissension inside and an extreme section terrorized Baghdad, instigating an unknown number of kidnappings and murders. Its attempts at unity with Egypt and Syria failed. To the general relief the regime was ended on 18 November 1963 in a gun battle in the streets of Baghdad. The moderate sections of the Baath joined with non-Baathist officers to suppress the militia forces used by the extreme section of the party.

A change had come over the public. Its expectations were more modest, but relief at the disappearance of the Baath regime was deep and widespread in the country. The new regime, predominantly Arab nationalist, entered on its career with the goodwill of the public. Order was restored: the rule of law prevailed again, except perhaps where communists were concerned. But dissensions arose and conspiracies were formed among the Nasserite sections of the Arab nationalists which led, almost by accident, to the appointment of a civilian to the post of Prime Minister under the Arifs. Abdul Rahman al-Bazzaz, a distinguished scholar, became the only civilian Prime Minister since the Revolution. In a notable period of eleven months he transformed the political atmosphere of the country. Free discussion and speech and a genuine desire to establish genuine representative government opened a prospect for the first time of a parliamentary democracy. Al-Bazzaz was the most popular, perhaps the only popular, leader since the Revolution. But the military officers by this time had acquired a vested interest in government and resented a civilian in the highest post. Al-Bazzaz was removed. The remaining period of the Arab nationalist regime was undistinguished. It had started with a great advantage, but had dissipated it by internal dissensions and by failing to follow up the great feat of al-Bazzaz in earning the trust of the Kurdish leaders and making peace in the north. No other government has been trusted by the Kurds since.

Then followed the *coup* by military officers in mid-July 1968. These aimed at a moderate regime, but were displaced by a Baathist conspiracy at the end of the month. This time the expectations of the public were negative in most quarters. The memory of the violence in 1963 had not died. The change was unpopular, and realizing this, the military–Baath resolved to purge political and administrative circles of all known opponents of the Baath. The results have been deplorable. Professor Elie Kedourie was wholly correct when, speaking of the seizure of power, he said: 'These officers, and their civilian colleagues, were a small conspiratorial group whose ideas were by no means shared by other members of the official class, let alone by the population at large'.[1]

This time the moderate section of the Baath, which played a useful role in November 1968, seems to have disappeared and in the last ten years Iraq has been ruled by a group of military officers and a totalitarian civilian party that stops at nothing to remain in power.

Economic Affairs

After the rise in oil prices in January 1974, international financial and economic affairs took a new turn. A very small group of countries laid claim to a much larger share of world income by virtue of their control over a natural resource on which the industrialized countries depended for the maintenance of their industrial activity, and the developing countries for the maintenance of their industrial and agricultural development programmes. The distinguishing feature of income from the extraction of natural resources is that most of it is rent—that is to say, income from ownership and not from effort and skill. The receiver of rents from the exploitation of wasting assets may be rich but is not necessarily skilled or otherwise well endowed. It therefore behoves a country in such a position to invest a good part of its income in acquiring skills and in developing alternative assets on which further income may be earned. Thus, in the oil-exporting countries their own economic development had to be given a high priority, even though some of the leaders and officials of some countries might give first place to the maintenance of their own power and others to the lining of their own pockets. For most countries, including Iraq, the new flow of riches was enough to accommodate all of these objectives within reason, and economic development became a central preoccupation of policy.

Like other countries, Iraq and the oil-exporting countries generally were inextricably linked with, or a part of, several worlds: the capitalist and communist industrial world from which the bulk of their imported goods, technology, and skills had to come; the international capitalist financial world, in which they had to hold the bulk of the financial assets derived from the sale of oil to this world;

and the less-developed industrializing world, which shared in varying degrees their poverty of skills, technological capacity, industrial infrastructure, and agricultural backwardness. Many of the oil-exporting countries looked on this last group of countries as their 'political constituency', so to speak, in their negotiations with the industrialized world. Finally, the Arab countries saw themselves as part of a wider Islamic world (with Iran and Indonesia) and a narrower Arab world; Iran looked forward to being a great power in Asia; Venezuela was a member of the Andean Pact; Nigeria was a powerful leader in West Africa. And of course for each of the individual countries there were crossroads where all, or some, of these several worlds met. Each of the countries had its own view of these different worlds and of its role within them.

Iraq and the Oil Company

Of all the oil-producing countries in the Middle East, outside the Maghreb, Iraq has had the least satisfactory relationship with her foreign concessionaires. In neither Kuwait nor Saudi Arabia, nor even in Iran, except during the Mossadeq interlude, were there any really serious difficulties between the oil concessionaire and the host country. But in Iraq there was always tension between the government and the IPC and, in particular, there was always an underlying resentment of the company among large numbers of politically conscious Iraqis. There were many reasons for this: the negotiations over the original concession terms were at times bitter, taking place before the country was fully independent and linked with the political shape and future of the new state; there was a dispute with the company over the extent of its territory and continual wrangling over money and over the rate of expansion of output. Latterly the demand for equity participation, a source of ill-feeling between government and company from the very beginning, was strongly revived. Moreover, since IPC output had to cross Syria to reach the Mediterranean, any conflict between the company and Syria which interfered with the passage of oil prejudiced Iraq, while any conflict between Syria and Iraq prejudiced the company. On this account, too, relations became strained at times.

But above all, the IPC was a British company and was widely identified with British 'imperialism', which in turn was held responsible by large groups of the politically conscious public, especially among the young, for the maintenance in power of a regime which resisted reforms in agriculture in the interest of landowning shaikhs and which pursued reactionary foreign policies. There is no question that Iraqis, even those who welcomed the foreign contribution to the oil industry and had no strong feelings against the governments of the time, felt that the sovereignty of the country was reduced by the power of the IPC, that the freedom of action of Iraqi governments was severely constrained by its presence, and in particular that governments had less control over economic policy than would have been the case had the industry not been in foreign hands. In this they were correct, for the interests of the oil company were not always identical with the interests of Iraq. At the same time, they much exaggerated the power of the IPC and underestimated the limitations on their own freedom of action imposed by the fact that their industry was but part of a very large international industry.

After nationalization of the IPC the government, with full control over the industry, had a much freer hand than before. The so-called 'strategic' north–south pipeline, or the Turkish pipeline, are examples in point, for it does seem unlikely that the IPC would have been happy about financing either of these lines in the circumstances of the time. Thus any Iraqi government would almost certainly have exerted increasing control over the company as time went on and would have insisted on a strong participation in its activities as soon as this became practicable; a 'revolutionary' government could hardly be expected to resist taking over completely.

Nevertheless, the expropriation of most of the IPC's concession area by the Qassim government in 1961 was premature. Although it went a long way towards satisfying the aspirations of the nationalists and the left wing, it brought stagnation to the oil industry for nearly a decade. The final nationalization of the IPC in 1972 completed for all practical purposes the assumption of control over its industry by the government, but since nearly every other oil-exporting country was doing the same thing without paying the cost of prolonged stagnation and conflict, it cannot be said that Iraq gained much by her own premature actions. Nor is the argument tenable that Iraq was a pioneer, blazing the trail for others to follow in achieving independence of foreign ownership, since others, though obtaining a similar independence, did not follow Iraq's path in doing so.

Domestic Policies

With the Revolution in 1958 the country branched out into many new directions, none of which fulfilled the expectations held at its inception and few of which can in retrospect be looked on as 'progress'. Land reform was undoubtedly a necessary condition for further advance in agriculture in a number of areas, especially in the south. But the precipitately executed Iraqi reform was a disaster, and agriculture continued to stagnate. The industrial nationalizations undertaken later did not have a disastrous effect on output although neither did they do anything to improve the efficiency of industry, since the government did not prove capable of establishing an effective organization for control and management.

The underlying purpose of the nationalizations was political and ideological and not economic, for they were designed to align the economic structure of Iraq more closely on that of Egypt as desired by the Nasserites, who were the chief architects of the new structure. It is not therefore appropriate to judge them entirely against economic criteria, even one related to the development of the Iraqi economy in itself. A socialist ideology of the kind espoused by the Nasserites in Iraq, and even more by the Baath party, had little room for the growth of a class of businessmen some of whom would undoubtedly amass considerable wealth and in any case would develop into a middle class which might at some point challenge military and single-party rule. With industry under its control the government and the party politicians would not only possess political power but would also be in a better position to prevent the rise of any independent economic power.

The rapid expansion of the public sector led of course to a rapid expansion of the state bureaucracy, which is an outstanding characteristic of the structure of the Iraqi economy. There is every reason to believe that the economists, 'technocrats', and others who were instrumental in 1964 in persuading the nationalist government to move in the direction of this particular type of socialism, were sincerely convinced that by doing so they were laying the foundation for a less exploitative society and perhaps a more efficient economy which would be more responsive to their well-meant plans for the transformation of the structure of the economy and a more rapid growth and modernization of industry. Success in this direction seems, however, to have been very limited; on the other hand, the measures undoubtedly did help to prevent the growth of an independent middle and upper-middle class with any effective economic base from which to challenge the government. The Baath perhaps appreciated this even more than the Nasserites, and continued to expand state ownership and ensure that the private sector in both industry and agriculture was confined to relatively small enterprises. The middle class in contemporary Iraq is composed primarily of urban-based government and party functionaries together with a new 'quasi class' of local contractors allied with the ruling bureaucracy.

Thus, if the political consequences of the 'socialist' economic measures were to strengthen the centralized control of the ruling oligarchy, the economic consequences were to weaken the efficiency of productive activity. In both industry and agriculture government destroyed an existing managerial and organizational structure by precipitately pulling out the existing ownership structure. In agriculture, this was done to protect a revolution; in industry it was done to enable the government quickly to reshape the Iraqi economy. In both cases, there was inadequate provision to ensure successful replacement of the managerial and organizational functions previously exercised by the displaced owners and managers, especially in agriculture. The Baath government after 1968 pushed compulsory co-operatives and other types of collective organization of farming even further. Collectivization of agriculture has a very poor record to show in any country and the Baath government in the past decade has displayed very little capacity for efficient organization in economic affairs. Nevertheless, it is apparently attempting to enforce on Iraqi agriculture this most difficult of all types of agricultural organization to implement.

In industry, similarly, nationalization was followed by the imposition of an unworkable bureaucracy, the inefficiency of which seems to have grown steadily more pronounced. The problem arises not because of the displacement of private by state ownership, but because of the heavy and cumbrous hand of bureaucracy which accompanied the latter. Not all forms of socialism require the obtrusive interference of ministries in the operating decisions of companies and the removal of nearly all vestiges of autonomy from the management of state enterprises. But the socialism of the Iraqi Baath is of the highly centralized type which must sacrifice economic efficiency to ensure political control. Only relatively small enterprises in the private and mixed sector have a significant degree of flexibility. Industrial investment and industrial output are growing with the rapid growth of the very large revenues accruing to the state. The favoured method for the implementation of projects is the delivery of factories built by foreigners on a 'turn-key' basis, a method which gets things built quickly but almost guarantees inefficient operation for a considerable time after the foreigners leave and has a minimal 'developmental' impact. In spite of the enormous investment boom much of the work is likely to prove abortive, but this will to a considerable extent be concealed so long as oil revenues pour in at a high rate, which will be for a long time to come.

International Economic Relations

With the 1958 Revolution Iraq became more international in her economic and political relations, establishing extensive links with the countries of Eastern Europe. As the country prepared to undertake the development of its own oil industry, these links became particularly strong, for only from these countries could Iraq expect to obtain the assistance needed to enable her to exploit effectively her resources. The international companies, which were the other important primary source of such assistance, having had their concessions expropriated, were, with the exception of the French, unwilling to assist Iraq—nor were they willing to permit anyone else to do so if they could legally prevent it. But once the IPC was finally nationalized and a settlement effected, there were signs that Iraq felt herself freer to adopt a more balanced approach towards Eastern and Western economic relationships and that the Western oil and other international companies were willing once again to undertake such operations as were desired by the Iraqi government, and profitable for the companies.

With some exceptions the governments of Iraq after the 1958 Revolution have, together with Libya and (to a lesser extent) Algeria, looked on themselves as 'radical' and 'progressive'. Iraq in particular has attempted to establish herself as the radical leader in the Arab world. To this end she has frequently attacked the conservative, traditional regimes in the area as well as those of Egypt and Syria when their policies diverged. As a consequence, her attempts to assert leadership in both OPEC and OAPEC have met with little success. At times her contributions to both of these organizations have been important, but for the most part she has been at odds with her fellow members, who often found her proposals unrealistic or unnecessarily militant and extreme. Having broken with her own concessionaire, she naturally wanted to encourage others to break with theirs, partly because of her general objection to foreign capitalist companies in the Arab oil industry. She also believed that her own interests lay in pressing for a common oil policy among the producing countries which would both raise prices and restrict output through quotas. Iraq's role in the 'oil' crisis following the October 1973 war was in part designed to force these issues and in part a consequence of her desire to ensure continued supplies of oil to Eastern Europe under her contracts with these countries; she increasingly depended on them for arms.

In the twenty years since the 1958 Revolution Iraq has received enormous oil revenues. These have permitted a substantial increase in the standard of living of the people, in social welfare, and in educational facilities, especially, but not exclusively, in the cities. They have sustained industrial development and the increase in skills associated with it at a reasonable rate. The civil service is better educated and the technocrats better trained, but the bureaucratic procedures are as clumsy and inefficient as ever. The countryside has changed, but slowly and in some places imperceptibly; in spite of increased mechanization, agricultural techniques are for the most part still backward and agricultural output fluctuates as heavily as ever, showing little long-run increase. There has clearly been economic development, but the present attempt to force the pace unduly is probably affecting adversely the underlying rate of genuine development.

On the other hand, for some years Iraq has been, and as we write these closing lines remains, in a state of arrested political development. Politics, in the constructive sense of free public debate and popular participation, is non-existent while the exercise of political power in government is autocratic, and has become increasingly ruthless, depending on the army, lacking the legitimacy either of tradition or of popular endorsement.

The criticisms of Iraqi governments in this study are far from being criticisms of the Iraqi people. None of their governments has been representative of the Iraqi people, least of all those since the Revolution. In fact, the tragedy behind Iraq's political history since independence lies in the waste of human resources, at a time when they were most needed, in the construction of a new state. It is not from a lack of able individuals capable of occupying key positions in the development of the country and in the conduct of its relations abroad that political growth has been arrested, but from the seizure and monopolization of political power first by army officers in the earlier stages, and more recently by a particular group among them and their civilian associates in a minority political party with totalitarian aims. The Iraqi people deserve better and we cherish the faith that the time will come when opposition will be accepted not only as a legitimate but also as a necessary part of government, when governments can replace each other peaceably in accordance with the will of the general electorate, without the rumble of tanks around the centre of the capital, and when the rule of law will cover every section of the community, including the President and the highest office-holders.

Note

1 Elie Kedourie, 'Continuity and Change in Modern Iraqi History', *Asian Affairs*, June 1975, p. 141.

Names of Provinces

In 1969 Iraq changed the names of many of the provinces (*liwas, muhafadhas,* governorates) and created some new ones. In 1976 she created two more new provinces. The names of the old provinces listed below are in column (1). When discussing the period before 1975 these names are used. Column (2) presents the names of the existing provinces.

Mosul	Nineveh	
	Dohuk	Dohuk, Arbil, and al-Sulaimaniya have been designated the 'autonomous region' since March 1974 when new laws were passed for Kurdistan.
Arbil	Arbil	
al-Sulaimaniya	al-Sulaimaniya	
Kirkuk	Tamim	
Diala	Diala	
Ramadi	al-Anbar	
Baghdad	Baghdad	
	Salahaddin	(created in 1976 from the northern part of the Baghdad governorate, centred on Takrit city and to include the *qadhas* of Takrit, Samarra, Balad, and Touz)
Kut	Wasit	
Hilla	Babylon	
Kerbela	Kerbela	
	al-Najf	(created in 1976 from the southern part of Kerbela governorate centred on al-Najf city and including the *qadhas* of Najf, Kufa, Abu Sukair, and the *nahiya* of Shabaka)
Diwaniya	al-Qadisiya	
	al-Muthanna	
Amara	Maysan	
Nasiriya	Thi-qar	
Basra	Basra	

Basic Data

Population: 11,505,000 of which:

27% of total in Baghdad governorate
10% in Nineveh governorate
8% in Basra governorate
12% in the 'autonomous region'

Area: 438,446 km^2
of which:

30% plains (including marshes and lakes)
10% terrain lands (between lowlands and high mountains)
21% mountains
38% deserts

National Accounts

Gross National Product, 1975 (Current Market Prices) ID 3,750.5 million
National Income *Per capita* ID 337.2

Gross Domestic Product, 1975 (Current Factor Cost)	
Distribution by Economic Sector	*Per cent*
Agriculture	7.5
Mining and Quarrying	57.6
Manufacturing, Construction, Electricity, Water	8.7
Transport, Trade, Finance	10.4
Public Administration and Defence	9.4
Other Services	6.4
Gross Domestic product at current factor cost	100.0

Annual Abstract of Statistics, 1976 Estimates

Petroleum Production: 1976
119 million long ton (2,422,000 b/d)
Source: *Annual Abstract of Statistics*, 1976

Government Finance, 1977
Estimated Revenue ID 5,988.4 million
Allocation to Development Plan: ID 83.2 million
ID 966 million (41%) for industry
ID 390 million (16.5%) for agriculture
Source: *MEES,* 28 March 1977.
Oil Revenues: ID 2,574.7 million (1976). $8,702.5m (ID=$3.38)
Source *MEED,* 3 June 1977, p. 22

Land, Agriculture, and Rural Population
Source: 1971 Agricultural Census as reported in *Annual Abstract of Statistics,* 1975, unless otherwise noted
Area Agricultural Holdings 5,725 million ha.

Land Use	000 ha.	
Winter crops	2,770	(2,726 fallow in summer)
Summer crops	372	(328 fallow in winter)
Palm & Fruit Trees	162	
Pasture	039	
Not cultivated previous year	1,730	
Not cultivable	430	
Cultivable not used	222	
	5,725	

Crops		
Barley & wheat	2,745	
Paddy	107	
Other	400	[In 1976 2,117,425 ha. were planted to wheat and barley, 53,172 ha. to rice and 26,852 ha. to cotton. Source: *Annual Abstract of Statistics*, 1976]
	3,252	
Oil seeds	26	
Legumes and pulses	55	
Cotton	35	
Tobacco & Tunbak	29	
Sugar	6	
Other	2	
Vegetables	97	
Fodder	25	

Farm Population		
Total:	3,973,045	
Number of households:	626,428	
Number of farmworkers:	2,110,593	
of which landholders (tenants & owners) and unpaid members of their household:	1,834,456	(44% female)
of which paid workers	276,137	(16% female)

Land holding

Owned (*mulk, tapu lazma*)	2,112
Managed temporarily by Agrarian Reform	2,273
Squatters	273
Waqf	853
Other	221
Total	5,732

Number of land holdings: 591,178 [A holding is a unit of operation and management—not ownership]

Size Distribution

hectares	*% of holdings*	
Without land	8.79	(i.e., squatters etc.)
Less than 1	1.18	
1 and less than 10	60.93	
10 and less than 100	28.54	
100 and less than 500	1.49	
500 and over	0.07	
	100.00	

Agrarian Reform

Sequestrated Land to 31.12.75	2.6m. ha.
Distributed Land from 1959–75	1.6m. ha.
Managed Temporarily by the Agrarian Reform 1974/75	1.3m. ha.

Source: *Annual Abstract of Statistics,* 1975

The original data are in the Iraqi units of measurement—the donum or *meshara*=.25 hectares. We have converted all figures to hectares for ease of international understanding.

(*Note:* the 1976 *Annual Abstract of Statistics* appeared after this book was in proof. We have been able to take account of the more recent figures only in a few cases where no calculations were required.)

Selected Bibliography

A large literature exists on the wide range of subjects and topics covered in the present study, which deals not only with economic and political developments in Iraq, but also with many aspects of intra-regional relations in the Middle East, with the place of Iraq and the Middle East in international affairs, and with the oil industry internationally as well as within the Middle East. It is not therefore practical to attempt here an adequate coverage of this literature and we have made no attempt to compile a bibliography for scholars. However, in addition to a list of the works actually cited we do include a short selection of the works consulted. We have not listed the ephemeral material, consisting largely of pamphlets, newspaper articles, and even leaflets, which are difficult to find and of use only for very special and limited purposes; nor do we include many of the numerous official publications and documents available. A number of the scholarly works we have cited have extensive bibliographies on the specialized periods or aspects of the subject with which they deal and to these we refer the interested reader. For the period since 1957 a great deal of the information used in our analysis comes from our own direct experience in the area and with its people.

Aaref, Hassan: *La Grande Bretagne en Egypte et en Irak,* Paris, 1939

Adams, Doris: *Iraq's People and Resources,* Los Angeles, 1958

Adamson, D.: *The Kurdish War,* London, 1964

Agwani, M. G.: *The Lebanese Crisis of 1958,* London, 1965

Albertini, Luigi: *Le origine della guerra del 1914,* Milan, 1926

Alnasrawi, Abbas: *Financing Economic Development in Iraq: the Role of Oil in a Middle Eastern Economy,* New York, 1967

Alwan, Abdul Salih H.: *The Process of Economic Development in Iraq, with Special Reference to Land Problems and Policies,* Unpub. Ph.D thesis, University of Wisconsin, 1956

Antonius, George, *The Arab Awakening,* London, 1938

Arab Baath Socialist Party, *Some Theoretical Principles Approved by the Six* [*sic*] *National Congress, October 1963,* Beirut, n.d.

Arab Baath Socialist Party–Iraq, *Revolutionary Iraq, 1968–1973. Political Report* adopted by the 8th Regional Congress of ABSP–Iraq, Baghdad, Jan. 1974.

Askari, Hossein, and Cummings, John: *Middle East Economies in the 1970s: a Comparative Approach,* New York, 1976

Atiyyah, Ghassan: *Iraq, 1908–1921: a Political Study,* Beirut, 1973

Al-Atraqchi, M. A. M. S.: *Statistical Analysis of the Pattern of Merchandise Foreign Trade of Iraq, 1948–62,* Unpub. Ph.D thesis, University of London (LSE), 1965–66

Al-Atrash, M. H. F.: *Monetary Policy in an Underdeveloped Economy, with special reference to the Experience of Egypt, Iraq, and Syria, 1951–58,* Unpub. Ph.D thesis, University of London (LSE), 1963

Baali, Fuad: 'Social Factors in Iraqi Rural–Urban Migration', *American Journal of Economics and Sociology,* Vol. 40, October 1966

Baer, Gabriel: 'Changes in Land Tenure Systems of the Middle East', *Middle East Development,* Jerusalem, 1968

Barraclough, G., and Wall, R.: *Survey of International Affairs, 1955–56,* Oxford, 1960

Al-Bazzaz, Abdul Rahman: *On Arab Nationalism,* London, 1965

Beaufre, General André: *Forces armées françaises,* Paris, April 1968

Becker, Abraham S., Hansen, Bent, and Kerr, Malcolm H.: *The Economics and Politics of the Middle East,* New York, 1975

Bedir Khan, Emir Kamuran: *La Question Kurde,* Paris, 1958

Berque, Jacques: *Les Arabes d'hier à demain,* Paris, 1960

Birdwood, Lord: *Nuri al-Said,* London, 1959

Brimmell, J. H.: *Communism in South East Asia,* Oxford, 1959

Brines, Russell: *The Indo-Pakistani Conflict,* London, 1968

Burrell, R. M.: 'Iranian Foreign Policy during the last Decade', *Asian Affairs,* February 1964, pp. 7–15

'Caractacus', *Revolution in Iraq,* London, 1959

Carré, Olivier: *Proche Orient entre la guerre et la paix,* Paris, 1974

Carrère d'Encausse, H.: *La politique soviétique au Moyen Orient 1955–1975,* Paris, 1975

Chamoun, Camille: *Crise au Moyen-Orient,* Paris, 1963

Chevalier, Dominique: 'Lyon et la Syrie en 1919: les bases d'une intervention', *Revue Historique,* Oct.-Dec. 1960

Churchill, Winston: *The Second World War,* Vol. III, London, 1950

Cohen, S. A.: *British Policy in Mesopotamia, 1903–1914,* Oxford, 1976

Colombe, Marcel: 'Le monde arabe au seuil de l'année nouvelle', *Orient,* No. 28, 1963

Colombe, Marcel: *Orient Arabe et le non-engagement,* Paris, 1973

Al-Dabbagh, Hashim: *Études statistiques sur le développement économique de l'Irak,* Baghdad, 1960

Dann, Uriel: *Iraq Under Qassem,* London, 1969

Davies, C.: *British Oil Policy in the Middle East. 1919–1932,* Unpub. thesis, University of Edinburgh, 1973

Dawn, C. Ernest: *From Ottomanism to Arabism: Essays on the Origins of Arab Nationalism,* Chicago, 1973

Demarchi, M., Mohanty, M., Ali, M., al-Azzawee, M., as-Saidi, S., and Isa, A.: 'Family Food Consumption Survey of Workers Belonging to the Brick Industry', *Journal of the Faculty of Medicine* (*Baghdad*), Vol. 5 (New Series), No. 4, October 1963

Demarchi, M., *et al.:* 'A Dietary Survey in Rural Areas of Baghdad', *Journal of the Faculty of Medicine* (*Baghdad*), Vol. 4 (New Series), No. 4, October 1962

Djamali, Muhammad Fadil: 'Retour sur le passé', translation by Marcel Colombe, *Orient,* 1969

Dowson, Ernest: *An Inquiry into Land Tenure and Related Questions,* Letchworth Garden City, 1932

Earle, E. M.: *Turkey, the Great Powers, and the Baghdad Railway: a study in Imperialism,* New York, 1924

Edmonds, C. J.: *Kurds, Turks and Arabs,* London, 1957

Fattah, Zeki M.: *Production, Capital Stock, Productivity and Growth in the Industrial Sector of an Oil Economy: Iraq 1960–1970,* Unpublished Ph.D thesis, Oxford University, 1976

Fenelon, K. G.: *Iraq; National Income and Expenditure, 1950–1956,* Baghdad, 1958

Fernea, Robert A.: 'Land Reform and Ecology in Post-revolutionary Iraq', *Economic Development and Cultural Change,* Vol. 17, No. 3, April 1969

Finnie, D. M.: 'Business in Basra and the Oil Industry', *Middle East Economic Papers,* 1956

Fisher, W. B.: *The Middle East,* 6th edn., London, 1971

Fleury, Antoine: 'La constitution d'un "bloc orientale"—le Pact de Saadabad', *Revue d'histoire de la deuxième guerre mondiale,* Avril, 1977

Flory, Maurice, and Mantran, Robert: *Les régimes politiques des Pays Arabes,* Paris, 1968

Food and Agriculture Organization: *Mediterranean Development Project, Country Study: Iraq,* Rome, 1959

Frye, R. N. (ed.): *The Near East and the Great Powers,* Cambridge, Mass., 1951

Gallman, Waldemar J.: *Iraq Under General Nuri, My Recollection of Nuri al-Said, 1954–58,* Baltimore, 1964

Gaulis, Berthe-Georges: *La question arabe,* Paris, 1930

El-Ghonemy, M. Riad: 'The Role of Land Policy in Agricultural Production and Income Distribution in the Near East', *Land Policy in the Near East,* published for the Govt. of Libya and FAO, 1967

Great Britain: Special Report by His Majesty's Government to the Council of the League of Nations on the Progress of Iraq During the Period 1920–31, HMSO, 1931

Al-Haidari, B. R. N.: *The Development of the Iraq Oil Industry and the Role of Iraq National Oil Company, 1925–74,* Unpublished Ph.D thesis, Polytechnic of Central London, 1976

Hameed, K. A.: Report *Manpower and Employment Planning,* Beirut, United Nations, 1975, mimeo

Haseeb, Khair al-Din: 'Plan Implementation in Iraq, 1951–57', *Studies on Selected Development Problems in Various Countries in the Middle East, 1969,* United Nations, 1969

Haseeb, Khair al-Din: *The National Income of Iraq, 1953–61,* London, 1964

Hashim, J. M.: *Capital Formation in Iraq, 1957–62,* Unpublished Ph.D thesis, University of London (LSE), 1966

Hashim, Jawad: *Development Planning in Iraq: Historical Perspective and New Directions,* Six Lectures, Baghdad, April 1975, mimeo

Hinsley, F. H.: *Nationalism and the International Order,* London, 1973

Hirszowicz, Lukas Z.: *The Third Reich and the Arab East,* London and Toronto, 1966

Holt, P. M.: *Egypt and the Fertile Crescent, 1516–1922,* London, 1966

Hurewitz, J. C.: *Diplomacy in the Near and Middle East: a Documentary Record,* Vol. II, Toronto and New York, 1958

International Bank for Reconstruction and Development: *The Economic Development of Iraq,* Baltimore, Md., 1952

International Bank for Reconstruction and Development/IDA: *Current Economic Position and Prospects of Iraq,* January 1969, mimeo

Ionides, M. G.: *Divide and Lose: the Arab Revolt, 1955–58,* London, 1960

Iraq, Directorate General of Industrial Planning: *The Industrial Sector of the Economy of Iraq,* Baghdad, June 1964

Iraq, Higher Committee for the Celebration of the 14th July Revolution:
The Iraqi Revolution in its Second Year, Baghdad, 1960
The Iraqi Revolution in its Third Year, Baghdad, 1961
The Iraqi Revolution in its Fourth Year, Baghdad, 1962

Iraq, Planning Board and Ministry of Planning: *The National Development Plan, 1970–74,* Baghdad, 1971

Iraq Irrigation Development Commission [The Haigh Commission]: *Report on the Control of the Rivers of Iraq and the Utilization of their Waters,* Baghdad, 1951

Ireland, P. W.: *Iraq,* London, 1937

Issawi, Charles, and Yeganeh, Mohammed: *The Economics of Middle Eastern Oil,* New York, 1962

Iverson, Carl: *A Report on Monetary Policy in Iraq, National Bank of Iraq,* 1954

Jalal, F.: *The Role of Government in the Industrialisation of Iraq, 1950–65,* London, 1971

Jargy, Simon: 'Le declin d'un parti', *Orient,* No. 11, 1959

Jargy, Simon: 'Une page d'histoire de la révolution irakienne: le procès Abd al-Salam Aref', *Orient,* No. 12, 1959

Kanaan, T. H.: *Input/Output & Social Accounts of Iraq, 1960–63,* Ministry of Planning, Baghdad, September 1965

Kedourie, Elie: *England and the Middle East,* London, 1956

Kedourie, Elie: 'The Kingdom of Iraq: A Retrospect' in *The Chatham House Version and Other Essays,* London, 1970

Kedourie, Elie: 'Continuity and Change in Modern Iraqi History', *Asian Affairs,* June 1975, p. 141

Kelidar, Abbas: *Iraq: the Search for Stability,* Conflict Studies, No. 59, London, July 1975

Kelsen, Hans: *The Law of the United Nations,* London, 1950

Kent, Marian: *Oil and Empire: British Foreign Policy and Mesopotamian Oil, 1900–20,* London, 1976

Kerr, Malcolm H.: *The Arab Cold War: Gamal 'Abd al-Nasir and his Rivals, 1958–1970,* 3rd edn., New York, 1971

Khadduri, M.: *Independent Iraq, 1932–1958,* 2nd edn., London, 1960

Khadduri, M.: *Republican Iraq,* London, 1969

Khadduri, M.: 'The Role of the Military in Iraqi Society', *The Military in the Middle East* (S. N. Fisher, ed.), Colombus, 1963

Kirk, G. E.: *The Middle East in War,* Oxford, 1953

Kuisel, R. F.: *Ernest Mercier, French Technocrat,* Berkeley, Calif., 1967

Kurmus, Orhan: *The Role of British Capital in the Economic Development of Western Anatolia, 1815–1913,* Unpublished Ph.D thesis, SOAS, University of London, 1974

Lacouture, Jean: *Nasser,* Paris, 1971

Lambelin, Roger: *L'Egypte et l'Angleterre vers l'indépendance: de Mohamed Ali au roi Fouad,* Paris, 1922

Langley, Kathleen: 'Iraq: Some Aspects of the Economic Scene', *Middle East Journal,* Vol. 18, No. 2, Spring 1964

Langley, Kathleen: *The Industrialization of Iraq,* Cambridge, Mass., 1961

Larcher, M.: *La guerre turc dans la guerre mondiale,* Paris, 1926

Lenczowski, George: *Oil and State in the Middle East,* New York, 1960

Lenczowski, G.: 'Iraq: Seven Years of Revolution', *Current History,* May 1966

Lepsius, J., *et al.* (ed.): *Die grosse Politik der europäischen Kabinette, 1871–1914,* Berlin, 1922–27

Lewis, Bernard: *The Emergence of Modern Turkey,* London, 1961

Lipschits, Issac: *La Politique de la France au Levant, 1939–41,* Paris, 1963

Little, Arthur D. (Inc.): *A Plan for the Industrial Development of Iraq,* Cambridge, Mass., 1956

Longrigg, S. H.: *Four Centuries of Modern Iraq,* Oxford, 1925

Longrigg, S. H.: *Iraq, 1900 to 1950,* London, 1953

Longrigg, S. H.: *Oil in the Middle East,* 2nd edn., London, 1961

Longrigg, S. H., and Stoakes, Frank: *Iraq,* London, 1958

Mabro, Robert: *The Egyptian Economy, 1952–1972,* Oxford, 1974

Mabro, Robert, and Radwan, Samir: *The Industrialization of Egypt, 1939–73,* Oxford, 1976

Mansfield, Peter (ed.): *The Middle East. A Political and Economic Survey,* 4th edn., London, 1973

Al-Marayati, Abid A.: *A Diplomatic History of Modern Iraq,* New York, 1961

Maurice, Maj.-Gen. Sir Frederick: 'Our Commitments in Mesopotamia', *The New Europe,* 18 March 1920

Mauriès, René; *Le Kurdistan ou la Mort,* Paris ,1967

Mejcher, Helmut: *Imperial Quest for Oil,* Oxford, 1976

Mikdashi, Zuhayr: *A Financial Analysis of Middle Eastern Oil Concessions: 1901–65,* New York, 1966
Monroe, Elizabeth: *Britain's Moment in the Middle East 1914–1956,* London, 1963
Moutran, Nadra: *La Syrie de demain,* Paris, 1916
McLachlan, K. S., and Donovan, M. (eds.): *The Developing Agriculture of the Middle East,* London, 1976
N'Dumbe III, Alexander Kum'a: 'Les buts de guerre d'Allemagne hitlérienne en Afrique', *Revue d'histoire de la deuxième guerre mondiale,* April, 1977.
Nevakivi, J.: *Britain, France and the Arab Middle East, 1914–20,* London, 1969
Nolde, Baron E.: *L'Irak, origines historiques et situation internationale,* Paris, 1934
O'Ballance, Edgar: *The Kurdish Revolt: 1961–1970,* London, 1973
Al-Pachachi, Nadim: *Iraqi Oil Policy, August 1954–December 1957,* Baghdad, 1958
Penrose, E. F.: 'Une année de coups d'état', *Orient,* No. 28, 1963
Penrose, E. F.: 'Essai sur l'Irak', *Orient,* No. 35, 1965
Penrose, E. F.: 'Une tentative de gouvernement civil en Irak', *Orient,* No. 39, 1966
Penrose, Edith: 'Money, Prices and Economic Expansion in the Middle East, 1952–60', *Rivista Internazionale di Scienze Economiche e Commerciali,* No. 5, 1962
Penrose, Edith: *The Large International Firm in Developing Countries: the International Petroleum Industry,* London, 1968
Penrose, Edith: 'The Development of Crisis' in *The Oil Crisis in Perspective* (R. Vernon, ed.), New York, 1976
Petran, Tabitha: *Syria,* London, 1972
Phillips, D. G.: 'Rural to Urban Migration in Iraq', *Economic Development and Cultural Change,* July 1959
Pichon, Jean: *Le partage du Proche-Orient,* Paris, 1938
Pichon, Jean: *Les origines orientales de la guerre mondiale,* Paris, 1937
Pingaud, A.: *Histoire diplomatique de la France pendant la grande guerre,* Paris, 1938
Pinon, René: *L'Europe et L'Empire Ottoman,* Paris, 1913
Poyck, A. P. G.: *Farm Studies in Iraq: an Agro-Economic Study of the Agriculture of the Hilla-Diwaniya Area in Iraq,* Wageningen, 1962
Qubain, F.: *Reconstruction of Iraq 1950–7,* New York, 1958
Rabinovitch, I.: *Syria under the Baath, 1963–66,* Jerusalem, 1972
Ramazini, Ronhollah K.: *Iran's Foreign Policy,* Charlottesville, 1975
Rasheed, Guzine A. K.: 'Development of Agricultural Land Taxation in Modern Iraq', *Bulletin of the School of Oriental and African Studies,* Vol. XXV, Part 2, 1962
Rondot, Pierre: 'Pour les Kurds d'Iraq, le temps de l'épreuve n'est pas fini', *Revue française d'études politiques mediterranéenes,* February 1976, pp. 57–60

Rondot, Pierre: 'Iraq: données constantes et modalités actuelles du jeu politique', *Revue française d'études politiques mediterranéenes,* February 1976, pp. 61–77

Rossi, Pierre: 'L'Irak devant la réforme agraire', *Orient,* No. 7, 1958

Rouleau, Eric: 'L'Irak à l'ombre des intrigues', *Le Monde,* 19, 20, 21 July 1973

Saab, Edouard: *La Syrie ou la révolution dans la rancour,* Paris, 1968

Salah, Zaki: *Mesopotamia (Iraq) 1600–1914: A Study in British Foreign Affairs,* Baghdad, 1957

Salim, S. M.: *Marsh Dwellers of the Euphrates Delta,* London, 1962

Salter, Lord: *The Development of Iraq: a Plan of Action,* Iraq Development Board, 1955

Sanders, L. von: *Five Years in Turkey,* London, 1927

El-Sayed, Raouf Abdel: *The Baghdad Pact in World Politics,* Geneva, 1971

Sayigh, Yusif: *Economics of the Arab World,* London, 1977

Schemeil, Yves: 'Le système politique irakien enfin stabilisé?', *Maghreb Machrek: Monde Arabe,* No. 74, 1976

Seale, Patrick: *The Struggle for Syria,* London, 1965

Sfer, Abdulla Pacha: *Le mandat français et les traditions françaises en Syrie et au Liban,* Paris, 1922

Al-Shawi, Hamid: 'Le Ba'th et l'armée en Irak et en Syrie: interpénétration et conflit', *Maghreb Machrek: Monde Arabe,* No. 71, 1976

Al-Shawi, Hamid: 'Le contenu de la contestation communiste en Irak et en Syrie', *Maghreb-Machrek: Monde Arabe,* No. 63, 1974

Shebab, F.: 'Iraq', *Bulletin of the Oxford University Institute of Statistics,* Vol. 21, No. 4, 1959

Stafford, R. S.: *The Tragedy of the Assyrians,* London, 1935

Stobaugh, Robert: 'The Oil Companies in the Crisis' in *The Oil Crisis* (R. Vernon, ed.), New York, 1976

Stocking, George: *Middle East Oil,* London, 1970

Suleiman, Hassan A.: *Industrial Productivity in Iraq with Special Reference to Selected Firms, 1953–63,* Unpub. Ph.D thesis, SOAS, University of London, 1968

Toynbee, Arnold (ed.): *Survey of International Affairs,* Vol. 1. *Islamic Affairs,* London, 1925

Toynbee, Arnold (ed.): *Survey of International Affairs, 1925. The Islamic World Since the Peace Settlement,* London, 1927

Toynbee, Arnold (ed.): *Survey of International Affairs,* London, 1934

Trevelyan, Humphrey: *The Middle East in Revolution,* London, 1970

United Nations, Economic and Social Office in Beirut: *Review and Appraisal of the Process of Decision-Making and Management in the Public Industrial Enterprises in Iraq,* Beirut, Oct. 1973, mimeo

United Nations, Economic Commission for Western Asia: *National Account Studies, Bulletin No. 1. Economic Growth of the ECWA Countries throughout the period 1960–75,* May 1977, mimeo

United Nations, Special Fund Project: *The Economic Status of Iraq,* Baghdad, April 1968

United Nations: *Studies on Development Problems of Selected Countries of the Middle East,* 1972

United States Federal Trade Commission, Staff Report: *The International Petroleum Cartel,* U.S. Govt. Printing Office, Washington, D.C., 1952

United States Senate, Committee on Foreign Relations, 93rd Congress, 2nd Session: *Multinational Corporations and United States Foreign Policy,* Hearings Parts 7, 8, U.S. Govt. Printing Office, Washington, 1974

Vanly, Ismet Chériff: *Le Kurdistan Irakien, entité nationale: Étude de la Révolution de 1961,* Neuchâtel, 1970

Vatikiotis, P. J.: *The Modern History of Egypt,* London, 1969

Vernier, Bernard: *Armée et politique au Moyen-Orient,* Paris, 1966

Vernier, Bernard: *L'Irak d'aujourd'hui,* Paris, 1963

Vernon, R. (ed.): *The Oil Crisis in Perspective,* New York, 1976

Viennot, J.-P.: 'L'idéologie du parti socialiste de la résurrection arabe', *Orient,* No. 29, 1964

Viennot, J.-P.: 'Le Ba'th entre la théorie et la pratique', *Orient,* No. 30, 1964

Warriner, D.: 'Land Tenure in the Fertile Crescent', a report presented to the Middle East Supply Centre, 1944, reprinted in C. Issawi (ed.): *The Economic History of the Middle East, 1800–1914*

Warriner, D.: *Land and Poverty in the Middle East,* London, 1948

Warriner, Doreen: *Land Reform and Development in the Middle East,* 2nd edn., London, 1962

Warriner, Doreen: *Land Reform in Principle and Practice,* Oxford, 1969

Weinberg, G. L.: *Germany and the Soviet Union, 1939–41,* Leiden, 1954

Weulersse, J.: *Le Pays des Alaouites,* Tours, 1940

Woodward, E. L. and Butler, Rohan (eds.): *Documents on British Foreign Policy, 1919–39*

Woodward, Llewellyn: *British Foreign Policy in the Second World War,* Vol. I, London, 1970

Zeine, N. Zeine: *The Struggle For Arab Independence,* Beirut, 1960

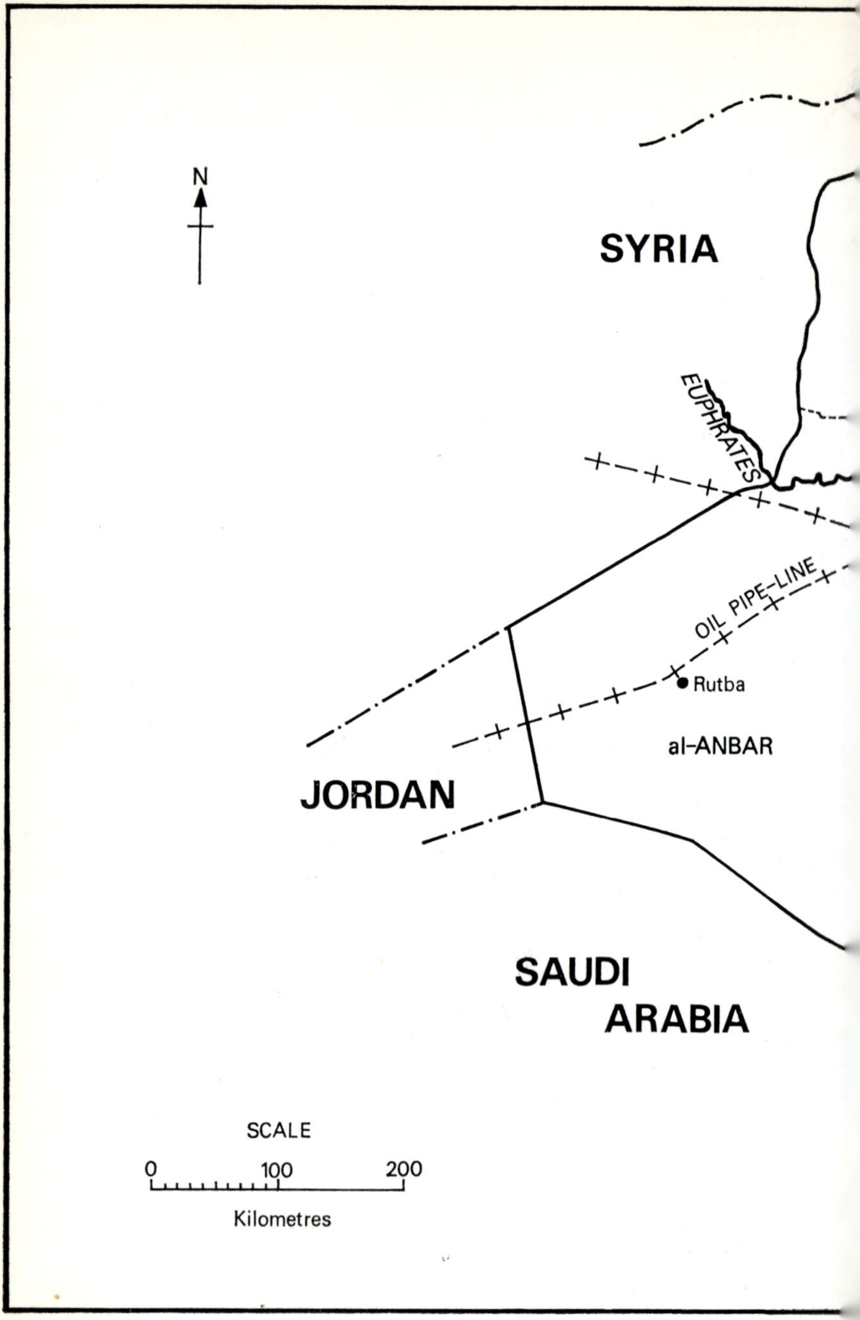

Iraq: General Map

TURKEY
Zakho
DOHUK
Dohuk
Barzan
Ruwanduz
ARBIL
Mosul
Arbil
SULAIMANIYA
NINEVEH
Kirkuk
Sulaimaniya
TIGRIS
KIRKUK
Takrit
Tharthar
Depression
Samarra
Khanaqin
IRAN
Haditha
Balad
BAGHDAD
Baquba
DIALA
Ramadi
Baghdad
Lake
Habbaniya
WASIT
MAYSAN
Kerbela
BABYLON
Hilla
Kut
KERBELA
Najf
Diwaniya
Amara
al-QADISIYA
THI-QAR
Samawa
Nasiriya
al-MUTHANNA
Basra
BASRA
KUWAIT
Fao
Kuwait
City
NEUTRAL
ZONE

Index